Comparative History
of Civilizations in Asia

Volume II: 1350 to present

Comparative History of Civilizations in Asia

EDWARD L. FARMER
University of Minnesota

GAVIN R.G. HAMBLY
University of Texas at Dallas

DAVID KOPF
University of Minnesota

BYRON K. MARSHALL
University of Minnesota

ROMEYN TAYLOR
University of Minnesota

Westview Press / Boulder and London

Copyright © 1986 by Westview Press, Inc.

Published in 1986 in the United States of America by Westveiw Press, Inc.; Frederick A. Praeger, Publisher; 5500 Central Avenue, Boulder, Colorado 80301

First published in 1977 by Addison-Wesley Publishing Company, Inc.

Library of Congress Catalog Card Number: 85-52370
ISBN: 0-8133-0356-7

Printed and bound in the United States of America

 The paper used in this publication meets the requirements of the American National Standard for Permanence of Paper for Printed Library Materials Z39.48-1984.

10   9   8   7   6   5   4   3   2

This book is dedicated to our children:

Amy	Jessica	Maximilian
Byron	Jim	Michelle
Charles	Joy	Sally
Dan	Judy	Sarah
Edward	Lara	Walter

A Note about Volume II

This volume begins with Chapter 9, "The Rise of Early Modern Empires in Asia." Readers who have used Volume I will notice that Chapter 9, as well as the Preface and Introduction, has been repeated here. The purpose of this repetition is to make the book more adaptable to a variety of classroom uses. While Chapter 9 is the logical place to end a survey of the traditional period, it is equaly essential as a starting point to the modern period. By repeating this section we hope to avoid a situation in which a student would be obliged to purchase both volumes in a single school term. The Preface and Introduction, which explain the conception and organization of the book, are repeated here for those users who are concerned with the modern period only.

Contents

List of Maps

Preface to
Volumes I and II

The day has long since passed when one could seriously question the desirability of including at least an introductory treatment of Asian history in the content of a liberal education. Yet the general reader, the student, or the teacher attempting to come to grips with the history of Asia is faced simultaneously with two formidable problems. The first is the need to assimilate a vast amount of unfamiliar information. The second is the need to order that information into meaningful units, to relate it to the rest of one's knowledge and to decide what is essential and what is less important. The purpose of this book is to help solve these problems by providing a broad framework and flexible method for thinking about the history of the peoples of Asia. The approach adopted, which involves the comparative study of civilizations, is described in detail in the Introduction. Here we will address the questions of why we have written such a book and how we think it can be used in teaching.

The Problem of Perspective
It is an understandable, if lamentable, fact that the curriculums and teaching resources of colleges and universities in the English-speaking world are heavily weighted toward the values and institutions of the European and American past. This condition is a natural result of the fact that the study of history, and to a lesser extent the other humanities and social sciences, has been motivated by a desire for self-understanding, by the search for a cultural self-image. Interest in other peoples and other traditions has been relegated to a secondary position. This has been particularly true of Asian studies, as a function of both physical and cultural remoteness from Western life. In recent decades, however, interest in the world outside the West has increased markedly and efforts have been made to include the history of most areas of the globe within the scope of a liberal education. In part at least this is due to the recognition that self-understanding is achieved through an understanding of the "other." Once one accepts the desirability of including Asian history in the undergraduate curriculum one is faced with formidable practical problems. Prominent among these problems is the question of scale. More than half of the people in the world are Asians. The size and diversity of Asia as a cultural unit is suggested by the fact that thirteen of the twenty principal spoken languages are Asian, while only six are of European origin.

The challenge for an introductory course in Asian history is how to give a meaningful account of this vast sector of the world, with less resources and less class time than is normally devoted to the cultures of the West. Two considerations, one theoretical and one practical, enter at this point. The first consideration is that Asia is too large, too complex,

Principal World Languages	Millions of Speakers	European	Asian
1. Mandarin	639		x
2. English	352	x	
3. Russian	226	x	x
4. Spanish	208	x	
5. Hindi	205		x
6. Arabic	121		x
7. Bengali	120		x
8. German	120	x	
9. Portuguese	120	x	
10. Japanese	109		x
11. Malay-Indonesian	93		x
12. French	87	x	
13. Italian	60	x	
14. Urdu	57		x
15. Punjabi	53		x
16. Telugu	53		x
17. Tamil	52		x
18. Korean	51		x
19. Marathi	49		x
20. Cantonese	47		x

Source: The World Almanac & Book of Facts 1975 (New York, 1974), p. 295.

and too diverse to be treated as a single unit in the way Europe or Latin America can be. It is necessary, therefore, for the purpose of analysis to divide Asia into smaller, more cohesive subdivisions. A reasonable division of the world into regions would separate Asia into five parts: West Asia, South Asia, East Asia, Southeast Asia, and Central Asia.

Region	North America	South America	Africa	Europe	Asia West	South	Southeast	East	Central
Area (Mil. Sq. Mi.)	9.4	6.8	11.5	3.7	2.5	1.6	1.7	3.9	7.7
Population (Millions)	335	206	374	659	130	724	297	956	158

Once Asia is broken into manageable and meaningful units the question arises as to how to treat several units at once. The approach offered in this series is to view the subdivisions of Asia from a comparative perspective.

The practical consideration that faces the instructor trying to teach a course covering the whole of Asia is the fact that no single individual scholar can hope to acquire a detailed familiarity with all areas of Asia. All too often the solution is to teach about China or India and let the rest go. The virtue of a comparative approach is to create flexibility by allowing one to extend inquiry from the relatively familiar to the relatively unfamiliar while retaining a balanced perspective.

How to Use This Book

This book is designed for use by an instructor who is more familiar with one subdivision of Asia than with the others. The organization of each chapter is intended to facilitate the extension of inquiry comparatively from known subject matter to the relatively unknown. Structurally, each chapter is composed of a "process" section (abbreviated P) and "pattern" sections (organized from west to east) describing historical events in the various subdivisions of Asia. For example, in Chapter 4 the process section (4.P) analyzes the formation of universal empires, while the patterns describe specific empires: the Achaemenids (4.1), the Mauryans (4.2) and the Ch'in-Han (4.3). This combination of process and patterns gives the reader a great freedom of choice in selecting a strategy for using the book.

The instructor need not follow the book section by section as it is printed. Instead his or her lecturing and reading assignments can be varied to use some or all of the chapters, some or all of the patterns within the chapters. The patterns within each chapter are in reality separable subchapters, which can be read in any order desired since they are numbered arbitrarily according to geographical position. The instructor should break up chapter assignments to meet the needs of a given course. We suggest a number of course formats in which the book could be used:

1. As it stands the book is an overview of all of Asian history from the eastern borders of Europe to the Pacific and from the birth of civilization to the present. The stress in this overview is placed on the identification of a number of significant stages of historical development in the life of civilizations and on clarification of the social and cultural subdivisions within Eurasia. On this scale there is no possibility of surveying in detail the history of each civilization. This overview has utility both for the beginning student who wants a sort of world map for future study and the advanced student who knows about one area and wants to extend his or her knowledge to others.

2. Less inclusively, one could survey just two civilizations using the processes as a basis for discussion and assigning only the two relevant patterns in each chapter. The instructor, of course, has the flexibility of choosing to lecture primarily on the area with which he or she is most familiar and perhaps assigning additional reading to supplement the text on the other area. Many variations are possible along these lines.

3. For a topical survey of one time period a course could be built around a single theme such as the universal religions discussed in Chapter 6. In this treatment the process portion of Chapter 6 would supply questions to be pursued in depth for a whole term. Chapter 3 on ethical protest and reform ideologies could be read for background, and the patterns in Chapter 6 could be supplemented by additional readings such as those suggested in the bibliography section appended to the chapter.

4. In the survey of a single area of Asia this book could be treated as a supplementary reading in which the process sections, particularly, might be used to formulate questions.

5. At a more advanced level, the process portions of the book could be used to provide a structural format for a seminar or discussion course. The patterns would supply minimum background for the discussion of unfamiliar areas, while the bibliographies would supply a starting point for those reading in depth on a given area and for those preparing papers.

6. The reader will note from the maps and the process format that the scope of this comparison could be extended beyond Asia to include all of Eurasia. That the patterns are confined to Asia alone is primarily a matter of practical considerations such as the amount of space required. Certainly lectures or readings on Western "patterns" (Rome, Christianity, etc.) would comfortably fit the structure of the comparison. Some instructors may wish to attempt such inclusions, which are often most stimulating. The authors have on numerous occasions benefitted in their own course from guest lectures by colleagues in ancient and medieval history. The last four chapters can likewise be expanded to a global range (Africa, Latin America, North America) since the processes associated with European maritime domination, nationalism, and modern change were not constricted by the confines of the Eurasian landmass.

The point of these remarks is to urge readers to use this book with flexibility according to their needs and circumstances. It is not intended to be a definitive account of all aspects of Asian history. Rather, it is intended as an introduction and as a tool to facilitate open-ended and comparative inquiry. Certain questions are raised in each chapter, and the descriptive material is necessarily oriented toward those questions. The reader should be prepared to challenge both the questions and the interpretations at any point. The value of the comparative format is not in the precision of the answers as much as it is in the way it formulates questions and clarifies basic assumptions in preparation for further study.

Bibliography

The scope of Asian history and the volume of scholarship on Asia defy any effort at definitive condensation. What we have tried to do in each chapter is suggest further readings that will provide practical beginning points to the reader who wishes to know more. In our selections we have usually included standard textbooks and reference works, and where possible we have indicated works available in paperback. For more detailed bibliographical guidance, however, more specialized works should be consulted. Among the most useful are:

Howard, Harry N., et al., eds., *Middle East and North Africa: A Bibliography for Undergraduate Libraries* (Williamsport: Bro-Dart Publishing Co., 1971), 80 pp.

Hucker, Charles O., *China: A Critical Bibliography* (Tucson: University of Arizona Press, 1962), 125 pp.

Mahar, J. Michael, *India: A Critical Bibliography* (Tucson: University of Arizona Press, 1964), 119 pp.

Silberman, Bernard S., *Japan and Korea: A Critical Bilbiography* (Tucson: University of Arizona Press, 1962), 120 pp.

Tregonning, Kennedy G., *Southeast Asia: A Critical Bibliography* (Tucson: University of Arizona Press, 1969), 103 pp.

Bibliography of Asian Studies, annual volumes published by the Association for Asian studies since 1971 (September 1970 issue). Prior to 1970 this work appeared as the fifth issue of the *Journal of Asian Studies.* This is the best source for recent Western-language works on Asia except for West Asia. However, one must look through each volume to get the publications of each year, and the citations do not contain annotations as do the critical bibliographies listed above.

Authorship

This book grew out of an undergraduate survey course taught for many years at the University of Minnesota. It was David Kopf's inspiration in 1967 to integrate the course by treating all Asia in a common format instead of assigning a given number of weeks to East Asia and a like number to South Asia. From that beginning four historians, specialists in modern India, premodern China, modern China, and modern Japan, became engaged in a collaborative teaching enterprise, which required each of us to expand the horizons of our teaching, to view our own areas of specialization from a comparative perspective, and often to engage in an extended, even heated, debate. Because no two history texts, particularly those dealing with different areas of Asia, treated history from a comparable perspective or in comparable units, we decided to develop our own teaching materials. In the most fundamental sense this book is a joint effort, the product of many continuing dialogues, and the writing itself has been a stimulating and rewarding experience. We were joined in the undertaking by Gavin Hambly of Yale University, who brought to the project a welcome familiarity with Iran, Central Asia, and Muslim South Asia. Writing and revision, which took five years and consumed a great deal of paper, was often interrupted by periods of research abroad and the normal strains of personal and professional life. Inevitably many changes were made in the design of the book and in the choice and definition of processes. While comments, suggestions, and criticisms were freely exchanged through several drafts, the primary responsibility for writing the individual sections was distributed as follows:

Edward L. Farmer: Introduction; 1.2 Harappan Civilization; 2.2 Aryan Civilization; 4.P Processes in the Rise of Universal Empires; 6.2 Hinduism; 9.P Processes of Early Modern Empires; 9.4 Ming and Ch'ing; 10.P Processes of Decline; 10.4 Decline of Ch'ing; 11.3 Western European domination in Southeast Asia; 11.4 Maritime Integration in China; 12.3 Disintegration in China; 13.3 Nationalism in Southeast Asia; 13.4 Nationalism in China; 14.3 Change in Southeast Asia; 14.4 Change in China.

Gavin Hambly: 4.1 Achaemenid Empire; 4.2 Mauryan Empire; 5.1 Parthians and Sasanids; 5.2 Kushanas and Guptas; 6.1 Islam; 7.1 Fragmentation in West Asia; 7.2 Fragmentation in South Asia; 8.2 Mongol Empire in West Asia; 8.4 Timur; 9.1 Ottomans; 9.2 Safavids; 9.3 Mughuls; 10.1 Decline of Ottomans; 10.2 Decline of Safavids; 10.3 Decline of Mughuls; 11.1 European Domination in West Asia; 12.1 Disintegration in West Asia; 13.1 Nationalism in West Asia; 13.2B Nationalism in South Asia among Muslims; 14.1 Change in West Asia.

David Kopf: 11.2 Western European domination in South Asia; 12.2 Disintegration in South Asia; 13.2A Nationalism in South Asia among Hindus; 14.2 Change in India.

Byron K. Marshall: 6.3 Buddhism (Japan portion); 7.5 Cultural Synthesis in Japan; 9.5 Tokugawa; 10.5 Decline of Tokugawa; 11.5 Maritime Integration in Japan; 12.P Processes of Disintegration; 12.4 Disintegration in Japan; 13.5 Nationalism in Japan; 14.P Processes of Change; 14.5 Change in Japan.

Romeyn Taylor: 1.1 Mesopotamian Civilization; 1.3 Shang Civilization; 2.1 Political Organization of Mesopotamian Civilization; 2.3 Shang and Chou China; 3.1 Hebrew Prophets and Zoroaster; 3.2 Mahavira and Buddha; 3.3 Reform Ideology in Chou China; 4.3 Ch'in-Han Empire; 5.3 Late Han and Three Kingdoms; 6.3 Mahayana Buddhism; 7.3 Fragmentation in Southeast Asia; 7.4 Fragmentation in China; 8.P Processes of Central Asian Domination; 8.1 Formation of Mongols; 8.3 Mongol Domination in East Asia.

Joint Authorship: *Farmer* and *Kopf*: 11.P Processes of Maritime Integration; 13.P Processes of Cultural Renaissance and Nationalism; *Kopf* and *Marshall*: 3.P Processes of Crisis and Ethical Protest; 6.P Processes of Universal Religions; 7.P Processes of Regional Fragmentation; *Kopf* and *Taylor*: 1.P Processes of Birth of Civilization; 2.P Processes of the Political Organization of Civilized Societies; 5.9 Processes of the Persistence of Empire.

Acknowledgments

Inevitably, in a project which has gone on as long as this one has, many people make contributions which the authors wish to acknowledge as best they can. The heroine of our entire effort has been Sue Cave, who, with occasional help from Kathy Cooper and Carley Albrecht, typed the entire manuscript at least three times, often at dazzling speed. The staff at Addison-Wesley understood what we were trying to do at the outset, brought the five authors together and set us to writing, and saw us through the long years of revision. Over the years our colleagues at the University of Minnesota have been tolerant of our struggles with a joint lecture course and an integrated manuscript. Among those who have lectured in the survey or made other contributions are Bernard Bachrach, Robert Berkhofer, Stephen Blake, Jerry Clinton, Stephen Dale, Tom B. Jones, Lothar Knauth, David Lelyveld, Richard Mather, Angus McDonald, Larry Moses, John Perry, Tom Noonan, Robert Poor, Stuart Schwartz, and Ira Spar. Our sternest and most constructive critics have been the teaching assistants who joined us in the classroom: Thomas Allsen, George Chang, Amalendu Chakraborty, Robert Dillard, Richard Heitler, Roland Higgins, Yun-yi Ho, Tai-yung Lin, Bonnie McKellar, Bruce Robinson, Patrick Roche, Kristina Kade Troost, Wallace Witham, and Dante Yip. Special thanks are due to Dorothy Larson and Lorraine Mix of Central Duplicating and Pat Burwell and Sandy Haas of the Cartography Lab of the University of Minnesota for expert help in many crucial points of production. The staff of the History Department at the University of Minnesota, particularly Gretchen Asmussen, Dennis Clayton, and Doreen Haven, gave institutional support and personal encouragement for which we are most grateful.

A Note on the Westview Edition

Our own experience in using this textbook since its publication and the many kind remarks from colleagues and students have reaffirmed our belief in the utility of the comparative approach for the study of Asian history. The growing interest in world history has made the book even more useful now than when it was first issued. We were greatly distressed, as were many others, when the first edition went out of print. We are therefore delighted that Westview Press has agreed to republish the book in paperback. The Westview edition is issued without change to the text. The relatively minor adjustments that might have been made to the original version were not large enough to justify the additional cost and delay that a complete recasting would have entailed.

E.L.F., G.R.G.H., D.K., B.K.M., R.T.

Introduction to Volumes I and II

The *Asian* in the title of this book indicates in a general way what part of the world is to be considered. Its use, however, may lead to certain misunderstandings unless its implications are examined. The conventional practice of dividing the Eurasian landmass arbitrarily into two "continents," Europe and Asia, along a line through the Ural Mountains reinforces the mistaken idea that Europe and Asia are equivalent historical entities. In fact, however, the Asian part is very much larger than the European and is the home of at least three civilizations. This means that while to study the history of Europe is to study one civilization, to study the history of Asia is to study several civilizations at once.

Because there is no single Asian civilization, it follows that there can be no uniform history of Asia. The familiar history of "Western civilization," which traces the evolution of a common cultural tradition from Greek and Roman origins through the Middle Ages to modern Europe and the United States, has no parallel in Asia. The history of Chinese civilization in East Asia or of Indian civilization in South Asia, to cite the two most obvious examples, would each be comparable to the history of Western civilization in Europe. Thus it becomes necessary to dispense with the notion of an Asian civilization and to distinguish several distinct cultural traditions, which shared the single common characteristic of being non-European. The problem is to decide which units to deal with and how to approach them. In this book Asia will be divided into five culture zones, three of which are clearly identified with civilizations, and their history will be treated comparatively.

Three cultural areas of Asia are historically comparable to Europe in the sense that major civilizations have evolved in them. Unfortunately, in the English language there are no common names for these areas as there is for Europe, a fact that makes it difficult to perceive their cultural unity. Consequently, we are forced to the expediency of labelling these civilizations by the geographical terms for the regions in which they developed: *West Asia, South Asia,* and *East Asia.* These terms, while graceless, at least avoid the parochialism of Europocentric terms (Near East, Middle East, Far East). They also avoid the imprecision and confusion of usages that derive from a single nation (Indian civilization, Chinese civilization) or religion (Islamic civilization). West Asia designates a polycentric culture zone that includes the Arabian peninsula, the Fertile Crescent, Turkey, Iran, and the southern flanks of the Soviet Union; by South Asia we mean the Indian subcontinent; while East Asia includes China and the adjacent territory of Korea, Japan, and Vietnam. Two other subdivisions of Asia, which have historically interacted with these areas, are *Southeast Asia* and *Central Asia.* Southeast Asia, while it was a meeting place and zone of interaction with the four major civilizations of Eurasia, displayed a high degree of cultural diversity and did not itself develop a unified civilization. Central Asia was generally inhospitable to the development of civilization, although in some parts of this region oasis cities flourished as local variants or blends of the major civilizations.

What do we mean by civilization? The term is used here not as a value judgment but to designate the largest distinct culture-bearing units—the evolving configuration of social norms, traditions, and institutions that came to be widely shared by the population of the major subdivisions of Eurasia. The reason civilizations are defined in this book in terms of the common and enduring culture of great regions is not to denigrate local cultures, much less national histories, which are the proper concerns of anthropologists and historians. The reason is to underscore the scale of the subject matter to be dealt with. We are looking only at the broadest outlines of historical development and generalizing about changes taking place through the entire span of human history and across the expanse of the world's most extensive landmass. It is simply not possible to pay detailed or consistent attention to local affairs.

The search for that which was widely accepted and enduring in Asian culture tends to lead one to elite culture, to the values and ideas that found expression and hence preservation in the written record of the literate classes. In this sense civilization is equated in large part with the "great tradition," or the high culture, of a region in contradistinction to local customs. This is not to say that ordinary people are of no interest or that what is noteworthy in human culture has been the product of the rich and powerful alone, for all classes of society have participated in the human experience and all have contributed to the cultural heritage. Nevertheless, it is the educated few who have tended to share common perceptions and practices over large areas. Just as Latin was known to educated individuals all over Europe, so classical Chinese served as a *lingua franca* among the speakers of many dialects in China as well as among the educated in Korea, Japan, and Vietnam. Moreover, our present state of knowledge regarding the history of the common people in Asian societies is very limited, and what information there is has often been filtered through the eyes of the literate class.

The formation of the great cultural traditions of Eurasia was a cumulative development that took place in historical time. While each civilization was unique, reflecting the particular circumstances of its situation, certain broad parallels are apparent which allow comparative generalization. In many cases these parallels may be the products of fundamental changes in economic organization, technology, social organization, or the accumulation and interpretation of traditional beliefs. For example, the development of agriculture played an important role in the origin of civilization; likewise, religions in each case helped shape basic social values; and in modern times, the complex of factors we call industrialization upset the traditional social order. The overview of Asian civilizations that follows assumes comparability and often seeks parallels on this very abstract level. However, several warnings are in order. First, no claim is made that all civilizations developed in the same stages and by reason of the same causes; in some cases the reader may be struck by similarities, while in other instances it is the differences that stand out. Second, we are not asserting that we have found the motivating forces that made civilizations the way they were, or even that the causal factors were the same in each case. Third, the reader is reminded that the comparisons ventured here are undertaken on the broadest scale and that an analysis that helps our understanding at the most general level may obscure it at a more detailed level. In this connection the reader should bear in mind the very loose and broad meaning we are giving to the word *civilization*. For example, while we may treat East Asia as a culture zone with a common civilization, generalizations about the whole area will not always hold true for all societies within it. Japan, for instance, shares many traits with China but differs from the latter sufficiently for it to be viewed as a distinct culture within the broader civilization. The problem is one of scale; the generalizations this comparative approach allows should not be endowed in the reader's mind with the sanctity of historical law.

To put the scale of this comparison into perspective, think of the entire history of Western civilization, and then consider how to organize a study of three other civilizations of a comparable magnitude. In such an undertaking, two approaches common to introductory history texts are precluded. The first is the consideration of national history. There are too many nations and peoples in Asia to attempt a coherent account of their histories within two volumes. The second approach, which might be useful if one were dealing with a single civilization, is the chronological survey. That survey format would not fit the history of Asia easily because of the diversity of the area. In place of these familiar forms of organization, a somewhat different framework will be employed here—selective comparison in chronological sequence. The structure and the terminology of this comparison need to be explained.

Process, Pattern, and Period

The comparative perspective is useful in studying Asian civilizations for two principal reasons. First of all, by treating the history of the civilizations comparatively, one underscores the differences among them and hence their separateness in a way that dispels the notion of an Asian unity. Second, comparison stimulates awareness of contrasts, raising questions about differences as well as similarities, questions that often would not occur if one were dealing with a single civilization. Thus, for example, if one studied only European history one might accept as "normal" and not question the fragmentation of the Roman empire into many states. But if one also considers the fact that the Chinese empire was reunited during the medieval period, one is prompted to try to account for the differences. The point here is not that a comparative method automatically yields answers to such questions, or that it can prove any particular theory of history, but merely that it helps to challenge assumptions and suggest fruitful questions. Another way to put it is to say that comparative history forces one to make basic concepts explicit. In this book the analytical concepts used to guide comparisons are called *processes* and the historical examples that are compared are referred to as *patterns*.

A *process* is a developmental phenomenon that can occur in different times and regions. It is described in broadly generalized terms so that the definition will fit various societies and cultures. An example of a process might be urbanization. One would find urban communities forming in all parts of the world at various times, although they would differ in appearance and the motive for forming them could vary widely. Thus one city might form as a castle town, another as a trading center, and a third as a place of worship. At the beginning of each chapter a process section will discuss a number of historical developments in the abstract to provide a guide or framework for the comparative sections to follow. For example, the birth of civilization will be discussed in terms of such processes as the development of agriculture, urbanization, and the invention of writing. We emphasize that the processes selected for discussion in each chapter are not fixed and rigid categories setting the limits on historical reality, or Platonic ideals representing the essence of the truth. Rather, they are commonsense formulations for the purpose of facilitating discussion. In this sense the processes are arbitrary; they are chosen on heuristic grounds. A different list of processes could have been used for most chapters, and each process could have been defined differently. In the case of urbanization, for example, the process can be conceived in a number of ways. Cities can be defined in terms primarily of trade, or the density of population, or their status in a political hierarchy. Each such alternative will produce a different process, which in turn will alter the comparison of cities in Japan, Iran, and elsewhere. The function of the processes, then, is to structure the comparison of civilizations in Asia and not to make a definitive statement about their history—still less to explain Asian history in causal terms.

Patterns, in the usage of this text, are the events in the particular subdivisions of Asia which are being compared. The beginnings of civilization, which will be discussed at the outset of Chapter 1 as processes, will then be viewed in three historical patterns: Sumerian civilization in West Asia, Harappan civilization in South Asia, and the Shang civilization in

East Asia. Whereas the processes are stated abstractly, the pattern sections are concrete and descriptive. It is the task of the reader to test the processes against the patterns in each case to see where there is similarity and where difference.

A third element in this scheme is *period*. Obviously, the comparable events in the history of various civilizations are not always going to be found in the same span of time. For this reason comparison must take into account the notion of period. In each chapter the reader will find a statement about the time period covered by each of the patterns. Sometimes the patterns will not even overlap in time. Evidence of the beginnings of civilization in Mesopotamia is much older than that of comparable developments in the Indus valley and northern China, so the patterns discussed in the first chapter will diverge chronologically. Generally speaking, the time periods diverge most widely in chapters covering the remote past and correspond most closely in those covering more recent periods, with the chapters covering the modern period overlapping broadly.

Chapter Topics

The comparison of civilizations in Eurasia entails certain assumptions about the classification of civilizations as cultural entities with uniform or similar attributes. A historical comparison entails assumptions about the relationships among the civilizations. The selection, arrangement, and interpretation of subject matter is influenced by assumptions about these questions. The perspective adopted here can be clarified by stating what it does not assume. First of all, we are not primarily concerned with seeking the origins of civilized values or institutions; we are not trying to trace civilization or its constituent elements back to some primal source. While the diffusion of cultural elements from one area to another is fully recognized, and even becomes a major theme of some chapters, the ancestry of a civilization is not a central concern of this work. Second, interaction among civilizations is not the focus. Contact between one part of Eurasia and another, the influence of one culture on another, is a constant and substantial portion of our picture, but it is not the interaction itself that is of primary interest, but the effects of interaction on the civilizations involved. Third, and by the same token, the uniqueness of each cultural tradition is not to be stressed. Most historians write about some aspect of their own historical tradition and thus are involved in developing a cultural self-image, a perception from the inside. While the comparative format recognizes both relatedness and distinctness, it is concerned less with grasping the peculiar essence of a particular civilized tradition than with generalizing about the common characteristics of a number of traditions.

The problem is to accommodate a comparative format to historical subject matter. A sociologist or a political scientist might be content to compare family structure or governmental institutions in various societies without regard to the historical epoch. This study, however, is historical in that the topics are arranged in a chronological order and the sequence of patterns contributes to the continuity of the whole. Since cultural traditions grow by accretion, it is important to see how they evolved over time. In this sense the earlier chapters are background to the later chapters. Thus, the ethical protest ideologies—which included, for example, that of the historical Buddha—are discussed in Chapter 3. These ideologies were later important in giving form to the universal religions— for example, Buddhism—dealt with in Chapter 6. Nevertheless, the reader is reminded that more attention has been given to the comparison across civilizations within each chapter than to the continuity within each civilization from one chapter to the next. In fact, the chapters are intended to cut across the flow of history at points of interest without promising to connect the spaces between in a uniformly detailed manner.

Another point to be clarified is that the chapters are not concerned with a uniform set of questions or perspectives. The scale of comparison differs—one chapter may deal with a thousand years, another with a half century; in some chapters an extended empire is the subject, while others might deal only with a small number of seminal thinkers. A further variation is introduced by the level of abstraction. Where the chapter on universal religions generalizes about the evolving faith of hundreds of millions of worshippers, the earlier account of ethical protest ideologies deals with the doctrines of a few individuals. Most important is the fact that the topics of various chapters pose different questions. A rough characterization of these differences in perspective can be presented in tabular form:

EVOLUTIONARY DEVELOPMENT	INSTITUTIONS	SOCIAL BREAKDOWN	ELITE VALUES IN CRISIS	REGIONAL INTERACTION
1. Birth of Civilization	4. Universal Empires	7. Regional Fragmentation	3. Ethical Protest	8. Central Asian Domination
2. Political Organization	6. Universal Religions	10. Decline of Empires	5. Persistence of Empire	11. Maritime Integration
14. Modern Change	9. Modern Empires	12. Cultural Disintegration	13. Renaissance and Nationalism	

The first two and the last chapter attempt to analyze the way that changing economic and social conditions affected culture. Three chapters deal with periods of unity, either political or religious, while three others consider periods of social breakdown and cultural disintegration. The perception of social crisis is the main topic of another three chapters, while regional interaction—including attempts to unify Eurasia—is the main theme of the remaining two.

Viewed sequentially, the chapters trace the evolution of human society in Asia by attempting to identify major points of change. Chapter 1 examines the processes by which civilization came into being, while Chapter 2 discusses the emergence of the state and kingship as a response to the problems caused by the growth of civilized society. In Chapter 3 we consider the protests and ethical prescriptions that were elicited in the first millennium B.C. by the incessant and escalating conflict among the newly evolved states. One solution to the dilemma, political unification on a basis as wide as the whole civilized world, or culture zone, was accomplished by universal empires, the subject of Chapter 4. The decline and collapse of universal empires were followed by attempts to resurrect them and to preserve their heritage (Chapter 5), but the more significant development was the rise of universal religions (Chapter 6), which promised mankind a new security independent of the structure of the state. A period of regional fragmentation (Chapter 7), rich in local cultural development, was followed by the heroic effort of the Central Asian peoples under Mongol leadership to unify the Eurasian world by military conquest (Chapter 8). Following the Mongol irruption, new empires (Chapter 9) were formed in the heartlands of the old civilizations. Their survival into modern times in a progressively weakened condition is the subject of Chapter 10. The extension of European activities by land and sea increased the intercourse between Europe and the civilizations of Asia, leading by the nineteenth century to the consummation of European domination over much of Asia (Chapter 11). This development, which hastened the introduction of forces of change, accelerated the cultural disintegration of Asian societies (Chapter 12). The response of Asian people to the ascendancy of Westerners assumed the form of cultural renaissance and nationalist movements (Chapter 13). In Chapter 14 the processes of modernization are examined in the context of their impact on the cultural traditions of Asian societies.

This brief summary should make clear that the chapter topics have been chosen to touch on a few periods of significant innovation and of crisis. The intent of this scheme is to give the reader an introductory grasp of some of the most interesting developments in the history of human societies in Asia and a framework with which to seek and sort out the vast store of information that further reading can provide.

The Geographical Setting

Now that the scheme of the book has been introduced, something about the setting in which these historical developments transpired remains to be said. The practice throughout the book will be to present the patterns in a geographical order moving from west to east. Here, some basic features of each culture zone of Asia will be reviewed and considered in order to orient the reader for the text that follows. The five subdivisions will be conventionally designated by the terms West Asia, South Asia, Southeast Asia, East Asia, and Central Asia.

West Asia is the name we use to designate the area commonly referred to in everyday English as the Middle East or the Near East—terms we abjure because they define the region from a European standpoint. (From the perspective of California or Hawaii, China is the "Near West" and Arabia the "Far West.") As a culture zone and a center of civilization, West Asia is less cohesive and more polycentric than either South Asia or East Asia. It is helpful to think of the area in terms of the three dominant regions that mark its poles—Iran (formerly Persia) to the east, the Arabian peninsula to the south, and Turkey, or Anatolia (the ancient Asia Minor), to the northwest. The physical dispersal of these subcenters of West Asia is an important feature of an area that has served to link Europe and Africa with Central Asia, South Asia, and East Asia by means of age-old caravan trails. In the northwest, Anatolia projects outward toward Europe in the shape of a rectangular peninsula bounded on the north by the Black Sea, on the south by the Mediterranean, and on the west by the Aegean Sea. The Sea of Marmara, with narrow straits—the Dardanelles to the south, the Bosporus to the north—links the Aegean to the Black Sea and physically separates Anatolia from Thrace, with Istanbul (originally Byzantium, later Constantinople) on the European side. Northeast of Anatolia, the Caucasus region lying between the Black Sea and the Caspian Sea connects West Asia with the Volga-Don steppes in what is now the Soviet Union. This region includes the Soviet republics of Georgia, Armenia, and Azarbayjan, which adjoin Turkey and Iran. Along the southern shore of the Caspian Sea run the Elburz Mountains, demarcating the northern extremity of the Iranian plateau, while to the east of the Caspian the arid region comprising the present-day Turkmen, Uzbek, and Tadzhik republics of the Soviet Union, bordering Iran and Afghanistan, acts as a glacis linking West Asia with the true steppelands of Central Asia beyond the Syr Darya. Iran, consisting of a vast plateau broken by ranges of mountains (of which the Zagros to the west and southwest have tended to insulate Iran to some extent from the course of events in Mesopotamia) is the prime link area of West Asia, with its eastern extension in what is now Afghanistan acting as a major funnel for intercourse with South Asia. Mesopotamia (now Iraq), the great agricultural basin between the Euphrates and Tigris rivers, lies at the center of West Asia, where the first Asian civilization was born. The Tigris and Euphrates empty their waters into the Persian Gulf, a body of water that is constricted at its mouth by the Strait of Ormuz and opens onto the Gulf of Oman and the Arabian Sea. These bodies of water, which have long provided avenues of commerce with the East, frame the eastern and southern coastline of the Arabian peninsula, a vast tract of desert and semiarid regions which lies between Mesopotamia and the northeastern coast of Africa. Separating the two continents is the Red Sea, on the eastern side of which is the region of the Hijaz with the important Muslim religious centers of Medina and Mecca. At the northern end of the Red Sea, Egypt is separated from Palestine by the Sinai peninsula, a heart-shaped body of land defined on the east by the Gulf of Aqaba and on the west by the Gulf of Suez, where canals have at various times provided a link with the Mediterranean. The Levant is the name given by Europeans

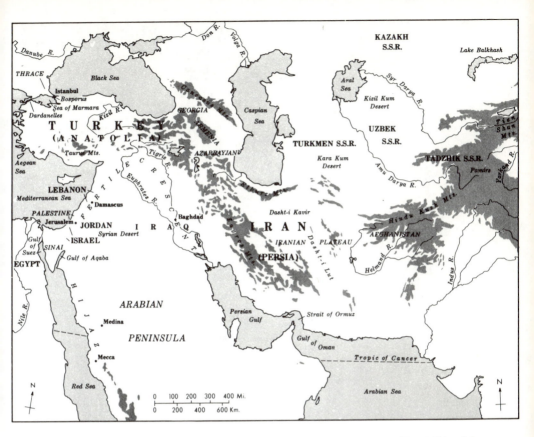

Map 1 West Asia

to the eastern coast of the Mediterranean, consisting of Syria and Palestine—the western arc of the curving belt of arable lands extending westward out of Mesopotamia known as the Fertile Crescent—and including the region long known to Christians as the Holy Land. The modern states of Jordan, Israel, Lebanon, Syria, and Iraq contain such historic centers as Jerusalem, Damascus, and Baghdad.

South Asia, the Indian subcontinent, has throughout its history interacted with West Asia and Central Asia along overland communication routes. India has also played a role as an intermediary in maritime trade between Southeast Asia and areas to the west, and South Asian values and institutions have made a profound impact on the culture of both peninsular and insular Southeast Asia. Natural barriers, the mountains of Tibet and western China and the nearly impenetrable jungles of Burma, have contributed to preventing direct commercial or military contact between India and China, but cultural contacts have been profoundly important, particularly the spread of Buddhism from South Asia to East Asia. For the purposes of this text, our focus in South Asia lies in the northern part of India, in particular the watersheds of the Indus and the Ganges rivers. This was the locus of the earliest civilized communities in South Asia and later of the greatest states. The Indus flows in a southwesterly direction from its headwaters in the Himalayan Mountains. The Indus plain is bordered on the west by the foothills that rise up to the mountainous massif of central Afghanistan and extend westward into the region known as Baluchistan, where they descend toward the Makran coast of the Arabian Sea some two degrees north of the Tropic of Cancer. Land routes lead westward from the Indus basin to Iran through Kandahar and, farther north, through Ghazni and Kabul. From the Kabul valley, passes lead northward

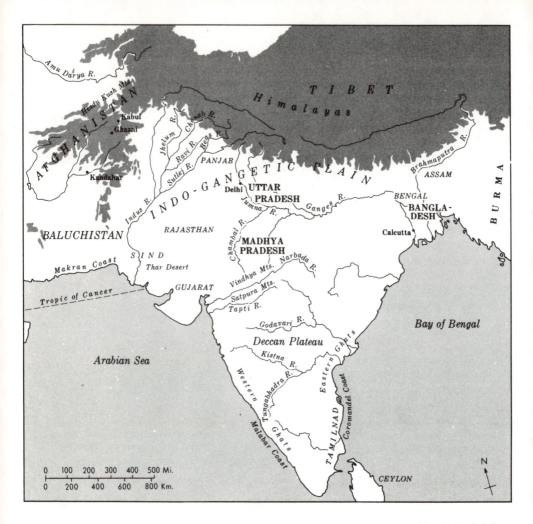

Map 2 South Asia

across the Hindu Kush Mountains into Central Asia. The major tributaries of the Indus flow across the Panjab, or "Land of the Five Rivers"—the Jhelum, the Chenab, the Ravi, the Beas, and the Sutlej. To the south the Indus region is cut off from the rest of the subcontinent by the Thar, or Great Indian Desert, and the arid portions of Rajasthan. From the Jumna, on which Delhi stands, and the upper reaches of the Ganges, the eastern arm of the Indo-Gangetic plain stretches some nine hundred miles to the sea near the modern city of Calcutta. The other major river of the north, the Brahmaputra, after leaving Tibet flows westward across Assam and turns south to form, with the Ganges, the vast deltaic region of Bengal, an important cultural subdivision of South Asia, currently divided between India and Bangladesh. The Narbada River, which flows west into the Arabian Sea, and the Vindhya and other low ranges running from west to east across the subcontinent have served to isolate the Deccan plateau and the far south of the peninsula from the north. The hilly terrain of much of central and southern India has tended to inhibit communication by land, prompting coastal peoples to turn to the sea. The Western Ghats, a range of mountains running close to the Arabian Sea, define the narrow coastal plain known in the far south as the Malabar coast. On the other side of the peninsula a wider coastal plain known as the Carnatic separates the Eastern Ghats from the Coromandel coast, facing the Bay of Bengal. The island of Ceylon, now the nation-state of Sri Lanka, which lies off the southern tip of the peninsula, is properly part of South Asia, but will play no part in our story.

Geographical factors have affected the history of civilization in South Asia in a number of important ways. The relative isolation of the southern coastal regions from the northern plains has meant that the former, which have had the most intensive contact with other cultures by sea, have had a relatively slight impact on the heartland of South Asia. In the north, exposure to invasion from West Asia and Central Asia has made possible repeated incursions into the Indian subcontinent by peoples who brought with them alien cultural influences, which constitute important elements in the pattern of South Asian civilization. In the Ganges region and in certain other areas, the rhythm of seasonal rainfall, the monsoon, caused by heavy rains drawn inland from the Indian Ocean by rising hot air in the warm season, followed by a dry period in the winter when cool air flows south from the Central Asian landmass, made possible an intensive rice agriculture and a dense population.

Southeast Asia includes both the arc of mainland Eurasia west of India and south of China and the thousands of islands of the Indonesian and Philippine archipelagos. Between China and Indochina, however, there is no sharp line of demarcation either in the form of a physical boundary or an historically stable political and cultural division. In the island world, common usage excludes Sri Lanka (Ceylon) on the west and Taiwan to the north from inclusion in Southeast Asia. From an analytical perspective, in terms of social and cultural history, a strong argument could be made for including those islands with their neighbors in Southeast Asia.

The dominant characteristic of the physical geography of Southeast Asia, and a fact that goes far towards explaining why a culturally uniform and politically organized society never developed in the area, is the fragmentation and dispersal of the habitable land over great distances separated by mountains and water. The land area of Southeast Asia totals some 1.5 million square miles, slightly less than South Asia, and yet this land extends over an area that is some two thousand miles from west to east and a similar distance from north to south. Most of the major rivers of mainland Southeast Asia originate in the eastern end of the Tibetan plateau, where they are flanked by the headwaters of the Brahmaputra and the Yangtze. The Irrawaddy and the Salween are the principal rivers that flow southward through Burma, reaching the Andaman Sea on the western side of the Malay peninsula. In Thailand the Chao Phraya (Menam), a relatively short waterway, enters the Gulf of Thailand near the modern capital of Bangkok. The principal river of Indochina, the Mekong, flows for half its length through China before it enters Laos, defining for a distance the border between that country and Thailand before it enters Cambodia and crosses South Vietnam in the area known in French colonial times as Cochin China, where it debouches into the South China Sea. Along its course the Mekong passes the present capitals of Luang Prabang and Vientiane in Laos and Phnom Penh in Cambodia. The Red River, which originates in southwest China, flows to the sea across North Vietnam, the area once termed Tonkin by the French, and then passes through the city of Hanoi before it reaches the Gulf of Tonkin, a body of water that is defined by the southern projection of the Chinese Luichow peninsula and Hainan Island.

In general, the mountains of the mainland run north to south between the rivers just described, a fact that, together with the prevalence of heavy jungle cover, contributes to the isolation of the valleys. Another isolating feature is the extremely extended coastline. The coastline of Burma runs south from Bangladesh in the Arakan Mountain region until it reaches the Irrawaddy River delta, where it runs briefly eastward to the south of the Pegu Range before turning south along the Tenasserim coast on the Malay peninsula. The Malay

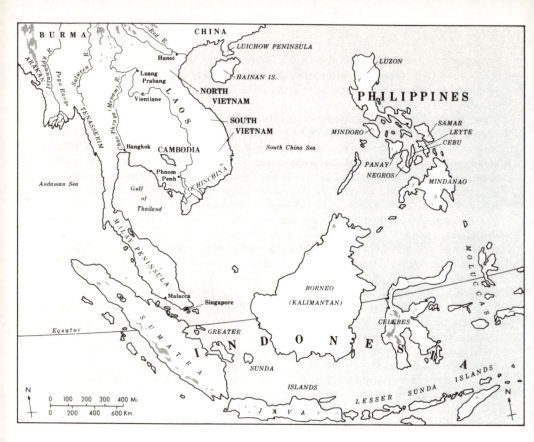

Map 3 Southeast Asia

peninsula is a long narrow arm of land that effectively lengthens the distance by sea between the western and eastern coasts of the mainland. As a consequence of this fact, such locations as Malacca and Singapore, at the tip of the peninsula, became strategic points for the control of sea-lanes and commerce. On the eastern side of the peninsula the Gulf of Thailand forms a southward-facing arc of coastline, while the elongated coast of Vietnam faces eastward toward the South China Sea. Since the political boundaries of Southeast Asia are of recent historical origin, the reader is advised that contemporary national terms are employed here for convenience purposes only.

The islands of the Indonesian archipelago are conventionally grouped into the Greater Sunda Islands, the Lesser Sunda Islands, Celebes, the Moluccas, and New Guinea (Irian). The Greater Sundas include the major islands of Sumatra, Borneo (Kalimantan), and Java. The Lesser Sundas and the Moluccas were important in the spice trade but have played a minor role in the history of Southeast Asian civilization. The principal islands of the Philippines are Luzon, Mindoro, Panay, Negros, Cebu, Samar, Leyte, and Mindanao. Southeast Asia lies on both sides of the equator, but only a tip of Burma extends north of the Tropic of Cancer. This fact, together with the abundance of rainfall, made wet-rice agriculture possible on the limited floodplains and deltas of the great rivers, but in mountainous areas the leaching effects of heavy rains often dictated a migrant slash-and-burn pattern of agriculture. Most important for cultural history, the accessibility of this fragmented landmass from the sea made Southeast Asia uniquely susceptible to the penetration of cultural influences from other parts of Eurasia. India certainly had the greatest impact, but Chinese institutions and values played a strong part in shaping Vietnamese culture, and Chinese commerce and immigration is an important feature throughout Southeast Asian history. Arab trade has long been important, and much of the population professes the Islamic faith. In modern times European and Japanese occupation and administration have introduced a further heritage of influences from those areas.

East Asia, by virtue of its physical location, was the most remote of the culture zones of Eurasia, but not isolated from the others. Its boundaries are indistinct. China, Vietnam, Korea, and Japan are the most important societies that have shared in a common East Asian civilization. The minority groups of southern and western China and the Tibetans, Mongols, and Manchus have periodically been drawn into the Chinese state and thus qualify as at least participants in the creation of the common cultural traditions of East Asia. Contact between East Asia and the other centers of civilization was limited by the great distance around Southeast Asia by sea, the mountains of western China, and the deserts of Central Asia. China proper is defined on the west by the Tibetan massif and on the north by the break between the steppe and sown, roughly along the line of the Great Wall. River valleys and their floodplains have provided the best locations for agriculture. In the south the Hsi (West) River meets the sea near Canton and Hong Kong. The Yangtze crosses the middle of China from the great Szechwan Basin in the west, through the lake country and the complex network of inland waterways, and past Nanking and Shanghai in the east. To the north, silt from the Yellow River (Huang Ho), which has altered its course north and south of the Shantung peninsula, has accumulated to form the north China plain, which stretches seven hundred miles from Nanking to Peking. Between the Yangtze and Yellow rivers is the transitional zone that marks off the warm south, where crops may be grown the year round, from the north, where cold air from Siberia makes winters frigid. In Manchuria the Liao River courses the wide valley east of the Greater Khingan Mountains and south of the Lesser Khingan Range. The Liaotung peninsula projects toward the Shantung peninsula to form the Po Hai, a northern annex to the Yellow Sea.

The Korean peninsula is demarcated by the Yalu River on the west and the Tumen on the east. The four main islands of the Japanese archipelago are, from north to south, Hokkaido (the last to be fully settled by Japanese), Honshu (the locus for most of the developments treated here), and the smaller islands of Shikoku and Kyushu. Formed originally by volcanic action, these islands are predominantly mountainous terrain. Both settled agriculture and urban life have occurred primarily on the coastal plains or in narrow valleys created by rivers debouching into the sea. The largest and most fertile of the plains are located on the island of Honshu, around the modern city of Tokyo and in the region of the neighboring cities of Osaka and Kyoto. These, and many smaller fertile plains, face the Pacific Ocean or the Inland Sea passage between Honshu and Shikoku and now, as in previous periods, have the highest concentration of population. Unlike China and other continental regions, there are no great rivers or, with the exception of Hokkaido, extensive grasslands for herding. Again with the exception of Hokkaido, the climate is made moderate by the warm ocean currents. One other geographical fact that has had important ramifications for Japanese history is its relative isolation. Over one hundred miles separate Japan from the tip of the Korean peninsula, the closest contact with mainland Asia. China lies several hundred miles southwest over rough waters. This has meant that the Japanese could interact with other East Asians, but it was difficult for outsiders to force that interaction or to incorporate Japan into a larger political unit.

Central Asia, or Inner Asia, is the expanse of steppes, deserts, and mountains that extend across Eurasia from the Caspian Sea and the Ural Mountains to Manchuria. Low rainfall and severe annual temperature variation made most of this area unsuitable for agriculture and therefore generally inhospitable to dense urban habitation. The peoples who lived in this region developed an economy and social organization based on a highly specialized form of animal husbandry. This style of life, which depended on seasonal migrations in quest of

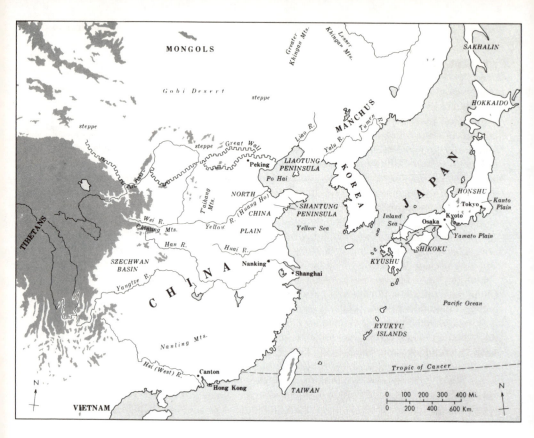

Map 4 East Asia

new grazing grounds, has been termed nomadic pastoralism. Where cities did occur in Central Asia, in the oases, on the river banks, and on the caravan routes, they were primarily extensions or outposts of the great sedentary civilizations (mainly Iranian and Chinese) on the fringes of Central Asia. The Volga River flows southward into the Caspian Sea. East of the Volga, in a north-south direction, lie the Ural Mountains, the conventional demarcation line between Europe and Asia. To the southeast lies the Aral Sea, fed by the Syr Darya (Jaxartes), which rises in the foothills of the Tien Shan Mountains, and the Amu Darya (Oxus), with its headwaters in the Pamirs. Across this region lay the land routes that connected West, South, and East Asia and passed through such ancient centers as Bokhara, Samarqand, Kashgar, and Khotan. East-west travel had to go north of the Tibetan plateau and either north or south of the Takla Makan desert, which lay between the Kunlun and Tien Shan mountain ranges. North of the Tien Shan Mountains lies the area to which the Russians have given the name of Semirechie, grasslands extending from the vicinity of Lake Balkhash in the west in the direction of the Altai Mountains to the northeast. Eastwards, beyond the pass known as the Dzungarian Gates, lie Dzungaria and Mongolia. Mongolia is bordered on the north by Lake Baikal and several mountain ranges, on the east by the Greater Khingan Mountains, and on the south by China, with the Gobi desert acting as a barrier separating them. Central Asia was important to the Eurasian civilizations in two respects. First of all, its caravan routes and oases facilitated the exchange of goods, peoples, and ideas between the centers of sedentary civilization. Second, it acted as a great reservoir from whence nomadic pastoralists, when mobilized for war, could strike at those same centers of sedentary civilization with devastating effect.

xxviii

BIBLIOGRAPHY

Bagby, Philip, *Culture and History: Prolegomena to the Comparative Study of Civilization* (University of California Press paperback, 1963), 244 pp. An effort to apply anthropological insights to the creation of definitions and guidelines for the comparison of civilizations.

Kroeber, Alfred L., *Anthropology* (New York, 1923; revised 1948), pp. 311-85. Chapters 8 and 9 of this work provide an influential early discussion of pattern and process which differs in some respects from the definitions employed here.

—————, *An Anthropologist Looks at History* (University of California Press paperback, 1963), 213 pp. Posthumous essays of a great anthropologist, including seven papers dealing with the comparison of civilizations.

McNeill, William H., *The Rise of the West: A History of the Human Community* (University of Chicago paperback, 1963), 828 pp. A brilliant and readable overview of Eurasian history with a tendency to stress interaction and influence among civilizations.

Redfield, Robert, *The Little Community and Peasant Society and Culture* (Chicago University Press, 1960), 182 pp. and 92 pp. The second of these combined essays contains some of the reflections of a noted anthropologist on the relationship between the local community and the civilization.

GLOSSARY

Civilization. The largest distinct cultural unit in human organization consisting of shared social norms, traditions and institutions persisting through historical time from one generation to the next. Usually this involves a "great tradition" fostered by a literate elite that consciously promotes the core values.

Culture zone. A subdivision of Asia characterized by common cultural traits, in some cases a common civilization.

East Asia. The western Pacific coast and islands including China, Japan, Korea, and sometimes Vietnam and extending inland to Tibet, Chinese Turkistan, and Mongolia.

Great tradition. The values and conventions of a dominant elite consciously propagated over a span of generations as the core of a civilized tradition. The great tradition is normally embodied in literature that is widely disseminated throughout a culture area, in contrast to a little tradition, which is embodied in the local community and tends to be orally transmitted.

Pattern. A particular instance of a generalized process of social change characterized by the influence of the physical location, historical antecedents, and social condition.

Period. The historical era or division of time in which a particular topic is discussed in this text.

Process. A characterization of social change in general terms without reference to a particular time and place, used for purposes of analysis and comparison of specific instances.

South Asia. The Indian subcontinent including the present-day territory of Pakistan, India, Bangladesh, and Sri Lanka (Ceylon).

Southeast Asia. The region south of East Asia and east of South Asia, including the arc of the Eurasian mainland from Burma to Vietnam and the islands of the Indonesian and Philippine archipelagos.

Steppe. Treeless, often arid plains of the Eurasian heartland.

West Asia. Known also as the Middle East or Near East, this area includes Turkey, Iran, and Arabia and the Fertile Crescent. For the purpose of this text, it also includes Afghanistan and the Soviet Central Asian Republics.

Early Modern Empires in Asia

1350 to 1850

Following a prolonged era of regional fragmentation and the brief experience of Central Asian domination, the principal culture zones of Asia were once again unified by great land-based empires. Included among these states of the period 1350 to 1850 were the Ottoman empire in West Asia, the Safavids in Iran, the Mughuls in India, the Ming and subsequent Ch'ing dynasties in China, and the Tokugawa regime in Japan. The Czarist Russian empire in northern Eurasia offers a counterexample with some Western cultural dimensions. The early modern empires resembled the universal empires of the ancient period in the sense that they were built upon a preindustrial agricultural base by hereditary military regimes employing foot soldiers and horsemen. They differed from their earliest predecessors, however, in that civilized society had grown in scale and complexity, considerable advances had been made in technology, and the passage of centuries had deepened the cultural traditions of each civilization. The universal religions, especially, tended to offer a measure by which Asians chose to define their civilizations. Early modern empires, in rationalizing their rule, gave special attention to this cultural dimension. The advent of printing and increased literacy made possible an intensive cultural policy on the part of the state. Early modern empires can be variously characterized as culturalistic or pluralistic, depending on their cultural policy and the foreign or indigenous origin of their rulers. In Anatolia a Turkish conquest group took up the Islamic banner in the long-standing hostilities with Christian Europe and others, and extended its holdings widely, bringing the Balkans as well as Egypt, Arabia, and Mesopotamia under its power. In Iran, a confederation of Qizilbash tribes consolidated a broad area into the Safavid empire, a state that patronized Shii Islam. The Mughuls, a name derived from the word "Mongol," were an essentially Turkish conquest group that controlled northern India through a pluralistic state system based on Muslim rule but incorporating indigenous Hindu elements. In China the Ming expelled the Mongols in the fourteenth century and established a centralized bureaucratic polity that promoted Confucianism as a state ideology. The Ch'ing dynasty, which was founded by invading Manchus after 1644, continued the essential outlines of Ming institutions. The Tokugawa regime in Japan was based on a carefully maintained balance of feudal lords held in check by a military hegemon who ruled while the hereditary imperial line was preserved in impotent isolation. In the broadest terms the early modern empires may be regarded as agents of cultural conservatism, reviving and preserving traditional values after the Mongol conquests. Social and political stability were among the outstanding achievements of these states, a fact that has often prompted Westerners to view Asian societies as static.

9

PROCESSES

The Creation and Maintenance of Early Modern Empires

a. Military conquest
b. Reunification of the culture area: control of frontiers
c. Domination of the economy and society

The Cultural Legitimation of Early Modern Empires

d. Promotion of the cultural tradition: culturalism and pluralism
e. Manipulation and modification of cultural forms

Consequences of the Formation of Early Modern Empires

PATTERNS

1. The Ottomans in West Asia

2. The Safavids in Iran

3. The Mughuls in South Asia

4. The Ming and Ch'ing Empires in China

5. Tokugawa Japan

9. EARLY MODERN EMPIRES

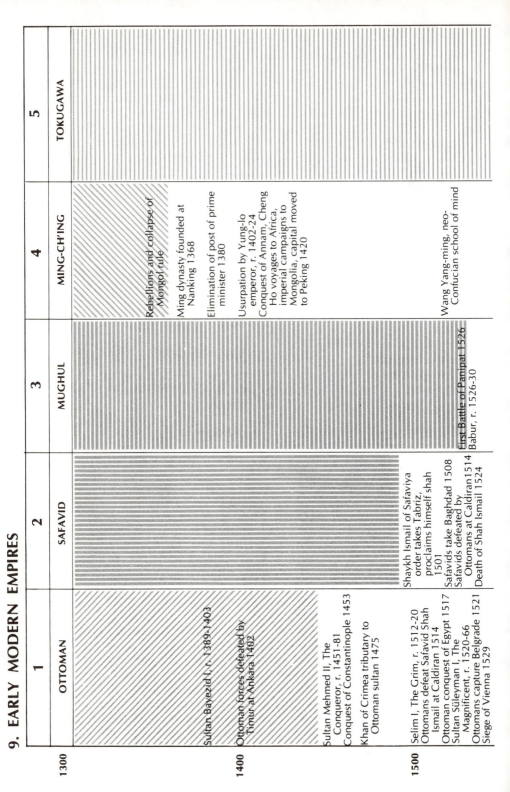

	1	2	3	4	5
	OTTOMAN	SAFAVID	MUGHUL	MING-CH'ING	TOKUGAWA
1300					
				Rebellions and collapse of Mongol rule	
				Ming dynasty founded at Nanking 1368	
				Elimination of post of prime minister 1380	
	Sultan Bayezid I, r. 1389–1403				
1400	Ottoman forces defeated by Timur at Ankara 1402			Usurpation by Yung-lo emperor, r. 1402-24 Conquest of Annam, Cheng Ho voyages to Africa, imperial campaigns to Mongolia, capital moved to Peking 1420	
	Sultan Mehmed II, The Conqueror, r. 1451-81 Conquest of Constantinople 1453				
	Khan of Crimea tributary to Ottoman sultan 1475				
		Shaykh Ismail of Safaviya order takes Tabriz, proclaims himself shah 1501			
	Selim I, The Grim, r. 1512-20 Ottomans defeat Safavid Shah Ismail at Caldiran 1514	Safavids take Baghdad 1508 Safavids defeated by Ottomans at Caldiran 1514			
1500	Ottoman conquest of Egypt 1517 Sultan Süleyman I, The Magnificent, r. 1520-66 Ottomans capture Belgrade 1521 Siege of Vienna 1529	Death of Shah Ismail 1524	First Battle of Panipat 1526 Babur, r. 1526-30	Wang Yang-ming, neo-Confucian school of mind	

	1600	1700	1800
	Nobunaga deposes Ashikaga shogun 1573		
	Hideyoshi establishes hegemony 1590		
	Tokugawa victory at Sekigahara 1600		
	Seclusion policy enforced 1620s and 1630s		
	Neo-Confucian college established 1630		
		Yoshimune as shogun 1716	
	Development of syncretic trends challenging orthodox neo-Confucianism		
	Factionalism at court intensified		
	Wei Chung-hsien, eunuch dictator		
	Peasant rebellions end Ming dynasty		
	Manchus establish the Ch'ing dynasty 1644		
	K'ang-hsi, r. 1662-1772, Chinese resistance in the south suppressed		
		Ch'ien-lung, r. 1736-95, patronage of Chinese scholarship	
		Rapid population growth Increased corruption	
		Spread of opium use	
	Humayun, r. 1530-40 and 1555-56 Second Battle of Panipat 1556		
	Akbar, r. 1556-1605		
	Jahangir, r. 1605-1627		
	Shah Jahan, r. 1627-58 Partial pacification of the Deccan 1636		
	Awrangzeb, r. 1658-1707		
	Awrangzeb leaves Delhi for Deccan 1681 Mughuls take sultanates of Bijapur and Golconda 1687		
		Death of Awrangzeb 1707	
	Ottomans take Tabriz and Baghdad 1534		
	Shah Abbas I, r. 1588-1629		
	Portuguese expelled from Hormuz 1622 Safavids reconquer Baghdad 1623 Baghdad lost to Ottomans 1638		
	Shah Abbas II, r. 1642-66		
		Shah Sultan Husayn, r. 1694-1722	
	Conquest of Baghdad 1534		

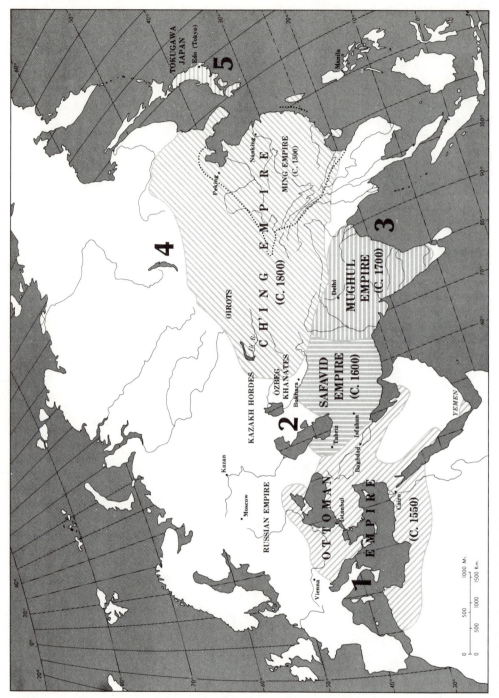

Map 37 Early modern empires in Asia

PROCESSES

Following the period of Central Asian domination, Asia came to be divided among a number of huge states that we call early modern empires. The era of these great empires lasted from around 1350 to 1850, and some of them persisted even into the twentieth century. Historically, these empires are significant both in terms of what preceded them and what came after them, for they provide a link between the earlier eras of regional cultural development and a more recent and familiar period of intensified global interaction. In their inception these empires constituted both an embodiment of the values of the cultural heritage derived from the historical experiences of universal empires and universal religions discussed in Chapters 4, 5, and 6, and a domestication of elements of Mongol rule considered in Chapter 8. In their demise, as will be seen in subsequent chapters, they constituted the forms of social organization that Western Europeans encountered in Asia in modern times and the institutional structures that conditioned the patterns of technological change and nationalism in Asia.

THE PERIOD

The early modern empires of Asia were roughly contemporaneous with the Portuguese, Spanish, Dutch, and English empires. Those empires were based on maritime expansion and differed in a number of fundamental respects from the Asian empires, which were formed by the control of contiguous land areas. For this reason the discussion of the European empires will be left to a later chapter in which they will be considered in terms of the interaction of civilizations under the title "Maritime Integration Under Western European Domination." The principal patterns to be considered here are: Safavid empire (1501-1722) in Iran; the Ottoman empire (1453-1918) formed by the Ottoman Turks in West Asia, eastern Europe, and northern Africa; the Mughul empire (1526-1739) in India; the indigenous Ming empire (1368-1644) and the foreign (Manchu) Ch'ing empire (1644-1911) in China. The Tokugawa state (1600-1868) in Japan was much more limited in size and cultural diversity than were any of the above but can fruitfully be treated under the same rubrics. The Russian empire (1480-1917) in northern Eurasia would be the most readily comparable "Western" example of an early modern empire.

In terms of the development of the various civilizations of Asia, the formation of early modern empires was in most cases a consequence of the experience of Mongol pressures in the preceding period. In some cases, notably China and Russia, the conquest and domination by Central Asians stimulated a reassertion of regional cultural values. To some extent, this response to external threats reflected a defensive or conservative psychology in which the peoples of a cultural area rallied to preserve the essential elements in their civilization from further intrusions. In other cases, especially the Safavids, Ottomans, Mughuls, and Manchus, Central Asian domination provided a model for the transformation of tribal organizations into empires through the conquest of civilized areas. Here, too, indigenous tradition played a significant role in defining the empire. The Safavid advocacy of an appeal to Shii loyalties helped to make Shiism the dominant faith in Iran. The Ottoman concept of the holy war against the unbelievers reinforced the historic sense of Islamic community in West Asia and northern Africa.

The early modern empires were vehicles of cultural resurgence in the sense that they reunified whole culture areas that had known unification before. In their scope the early modern empires were comparable to the universal empires of the ancient period. In a historical perspective, however, the two groups of empires differed markedly. In the first place, the universal states of the first millennium B.C. unified culture areas in a way that was without precedent, and by so doing shaped the subsequent development of the civilization in a unique way. All empires that followed, the early modern empires included, were constrained by established precedent and to varying degrees defined themselves retrospectively in terms of their predecessors. Secondly, the very fact that each culture area had experienced periods of relative political integration and division limited the claims that could be made for a new empire in the early modern period.

The significance of the early modern empires is perhaps best revealed by the degree to which they embodied developmental changes that were cumulative throughout history. Like the universal empires of the ancient period, the early modern empires were land empires based on a predominantly agricultural economy. The early modern "preindustrial" economy had evolved through incremental changes far beyond the stages reached in the pre-Christian era. Growth in population, increase in land area under cultivation, and improvements in techniques, tools, and seeds meant both that the total agricultural output was greater and that a greater portion of it was available to support nonagricultural activities. Likewise in industry, while the use of inanimate power sources and capital accumulation did not reach the stages of rationalization that characterized the industrial revolution, there were substantial advances in technologies, such as mining, smelting, weaving, pottery, silk production, paper making, boat building, architecture, chemicals, and weaponry. Applied to an activity like warfare, these incremental advances gave the early modern empire capabilities that surpassed previous eras in terms of equipment, techniques, and the scale of operations.

A most important technological advance in the early modern period was the development of printing, which significantly facilitated the collection, storage, and dissemination of information. The growth of a relatively large and sophisticated literate class, which staffed the elaborate bureaucracies of the early modern empires, made it possible for those regimes to pursue active managerial roles in their societies, particularly with regard to cultural and ideological affairs. While physical sciences, technology, and industrial practices did not undergo the open-ended, intentional, and cumulative rationalization that was characteristic of a later stage of modernization, advances in the social-control capabilities of the early modern empires were unprecedented. The fact that control was aimed primarily at social stability has often prompted Westerners, thinking in terms of economic development or an even vaguer notion of "progress," to regard Asian societies as static or stagnant. A better view would be to see the size and endurance of the great Asian empires as positive achievements in the management of the social environment. If one includes in the definition of modernization the enhancement of control over the human as well as the natural environment, then the political integration and bureaucratic organization of the early modern empires appear as significant developments.

THE CREATION AND MAINTENANCE OF EARLY MODERN EMPIRES

a. Military Conquest

Early modern empires were founded in all cases by military conquest. In some instances the conquest was the result of invasion by an outside or peripheral element (such as the Ottoman Turks in West Asia or the Manchus in China), and in other instances of unification by an indigenous group driving out foreign elements (the Ming founder in China) or success in internal warfare (Tokugawa Japan). In any case, the new ruling group faced the task of converting itself from a military machine into the core of a stable and reasonably efficient bureaucratic state. The goals of the ruler were paramount and the viability of the new regime depended on the ruler's ability to accomplish his goals within the conditions of the society he conquered. Such factors as the cultural and ethnic homogeneity of the society, the availability of resources, the strength of potential rivals, and geographical conditions influenced the character of the resulting regime.

b.   Reunification of the Culture Area: Control of Frontiers

One of the primary objectives in the formation of an empire was the control of the frontier areas. Insofar as the empire was the instrument for the preservation of civilization, the defense of its perimeter may be considered to have been its paramount function. From this perspective, the empire was—in its most essential form—an instrument for delineating and enforcing the boundaries of a culture area. Stabilization of frontiers could take many forms, from defensive policies of exclusion aimed at keeping barbarians out to aggressive policies of inclusion by conquest, annexation, and assimilation. In addition to military activity, frontier arrangements involved the monitoring of travel, of trade, and of cultural contacts between the interior of the empire and the outside. As we shall see, the nature of frontier stabilization varied with the nature of the regime.

The ability to control territory and define frontiers—essential for any political system— was a function of power. It must be stressed that the early modern empires began as regimes of military conquest and always retained the configuration of military dictatorships. Once in power, the military apparatus was augmented by the creation of civil organs and programs to increase acceptance and support. Nevertheless, military power was always held in reserve. The degeneration of the military or rulers who neglected military affairs often imperiled the state. Usually there were special institutions that tied the military establishment to the ruler, such as a special royal guard composed of elite forces loyal to the ruler himself. Strict measures were designed to keep this group separate from powerful interests in the bureaucracy or the nobility. In extreme cases this royal guard might be composed of foreign elements, like the Swiss Guards who protected the Pope in the Vatican.

Military organization and technology in the early modern period showed clear signs of Mongol influence. The great innovations of the period of Central Asian domination were reflected in mixed forces, including infantry, mounted archers with increasingly effective armor, and siege-warfare specialists, organized in decimal units and coordinated through rapid signal and relay communications systems. Another feature that became characteristic of warfare during the thirteenth and fourteenth centuries was the increasing use of gunpowder and the development of artillery, which gave a relative advantage to imperial power at the expense of local autonomy.

c.   Domination of the Economy and Society

Unification of the physical territory of an entire culture area under a single political authority—which was the continuing task of the ruler of an early modern empire—was possible only so long as the ruler could draw on the energies of the peoples under his rule. Reduced to the simplest terms, the politics of the early modern empire may be understood as a process by which the ruler attempted to exert his control over the society and extract from it the resources he needed. By resources we mean all the goods and services the ruler used to carry out the activities of the state: money, food, raw materials, manufactured products, manpower, and specialized talent. Social control includes measures that elevated the ruler above the rest of society and specified the forms of obligation and support that each sector in the polity owed to the state.

The total wealth at the disposal of any society and the way it was distributed within the society determined to a large extent what scale of a state could be supported. It was in the ruler's interest to have resources in as "free" a state as possible—that is, to have them available when needed and not become the preserve of some specialized group that might withhold support. This was a frequent source of conflict within the empire as the ruler tried

The military might of early modern empires owed much to Mongol experience with cavalry warfare.

9.1 The army of the Ottoman sultan, Süleyman the Magnificent (1520-66), crossing the river Drava in Hungary, 1566. Ottoman Turkish miniature, sixteenth century. The *sipahis* are crossing the river under the eyes of the sultan while the Janissaries wait on the left bank. Courtesy: Chester Beatty Library, Dublin.

9.2 A Qizilbash horseman of the seventeenth century. It was by means of the highly mobile cavalry provided by the nine Turcoman tribes known as Qizilbash ("Red Heads") that the Safavids acquired control of Iran and kept their Ottoman, Özbeg, and Mughul neighbors at bay. Source: J. Chardin, *Voyages du Chevalier Chardin, en Perse,* ed. Langles (Paris, 1811), Plate 29.

to consolidate his control over major resources. Normally the ruler of a bureaucratic empire would draw whatever goods and services he needed from his empire by means of a system of taxation and compulsory service. When the needed resources were the special preserve of some vested interest group, the ruler would be obliged to engage in a power struggle with competitors. For example, if monasteries held too much money in their treasuries or were keeping too much land off the tax roles or too many men out of military service, the ruler might find it necessary to enact laws restricting the operations of religious groups. Similarly, rich landlords and merchants could find themselves the victims of confiscatory policies. With specialized kinds of resources the bureaucratic regime usually organized its own source of supply in the form of state monopolies, mines, arsenals, horse farms, and the like.

One of the greatest powers the ruler of the bureaucratic empire possessed was control over the symbols of status. Rule was generally hereditary, and the royal house reserved special titles of kingship to its own line, which assigned it a unique role in the society and often characterized the ruler in terms of the welfare of the entire society as an agent of divine power or a link to the cosmic order. Close supporters of the ruling house might be given titles of nobility and social privileges. Being able to determine who would enjoy the most important ranks and privileges gave the ruler a powerful device for winning capable, ambitious, and powerful people over to his cause. Religious orders, feudal orders, tribal and other groups that still commanded great respect in the society represented limitations on the ruler's control over status and thus provided alternative modes of advancement for ambitious individuals which might not involve service to the regime and might even involve activities contrary to the imperial interests.

In the early modern society the bulk of the populace occupied mean or servile positions, variously characterized as peasants, serfs, slaves, retainers, or servants. Since the amount of wealth available was less than in a predominantly industrial society, the nonlaboring classes—especially the ruling elite, the military leadership, and religious authorities and scholars—represented a tiny segment of the total population. Consequently, the gap in standard of living between the elite and the mass of the commoners was correspondingly great. Strict enforcement of class distinctions was necessary to assure stability. Commoners and members of the lower classes were forbidden to take part in political activities. It was in the interests of the ruler and the state to discourage social change and to reinforce social distinctions that kept most of the populace in submissive roles. Special attention was given to recruiting and training talented individuals for service in the bureaucracy. Often the state organized its own training system to provide a supply of officials. An officialdom based on talent was a major asset to the centralized state because the individuals involved owed their allegiance to the state that recruited them and they lacked the security of a hereditary class.

THE CULTURAL LEGITIMATION OF EARLY MODERN EMPIRES

The rulers of early modern empires consciously and systematically sought to legitimize their rule by appeal to religious and ideological traditions. Thus, an emperor might claim to rule on behalf of a god or to be an authority in spiritual or ideological questions. Motivations for such claims could vary in individual instances, from the most cynical expediency to sincere conviction that a ruler was acting as an instrument of divine will. If we view this same matter from the perspective of the cultural tradition—from the point of view of religion, ideology, or other elite culture forms—the legitimation of the ruler takes on great importance. Where the ruler was successful in adapting cultural symbols to political ends, the whole corpus of cultural values could become politicized in the sense that they became so tied to the state that they no longer had an independent course of development. Political considerations and the interests of the state became prime determinants in the direction of cultural change. Where this tendency was most pronounced, the core values of the civilization were thought to be embodied in the institution of the early modern empire, and the demise of that empire was viewed as a blow to the civilized tradition itself. It is for this reason that we need to pay particular attention to the cultural orientation of the early modern empire.

d.   Promotion of the Cultural Tradition: Culturism and Pluralism

In the creation of the early modern empire the rallying cry around which the society was to be united and a new polity formed was a sense of common culture either in the form of a religion or a state ideology. This culture provided the basis for a strong sense of identity and a distinction between the dominant group in the empire, which considered itself to be civilized, and outsiders, who were thought to be barbaric and a threat to civilization. The founding of the empire was infused with a sense of mission—the salvation and preservation of the cultural heritage.

Because the empire was inspired by a sense of mission, there was a strong tendency for the state to promote an orthodox religion or ideology. In practice, this orthodoxy might have extended only to certain classes of the population that were more politically potent and active. Where a church or religious leadership already existed, the state would forge links to those groups, often co-opting them into service to the throne. The state could either patronize existing institutions and organizations or form new ones. State schools and academic institutions elaborated and propagated orthodox values.

The form that cultural policy took was often determined by the relative cultural uniformity of the empire. Two types of orientation may be identified. Those empires that were based on culturally homogeneous societies we may call culturistic empires. Those that included diverse cultural elements we may characterize as pluralistic empires. The degree of cultural diversity influenced greatly the policies of the empires in a number of areas. In general, the more uniform, or culturistic, empires were those that were formed in response to external threats to a civilized area. These empires tended to place the greatest emphasis on tradition and the preservation of the heritage of the past. Internally there was a strong tendency for state policy to encourage cultural uniformity within the society and suppress deviance and change. Externally, the culturalistic state was defensively oriented and shunned extensive contact with outside influences. Examples of culturalistic states would be Safavid Iran, Ming China, and Tokugawa Japan.

The pluralistic empire by definition was one that incorporated diffuse cultural elements. Often these empires were the products of conquest. The ruling group was composed of outsiders who had to accommodate themselves to the culture of the people and the region they subdued. Cultural policy in these empires had to be flexible enough to accommodate to the differences of a mixed society and yet support the position of the rulers. In some cases, this could be accomplished by the rulers becoming cultural converts and then patrons of the indigenous culture. This placed the conqueror in the position of acting as the custodian of someone else's heritage. Inevitably, the result was a considerable reinterpretation of that heritage and particularly the suppression of those elements that were least congenial to the conquest group. Another development not uncommon to this situation was a tendency for these converts to take extreme and uncompromising views of their new faith. Internally, pluralistic empires were characterized by special administrative arrangements to accommodate the machinery of government to a mixed society. The imposition of an outside ruling group on top of a conquered society led to ethnic or racial stratification in which various classes could have distinct religious values, social customs, and even languages. Often the government found it necessary to utilize more than one language in official documents, staffing bureaucratic posts with multiple sets of officials, translators, and interpreters.

Externally, the pluralistic empires were more prone to expansion and wars of conquest. Ideologically, the rulers of pluralistic empires had to rationalize their rule in terms of universal sanctions that would justify their initial conquests. In the extreme case this could lead to the claim that the ruler was spreading a true faith and therefore had a right and duty to continue annexing new territories. Where the pluralistic empire could not easily convert subject peoples it could encapsulate them within its boundaries by allowing them varying degrees of self-rule. Examples of pluralistic empires are the Ottomans in West Asia, the Mughuls in India, and the Ch'ing in China. The Ottomans were a Turkish people who used Islam to justify widespread conquest of Islamic and non-Islamic peoples. The Manchus, who invaded China to form the Ch'ing empire, became ardent proponents of Chinese culture but also controlled vast areas of Manchuria, Mongolia, and Central Asia beyond China proper. The Mughuls are of particular interest because of the conflicting demands of the Hindu and Islamic cultural elements in their environment and because of the varied cultural policies of early Mughul rulers.

e.   Manipulation and Modification of Cultural Forms

Where the early modern empire entered into the promotion of cultural values, it did so for political purposes. The patronage of culture by a bureaucratic state led inevitably to the modification of cultural forms. In the simplest cases, this modification of cultural values by political influences might have been nothing more than a reflection of the personal whims of a given monarch. A ruler who liked a particular style of architecture or painting might have chosen to patronize practitioners of that style at the expense of others. In other cases, the influence of state patronage took on a more systematic and penetrating character. Particularly in areas of religion and ideology, state patronage was selectively directed toward those thinkers and doctrines that were most supportive of the ruler's position. Patronage inevitably led the state to the practice of thought control. This could include such methods as the suppression of certain parts of the inherited tradition, the banning of heterodox interpretations of sacred texts, the persecution and elimination of heretical thinkers, the supervision of education, book burning, the patronage of orthodox scholarship, and various measures to discourage contact with other societies.

This intervention of the state into the realm of cultural values was by no means a new development with the early modern empires. What was new in the early modern period was the systematic, rational, and explicit character of state cultural policy. The state now saw itself as a legitimate custodian of tradition and took an active hand in modifying and manipulating tradition to state ends. The increase in literacy and the accumulation and circulation of printed material made it necessary for the state to be more active in these areas than had been the case in earlier ages.

CONSEQUENCES OF THE FORMATION OF EARLY MODERN EMPIRES

The processes of political control and cultural promotion discussed here were not essentially different from the core activities of other political systems. What was outstanding in the case of the early modern empires was the intensity and the persistence of the exercise of centralized political control. The result of this prolonged experience of political union was often to freeze the cultural forms of an area in such a manner that core values of the civilization became imbedded in the institutions of the empire. This very much influenced the direction in which the civilizations developed in the subsequent era of technological change, European intrusion, and nationalism. Those empires, like the Ch'ing, the Tokugawa, or the Russian, that showed the greatest stability lasted the longest but eventually faced the most extreme transformation of cultural forms. Confucianism died with the emperorship; samurai institutions with the shogunate. Those empires with the most pluralistic social bases, like the Mughuls and the Ottomans, displayed the lowest levels of national or group consciousness (as distinguished from religious affiliation). In other words, where the state was least influential, the cultural traditions were least threatened by its passing.

PATTERNS

1. THE OTTOMANS IN WEST ASIA

The Establishment of the Ottoman Empire

The early growth of the Ottoman sultanate has been briefly described in Chapter 8. One of several *ghazi* principalities that arose in western Anatolia upon the ruins of the former Seljuk sultanate of Rum, it had, by the second half of the fourteenth century, eliminated all would-be rivals and was already a formidable power in southeastern Europe. Sultan Bayezid I (r. 1389-1403) advanced the Ottoman frontier deep into the Balkans while maintaining a fairly effective blockade against Constantinople itself, which he would have surely conquered but for the intervention of Timur. In Asia he extended Ottoman rule into eastern Anatolia and seized the Mamluk frontier towns in the upper Euphrates valley, although by so doing he provoked the hostility of Timur, who brought the sultan's forces to bay at Ankara (1402), where Bayezid suffered the humiliation of defeat and capture. In the wake of Timur's destructive thrust into western Anatolia there occurred a temporary lull in the hitherto uninterrupted course of Ottoman expansion, and the next half century was characterized first by internal consolidation and then by renewed expansion in the Balkans.

It was Mehmed II (r. 1451-81), known as The Conqueror, who made the Ottoman Turks the dominant power in the eastern Mediterranean. In 1453 he besieged and captured Constantinople, which he renamed Istanbul and which now replaced Edirne in Thrace as capital of the empire. Master of both shores of the Bosporus, he vigorously pursued his goal of naval hegemony at sea as well as military hegemony on land, so that by 1477 Ottoman galleys were cruising in Venetian home waters while in 1480 an Ottoman expeditionary force actually seized the south Italian port of Otranto. In the Balkans the Ottoman grip over Greece and Serbia was tightened, while the northern frontier was extended, at least nominally, to the line of the Dniester. Symptomatic of the growing prestige of the empire, in 1475 the Tatar khan of the Crimea acknowledged the sultan as his overlord. In the east, Mehmed embarked upon the pacification of central and eastern Anatolia, but here he encountered fierce resistance from the Turcoman tribes of the region, which opposed both the establishment of the relatively centralized Ottoman administrative system and also a Sunni orthodoxy hostile to the syncretic folk-Islam of the nomads. They turned for assistance to Uzun Hasan (1453-78), ruler of the Ak-Koyunlu Turcoman confederacy, but Mehmed defeated him in 1473, thereby temporarily stabilizing a dangerously volatile frontier region.

After the exertions that characterized the reign of Mehmed the Conqueror, the reign of his successor, Bayezid II (r. 1481-1512), constituted a much-needed breathing space. The pace set by Mehmed had been too demanding and by the time of his death the treasury was depleted, the army mutinous, and the civilian population seething with discontent. Not that Bayezid's reign was a period of peace. The first decade of the sixteenth century saw the spectacular rise to power in Azarbayjan and eastern Iran of Shah Ismail, founder of the Safavid dynasty, and his vigorous dissemination of Shiism among the heterodox Turcoman tribes of eastern Anatolia, thus once again presenting the Ottoman empire with a serious threat to the security of its eastern marches. Bayezid failed to appreciate the nature of the danger but his son and successor, Selim I (r. 1512-20), did. Advancing eastward with a formidable army, he systematically massacred the Shii Turcoman tribes of central and eastern Anatolia and extirpated heterodoxy wherever he found it. In 1514 he forced Shah Ismail to give battle at Caldiran, in Azarbayjan, and there his artillery and the Janissaries, armed with handguns, routed the Qizilbash cavalry in an encounter as decisive as any in history. After plundering Tabriz, the Safavid capital, he withdrew southwestward to complete the pacification of eastern Anatolia. In so doing he trespassed on the northern marches of the Mamluk sultanate of Egypt, and a confrontation between these two great Turkish states became unavoidable. In 1516 Selim defeated the Mamluk army near Aleppo in northern Syria and then proceeded to march on Egypt, occupying Damascus and Jerusalem in the course of his advance. In Aleppo he had taken under his protection the descendant of a long line of titular Abbasid caliphs who had been pensioners of the Mamluk government since the fall of Baghdad to the Mongols in 1258. In Cairo, in 1517, he received the submission of the sharif of Mecca, who presented him with the keys of the Holy Cities of the Hijaz. He thus became the supreme ruler of the Muslim world in a way no ruler had been since the greatest days of the Abbasid caliphate of Baghdad.

Prior to the reign of Selim I the Ottoman Turks had possessed more territory in Europe than in Asia and much of their energies had been consumed by internal pacification and frontier warfare in the Balkans. Selim's Asian campaigns, however, changed the ethnic and communal composition of the empire, as a result of the acquisition of Syria, Palestine, and Egypt, areas inhabited mainly by Arabic-speaking Muslims. Thus, the Ottoman empire became in a geographical as well as in a spiritual sense the successor to the Umayyad and Abbasid caliphates and it only remained for Süleyman I (r. 1520-66), known to the Turks as the Lawgiver and to Europeans as The Magnificent, to complete his father's work with the conquest of Baghdad and the annexation of Iraq. The reign of Süleyman, although it did not mark the maximum extension of the imperial frontiers, is rightly regarded as constituting the apogee of Ottoman imperialism. In 1521 Belgrade was captured, followed in 1522 by the fall of Rhodes. In 1526 the greater part of the former kingdom of Hungary was incorporated into the empire as a vassal state, and in 1529 an Ottoman army was encamped beneath the walls of Vienna. This triumphal progress continued into the 1530s with the capture of Algiers and Tunis in the west and Baghdad in the east.

The last three decades of Süleyman's reign seem to have seen some perceptible loss of vigor, although successful campaigns continued to be mounted against the Safavids in the southern Caucasus region, the Habsburgs in Hungary, and the Venetians at sea. In the 1550s Tripoli in modern Libya and Bahrayn in the Persian Gulf were added to the empire, and due partly to the conquest of the Yemen earlier in the reign, the Ottoman Red Sea fleet penetrated into the Arabian Sea to measure itself against its Portuguese foes. These achievements, however, seemed to necessitate a greater degree of exertion than in the past, and in fact the empire was fast approaching a point where its resources were becoming visibly overstrained. Even before Süleyman's death there were ominous signs that the best days of the empire were over. In 1552 the Ottoman fleet in the Persian Gulf failed to dislodge the Portuguese from Ormuz. The Russian seizure of Kazan in 1552 and of Astrakhan in 1554 eliminated two weak but friendly Muslim regimes on the Volga, cut the Ottoman line of communication with the Özbeg khanates in Central Asia, and marked the beginning of the Russian advance into areas hitherto within the Ottoman sphere of influence. Most striking of all, the prodigious effort made by the Ottomans to conquer the island of Malta, the headquarters of the Knights of St. John, who earlier had been expelled from Rhodes, met with complete disaster.

The Reunification of Islamic West Asia and the Eastern Mediterranean Basin
Unlike the other empires of the early modern period described in this chapter, the Ottoman empire was not an exclusively Asian phenomenon since it was also felt as an imperial

Map 38 The Ottoman empire, about 1600

presence in Europe and Africa. The rise and fall of the Ottoman empire is therefore part of the history not only of West Asia, where the consequences of its demise are still apparent today, but also of North Africa and of southern and eastern Europe. It has long been a weakness of Europocentric historians that they have failed to take cognizance of the role of the Ottomans within the framework of the European experience, whether in a purely military and diplomatic context or, although more difficult to assess, in terms of social and cultural development. At this juncture it is perhaps not altogether inappropriate to compare, however superficially, the story of the emergence of the Ottomans as a world power between the second half of the fifteenth century and the first half of the seventeenth century with that of the Spaniards during much the same period. Both empires owed their beginnings to the military exploits of a frugal, hardy people occupying an arid and relatively infertile country, the high *mesta* of Castile and the western extension of the Anatolian plateau. Both peoples were habituated to the fervor and ferocity of crusading warfare in the marches that separated rival cultures, and both were capable of experiencing intense spiritual exaltation in the service of their faith. The Ottoman Turks and the Castilians were alike in the way they erupted from a poverty-stricken hinterland to dominate richer

419

neighbors, to acquire control over the alien element of the sea and, finally, to become masters of vast and far-flung territories. Both, notwithstanding a genius for war and no small talent as proconsuls, lacked the manpower resources, the bureaucratic and fiscal expertise, and the commercial aptitudes to sustain the great adventure, and both were compelled to enlist the support of their subject peoples, the Turks utilizing the services of Serbs, Bosnians, Moldavians, Greeks, Armenians, and Jews just as the Castilians utilized the services of Catalans, Italians, Germans, and Flemings. If the armies and fleets of the king of Spain were a microcosm of the plural composition of the Habsburg empire, so too were the military forces of the sultan representative of the ethnic diversity of the Ottoman empire—the Janissaries recruited from Serbs, Albanians, Bosnians, and Bulgarians; the cavalry composed of Turks, Kurds, Wallachians, Moldavians, and Tatars; and the galleys manned by Greeks, Dalmatians, and Algerians. If Spain at the height of its power occasionally entrusted supreme military authority to foreigners, the Ottoman admirals too included more than one Christian renegade, while the Albanian ancestry of the Köprülü family of grand *vazirs* was typical of the higher echelons of the bureaucracy.

For the greater part of the sixteenth century and especially during the reign of Süleyman I, the Ottoman empire constituted the greatest concentration of military power from the Atlantic to the Pacific, a military power far more formidable than that of the contemporary Habsburg empire in Europe and America or of the Ming empire in East Asia. Outside China, the Ottoman sultan was the head of what was probably the most complex imperial administration to evolve between the fall of Rome and the emergence of the European colonial empires of the nineteenth century. The empire's maximum extent, measured in terms of the modern states that have arisen upon its ruins, was truly impressive. In Asia the sultan's rule extended over present-day Turkey, Iraq, Syria, Lebanon, Israel, Jordan, and much of the Arabian peninsula, including the Yemen. In Europe it extended over Greece, Cyprus, Albania, Yugoslavia, Bulgaria, Rumania, the greater part of Hungary and, in the Soviet Union, much of the Ukraine, the Crimea, and the western and southwestern flanks of the Caucasus region. In Africa it included Egypt and the coastal zones of Libya, Tunisia, and Algeria. The Mediterranean was virtually a Turkish lake, as were the Black Sea, the Persian Gulf, and the Red Sea. Ottoman galleys raided the Mediterranean shores of Italy, France, and Spain with impunity, but they also attempted to challenge Portuguese hegemony off the Horn of Africa and as far east as Gujarat. For sixteenth century Europeans the military might of the Ottomans, the secrecy and effectiveness with which they conducted their affairs, the mystery and awe that surrounded the sultan's government, and the knowledge that the principal *raison d'etre* of the empire was to wage war upon infidels and enslave them, all contributed towards a sense of psychological inferiority offset only by the counterbalancing spirit of Christian fanaticism.

The Organization of the Ottoman Empire

Deriving its institutional origins from the Turcoman *ghazi* principalities of central and western Anatolia but also from the earlier Seljuk sultanate of Rum, the Ottoman state system combined with this Turkish legacy older Islamic traditions derived from the Umayyad and Abbasid caliphates and also some aspects of the very different Byzantine heritage. Thus the Ottoman sultan personified the traditional leadership of a *ghazi* warlord, older and more remote traditions of Central Asian Turkish sovereignty, the Islamic ecumenicalism of the Abbasid caliphs, and the Caesaro-papalism of the Byzantine emperors. Originally the sultan's authority had been upheld by the bands of Turkish *ghazis* who had flocked to fight in the holy war against the Byzantines, but these had gradually been replaced by regular cavalry *(sipahis)*, which, notwithstanding the fame of the Janissary infantry, probably remained the most important element in the Ottoman army down to the period of imperial decline in the early seventeenth century. These *sipahis* were of two kinds. The first constituted, with the Janissaries, the sultan's standing troops and were a part of the sultan's slave household. The second, often referred to by historians as the "feudal" *sipahis,* were stationed in the provinces but were available for active service during specified periods. In lieu of salary they received a grant of land known as a *timar,* which was exempt from revenue payment and by means of which they maintained themselves and provided their own weapons and mounts. When the *timar* exceeded a certain size they were also required to maintain a specified number of troops to accompany them when they went on campaign. Clearly, there was a great loss of potential revenue to the central exchequer from the *timars* granted to the "feudal" *sipahis* but, in compensation, the empire was able to maintain a very large body of cavalry without the necessity of making cash disbursements. In addition to the regular cavalry, the Ottoman army also included irregular cavalry units that served without pay, maintaining themselves by ravaging the enemy's countryside. Somewhat similar to these troops were the irregular cavalry forces provided by the voyevods of Wallachia and Moldavia and by the Tatar khan of the Crimea, useful auxiliaries who accompanied the Ottoman army on its European campaigns and also, in the case of the Tatars, on expeditions into the Caucasus.

The Ottoman cavalry vastly outnumbered the infantry but it was the celebrated Janissaries *(yenicheri,* "new troops") who were regarded as the crack troops of the empire and whose advance onto the battlefield usually filled their foes with the utmost consternation. While the "feudal" *sipahis* were freeborn Muslims, the Janissaries, who carried firearms and who, in the days of the warrior sultans, were subjected to an exacting training and discipline, were all recruited by means of the *devshirme.* The *devshirme* was the name given to the levy of male children from the Christian population of the Balkans, an operation that was undertaken every three to seven years, according to need. Recruitment was restricted solely to agricultural communities, with urban families and families with only one male child being exempted. The majority of boys recruited by the *devshirme* were trained as soldiers and entered the Janissary corps, although some of the more intelligent and those who showed little aptitude for bearing arms were separated from the rest and educated in the palace school as personal attendants upon the sultan and as elite administrators. Severed from their Christian surroundings at an early age and carefully instructed in the Muslim faith, in which they frequently became more zealous than freeborn Muslims, these *devshirme* children were meticulously trained to become members of the military and governing elite of a regime dedicated to war and the propagation of the faith.

Whether as soldiers or bureaucrats, the sultan's slaves *(kapikulus)* constituted the ruling elite of the empire, yet they remained his creatures from beginning to end and their power and position were entirely dependent on his goodwill. To this extent they were a "slave nobility" such as had been the governing elite of the early Delhi sultanate and Mamluk Egypt. Under the direction of the grand *vazir,* himself almost invariably of slave origin, the higher echelons of the administration were staffed exclusively by *kapikulus,* as were the more important administrative posts in the provinces. The largest provincial divisions were known as *beylerbeyiliks,* each of which was in the charge of a *beylerbeyi,* and these, in turn, were subdivided into *sanjaks,* administered by a *sanjak beyi.* Like other Muslim rulers, the Ottomans deliberately established institutional checks and balances to prevent the abuse of power by provincial officials. This was done by creating parallel hierarchies of authority in the provinces. From the sixteenth century onward, the *shaykh al-Islam,* as head of the *ulama* of the empire, acquired the right to recommend the appointment and dismissal of the provincial *qazis,* and the latter therefore showed little hesitation in complaining to Istanbul regarding the conduct of *beylerbeyis* and *sanjak beyis.* In addition, the central fiscal bureau in the capital appointed an official to administer the crown lands in each province, while yet another official superintended the lands granted as *timars* to the "feudal" *sipahis*. Most important of all, the *beylerbeyis* did not have direct control over the provincial garrisons.

In its greatest days Ottoman provincial administration appears to have been a highly efficient system, its severity mitigated by an elaborate set of checks and balances and by some sense of an imperial mission on the part of the highly trained and hand-picked *kapikulus*. The maintenance of administrative stability and continuity at the lower levels was dependent on a careful recording of rights and obligations, based on census and cadastral registers, which in their complexity and accuracy went far beyond those of earlier Islamic empires. The character of administration in the higher echelons depended very largely on the degree of the control exercised by the central government. Much, too, depended on the capacity and temperament of the individual sultans. Hardly less important was the influence of the grand *vazir* but he was not without rivals, of which the most obvious was the *shaykh al-Islam*, since, if the grand *vazir* was the deputy of the sultan in all executive matters, the *shaykh al-Islam* was his deputy in the spiritual sphere. Both, however, faced serious competition for the sultan's ear within the Topkapi Sarayi, the elaborate complex of buildings located on the promontory lying between the Golden Horn and the Bosporus, which housed both the imperial family and the government itself. The first of these would-be rivals for power was the *valide sultan*, or mother of the reigning sultan, and the second, who was also the principal agent of her authority, was the *kizlar aghasi*, or chief of the black eunuchs. Somewhat less influential, because his domain lay outside the forbidden precincts of the harem, was the *kapi aghasi*, or chief of the white eunuchs, who was directly responsible for the training and discipline of the slaves selected to become administrators or personal attendants upon the sultan. Finally, outside the Topkapi Sarayi itself, the *yenicheri aghasi*, or commander of the Janissaries, exercised great influence in the counsels of state by virtue of the physical force available at his disposal.

Ottoman Control over the Resources of the Empire

Among the great continental empires of the early modern period, that of the Ottomans was of quite exceptional ethnic, cultural, and sectarian diversity. In terms of manpower its population was enormous and was rapidly expanding throughout the sixteenth century, especially in the cities, which included what were then some of the largest metropolitan centers of the world—Istanbul, Cairo, and Baghdad. The Ottoman empire also contained large non-Muslim communities, especially in the Balkans, and these were organized into virtually autonomous *millets*, living according to their own traditional beliefs and laws, the latter administered by religious leaders who were also the official intermediaries between their coreligionists and the sultan's government. The majority of these non-Muslim subjects of the empire were agriculturists (Serbs, Bosnians, Bulgarians, Hungarians, etc.), but certain communities, especially the Greeks, the Armenians, and the Jews, occupied an important and in some areas a dominant position in the commercial life of the empire. When the Ottoman administration was functioning effectively, the non-Muslim minorities probably enjoyed a far greater degree of physical security than any minority could have hoped for in contemporary Europe. When the Jews were expelled from Spain in 1492, for example, many of the refugees sought sanctuary and later acquired great wealth and prosperity in the sultan's domains. In those parts of Hungary incorporated into the empire during the sixteenth century, Protestantism spread rapidly under Ottoman rule, where converts were secure from the persecution suffered by their coreligionists under Catholic Habsburg domination. Nor should it be forgotten that at the time of the initial Ottoman thrust into Serbia and Bosnia, the Orthodox Christian population, fearful of the Catholic zeal of the rulers of Hungary to the northeast, welcomed the coming of the Turks as the lesser of two evils. Unfortunately, European dread of Ottoman power during the sixteenth and seventeenth centuries, combined with nineteenth and twentieth century European sentiment in favor of the subject Christian nationalities of the empire, have created an almost ineradicable legend of Ottoman oppression, which, at least in the great days of the empire, is not borne out by modern research.

The great majority of the subjects of the sultan, whether Muslim or Christian, were agriculturists who supported the state by the payment of land revenue, unlike the tax-exempt *timar*-holding *sipahis,* the tribute-paying nomads, and the urban population, upon which various cesses were levied. The land itself was regarded as belonging to the state. The *timar*-holder was not a landowner in the European sense of the word and possessed only qualified occupancy rights, such as the right to collect the revenue instead of the government doing so. The cultivator, whether he worked on crown land or on a *timar,* enjoyed the status of a hereditary tenant who, although he could not dispose of the land at will except to his legal heirs, could not be dispossessed so long as he paid the revenue demand or its equivalent. It is impossible to generalize with regard to the actual conditions under which the cultivator lived without specific reference to period and area, but it is probably fair to say that the *timar* system brought *timar*-holder and cultivator into a more intimate relationship than would have been the case had the countryside been administered directly by officials of the central government or, as happened subsequently, by tax farmers. Many *timar*-holders maintained a paternal attitude towards their cultivators (*timars* varied greatly in extent and most *timar*-holders, when not on campaign, must have lived rather in the style of poorer knights in medieval Europe), and until the rapid expansion of population during the late sixteenth century there was a shortage of cultivators rather than pressure on land. Thus the *timar*-holders competed with each other to secure a sufficient labor force to work their estates or to extend the area already under cultivation. Moreover, since the *timar*-holder enjoyed a hereditary status, he was not tempted to bleed dry his *timar* in anticipation of a future transfer to another area, as happened in the case of Mughul India.

Ottoman Cultural Legitimation and the Islamic Tradition

The Ottoman sultan and his government were heirs to diverse, even rival, traditions—the *ghazi* principalities of Anatolia and the Byzantine empire, Central Asian nomadic sovereignty, and Abbasid sacerdotalism. In consequence, the Ottoman empire was perhaps especially receptive to outside influences, its cosmopolitan character being exemplified by the diverse social origins of the ruling elite and by the ethnic composition and life-style of the population of Istanbul, which by the beginning of the sixteenth century may well have numbered nearly 200,000 persons. With regard to their place in the Islamic world order, the Ottomans saw themselves as embodying the culmination of almost a thousand years of history, and they were for the most part condescending, if not overtly hostile, towards other Muslim states. Undoubtedly, the period of Ottoman greatness was also a period when Islamic intellectual life everywhere was becoming somewhat torpid, but several Ottoman rulers left a reputation as bibliophiles, as patrons of traditional scholarship, and as founders of lavishly endowed colleges, hospitals, and asylums. The Ottoman regime stimulated the growth of an impressive historiographical tradition and also encouraged the study of geography, mathematics, and astronomy. Mehmed II took into his service an astronomer, trained at Ulugh Beg's observatory in Samarqand, who established in Istanbul a tradition of scholarship in mathematics and astronomy which culminated in the construction of a short-lived observatory in Galata in 1577. Court poetry drew heavily, at least initially, from the classical Iranian masters so that even Selim I, although he was a relentless foe of the Safavids, wrote his verses in Persian (while, paradoxically, Shah Ismail wrote in Turkish, in order to spread his Shii doctrines among the Turkish-speaking tribes of Anatolia). Ottoman painting, on the other hand, owed much less to Iranian influences, and the robust and realistic vision of the Ottoman miniaturists is in striking contrast to the limpid elegance of their Safavid and Mughul contemporaries. No less distinctive than Ottoman painting was the Ottoman architectural achievement, which reached its stylistic apogee in the imperial mosques of Istanbul built by the great Sinan (d. 1588). It is an architectural tradition that is quite distinct from that of the Arab world, Iran or Muslim India, but in its monumentality and its spatial effect it seems to epitomize the formal grandeur of this greatest of all Islamic empires.

2.   THE SAFAVIDS IN IRAN

The emergence during the first half of the sixteenth century of the three Islamic empires of the Ottomans, the Safavids, and the Mughuls was a interrelated development—as was also their decline during the first half of the eighteenth century. The central geographical position of the Iranian plateau ensured that the behaviour of the Safavid dynasty would serve as the principal catalyst for both these processes.

It has already been noted that among the consequences of the disintegration of the Timurid empire during the fifteenth century were: (1) the substitution of the Özbegs for the Timurids as the rulers of Mawarannahr (hereafter to be referred to as Turkistan) and part of Khurasan; (2) the gradual recovery of the Ottoman sultanate after Timur's victory at Ankara in 1402; and (3) the attempts made first by the Kara-Koyunlu Turcomans and then by the Ak-Koyunlu to fill the power vacuum left by Timur's ravages in western Iran, Iraq, and eastern Anatolia. Both attempts failed but they pointed the way for the Safavids, who, in part at least, built upon Timurid, Kara-Koyunlu, and Ak-Koyunlu foundations. Yet in one respect the Safavids were unique: they enlisted the military resources of a powerful tribal confederacy, the Qizilbash, to assist in the spread of their own particular form of "Twelver" Shiism.

The Establishment of the Safavid Empire

The Safavid regime was founded on three distinct, yet interconnected, elements. First, there was the charismatic leadership of the *murshid,* or spiritual director of the Safaviya order, the future Shah Ismail (d. 1524), who seems to have regarded himself as a living and hereditary incarnation of God. Second, there was the military support provided by the nine Turcoman tribes that formed the Shii confederacy known as the Qizilbash ("Red Heads"), a nickname deriving from the red headdress with its twelve points (symbolizing the Twelve Imams) which they wore as a sign of their allegiance to their *murshid,* Ismail, towards whom their chieftains assumed the role of disciples. Third, there was the support of the Shii urban population organized into solidarity groups (*futuwwa*). It seems unlikely that prior to the beginning of the sixteenth century Shiism was the faith of the majority of the population of Iran, but throughout the Il-Khanid and Timurid periods Shiism had been spreading unobstrusively, especially among the urban population. Even during the first half of the fourteenth century certain cities in central Iran—Ray, Qum, and Kashan, for example— were regarded as Shii strongholds.

Ismail attracted a following as much by his brilliant exploits as a warrior as by his spiritual charisma as a Sufi *murshid.* Starting from his base at Ardabil in eastern Azarbayjan he obtained possession of Tabriz in 1501, where he proclaimed himself shah, and thereafter brought the former Ak-Koyunlu territories in western Iran, Iraq, and eastern Anatolia under his control. The capture of Baghdad in 1508 marked the culmination of a process whereby yet another Turcoman dynasty had come to dominate the heartlands of West Asia. What made this new regime different from its predecessors and in a special sense "revolutionary" was its messianic Shiism, which demanded both the forceful propagation of Shii beliefs and the no less vigorous persecution of the recalcitrant Sunni population now living under Shii rule.

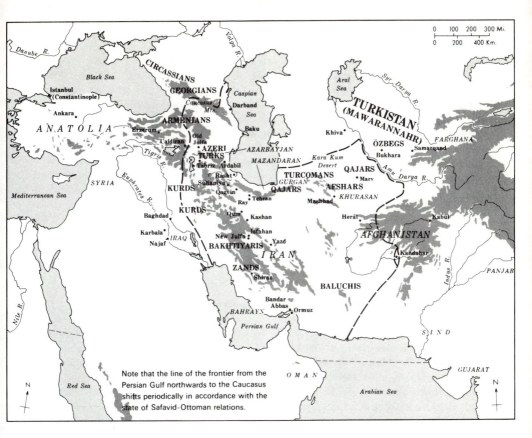

Map 39 The Safavid empire, about 1600

While Shah Ismail was pursuing his conquests in the west, the Özbeg chieftain, Muhammad Shaybani, was engaged in the annexation of the remaining Timurid principalities in Turkistan, where he seized Samarqand in 1500. Among the refugees who fled before the Özbeg advance was Babur, a descendant of Timur and a former ruler of Farghana and, very briefly, of Samarqand. In 1504 he established himself in Kabul in eastern Afghanistan. Here he remained until 1526, when he embarked upon the conquest of northern India, where he laid the foundations of the Mughul empire. Meanwhile, in 1507, Muhammad Shaybani gained possession of Herat in Khurasan, the last major center still controlled by the Timurids. A direct conflict between Muhammad Shaybani and Shah Ismail now became inevitable and their personal antagonism was reinforced by sectarian rivalry. While Shah Ismail harried the Sunnis, driving eminent *ulama* and scholars to seek refuge in Özbeg or Ottoman territory, Muhammad Shaybani reciprocated by persecuting the Shiis. Finally, in 1510, the Safavids and Özbegs met in battle near Marv and Muhammad Shaybani was defeated and killed.

Having had Muhammad Shaybani's skull made into a drinking cup, Shah Ismail sent the Özbeg's headless corpse, stuffed with straw, to the Ottoman sultan as a gratuitous insult. Selim I (r. 1512-20) accepted the challenge and in 1514 marched eastward, allegedly massacring 40,000 potential supporters of the Safavid cause among the Turcoman tribes of Anatolia and laying waste the Safavid ancestral homeland of Azarbayjan. At Caldiran the Ottoman artillery and the discipline of the Janissaries inflicted a crushing defeat on the

425

Qizilbash forces. Tabriz, Shah Ismail's capital, was occupied, but thereafter the Safavid "scorched earth" policy discouraged further Ottoman penetration into Iran. Shah Ismail continued to reign for another ten years until 1524, but both his personal self-confidence and his charisma among his followers had experienced an irrevocable setback.

Between 1524 and 1588 the Safavid empire was again and again hard pressed both by the Ottomans in the west and by the Özbegs in the east. Ottoman armies four times invaded Azarbayjan during the reign of Sultan Süleyman (1520-66) and in 1534 both Tabriz and Baghdad were occupied, and Iraq was incorporated into the Ottoman empire. Under the greatest of the Safavids, Shah Abbas I (r. 1588-1629), this trend was reversed, the northern frontier was secured against the Özbegs, and in 1623 Baghdad and much of Iraq passed back into Safavid hands. The shah's death, however, and the incapacity of his successor tilted the scales once more in favor of the Ottomans, and Baghdad was lost again in 1638. There followed a further revival under Shah Abbas II (r. 1642-66) but thereafter the Safavid empire sank into incurable lethargy during the long reigns of Shah Sulayman (1666-94), a drunken recluse, and Shah Sultan Husayn (1694-1722), a pious debauchee.

The Safavid Reunification of the Iranian Culture Zone

In retrospect, the Safavid period can be seen as the first phase in the emergence of modern Iran, the period when the present-day frontiers (allowing for some loss of territory during the nineteenth century) took shape and when Shiism was adopted as the religion of the majority of Iranians. The Safavids themselves, however, were not concerned with building a nation-state. Rather, Shah Ismail and his successors sought to create a traditional type of Islamic empire centering on the Iranian plateau but extending into the Fertile Crescent, the steppe zone of Anatolia, and even Turkistan. Had they been successful, the Safavid empire would have resembled in area and also to some extent in organization the earlier regimes of the Seljuks and the Il-Khans. Because they failed, and because twentieth-century Iranian historiography identifies the Safavid period with the resurgence of Iranian values after centuries of foreign domination by Arabs, Turks, and Mongols, the range of the Safavids' imperial aspirations has tended to be obscured by the more obvious success of their Ottoman and Mughul contemporaries. It is therefore worth stressing that whenever the Safavid shahs commanded sufficient resources, they invariably sought to extend their frontiers. At such times they probed deep into Anatolia and the Caucasus region, including Georgia. They held Baghdad and much of Iraq from 1508 to 1534 and again from 1623 to 1638. In 1511 and 1512 Shah Ismail dispatched troops into Turkistan and in 1602 Abbas I occupied Bahrayn. The Safavids always regarded the Kandahar province (claimed by the Indian Mughuls) as rightly theirs, and they were masters of the city for extended periods between 1556 and 1711. All this suggests that, far from containing their ambitions within the Persian-speaking lands of the Iranian plateau, the Safavids fitted the traditional pattern of empire builders in West Asia. It was their misfortune that there should have emerged so even a balance between their own forces and those of the Ottomans, Özbegs, and Mughuls in those vaguely defined frontier marches that constituted their mutual zones of expansion.

That the Safavids were able to hold their own against the Ottomans and the Mughuls, who possessed far greater resources than they did, was due partly to the rugged frontier terrain and partly to the fighting qualities of the Qizilbash tribes. Yet the military organization of the early Safavids was unsatisfactory on at least two counts: the irregular cavalry forces led by the Qizilbash chieftains did not perform particularly well in the face of artillery or regular troops and, far worse, their loyalty lay first and foremost with their own chieftains, who competed fiercely among themselves and sometimes against the throne itself in their quest for offices at court as well as provincial governorships. It was for this reason that Shah Abbas I endeavored to substitute for the Qizilbash tribal levies regular units upon which he could rely in a crisis without any fear of divided loyalties. He therefore established a corps of *ghulams* (the Persian equivalent of the Arabic *mamluk*) modeled on the Ottoman Janissaries and recruited from Georgian, Armenian, and Circassian slaves under the command of an officer who came from a non-Qizilbash background.

Following their exposure to Ottoman artillery fire in 1514, the Safavids gradually developed an artillery arm, although handguns had been known even during the Ak-Koyunlu period. Shah Abbas I, as part of his general policy of reforming and centralizing the military organization of the empire, greatly expanded the artillery and established a regiment of musketeers recruited from among the sedentary population. He also strengthened his exposed northeastern frontier while at the same time pursuing a policy of "divide and rule" among the tribal population by the enforced migration of turbulent elements to serve as a first line of resistance to Özbeg or Turcoman raiders from across the Amu Darya or the Kara Kum desert. In this way several Kurdish tribes were transferred to northern Khurasan, while two branches of the powerful Qizilbash tribe of Qajars were settled in Gurgan and Marv respectively. The Gurgan Qajars would provide the ruling dynasty in Iran between 1779 and 1925. Unlike the Ottomans, but like the Indian Mughuls, the Safavids appear to have been largely oblivious of the significance of sea power. When Shah Abbas I determined to expel the Portuguese from the island of Ormuz in 1622 he relied on ships of the British East India Company for offshore support.

The Organization of the Safavid Empire

As in the case of the other Islamic empires of the early modern period, the Safavids freely adopted the administrative structures of preceding regimes, although these had to be modified to take into account the peculiarly theocratic character of an empire founded by a militant Sufi order and also the dominant position of the Qizilbash *amirs,* who formed the higher echelons of the ruling elite. Otherwise, the Safavids were not particularly innovative in their administration, following precedents set by the Timurids, Kara-Koyunlu, and Ak-Koyunlu and clinging to well-established Irano-Islamic bureaucratic traditions. An exception to this, however, was the position of the *ulama,* which was bound to be highly ambiguous under a ruler such as Shah Ismail, who regarded himself, and was presumably regarded by many of his subjects also, as a divine emanation. It was the duty of the principal religious functionary, the *sadr,* and his provincial deputies to ensure the propagation of the official Shii faith, to supervise the conduct and teaching of the *ulama,* and to manage religious endowments. Much has yet to be learned regarding the social background, local connections, and economic position of the Safavid *ulama.* During the early years of the regime it appears that there did not exist in Iran a sufficient number of qualified persons to spread the new faith so that Shii divines had to be imported from the Arab world, especially from Bahrayn and Syria. But whether foreign- or native-born, the *ulama* of the early Safavid period were probably more closely supervised by the central government than had ever been the case before.

At the head of the civil administration stood the *vazir,* among whose functions the assessment, collection, and disbursement of the revenue took first place. Under him was an elaborate hierarchy of officeholders—secretaries, chancellery clerks, revenue assessors, and collectors—constituting that typical Iranian bureaucratic framework that both the Seljuks and the Il-Khans had recognized to be a prerequisite for ensuring a regular flow of revenue and an orderly administration. These Iranian officials were often objects of intense suspicion and hostility among the Qizilbash *amirs,* who claimed a virtual monopoly of the most important offices of state, including the provincial governorships. The *amirs* understood very well that the Iranian bureaucratic structure constituted a rival nucleus of power within the empire and that one of its functions was to maintain and extend the shah's authority at their expense and also to check their predatory activities, which were frequently exercised at the expense of the shah's own subjects rather than at that of his enemies. Prior to the accession of Shah Abbas I in 1588, the brute force that the Qizilbash *amirs* could bring to bear generally prevailed in their conflicts with the bureaucracy, due to their all-important role as military commanders and also to their grip on the great offices of state. For the Qizilbash *amirs* it was intolerable that Iranians should be appointed to the latter posts, and during the sixteenth century there were several instances of Iranians holding high office being abandoned in battle or even assassinated by the Qizilbash *amirs*. When, therefore, Shah Abbas I set about restructuring the Safavid state and its military establishment, he was striking not only at the ubiquitous turbulence of the Qizilbash chieftains among themselves but also at the destructive rivalry between the Turcoman and Iranian components of the ruling elite, a rivalry that also to some extent reflected cultural, ethnic, and even linguistic differences. Even down to the nineteenth century the Qajar dynasty, one of the original nine tribes of the Qizilbash, was Turkish speaking.

Under the Safavids Iran was divided into relatively small provinces ruled by Qizilbash governors, who provided for their military contingents and for the salaries of the local officials out of assignments on the land revenue. In each province the administrative hierarchy was modeled on that of the central government and was headed by a provincial *vazir* responsible for civil and fiscal administration. Khurasan, on account of its great size, its exposure to invasion by the Özbegs, and also because it was the traditional appanage of the heir apparent, had a somewhat more elaborate administrative structure, with a principal *vazir* stationed at Herat, where the heir apparent held court, and with subordinate *vazirs* in important local centers such as Mashhad and Sabzavar.

Safavid Control over the Economic and Human Resources of the Empire

The Safavids governed a society in which a substantial segment of the people were pastoralists and nomads or seminomads while the remainder were either sedentary agriculturists or town dwellers. Neither the relative size of the pastoral element nor the size of the population as a whole can now be known. The overwhelming majority of Iranians, however, lived in villages or tribal encampments and were engaged in cultivation of the land or animal husbandry, which provided the bulk of the revenue.

Safavid rule must have pressed fairly hard on the rural population, since the period was one in which the rigorous methods of land-revenue administration, initiated long before under the Seljuks and Il-Khans were further intensified by the centralizing trends of Safavid government. Like their predecessors and also their Mughul contemporaries in India, the Safavids endeavored to keep up their military establishment by making direct payments to the military commanders out of the central treasury. This proved impracticable and so they were forced to resort to the allotment of *iqtas*, or "revenue assignments." These went mainly to the members of the Qizilbash ruling families and, as had happened under previous regimes, such assignments showed an unfailing tendency to develop into personal and hereditary fiefs, which could be resumed by the crown only with very great difficulty. Unlike Mughul India, however, land in Safavid Iran was a marketable commodity and proprietary right was widely recognized, despite the theory that the shah was the sole owner of the soil. One peculiarity of the Safavid period was the transfer of large areas of land into clerical hands. Not only did the Shii shrines such as that of the Eighth Imam at Mashhad or that of the Safaviya order at Ardabil acquire extensive endowments, but the Shii clergy, owning land individually, became a major component of the landowning class.

The assessment of the land revenue varied from reign to reign and from province to province, but at its most favorable it may have been as little as one-quarter of the annual produce. Crop sharing was the normal method of payment in most areas, but cash payment probably prevailed on land in the vicinity of an urban center that could provide an accessible market for surplus produce. Over most of the Iranian plateau water for the soil could be obtained only by means of artificial irrigation, which had to be paid for. Sometimes the government granted advances or remitted revenue in order to extend the area under cultivation or to offset the consequences of drought, famine, or some other disaster. Apart from the hardships and misfortunes that were normal occurrences in the life cycle of the cultivator, he was also exposed to the fourfold miseries of forced labor, illegal exactions from his landlord, illegal exactions from government officials, and maltreatment at the hands of passing military or tribal contingents.

The Safavids were well aware of the advantages to be derived from actively encouraging commerce and indigenous manufacturing skills. Protection was extended to merchants and craftsmen, and it was partly in recognition of their commercial skills that Shah Abbas I transferred the Armenian population of Julfa in Armenia to a suburb of Isfahan, New Julfa, where they lived under the shah's special protection. The period as a whole saw the culmination of a long tradition of Iranian skill in the weaving, dyeing, and finishing of sumptuous cloths—brocades, velvets, damasks, cloth-of-gold, etc. In the Caspian provinces of Gilan and Mazandaran the silk-weaving industry flourished under royal patronage, and so did carpet weaving. Hostile relations with the Ottoman empire and the Özbeg khanates adversely affected Iranian participation in the traditional transcontinental caravan trade, which in any case was now in decline as a result of the opening of maritime trade routes between Europe and China. The Safavids therefore actively encouraged European merchants to trade in Iran, and Shah Abbas I founded the port of Bandar Abbas on the Persian Gulf, which serviced the important maritime trade with Gujarat and the Deccan sultanates, as well as with the Dutch and the British. Desire to stimulate trade resulted in the building of the many monumental caravanserais which are still to be seen along the old trade routes crossing the Iranian plateau and which are invariably ascribed by the local population to the beneficence of Abbas I, who also laid an impressive causeway across the low-lying countryside of Mazandaran.

Although the urban history of the Safavid period has yet to be written, it seems clear that some cities prospered exceedingly, especially manufacturing centers and those centers located far from the frontier regions, such as Isfahan, Kashan, Yazd, Qum, and Qazvin. So also did Mashhad, a major pilgrimage center, and some of the new foundations on the Caspian. On the other hand, the great commercial and cultural centers of Tabriz and Herat, repeatedly beseiged by Ottoman or Özbeg armies, probably declined in prosperity and population between 1500 and 1700, as did also the former Il-Khanid metropolis of Sultaniya. Tabriz had been the first capital of the dynasty, but its proximity to the Ottoman frontier led to its replacement by Qazvin. Later, Shah Abbas I transferred the capital to Isfahan, a more central and secure location, although both Qazvin and Tehran, already in existence in the Timurid period, were better placed as vantage points for watching the vulnerable northwestern and northeastern frontiers. Under the Safavids the cities enjoyed a certain measure of de facto self-government, as exercised by the more prominent ulama, the wealthier merchants, and long-established landowners in the neighborhood. The shah's authority was represented by a functionary known as the kalantar, who was a local man of consequence whose appointment was confirmed only after the heads of each quarter of the city had signified their approval. These latter were the real link between government and the urban population and it was they who provided the local knowledge necessary for assessing the allocation of taxes in each quarter. In return, they were the recognized channel for the expression of local grievances.

Safavid Promotion of the Iranian Cultural Tradition

The genesis of the Safavid empire lay in the unusual conjunction of a Turcoman tribal confederacy with a militant Shii Sufi order, although neither provided a particularly firm institutional base upon which to build. The Turcoman Qizilbash element in the empire tended to reduce all but the most vigorous rulers to the status of a mere *primus inter pares,* while once it became clear that the external danger to the empire came from the Ottomans and the Özbegs, Turks by race, culture, and language, there was a real need for the Safavids to disassociate themselves from their arch-foes by playing down their own Turkish origins. The Shii factor led to emphasis on the (probably spurious) descent of the Safavids from the Fifth Imam and ultimately from Ali and Fatima. To the clerical classes and to the pious in general this illustrious Arab genealogy was a source of deep satisfaction, but it did not in itself provide the kind of dynastic legitimation needed by a regime hard-pressed internally by turbulent and aspiring chieftains and by enemies beyond the frontiers with no less pretentious claims to world domination. Thus the Safavid rulers relied less and less on their position as leaders of the Qizilbash confederacy and on their charisma as *murshids* of the Safaviya order, identifying rather with those ancient traditions of Iranian absolutism that had managed to survive since Sasanid times throughout centuries of foreign domination. Those traditions, partly bureaucratic and institutional, partly literary and cultural, and always placing great stress on the charisma of monarchy, had reemerged briefly between the ninth and eleventh centuries under the patronage of Iranian dynasties such as the Saffarids, Samanids, and Buyids. Thereafter, the tradition had been taken over by the Turkish Ghaznavids and Seljuks and even by the Mongol Il-Khans and the Turco-Mongol Timurids. This was the tradition that the Safavids, at least from the time of Shah Abbas I, made their own. Consciously or unconsciously, the dynasty identified increasingly with its Iranian subjects, while the gorgeous trappings of kingship, designed to impress even those visitors who knew the courts of the Ottoman sultan or the Mughul padshah, provided the facade behind which lay an increasingly authoritarian and centralized regime.

Shah Abbas I beautified and enlarged his capital, Isfahan, in order to vie with and even outshine the splendor of Ottoman Istanbul. Certainly he planned on a truly imperial scale, and there can be little doubt that his example influenced the Mughul padshah, Shah Jahan, when the latter planned a new capital at Shahjahanabad (now Old Delhi) two decades later. Iranian architecture under the Safavids likewise evolved what may be called an imperial style. The architectural forms were less original than those of Seljuk or Il-Khanid times and the color and design of the tilework was less brilliant than Timurid decoration at its best, but the overall effect was one of sumptuous and dazzling opulence. Much the same may be said of the miniaturist's art, which, except during the early sixteenth century, never equalled that of the great masters of the Timurid period.

One important adjunct of the shah's authority was the support of the clerical classes. As Safavid rule stabilized itself and Shiism became the faith of the majority of the shah's subjects, the standing of the *ulama* in society rose accordingly, both in terms of their politico-religious influence with the masses and also in terms of their economic leverage. The regime recognized and supported this great growth in clerical power and pretensions. The authority of the *ulama* as a whole was upheld, individual teachers and theologians enjoyed royal favor, and Shii devotional literature was generously patronized. Unlike almost all previous regimes, whether indigenous Iranian, Turkish, or Turco-Mongol, the Safavids gave little or no encouragement to the composition of poetry, which over the centuries has been one of the crowning glories of Iranian civilization. The reason for this omission is clear. Poetry had long been closely associated with Sufism but now Sufism, apart from that manifested in the Safaviya and related orders, was positively discouraged and from time to time persecuted. Under the Safavids there emerged an alliance between the shah and the Shii clergy which served to counterbalance the less dependable alliance between the shah and the tribal ruling elite.

3. THE MUGHULS IN SOUTH ASIA

The Establishment of the Mughul Empire

In two decisive battles, against the Lodi Afghans at Panipat in 1526 and against a confederacy of Rajputs at Khanua in 1527, Babur laid the foundations of Mughul rule in India. At the time of his death in 1530 the frontiers of this new empire bounded an area that included the Panjab, the plains of the Jumna and the Ganges eastward into northern Bihar, and the country south of the Jumna and the Chambal as far as Gwalior. It also included the Kabul valley and much of what is now southeastern Afghanistan.

The term Mughul, as applied to Babur, his followers and descendants, is a misnomer now too firmly established to be dislodged, but a misnomer nonetheless. In Persian, *mughul* means "Mongol" (e.g., the race of Chingiz Khan and his descendants and especially the Il-Khanid dynasty), while *mughulistan* means "the land of the Mongols," the name traditionally given to the steppe region beyond the Syr Darya and, today, to the Mongolian People's Republic. Babur was not a Mongol but a Turk and his native tongue was the Turkish language known as Chaghatay, although he had Mongol ancestors on his mother's side, descended from Chingiz Khan's second son, Chaghatay. However, in this instance it was the paternal descent from Timur that mattered most. It was Timur's throne of Samarqand that Babur had aspired to seize in his adventurous youth, and it was as Timur's heir that he claimed the sultanate of Delhi on the strength of Timur's conquest of 1398. Strictly speaking, therefore, Babur and his descendants should be known as Timurids. In India they were frequently referred to as Chaghatays, but European travelers of the sixteenth and seventeenth centuries picked up the term Mughul, which was widely used to distinguish the foreign Muslim ruling elite from Indian-born Muslims, and the term is now sanctified by long usage. It is important to remember, however, that the Mughuls were Turks, like the majority of the earlier Muslim invaders of India, although they had undergone a much greater degree of Iranicization before entering the subcontinent than had any of their predecessors.

Under Babur's son, Humayun (r. 1530-40 and 1555-56), the empire, still unconsolidated, first expanded rapidly and then contracted. Having recklessly overextended his conquests, Humayun and his Mughuls were expelled from India in 1540 by the Afghans already settled in the Gangetic plain and were forced to seek temporary asylum in Safavid Iran. In 1555 Humayun made his way back to Delhi where he died in the following year, so that the work of reconquest and reconstruction had to begin all over again, under the nominal leadership of Humayun's thirteen-year-old son, Akbar (1556-1605). After a decisive victory, again at Panipat, over combined Afghan and Hindu elements, there was a short lull before the young ruler came into his own. Then, from 1561 until his death in 1605 the momentum of expansion continued unabated for four decades, advancing the Mughul frontier far beyond the Narbada, traditional southern boundary of north Indian empires. One by one, the sultanates of Malwa, Gujarat, and Bengal were annexed, as were areas such as Gondwana and Orissa in which the Muslims had hitherto taken little interest. To the north and west of the Panjab, the Kashmir valley was occupied, Mughul rule in the Kabul valley was strengthened to protect that strategic area from the formidable Özbeg ruler of Bukhara, Sind on the lower Indus was annexed, and Kandahar was acquired through the good offices of a defecting Safavid governor. At the same time, a nominal overlordship was asserted over the Pathan, Baluchi, and Brahui tribes of the northwestern frontier region.

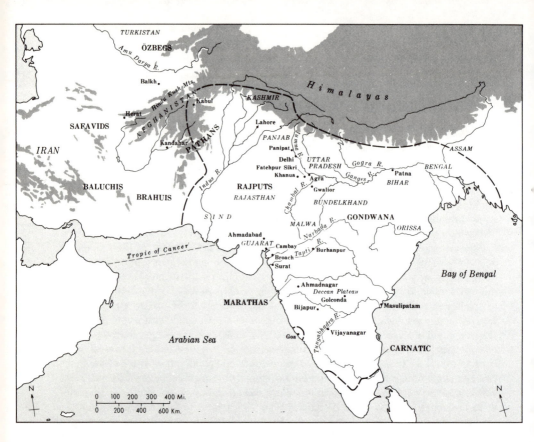

Map 40 Maximum extent of the Mughul empire under Awrangzeb, about 1700

These acquisitions can all be seen as part of a familiar pattern of expansionist dynamics. But while Akbar, like his predecessors, sought to enlarge the area under his rule, he was confronted within his own territory by the problem of the Rajputs, warlike and independent Hindu chieftains who occupied strategic fortresses or fortress cities not only in Rajasthan itself but also in Malwa and Bundelkhand. The retention of independence by these Rajput chieftains had always posed a threat to the Muslim rulers of northern India, first to the sultans of Delhi and later to the sultans of Malwa and Gujarat. Unless the Rajputs could be subjugated it was impossible for a Delhi-based regime to hold with complete security Gujarat, Malwa, and the highway to the Deccan. From apparently quite early in his reign, Akbar understood the significance of the Rajput problem and he dealt with it pragmatically, eliminating one Rajput stronghold after another with ferocious determination while shrewdly providing opportunities for the less recalcitrant Rajput chieftains to be co-opted into the imperial system by granting them positions of trust and honor.

During the last decade of his life Akbar felt his position in the north to be sufficiently strong for him to attempt to extend his empire into the Deccan, presumably with the ultimate intention of bringing the whole of peninsular India under Mughul rule. By the close of the sixteenth century the position in central and south India had changed radically from what it had been at the beginning of the century. The Bahmanid sultanate of the Deccan had disappeared and so had the Hindu kingdom of Vijayanagar south of the Tungabhadra River. No single state had arisen as successor to either, and compared to the Mughul empire, the sultanates of Ahmadnagar, Bijapur, and Golconda, the three principal regimes to emerge in the south, possessed only modest resources in terms of their military establishments. They did enjoy, however, substantial advantages in the difficult terrain and the tenuous line of communications which would face any invader whose base lay so far north as Delhi. Even the ablest of Mughul rulers seriously underestimated the difficulties involved in advancing southward.

From 1691 onward, Akbar sent envoys and armies to the south, but the rulers of the Deccan, divided though they were among themselves, resisted Mughul domination. Under Akbar's successor, Jahangir (r. 1605-27), a somewhat lethargic ruler, the pace of expansion slowed down while the empire enjoyed a breathing space in which to consolidate the gains of the previous half century. There followed a further burst of energy during the reign of Jahangir's successor, Shah Jahan (r. 1627-58), a vigorous expansionist. Shah Jahan set great store on regaining Kandahar, which had passed temporarily into Safavid hands in 1622. This he accomplished in 1638, but lost it again in 1648, and neither of the costly expeditions sent to recover it in 1649 and 1652 was successful. Shah Jahan also sent an expedition north of the Hindu Kush in 1646 to seize the Özbeg outpost of Balkh but without lasting success. Shah Jahan's attempts to recover the ancient possessions of his family in Central Asia were failures, but they were offset by his successes in the south, where the sultanates of Ahmadnagar, Bijapur, and Golconda were all brought to terms by 1636. Thereafter, the region stretching southward from the Narbada to the northern frontiers of Bijapur and Golconda was formed into a single viceroyalty (of which the core was the former sultanate of Ahmadnagar) over which Shah Jahan appointed as viceroy his third son, Awrangzeb, who served there from 1636 to 1644 and again from 1653 to 1657. Awrangzeb directed his considerable energies to pacifying and establishing effective control over the Mughul Deccan, but he never lost sight of his ultimate objective—the annexation of the two independent sultanates to the south. In 1656 his opportunity came when he intervened in a dispute between the sultan of Golconda and his Iranian general, Mir Jumla, who had recently conquered the Carnatic, the coastal area lying between the Eastern Ghats and the Bay of Bengal. Awrangzeb invaded the sultanate and was about to occupy Golconda itself when he received orders from Delhi to desist, sent by his father at the instigation of his jealous elder brother. A settlement was negotiated with the sultan, and Mir Jumla transferred his allegiance to Delhi, where he became imperial *vazir* and an influential partisan of Awrangzeb. In the following year, Shah Jahan's advancing senility provoked the long-expected contest for the throne among his four sons, from which Awrangzeb (r. 1658-1707) eventually emerged as sole ruler, having in the meantime rid himself of his brothers and several nephews.

Awrangzeb proclaimed himself padshah in 1658, but his father, Shah Jahan, survived as a prisoner until 1666. In consequence, notwithstanding his already considerable reputation as a general, the usurper felt the need to prove himself his father's equal and to conciliate the ruling elite by providing them with opportunities for patronage and personal enrichment such as they had enjoyed during previous reigns. For some years, therefore, the imperial court continued to be the setting for magnificence and extravagance on a scale comparable to Shah Jahan's time, while costly missions were dispatched to Mecca and to the courts of various Muslim rulers. Meanwhile, expansion into Assam on the northeast frontier, undertaken by Mir Jumla, provided substantial rewards in glory and plunder for the military classes. No doubt during these first decades of the reign Awrangzeb continued to think in terms of further aggression against Bijapur and Golconda, but affairs in the north engaged his attention until 1681. This was partly the result of his own high-handed dealings with the Pathan tribes across the Indus and with the Rajputs, hitherto an undoubted source of strength to the empire. Historians have traditionally attributed Awrangzeb's alienation of the Rajputs to his general aversion to Hindus but his motive may have been primarily fiscal, believing that the elimination of this particular component of the ruling elite was a price

worth paying for easing the overall pressure on patronage and revenue assignments. In any event, by 1681 patched-up settlements with the Rajputs and with the tribes of the north-western frontier region enabled him to turn his attention once more to the Deccan and he abandoned Delhi for the south, never to return. For the remaining twenty-six years of the reign he remained in the Deccan, where he achieved his life-long ambition of conquering the sultanates of Bijapur and Golconda but where he failed to solve a greater problem, the intransigence of the warlike Marathas who occupied the rugged terrain of the northwestern Deccan, where they had been subjects of the former sultans of Ahmadnagar. It was a failure that contributed substantially to the ultimate disintegration of the empire.

The Mughul Unification of the Indian Subcontinent

The history of the Mughul empire from the first battle of Panipat (1526) to the annexation of the sultanate of Golconda (1687) covered a span of 160 years, and although expansion was to bring almost the entire subcontinent under Mughul rule—at least nominally—it would be unwise to postulate that the Mughuls envisaged themselves as fulfilling some kind of "manifest destiny" to which, as rulers of India, they were bound to aspire. The Mughuls were aliens in India and the traditions of the dynasty were characteristically Turco-Mongol and Central Asian. In attacking the Delhi sultanate, Babur saw himself reclaiming a lost appanage of the Timurids, but he probably also viewed it as being of less worth than Samarqand and the ancestral homelands of his dynasty north of the Hindu Kush and of the Amu Darya, now in the hands of the Özbegs. It took the Mughuls a long time to accustom themselves to a purely Indian role. Babur, Humayun, and Akbar were all compelled to keep a watchful eye on what was happening north of the Hindu Kush. There was an ongoing awareness of the exposed frontier with the Özbegs and the Safavids and also of the strategic importance of the country lying between the Indus and Kabul. In his costly wars against Balkh and Kandahar, Shah Jahan was reaffirming (although for the last time) the dynasty's historic preoccupation with Central Asia.

In India itself, by way of contrast, the Mughuls encountered no rivals for hegemony: only refractory centers of local power (such as the Rajput principalities) or decaying sultanates such as those of Bengal and the Deccan whose inherent weakness made them tempting objects for aggression and whose inability to control their own frontier regions provided opportune pretexts for intervention. The Mughuls occupied these power vacuums one after another not because they possessed a compulsive urge to bring the entire subcontinent under a single rule but because the Mughul dynasty, like all such dynasties, was naturally predatory (Akbar declared on one occasion: "A monarch should be ever intent on conquest; otherwise, his enemies rise in arms against him. The army should be exercised in warfare, lest from want of training they become self-indulgent.") and because it could maintain itself only by the continuous acquisition of new sources of revenue and land with which to reward its followers.

The Mughul war machine included such disparate elements as the highly mobile mounted archers who had been the shock troops of former Turkish invaders of India, the massed infantry and elephants of traditional Hindu warfare, and also artillery. Notwithstanding assertions to the contrary, firearms in India were not a Mughul innovation, for they were already known in the sultanates of Gujarat and the Deccan. In general, the Mughuls made rather ineffective use of both artillery and handguns, being content to employ mostly foreigners—deserters from the Ottoman provinces or European renegades—as artillerymen and gunsmiths. Artillery was valued mainly for siege operations

---

9.3 Mughul siege guns being dragged into position at the siege of the Rajput fortress of Ranthambhor, Rajasthan, in 1568. Mughul miniature, late sixteenth century. Courtesy: Victoria and Albert Museum, London.

and so, as in the case of the Ottoman empire, there was a tendency for cannon to get larger and larger, but also more clumsy and difficult to handle. At the beginning of the eighteenth century, for example, some cannon were removed from the Lahore fort which were so heavy that it took 250 oxen and five or six elephants ten days to move them a distance of three or four miles.

The Mughul empire in its great days did not, except perhaps in the first decade of its existence, depend on the support of a single group in the way that the early Safavid empire depended on the Qizilbash. Rather, the strength of the Mughul empire lay in the diversity of its ruling elite, the loyalty of which was assured so long as it had access to a continuous flow of titles and honorifics, appointments and revenue assignments. The initial conquests had been the work of a fairly homogeneous Iranicized Turco-Mongol military elite, confronting two preexisting power groups that had dominated northern India for the preceding century or more—the Afghans and the Rajputs. During the sixteenth century both these groups were gradually co-opted into the new Mughul system, although not without some show of resistance from the resentful Afghans, who regarded the Mughuls as having supplanted them, and also from those Rajput clans that saw their traditional Rajput rivals already well entrenched within the new order. At the same time, the opportunities for enrichment provided by service in the Mughul army or bureaucracy tempted many enterprising soldiers of fortune, *ulama,* and scholars to immigrate into India from the Muslim lands to the northwest, especially from Bukhara and the surrounding regions. Immigrants from Bukhara were mainly Turks and therefore Sunni, in contrast to the immigrants from Iran, who were Shii. Numerically, the Iranian immigrants were in a minority but they included some of the ablest among the newcomers. Sometimes the immigrants were political or religious refugees, but irrespective of the reasons that brought them into India (then regarded as a land of opportunity), their departure from their homeland constituted a veritable drain of talent, which in the case of Safavid Iran in particular must have contributed to the prevailing decline of the late seventeenth century. These Turkish and Iranian immigrants were the backbone of the Mughul system, but during the seventeenth century the Mughul advance into the Deccan led to the recruitment of new groups into the ruling elite—Deccani Muslims who had formerly served the sultans of Ahmadnagar, Bijapur, and Golconda, and also Hindu Marathas.

The Organization of the Mughul Empire

While the size and complexity of Mughul administration far exceeded that of the Muslim regimes that had established themselves in India between the thirteenth and sixteenth centuries, it is important to stress that the Mughuls built upon preexisting foundations. Akbar was not the first Muslim to rule an extensive area of the subcontinent and devise an elaborate bureaucracy to collect the land revenue and maintain order. The organization of the Mughul empire as it emerged in the second half of the sixteenth century was rooted in the traditions of the Delhi sultanate, but it also—like all the later Islamic empires—derived much of its institutional structure and its dynastic life-style from a common Turco-Mongol heritage. The decimal chain of command in the army, for example, was based on Chingizkhanid practice, and when Shah Jahan styled himself Lord of the Fortunate Conjunction of the Planets he was deliberately reviving the title used by his famous ancestor, Timur. But it is not enough to emphasize the Mughuls' Central Asian antecedents and the heritage of the Delhi sultanate. A number of features of Mughul government—the functions of the *vazir,* for example, and the separation of the revenue administration in the provinces from the executive arm—derived from long-established practices going back to the great days of the Abbasid caliphs in Baghdad. It is less easy to detect truly indigenous elements in the Mughul system of government in the higher echelons, although the fact that the land revenue was assessed and collected mainly by subordinate Hindu officials ensured that the modes of control and coercion at subdistrict and village level followed traditional patterns.

As in the case of the Ottomans and the Safavids, it is convenient to divide the power structure of the Mughul empire into two distinct hierarchies, one religious and the other bureaucratic. The plural composition of Indian society and the diversity of the Mughul ruling elite (Indian and non-Indian, Muslim and Hindu, Sunni and Shii) necessarily involved some relaxation of the application of the *Sharia*. Partly in consequence of this, the *ulama* under the Mughuls enjoyed less prestige than they did in other Islamic empires. This was due not only to the peculiar situation of Islam in India as a minority religion but also to the place of the *ulama* in Indo-Muslim society. The power of the *ulama* in traditional Muslim society was based on the influence they exercised over the entire "community of believers," which in turn gave them political leverage to put pressure on the state or its representatives. In India, however, where the Muslims had always been a minority, the *ulama* were far more dependent on the goodwill and the patronage of the state than were the clerical classes in the Muslim lands farther west, and this necessarily bound them to the reigning sultan, who alone could assure them of such practical necessities as official posts, pensions, and revenue assignments. At the same time, leadership of the Muslim community as a whole had long been preempted by the Sufis, a tradition going back to the great Chishtiya *murshids* of the thirteenth and fourteenth centuries. Under the Mughuls the *ulama*, therefore, continued to be an "establishment" clergy, widely regarded as being venal and time serving.

The head of the *ulama* in Mughul India was the *sadr* or *shaykh al-Islam*, who had charge of religious endowments and institutions of religious learning. Muslim law was administered by a chief *qazi*, sometimes the same person as the chief *sadr*, to whom all provincial *qazis* were subordinate. The relationship of these officials to the padshah was necessarily an ambiguous one and demanded discretion on both sides. In 1578-79, for example, the behavior of the *ulama* at court so irritated Akbar that he assumed certain functions—the reading of the *khutba* and the handing down of judicial decisions based on his own interpretation of religious law—which in turn deeply offended orthodox opinion. Under more conventional rulers such as Shah Jahan and Awrangzeb the *ulama* enjoyed a somewhat higher prestige than under Akbar. Nevertheless, even then, the distribution of power among the ruling elite of the empire and the great personal prestige enjoyed by the Sufis in Indo-Muslim society gave the *ulama* less importance than might have been expected. Significantly, the disintegration of the empire did not result in an increase in the influence or authority of the *ulama* such as the Shii *ulama* in Iran gained from the decline of the Safavids.

Mughul India was governed by a service nobility in which every nobleman held a military rank called a *mansab* and was consequently known as a *mansabdar*. This rank was determined by the number of troops the nobleman was required to maintain on a war footing. The most junior *mansabdars* maintained a mere ten men while in Awrangzeb's reign there were *mansabdars* who maintained as many as seven thousand. A *mansabdar* might have exclusively administrative duties—as a revenue official, for example—but he remained part of a military hierarchy in which promotion was measured by the number of troops attached to each *mansab*. Only the *ulama* were outside the system, and even Hindu tributaries such as the Rajput Maharajas held *mansab* ranks. It was a highly effective system since it provided a steel framework within which the entire military and civil administration (apart from the judiciary) operated.

Mansabdars were recruited from various social and ethnic backgrounds ranging from immigrants and local supporters to erstwhile foes, and included both princes of the imperial house and also self-made men such as Mir Jumla, who had started life as an oil-merchant's son in a village outside Isfahan. One category was, however, almost wholly unrepresented—persons of slave origin. Unlike their Ottoman and Safavid contemporaries or the former sultans of Delhi, the Mughuls apparently had no use for *mamluks.*

It had been Akbar's intention that every *mansabdar* should receive his salary in cash, the logical consequence of his intention that the land revenue should be paid in cash. This, however, proved impossible. Instead, *mansabdars* were granted territorial revenue assignments known as *jagirs* on which they were required to collect the land revenue for the government, deducting an agreed amount to cover their salary, including the maintenance of their troops and the cost of collection. A *mansabdar* might be granted *jagirs* in several different provinces, sometimes in localities remote from where he was serving. Necessarily, therefore, he was compelled to employ agents to administer these *jagirs* on his behalf. Even so, the government was determined to prevent *jagirs* from being converted into private fiefs and so they were systematically transferred from one officeholder to another every three or four years.

The higher echelons of the administrative system were closely supervised by the rulers in person, and the ablest padshahs—Akbar, Shah Jahan, and Awrangzeb—were very much in control. Under their watchful direction the *vazir* (sometimes known also as the *diwan*) supervised the entire bureaucracy and especially the revenue-collecting arm of the government, while other great officeholders were in charge of the military commissariat, the administration of the imperial household, and various secretariats.

In the middle years of Akbar's reign the empire was divided into twelve provinces, known as *subahs,* but these increased in number with the later conquests until by 1687 they numbered twenty-one. Differing from each other in extent of area, size of population, and revenue yield, their boundaries were for the most part predetermined by the historical growth of the empire. There were also, however, extensive tracts of country which were excluded from the provincial structure and left in the hands of local rulers on condition that they paid tribute regularly. Such areas usually consisted of jungle or hill country considered difficult to control and unlikely to be very remunerative in terms of their revenue yield.

In charge of each province was a governor, known as a *subahdar,* who headed the administrative hierarchy of district officers responsible for upholding the padshah's authority. The *subahdar* did not, however, appoint the district officers to their posts. They, like the police officials in charge of the larger towns and the commandants of important fortresses in the provinces, were all appointed from Delhi itself. The prime function of all these officials and also of their subordinates at subdistrict level was the maintenance of law and order of a rough-and-ready kind. They played no part whatever in the most important function of government—the assessment and collection of the land revenue. This was separately administered by a provincial *diwan,* who was appointed by and was solely answerable to the imperial *vazir,* or *diwan,* in Delhi. Under the provincial *diwan,* throughout the districts and subdistricts, there was a skilled staff, composed mainly of Hindus, which determined the amount of the land revenue to be paid and supervised its collection. The majority of subdistrict officials were local men and in many cases the office became hereditary.

Mughul Control over the Economic and Human Resources of the Empire

The overwhelming majority of the subjects of the Mughul padshah were engaged in agriculture, living in relatively stable village communities where land was not a marketable commodity and where contacts with the outside world were few. The state impinged on the village communities to obtain revenue but for hardly anything else. Throughout the empire it was the custom for the government to demand a proportion of the crop or its equivalent in cash, but while this proportion had fluctuated under former dynasties it had rarely reached the level exacted by the Mughuls, which was one-third of the crop during the second half of the sixteenth century and one-half a century later. Under Mughul rule areas directly administered from Delhi were divided for revenue assessment purposes into two distinct categories: crown lands administered by state officials, and revenue assignments (jagirs) administered by the jagirdars or their agents.

Unlike the townsfolk, of whom a substantial minority were Muslims and therefore subject to the Sharia administered by the qazi, most cultivators were Hindus who conducted their lives in accordance with Hindu religious traditions upheld by the local brahman or embodied in the consensus judgments of the village council of elders. For the bulk of the population, therefore, the sole link between the imperial government and themselves—at least under normal circumstances—was the payment of the land revenue, while at subdistrict level the revenue officials were generally Hindus and local men. Thus the average villager was no more likely to come into contact with Mughul officialdom than he was later to come into contact with British officialdom. But if the cultivator saw little of the pomp and splendor of Mughul rule he nevertheless felt its weight upon his shoulders, and all the evidence points to the conclusion that Mughul rule pressed upon him very heavily indeed. The available statistics are exceptionally difficult to interpret for purposes of comparison with earlier or subsequent regimes, but what does seem certain is that the revenue demand, heavy enough during the sixteenth century, had increased substantially by the second half of the seventeenth century and that, concurrently, serious abuses had crept into its administration, especially in the form of illegal exactions by the revenue officials themselves.

Inspired by the vigorous administrative reforms undertaken by Sher Shah Sur (r. 1540-45), an Afghan predecessor who reigned in Delhi all too briefly, Akbar and his advisers devised an improved system of revenue assessment and collection, which was probably superior to anything hitherto known in the subcontinent. The principles upon which this system was based were (1) the accurate measurement and classification of all land under cultivation, (2) fixed rates of assessment made, wherever possible, with the actual cultivator of the soil, and (3) payment in cash rather than kind, wherever market conditions allowed. Admirable as these principles were, they had to be modified to a very considerable extent in the interests of administrative expediency. The accurate assessment of the revenue demand envisaged by this system necessitated the creation of an extensive subordinate bureaucracy that required constant supervision from above. Revenue settlements made with the cultivators were extremely laborious to administer in comparison with settlements made with intermediaries, whether village headmen, local notables, or revenue farmers. Cash payments were possible only where a cash economy was already well established at village level. Above all, it was not possible to find the ready cash to cover the day-to-day cost of running the court and government and in particular to pay the salaries of the mansabdars. Hence, even during Akbar's lifetime the regime was forced to fall back on the time-honored device of making revenue assignments—the jagirdari system.

Surviving instructions to Mughul revenue officials invariably include passages to the effect that the cultivator should be treated with justice and consideration, and it was certainly in the long-term interests of the empire to encourage expansion of the area under cultivation, with a view to a future increase of revenue. But the mansabdar who had received a temporary revenue assignment that he knew was to be transferred to a fellow mansabdar within three or four years felt no incentive to invest in the future prosperity of his jagir. On the contrary, it was in his interest to squeeze the maximum profit out of it in the shortest possible time. For this reason the jagirdari system, excellent as it was as a political device for preventing the growth of local bases of power among the mansabdars, was ruinous for agriculture.

It is curious to note how many European visitors to India during the seventeenth century, coming as they did from countries where the lot of the peasant was far from idyllic, nevertheless commented on the brutal treatment of the Indian villager by the agents of the government. It seems clear that, notwithstanding the professed concern of the Mughul government for the welfare of the cultivator, the fiscal needs of the regime were virtually insatiable and those who could not or would not meet the revenue demand were savagely punished. Apart from being beaten and tortured, cultivators who defaulted on their revenue payments, or the members of their families, were frequently sold into slavery. Sometimes widespread and persistent oppression by revenue officials provoked an uprising over an extended area and when this occurred the revolt would be put down with exemplary ferocity, a ferocity that generally far exceeded that shown in the case of outbursts of insubordination and fractiousness on the part of dissident nobles.

It should be stressed, however, that exemplary punishment for rebels was a response to the rather limited means of coercion that were, under normal circumstances, available to the authorities. The Mughul regime in its prime possessed a highly effective military machine, which was certainly more powerful than anything known in India before the sixteenth century, but it lacked the means to undertake the constant regulation of its subjects in the form of law-enforcement agents and basic statistical information such as enables even democratic governments in the twentieth century to exercise an all-pervasive authority over the lives of their subjects. Inadequate communications, a relatively small administrative cadre, the dispersal of regular troops over a vast area, shortage of ready cash, and the need for tacit support from the population as a whole resulted in the exercise of some degree of restraint in all aspects of government in which the acquisition of revenue was not directly involved.

One severe burden traditionally endured by the cultivator in premechanized societies—forced labor—seems to have been rather limited in Mughul India. The regime undertook few hydraulic or irrigation schemes except in the immediate vicinity of Delhi and Lahore, and the lavish building of palaces, mosques, and mausoleums appears to have been done by hired laborers. Another traditional abuse, the conscription of peasants to assist in the transport of military supplies and grain for the army, seems to have been rather rare, being undertaken normally by occupational groups such as the nomadic Banjaras, who supplied grain for Indian armies on the move well into the nineteenth century. It should, however, be stressed that the Mughul period was as accustomed to the prevalence of chattel slavery as were the preceding two millennia of Indian history, although the presence of a large slave population was less obvious than in some other societies because the overwhelming majority of slaves were employed in domestic service.

Mughul rule pressed much more lightly upon the urban population, which apart from the payment of miscellaneous taxes and customs dues, contributed much less in the way of state revenue than did the agricultural population. Under the Mughuls, urban life continued to flourish, as it had done throughout the three preceding centuries of Muslim rule. Great manufacturing centers such as Patna and Ahmadabad, ports such as Broach, Cambay, and Surat, and towns located on important trade routes such as Burhanpur on the Tapti prospered and expanded along with the imperial capitals of Agra, Delhi, and Lahore. Many small towns mushroomed into important local centers, especially in the area between the Jumna and the Gogra in what is now Uttar Pradesh. It has also been suggested that Akbar's endeavor to enforce the payment of the land revenue in cash stimulated the emergence of nuclear townships, where grain dealers, money lenders, money changers, *jagirdari* agents, and local officials gathered for convenience and perhaps security.

Mughul urban prosperity was based largely on a growth in the demand for manufactured commodities of all kinds. This demand was partly a natural consequence of the creation of the Mughul empire itself, which had brought into being a vast free-trade area in which merchants and their goods could pass with relative ease and safety over vast distances from Kabul to the Deccan and from Gujarat to Bengal. It was also a response to the insatiable demand for luxury commodities on the part of the exceedingly affluent ruling elite. In addition, there was a growing foreign demand for Indian manufactured goods, especially textiles, which were sought after not only in the traditional marts of West Asia and of the lands bordering the Indian Ocean, but also in increasing quantities by the European traders who now began to frequent the ports of the subcontinent and even some of the manufacturing centers up country, rubbing shoulders with their Arab, Iranian, Armenian, and Indian competitors.

The Mughul regime well understood the value of merchants and bankers. It therefore encouraged them, protected them, and even went into partnership with them, having perhaps more need of these useful subjects than they had need of any such imperial superstructure. In any event, the creation of an empire that in course of time came to include the greater part of the subcontinent, together with the establishment of an orderly administrative system, served to boost trading activities of all kinds, as did government initiative in repairing and making safe the main commercial arteries of the country, in the construction of bridges, caravanserais and milestones, and in the attempted standardization of currency, weights, and measures. All these activities favored the commercial classes. In addition, the Mughuls involved themselves directly in the affairs of those same commercial classes in three specific spheres of activity. First, they maintained workshops, often located within the fortress-palaces of their capital cities, where luxury commodities and, in particular, textiles were manufactured under the direction of state officials, a practice emulated by many of the wealthier *mansabdars*. Second, they invested directly in a wide range of capitalist activities, including maritime ventures across the Arabian Sea and the Bay of Bengal. That a *mansabdar* with a commercial background such as Mir Jumla should have gone into partnership with local merchants and also established monopolies in certain commodities was only to be expected, but similar enterprises were also undertaken by members of the ruling house, including some of the women in the imperial harem. Third, the regime was frequently compelled to turn to the capitalist classes for loans in times of emergency, such as at the outset of a campaign. It also sought from them bills of exchange for the transfer of large sums of money over great distances, as when tribute was to be sent from Golconda to Delhi or when the land revenue collected in the province of Bengal was needed to pay troops operating in the southern Deccan.

Under such circumstances, the commercial and banking classes seem to have flourished under Mughul rule. The same can hardly be said of the urban proletariat, steadily growing in number in consequence of an unregulated drift to the towns, where the squalor of the slums might be regarded as preferable to the exactions of the government's revenue officials in the villages. Artisans were paid virtually subsistence wages, and the more skillful were subjected to periodical seizure by nobles who sought their services, often *gratis*, in their own factories. Vast numbers of persons, both in towns and villages, were engaged in the manufacture of textiles, of which cotton weaving undoubtedly employed the most.

Mughul bureaucracy, whatever its achievement in the coercion and manipulation of a vast and diverse population, provided little or nothing in the way of assistance or security for these people, beyond maintaining order of a rather heavy-handed kind. The government's revenue demands and the additional exactions of its servants left the cultivator little or no margin to protect himself against the onset of bad times, and much the same may be said of the pitiful wages of the weaver or unskilled laborer. Both cultivator and artisan alike were exposed to the violence and rapacity of those above them, and both were the first victims of those periodical natural disasters such as drought or famine against which the age knew no protection.

Mughul Cultural Legitimation and the Indian Cultural Tradition

The Safavids, as was shown in the preceding section, acquired cultural legitimation first by linking the fortunes of the Safaviya Sufi order with a tribal Turcoman confederacy, the Qizilbash, and then by gradually identifying their interests with those of their Iranian subjects. The result was to link the dynasty with messianic Shiism, with ancient traditions of Iranian absolutism, and with the Iranian sense of cultural identity and its corollary, the Iranian sense of antagonism towards Ottoman and Arab neighbors. In the case of the Ottomans, the sultan, engaged in *jihad* ("religious warfare") against the infidel in Anatolia and the Balkans, was able to stand forth as the supreme *ghazi*, or "fighter for the faith." In course of time this role was enlarged, first by taking over the imperial Byzantine heritage and then that of the long-defunct Abbasid caliphate of Baghdad. By way of contrast, the Mughuls were confronted by peculiar difficulties in acquiring cultural legitimation as the *de facto* rulers of the subcontinent. Nowhere in their past could they claim a spiritual charisma such as the Safavids claimed through their descent from the *shaykhs* of Ardabil. The role of *ghazi* was inappropriate in a land where, notwithstanding the fact that the majority of the population was non-Muslim, Muslim states had been in existence for three centuries and which, except at its peripheries, was regarded as an extension of the Muslim world of West Asia. Yet the heritage of the sultans of Delhi did not offer an attractive source of legitimation either. The sultans, it is true, had sometimes assumed the role of *ghazis,* but the chronicles of their reigns seem to be mostly tales of unrighteous tyrants and bloody usurpations. Moreover, with one exception, the sultans of Delhi had never claimed to be more than lieutenants of the Abbasid caliphs. They had humbly styled themselves "Helper of the Commander of the Faithful," and Indo-Muslim coins had continued to be struck in the name of the last caliph long after the Mongol sack of Baghdad in 1258. This was hardly an appealing tradition to conquerors with such pretensions as the Mughuls, and indeed they had at hand a far more persuasive tradition of cultural legitimation—that of their Turco-Mongol ancestors, the Chingizkhanids and the Timurids, with their lofty claims to universal empire. This was a tradition of empire in the true sense of the word, a tradition of mastery over men, without regard to geography, race, or creed, and it was reinforced by the folk memory and life-style of the dynasty and its followers and also by that Iranian historiographical tradition, going back to the thirteenth century, which had been brought into existence largely to serve first the Chingizkhanid Il-Khans and then the Timurids.

Significantly, Babur adopted the title of padshah not when he conquered the Delhi sultanate in 1526 but some twenty years earlier, at the time of the death of the senior ruler of his house, Sultan Husayn Baykara of Herat. It was an unusual title since the Timurids (apart from Timur himself, who was content with the title of *amir*) were traditionally styled mirza and occasionally sultan. It seems that in assuming the title of padshah, Babur was proclaiming himself head of all those ruling lineages and clans throughout Central Asia to whom he was related, whether Timurid or Chaghatay. It was with just such a claim, supported by a pedigree to match it, that he and his descendants built up their empire in India, operating within the traditional framework of the steppe empires of their Turco-Mongol ancestors.

For many years the Mughuls and their Central Asian followers continued to regard the Indian subcontinent as an alien environment, due partly to the strength of the cultural heritage they had brought with them from the lands beyond the Indus and partly to their instinctive rejection of the climate, living conditions, and patterns of behavior which they met with in India and which Babur denounced in his memoirs in no uncertain terms. Above all, there was that antipathy between the Islamic and the Hindu world view which has been a continuous factor in shaping the attitudes of Indian Muslims from the time of Sultan Mahmud of Ghazni and al-Biruni down to the twentieth century.

In dress, diet, and in many other respects the Mughuls only slowly and very partially adapted themselves to an Indian life-style. Persian remained the language of the imperial court, of higher administration, and of polite learning, while as late as the reign of Awrangzeb the imperial princes and princesses were still taught Chaghatay Turkish. The Persian poetry written in India continued to mirror the tastes of Shiraz or Herat, and virtually everyone in the long list of poets attached to Akbar's court was a foreigner. Akbar's favorite authors were the classical masters of Iran—Firdawsi, Rumi, Sadi, and Hafiz—and it is arguable that his intellectual predilections, like his eclecticism in religious matters, his lavish patronage of the arts, his magnificent life-style, and his openhanded generosity to suppliants and supporters were a legacy of his Turco-Mongol ancestors rather than a response to a specifically Indian situation.

In general, the imperial family and the foreign nobility did not marry Hindus (Akbar's marriage alliances with Rajput princesses were exceptions which proved the rule) or even Indian Muslims, carefully choosing their sons' brides from other foreign families. Babur, Humayun, and Akbar were of partly Turco-Mongol and partly Iranian descent. Jahangir, however, had a Rajput mother, and so had Shah Jahan. Shah Jahan, in turn, married an Iranian, in whose memory he built the Taj Mahal at Agra, and so Awrangzeb was Iranian on his mother's side. Two centuries later, European visitors at the court of the last Mughul padshahs commented upon their pale complexions and Central Asian features.

Against all this, however, must be weighed the consequence of the rulers having harems inhabited by Indian concubines and slave girls, being surrounded by Hindu servants and retainers, and being exposed to the novelties—sexual, dietary, and recreational—of an Indian milieu. In music and dancing, painting and architecture, indigenous influence proved especially pervasive. By the reign of Jahangir, for example, miniature painting had emancipated itself from the constricting traditions of the Safavid court and had evolved a distinctly Mughul style, as much Indian as Iranian. Pre-Mughul Muslim architecture in India had long shown a tendency to draw inspiration from Hindu forms and decorative motifs, a process that reached its culmination in the sixteenth century in Akbar's new foundation of Fatehpur Sikri.

It was in the sphere of religious life that the polarization of attitudes—indigenous versus foreign—found most complete expression. This was expressed not so much in terms of Hinduism versus Islam as in terms of Sufi heterodoxy versus Sunni orthodoxy. Tracing its origins back to the days of the great Chishtiya *murshids* of the early Delhi sultanate, Sufism in India had assumed during the fifteenth and sixteenth centuries increasingly syncretic and esoteric forms, of which the religious eclecticism of Akbar's court was only one manifestation. Whether these developments should be regarded as the direct consequence of Hindu influence or of a fluidity peculiarly characteristic of Islam in a frontier setting (e.g., in the marches of Byzantine Anatolia or in Southeast Asia), they posed an undoubted threat to Sunni orthodoxy and, by implication, to Muslim political domination. A predictable reaction, therefore, occurred at the close of the sixteenth century, spearheaded by a Sufi order new to India, the Naqshbandiya, which in Bukhara, its home territory, had long been celebrated for its close association with the ruling elite (in contrast to orders like the Chishtiya) and for a spiritual discipline somewhat at variance with the liberal Sufi traditions of the subcontinent. The most effective spokesman of the Naqshbandiya position was Shaykh Ahmad Sirhindi (1564-1624), who cast himself in the role of a millennial renovator of Islam (a thousand years having passed since the *hijra*, the Prophet's flight from Mecca to Medina), much to the apprehension of the self-indulgent Jahangir. The success of his movement, however, probably owed as much to the conventional piety of Jahangir's successors, Shah Jahan and Awrangzeb, as to the work of the *shaykh* himself. Neither during the seventeenth century nor later were these polarizing tensions and conflicts within the Indo-Islamic tradition resolved, and they have come to be seen in retrospect as aspects of another conflict, between those who were willing to adapt and to acculturate themselves to

443

the Indian situation and those who were not. It seems unlikely, however, that contemporaries would have seen the problem in such terms. Rather, they would have seen it in the light of the age-old problem of integrating the personal vision of the Sufis into the rigid framework of the Sunni great tradition.

4. THE MING AND CH'ING EMPIRES IN CHINA

In China the period that followed the era of Central Asian domination is conventionally designated by the names of the two dynasties that succeeded the Mongol Yuan. These dynasties, the Ming (1368-1644) and the Ch'ing (1644-1911), are thus the Chinese counterparts of the early modern empires that existed in the other subdivisions of Asia. In viewing the Ming and Ch'ing dynasties as early modern empires two questions at once arise: (1) How are these regimes different from other dynasties in earlier periods of Chinese history? (2) What is the difference between the Ming and the Ch'ing—should we think of them as distinct or as a single block?

The answer to both of these questions flows from the processes defined at the outset of this chapter. First, in designating an early modern period we are specifically referring to the post-Mongol period and asserting that the regimes that supplanted the Central Asian conquest empires were different from those that went before. There were three types of differences: those resulting from the continuation or adaptation of institutions or practices from the period of Central Asian dominance, those that were part of a reaction to Central Asian dominance, and those that stemmed from ongoing changes within the societies. In the Chinese case it will be seen that the post-Mongol dynasties were different from the pre-Mongol dynasties in a number of significant ways. In general, the elements to be stressed relate to the influence of the political structure upon the society and the tendency for essential cultural values to be shaped by political forces. Second, the Ming and Ch'ing empires both fall into the period designated and both illustrate the trends associated with the early modern empire. However, since these two states were of fundamentally different origins—the Ming was the last indigenous Chinese dynasty while the Ch'ing was a Manchu conquest empire—it will be necessary to discuss them separately in order to understand their separate contributions to the evolution of political institutions and cultural forms. The Chinese state will be viewed as a culturalistic empire and the Manchu state as a pluralistic empire.

The Chinese Ming Empire

Mongol rule in China lasted less than a century after the establishment of the Yuan dynasty in 1279. By the 1340s the empire was torn by dissension and civil disorder at every level: factionalism among the ruling group itself led to fighting over the throne, regional commanders defied central authority, local gentry organized their own security forces, and Chinese peasants rose in armed rebellion. It was peasant rebellion that ultimately dismembered the Yuan. In revolt equally against the harsh exploitation of a ruthless landlord class and the oppressions of a foreign Mongol regime, the common people were inspired by the millennarian doctrines of secret societies which promised them deliverance from the suffering of the traditional order. These organizations, of which the White Lotus Society was the best known, existed deep within the body of peasant society and there harbored values and beliefs strikingly at odds with the high culture of the Chinese elite classes—the ideology of the Confucian state. By the mid-fourteenth century there was widespread belief in a Prince of Brightness (Ming Wang) who would appear and save the world. This doctrine, which combined elements of Maitreya, the popular Buddha of the Future, with traces of Manichaeanism (the West Asian religious dualism, in Chinese *ming chiao*), was combined by the rebels with the demand for the restoration of the Sung dynasty.

Chu Yuan-chang (1328-98), the founder of the Ming empire, started his career as a member of one of the rebel bands. Like the Han founder some fifteen centuries before, he began life as a peasant and was only the second such person in history to rule China. Orphaned and destitute, Chu Yuan-chang spent some of his early years as a wandering monk, begging for his food. Shrewd and ruthless, he rose rapidly once he joined the rebels. A cautious but adequate military strategist and a better judge of men, he soon attracted a large following. Establishing his seat at Nanking on the southern bank of Yangtze, he set about the business of destroying his rivals and annexing territory. Motivated in part by a strong hatred of the landlord class and ever mindful of his own experience of poverty, Chu Yuan-chang took stern measures to prevent his soldiers from harming the common people. Partly because of this solicitude for the peasantry but also because of good generalship and the centrality of his location, Chu Yuan-chang was able to eliminate competing Chinese leaders with regimes similar to his own. Initially, he maintained his allegiance to the secret society elements and to the fledgling state of Sung, which they had created. At the same time he set about building an administrative apparatus of scholars, gentry members, and former Yuan civil servants. By 1367, when he sent his armies north to sweep the Mongol remnants from China, he was ready to disavow his connections with the secret societies and their heterodox doctrines and put himself forward as a champion of orthodoxy qualified to take the Chinese throne. In 1368 he became the first emperor of the Ming dynasty. The name Ming was an ingenious touch, because its meaning—"brightness"—could be variously interpreted as referring to the popular notion of a savior—the Prince of Brightness, Ming Wang—or to a Confucian value (perfect understanding). A gesture in the direction of Sung restoration was made in the same year when the new ruler proposed to make Kaifeng, the first Sung capital, an imperial city (the plan was never realized).

Once in power Chu Yuan-chang devoted his energies to the task of reuniting the Chinese peoples into a single state. Faced with the problem of holding power and building an administration, the Ming founder soon forgot the radical ideals of the peasant movement in favor of an orthodox Confucianism. Thus did potential social revolution turn to cultural conservatism once power was attained. Chu Yuan-chang spent thirty years on the throne, designing and redesigning the institutions that would make his house and government endure. In this enterprise he borrowed freely from the Mongol example as well as from precedents in the Chinese historical record.

Domination over Society and Economy

Imperial domination over Chinese society was guaranteed by an elaborate prescription of the status of all strata of Chinese society. Rule was the monopoly of the imperial family. All offspring of the founder were granted hereditary titles as princes or princesses and were supported by government stipends. Succeeding generations were granted lesser titles. All were barred from government service or any useful occupation. By the end of the Ming, the ranks of the royal family had swollen to more than 100,000 members. The generals who participated in the founding, originally peasants, were converted into a hereditary nobility that intermarried with the imperial clan. Forced to reside in the capital, this group of loyal supporters became a pool from which military commanders were drawn. Actual military forces were scattered about the empire in small guard units organized on a decimal system of Mongol origin. When campaigns were ordered, generals were sent out from the capital to command the troops of the guard units. In this manner a commander was prevented from developing more than temporary ties to his troops. Moreover, the retention of his family in the capital as virtual hostages encouraged the general's loyalty in the field. Beneath this hereditary stratum of the Ming ruling elite lay the two traditional divisions of Chinese society—the gentry and the commoners. The status of the gentry—the wealthy and influential class of literati that had been growing in number ever since the Sung period—was formally fixed by the government through the device of the examination system. Success in passing a government examination conferred a degree, and with the degree went a special social status that extended to the members of the degree-holder's family. Elaborate sumptuary laws specified in detail the clothing and life-style appropriate to each level of society. Nobles and gentry members might wear silk gowns and ride in sedan chairs, while peasants were obliged to wear cotton and to walk. Tax and labor-service regulations and criminal laws were likewise specifically favorable to the upper classes.

The vast bureaucratic apparatus that the Ming founder assembled to run his empire was probably the most sophisticated administrative organization created anywhere up to that time. Organized into the traditional tripartite divisions of civil, military, and censorial elements, it was staffed throughout by salaried officials recruited into imperial service on the basis of merit and dependent on the emperor's trust for continuance in office. Military administration was divided among five regions and numerous military commissions. Civil administration adhered to the traditional units of provinces, prefectures, and counties, while the small body of censors circulated throughout the government and the empire monitoring the efficiency of administration, investigating, criticizing, and exposing all sorts of abuses.

Manpower for the administration was recruited through the traditional examination system, which was now elaborated and regularized on a scale that surpassed the practice of earlier dynasties. Examinations were held in three-year cycles starting at the county level, then moving to more stringent elimination rounds at the provincial level and then at the capital, where the final runoff was held under imperial supervision within the Forbidden City. Degrees were awarded at all three levels, and placing first in the palace examination was a guarantee of fame and fortune for life. Such was the prestige associated with success in the examination system that families of any wealth and ambition whatsoever tutored their sons for the competition. Passing even at the lowest level brought the reward of gentry status. Winners of the higher two degrees might reasonably expect to be appointed to government service. So desirable were the rewards of the degree system and so totally did the degree holders dominate Chinese society that it was not uncommon for ambitious men to spend decades in preparation and attempt repeatedly to pass the examinations. Far more rigorous and restrictive than even the most advanced graduate training in our own degree-conscious society, the examinations drove many to nervous collapse, madness, or suicide. Administration of the examinations was scrupulously fair and every effort was made to avoid cheating or bias of any kind. Examinees were sealed up in cubicles while they wrote their examinations and their papers were coded to preclude favoritism on the part of the judges. Quotas at the provincial level restricted the number of successful graduates, the largest number being assigned to the capital and the richest and most culturally developed areas in the lower Yangtze. The average number of doctorates (the highest degree) awarded in the ninety triennial metropolitan examinations was about 275. In all, the civil service consisted of some ten to fifteen thousand degree holders in eighteen grades, whose careers were carefully regulated. Laws of avoidance kept them from serving in their home districts, thereby reducing the chance of conflict of interest. Efficiency reports evaluated their performance and transfers took place at regular intervals. The effect of recruitment through the examination system was to guarantee the emperor a continuous supply of talented and willing administrators and to preclude the development of entrenched opposition. All officials served at the emperor's pleasure and none held hereditary claim to high office. To continue in office, a family had to educate sons who could pass the examinations—a feat that few could sustain over very many generations. So stable and well regulated was the Ming administration that it operated without major change for more than 250 years.

Mobilization of resources in Ming society was related to the social policy of the Ming government. Just as the nobility monopolized command over military forces, so the gentry supplied administrative talent for the bureaucracy. Lower classes, precluded from participating in government affairs or the political process, were also expected to support the state. The populace was divided into military households, artisans, and commoners. Military families were obliged to supply sons for service in the armed forces. Artisans served terms of rotation as skilled craftsmen on government construction projects. The great bulk of the population, the commoners, were obligated to pay grain taxes and perform labor service. At the founder's behest a comprehensive survey of all the agricultural land in the empire was carried out, along with a census of the population. Compiled for tax purposes, the land survey consisted of annotated diagrams depicting each parcel of land. The "yellow registers" of the census, first completed in the 1390s, described a population of about 60 million persons—a population that was to climb as high as 150 million by the year 1600. Taxation was assigned by quotas at the county level according to the wealth of the area. The basic grain tax, which the peasants paid in two annual portions, was collected by "tax captains," who were chosen from the wealthiest families in each area. This policy, which in effect placed control of landed wealth in the hands of the local elite, was one of the foundations of Chu Yuan-chang's accommodation to the landlord gentry class. It prompted the charge from one modern Chinese historian that Chu had "sold out" the peasantry. At the most local level the peasants were organized in the traditional *li-chia* system—groups of 10 and 110 households that rotated the duties of tax collection and labor service among their members, relieving the government of the need to extend its own agencies down as far as the village level.

One feature of the Ming government which differed decisively from earlier Chinese dynasties was the centralization of power at the top, particularly in the person of the emperor. Organizationally, the most important innovation was the elimination of the office of prime minister. Traditionally, the power of the Chinese emperor was partially balanced by that of the prime minister, who headed the bureaucracy and provided continuity of executive control over government operations. Acting on a report that his highest official was planning a coup d'etat, the first Ming ruler executed his prime minister in 1380 and eliminated for all time the office that the offender had occupied. This event initiated a thorough reorganization of the government in which all of the highest official posts were eliminated. The result of these changes was that the emperor made himself the sole central source of coordination for both the civil and military sides of the government. Reporting directly to him were the five military commissions and the six civil ministries of personnel, revenue, rites, war, justice, and works. All executive coordination had now to come from within the palace. Eventually the emperor appointed civil officials to the various administrative halls within the palace to handle the enormous flow of documents. These officers, called grand secretaries, gradually evolved enormous power and prestige, at times exercising control over the government like that of a prime minister. Unlike prime ministers, however, they were not a check on the ruler but agents of imperial power. Reorganization of the government was accompanied by a prolonged series of purges that eventually put to death twenty or thirty thousand persons suspected of plotting against the emperor. In large part this bloodletting was an outgrowth of the founder's paranoia, but it may also reflect to some extent the brutalization of Chinese life under Mongol rule. The first Ming ruler was, after all, a peasant who had risen to the throne through armed struggle. It was not uncommon for high officials to be fatally beaten right in the court. The emperor is even quoted as having threatened to put a few individuals to death with his own hands. Doubtless some of his fury came from his hatred of the literati and the fact that he had to deal with them in order to rule. On one occasion he had the skin of an official caught pilfering funds stuffed with straw and hung up outside the office as a warning to others. These changes in imperial rule, both institutional and behavioral, are often referred to as Ming despotism. They represented a marked departure from the more temperate and decorous style of the Sung court.

Promotion of the Cultural Tradition

The Ming empire was a culturalistic empire in the sense that its territory encompassed little more than China proper. Its ruling group came to power by expelling the foreign Yuan house so that Chinese self-rule could be reestablished. Reviving a sense of Chinese identity and unity required considerable effort. North China, after all, had been under non-Chinese rule for more than two centuries, parts of it for four centuries. It is little wonder that the new government found it necessary to decree that all Chinese should return to the dress style of the T'ang dynasty and that the practice of Mongol customs and the use of Mongol surnames be discontinued. The Ming regime was based in south China, at this time the Yangtze region (an area Marco Polo had referred to as Manzi, in effect a separate country from the north). In a sense the founding of the Ming was a reassertion of the rich and culturally developed south. It was the first regime ever to rule north China from a capital south of the Yangtze.

Military policy is revealing of the cultural claims of the Ming empire. With the exception of the Liao River valley in the northeast (Manchuria), the northern frontier followed the general contours of the Great Wall, with only purely military installations "beyond the passes." The Ming made no attempt to rule Mongolia as the Mongols had ruled China. The empire was defined essentially in terms of the location of the Chinese population. Peripheral states and tribes were dealt with through a combination of diplomatic and military means but were not incorporated in the territory of the empire. A huge military establishment was maintained across north China with the sole aim of preventing a return of the Mongols. Chu Yuan-chang was obsessed with the danger of a Mongol comeback. He sent his best generals to the north and later stationed his sons in princedoms along the frontier so they could patrol the border.

The Ming state was a Confucian state. So thoroughly had Confucian values colored Chinese history, literature, and statecraft that anyone who governed in China by Ming times was obliged to explain his actions in terms of Confucian prescriptions. In the Ming case the vigorous effort to unify China and to rationalize its administration had the effect of pushing Confucian norms deeper into society than had previously been the case. The examination system was more extensively used than it had been in earlier dynasties. It was under the Mongols that the neo-Confucian *li-hsueh* of Chu Hsi became the core curriculum for the examinations, in effect making ideological purity a prerequisite for government service. Perhaps because he harbored such hostility to the upper classes, the first Ming emperor greatly opened access to the examination system by establishing schools at the local level throughout China. Various imperial codes aimed at bringing Chinese society into conformity with imperial ideals and there stabilizing it. The classification of the population, already alluded to, was part of this effort. An imperial will was issued by the founder governing the affairs of the royal family. Designed to protect the throne, it stipulated the order of succession, regulated the movements of the princes, and specified distinctions between their ranks. For the populace at large there was a comprehensive Ming Code, which covered both criminal law and sumptuary social regulations. The emperor also issued a number of Grand Pronouncements, which covered a wide range of criminal and economic issues. These were in the form of imperial warnings against certain kinds of abuses. Mere possession of these documents entitled the bearer to reduction of criminal sentences by one degree.

The founder's death in 1398 was followed by a period of civil war in which the prince who was stationed at the old Mongol capital at Peking turned his army south and seized the throne from the rightful heir. The usurper, Yung-lo (r. 1402-24), made a number of important changes in Ming government. First, his efforts to rationalize his usurpation of the throne led to drastic alteration of the historical record. The whole reign period from 1399 to 1402 was simply erased. Many historical documents were forged and many more destroyed. Imperial influence in literature reached a new stage with the compilation of the *Yung-lo Encyclopedia* in some twenty-two thousand chapters. Selecting words for inclusion provided an opportunity to search out and destroy undesirable literature. Many officials found their loyalties to the preceding ruler hard to overcome, and the usurper had to make extensive use of less scrupulous agents like the palace eunuchs. This practice led later to the most serious abuses of Ming government.

Second, Yung-lo carried out an extraordinarily aggressive foreign policy that extended Ming influence in all directions at the same time. The emperor's attention to foreign affairs may well have been part of an effort to bolster his prestige by increasing the number of states that paid him tribute. Toward the south he sent his armies into Annam and annexed it as a province. By sea a series of great maritime expeditions was sent out under the direction of the Muslim eunuch Cheng Ho. Using huge, oceangoing junks that carried thousands of soldiers, the expeditions, seven in all, sailed to Southeast Asia, India, Persia, Arabia, and the east coast of Africa. States visited were encouraged to send tributary missions to the Chinese court and some rulers who resisted were attacked. Coming a century before the first European ships reached China, the expeditions reveal Ming technological sophistication in the early fifteenth century. The Yung-lo emperor also undertook a series of five military expeditions into Mongolia. These he led himself. The largest armies numbered more than half a million men and drove as far into the steppe as Karakorum. None of these aggressive efforts expanded Chinese territory. Annam proved ungovernable and had to be given up in the 1430s. The voyages were discontinued at about the same time. Imperial expeditions in the north harassed the Mongols but could not control them. A subsequent emperor, campaigning north of the Wall, was even taken prisoner by the Mongols in 1449.

The third accomplishment of the Yung-lo period was to move the capital to Peking in the north, thus enabling the emperor to keep a closer control over his frontier defenses. Considerable costs were involved, however, for the Grand Canal had to be reopened to bring grain from south China to support the capital at Peking. A more subtle cost was the removal of the government apparatus from the Chinese heartland to the site of what had previously been an alien political center.

Late Ming Developments

The first Westerners to report extensively on China in the sixteenth century were astounded at the orderliness and stability of Chinese society. No doubt this was due in large part to the conscious effort of the Ming government to control change and impose its pattern on Chinese society. Its mere survival as an institution for nearly three centuries testifies to its success. Nevertheless, changes did come with the passage of time. If one compares early Ming China with China of the late Ming, one sees that both the government and the social order were drastically altered. Since the focus of our attention is the impact of the early modern empire on Chinese civilization, and not the fate of the Ming empire as such, it will suffice here simply to note the sort of forces at work in late Ming times as a background to the Manchu invasion and the founding of the Ch'ing dynasty in 1644.

Already in the fifteenth century, drift was apparent in the higher reaches of Ming government. Weak emperors were controlled by ambitious eunuchs who elaborated the imperial bodyguard into a vast secret police apparatus that could terrorize the entire civil service. The number of eunuchs mounted to the tens of thousands. They busied themselves

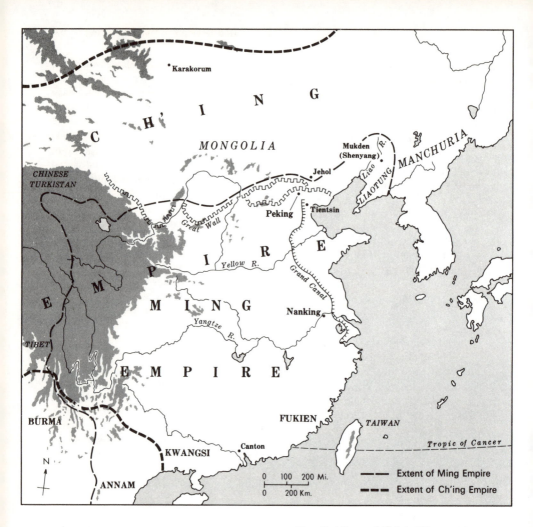

Map 41 Ming and Ch'ing China, 1400-1700

throughout the empire appropriating land that was converted into eunuch-run "imperial estates," making the palace establishment a state within a state. As the central government lost its vigor, it also lost touch with changes in Chinese society. Powerful forces were at work in south China—the wealthy and populous area along the lower Yangtze. The volume of trade increased, urban populations grew, and the whole economy became monetized. What had been a grain economy now became a money economy as labor service and tax payments in kind were converted to payment in silver. Silver flowed into China from the great mines of Mexico as the growth of external trade provided the first preview of the European and American maritime commerce to come.

Remote in the north, dependent on the grain shipments up the Grand Canal for its sustenance, the Ming court was ill-suited to convert its fiscal machinery to the demands of a new economic reality. In the sixteenth century, when new Mongol threats materialized in the north, the government discovered that its old hereditary military system was no longer adequate. It became necessary to raise revenues and hire a whole new army. Piecemeal reforms were instituted and the government muddled through, but not without placing strains on its own cohesion as well as the tolerance of the peasantry, who were asked to bear additional burdens in a tax structure now grossly inequitable.

Changes in the economy and the society were mirrored in art and literature. An acquisitive wealthy class demanded the symbols of cultured existence even when the substance was lacking. The volume of porcelain production, for example, rose to satisfy an expanded market, but the quality fell. Austere and refined motifs of the early wares gave way increasingly to the vulgar symbols of long life, wealth, and happiness. Paintings, too, were turned out in greater number but increasingly by mere copyists to grace the walls of uncultured consumers. Printing reached great heights in the Ming, especially techniques of illustration and color printing. Here also quantity was at odds with quality. Many of the Ming editions were poorly edited and full of mistakes—printed more for display than for reading. One of the liveliest areas of literature was popular colloquial fiction. The growth of literacy is no way better evidenced than in the conversion of storytellers' tales into vernacular novels. Stories like *All Men Are Brothers* and *Monkey*, which had long been part of an oral tradition, appeared as books in the late Ming. Short stories were also extremely popular. The facts that these novels were written in a style that approached the spoken language and that some of them, like *Chin P'ing Mei (Golden Lotus)* and *Jou Pu Tuan (Prayer Mat of Flesh)*, were overtly pornographic is indicative of the breakdown of Confucian standards.

So unsure did people become about the norms of behavior that handbooks for everyday conduct were written to tell people how to manage their affairs. Morality books were written as guides to ethical action, and "ledgers of merit and demerit" allowed the reader to score his behavior by totaling up points for good deeds and bad. Another aspect of the confusion about values was the continuing tendency for elements of Confucianism, Buddhism, and Taoism to be fused together as the distinctions between the "three teachings" became blurred. The popular traditions, Buddhism and Taoism, interacted with the elite tradition, Confucianism, with influences running both ways. Elite patterns were emulated by lower classes but the literati were also receptive to new values. These developments can best be seen in the realm of philosophy.

The greatest philosophical thinker of the Ming period was Wang Yang-ming (1472-1529), who is credited with bringing to fruition the second major branch of neo-Confucianism, the School of Mind *(hsin hsueh)*. By the end of the fifteenth century the orthodox interpretations of Chu Hsi's *li-hsueh* school had lost their vitality and intellectual appeal, although students continued to memorize the orthodox commentaries so that they could pass the examinations and become degree holders. Orthodox learning was a badge of ideological conformity to the state but it could not answer the pressing intellectual and moral questions of the day. Confucian scholars were tormented by the demands of loyalty to a state that had grown corrupt and was at times the antithesis of the Confucian ideal. The effect of Wang Yang-ming's innovation was to move the locus of moral and epistomological authority from an externally discovered principle *(li)* to an internal source: the mind *(hsin)*. For Wang, the universal principles of which Chu Hsi had spoken were the same as the true substance of the mind and therefore could be discovered by looking inward. This innovation had two major implications: (1) much formal book learning and scholarship could be dispensed with since the truth could be attained through introspection, and (2) since it was no longer necessary to be a learned scholar to gain enlightenment, the way was open to sagehood for the common man.

Wang Yang-ming led an active career as a high official, distinguishing himself in military pacification work by putting down rebels and insurgent tribal groups in South China. For him there was no conflict between the dictates of his mind and the social demands of his role as an official in the service of the emperor. He did not question that the norms that were enshrined within the mind were the same as those that orthodox thought approached through the "investigation of things" or through conventional scholarship. Inevitably, however, Wang's thought, with its emphasis on the mind and on quiet sitting, meditation akin to that practiced by Taoists and Chan (Zen) Buddhists, led later thinkers further and further from orthodoxy and official careers. The changes in Chinese philosophy after Wang Yang-ming were so great in the sixteenth century that they have been characterized as a near revolution in thought. Doctrines of the School of Mind were transmitted, studied, and discussed in academies, centers of Confucian learning that sprang up throughout China in the Ming. By the latter half of the sixteenth century something approaching a counterculture had emerged. Popularization of revitalized Confucianism was manifested in mass meetings, complete with group singing and uplifting speeches by itinerant evangelists. Eventually, radical thinkers emerged who broke out of the Confucian mold entirely. Where Wang Yang-ming's thought had sought a kind of psychic adjustment to the conflicting demands of conscience and duty in a corrupt society, these thinkers attacked the society and its institutions. The most outspoken of them were hunted down, jailed, and put to death or driven to suicide.

The philosophy of Wang Yang-ming represented a major innovation within Confucianism but it failed to overturn the orthodox li-hsueh school. Wang's most lasting influence was felt not in China but in Japan (where he is known as Ōyōmei). In China Wang's thought was attacked by orthodox thinkers as Buddhism in disguise. By the beginning of the seventeenth century an intellectual reaction had set in and conservative Confucians tried to restore strict moral standards to the decadent government. Organized around academies like the Tung-lin, they soon became enmeshed in the factional struggles of the court involving rival groups of officials and eunuchs in unstable alliances.

Ming politics reached bottom in the 1620s with the emergence of the eunuch dictator Wei Chung-hsien (1568-1627). Utterly unscrupulous, Wei rose to power in the palace establishment through manipulation of a child emperor and quickly established control over both the police apparatus and the fiscal machinery of the state. All who resisted him were subjected to persecution. A blacklist was drawn up of those, such as the Tung-lin faction, who dared to criticize his actions. Government was perverted utterly. At the height of his power officials throughout the empire competed to build temples to his honor while students in the imperial academy compared him to Confucius. As the Ming government degenerated, the Chinese people rose in armed rebellion. Massive peasant uprisings swept the northern and western provinces in the 1630s and early 1640s. Rebel leaders like Li Tzu-ch'eng (d. 1645) and Chang Hsien-chung (1605-47), after years of bloody campaigning, assumed imperial titles in direct challenge to the Ming house.

Manchu Conquest and Establishment of the Ch'ing Dynasty

With the Manchu seizure of Peking in 1644 China entered upon another era of foreign rule, which was to last until the twentieth century (1911). In subsequent chapters we shall have cause to notice various ways in which the fact of foreign rule influenced China's response to forces of change and inhibited the development of Chinese nationalism.

Unlike the Central Asian Mongols, the Manchus were descended from tribes of hunter-fisher peoples in the forested slopes of the Liaotung area northeast of China. Of Jurched stock, they were related to the founders of the Chin dynasty (1115-1234), which had ruled north China in pre-Mongol times. Under the Ming the Manchus were nominally organized into a commandery on the Chinese frontier. As Ming power declined this tribal group transformed itself from the status of a tributary loosely affiliated with the court to an independent and aggressive state. Much of the later Manchu success is traceable to the fact they were able to devote several decades to state building in the relative security of Manchuria before they invaded China. In this incubation period they enjoyed an advantage over the Chinese rebels who were obliged to build their regimes within China proper in territory contested by the Ming.

The most remarkable aspect of the Manchu conquest of China was the almost total social and institutional transformation that the Manchus underwent. In but half a century they developed from a loose group of tribes into a highly mobilized war machine with an administrative arm capable of managing the largest empire on earth. Many of the processes of the formation of hybrid barbarian-civilized empires discussed in the preceding chapter were repeated in this transition. The Manchus survived their transition and erected a state that long outlived any the Mongols attempted. Essential to the effort was a judicious and pragmatic blending of traditional tribal elements, Chinese bureaucratic institutions, and outright innovations.

The first steps were taken around 1600 by Nurhaci (1559-1626), who unified the Jurched tribes and created a flexible military organization. Called the banner system, this involved the division of his fighting forces into units designated by colored flags. The four initial units were expanded to eight by adding borders to the banners, and later eight Mongol and eight Chinese banners were added. The size of the banner units grew to encompass the whole Manchu and allied population and the function was generalized to include a variety of administrative matters. In this way tribal organization was gradually displaced by more rational and bureaucratic forms and the entire society was mobilized for service under a central leadership. Nurhaci extended his territory and fought enough battles with the Ming to control the area east of the Liao River. He established his capital at Mukden (Shenyang).

The Manchus were keenly aware of the superiority of Chinese governmental organization. They therefore set out in a very systematic way to learn as much as they could from the Chinese. As they came into control of towns and cities in the Liaotung area and as Ming forces surrendered to them in battle, Chinese officials and officers were induced to teach them the arts of government. A new written script was created for the Manchu language and numerous Chinese texts were translated. Nurhaci's successor, Abahai (1592-1643), set up a civil administration in the Chinese style with six boards, slightly modified to accommodate Manchu princes in the top positions.

It is often true in politics that the essence of political authority resides more in the imagery of power than in its substance. Nowhere was this better appreciated than China, where Confucian political culture explicitly stressed the importance of the "rectification of names." This matter is worthy of our attention for it has to do with the relationship between the Manchus and the Chinese cultural tradition. If the Manchus were to conquer China and rule it they had to create an image of legitimacy. Nurhaci had originally called his state Chin in reference to the earlier conquest dynasty. This title Abahai changed in 1636 to Ch'ing ("pure"), suggesting a reform much needed in China. The term Jurched and the name of the old commandery were suppressed and the new term Manchu was coined to obscure the fact that the Ch'ing had once been tributaries of the Ming. The greatest boon to the Manchus came in 1644, when the rebel Li Tzu-ch'eng entered Peking and the Ming emperor committed suicide. This spared the would-be invaders the onus of extinguishing a legitimate Chinese rule. The Manchus by this time had conquered most of the territory north of the Great Wall and were poised to invade China. The Ming Chinese general who was guarding the passes against the Manchus, Wu San-kuei (1612-78), now invited the Manchus to enter China and attack Li Tzu-ch'eng. This allowed the Manchus to pose as the agents of order and orthodoxy even as they occupied the Ming capital.

Domination over Chinese Society

Control over the empire and acceptance by the Chinese was not quick in coming to the new Ch'ing dynasty. Before entering China the Manchus built alliances with the peoples on their flanks, the Koreans and the Mongols. Initially this multiethnic military alliance controlled only north China as a civil administration was gradually elaborated. In the southern provinces a number of regional satrapies were tolerated for several decades under such Chinese collaborators as Wu San-kuei. A series of Ming princes offered token resistance along the seacoast and southern frontier. Wu San-kuei pursued the last of these pretenders into Burma and brought him back for strangulation. The most colorful of the Ming loyalists was a half-Japanese pirate named Cheng Ch'eng-kung (1624-62), better known to Europeans as Koxinga. He fought for the Ming cause along the coast south of the Yangtze and then was forced across the strait to Taiwan, where he defeated the Dutch and took over the island. The Manchu conquest of China was not completed until 1683, by which time the regional satraps and Ming pretenders had been eliminated and Taiwan taken. Nearly forty years had elapsed since the fall of Peking.

Initially the Manchus were obliged to utilize such persons as were willing to collaborate with them. One of their first Chinese grand secretaries, for example, was an official who had done some of the dirty work for the eunuch Wei Chung-hsien. Wu San-kuei was a temporary ally. Another example is Koxinga's father, Cheng Chih-lung (1604-61). A political opportunist, he touched all the bases in a western Pacific community where Portuguese, Spanish, and Dutch intermingled freely with Chinese and Japanese and commerce shaded indistinguishably into piracy. A native of Fukien, he was baptized Nicholas Gaspard in Macao before going on to Manila, Taiwan, and Japan, where he married. Becoming a pirate he operated out of Taiwan against both the Chinese and the Dutch. Later he went over to the Ming and worked for them against the pirates. After the fall of the Ming he served a Ming pretender briefly and then defected to the Manchus. Residing in Peking, he came under suspicion when his son continued to lead the fight against the Ch'ing. Eventually he was imprisoned and executed.

Reliance on allies such as these could not guarantee the Ch'ing rulers continued control over China. Since the Manchus were outnumbered by their subjects on the order of a hundred to one, the durability of their government depended on their ability to recruit capable Chinese administrators into their service. The system that resulted was a Manchu-Chinese dyarchy, or dual form of government. Basically, the Ch'ing continued the Ming organization of civil administration with Manchu control elements added at the top. The highest positions were divided among Manchus, some Mongols, and reliable Chinese, many of whom descended from earlier collaborators in Manchuria. Governors of provinces were typically Chinese officials, but imposed upon them, usually with responsibility for two provinces, were governors general (normally Manchus), whose concurrent reports provided the emperor with a reliable check on the Chinese. Another safeguard in the provinces was the presence of banner forces under Manchu command. In the central government the heads of the six boards, or ministries, were staffed by two officials, one Manchu and one Chinese. The Chinese provided bureaucratic expertise while the Manchus guaranteed political reliability. The highest organ continued to be the grand secretariat, which the early Ming emperors had developed as an agency of the throne. In the early eighteenth century a new body was superimposed at the top. Called the Grand Council (literally "military plans office"), it consisted of a select group of grand secretaries who met informally with the emperor to decide the most sensitive issues. This marked the culmination of a number of steps by which the emperors tightened their hold over the administration by channeling the flow of the most sensitive secret reports directly into the palace.

Patronage of Chinese Culture

Because it was a conquest dynasty, the Ch'ing can be classified as a pluralistic empire. Although the Ch'ing continued Ming institutions in a wholesale manner, it nevertheless differed from its predecessor in a number of fundamental respects. For one thing, its territory included vast tracts of Mongolia and Central Asia. Peking, at the northern edges of the Ming, was in the southern half of the great eighteenth century map of the Ch'ing empire. The Ch'ing ruler, like other conquerors before, extended his rule both north and south of the Great Wall. Court business was conducted in two languages—Chinese and Manchu—and court documents were prepared in bilingual form. The Manchu homeland was maintained as a preserve for the tribal peoples and Chinese settlement there was restricted for the first two centuries of the dynasty. Mukden continued to rank as a subsidiary capital, while Jehol, just beyond the Wall, was the site of a summer palace. Relations with areas such as Mongolia, Tibet, and Chinese Turkistan were handled through a Superintendency of Dependencies, which paralleled the civil organs for China proper. In military terms the Ch'ing were not content as the Ming had been to rule just China. Frontiers were expanded vigorously—especially in the north and west, where aggressive campaigning continued into the middle of the eighteenth century.

In matters of cultural policy the Ch'ing rulers carefully nurtured different traditions to meet the needs of their pluralistic empire. To keep alive their own customs they encouraged the use of the Manchu language and even established an examination system in Manchu similar to that in Chinese. An important part of Ch'ing policy toward Central Asian subjects was imperial patronage of Lamaism, a faith that was important to Mongols as well as Tibetans. Toward the Chinese, of course, the Manchus presented themselves as champions of Confucian values. Much of their success in building a permanent empire on Chinese soil was due to the fact that early emperors, K'ang-hsi (r. 1662-1722) and Ch'ien-lung (r. 1736-95) in particular, were able to demonstrate great proficiency in Chinese learning. Tireless administrators who personally handled heroic quantities of documents, these men approached the ideal of Confucian kingship. They were equally familiar with civil and military administration; they wrote poetry and patronized the arts. K'ang-hsi was the first Manchu ruler to travel south to the Yangtze region to inspect the conditions of the Chinese heartland and enhance his prestige among the Chinese literati.

The Ch'ing revived the civil-service examination system of the Ming which continued the patronage of Sung neo-Confucianism. The works of Chu Hsi were reprinted under imperial sponsorship during the K'ang-hsi reign. Resistance to Manchu rule by Ming scholars was widespread. It was several decades before special imperial examinations were held as a device for recruiting Chinese scholars to take part in the compiling of the official history of the Ming dynasty (Ming-shih). Some refused to take part, others did so under duress, while many who participated were tormented by the conflict between a desire to accurately record the history of their dynasty and a revulsion at collaboration with a foreign conqueror. The resulting Ming-shih was not completed until the 1720s. It is regarded as one of the most accurate of the twenty-four official histories. Still, the Ming-shih is purposely obscure on a number of points dealing with the Mongols and the Manchus.

Imperial patronage of scholarly activity not only bound scholars to the state, it also gave the state an opportunity to shape the content of learning itself. So boldly did the Manchu rulers act in this regard that the whole picture of modern Chinese history was distorted by their efforts. The K'ang-hsi emperor undertook projects of the same scale as had the early Ming rulers. The great illustrated encyclopedia, Ku-chin t'u-shu chi-ch'eng, ten thousand chapters, completed in 1725, ranks with the Yung-lo Encyclopedia as an effort to summarize all knowledge. The K'ang-hsi Dictionary (1716) contains definitions for forty-seven thousand individual Chinese characters arranged according to a list of 214 radicals (parts of characters) and then ranked by the number of brush strokes used in writing the characters. This system of classification, which functions as alphabetical ordering does in our language, has remained a standard feature of Chinese ever since. In the Ch'ien-lung era an even grander project was undertaken. This was the compilation called Ssu-k'u ch'uan-shu, or Complete Books of the Four Treasuries. Occupying an editorial board of 361 scholars from 1773 to 1782, the final manuscript consisted of more than seventy-eight thousand chapters arranged under the four traditional categories of classics, history, philosophers, and belles lettres. As important as the collection itself was the selection process involved in its creation, for it provided the opportunity for a massive purge of Chinese literature. Rare works were actively solicited from throughout the empire, brought to Peking and examined. Only 3,461 books were eventually copied into the manuscript, but all of the works were described and evaluated in a catalogue that contained more than ten thousand entries. Hand in hand with this scholarly survey of Chinese literature there proceeded an equally thorough effort to identify, collect, and destroy all works offensive to the Manchu house. In the 1780s a Bureau of Book Censorship was set up and an *Index* of banned books issued which contained more than two thousand titles. Proclamations were issued, homes and libraries searched, and books seized for burning in every province.

The fact that systematic purges of Chinese literature came after more than a century of Manchu rule reflects the change in political conditions. The policies of the K'ang-hsi emperor in the late seventeenth century were patronizing toward the Chinese scholars and aimed at drawing them into government service. Considerable tolerance was involved. The great Ming scholar and loyalist Huang Tsung-hsi (1610-95), for example, refused to join in the compilation of the *Ming-shih,* but the emperor ordered that his works be made available to the editorial board. In this way, Huang's resistance was overlooked and his learning acknowledged by the Manchu ruler. By the 1770s Ch'ien-lung realized that the scholarship of the preceding century contained many elements dangerous to Manchu supremacy. Works that dealt with Ming history, border affairs, defense, conquest dynasties or that contained even the most subtle criticisms of Manchu rule were ruthlessly suppressed. One result of the suppression was to obscure or distort the portrayal of early modern Chinese history. Only in the last few decades have copies of banned works been discovered and reprinted and scholars set about the task of reconstructing the story of Ming history.

Another effect of Ch'ien-lung's book burning was to deflect Chinese scholarship away from sensitive issues. Already by the end of the Ming, scholars were in reaction against the idealism of the Wang Yang-ming school, which stressed the mind. Late Ming and early Ch'ing scholarship turned increasingly to concrete subjects like geography, history, and bibliography. The result was Ch'ing empiricism—a rigorous and systematic scholarship that was protoscientific in its rules for collection of data, use of evidence, and citation of sources. It did not include experimentation, however, and there was little interest in the realm of nature. The favored subject matter was the literary tradition itself, and some of the greatest achievements were in areas like philology, phonology, lexicography, and textual analysis of the classics. Thus by the twin sanctions of sponsorship and suppression, the Manchu state was able to channel the energies of the Chinese literati into harmless endeavors. As scholarship became less relevant to the issues of the day it also declined in vigor and creativity.

In China the era of the early modern empires saw a continued development of the centralized power of the imperial state. The Ming, which arose in response to Mongol rule, was self-conscious in its culturism. The state took an active role in the promotion of Chinese high culture and in stabilizing the social and administrative institutions of the empire. The jurisdiction of the Ming was essentially China proper, an area the state governed and defended as a self-contained island of cultural superiority. The Manchu conquest in the seventeenth century reduced the Chinese to the status of a subordinate, though large, majority within a pluralistic Ch'ing empire. The Manchu rulers assiduously adopted and promoted the Ming forms but transformed them to the needs of a foreign rule. The result in the first century and a half was a prosperous empire under stable and capable administration. Under the Ch'ing government, China attained in the eighteenth century its greatest prosperity—perhaps the greatest wealth known to any society in history up to that time.

Internal peace and moderate levels of taxation contributed to a doubling of the population from 150 million to more than 300 million by the end of the century. In subsequent chapters we will have cause to note that the very successes of the Ming and Ch'ing governments created problems for China in the nineteenth century. Ming institutions worked so well that innovation was hard to justify or even to conceive, Manchu cultural policy was so effective that the Chinese were tardy in developing a sense of nationalism, and the growth of population undermined the prosperity of the whole society.

5. TOKUGAWA JAPAN

During the era of Mongol dominance in China and other parts of Asia, Japanese society remained largely outside the historical developments on the Eurasian continent. Although the abortive attempts at invasion by Mongol naval forces at the end of the thirteenth century perhaps played a role in further weakening the Kamakura government, there was no foreign conquest and the major currents in Japanese history down to the sixteenth century were primarily indigenous in origin. Nevertheless, the creation of the Tokugawa early modern empire at the turn of the seventeenth century does in numerous ways resemble the rallying of other Asian societies to restore cultural stability after an extended period of turmoil.

From the middle of the fifteenth century the tempo of change within Japanese society had increased dramatically. Foreign trade had stimulated the growth of the domestic economy, and cities and towns had sprung up outside the framework of the older social structure. Social and geographical mobility had increased to produce a much more fluid society. Contact with the outside world reached new proportions in Japanese history and in the late sixteenth century Europeans for the first time appeared on the scene, albeit in small numbers and with limited impact. These developments were accompanied in the fifteenth and sixteenth centuries by a breakdown in the political system and near anarchy, as the warrior elite became locked in protracted struggles for power. Thus the Tokugawa regime can be viewed as the result of a concerted effort at cultural conservatism, an attempt to stem the tide of change by reasserting the older ideal of a government capable of dominanting social and cultural life. As such it was an effort that did slow the tempo of change in certain sectors and largely reverse the process by which Japan had become increasingly involved in the outside world. It is this aspect of early modern Japanese history that will be emphasized here, leaving to later chapters the more dynamic story of how the changes in the Tokugawa period paved the way for the modern transformation of Japan of the nineteenth and twentieth centuries.

Creation and Maintenance of the Tokugawa State

The Tokugawa regime in Japan, like other early modern empires in Asia, was first established through military might. From the fifteenth century on the Japanese military elite, described in Chapter 7, had engaged in almost incessant conflict in the attempt to create a stable configuration of political power. In the early stages, from about 1330 to about 1460, it was primarily the regional overlords, the heirs of the military governors of the Kamakura period, who struggled among themselves for the position formerly held by the Minamoto, a position that continued to elude the Ashikaga despite their claims to the title of shogun. After the middle of the fifteenth century central authority became a myth to which few bothered to pay even lip service, and for a century effective control over regions as large as the old provincial units proved beyond the capacities of most competing warlords.

Political power had become fragmented to the point where stability and peace were at best temporary phenomena, achieved only in local areas constantly defended by force of arms. Political authority was thus largely equated with military force. The synthesis of familial and bureaucratic norms that had aided in holding together the political system of the previous era gave way to something resembling very closely the feudalism of medieval Europe, the significant political groupings being local networks of fighting men tied together by the institutions of vassalage and fiefs. These shifting alliances based on feudal vassalage were too unstable and the ghost of a single national hegemony too strong an ideal to permit a lasting equilibrium, and in the late sixteenth century the struggles for power entered a new stage. Although firearms introduced via the Portuguese played a small role in these struggles, the key factors here were new types of regional leaders who utilized new institutional arrangements to more fully mobilize the economic, social, and military resources of their domains to piece together larger and more stable territorial bases. The three most successful of these leaders were Oda Nobunaga (1534-82), Toyotomi Hideyoshi (1537-98), and finally Tokugawa Ieyasu (1542-1616).

Oda Nobunaga had been a relatively obscure warrior leader with a small local base near the present-day city of Nagoya and the vassal of a warlord with an expanding territory in eastern Japan. In the fashion that had become increasingly prevalent in the late Ashikaga period, Nobunaga turned on his liege lord and usurped control over his network of vassals. He then marched on the imperial city of Kyoto, established dominance over central Japan, and eventually deposed the last Ashikaga shogun in 1573. Although Nobunaga died in the struggle to expand his authority at the expense of other regional hegemons, his power base passed intact to Toyotomi Hideyoshi. Hideyoshi, whose rise from the peasantry to become Nobunaga's chief lieutenant illustrates the openness and fluidity of the social structure at this time, was an extraordinarily gifted military leader, and by the early 1590s the rival leagues of warlords in the eastern and southwestern regions of Japan were forced to acknowledge Hideyoshi's supremacy. His hold over the country was extremely tenuous, however, and his death in 1598 threatened to pitch Japan into a new round of bloody conflict. It was only after another of Nobunaga's former vassals, Tokugawa Ieyasu, combined crucial victories in the battle of Sekigahara in 1600 and the siege of the castle of Hideyoshi's heir in 1615 with skillful political compromises that the great regional leaders of the country were convinced that little was to be gained by further recourse to arms.

It is important to note that Ieyasu's military victories did not eliminate his opposition. The settlement that created the Tokugawa regime was a series of compromises, a fact that is a key to understanding the political life of Japan over the next two and a half centuries. Whatever Ieyasu's own ambitions and views of the ideal political system may have been—and it is quite possible that he did not envisage a highly centralized bureaucratic state since his own experience and that of his contemporaries was limited to the feudal milieu of his times—his forces simply did not have the strength to destroy the other warlords within the country. The advantage he did possess over his rivals rested on a larger network of alliances, family ties, and feudal vassalage linking the Tokugawa house with other military lords. This network was strong only so long as Ieyasu's own vassals were assured of their rightful status as feudal lords and hence of a measure of autonomy within their own domains or fiefs. The military supremacy of this network over the rival leaders of the northeast and southwest was sufficient to persuade them to pay homage to the Tokugawa, but, again, only so long as these lords were not forced to choose between losing control over their own domains, on the one hand, and a new round of battles on the other. In short, the Tokugawa in the early seventeenth century did not have the capacity nor perhaps the will to create a truly centralized state; rather, Ieyasu sought a grand compromise in which the more powerful of his own vassal lords and those outside his network were confirmed as rulers within their own territories in return for accepting Tokugawa overlordship and authority in matters of overall national policy.

As a consequence of this compromise, the political map of Japan between 1600 and

1868 remained a patchwork quilt. The largest single area, comprising approximately a fifth of the country and a third of the population, consisted of Tokugawa houselands administered directly by Tokugawa officials and liege vassals. The bulk of the land and its peoples, however, was divided into over 200 semiautonomous domains administered by lords over whom the Tokugawa shogun's influence varied greatly. The majority of the very largest domains were held by the descendants of the warlords classified as *tozama*, or "outside lords," who had originally resisted Tokugawa hegemony. Their size, the tradition of independence, and their strategic geographical position (the more important were located in the southwest, outside of the central regions around Kyoto and Tokyo) gave them considerable autonomy, although they were largely excluded from any role in the formulation of Tokugawa policy. The second category of domains were governed by *fudai*, or "inside lords," the heirs of men who had early sworn personal allegiance to Ieyasu. The more important of these "inside" lords sat in the higher councils of the Tokugawa shogun and provided the administrative leadership for the regime. The remainder of the *fudai* lords participated at lower levels in the Tokugawa government and were also subject to closer supervision over the internal affairs of their domains.

Despite the basically decentralized character of the political system that took shape in Japan during the early seventeenth century, there were critical restrictions placed on the lords in their semiautonomous domains, and certain key powers were reserved to the Tokugawa central government in Edo (modern-day Tokyo). Given the Tokugawa's direct control over a large share of the nation's resources and people, these powers and restrictions constituted a significant degree of centralized power, and a complex system of interlocking checks on the activities of the lords, whether "outside" or "inside," served to create a political equilibrium in which Tokugawa hegemony could be maintained for over two and a half centuries. These restrictions included prohibitions against expanding military fortifications or forming political alliances through marital ties. Perhaps the most significant of these, however, was the system of alternate attendance, under which all lords were required to be present in Edo for specified periods of time to pay homage to the Tokugawa shogun. This served both to siphon off some of the economic means of challenging Tokugawa supremacy—the heavy expenses incurred in the long journeys to and from and the maintenance of large mansions in Edo were a continual drain on the finances of the lords—and as a thinly veiled hostage system. When the lord himself was not present in Edo, other members of his family were to reside there both as symbolic acknowledgement of submission to Tokugawa overlordship and as a concrete guarantee of good conduct.

Reunification of the Cultural Area

One of the most important of the powers reserved to the central government was that of making foreign policy, a power the Tokugawa utilized to further ensure stability and shield against disrupting influences. By the middle of the seventeenth century the Tokugawa had all but cut Japan off from intercourse with the outside world. Vessels were limited to sizes suitable only to coastal shipping, and Japanese who traveled abroad were subject to permanent exile or severe punishment. Foreigners, with the exception of some Chinese merchants and employees of the Dutch East Indies Trading Company, which was permitted a specified number of voyages per year, were forbidden to land on Japanese territory. Even the Dutch were allowed outside their trading factory in Nagasaki only to report to Edo upon shogunate demand. This policy of isolation was a radical reversal of trends in the late sixteenth century toward greater involvement in the wider world. Japanese pirates then had flaunted Ming authority on the China coast, while merchants had sought profits as far abroad as Southeast Asia, and adventurers had sold their military skills in the service of both sides in the conflicts that accompanied European probes in that part of Asia. This outward

Map 42 Tokugawa Japan, about 1700

thrust had culminated in the 1590s when Hideyoshi, combining an ambition for conquest with a shrewd plan for diverting his rivals' attention from domestic politics, had launched two ill-fated expeditions up the Korean peninsula.

During this period, Hideyoshi and others welcomed the European traders and their missionary companions, exhibiting great interest in the goods, technology, and even ideas carried with them. The details of this early interaction with the West will be discussed in a later chapter; here our concern is with the reasons the Tokugawa insisted on decision-making power in foreign affairs and why they utilized it to enforce an almost total ban on interaction with the world. Stated in simplest terms, foreign contacts posed an internal and an external threat. The external threat was vividly described for them by the accounts of European military victories elsewhere in Asia—accounts supplied in part by competing Europeans who sought to advance their own nation's interests in Japan by warning the Japanese of their rivals' greed. The internal threat was posed in part by the fact, dictated by simple geography, that foreign contact had taken place first in the southwest domains of the *tozama*, or "outside," lords. Profits from trade and military advantages from European weapons were seen by the Tokugawa as potentially undermining its own supremacy. Even the conversion of members of the elite to the Christian faith appeared a political threat insofar as it served to forge new ties between anti-Tokugawa forces. Although the To-kugawa did keep the door slightly ajar for a small volume of trade via the Dutch, its own views of the role of commerce in the economy precluded any serious interest in the long-range possibilities of foreign trade. Hence, on the balance there was little to be gained and much, in the form of disruption of the newly established balance of power within Japan, to be lost by foreign contacts.

Domination of Economy and Society

Having eliminated foreign trade as a major factor, the Tokugawa also consolidated its control over other aspects of the economy. Its general view of economics was derived from the experience gained in successfully mobilizing resources for the military campaigns of the late sixteenth century. What adaptations were needed for peacetime were made ad hoc or suggested by Chinese neo-Confucian precepts. Agriculture was seen as the all-important foundation for strong government and an affluent society, and following the lead of Hideyoshi the new regime took steps to ascertain precisely what the land would produce and to routinize tax collections. Direct Tokugawa control, however, applied only to its own houselands. Although the various lords were required from time to time to contribute to such special projects as the rebuilding of the imperial city of Kyoto or the repair of fire damage in Edo, there was no systematic taxation of their domains by the shogunate. On the other hand, the estimated yield of the Tokugawa lands in the early period amounted to as much as 25 percent of the whole country's agrarian production. Revenue from this for the most part flowed directly into the Tokugawa treasury, since by the end of the seventeenth century few of the Tokugawa liege vassals had any direct economic power over their fiefs. Tax policy was set by the shogunate councils, collected by agents of the shogunate, and stored in shogunate granaries. Levies on the peasantry in the form of labor services were also controlled from the castle town. Most vassals who held title to specified villages as fiefs merely collected their income from the granary officials. The campaigns of Nobunaga and Hideyoshi had earlier broken the economic power of the central Buddhist temples and Shinto shrines, and these too were now supported by payments from revenue collected by shogunal officials. Although in large part autonomous, the various lords within their own domains followed a similar pattern, imposing a more centralized control over agrarian production by removing their vassals from the land and substituting stipends for fiefs of the type common in earlier periods.

Commerce as such was not viewed as a source of regular revenue by the Tokugawa government. It was seen rather as potentially disruptive to a smoothly functioning, agrarian-based economy and subjected to a wide variety of restrictions, particularly with regard to merchant activities in the rural areas. The prohibition on merchants acquiring land was indicative of the Tokugawa attempt to separate urban commerce from rural agriculture and keep important resources in its own hands. The Tokugawa was therefore careful to bring the major urban centers of consumption and trade under its own direct supervision, for political as well as economic reasons. Thus Kyoto (the seat of the imperial court and an important consumption center), Osaka (which had replaced its neighbor Sakai as chief port along the inland sea), Nagasaki (the only outlet for foreign trade), as well as the Tokugawa castle town of Edo were administered by Tokugawa officials. None was allowed opportunity to develop the type of independence found in Western European cities. Whereas large merchant houses did achieve a position of influence over the economy, they were forced to operate in a political atmosphere basically hostile to com-mercial interests. Even the fact that the Tokugawa did not regularly tax trade was partially offset by the practice of forced "loans," licensing fees, and even outright confiscation in some instances. These practices were imposed on an irregular basis and were at times compensated for by grants of monopolies, but they are evidence that the Tokugawa was far more concerned with keeping the activities of the merchant class within limited channels than with promoting its growth. The ultimate failure of this attempt is an important part of the story of the decline of the Tokugawa system.

The Tokugawa, moreover, recognized the strategic importance of some economic goods and placed them under tight control. The chief sources of precious metals for coinage—which was one of the important economic powers reserved to the central government—were monopolized by the shogunate, whose officials supervised the production and minting of gold, silver, and copper. The resulting opportunities for manipulation of currency, although in the long run detrimental to Tokugawa economic stability, were frequently made use of for short-run goals.

Despite the severe limitations on political freedom and the many harsh features of government in the Tokugawa period, there were very real restraints on shogunal power both in principle and in practice. The nature of the relationship to the imperial throne gave political authority a dualistic character; even though the emperor in Kyoto was a puppet, his mere existence prevented the shogun from acquiring the full status of national monarch. While Japanese feudalism had never developed the concepts of contractual rights that came to be present in European vassalage, the status of samurai was an honorable one, and no lord could ignore entirely the claims upon his benevolence if his authority was to remain legitimate (hence, for example, when the Tokugawa and other lords in economic difficulties resorted to reductions in the stipends of their samurai retainers, they also resorted to such euphemisms as "loans" to soften the impact). In practice, there were more tangible restraints on Tokugawa despotism. As noted above, the continued existence of domains economically and militarily independent of the shogunate meant that political power remained somewhat fragmented in Japan. While able to dictate policy on foreign affairs and require lords to pay homage at the castle in Edo, even Ieyasu at the height of his military victories had been cautious about direct interference into the internal affairs of the larger outer domains.

If we shift the focus from the Tokugawa as a national government and consider the shogunate and the domain governments as parts of a single political system, we do see a number of features that combined to give the elite in power greater control over Japanese society than any previous regime had achieved.

One development, or set of developments, that made this social control possible was the rapid growth of bureaucratic institutions and techniques. Both the shogunate and the individual domain governments built upon the advances inherited from the late sixteenth century in their efforts to mobilize human and material resources. The responsibility for such administrative functions as finances, religious affairs, urban government, mining and other monopolies, as well as military matters, was divided among hierarchically structured offices operating according to routinized procedures. Hereditary rank within the samurai class was still the essential qualification for official positions; but since the pool of samurai at any given level was larger than the number of offices to be filled, it was usually possible to pass over the obviously incompetent and select officials from among those with the proper rank who exhibited particular merit. On the other hand, promotion across hereditary rank lines remained uncommon, although here again consideration of competency or political favoritism sometimes prevailed over the strict adherence to hereditary status. By the late Tokugawa period there was also greater concern for training appropriate to the specialized functions to be assumed by these samurai civil servants. On the whole, although the Tokugawa bureaucracy was far less developed in terms of specialization of function, codification of regulations, or recruitment according to impersonal standards than either the contemporary Chinese or twentieth century Western standards, there had been a marked departure from the style of administration of medieval Japan.

The country was also now far more effectively knit together by means of communication than it had ever been in Japanese history. The mountainous terrain and the dictates of military defense hindered road building (rivers were often left unbridged in order to prevent the easy movement of troops and checkpoints were established to control illegal travel), but overland transportation did improve greatly with such major arteries as the Tokkaido road linking Edo and Osaka. In addition to providing for administrative needs, the major roads were well traveled by merchants, pilgrims, and tourists, giving rise to thriving post towns where innkeepers, prostitutes, bearers, and money changers competed to make the journey more comfortable, if also more expensive. The shipping of foodstuffs and other commercial goods was cheaper by sea, and by the beginning of the eighteenth century a well-developed system of coastal routes encircled the islands. The annual arrival in Edo of the first barrels of premium *sake* wine from the Osaka region became a festive occasion with public acclamation for the captain who won the race. One of the chief stimuli for this vastly increased movement of people and goods through the country was the alternate attendance system created as a political device for controlling the feudal lords. Facilities for both land and sea transportation were necessary to accommodate the large entourages of the lords' processions to Edo, and the heavy costs were offset by shipping tax grain and other domain products to Osaka or Edo for the urban markets.

The flow of elite and their samurai retainers in and out of Edo also stimulated a national exchange of information, ideas, and fashions, serving to reduce regionalism and parochialism. The most significant development in this process of knitting Japanese society more closely together, however, was the dramatic increase in literacy. Bureaucratic requirements for record keeping and the neo-Confucian faith in moral education transformed the unlettered, unpolished swordsman of the medieval battlefield into a literate official capable of producing formal reports and, when the occasion demanded, quoting the appropriate Confucian precept. Literacy became increasingly common among the general populace as well; it has been estimated that by the end of the Tokugawa period the majority of all males routinely experienced some formal schooling. Journalism as such did not develop until after Western influence, but by the end of the seventeenth century there was a thriving publishing industry meeting the demand for theatre announcements, advertising handbills, travel guides, and earthy novels, as well as the more solemn works on moral inspiration and success through crop selection. Thus, despite the self-contained character of the separate domains and the many legal restrictions on travel by the lower classes, information moved relatively freely throughout Japan and promoted a higher degree of cultural homogeneity.

From the point of view of those in political power in Japan, however, communications were most often conceived of as another means of furthering social control. The effort at controlling status in particular gave the Tokugawa regime some of its most marked characteristics. Ieyasu and his successors, as well as the lords of the various domains, were acutely sensitive to the political importance of rank, titles, and honors, including those associated with the imperial court and the Buddhist and Shinto establishment, even though these structures had lost the substance of economic or political power. In general, the good society was equated with stability, and stability was thought best achieved by strict maintenance of hereditary status. This was sought not only within the ranks of the samurai class but within the functional divisions of the larger society. Hence, the samurai class took on the character of a closed caste with very little movement across the line between it and the general populace. The late sixteenth century practice of removing warriors from the land and stationing them permanently in castle towns became the almost universal rule in the

9.4

Symbolic of the social stratification of early modern societies are the fortifications which protected the governmental elites of China and Japan.

9.4 Corner of the Peking city wall. In the Ming period the earthern walls of the former Mongol capital were strengthened and faced with brick. Numerous city walls were built in the Ming and portions of the Great Wall were refurbished and garrisoned. Source: Sir Charles Eliot, *Letters from the Far East* (London, 1907).

9.5 The "White Heron" castle at Himeji is one of the most impressive extant examples of the headquarters of Japanese daimyo lords. Built at the turn of the seventeenth century as a military fortress, it was even more an expression of the vast wealth and power held by the samurai leaders of the early modern period. Courtesy: Japan Information Service, Consulate General, San Francisco.

9.5

seventeenth century, although the domain of Satsuma was a notable exception. The peasantry, which had included large numbers of part-time participants in medieval warfare, were stripped of their weapons and legally bound to agrarian pursuits within their native villages. A system of official registration and passport requirements for domestic travel was devised to impede both occupational and geographical mobility. Prohibitions against selling or dividing land and establishing new families without parental consent, and sumptuary laws to curtail conspicuous consumption, were also aimed at creating social stability. In the same fashion the merchant and artisan classes within urban areas were subjected to measures intended to enforce the status quo. In the long run, as economic changes provided incentive for migration to the cities and expanded commercial opportunities in the rural hinterland, these legal checks were less and less effective, and it proved impossible to maintain in actuality the official hierarchy of social prestige. Nevertheless, considerable attention and energy were given to this elaborate attempt at social engineering, which contributed greatly to the longevity of the Tokugawa system.

Cultural Legitimation

No regime rules long by military might alone, and an essential pillar in the Tokugawa political structure was its claim to legitimacy. Although this came to be most frequently articulated in terms of the Chinese neo-Confucianism that the Tokugawa adopted as official orthodoxy, the three most important sanctions invoked in this appeal for respect stressed continuity with basic elements in Japan's own political history. The title of shogun and the style of the shogunate as a government derived from the Kamakura period and had clear historical precedents. The Tokugawa also emphasized the ideal, if not the reality, of the shogun's role as agent of the imperial throne; they took great pains to restore the material symbols of court life in Kyoto, thereby reversing the long trend toward obscurity that had marked the medieval period and reviving a substantial measure of prestige, if not power, for the throne. This outward show of respect for the throne as the fountainhead of authority in Japanese political culture bolstered the Tokugawa's own position as interpreter of the imperial will and permitted the shogunate to claim a national hegemony without violating the sanctity of the imperial dynasty. Third, the Tokugawa made full use of the values of *bushido*, the code of the heroic warrior of the late Ashikaga period, in invoking the principles of feudal vassalage. The shogun stood at the apex of the vertical chains of lord-vassal relationships. The swearing of homage by the various lords in theory was an acknowledgement of Tokugawa overlordship over all samurai. This combination of appeals to historical precedent, the sacrosanct character of the throne, and central values of the military class, once systematized in neo-Confucian terms, formed a potent ideological justification for Tokugawa rule which was not seriously challenged until the mid-nineteenth century.

The Tokugawa preoccupation with political and social control was matched by its concern for cultural activities. As already noted, its own legitimacy rested in part on the prestige of the imperial court, which had suffered a decline during the long period of political turmoil. Tokugawa patronage of the court served to prevent further decline and to an extent stimulated a revival of classic court culture. In addition to restoring physically much of the old capital at Kyoto, the Tokugawa shoguns and the local lords lavished wealth and energy on building new urban centers dominated by monumental castle architecture. Furnished with richly decorated screens and other art work, these castles of the late sixteenth and early seventeenth centuries were intended as much to symbolize political authority as to protect against military attack. This symbolic function is even more apparent in the mausoleum built for Ieyasu at Nikko—a shrine complex of almost incredible ornateness dedicated to the glorification of the Tokugawa founder. In a similar fashion, official patronage of the Shinto and Buddhist religious establishments was intended to preserve and control traditional cultural values and to give substance to the Tokugawa claim to have restored peace and order. The greater patronage, however, went to neo-Confucianism.

Ieyasu employed, as did other warlords, a number of learned men to aid in the bureaucratic tasks of civil administration and to advise in the formulation of new policy. Buddhist priests had played this role in earlier periods but the bitter struggle with Buddhism as a secular power and the absence of political doctrine appropriate to the new Tokugawa structure turned the feudal elite in the direction of neo-Confucian scholars. Although always subordinate to the regular samurai officialdom and never achieving the direct influence of the Confucian literati in China, these scholar-advisers played an important part in establishing the world view that was to remain the orthodox social and political view until the mid-nineteenth century. They provided philosophical underpinnings to the feudal code of *bushido,* systematizing the amalgam of traditional values in Confucian terms, and supplied historical precedents for justifying Tokugawa policy. Their greatest influence came in the educational institutions where the process of civilizing and preparing the warrior class for its role as a political and cultural elite took place. The Confucian academy established in Edo with Tokugawa subsidies in the seventeenth century became the seat of orthodox interpretations of social doctrine.

Although the means available to the Tokugawa shogunate to enforce, whether through coercion or co-option, cultural uniformity were somewhat limited by the decentralized pattern of local political power, the Tokugawa state can nevertheless be characterized as culturalistic. Japanese society, effectively sealed off from the larger world by geography and foreign policy, was racially, ethnically, and linguistically quite homogeneous. The local lords, moreover, shared a common interest in measures conducive to maintaining their collective hegemony. Thus there was a marked tendency toward common cultural policies in the various domains.

This orientation toward culturalism, however, did not mean the total absence of intellectual diversity. Despite strict bans on Christianity and occasional attempts to eliminate domestic heresies, heterodoxy continued to flourish throughout the Tokugawa period. Here again the autonomy of the various powerful domains was conducive to an intellectual diversity, which was tolerated by the political elite so long as it was not seen as posing a direct challenge to the status quo. The problems of synthesizing Chinese and Japanese cultural values—for example, the contradiction between the Confucian stress on merit and the Japanese system of hereditary status—kept alive a certain tension that resisted the imposition of intellectual uniformity. This was further fed by the ferment that accompanied the growth of a new urban culture semiindependent of the feudal elite.

The diverse aspects of Japanese intellectual life in the Tokugawa no doubt made the society somewhat open to novel ideas. Certainly, despite the restrictions on contact with the Europeans, curiosity about "Dutch learning" continued among Japanese, and this in turn is indicative of a considerable degree of ambivalence inTokugawa views of the outside world. The official policy of self-containment was itself contradicted by the acceptance of a neo-Confucian orthodoxy that was foreign in origin. It may be argued as a generalization that, because of this diversity and the nature of the cultural relationship with China, Tokugawa intellectuals never achieved the degree of self-assuredness or confidence in cultural identity that characterized their Chinese counterparts. In any case, as we shall see in a later chapter, intellectual heterodoxy increased toward the end of the Tokugawa period and was directly related to the flexibility with which Japanese society responded to the Western challenge in the nineteenth century.

Consequences of the Formation of the Tokugawa State

Assessments of the Tokugawa period in the overall unfolding of Japanese history have varied considerably. Some historians, often working from an evolutionary model of socioeconomic development drawn largely from the European experience, have seen the formation of the Tokugawa regime as a major setback. In their view it represented a "refeudalization" of Japanese society that curtailed social development by reimposing samurai control over "free" cities and an independent peasantry, thus freezing the society at a "medieval" stage of history and delaying its entry into modernity by several centuries. This view has been sharply criticized by others who would challenge both the Europocentric conceptual premises and the accuracy of the claim that sixteenth century Japanese society was as highly developed as this interpretation would imply. There is somewhat more agreement among historians regarding the consequences of the Tokugawa policy of seclusion. Certainly the Japanese did cut off themselves from the stimulus of cross-fertilization that played such a large role in the early modern technological and economic advances of Western Europe. Moreover, to the extent that such traditional values as respect for hierarchical authority and vertically organized groups were embedded in the institutions of Tokugawa state, this period can be viewed as one in which older cultural patterns were hardened in a manner that precluded some alternative directions for cultural growth even after the onset of industrialization ushered in by late nineteenth century contact with the Western world.

As we shall see in later chapters, however, Tokugawa society did not stagnate to the extent that such interpretations might imply. On the contrary, despite the intentions of the Tokugawa elite, many of the trends within Tokugawa history were to pave the way for the modern transformation of Japan. To the extent that this was true, the Tokugawa heritage must be seen in a different light.

CONCLUDING REMARKS

The early modern empires that followed the period of Central Asian domination were notable for their stability and longevity. They differed, however, in the extent to which they continued the pattern of the Mongol achievement. In West Asia, Turkish tribal federations formed three Muslim conquest empires. The Ottomans, championing the cause of Sunni orthodoxy, captured control of the old Muslim heartland and waged a vigorous holy war on the periphery of a vast and diverse empire. In Iran, the Qizilbash tribes built the Safavid state on the foundation of a preexisting Iranian society. Farther east the Mughuls, following Timurid precedents, failed in Central Asia but succeeded in India in creating an empire of unprecedented wealth and power. In East Asia the Ming empire represented the reverse of the tribal conquest model, since it was the result of the Chinese expelling the Mongols from south of the Great Wall. The following Ch'ing regime, however, was again an instance of a tribal federation conquering a sedentary population. In Japan, the Tokugawa state was the product of internal civil war and cannot be attributed to Central Asian influences.

These empires may be compared by asking what was the basis of their power and how they were integrated politically. The Ottomans built a central core of military forces and administrators by the training and enslavement of youths levied from the subject population, which was allowed to remain divided in terms of custom, religion, and language. Safavid power was based on an uneasy combination of Qizilbash tribal forces and an Iranian administrative apparatus. How did the Ottoman administration compare with that of the Mughuls, where an effort was made to prevent the entrenchment of supporters in specific locations? Or how would these cases contrast with Japan and Iran, where tribal chieftains and "inner" and "outer lords" held lands and loyalties at the local level which were a check on the power of the central government? How does one account for the fact that Ming China avoided the formation of such a regional military elite? How would the Ming case compare with that of the Ch'ing in regard to the control of the military establishment?

How did the structures of the early modern empires affect their cultural policies? Could one argue that the success with which the Safavids and the Ming vigorously promoted Shiism and neo-Confucianism, respectively, can be explained by the fact that they controlled areas of relative cultural uniformity? To what may one attribute the failure of the Mughuls to develop a strong state ideology? How were intellectual and religious elites integrated into the regime? What factors account for the relatively defensive postures of the Safavids, Ming, and Tokugawa and the more expansionist tendancies of the Ottomans, Mughuls, and Ch'ing?

A further set of questions can be asked regarding the social and economic life of these societies. Each case varied in the degree to which the regime systematically attempted to control mobility within the social hierarchy and regulate relations between various classes and status groups. Moreover, although the Tokugawa in Japan was an extreme example of an effort to circumscribe some types of commercial activity, other regimes also attempted to channel economic behavior into acceptable patterns. What factors account, for example, for the different policies toward foreign trade, a topic of particular importance in Chapter 11? To what extent was mercentile wealth convertible into social status and political influence?

BIBLIOGRAPHY

9.P EARLY MODERN EMPIRES: PROCESSES

Eisenstadt, Shmuel N., *The Political System of Empires* (Free Press paperback, 1969), 524 pp. A monumental analysis of the forces at work within "historical bureaucratic societies," with material drawn from a wide spectrum of examples. The same author has produced many articles or related subjects, all challenging reading.

Parsons, Talcott, *Societies: Evolutionary and Comparative Perspectives* (Prentice-Hall paperback, 1966), 120 pp. A theoretical analysis of political organization; it assigns the empires of China, India, and Islam to the same category as Rome, that of historic intermediate empires.

Toynbee, Arnold J., *A Study of History,* Vol. 7A, *Universal States* (Oxford University Press paperback, 1963), 379 pp. Full of insights from the perspective of a great overview of human history.

Weber, Max, *The Religion of China: Confucianism and Taoism* (Free Press paperback, 1964), 308 pp. English translation of a great German social theorist considering the role of ideological values in the organization of premodern Chinese society.

Wittfogel, Karl A., *Oriental Despotism* (Yale Press paperback, 1963), 556 pp. A controversial but often stimulating theory of totalitarian states; much of the data drawn from Chinese history.

9.1 THE OTTOMANS IN WEST ASIA

Gibb, Hamilton A. R., and H. Bowen, *Islamic Society and the West,* 2 vols. (London, 1950), Vol. 1, pp. 19-173. An in-depth analysis of the governing institutions of the Ottoman empire.

Holt, Peter M., *Egypt and the Fertile Crescent, 1516-1922. A Political History* (Cornell University Press paperback, 1966), pp. 1-57. A straightforward account of the Ottoman conquests in Asia.

Inalcik, Halil, "The Rise of the Ottoman Empire," *Cambridge History of Islam* (Cambridge, 1970), Vol. 1, pp. 295-323. A reliable narrative, by one of the leading authorities.

————, *The Ottoman Empire: The Classical Age, 1300-1600* (New York, 1973), 202 pp. A detailed analysis of institutions, to be read in conjunction with the same author's narrative account, listed above.

Lewis, Bernard, *Istanbul and the Civilization of the Ottoman Empire* (Norman, Oklahoma, 1963), 176 pp. A brilliant evocation of Istanbul in its age of splendor.

Lewis, Raphaela, *Everyday Life in Ottoman Turkey* (New York, 1971), 197 pp. A vivid reconstruction of social life, with illustrations.

9.2   THE SAFAVIDS IN IRAN

Blunt, Wilfred, *Isfahan, Pearl of Persia* (New York, 1966), 208 pp. A popular account of the history, monuments, and social life of the Safavid capital, lavishly illustrated.

Lambton, Ann K.S., "Islamic Society in Persia," in L. E. Sweet, ed., *Peoples and Cultures of the Middle East,* 2 vols. (New York, 1970), Vol. 1, pp. 74-101. A succinct overview by a leading scholar, stressing urban patterns, especially during the Safavid and Qajar periods.

————, *Landlord and Peasant in Persia* (Oxford, 1953), pp. 105-128. Discusses the impact of the Safavids upon preexisting agrarian relationships.

Mazzaoui, Michel M., *The Origins of the Safavids* (Wiesbaden, 1972), 109 pp. A monograph of seminal importance, recommended only for the advanced student.

Nasr, Seyyed Hossein, ' Ithnā 'Asharī Shī'ism and Iranian Islam," *Religion in the Middle East,* ed. A. J. Arberry, 2 vols. (Cambridge, 1969), Vol. 2, pp. 96-118. A brief introduction to Shiism in Iran.

Savory, R. M., "Safavid Persia," *The Cambridge History of Islam,* 2 vols. (Cambridge, 1970), Vol. 1, pp. 394-429. The best account of the dynasty available in English.

9.3   THE MUGHULS IN SOUTH ASIA

Ahmad, Aziz, *Studies in Islamic Culture in the Indian Environment* (Oxford, 1964), pp. 22-54 and 167-200. Scholarly essays on Indo-Islamic civilization in the Mughul period. Strongly recommended.

Ali, M. Athar, *The Mughal Nobility under Aurangzeb* (New York, 1970), 174 pp. The best account available of the governing institutions of the Mughul empire.

Ikram, Sheikh Mohamad, *Muslim Civilization in India* (New York, 1964), pp. 134-253. The best general account.

Mujeeb, Mohammed, *The Indian Muslims* (London, 1967), pp. 236-388. A leisurely narrative by a scholar of great learning and perception.

Sharma, Sri Ram, *The Religious Policy of the Mughul Emperors* (New York, 1962), 185 pp. Attempts to assess the significance of the various measures initiated by the first six Mughul rulers with regard to matters of religion.

Spear, Percival, "The Mughul *Mansabdari* System," in Edmund Leach and S. N. Mukherjee, eds., *Elites in South Asia* (Cambridge, 1970), pp. 1-15. A lucid introduction to a complicated institution.

9.4   THE MING AND CH'ING EMPIRES IN CHINA

de Bary, William Theodore, ed., *Self and Society in Ming Thought* (Columbia University Press paperback, 1970), 550 pp. Monumental work on late Ming intellectual history with articles describing the revolutionary trends in Chinese thought in the sixteenth and seventeenth centuries.

Fairbank, John K., Edwin O. Reischauer, and Albert M. Craig, *East Asia: Tradition and Transformation* (Boston, 1973), 969 pp. Chapters 8 and 9 give the best textbook account of Ming and Ch'ing China.

Hsu, Immaneul C. Y., *The Rise of Modern China* (New York, 1970), pp. 1-121. The best textbook account of the early Ch'ing empire with bibliographies at the end of each chapter.

Hucker, Charles O., *The Traditional Chinese in Ming Times (1368-1644)* (University of Arizona Press, 1961), 85 pp. Brief but informative description of the Ming empire, stressing the political organization.

Michael, Franz, *The Origin of Manchu Rule in China* (Baltimore, 1942), 127 pp. Describes the transformation of the Manchu tribal society for the purpose of conquest of the Chinese empire.

Wu Ching-tzu, *The Scholars* (Grosset and Dunlap paperback, 1972), 721 pp. English translation of the satirical novel aimed at the actions of Chinese literati and officials of the Ming.

9.5 TOKUGAWA JAPAN

Dore, Ronald P., *Education in Tokugawa Japan* (Berkeley, 1965), 346 pp. A brilliantly written analysis of the central values and the relationships between hereditary status, education, and the social order.

Hall, John W., *Government and Local Power in Japan, 500-1700* (Princeton, 1966), 446 pp. A careful analysis of the institutional innovations and the underlying political dynamics that produced and supported the Tokugawa regime is contained in Chapters 12 and 13.

Hall, John W., and Marius B. Jansen, eds., *Studies in the Institutional History of Early Modern Japan* (Princeton University Press paperback, 1970), 396 pp. Parts 1-3 include seminal articles on various political and social aspects of the seventeenth and eighteenth centuries.

Sansom, George B., *A History of Japan, 1334-1615* (Stanford University Press paperback, 1960), 462 pp. Chapters 17-26 of this standard survey describe the centralization of power achieved by the military coalition eventually headed by Tokugawa Ieyasu.

————, *A History of Japan, 1615-1867* (Stanford University Press paperback, 1963), 270 pp. Although not of the quality of the first two volumes in this series, Chapters 1-9 give a concise description of the Tokugawa political and social systems as they took shape in the seventeenth century.

Tsunoda, Ryusaku, *et. al.*, comps., *Sources of Japanese Tradition*, Vol. 1 (Columbia University Press paperback, 1964), 506 pp. Chapters 15-21 are well annotated translations from early Tokugawa materials.

GLOSSARY

Amir. Generally, a military commander or governor; occasionally a sovereign title, as in the case of the amir of Bukhara.

Ashikaga. A family of military aristocrats who held an increasingly tenuous hegemony over Japan between 1333 and 1573, giving their name to that historical period.

Banners. Military-political units of Manchu society formed in mobilizing for the conquest of China; later hereditary garrisons, some containing Chinese and Mongols.

Caliph (Arabic, **khalifa**). Originating with the title of the Prophet Muhammad's successor, Abu Bakr, Khalifat Rasul Allah, "Successor of the Messenger of God." The caliph was the head of the Islamic *umma,* "the community of believers," and was referred to as *amir al-muminin,* "commander of the faithful."

Chaghatay (d. 1241). Second son of Chingiz Khan and founder of the Chaghatay khanate in Central Asia; also, Chaghatay Turkish, the language spoken in that Khanate and the precursor of the present-day Ozbeg.

Cheng Ho. A Muslim eunuch who led Chinese imperial maritime expeditions to South Asia, Arabia, and the eastern coast of Africa in the early fifteenth century.

Chu Yuan-chang (1328-98). Founder of the Ming dynasty, which expelled the Mongols from China and increased the power of the emperor; the second peasant to rule China.

Confucianism. A social and political philosophy based upon the doctrines of Confucius (sixth century B.C.), this became the ideology of an elite bureaucratic-scholar class and the official learning promoted by the imperial Chinese state.

Deccan. The great tableland of central India. The Narbada River was traditionally regarded as constituting the dividing line between the northern India and the Deccan plateau.

Devshirme. The system whereby the Ottoman empire recruited slaves for the administration and the army by levying a child tribute upon the Christian provinces in the Balkans (Rumelia.)

Edo (Tokyo). The castle city that was built as headquarters for the Tokugawa at the end of the sixteenth century and grew into the largest city in the world. Renamed Tokyo ("Eastern Capital") in 1868 when the imperial court took possession of the Tokugawa castle.

Eunuch. A castrated male used in China, India, and West Asia as imperial servants and harem guards; during the Ming period they often exercised great political influence.

Fudai daimyo. Regional leaders who held fiefs from the Tokugawa and, in addition to being lords over their own domains, served as councillors and administrators within the Tokugawa central government; hence referred to here as "inner lords."

Futuwwa. Associations or solidarity groups, generally composed of young Muslim males drawn mainly although not invariably from the poorer elements of the urban population.

Ghazi. A warrior living in the frontier areas of the Muslim world and engaged in holy warfare *(jihad)* against non-Muslims.

Hijra. The flight of the Prophet Muhammad from Mecca to Medina in 622, an event that marked the beginning of the Islamic calendar.

Iqta. The revenue assignment of a certain area, generally granted in exchange for military service.

Jagirdar. The holder of a *jagir,* or revenue assignment, in Mughul India.

Janissaries (from Turkish, *yenicheri,* "new troops"). Technically slaves, recruited by means of the *devshirme,* or child tribute, levied upon the Christian population of the Balkans. The Janissaries were the best disciplined and most feared troops of the Ottoman sultans, especially during the centuries of imperial expansion.

Jihad. The holy warfare that Muslims were enjoined to wage against non-Muslims.

Kamakura. The historical period from 1185 to 1333, so named because the Minamoto shoguns who held power had their headquarters in this city in eastern Japan.

Kapikulus. The personal slaves of the Ottoman sultans.

Khurasan. Formerly a vast area extending northeastward from the central Iranian desert to the Amu Darya River, with its metropolitan centers located at Nishapur, Marv, Herat, and Balkh. Today Khurasan consists of a province in northeastern Iran, bordering the U.S.S.R. and Afghanistan, and with its capital at Mashhad.

Khutba. The sermon given in the congregational mosque on a Friday, in which are included prayers for the well-being of the ruler. The usual proof of sovereignty in Islam is to have one's name read in the *khutba* and impressed upon the coinage.

Mamluk. A slave-soldier, generally although not exclusively a Turk, a Georgian, or a Circassian.

Manchus. A tribal hunter-fisher people from the region north of the Korean peninsula who adopted Chinese techniques of statecraft and conquered China in the seventeenth century.

Mansabdar. The holder of a *mansab*, a salaried rank in the administrative hierarchy of the Mughul empire.

Mawarannahr (literally, "that which lies beyond the river"). The Arabic name for the area lying between the Amu Darya and Syr Darya rivers, and including the cities of Samarqand and Bukhara. Known in ancient times as Sogdiana, the "land of the Sogdians," and to the Greeks as Transoxania, "the land beyong the Oxus" (i.e., the Amu Darya), it was generally referred to in the nineteenth century as Russian Turkistan.

Millet. A non-Muslim religious community living under the protection of a Muslim state (especially the Ottoman empire) and maintaining a considerable degree of internal autonomy under its own religious leaders.

Murshid. A Sufi teacher, also known as a *shaykh* or *pir*.

Nurhaci (1559-1626). The Manchu leader who unified the tribes and built the military organization that later conquered China.

Özbegs (also, **Uzbeks**). A Turkish people who, since the second half of the fifteenth century, have occupied the area between the Syr Darya and Amu Darya rivers (formerly Russian Turkistan and now divided between various Central Asian republics of the U.S.S.R.

Qazi. The Islamic judge who administers the Sharia.

Qizilbash (Turkish, "red head"). A confederacy of nine Turcoman tribes assembled by Shah Ismail Safavi and thereafter forming the dominant military class of the Safavid empire. Among the Qizilbash tribes were the Afshars and the Qajars, who provided the dynasties that succeeded the Safavids. The nickname Qizilbash refers to the peculiar red headdress (with twelve points in honor of the twelve Shii imams) worn by the followers of Shah Ismail.

Sharia. The Law of Islam, derived from the Quran, the *Hadith*, or *Sayings of the Prophet*, and the analogical interpretations of the jurists.

Shaykh al-Islam. The title held by the chief religious dignitary of the Ottoman and Mughul empires.

Shiis. Those who follow the *shia* (or "party") of Ali, Muhammad's son-in-law and the fourth caliph of the Muslims. The Shiis, although subdivided into a number of sects, constitute the largest minority group (as opposed to the Sunni majority) within Islam, and are today chiefly to be found in Iran and Iraq.

Shogun. An old court title given to imperial commanders in chief but adopted by the leading military family in the Kamakura period (1185-1333) and subsequently by the Ashikaga and then Tokugawa Ieyasu to signify their national hegemony.

Sipahi (Persian "soldier," hence the Anglo-Indian term, sepoy). In the Ottoman empire the *sipahi* was a cavalryman who maintained himself, his horse, and arms, and in some cases mounted retainers out of a revenue assignment known as a *timar*.

Subahdar (also **nawab**). A Mughul provincial governor; the officer in charge of a *subah*, the largest unit of administration in the Mughul empire.

Sufi. A dervish or mystic. Hence, Sufism, Islamic mysticism.

Sultan. A ruler, "one who exercises power"; the title adopted by territorial rulers in the Muslim world from the eleventh century onwards.

Sunnis. Those who follow the *sunna*, or "practice," of the Prophet Muhammad; the majority community in the Islamic world.

Timar. A revenue assignment in the Ottoman empire for the maintenance of a *sipahi*, or cavalryman.

Tokugawa Ieyasu (1542-1616). The leader of a large military coalition who triumphed over rival lords to found the Tokugawa regime; he assumed the title shogun in 1603.

Tozama daimyo. Regional leaders who were confirmed as lords of their semiautonomous domains after agreeing to accept the Tokugawa as their leige lord and national hegemon. They were largely excluded from the inner council of the Tokugawa central government, hence the term "outer lords."

Turcoman. A term of unknown origin. One explanation of its derivation links it to the Persian *Turk manand,* meaning "Turk-like." Although appearing at different times in different areas, the Turcomans generally spoke a West Turkish language, retained memories of a pastoral-nomadic background, and displayed a life-style of a kind associated with Turkish peoples over an extensive area of West and Central Asia.

Turkistan (literally, "the land of the Turks"). A term sometimes used to describe all those areas of Central Asia inhabited by Turkish peoples. During the nineteenth century, the term Russian Turkistan was applied to the area between the Amu Darya and Syr Darya rivers, together with the steppe region beyond the Syr Darya. The term Chinese Turkistan was used to describe the Tarim basin, modern Sinkiang.

Ulama. The Arabic plural of *alim,* meaning a scholar trained in the Islamic "sciences." Collectively, the *ulama* enforced the Sharia and determined the social norms that governed the life of the Muslim community as a whole.

Vazir. The minister of a Muslim ruler. In fact, a ruler might appoint concurrently two or more *vazirs* to have charge over different areas of administration, but the term is usually applied in the sense of a chief minister, as with the Ottoman "grand vizier."

Wang Yang-ming (1472-1529). Chinese bureaucrat and thinker who developed the School of Mind, an introspective and individualistic trend in Confucianism symptomatic of social changes in south China.

Yuan (1279-1368). Dynastic title for the period of Mongol rule in China; the first period that all of China came under foreign rule.

10

Decline of Early Modern Empires

Decline of Early Modern Empires

1650 to 1850

The early modern empires that dominated most of Asia from the fourteenth and fifteenth centuries were notable for their durability and for the degree of stability they brought to Asian societies. Before considering the modern demise of these traditional states it is important to bear in mind that these polities were weakened by corrosive internal forces long before they collapsed. In particular it should be noted that maritime contacts between Western Europeans and Asians began in the early sixteenth century, and in most cases centuries passed before European power dominated Asian societies. Thus the decline of the Asian empires cannot be attributed solely to external (Western) causes but must be seen as the consequence of institutional aging. At the heart of the early modern empire was a hereditary ruler. Frequently a lapse in the vigor of the ruling house itself marked the first weakening of the central government. Inefficiency in the bureaucracy and the military organs lessened the state's ability to control resources and defend its territory. Preexisting strains in the empire, such as ethnic differences and ideological conflicts, could in times of stress contribute to a crisis. Population growth, economic pressure, and foreign invasion are additional factors that might test the strength of the established order. In West Asia the Ottoman empire declined slowly in the seventeenth and eighteenth centuries as the military advantage began to tilt adversely. Fragmentation of the empire took place as European territories were given up, northern African holdings asserted their independence, and the Wahhabiyya movement in Arabia challenged the authority of the Ottoman sultan. In Iran the Safavid empire was undermined by the emergence of local power holders and the prestige that came to be accorded to the *mujtahids* as Shii spiritual authorities. The dynasty was ended in the early eighteenth century when Nadir Shah deposed the last Safavid ruler. The decline of Mughul rule in India was well advanced by the early eighteenth century. The resources of the state were strained by prolonged warfare on its frontiers and fragmented through the granting of tracts of revenue lands to supporters of the padshah and the tendency of these clients to pursue their own interests. Hindu-Muslim tensions imposed limits on the ideological solidarity the Mughuls could attain. In China peace and prosperity in the eighteenth century contributed to population growth, excess of luxury and corruption in the government and at court, and eventually to the malaise evidenced by widespread opium addiction. Peasant rebellions and foreign invasions led to profound crises in the nineteenth century, which the Manchu ruling house survived in a state of weakness. In Japan the stability of the Tokugawa system led to gradual internal changes. Commercialization of the economy, worsening of the government's fiscal position, and a slippage in the prestige of the military rulers all eroded Tokugawa supremacy.

10

PROCESSES

Institutional Decline

a. Degeneration of hereditary rule
b. Administrative inefficiency
c. Weakening of the military
    establishment

Social and Cultural Change

d. Ethnic and class conflict
e. Ideological change
f. Population growth

External Pressures

g. External economic pressures
h. Invasion

PATTERNS

1. **Decline of the Ottomans in West Asia**

2. **Decline of the Safavids in Iran**

3. **Decline in the Mughuls in South Asia**

4. **Decline of the Ch'ing Empire in China**

5. **Decline of the Tokugawa in Japan**

10. DECLINE OF EARLY MODERN EMPIRES

	1	2	3	4	5
	OTTOMAN	SAFAVID	MUGHUL	CH'ING	TOKUGAWA

Timeline (years, top to bottom): 1450, 1500, 1550, 1600, 1650

OTTOMAN:
- Death of Süleyman The Magnificent 1566
- Sultan Murad IV, r. 1623-40
- Baghdad lost to the Safavids 1623
- Ottoman Turks recapture Baghdad 1638
- Köprülü Mehmed Pasha, *vazir* 1656-61
- Köprülü Fazil Ahmad Pasha, *vazir* 1661-76
- Ottoman Turks besiege Vienna 1683

SAFAVID:
- Death of Shah Abbas I 1629
- Shah Abbas II, r. 1642-66
- Shah Sulayman, r. 1666-94

MUGHUL:
- Surat sacked by Shivaji's Marathas 1664
- Second Maratha sack of Surat 1670

TOKUGAWA:
- Establishment of Tokugawa rule 1600

	Ottoman / Arab	Iran	India	China	Japan
1700	Treaty of Carlowitz 1699 Sultan Ahmad III, r. 1707-30 Treaty of Passarowitz 1718	Shah Sultan Husayn, r. 1694-1722 Afghan sack of Isfahan; Russia invades Azarbayjan and Gilan 1722 Nadir Shah invades Mughul empire, sacks Delhi 1739	Awrangzeb leaves Delhi for the Deccan, 1681, dies 1707 Muhammad Shah, r. 1719-48 Nadir Shah invades, sacks Delhi 1739	Domestic tranquility, prosperity, and rapid population growth Ch'ien-lung, r. 1736-95	Yoshimune as shogun 1716-45
1750		Ahmad Shah Durrani, r. 1747-73, establishes Durrani empire centered on Afghanistan Karim Khan Zand rules in Fars 1750-79 Aqa Muhammad Khan proclaims himself shah, establishes Qajar dynasty 1796	Ahmad Shah Durrani sacks Delhi 1757; defeats Marathas in Third Battle of Panipat 1761 British East India Co. is granted *diwani* of Bengal 1765	Growing volume of European trade at Canton White Lotus Society rebellion Spread of opium addiction	Tanuma in power, increased unrest 1764-86 Russian pressure 1792
1800	Treaty of Küchük Kaynarja 1774 Death of Wahhabiya movement founder 1792 French invasion of Egypt 1798 Wahhabis occupy Mecca and the Hijaz 1803 Egypt under Muhammad Ali Pasha, r. 1805-48 Sultan Mahmud II, 1808-39		Lord Lake enters Delhi 1803	Unfavorable balance of trade	British pressure, 1810-30 Famine, Osaka riots 1833-37
1850			Bahadur Shah II, r. 1837-58 Delhi taken by British 1857; Bahadur Shah tried deposed and exiled 1858	Opium War, British aggression resulting in unequal treaties and opening of ports Taiping Rebellion, 1850-64 T'ung-chih, r. 1862-74, conservative restoration, limited innovation and reform	Perry's demands 1853 Fall of Tokugawa 1868
1900					

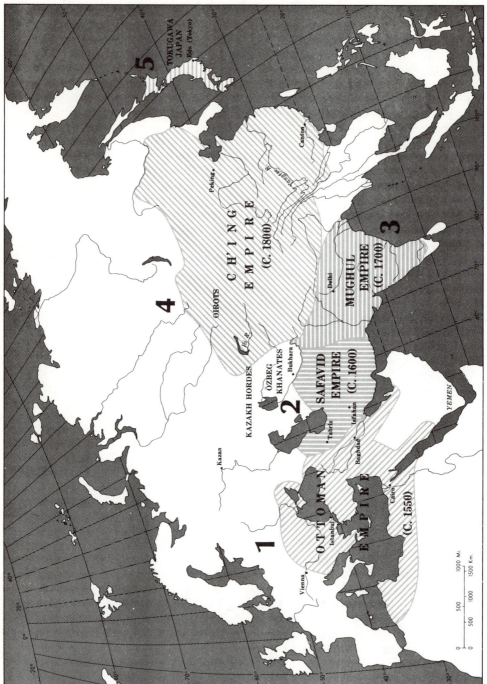

Map 43 Decline of early modern empires

PROCESSES

The early modern empires described in the preceding chapter represented efforts to impose political cohesion and stability upon Asian societies in the post-Mongol period. With varying degrees of success, regimes linked their fortunes to the core values of their respective cultural areas. It was this configuration of empire and cultural tradition that characterized the Asian civilizations in the early modern period. The susceptibility of Asian civilizations to external influences or to internal mutations was governed in large part by the strength and stability of the empires. Where the state, the social structure, and the value system were well balanced, the empire tended to be impermeable to external influences and rigidly resistant to change. The weak and unstable empire was more porous to the elements of change. For this reason the consideration of the processes of decline in early modern empires constitutes a logical prerequisite to a discussion of the period of European domination and influence.

If we take the effect of European influence as a measure of change in Asia, it is clear that the penetration of that influence into a given society was a function of the relative power on the two sides. Thus, while there was increasing interaction between Europe and Asia from around 1500 A.D., the first few centuries of that interaction must be characterized as a period of *contact*. The Asian empires were still vigorous and European forces still too weak, culturally, economically, and militarily, to effect significant penetration. Only two or three centuries later, depending on the area, would it be accurate to speak of European *domination*. One factor was the growth of European strength while the other was the decline of the Asian empires.

THE PERIOD

The decline of the early modern empires took place approximately in the period 1650-1850. The principal empires that will be discussed in this chapter are the Safavid (1501-1722) in Iran, the Ottoman Turks (1453-1918) in West Asia, the Mughuls (1526-1739) in India, the Ch'ing (Manchu, 1644-1911) in China, and the Tokugawa (1600-1868) in Japan. The Russian empire in northern Eurasia resembled them in many essentials.

The modern European empires—Portuguese, Spanish, Dutch, and English—overlapped in span of time with the Asian empires but differed fundamentally from them. The European empires were maritime and global in character, while the Asian empires were primarily land-based unions of contiguous territory. Created after the period of Central Asian domination, the Asian empires were policed and administered with the assistance of institutions like cavalry and mounted couriers, geared to the capabilities of the horse. The seaborne empires, dependent on ships, were influenced by rapid changes in naval technology which had no parallel in the realm of equestrian technique, where Mongol innovations were never surpassed. Although all empires derived sustenance from trade, landed empires tended to give more attention to settled agriculture while commercial interests were pronounced in maritime empires. The dispersed and diverse operations of the maritime empires required more active maintenance than did those of landed empires, where physical propinquity encouraged cultural homogeneity often to the point where political unity was regarded as normal and disunity as abnormal.

The strength of the early modern empires was taxed by various changes that in themselves were neither inevitable nor, once they occurred, beyond remedy. These processes of decline appeared in differing orders and combinations as conditions dictated, and they endangered the existence of an empire usually only gradually as their effects gained momentum. The demise of the empire in most cases followed the imposition of European domination (Chapter 11), a domination that its own prior decline facilitated, and culminated in a phase of drastic change amounting to cultural disintegration (Chapter 12). The processes of the decline of an empire may be arranged in three categories: weakening of its basic institutions, disruptive change in its social and cultural forms, and external pressures.

INSTITUTIONAL DECLINE
The institutional structure of the early modern empire was designed to perpetuate political unity, uphold cultural norms, and arrest social change in the territory under its control. Formed by conquest , the empire was the creation of a military elite whose heirs continued to enjoy a monopoly on armed force and maintained their control through a hereditary rulership. Centralizing political power, the imperial government formed a bureaucratic administrative structure to regulate its vast holdings and to extract needed resources from the economy. Suppression of opposition and defense of the frontiers were necessary functions of the military organs the ruler controlled. Institutional decline encompasses numerous kinds of change that weakened the three fundamental institutions: the ruling house, the civil administration, and the military.

a. Degeneration of Hereditary Rule
An inherent weakness of the early modern empire was the fact that political authority was centralized about the throne of a hereditary ruler. In most cases the empire was founded by vigorous military leaders who exercised power personally. This left the possibility that successors to his line might prove less capable both in war and in administration. Mechanisms of succession and preparation for rule were of great importance. In the cases of the Chinese and the Ottoman empires, the influence of eunuchs and female relatives in the imperial harem was blamed for the corruption of many palace-bred princes. In the Mughul empire a practice of open competition for the throne favored the succession of good fighters but only at the price of considerable unrest. In cases where the ruler was not personally competent there was usually an arrangement for power to be exercised by some minister or servant on the emperor's behalf. This fact explains the ability of empires to function without the guidance of their normal leaders. However, early modern Asian empires never solved the problem as effectively as the evolution of constitutional monarchies and elective governments did in Europe. The hereditary ruler remained the unique source of legitimate authority, and this fact always limited the extent to which ministerial power could be realized or rationalized.

b. Administrative Inefficiency
Early modern empires were dependent for their sustenance on bureaucratic organs that could raise the revenues needed to support the ruling elite and the military organs. Bureaucracies created for the ruler's benefit at the founding of an empire could, over time, develop into powerful self-serving interest groups accumulating wealth at the expense of both ruler and ruled. One common tendency was the development of competitive factions that fought for the ruler's favor. A related tendency was the use of influence by privileged groups to maximize their economic welfare through tax evasion. Both of these trends contributed to increased corruption, which impeded strict enforcement of statutes, accurate surveys of land, and efficient transmittal of tax receipts. Particularly common was a tendency for the tax base to shrink in such a way that the wealthy escaped taxation while levies on the peasantry were increased.

c. Weakening of the Military Establishment
In the early stages of an empire's existence the founders faced the problem of converting their army of conquest into a garrison force that could maintain the ruler's position and defend his frontiers. Insofar as this military establishment incorporated feudal or tribal

elements, there existed the possibility that loyalties to the ruling house would change in subsequent generations. Insofar as the military forces were dependent on recruitment of manpower, shifting social attitudes and improved economic opportunities could make other occupations more appealing than military service. Prolonged periods of peace and stability generally led to the neglect of the military establishment. By the eighteenth century, European advances in military technology threatened the survival of traditional Asian military organizations. Often it was the creation of new military forces, in the midst of war, that introduced instability into the empire. Such forces might upset the delicate balance of central and regional power, might threaten certain vested interest groups, might lack the political reliability of older forces, and often required great amounts of money for their support.

SOCIAL AND CULTURAL CHANGE

It was stressed in the preceding chapter that the early modern empires strove to retard social change and to preserve core cultural values. The supremacy of the ruling group in the society was maintained by active policies that enhanced the position of the elite by rewarding behavior supportive of the regime and penalizing behavior subversive of it. These arrangements were rationalized and legitimized by appeal to the values of the dominant cultural traditions, the symbols of which the state manipulated to serve its own purposes. As time passed, all of these means of preserving cultural orthodoxy were gradually undercut by currents of cumulative change.

d. Ethnic and Class Conflict

Fragmentation within an empire could develop along class, religious, ethnic, or regional lines. At the inception of the empire the founder usually granted hereditary positions to reward his closest military supporters. Over decades and centuries other groups such as officials, religious leaders, and merchants might emerge to challenge the position of the old elite. In a bureaucratic empire power frequently accumulated in the civil administration, particularly when the ruler was inactive, in such a way that chief ministers could rival nobles, palace functionaries, and relatives of the ruler in the competition for wealth. Commercial elements, local landowners, and tribal leaders had their best opportunities to advance their interests at times when the ruler was obliged to bargain for support. Under the pressure of internal rebellion or external aggression the ruler might be obliged to grant special favors to those who could give him military and financial support on an emergency basis. In this way tribes might gain a degree of independence; tax farmers might gain license to exploit the peasantry; or merchants, special consideration before the law. A more extreme form of social cleavage was rebellion, in which a sector of the population, whether a religious group, an ethnic minority, or a broad section of the peasantry, forsook its normal political passivity and openly challenged the ruler. Foreign encroachment, ethnic or cultural conflicts, economic pressure, or administrative inefficiency could all combine at times to provoke elements of the populace to armed insurrection.

e. Ideological change

In a state that justified its rule in terms of an orthodox ideology or religion, changes in values could threaten the ruler's image of legitimacy. When aberrant doctrines and interpretations were expressed, they presented challenges to the regime's ability to exercise thought control. In some cases, radical criticism of the ruler and the traditional order might come from within the orthodox tradition itself, like that of some sixteenth and seventeenth century neo-Confucianists in China, or challenge might take a regional cultural form, like the Wahhabi movement among the Arabs. In extreme cases, cultural change involved a shift of political loyalties and was often tied to rebellion. When popular religion furnished the ideology of peasant or tribal uprisings, it provided a foil to the orthodox values of the elite. Sometimes it was the Christian doctrine spread by Western missionaries that subverted the loyalty of the empire's subjects.

f. Population Growth

The rapid increase in population, which took place in many parts of Eurasia in modern times, had a disrupting influence on social and political structures wherever it occurred. Ironically, the very stability and tranquility of early modern empires may have contributed as much to population growth as did changes in hygienic practices or the introduction of new food crops from the Americas. The doubling or tripling of the population of a given area posed acute problems of administrative control, altered the ratio of mouths to land, affected occupational patterns and social stratification, and perhaps resulted in significant migrations.

EXTERNAL PRESSURES

In addition to the processes of internal decline outlined above, the early modern empires were subjected to external pressures that became so intense in the nineteenth century that it was no longer possible to maintain the integrity of the frontiers. To some extent these processes anticipate the subject matter of the next chapter, since European expansion often constituted the external pressure.

g. External Economic Pressures

Developments in interregional trade, commerce, and industry sometimes had adverse effects on the early modern empires which the rulers were unable to counter. The development of European sea routes around Africa and later through the Suez Canal, for example, diverted an enormous and lucrative trade from the traditional land routes through Ottoman territory. European demands for such Asian products as tea, silk, and porcelains from China diverted considerable commercial activity toward coastal trading centers and by so doing altered the patterns of domestic agriculture and trade. The introduction from the sixteenth century on of precious metals from the Americas drastically affected the currencies of the Asian empires. The Chinese economy was converted to a silver standard and the Ottomans were obliged to issue several new currencies.

h. Invasion

Threats to the territory of the empires required responses. In the case of invasion an actual contest for control of territory could develop, which would test the ability of the state to meet its fundamental responsibilities. Foreign war, whether with Europeans or other Asians, made harsh demands on the ruler, the military apparatus, and the resources of the empire, often in such a way that the ruler had to make substantial concessions in order to mobilize support.

The processes identified here serve to illustrate the forces of decline at work in the fiber of the Asian empires in modern times. It must be stressed that not all the processes were manifested in every area and that the pattern of decline was different in each empire. In general, however, it is valid to say that decline passed through phases from a period of mere institutional weakness, through a crisis phase, in which the empire's existence was threatened by factors such as rebellion or invasion, to a period of disintegration corrosive of the very conditions under which the great empires existed. In the crisis phase the empire could have come to an end and been replaced by another empire. In the disintegration phase fundamental social changes, such as industrialization, made the creation of a comparable new empire impossible.

PATTERNS

1. DECLINE OF THE OTTOMANS IN WEST ASIA

Institutional Decline

The first ten Ottoman sultans down to Süleyman the Magnificent had all been talented rulers and a few had been outstanding by any reckoning. With Süleyman's death in 1566 degeneration seems to have set in, and apart from the dynamic personality of Murad IV (r. 1623-40) no ruler of ability succeeded to the throne until the accession of the would-be reformer Selim III in 1789. There was, however, a brief revival of *fin de siècle* court culture during the reign of Ahmad III (1703-30) in the so-called *Lale Devri*, or "Tulip Age," remarkable for a fashionable preoccupation with the cultivation of the tulip. The decline in the caliber of the Ottoman sultans can hardly be regarded as fortuitous and must be attributed to the deliberate policy of confining the ruler's male children in the imperial harem where, reared amid the intrigues of rival wives and eunuchs, they grew up without experience of administration, civil or military, and where, upon the death of their father, the eldest usually arranged for the strangulation of his siblings. Paradoxically, the Ottoman system of government, even in its decline, continued to recruit some remarkable administrators, but even outstanding grand *vazirs* were unable to provide the charisma and the kind of leadership that only members of the imperial house could be expected to possess.

To contemporaries, Ottoman decline was all the more striking because, in terms of its organization and resources, the empire had hitherto seemed so powerful and unassailable. Ottoman statesmen were among the first to recognize this decline for what it was. Unfortunately, their remedies were essentially traditional ones, maintaining that if only the governing institutions of the empire could be restored to the state in which they had been during the golden age of Selim I and Süleyman I, then all would be well once again. Naturally enough, the most obvious aspect of Ottoman decline was the loss of that reputation for military invincibility, which, whether regarded as cause or effect of the decline of the empire, necessarily involved contraction of territory, revenue, resources, and manpower.

In decline, the superb military machine that had been built up around the *ghazi* frontier tradition found itself at a definite psychological disadvantage, although it would be a mistake to underestimate the military capacity of the Ottomans even in this grim period of imperial retreat. If, during the seventeenth and eighteenth centuries, the Ottoman armies found themselves at a decided disadvantage in facing their Austrian and Russian foes such as they had not experienced during the sixteenth century, this was because European military technology and organization had caught up with and rapidly outstripped them, while the logistics of campaigning against the Safavids were always debilitating unless the shah's troops could be swiftly brought to bay in a formal engagement. Notwithstanding a monotonous succession of defeats and atrocious mismanagement at the rear, the Turks remained, as they have always been, magnificent fighters, as those commanders who fought against them on numerous occasions, such as Potemkin and Suvorov, readily attested. Nor should it be assumed that in this period the Ottomans were invariably on the defensive. During the 1660s and 1670s, for example, the Köprülü grand *vazirs* launched successful counterattacks into Hungary and the Ukraine, and as late as 1683 an Ottoman army besieged Vienna for the last time.

The victories of Mehmed II, Selim I, and Süleyman I had been achieved by a combination of two elements: the "feudal" *sipahi* cavalry, who maintained themselves out of the revenue derived from their *timars*, and the *kapikulus*, or slave troops, of the sultan's household, among whom the Janissaries, recruited by means of the *devshirme* and maintained out of the central treasury, were the most important. Throughout the sixteenth century, however, the rapid spread in the use of both handguns and artillery, especially among the emergent

European nation-states, created a revolutionary situation. Governments were now compelled to substitute regular troops, trained in costly weapons that only the state itself could provide, for the old-style irregular levies, which were often composed of part-time soldiers and which generally provided their own weapons and mounts. A major consequence of this development was to impose a new and exceedingly heavy financial strain upon governments everywhere, calling for new sources of income to offset the ever-rising cost. The Ottoman government reacted by allowing the "feudal" *sipahis* to decline in number and importance, in the belief that they were of only limited value against disciplined European infantry, and by increasing the numbers of the *kapikulu* standing troops. But the Janissaries, at all times prone to violence, now became a highly volatile element in the state, so that one abiding and exceedingly dangerous feature of the period of Ottoman decline was the habitual interference of the Janissaries in the day-to-day government of the empire in the form of mutiny, mayhem in the streets of Istanbul, the massacre of their opponents, and even on occasion the murder of the sultan.

Another aspect of Ottoman military decline was an obvious unwillingness to innovate in the field of military technology, and this apparent fossilization in the seventeenth century is all the more surprising when it is recalled that in the fifteenth century it was Ottoman readiness to innovate that gave them the edge over all their opponents. In artillery warfare, for example, the Ottomans had always shown an unhealthy tendency to think of cannon in terms of sieges and static mountings, and in the period of decline their fieldpieces grew larger and larger in girth and almost impossible to maneuver, a development that was to have its counterpart in Mughul India. In the same way, Ottoman naval ascendancy in the Mediterranean in the late fifteenth and early sixteenth centuries had been lost a century later when, with the substitution of sailing vessels for the traditional war galley, the Ottomans failed to adopt the superior naval technology of the Atlantic powers. Thus, an inability to keep up with recent developments in military technology, a shrinking revenue base from which to support an increasingly costly army, neglect of the *sipahi* cavalry, and the deterioration of the Janissaries all contributed to the decline of the Ottomans as a military power.

Institutional decay in the once invincible Ottoman army had its counterpart in the decay of the system of civil administration, which in its heyday in the early sixteenth century had known no equal except in China and ancient Rome as a model of a preindustrial bureaucracy. Certainly, the system did not collapse overnight and, even in decay, it continued to recruit dedicated and energetic administrators. In the second half of the seventeenth century, for example, the empire gained a respite of two decades thanks to the talents of the Albanian Köprülü family, in whose time the grand *vazir's* residence, the Bab-i Ali, or "Sublime Porte," became the *de facto* headquarters of the administration. Köprülü Mehmed Pasha (1656-61) and his son, Köprülü Fazil Ahmad Pasha (1661-76), rank among the greatest of Ottoman grand *vazirs*, while Kara Mustafa Pasha (1676-83), who commanded the last assault on Vienna, belonged to the same family. In general, however, the old system of government constructed around the sultan's slave household was already in jeopardy by the close of the sixteenth century and thereafter the bureaucracy showed distressing evidence of incompetence and corruption. These developments should not be explained away in conventional phrases regarding the inevitable decay of great empires. Rather, the importation of silver into the empire from the Americas, which seems to have begun in the 1580s, coinciding with rising military expenditure, triggered off an ongoing fiscal crisis in which the bureaucracy, its standard of living and its prestige endangered, began to lose both its sense of moral purpose and its financial integrity.

One aspect of this fiscal crisis proved exceptionally deleterious in the provinces of the empire. In a desperate quest for increased income, the government proceeded to appropriate the *timars* of the "feudal" *sipahis,* which were then placed in the charge of revenue

10.1 Ottoman Janissaries, early seventeenth century engraving. During the period of Ottoman decline the mutinous conduct of the Janissaries frequently forced the government to abandon necessary but unpopular reforms and sometimes led to the overthrow of the sultan or his ministers. Courtesy: Picture archives of the Austrian National Library.

farmers who administered them directly on behalf of the crown. The spread of revenue farming, which soon became hereditary, and the growth of vast rural *latifundia* inevitably weakened Istanbul's control over the provinces, where quasi-independent congeries of power began to accumulate in the hands of local notables and landholders whose wealth and authority owed little or nothing to the imperial system. In such circumstances, ambitious pashas and their subordinates, and also those who wanted to maintain a clean record and avoid trouble, came to terms with the realities on the spot. It was a process to be found in Safavid Iran and Mughul India as well, but if some of these centrifugal forces went further under the Ottomans, the greater resilience and and durability of the superstructure enabled the empire itself to endure for far longer.

External Pressures
No single date can be taken as a symbolic or actual moment marking an irrevocable turning point in Ottoman affairs. There was nothing comparable to the sack of Safavid Isfahan in 1722 or of Mughul Delhi in 1739. The process was one of slow attrition, resulting from the steady erosion of Ottoman military power, evinced by a succession of disastrous campaigns, offensive as well as defensive, waged against the Christian powers of Eastern Europe. Traditionally, 1683, the year in which the Ottomans were driven back from the walls of Vienna for the last time, is taken to mark a major turning point in Ottoman fortunes, but by then the loss of absolute military superiority over both European and Iranian foes was already a century old, and some symbolic significance may perhaps be attributed to the fact that in a treaty as early as 1606 the sultan acknowledged the imperial title of the Habsburg emperor, thereby recognizing him as an equal. More significant as pointers to absolute rather than to relative decline were the terms of the treaties of Carlowitz (1699) and Passarowitz (1718) with Austria, the former being the first occasion when the Ottoman empire undertook peace negotiations as a defeated party, and of those with Russia, of which the most humiliating was that of Küchük Kaynarja in 1774.

Military disasters on the frontiers necessarily had repercussions of one kind or another throughout almost every province of the empire, but this was only to be expected in view of the plural composition of the subject population and the extreme diversity of regional and communal interests. Predictably, the more inaccessible mountain and desert tracts were among the first to become unmanageable, especially when such areas were inhabited by tribal groups who were ever on the watch for any signs of a weakening of control from the center. In more closely administered areas the picture was rather different but no less serious from the viewpoint of Istanbul, although it is interesting to note that it was not in the Balkan provinces of Rumelia, the scene of protracted frontier wars with the Christian powers, but in the Asian and African provinces that the drift towards autonomy and, spasmodically, rebellion first became apparent. The tendency for the provincial notables and landholders to compete for power and influence against the local representatives of the imperial government has already been noted. In Anatolia the *dere-beyis,* hereditary feudal chieftains, had become virtually their own masters by the close of the seventeenth century although they continued to recognize the sultan's authority. Their long-standing family links with the areas they controlled often gave their rule a distinctly paternal character, but in this respect Anatolia was the exception rather than the rule in the Asian provinces of the empire.

Over vast areas authority was exercised by independent-minded representatives of the sultan's government, generally ambitious pashas who reckoned that Istanbul was too far away from them to be interfered with. Some of these developments had already been foreshadowed as early as the late sixteenth and early seventeenth century, although the significance of these first abortive breakaway movements should not be overstressed. In the Maghrib the remote provinces of Algiers, Tunis, and Tripoli, never very closely assimilated to the imperial system, went their own way under local rulers who asserted an ever greater degree of independence. In Egypt there was a series of military revolts culminating in that of 1609, although even after its suppression the province remained very much in the hands of the descendants of the former Mamluk ruling class. In the Fertile Crescent a Druze chieftain ruled the area around Mount Lebanon as a virtually autonomous principality between 1590 and 1635; Baghdad was reoccupied by the Safavids between 1623 and 1638; and Basra was ruled by an independent local dynasty between 1596 and 1668. On the farthest frontier of the empire, Yemen passed out of Ottoman control in 1635.

These first trends towards provincial fragmentation were apparently countered by the vigorous policies of Murad IV, who captured Baghdad in 1638, and of the Köprülü grand *vazirs,* at least as far as the Fertile Crescent was concerned, but during the eighteenth century the process of fragmentation began again. Perhaps the strongest and most resilient of these local despotisms was that centered upon Baghdad, where the Ottoman governor, Hasan Pasha (1704-23), and his son, Ahmad Pasha (1723-47), ensured their *de facto* independence by recruiting a large force of Georgian *mamluks.* Between 1749 and 1831, when the pashalik of Baghdad was forcibly reintegrated into the empire, a succession of *mamluk* adventurers made themselves masters of the province, a situation the sultan's government felt compelled to recognize since it was unable to do anything to prevent it. In the western part of the Fertile Crescent there were somewhat similar developments, tempered by the relative proximity of Syria to the capital of the empire, the divisive factor of tribal and urban rivalries upon which the government relied to confuse and weaken its opponents, and the fact that none of the would-be despots succeeded in creating an infrastructure of *mamluk* backing in the way the pashas of Baghdad had done. In Egypt the authority of the Ottoman viceroy had long been utterly ineffective as a result of the factional excesses of the dominant neo-*mamluk* families and the turbulence of the troops composing the Ottoman garrison.

In general, these local despots, apart from the rather special circumstances of the *dere-beyis* of Anatolia, personified no regional or nationalist movement of revolt against the central government but simply a time-honored lust for dominion. Very different in character, however, was the movement of the Wahhabiya in Arabia. Muhammad ibn Abd al-Wahhab (d. 1792) was a puritan reformer of the orthodox Hanbali sect who sought to restore the Islam of his day, which he judged to be debased and degenerate, to what it had supposedly been during the lifetime of the Prophet and the "Four Righteous Caliphs." This goal he came near to achieving, at least in the Arabian peninsula, as a result of his close alliance with Muhammad ibn Saud, a bedouin chieftain in Najd, and his successors, ancestors of the founder of the present-day kingdom of Saudi Arabia. The Wahhabiya movement, at least in the first half century of its existence, constituted a most serious threat to Ottoman rule. In the first place, the Wahhabi raiders, bursting upon the cultivated regions of the Fertile Crescent from their fastnesses in inner Arabia, enjoyed an overwhelming strategic advantage over their opponents, as had the first Muslims centuries before when they had struck at the adjacent provinces of the Byzantine and Sasanid empires. Iraq, in particular, was very vulnerable to Wahhabi attacks, and in 1802 the Shii pilgrimage city of Karbala was taken and its inhabitants put to the sword. In the west, the Hijaz proved no less vulnerable than Iraq and in 1803 Mecca itself was sacked, as was Medina two years later, in an outburst of puritanical zeal against what the Wahhabis regarded as a falling away from the pristine ideals of the Prophet's lifetime. In 1807 the Saudi ruler even dared to forbid the Ottoman pilgrim caravan to enter the Hijaz. Thus, the Wahhabiya represented a clear politico-military threat to the imperial system. Even more dangerous, however, was their theological challenge to the Ottoman regime, since they denied the claim of the Ottoman sultan to be the universal caliph and they uncompromisingly denounced the Ottoman religious establishment, embracing both the *ulama* and the dervish orders.

The fanatical spirit of the Wahhabiya was a force with which the Ottoman empire in its decline was quite unfit to deal. This task fell to the ingenious Albanian adventurer Muhammad Ali Pasha, who, in the wake of the French invasion of Egypt between 1798 and 1801, made himself master of that country, and its first modernizer. Among his major innovations was the creation of a European-trained army, and between 1811 and 1818 he used it to drive the Wahhabis out of the Hijaz. During 1831-32 his troops, led by his son Ibrahim, occupied Syria and invaded Anatolia, compelling the sultan, Mahmud II, to recognize him as ruler of Syria as well as Egypt. When, in 1839, Mahmud attempted to expel Ibrahim's forces from Syria, the imperial army received a crushing defeat so that only the timely intervention of the European powers, fearful of the consequences of Ottoman fragmentation, prevented the dismemberment of the empire. Yet it is a paradox of nineteenth century Ottoman history that the high-handed rule of Muhammad Ali Pasha and his son in Syria, and likewise that of the *mamluk* pashas of Baghdad, toppled by Mahmud II in 1831, did much to pave the way for the introduction of the Tanzimat reforms into the long-neglected Asian provinces.

Social and Cultural Change

The processes of disintegration at work in the Ottoman empire are more perceptible than in the case of either Safavid Iran or Mughul India, although much more detailed research has still to be done on this subject. Some of these problems—the effect of the importation of American silver, the rising cost of government, the depopulation of the countryside—were by no means a unique feature of Ottoman rule, but applied in a varying degree to a large part of the Mediterranean world—Spain, southern Italy, the Maghrib. In the period of Ottoman decline there was, however, one problem that lay at the root of all others: a phenomenal growth in population during the sixteenth century, which rapidly outstripped the availability of agricultural land. So far as is known, neither Safavid Iran nor Mughul India experienced a comparable pressure.

The prosperity of the Ottoman empire was undoubtedly affected adversely by the European discovery of the sea routes to India and China, which resulted in a decline in both the traditional caravan trade across West Asia and in the maritime trade of the Persian Gulf, the Red Sea, and the eastern Mediterranean, especially the highly remunerative trade in spices, in which the role of middleman between Asian producer and European consumer had been especially profitable. This process certainly did not take place overnight but it was no less disastrous for being gradual.

But the European oceanic voyages of discovery affected the Ottoman empire in another way, perhaps even more disastrous than the loss of its role as middleman in the spice trade. The basic currency throughout the empire had always been silver, of which, from time to time, there were occasional shortages. Ottoman rulers, like their contemporaries elsewhere, endeavored to remedy the situation by forbidding the export of bullion and by debasing the coinage, ineffective measures that had their counterpart in early modern Spain and England. From the last quarter of the sixteenth century, however, the flood of cheap silver (and, to a lesser extent, gold) from the New World began to have a catastrophic effect upon the entire fiscal structure of the empire, a situation with which the Ottoman sultans were no better able to deal than were the Spanish Habsburgs. Beginning with the devaluation of 1584, there was unleashed a continuous financial crisis in the face of which all attempts at administrative reform were doomed to failure and against which must be measured all assessments of the cause of Ottoman decline. Latin American silver, as it poured into the empire, fell in value while forcing up the price of gold, resulting in further debasement and devaluation. Among the most striking consequences of the fall in the value of silver was the staggering increase in the cost of government, due to the fact that the fiscal crisis coincided with the expansion in the size of the regular army, and also a decline in the standard of living of those people, such as government officials, who received fixed salaries and those whose income was derived from such sources as *timars* and religious endowments.

Another element in the weakening of the fabric of Ottoman society was its failure to adopt new technology. The failure to innovate in the sphere of military technology has already been emphasized but the overall picture was the same in every other sphere—in manufacturing and industrial processes, in modes of transportation and, most disastrous of all, in agriculture. Methods of agriculture remained at a primitive level, while the drift of cultivators from the country to the towns resulted in rural depopulation and a contraction of the total area under cultivation. This drift from the land was primarily a consequence of the exploitation of the cultivator by new landholding elites comprised of hereditary revenue farmers and owners of vast *latifundia,* who were often absentees and whose social roles were very different from those of the former *timar*-holding families whom they had displaced. The emergence of this new order in the countryside was accompanied by an almost complete loss of direct control over the cultivator by the agents of the central government, as evinced by the abandonment of the former practice of compiling land surveys and census reports, developments that also occurred in Mughul India at about the same time.

Beyond this must be noted a phenomenon not readily explicable—the spreading of a mood of intellectual torpor, which seems to have pressed like a dead weight upon all reforming and innovative measures, notwithstanding the ability and intelligence of many individuals in the higher echelons of the administration and also notwithstanding signs of continuing vigor in certain rather narrow intellectual fields, such as historiography and poetry. In the first volume of this work the high degree of receptivity of Islamic civilization to external influences and ideas has been stressed as a significant feature of the early Islamic centuries. During the period from the thirteenth century onwards, when West Asia was dominated by Turco-Mongol tribal regimes, Islamic thinkers seem to have turned inward and to have cut themselves off from all alien influences, becoming preoccupied with mysticism and quietism. This process seems to have been intensified under Ottoman rule, as if the age-old Muslim sense of innate superiority over the non-Muslim world, and especially barbarian Europe, was magnified by the Ottomans' knowledge of their overwhelming military superiority over their adversaries. Their empire, as it has been described in the preceding chapter, centered on the concept of the *ghazi* state and stressed the virtues of the soldier, the missionary, and the frontier colonist. Commerce and all ancillary occupations were despised as being fit only for non-Muslims—Christians and Jews—and even when, in later centuries, some Turks took up these occupations long associated with non-Muslims, the occupations themselves continued to be despised. Thus the Ottoman bourgeoisie—merchants, financiers, entrepreneurs, and professional people of various kinds—possessed very little political leverage and if, as was often the case, they belonged to one of the minority religions, they were also by definition second-class subjects. Yet, in early modern Europe, these were the very classes that were contributing most to the modernization of methods of government and the development of public finance, the encouragement of education and invention, the growth of wealth and, in time, the introduction of the industrial revolution. They had no place in traditional Ottoman society.

2. DECLINE OF THE SAFAVIDS IN IRAN

Institutional Decline

The process of decline in all three of the great Islamic empires of early modern times showed a striking similarity in broad outline, even if the specific elements varied in accordance with local circumstances. As in the case of the emergence of these empires, it was Safavid Iran that served as the catalyst in accelerating the process of decline.

10.2 A scene in the Madrasa-ye Chahar Bagh, Isfahan, a lavishly decorated theological college built by Shah Sultan Husayn (1694-1722). An extravagant court and ostentatious piety characterized the last Safavid shahs, who lacked the qualities of leadership needed to control Iran's turbulent tribal population.
Source: E. Flandin and P. Coste, *Perse Moderne* (Paris, 1856), Plate 49.

The lifespan of the Safavid dynasty covered almost two and a quarter centuries between 1501 and 1722, yet after the death of Shah Abbas I in 1629 the line included only a single ruler of caliber, Shah Abbas II (r. 1642-66), while the remainder were nonentities or worse. During the last fifty-six years of Safavid rule the throne was occupied by two of the most ineffective rulers in the whole history of Iran, Shah Sulayman (r. 1666-94) and Shah Sultan Husayn (r. 1694-1722). It is difficult, therefore, to avoid the conclusion that a prime cause of the decline of the empire lay in the feeble personalities of the later Safavid shahs. Ironically, this feebleness was partly the fault of Shah Abbas I, who, in his determination to prevent the ruler's offspring from becoming focal points for unrest or rebellion and also to minimize the chances of a struggle for the succession at the death of each ruler, adopted the Ottoman practice of immuring the heir to the throne and his sibling brothers in the imperial harem. Here, enmeshed in a web of court intrigue and guarded by eunuchs bent on furthering their own interests, they grew up devoid of any experience of public affairs or the country over which they might one day be called upon to govern. This innovation of incarceration within the harem was in striking contrast to the practice of earlier rulers such as the Seljuks, the Timurids, or even the early Safavids, all of whom appointed their male children to provincial governorships, where, supervised by an experienced guardian, they enjoyed some scope for developing their potential as administrators and as commanders in the field.

Rulers educated like the later Safavids in so enervating an environment naturally showed little aptitude for military matters. The centralizing policies of Shah Abbas I (r. 1588-1629) had given the empire a more effective military establishment than it had ever possessed during the preceding period when the chieftains of the Turcoman confederacy of the Qizilbash had dominated public affairs, but firm leadership from the throne was still a prerequisite. If, however, the ruler proved to be a mere figurehead, it mattered little whether the war machine was in the control of Qizilbash chieftains or Georgian *mamluks,* since both had their own axes to grind. The same was true of the civil administration and of local government in the provinces. Prior to the time of Shah Abbas I the provincial administration had been the preserve of the Qizilbash chieftains, who maintained a rough-and-ready kind of order, keeping their provinces quiet and not permitting too much surplus revenue to pass into the central treasury, which provided for the upkeep of the shah's household out of income derived mainly from crown lands. In consequence, however, of the reforms introduced by Shah Abbas I, which included the creation of a large standing army, it became necessary to find new sources of income for the state. One device was to reduce the number of provinces administered by Qizilbash chieftains and to replace the latter by royal officials, who would be intent only on transmitting the maximum revenue to the treasury and who would in effect treat the provinces as crown lands. In the course of so doing they bled the country dry in a way the former Qizilbash governors had rarely done. They were encouraged in their extortions by the all-powerful court eunuchs, who, in company with the shah's current favorites and the occupants of the imperial harem, interferred in the most deleterious way in the day-to-day government of the empire, especially during the reigns of Shah Sulayman and Shah Sultan Husayn. The administration at all levels now became lax, corrupt, and exceptionally oppressive. The financial needs of an extravagant court invariably exceeded the income available, while members of the ruling elite, increasing in number from generation to generation, were forced into acute competition with one another for a steadily diminishing share of available resources. This was one factor among several that accounted for the steady drain of talented manpower out of Iran and into India, a characteristic feature of the later Safavid period.

Ineffective control by the central government encouraged the establishment of local concentrations of power in areas beyond the reach of the shah's displeasure. These local concentrations of power were sometimes personified by an ambitious governor of a remote and self-supporting province, by a tribal khan secure in the loyalty of his kinsmen and followers, or by a marcher lord who recognized the shah's writ only when he was dealing with such men as Shah Abbas I or Shah Abbas II. Once it became clear that the central government no longer possessed the will or the ability to maintain order and uphold justice, humble folk voluntarily submitted themselves to such masters—often little better than bandit chieftains—hoping thereby that they would be permitted to till their fields, repair their irrigation channels, and work at their looms in relative security.

There was a parallel development in the way in which the Shii *ulama* gradually came to replace the ruling house in the popular view as the true source of legitimation. In the lifetime of the founder of the dynasty the shah had been regarded as a semidivine figure. During the reign of Shah Abbas I he had come to embody the traditional Iranian concept of the monarch as supreme warlord and judge, thereby reflecting the solid achievements of that remarkable personality. Under the later Safavids, however, no such charisma attached itself to the person of the ruler. Instead, the awe and authority that in former times had encased the shah were transferred to the *mujtahids,* the exponents of Shii doctrinal orthodoxy and the interpreters of Shii Muslim law. The mass of the population no longer expected much good from the representatives of government, now increasingly regarded by the *ulama* as constituting an illegitimate authority. While they awaited patiently the reappearance of the Hidden Imam, ordinary folk looked to the *mujtahids* for guidance and strength in what was to prove a period of extreme anarchy and oppression lasting throughout the entire eighteenth century. So long as the Safavid empire remained intact the *mujtahids* generally resided in Isfahan, but following its demise they scattered, some taking up residence in the shrine complexes in Qum and Mashhad while others prudently established themselves in Najaf and Karbala, Shii pilgrimage centers under the jurisdiction of the Ottoman pasha of Baghdad. From this safe retreat they took it upon themselves to denounce the crimes and follies of successive rulers of Iran without fear of punitive reprisals.

Social Conflict and External Pressures

In response to the disintegration of the governing institutions of the Safavid empire, regional and communal tensions, long suppressed or concealed, began to surface. In comparison with the Mughul and Ottoman empires, Safavid Iran may seem to have enjoyed a relatively favorable degree of racial, linguistic, denominational, and cultural coherence, but appearances were deceptive. Ethnically, the population included Iranians, Kurds, Turks and Turcomans, Baluchis, Georgians, and Armenians. Linguistically, Persian was spoken by the majority of the population but there were also substantial Kurdish- and Turkish-speaking minorities as well as smaller groups speaking Arabic, Baluchi, and various Caucasian languages. The majority of the shah's subjects were Shii Muslims, but the Kurds in the west, the Baluchis in the southeast, and the Arabs who inhabited the Persian Gulf region were Sunni, while many towns contained Christian, Jewish, and Zoroastrian communities. There was little sense of allegiance to empire or state, let alone nation. A man's loyalty was directed primarily towards his family and local community. He identified with his occupational group, the quarter of the town in which he lived, even with the town itself, but not with the country as a whole. There was, of course, nothing new in all this, but such diversity further weakened the social fabric at a time, such as during the early eighteenth century, when the institutional framework was collapsing and when the regime was being subjected to violent external pressures. Thus it was certain that rebellion and foreign invasion, when they occurred, would stimulate not only predictable manifestations of personal greed and ambition but also more dangerous regional, communal, and particularist rivalries.

The actual catalyst for the collapse of the empire occurred in the remote eastern provinces where Afghan tribesmen, having first gained possession of Kandahar and Herat, began raiding deep into central Iran without encountering any effective resistance. Finally, in 1722, they captured Isfahan, the imperial capital, which now experienced recurring devastation, massacre, and famine. Meanwhile, news of the fall of the Safavids had whetted the appetites of predatory neighbors, and while Russia seized Darband, Baku, and Rasht on the Caspian Sea, Ottoman armies advanced from Baghdad into Kurdistan and from Erzurum into Georgia and Azarbayjan.

It was at this moment of peril that there appeared one of those "savior" figures who have periodically arisen in times of crisis to rescue Iran from anarchy and disintegration. The newcomer was a Turcoman of the Afsharid tribe (one of the original nine tribes of the Qizilbash confederacy) who undertook the reunification of the country in the name of the Safavid dynasty by first expelling the Afghan invaders and by then doing the same to the Russians and the Ottomans. Finally, in 1736, he disposed of the reigning Safavid shah, a mere puppet in his hands, and proclaimed himself ruler as Nadir Shah, founder of the Afsharid dynasty. The fiction of Safavid rule, which had been carefully upheld since 1722, was thus brought to an end although for several more decades Safavid pretenders regularly made their appearance on the scene.

Nadir Shah (r. 1736-47) was the last of a long line of Central Asian conquerors to become a folk legend in consequence of his bloody victories and appalling holocausts. For a brief period he made Iran once again the center of an empire extending from the Caucasus and the Tigris as far east as Delhi. Again and again, he harried Ottoman Iraq and the eastern marches of Ottoman Anatolia; he raided deep into the Caucasus region; he invaded the Panjab and captured the Mughul padshah, Muhammad Shah (r. 1719-48); he occupied the khanates of Khiva and Bukhara and compelled the submission of their rulers; he built a fleet in the Persian Gulf and sent an expedition against Oman. Everywhere he treated the conquered with a savagery worthy of Timur himself (as in the sack of Delhi in 1739), but his own subjects reaped few benefits from his triumphs, from the plunder of captured cities and the fabulous treasure of the Mughuls. He apparently had little idea how to consolidate his empire, although, laudably, he attempted to end the traditional Shii-Sunni rivalry that had so long bedeviled Irano-Ottoman relations, and when he was assassinated in 1747 he left behind no durable administrative structure upon which his successors could build.

The eastern part of Nadir Shah's empire passed into the hands of an Afghan chieftain, Ahmad Shah Durrani (r. 1747-73), who ruled from the upper Amu Darya southward into Sind and who, on several occasions, invaded the Panjab and entered Delhi as a conqueror. The western provinces of Nadir Shah's empire were divided among rival tribal chieftains, Afsharid, Qajar, Zand, and Bakhtiyari. Iran now entered upon a period marked by regional fragmentation and anarchy, the abandonment of cultivation in some areas and a reversal to pastoralism in others, contraction of the urban population, and a markedly low level of cultural life. Some semblance of civilization was preserved in Fars, where Karim Khan Zand (r. 1750-79) made his capital, Shiraz, a haven of tranquility, but after his death his line was exterminated by the ferocious Qajar eunuch Aqa Muhammad Khan, whose family continued to rule Iran down to 1925.

Aqa Muhammad Khan (r. 1779-97) set about the resuscitation of the former Safavid empire by eliminating all potential rivals, reabsorbing the lost provinces, and reconquering Georgia. He also endeavored to restore the administrative framework that had all but vanished in the half century or more that followed the demise of the Safavids, and to provide favorable conditions for a revival of agriculture and commerce. These substantial achievements were made possible by an alliance between the Qajars and the tribes of the north and the northwest, especially those of Mazandaran and Kurdistan, but also by the military talent and political finesse of Aqa Muhammad Khan himself, who assumed the title of shah in 1796. Had Iran entered the nineteenth century, a period marked by acute Anglo-Russian rivalry in the area, in the fragmented and anarchic condition that prevailed during the eighteenth century, it is certain that foreign conquest (as in the case of Mughul India) or partition into spheres of influence by the European powers, and possibly permanent Balkanization, would have followed. That Iran escaped this fate is due in large measure to the work of this able, although repulsive, personality.

Social and Cultural Change

It is not easy to relate the events just described to the more general corrosive influences at work in the Safavid and post-Safavid periods. There is not, for example, any evidence of accelerated population growth with its attendant pressures; rather, the opposite. During the eighteenth century, in particular, it seems probable that the overall urban population contracted, that less land was under cultivation than formerly, and that additional tracts were absorbed into the tribal economy and given over to pasture in a period characterized by a great resurgence of tribal autonomy.

One factor that undoubtedly had a detrimental effect on Iran between the opening of the sixteenth century and the close of the eighteenth century was the development of the maritime trade routes between Europe and East Asia, which rendered obsolete Iran's age-old role as an intermediary on the caravan route (the famous Silk Road) between China and the Mediterranean. What this loss meant to the economic life of the country cannot now be assessed quantitatively, but it may have been offset to some extent during the Safavid period by a growing European demand for Iranian manufactured goods, especially textiles, silks, and carpets. Iran did not, however, experience in this period the full force of European expansionist activity, apart from the Portuguese intrusion at Ormuz between 1507 and 1622 and the brief Russian incursion into Gilan in 1722-23. Europeans made their way to Iran in quest of trade and even military support against the Ottomans, but they came as suitors. From a military point of view Iran was more inaccessible than either the Mughul or the Ottoman empires, whether approached by way of Bandar Abbas in the Persian Gulf or across the Caspian or the Caucasus. In the eighteenth century such intercourse with Europe as had occurred under the Safavids decreased markedly. It took the global strategy of the Napoleonic wars and the supposed Franco-Russian threat to the British possessions in India to draw Iran into the mainstream of European Great Power diplomacy.

When, at the beginning of the nineteenth century, a succession of European diplomatic missions to Iran sent back reports and travelers' accounts of that country and its people, they were describing a large area on the map of Asia which had hitherto remained impervious to European influence. The general impressions they recorded differed little from those of their predecessors two hundred years earlier. Agricultural techniques, methods of hydraulic irrigation, manufacturing processes, and handicraft skills all exemplified the cumulative effort and ingenuity of centuries of patient adaptation unaffected by technological innovations from Europe. Most striking of all, wheeled vehicles were virtually unknown on account of the rugged terrain. The only evidence of a more modern technology was the use of firearms, but even here it was the Ottomans rather than the Europeans who had served as exemplars.

3. DECLINE OF THE MUGHULS IN SOUTH ASIA

The decline of the Mughul empire can be viewed in terms of a fiscal crisis of the late seventeenth century which necessarily imposed intolerable pressures on the institutional structure. These pressures were accentuated after 1712 by the absence of any ruler of even moderate competence. It was during the long reign of Muhammad Shah (1719-48) that the empire disintegrated physically beyond the possibility of restoration or reconstruction. A symbolic date for the passing of the empire as an effective power is 1739, when Nadir Shah entered and sacked the imperial capital, although remnants of the imperial system persisted well into the nineteenth century.

As in the case of the Safavids, deterioration in the caliber of the later Mughul padshahs was a major element—perhaps the decisive element—in the decline of the empire. The first six Mughul padshahs had all been in one way or another impressive figures, and in the case of three of them—Akbar, Shah Jahan and Awrangzeb—exceptionally able. The seventh, Bahadur Shah I (r. 1707-12), was of above-average ability but he succeeded his father, Awrangzeb, at the advanced age of sixty-three and died within five years of his accession. Thereafter, the rot set in with a succession of titular sovereigns manipulated and then discarded by rival factions among the *amirs,* who seem to have understood that in terms of personality not one among the numerous candidates for the throne was likely to impose a check upon their reckless exploitation of the empire's resources. Paradoxically, the Mughuls had avoided the mistake made by the Safavids and the Ottomans of keeping members of the imperial family immured within the harem. Traditionally, the male children of the reigning padshah were appointed at an early age to provincial governorships and in this way they acquired practical skill in administrative and military matters. At the same time their appetite for the throne was thereby whetted, often to a point beyond conceal-ment. One consequence of this policy was that during the last years of a reigning padshah's life or at his death the empire was liable to witness a bloody struggle for the succession among his sons and grandsons. This happened during the last years of Jahangir's reign, during the dotage of Shah Jahan, and at the death of Awrangzeb. On the positive side, there was a widespread assumption, possibly true, that such bloodletting was a contest in which the ablest contender was bound to win. Certainly, all other things being equal, the victor was likely to be the most talented commander in the field and also the man who enjoyed the broadest spectrum of support among the principal *mansabdars.*

By the close of the seventeenth century, however, this rough-and-ready system of natural selection had broken down. Awrangzeb, dying at the age of eighty-nine, left behind him, like his ancestor Timur, three generations of competitors for the throne. His three surviving sons, bullied and spied upon by a suspicious father fearful lest they reenact his own revolt against his father half a century before, lacked his outstanding qualities. His grandsons and great-grandsons were nonentities, most of whom died violently and were buried in obscuri-ty. One such great-grandson was Muhammad Shah (r. 1719-48), who was placed on the throne by the Sayyid brothers, kingmakers *par excellence* among the *amirs,* who had already disposed of several unsatisfactory predecessors. But Muhammad Shah, although pleasure loving and feckless, was as crafty as the men who sought to make him their tool, and he possessed a remarkable capacity for survival. Within a year of his accession he rid himself of both the brothers and thereafter reigned for nearly three decades, displaying a singular resilience in the face of misfortune for which he has not hitherto received due credit. His two successors proved helpless puppets manipulated by a mercurial *vazir,* who ultimately murdered them both. Subsequently, Shah Alam (r. 1759-1806) only retained his throne first as a client of the *subahdar* of Awadh, then of the Marathas, and finally of the British, who entered Delhi as conquerors in 1803. The last two rulers of the line, Akbar II (r. 1806-37) and Bahadur Shah II (r. 1837-58), were confined to the Red Fort in Delhi and the gardens in the vicinity of the city as British pensioners. The latter, deposed after the rebellion of 1857, was exiled to Rangoon, where he died in 1862.

Even before the death of Bahadur Shah I in 1712 the Mughul military machine had deteriorated markedly in quality. It has already been stressed that the Mughul conquest of India had not coincided with any obvious innovations in military strategy or technology. The Mughuls had won their empire in much the same way as had earlier Turkish dynasties—by skillful leadership on the part of commanders who knew how to employ to maximum advantage the fine horsemanship, mobility, and élan of their predominantly Turkish following. From the outset the Mughuls had used handguns and artillery but neither with great success except in siege warfare. For the most part, battles in India in the sixteenth and seventeenth century were still won from the saddle, and it was in this way that the Mughuls established a reputation for overcoming their Indian foes which drew men to their service. Volunteers came from far beyond the Indus and the Hindu Kush to win honor and riches on the battlefields of India, and the Mughul army was continuously being replenished by fresh accretions of manpower, including defeated enemies such as the Afghans, Rajputs, and Marathas, all of whom were co-opted into the system. But by the middle of the seventeenth century there were signs that all was not well. Shah Jahan's costly and ineffective expeditions against Balkh (1646-47) and against Kandahar (1649 and 1652) had seen the Mughuls seriously mauled by their Safavid and Özbeg rivals, and neither the pacification of the rebel Pathan tribes beyond the Indus early in Awrangzeb's reign nor the attempt to annex the Rajput principality of Marwar added much luster to Mughul arms.

Far more debilitating was the war of attrition in the Deccan, conducted by Awrangzeb in person between 1681 and 1707, for it was in these arduous and indecisive campaigns against the Marathas that the empire quite literally bled to death. For much of the time the Mughuls appeared to retain the upper hand, but in retrospect it is clear that the reality was altogether different. This was because they were operating in a most difficult terrain, with their lines of communication with the north dangerously overstretched and with their war machine disintegrating as a result of a contraction of financial resources. In the first decade of the eighteenth century the empire still possessed able commanders and some fine troops, but treachery, war weariness, and indifference on the part of perhaps a majority of the *mansabdars* were as effective as the Marathas themselves in rendering impossible Awrangzeb's dream of annexing the entire peninsula. Symptomatic of the general decline, most Mughul commanders, when confronted by Maratha guerrilla tactics, proved incapable of adopting new methods of fighting. While the Marathas placed emphasis on mobility and maneuverability, intimate knowledge of the country, the well-laid ambush and the swift retreat, the Mughul army had come to resemble a ramshackle city on the move. Encumbered with superfluous baggage, animals, and camp followers, it stripped bare the country through which it passed so that it was more dreaded by its friends and those whom it was supposed to protect than by its nimble, elusive foes.

Incomprehensibly, the Mughuls virtually ignored the strategic potentialities of sea power. Indian merchants, with capital that was often provided by members of the imperial family or of the ruling elite, undertook commercial ventures overseas and the Mughuls themselves knew well the importance of the sea route to the Hijaz, to Egypt, and even to Europe. Yet all this notwithstanding, they never took to the sea, as the Ottoman Turks had done. When at last they perceived the seriousness of the threat presented by the Europeans, and also by the Marathas, their response was limited to buying the support of the piratical Sidis of Janjira, who were no match for the new masters of the Indian Ocean. This failure to recognize the importance of sea power ensured that, with the decline of the Mughul empire, no indigenous power in India would be capable of challenging European command of the seas.

The financial stringencies and organizational weakness of the late Mughul army were closely linked to the general decline of administrative standards throughout the empire. The Mughul empire, like all the Islamic empires that had preceded it in India and West Asia, depended in the last resort on unremitting attention to the day-to-day business of government by the ruler or, if not by the ruler himself, by a no-less-zealous deputy. This was the way in which Akbar had made his will effective over vast areas, as had Shah Jahan in his younger days. Awrangzeb too understood very well this need for personal supervision, but in his case he made the virtue a vice with his suspicious nature and his preoccupation with bureaucratic detail. Moreover, the transfer of the imperial court and administration to the

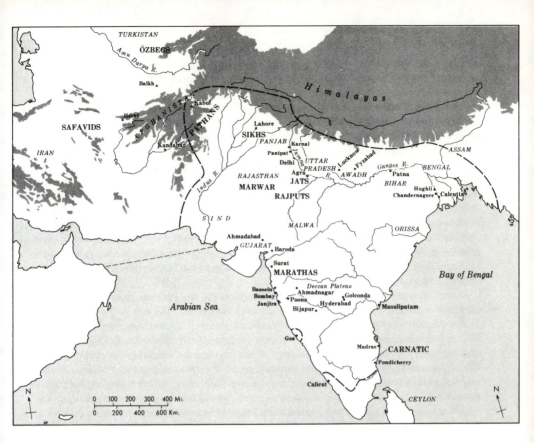

Map 44 The Mughul empire, eighteenth century

Deccan in 1681 meant that the northern part of the empire was left in the charge of provincial officials who were now freed from direct supervision by the padshah or his ministers. No doubt the full implications of this were not appreciated at the time of the move southward, or faced up to afterwards when their effects became clearly apparent, but it is possible to date from this time a tendency for the *subahs* to become *de facto* independent satrapies. In any case, during the latter part of Awrangzeb's reign provincial officials who enjoyed the padshah's confidence retained the same office for far longer than had been the case in the past, notwithstanding the fact that this went against traditional policy, which was to transfer the *mansabdars* from one post to another after relatively short periods of tenure in each post. Clearly, in the conditions of the late seventeenth century something had to be sacrificed to the overriding need for maximum revenue yields, which in turn called for a high degree of continuity in provincial administration. In the case of Gujarat, for example, one *subahdar* held office for ten years between 1672 and 1682, and another for sixteen years between 1685 and 1701. Similarly, in the case of Bengal, Awrangzeb's uncle was *subahdar* from 1664 to 1677 and again from 1679 to 1688, while another *subahdar* held office for nine years between 1698 and 1707.

The disintegration of the *mansabdari* system as it had evolved during the late sixteenth and early seventeenth century was not, however, due exclusively or even mainly to Awrangzeb's absence in the Deccan and his consequent inability to supervise the administration of the core provinces of the empire. The problems were more profound and more pervasive than the merely temporary evils arising from the age or absence of the padshah, which could, after all, be set right again once the empire passed into the hands of a younger and more energetic ruler. But incurable malaise lay in the *mansabdari* system itself and in the revenue system that sustained it, both cause and consequence of a fiscal crisis that enveloped the entire empire in the second half of the seventeenth century. Before we consider the implications of this crisis for the *mansabdari* system, two aspects of Mughul government deserve emphasis. First, the financial resources of the empire, although very great, were relatively inelastic. Revenue was derived from a variety of sources, including import and transit duties, and a variety of miscellaneous taxes, but the greater part was provided by agriculture. The income from this source, while it might fluctuate in consequence of good or bad harvests, drought or flooding, and the way in which it was collected, could be expanded only by taking a greater share of the crop or by increasing the area of land under cultivation. Awrangzeb himself ordered the revenue officials to encourage the cultivators to bring more land under cultivation and to punish those who abandoned their fields, but his concern suggests that the total area under cultivation, if measured by the revenue yield, was no longer expanding and that there was a drift of cultivators from the countryside to the towns.

At the same time, Mughul government throughout the seventeenth century was extravagant and wasteful. The splendor of the court and the opulent life-style of the *mansabdars*, whose wealth was derived mainly from government service, have been recorded in detail by numerous European travelers in seventeenth century India. Shah Jahan's lavish expenditure on building, including the construction of a new capital at Shahjahanabad (now Old Delhi), his expeditions against Balkh and Kandahar, and his campaigns in the Deccan were a great drain of wealth. When Awrangzeb seized the throne it was necessary for him to follow in his father's footsteps if he were to retain the support of the *mansabdars* who had made possible his usurpation. Notwithstanding Awrangzeb's later reputation as a royal dervish, the Mughul court remained long after 1658 much as it had been during Shah Jahan's reign, and the new ruler felt compelled to prove himself by continuing the aggressive and expansionist policies of his predecessor. Expeditions against Assam, the frontier tribes beyond the Indus, Marwar, and then the Deccani sultanates necessitated the maintenance of a huge military establishment. Since the government's needs were without limit and the sources of revenue were so inelastic, the pressure on the cultivators increased steadily. If one aspect of life in seventeenth century India was noted by nearly all foreign observers, it was the oppression of the cultivators by government officials determined to squeeze out of them the maximum revenue.

It may be argued that the Mughul empire was far from being unique in that the cost of the army and the administration, the maintenance of a sumptuous court, and the affluence of the ruling elite were all sustained by the labor of the cultivator. Yet, in one respect, the Mughul regime may well have been more oppressive than previous regimes in the subcontinent or on the Iranian plateau, despite the fact that Mughul administrative practice had to some extent been modeled on that of its predecessors. The *mansabdari* system, as previously described, worked best when *mansabdars* received their salaries in the form of cash payments. In fact, however, this had proved impossible, even during the sixteenth century, and throughout the seventeenth century the normal practice was for salaries to be paid in the form of *jagirs*. It will be recalled that a *jagir* was a revenue assignment on a particular area of land on which the *mansabdar* or, since he himself was usually posted far from his *jagir* in some other part of the empire, his agent collected the land revenue and his expenses, but was vested with no property rights in the soil. It had never been intended that the *mansabdars* should develop local connections or acquire a prescriptive right to control a particular area, and to ensure that this should not happen, *jagirs* were constantly being transferred from one *mansabdar* to another. This was a most effective way to ensure that no *mansabdar* built up local influence or established a family connection with lands assigned to him as *jagirs,* but it also ensured that he felt not the slightest interest in the long-term prosperity of those *jagirs.* Rather, it was in his interest to extract the maximum profit from the land in the shortest possible time. There was thus not the slightest incentive to spare the cultivator. In the preceding section it was stated that in Safavid Iran the Qizilbash provincial governors, however oppressive their individual actions might have been, had a vested interest in the prosperity of their provinces, while, in contrast, the officials who administered the crown lands on behalf of the shah were concerned only with squeezing the maximum revenue out of the cultivators. In Mughul India, too, it was government practice to show a short-term preoccupation with obtaining the maximum revenue at the expense of long-term gains, including extending the area under cultivation. Agriculture suffered accordingly.

This defect was inherent in the system from the outset, but it was compounded many times over by the need for an expanding supply of *jagirdari* land to be available for assignment. The Mughul ruling elite, institutionalized by the *mansabdari* system, multiplied throughout the period between the accession of Akbar and the death of Awrangzeb. It has been calculated that under Akbar there were 1,658 *mansabdars;* under Jahangir, 2,069; under Shah Jahan, 8,000; and under Awrangzeb, 11,456. This increase was partly the result of territorial expansion, which necessitated a larger administrative cadre, and partly the result of a common tendency for bureaucracies to swell their ranks, but two further factors deserve consideration. With the passing of each generation the number of those with expectations of acquiring *mansabdari* status increased proportionately. A *mansabdar* owed his wealth and social standing to his rank in the imperial bureaucracy, but the *jagirdari* system prevented him acquiring hereditary rights in the land, and in any case his property, in theory at least, reverted to the crown at his death. The only way, therefore, for him to provide for his sons was to ensure that they too became *mansabdars* since no other form of occupation was open to them. This factor alone would account for the growth in the number of *mansabdars* from decade to decade, but the increase was compounded by the Mughul tradition, inherited from previous Indo-Muslim dynasties, of encouraging the immigration into India of Muslim adventurers from Turkistan, Iran, and West Asia. Such persons, highly prized in India as soldiers or administrators, were generally appointed *mansabdars* on their first appearance at court by rulers who gloried in a reputation for generosity and openhandedness. Internal enemies such as the Afghans, Rajputs, and Marathas were treated in much the same way. Implacable foes were eliminated but those who showed themselves to be conciliatory were co-opted into the system, as Akbar had done with the Rajput Maharajas and as Awrangzeb attempted to do with the Marathas.

The effect of all this was an increased demand for *jagirs* among an expanding number of *mansabdars,* and at least one element in Shah Jahan's and Awrangzeb's determination to annex peninsular India must have been a belief that the acquisition of this vast area would solve the otherwise insoluble problem of the shortage of *jagirs* in the north. Indeed, even before the crisis phase was reached in the late decades of the seventeenth century, the pressure on existing sources of revenue and the need for more *jagirs* had provided the incentive for campaigns of imperial expansion. Annexation, in theory at least, meant more revenue for the state and more land available for assignment as *jagirs.* In the case of the advance into the Deccan, however, such gains were not forthcoming. One reason for this was that the campaigns proved extremely costly. Another was that, although the Mughul ruling elite anticipated that victory, when it came, would mean a lavish handout of new appointments and *jagirs,* both had to be shared with the tenacious ruling elites of the former sultanates, whose submission had been conditional upon the assurance that they would be allowed to retain a part or all of what had formerly been theirs.

By the late seventeenth century the Mughul government had neither sufficient cash in hand to pay its troops in the field nor sufficient *jagirs* to satisfy the expectations of the *mansabdars*. Various devices were attempted to alleviate the situation. One was to demand a higher revenue from the cultivator. Another was to require that the *mansabdars* give gifts of money to the ruler whenever they were promoted or appeared at court. Another was to calculate payment of salary on the basis of ten or even six months instead of twelve. When no *jagirs* were available, a *mansabdar* had to be content with the promise of the first claim to a specific *jagir* already assigned to someone else but likely to become available at some date in the future. Needless to say, none of these measures had any effect: the army remained unpaid and mutinous and the *mansabdars* became impecunious and desperate. The latter now looked to their own interests more and more and to the imperial service less and less. For them, one solution to the problem was to come to terms with the enemies of the empire. A Mughul general, for example, might drag out the siege of a Maratha fortress that he could have taken months before in order to extend the period of his command or while he watched for a chance to steal a march on his rivals in the imperial camp; or he might establish an understanding with his Maratha opponent so that, in a crisis, he could rely on his assistance or, at least, his inactivity. Another solution was for a group of *mansabdars* to cooperate together in pursuit of mutually advantageous goals or in order to counter the ambitions of other factions that they regarded as a threat to their position. Such groups were often related by marriage, clientage, or ethnic origin: the foreign *mansabdars* banded together against the Indian-born *mansabdars,* both Muslim and Hindu, while those who came from Iran and were Shii intrigued against those who came from Turkistan and were Sunni. By the beginning of the eighteenth century it was the *mansabdar's* place in a well-defined hierarchy of client-patron relationships, not the padshah's favor or the *mansabdar's* appointment, that gave him political power and leverage, although each faction fought hard to monopolize what were judged to be the most important of the great offices of state.

These tensions and rivalries apparently did not manifest themselves in any ideological form other than the traditional rivalry between Muslim and Hindu, Sunni and Shii. This may have ben been partly due to the fact that the Mughul empire, unlike the empires of the Ottomans and Safavids, never included any distinct ideological component of a quasi-religious nature. Significantly, Mughul authority was toppled not by those movements of agrarian and sectarian unrest that surfaced in the late seventeenth and early eighteenth century but by the combined pressure of irresponsible and power-hungry *mansabdars* operating from within the system, Maratha raiders from the south sweeping all before them, and invading Iranians and Afghans from beyond the northwestern passes, all of whom took advantage of the administrative paralysis of the empire and, after 1712, the weakness of the throne itself to seize whatever they could get. Those who now tore the imperial structure apart did so in quest of revenue, plunder, and power, and they did so because the empire itself could no longer legitimately provide them in the way it had done in the past.

External Pressures

Throughout the first two hundred years of their rule, the Mughuls never experienced the kind of external challenge experienced by the Safavids and the Ottomans. On the northwest frontier of the empire some danger was apprehended from the Özbegs but this never materialized, and the struggle with the Safavids for Kandahar lay well outside the subcontinent. Within India itself the Mughuls were invariably the aggressors, and although the Marathas in the late seventeenth century eventually turned the tables on them and assumed much the same aggressive and predatory role, they did so from within the boundaries of the empire as an unabsorbed element within the imperial system. During the sixteenth and seventeenth centuries the Europeans acquired an absolute hegemony over Indian territorial waters but they never constituted a challenge to the continental power of the Mughuls, towards whom they generally assumed the role of suppliants for favors. By the second quarter of the eighteenth century, however, decline was far advanced, and when in 1739 an external assault came it revealed beyond any possibility of doubt that the Mughul empire as it had existed for the preceding two centuries was finished.

The career of the Afsharid chieftain Nadir Shah has been described in the preceding section. His role in the history of northern India was brief, bloodthirsty, and definitive. He followed in the footsteps of earlier invaders from the northwest and the resistance offered to his advance was little more than nominal. Nadir Shah followed up his decisive defeat of the Mughul army at Karnal in 1739 by marching on Delhi, with Muhammad Shah accompanying him as a prisoner. On his entry into the city he occupied the Red Fort, seized the vast treasure accumulated by the Mughuls over the past two centuries, and had his name read in the *khutba*. On the pretext that his troops had been molested by the citizens of Delhi he ordered a general massacre and the systematic sack of the city. Prior to his departure he compelled Muhammad Shah to cede to him the three northwestern *subahs* of Sind, Kabul, and the Panjab, and then withdrew, taking with him a legendary booty, including the fabled Peacock Throne.

The news of the sack of Delhi reverberated throughout northern India, signifying for contemporaries the end of an epoch. To the former Mughul ruling elite throughout the provinces, to the predatory Marathas, to the rebellious and the discontented everywhere it relayed the same message—the Mughul empire was no more. To the Muslim community as a whole it seemed to herald the doom of Islam in the subcontinent. Within the imperial metropolis itself the self-destructive rivalries among the Mughul ruling elite, which had been evident for decades, continued with undiminished virulence. Beyond the walls the surrounding districts passed into the hands of rebellious communities driven into revolt by unrelenting fiscal oppression or simply reacting to the prevalence of anarchy and violence. South of Delhi and around Agra it was the Jats. In the eastern Panjab it was the Sikhs, a reforming sect of Hindus sporadically persecuted by the Mughuls. Everywhere communities in outlying areas asserted a *de facto* independence in response to the collapse of the imperial system. To cap it all, there were further invasions from across the Indus. Nadir Shah had been assassinated in 1747 but the eastern marches of his empire had fallen to the Durrani Afghan chieftain, Ahmad Shah, who penetrated northwestern India on a number of occasions and in 1757 sacked Delhi hardly less savagely than Nadir Shah had done. There was little enough for the Marathas to plunder when they forced their way into the city in 1760 and even less when Ahmad Shah returned a year later.

By this time, however, the Marathas had become the principal actors on the Indian stage. Originating in the northwestern part of the Deccan, they had constituted an important element in the former sultanate of Ahmadnagar (1491-1633), where they had enjoyed a considerable degree of autonomy. The Mughul conquest of the sultanate, however, which began in the last decade of Akbar's reign, threatened to undermine their relative freedom of action. With the sultans of Ahmadnagar, the Maratha chieftains had arrived at a mutually advantageous *modus vivendi* but it was impossible to maintain it once the sultans were replaced by the Mughuls, who viewed annexation in terms of increased revenue for the central treasury and of *jagirs* and offices for their followers. In the course of the transition to Mughul rule the preexisting administrative structure disintegrated and out of this turmoil emerged Maratha chieftains such as Shahji and his son, Shivaji, who were intent on asserting a *de facto* independence of imperial authority. The Mughuls at all times were prepared to co-opt the Marathas into their system in exactly the same way they had co-opted the Rajputs and the Afghans, and it has been estimated that between 1679 and

1707, 16.7 percent of the *mansabdars* of the empire consisted of Marathas. However, Maratha society, unlike Rajput society, was not organized by clans. In effect, every prominent Maratha decided for himself whether or not to throw in his lot with the Mughuls, and frequently he found it more profitable to remain outside of and hostile to the imperial system. In any case, the Mughuls were unable to offer sufficient inducements to the Marathas to bring all of them over to their side. It was this intransigent element that first rallied to the cause of Shivaji and his son, Shambhuji, and then to the peshwas, or chief ministers of Shivaji's descendants, in Poona.

Shivaji (r. c. 1659-80) was an outstanding guerrilla leader in a region where the terrain was generally unsuitable for the traditional methods of northern Indian warfare. At first his main antagonist was the sultan of Bijapur, but he was soon in conflict with the Mughuls. In 1663 he achieved prominence with a successful night attack on the camp of the Mughul viceroy of the Deccan, Awrangzeb's uncle, and in 1664 he sacked the port of Surat, the great Mughul emporium on the west coast. Initially, Awrangzeb seems to have regarded Shivaji as an enterprising Hindu chieftain who possessed exceptional nuisance value. He therefore attempted to co-opt him into the imperial system but the attempt failed, and after sacking Surat a second time in 1670 Shivaji declared himself an independent ruler. Following Shivaji's death in 1680, Awrangzeb and his commanders endeavored to suppress this kingdom-within-a-kingdom, which lay athwart the lines of communication between northern India and the newly conquered sultanates of the Deccan, but although Awrangzeb captured and executed Shivaji's son, Shambhuji, and for many years retained his grandson, Shahu, as a hostage, Maratha resistance continued unabated.

During the long reign of Shahu (1708-49) *de facto* authority over the Marathas, now a formidable confederacy of predatory chieftains eager to plunder the defenseless Mughul provinces, shifted from the ruling Maratha dynasty, descendants of Shivaji, to their chief ministers, or peshwas, who established their headquarters at Poona. It was the greatest of the peshwas, Baji Rao I (r. 1720-40), rather than Shivaji, who laid the foundations of a Maratha empire that might have become a reality had not the bickering and jealousy of rival Maratha commanders in the field and, later, the generalship of Ahmad Shah Durrani undone almost everything Baji Rao had worked for. Even so, his achievement was an impressive one. He led Maratha armies into Malwa and Gujarat, permanently severing those provinces from the control of Delhi. He sent his raiders as far north as the banks of the Jumna and when their further progress was threatened by the advance of the nizam of Hyderabad from the south, he vigorously drove off this most dangerous of adversaries. In 1739 he rounded off a brilliant career of conquest by expelling the Portuguese from their fortress of Bassein. At the time of his death a year later it seemed as if his son and successor, Balaji Rao I (r. 1740-61), would eventually have the whole of India within his grasp. But Balaji Rao, although an able ruler, proved less energetic than his father and in 1761 the main Maratha army was brought to bay at Panipat by Ahmad Shah Durrani and crushed in one of the most complete and decisive battles of the eighteenth century. The Maratha confederacy was shattered, each chieftain now going his own way and pursuing his own course of personal aggrandizement. Ahmad Shah, as usual, withdrew towards Kabul before the onset of the summer heat and neglected to consolidate his victory. He thus cleared the stage for the British advance. But for Panipat, India in the late eighteenth century might well have been dominated by a powerful military regime headed by the peshwas in Poona, and the course of European penetration into South Asia could well have followed a quite different course.

In the middle of the eighteenth century the truncated Mughul regime surviving in Delhi was caught in the cross fire of Marathas from the south and Afghans from the northwest. Moreover, the Maratha seizure of some of the richest provinces of the empire, especially

10.3 A body of Maratha cavalry. The cumbrous Mughul armies of the eighteenth century were no match for these lightly armed, highly mobile troops. Courtesy: The British Library.

Gujarat, with the consequent loss of revenue, made further initiative on the part of the Mughul court out of the question. Over wide areas of central and northern India the imperial administration of former days was swept aside and local officials, where they managed to survive at all, came to terms with new masters. In areas relatively remote from Maratha incursions provincial governors recognized that their only hope for survival was to strike out on their own as independent rulers. In most instances they continued to recognize the titular sovereignty of the padshah in Delhi, sending occasional revenue payments and presents in return for confirmation of their *de facto* independence, but they identified increasingly with the provinces that had now become their petty kingdoms, seeking alliances with influential local elites and sometimes patronizing the regional culture. In this way, the *subahdar* of the Deccan became nizam of Hyderabad and an independent ruler in all but name, as did the *subahdars* of Awadh and Bengal. The title of *subahdar* fell into disuse, to be replaced by that of *nawab*. It was with the rulers of these successor states of the Mughul empire—the nawab of Bengal and the nawab of the Carnatic, the nawab vazir of Awadh, and the nizam of Hyderabad—that the European trading companies negotiated and intrigued in that period of intense rivalry that preceded the establishment of British hegemony in the late eighteenth century.

Economic Trends and Early Western Contacts

The lack of sophistication that has hitherto characterized much of the historical writing relating to this period, and the general neglect of Indian social and economic history, make it extremely hazardous to attempt to link the process of decline outlined above to broader movements of social transformation. Historians still do not possess a very clear idea about what was happening below the surface of Indian political life during the seventeenth and eighteenth centuries. They assume, but without any figures to support the assumption, that the population of India in 1600 was somewhere around 100 million, in contrast to 300 million in 1900. This assumption presupposes a continuous expansion of population during the intervening three centuries, but it is impossible to know whether this expansion continued at a steady rate during the period of Mughul decline. Did, for example, that process of decline affect the growth rate in any way? Or, on the contrary, did the growth rate have any impact on the overall process of decline? These are questions to which, in all probability, historians will never be able to find precise answers.

Much the same kind of uncertainty applies to our knowledge of the economic infrastructure of late Mughul India. Historians have assumed that endemic warfare, raiding and counterraiding across wide stretches of country, and the breakdown of the administrative system must have had an adverse effect on agriculture, perhaps resulting in an overall contraction of the total acreage under cultivation. There is, however, little data to support this assumption and if, indeed, this were true of some areas, the phenomenon was certainly not universal. Pursuing the same line of reasoning, a shrinkage in urban population might be expected but, again, evidence is lacking. Presumably the population of the great metropolitan centers of the empire—Delhi, Agra, and Lahore—declined, but an impressive number of medium-sized cities—such as Poona, Baroda, Hyderabad, Fyzabad, and Lucknow—flourished and grew, stimulated by the presence of local courts.

With regard to commerce, a great deal is known from the surviving records of the European trading companies about the market conditions in the vicinity of the European settlements and of those commodities that were of particular interest to the Europeans. Of the situation throughout the subcontinent much less is known, although some writers have assumed that the period of Awrangzeb's campaigns in the Decca, followed by the chaotic conditions of the early eighteenth century, resulted in a contraction of commerce and perhaps also of credit over wide areas. As for India's international commerce, now directed primarily towards Europe, there can be no question of European economic pressures adversely distorting indigenous trading patterns at this time. The textile industry in certain areas was, however, greatly stimulated by the European demand for Indian textiles, and some of the Indian merchants and bankers who were connected with the European factories began to lay the foundations of future fortunes.

Down to the middle decades of the eighteenth century the Europeans in India consisted mainly of two categories, traders and military adventurers. During the greater part of the seventeenth century European commercial activity centered upon indigenous entrepots such as Surat, the most flourishing port of the Mughul empire prior to its sack by Shivaji in 1664; Masulipatam, principal outlet of the sultanate of Golconda; and up-country centers such as Ahmadabad and Patna. Towards the end of the century, however, the European settlements themselves were gaining in commercial importance, including British Calcutta and Madras (Fort St. George) and French Pondicherry and Chandernagore. The period of Mughul decline saw the European factories and the local representatives of Mughul authority increasingly at loggerheads, but down to the middle years of the eighteenth century the Europeans only crossed Indian rulers at their peril. Shah Jahan's ruthless punishment of the Portuguese of Hughli in 1632 for their slave-raiding activities was an extreme case, but Awrangzeb made life thoroughly uncomfortable for the English in Bengal between 1686 and 1690, while Baji Rao's treatment of the Portuguese in 1739 was a warning to all the settlements on the west coast to treat the Poona regime with respect.

The other main category of Europeans to be found in India in this period was composed of military adventurers. The Mughuls, the Deccani sultans, the Marathas, and the various successor regimes of the Mughul empire all employed a small number of Europeans in their service. The majority of these were artillerymen but some were artificers skilled in the casting of cannon, while a few were surgeons and physicians. Some of these men were adventurers seeking to sell their swords to the highest bidder. Others were deserters from the European settlements, men who had jumped ship or had escaped the Inquisition at Goa. Many, perhaps most, adopted a partially Indian life-style and a few became converts to Islam. Their importance lay in the fact that, apart from Jesuit missionaries and the official representatives of the European companies, they were the first and for a long time the most conspicuous Europeans with whom Indians had any dealings. They also had an importance far beyond their numbers on account of their role in the introduction into India of European military discipline and technology. Throughout the eighteenth century, in particular, such men were to be found in the employment of all those Indian rulers who sensed the superiority of European military organization and tactics. A few commanders took a personal interest in the application of European technology to the conditions of Indian warfare, but most were content to leave the matter in the hands of European renegades. But Indian rulers were neither ignorant of European methods of fighting nor unwilling to take advantage of new ways. At the battle of Panipat in 1761 between the Marathas and the Afghans there was a Muslim soldier of fortune in the Maratha ranks who had been trained by the Marquis de Bussy in Hyderabad and whose troops were described as fighting in the European manner. Later in the century, the great Maratha chieftain Sindhia (d. 1794) maintained an impressive establishment of European-officered regiments trained in the French style and commanded by Benoit de Boigne, a Savoyard soldier of fortune. But whether they were merchants or soldiers, the point about Europeans in India in the two and a half centuries that separated the arrival of Vasco da Gama at Calicut in 1498 from Shah Alam's grant of the *diwani* (the right to collect the land revenue on behalf of the padshah) of Bengal, Bihar, and Orissa to the East India Company in 1765 was that they operated *within* the system, their activities being strictly regulated by Indian rulers or their local representatives.

4. DECLINE OF THE CH'ING EMPIRE IN CHINA

It happens that there were two early modern empires in China: the native Ming dynasty and the Manchu Ch'ing. As we have already seen, the decline of the Ming regime did not lead to a fundamental alteration of social conditions in China but rather to a successor that resembled it in many important respects. The Manchus' conquest state was consciously built on the Ming model. So well did it succeed that many elements in the traditional order took on a rigid and inflexible cast. When the Ch'ing, in turn, declined there was to be no adaptation to a new imperial order. Rather, decline proceeded on to disintegration as the central institutions embodying the core values of Chinese civilization were sundered apart and collapsed.

The decline of the Ch'ing empire was thus a stage in the journey to the end of what is referred to as the imperial era in Chinese history. In a sense the demarcation of a decline phase is arbitrary, since we know in retrospect that the Ch'ing was not followed by another dynasty. Yet the distinction is worth making, for the Ming example suggests that there might have been points at which another imperial order could have been erected from traditional elements and subsequently a point after which that was less feasible. One of the purposes in a discussion of decline in the early modern empire in China is to try to identify which factors were simply a threat to the Ch'ing empire and which factors undermined the very foundations of the imperial system. Another purpose is to show how the decline of the Manchu regime facilitated the intrusion of European power and Western influences into the Chinese cultural sphere.

The Ch'ing empire, founded in 1644, reached the peak of its vigor in the middle of the eighteenth century. Judged in terms of its overall wealth and the living standard of the upper class, China was one of the most prosperous societies the world had known. Traditional labor-intensive agricultural techniques were highly developed in a stable social and political order keyed to the management of a preindustrial economy. Content to limit mercantile activity to a government-regulated trade through specified southern ports, the court benefitted from a net inflow of silver which continued unabated through the sixteenth, seventeenth, and eighteenth centuries. Aggressive on the frontiers, pushing Ch'ing influence into Tibet and Central Asia, the Manchus maintained domestic tranquility for the most of the eighteenth century. One consequence of these happy circumstances was a sudden growth in the Chinese population. A society that had consisted of 150 million members around 1700 grew to 313 million by 1794 and 430 million by 1850. An account of the decline of the Ch'ing empire can begin with this doubling of the population and the pressure it must have placed on resources and services. But after the middle of the nineteenth century it is fair to ask if the population had not reached a point that over-reached the managerial capabilities of the traditional order.

The first phase of Ch'ing decline took place in the period 1775 to 1850. After 1850 the dynasty entered a crisis period in which its survival, challenged by the twin evils of external aggression and domestic rebellion, was in doubt. At a later point, 1895 perhaps, we may say that the imperial system was beyond salvation and characterize developments of the time in terms of processes of social and cultural disintegration.

Institutional Decline

Both the peak and the downturn in Ch'ing fortunes came during the rule of the Ch'ien-lung emperor, whose reign spanned more than half a century (1736-95). Ch'ien-lung was one of the two greatest monarchs of the Ch'ing and already during his life the decline of the hereditary rule was apparent. An exceptionally vigorous and capable administrator in his youth, he abdicated after sixty years on the throne and continued to rule in fact until his death three years later. Corruption among the official establishment became increasingly widespread after the middle of the century. This is nowhere better illustrated than in the career of the imperial favorite, Ho-shen (1750-99).

In 1775, Ho-shen, a young Manchu bannerman assigned to the Imperial Equipage Department, caught the eye of the emperor, then forty years his senior. Whatever the nature of the old man's fascination with Ho-shen—there are stories that suggest a sexual attraction—he heaped favors and governmental powers upon his new protégé. In the space of a few years Ho-shen was given some of the highest and most lucrative offices in the empire. He became president of the Board of Personnel—a post that allowed him to control appointments throughout the empire. He was made a grand secretary and so became privy to all the most sensitive affairs of state. He had easy access to the palace, he was given noble titles, and his son was married to the emperor's favorite daughter. A man of little education and no discernible virtues, he extended unrestrained influence into all areas of government. The emperor resisted all efforts to impeach him. Ho-shen acquired enormous wealth, mostly through rake-offs from the customary tribute payments that officials throughout the empire sent to the throne. These unofficial gratuities, which grew in volume, were an early symptom of the corruption of the bureaucracy and at the same time a stimulus to rapacity as officials tried to squeeze greater amounts from the taxpayers within their jurisdictions. When Ch'ien-lung died in 1799, Ho-shen came immediately under attack and was allowed to commit suicide. His fortune, built up in less than three decades, included much land and many pawnshops, thousands of gold vessels and millions of ounces of silver. Its total value has been estimated as the equivalent of more than a billion dollars.

While Ho-shen's lurid career was symptomatic of the demoralization that pervaded the court circles, far more fundamental and extensive forms of corruption were at work in the vitals of the Ch'ing economy: the agricultural tax system. The most important resources available to the Manchu regime were the land taxes and labor service (corvée) levied on the Chinese peasantry. In 1713, in a time of prosperity, the emperor tried to fix a permanent limit to these exactions so as to guarantee the well-being of the populace. This proved to be highly unrealistic. As the style of official life changed, the demand for tribute payments and customary fees in governmental circles created needs for additional revenue which were eventually passed on down the line to the peasant producers. At the same time, the growth of population increased the competition for the fruits of agricultural endeavor. Although the size of bureaucracy grew more slowly than the population, the ranks of the gentry class as a whole were swollen. Ever larger numbers of degree holders had to find semiofficial or unofficial positions appropriate to their class. Some acted as intermediaries between the commoners and the officials, using their skills and influence to profit from both sides. They could blackmail officials by threatening to report irregularities and they could trade on the influence of powerful clans to negotiate lower tax rates, collecting a broker's fee—called "lawsuit rice"—for their services. The use of political and social influence by wealthy families to reduce their tax obligations led to a progressive shrinkage of the tax base. Since tax quotas were set by district, the officials had no alternative but to make up the deficits of the large households by increasing the levies on the small households. Many forms of exaction were used to increase the peasant's burden, including fees for transportation, fees for spoilage, inaccurate measuring, and discriminatory ratios of conversion from payment in kind to payment in money. By 1800 government revenues were threatened in a number of areas and the burden that fell upon the poorest elements in the population became unbearable.

One sign of the mounting distress in the countryside was the emergence in the 1790s of peasant rebellions in north and central China. Led by secret society elements of the White Lotus Society, which had served as a vehicle for popular discontent and antiforeignism since the Mongol conquests of the thirteenth century, the rebels organized armed bands at

現在匕聚營山縣屬箕山已令朱射斗牽制不
致遠颺今冊文傳等既俗奔赴巖峯灘一帶難
免不與羅其清歸俾必須分捘剿辦不使得均
德北寵又不致冊文傳與羅其清合夥方可期
殲除一股再圖別股努德楞泰當即帶兵由玉
山一帶兜努惠齡恒端由立山一
帶截巢冊文傳等即於初七日分路進兵努惠
齡恒瑞於初九日馳抵黑馬山據弁報稱
才傳龍紹周等股賊匪逃至老林場山梁屯踞
努才惠齡等細心籌議既冊文傳等據此山梁當
就現有兵力由西北面兜剿不使寵赴箕山與
羅其清全俾再行截剿高均德各股廢不致顧

10.4 A memorial endorsed by the Chinese emperor in 1798. The text reports on efforts to suppress the White Lotus Rebels. The emperor's endorsement (red in the original) has blotted out the names of the rebels and put circles next to those of officials. This rebellion demonstrated the weakness of the traditional banner forces after a prolonged period of internal peace. Courtesy: Collection of the National Palace Museum, Taipei, Taiwan, Republic of China.

the local level but failed to threaten the Manchu dynasty. This was but a preview of a string of uprisings that was to plague the Ch'ing in the nineteenth century. Ineffectual Manchu efforts to suppress the rebellion gave the first indications of the weakening of the military establishment. Hampered initially by the meddling of Ho-shen, the suppression campaign experienced success after 1799. Some of the pacification techniques used—organization of local militia, construction of stockades, relocation of the farming population in walled towns, and stripping the countryside of food supplies—are familiar in our own day.

Social and Cultural Change

Sensitive and reflective minds among the Chinese scholar class detected signs of a growing crisis toward the end of the eighteenth century. The geographer and scholar Hung Liang-chi (1746-1809), for example, wrote (in 1799, after Ho-shen's downfall) criticism of official corruption and even of the emperor's conduct. Such forthrightness earned him exile to Ili in Chinese Turkistan and nearly cost him his head. Because he noted the increase in China's population and speculated on its implication for living standards, Hung has been cited as "the Chinese Malthus." The title is undeserved, however, since Hung's reflections were not formulated with the same rigor as were those of his English contemporary, nor did they influence subsequent discussion of practical policy. A more significant line of scholarship was that known as the School of Statecraft, which flowered in the early nineteenth century. Reacting against the bookishness of early Ch'ing "empiricism" and the backward-looking "Han learning" of the scholars, like Hung, who took part in the great imperial compilation projects of the Ch'ien-lung period, the advocates of statecraft concentrated on practical questions of government. They were motivated by a sense of urgency stimulated by mounting evidence of Ch'ing decline. The best example of this trend was the historian and geographer Wei Yuan (1794-1856). Both a scholar and a man of action, Wei made practical contributions in the areas of salt administration, grain transport, and flood control. He was one of the first to recognize the importance of the West. His illustrated *Gazetteer of the Countries Overseas* (1844) was written to inform the Chinese about the Europeans who were beginning to make serious inroads into the empire. Given the rigidity and conformity in the intellectual world of the time, Wei Yuan and the Statecraft School had little effect on official thinking or the climate of opinion generally. Paradoxically, it was his classical scholarship that was to make the greatest contribution to intellectual change. Wei Yung was an advocate of the New Text school of Confucianism—a term that refers to the fact that there were two versions of the Confucian classics argued over by scholars since the ancient period. The discrepancies between the two versions were to be exploited by intellectual innovators in the 1890s, as we shall see in Chapter 13.

The most ominous symptom of the coming crisis in Chinese society was rapid spread of the use of opium. This was one sign for alarm that was recognized, and vigorous efforts were taken to deal with the problem. Long known as a medicinal drug (it is used to treat diarrhea), it began to be smoked as a narcotic in the seventeenth century. The practice was taken up during the eighteenth century by individuals in all walks of life. Prohibitions on selling and smoking opium were handed down by emperors from the 1720s to the 1820s, but the use of the drug continued to grow. The emperors and their advisers viewed the drug addiction as a sign of moral decay and acted accordingly. The failure of their efforts to stamp out the problem revealed further weaknesses in the fabric of society.

Opium was a question that had many facets: (1) addiction itself was a symptom of psychological distress of the users; (2) the failure to prohibit its use was a sign of corruption—indeed, official corruption fed on the drug trade; (3) the major source of supply was through smuggling from abroad—a fact that gave the suppliers (the British) a strong motive to break down Ch'ing control over frontiers and trade; and (4) the volume of the trade grew to the point that it was a drain on the economy. Some opium was grown in south

China but the bulk of it came by sea from India and Turkey. Since it was contraband, it bypassed the only legal port for foreign vessels, Canton, and was off-loaded at points along the coast. Opium extract, taken from the seed pod of the poppy, was packed in chests (of 133 or 160 pounds) for shipment to China. Demand rose rapidly from an average of less than two thousand chests per year in the 1790s to more than thirty-five thousand chests in the 1830s. Prices ranged anywhere from $500 to $2,000 per chest depending on quality and demand. The drain on the Chinese economy was enormous. Totaling several million ounces of silver per year, it reversed the balance of trade that had made China wealthy in the preceding centuries. Opium was picked up on the coast by smugglers' boats, known because of their many oarsmen and high speed as "fast crabs" and "scrambling dragons," while payment was made to British merchants in Canton. The Chinese thought that the silver outflow was worse than it actually was because they did not see that other capital was coming in at Canton to take advantage of the high interest rates.

The opium problem came to a head in the 1830s. After extensive discussion, in which some counseled legalization to bring the trade under government regulation, the emperor decided on a policy of total prohibition. Importation, cultivation, sale, and consumption were all to be punished by death. The tragic hero of this misguided effort to purge the empire of an evil habit was a Chinese official named Lin Tse-hsu (1785-1850). A capable and experienced administrator as well as an advocate of the School of Statecraft, Lin was personally incorruptible, loyal to the throne, and adamantly opposed to opium. In 1839 the emperor dispatched Lin to Canton as a special imperial commissioner with orders to halt the drug trade. In Canton Lin proceeded to halt trade, to publicly destroy some twenty-one thousand chests of surrendered opium, and to put pressure on foreign merchants to sign pledges not to continue the illegal traffic. The result of Lin's initial succes was to provoke the British to a test of strength. When English naval vessels blockaded key points up and down the China coast, Lin Tse-hsu fell from favor and was banished to Ili. In the warfare that continued on and off between the British and the Ch'ing for the next twenty years, the Manchus were forced to make many concessions that significantly eroded their sovereignty. The opium trade continued.

Up until the 1840s the accumulating problems of popular unrest, official corruption, and foreign pressure indicated that the Ch'ing regime was in an advanced stage of decline, but they still did not constitute a threat to its survival. After 1850 the dynasty had to fight to stay alive. The principal dangers were the classic twins of dynastic decline: internal rebellion and external aggression.

At mid-century China was torn apart by rebellions. North of the Yangtze territory was held by the Nien rebels (1851-64), while Muslim groups broke away in the southwest (1855-73) and northeast (1862-78). The greatest rebellion of all, the Taiping (1850-64), seized the richest and most populous provinces south of the Yangtze and threatened the dynasty. There were rebellions of all types: religious groups (Muslims), ethnic minorities (Miao), secret society and bandit operations (the Nien, the Small Sword Society), and a full-scale millennarian social revolution (the Taiping). The causes of rebellions were the oppressive conditions of life in the lower strata of Chinese society and the dissatisfaction of marginal elements with that life. Such conditions were not new in the 1850s. What made the rebellions possible were (1) the failure of the government to perform its normal pacification activities effectively and (2) the erosion of respect for Manchu authority.

The story of the Taiping Rebellion (some call it a revolution) illustrates a number of elements in the process. The Taiping movement originated in the southernmost part of China, Kwangtung province, far from the capital and also the area (around Canton) most exposed to foreign influences. Local conflicts at the clan and village level between native Cantonese and Hakkas (literally "guest households"—a group that had migrated south some centuries earlier but retained distinct cultural traits) made chronic partisan warfare a way of life. Already at the time of the opium crisis, gentry and populace formed their own militia units to take action against the foreigners. Such popular activism, in fact, was one of the elements that made it difficult for Manchu officials to make concessions to Western demands. The repeated humiliation of Manchu banner forces at the hands of the Europeans eroded respect for the dynasty and heightened the feeling of dissatisfaction with the government. Hung Hsiu-ch'uan (1814-64), the founder of the Taiping movement, was a Hakka who tried to raise himself to gentry status through the governmental examination system. Frustrated by repeated failures to pass the lowest examination, Hung underwent a mental breakdown in which he had visions of himself in Heaven being charged with the mission of eradicating evil spirits. Some years later (1843) Hung connected his vision with some Christian tract literature that Protestant missionaries were then distributing in Chinese translation. Hung concluded that he was God's son and the younger brother of Jesus and that his mission was to save China. Quickly Hung set about studying Christian doctrine, developing his ideology, and converting friends and relatives. Although he had some contact with an American southern Baptist missionary in Canton, his knowledge of Christianity remained limited and he made as much use of traditional Chinese texts as he did of the Bible.

Moving to the adjacent province of Kwangsi, Hung Hsiu-ch'uan and his followers founded an Association for God Worshippers, recruiting new members from the poorest elements: landless peasants, charcoal workers, porters. Famine and a secret society uprising in 1840-50 led to widespread banditry and disorder. Hung's followers swelled to more than ten thousand and he began to prepare for armed insurrection. In 1851 he proclaimed the Heavenly Kingdom of the Great Peace (T'ai-p'ing t'ien-kuo, "great peace," a phrase from the Confucian classics) and himself took the title Heavenly King. Gathering momentum as they went, the Taiping forces fought their way north to the Yangtze and by 1853 took the southern capital at Nanking (renamed T'ien-ching, "Heavenly Capital"). A probe north of the Yangtze was turned back before it could threaten the Manchus in Peking. The Taipings then settled down in Nanking, which they held for more than a decade. Although they never built a very cohesive administrative apparatus, the Taiping rebels did establish a regime that was a rival to the ruling dynasty and they did hold many of the richest provinces in the south, choking off revenues that the Ch'ing needed to survive.

The most enticing aspect of the Taiping movement is the fact that it projected, in theory at least, a radically different model for the organization of Chinese society. Such an undertaking was not attempted again until the establishment of the People's Republic in 1949. First of all, the Taipings rejected Confucian values and denied the authority of the classics, which rationalized the traditional social order. Instead, they put forward their own Christian doctrines and recognized the authority of the Bible and direct revelations from God to Hung. Second, their order was a communal one in which all were part of a religious community, property was jointly held, and equality of the sexes was recognized. Third, the entire population was to be organized in groups of twenty-five families under officers who managed all their affairs, conducted church services, and acted as military commanders. Fourth, they succeeded in creating a puritanical atmosphere, attacking vices like opium smoking, drinking, and foot binding and building up a fighting morale that contrasted starkly with that of the imperial forces.

The liabilities that caused the Taipings to fail can be stated in both negative and positive terms. In a single decade they were simply unable to establish a stable new social order. Much of their administration did not go beyond military action and exaction of wealth from the countryside. Their leadership, furthermore, was unstable. Hung Hsiu-ch'uan himself was a withdrawn and erratic figure able neither to lead nor to discipline the other "kings," who fell to feuding among themselves. Against the Taipings were arrayed the most powerful interests in Chinese society. Because it would have eliminated the land system and the

Confucian orthodoxy, Taiping doctrine struck directly at the core values of the gentry-official class. That group was able to dominate Chinese society by virtue of its ownership of land and its monopoly on learning. Under other circumstances the gentry might have been turned against the Manchus—certainly they had no love for a foreign ruling house. But when their own position was threatened, the gentry had little choice but to rally to the Ch'ing standard. The Manchu Ch'ing, cynical patrons of the cultural tradition, became the embodiment of orthodoxy and so won the unflinching support of the Chinese elite, who turned on their countrymen to suppress the rebellion. Thus was nationalism defeated in China: the Chinese were divided along class lines while the empire was reunited on the basis of cultural orthodoxy.

One by one the Ch'ing armies had been defeated or proved ineffectual by the rebels. In desperation, the Manchu court was obliged to trust its fate to a new class of Chinese leaders. First among these men was the administrator-turned-soldier Tseng Kuo-fan (1811-72). Ideologically motivated by loyalty to the throne and a desire to preserve the Confucian system, Tseng built the first regionally based, Chinese-led army. His lieutenants, most notably Tso Tsung-t'ang (1812-85) and Li Hung-chang (1823-1901), were later to repeat the process elsewhere. The essence of Tseng's accomplishment was to knit together a large force from the militia units that were already being formed locally by elements of the gentry class for their own protection. Great emphasis was placed on building up a network of loyalties between the officers and their subordinates, ideological indoctrination, and a program of social reconstruction. The resulting Hunan Army was supported by local revenues raised through the provincial government. Tseng Kuo-fan's forces were turned against the Taipings and the Nien and deserve most of the credit for their suppression. New regional forces of this kind were under Chinese, not Manchu, command. They made possible the Ch'ing survival, but at great expense. Regionalism now emerged as provincial revenues that had once been at the disposal of the central government were consumed locally and Chinese officers commanded the strongest armies where once Manchu banners had been supreme.

External Pressures

At the very moment when the internal rebellions were at their peak, the Ch'ing empire was subjected to unprecedented foreign pressure. In the debacle of the Opium War (1839-42), the Chinese commissioner Lin was succeeded by a series of Manchus from the imperial clan who could better represent the emperor in sensitive negotiations with the Western barbarians. There was no precedent in Chinese history for a vital threat to the empire coming from the seas. The historically strategic frontier had always been the northern border. The Manchus, having themselves conquered China from the north, framed their own military thinking in those traditional terms. When the superiority of Western naval power was demonstrated in battle, they had no choice but to make concessions. Still, the court failed to recognize, or refused to admit, the seriousness of the Western threat. In the face of the emperor's contempt for the Westerners and the superiority of their arms, the Manchu negotiators often found themselves in the most untenable position. They were reluctant to report to the emperor the entire truth about the weakness of the Ch'ing position, and yet, at the same time, they had to satisfy the demands of the British. Reports to the throne were not always entirely candid. The emperor, for his part, promised more in treaty settlements than he was willing to give up in practice. This proved to be a grave miscalculation.

Important concessions in the settlement of the Opium War included the granting of the island of Hong Kong to the British as a permanent base and the opening of five ports for trade and residence by British merchants. The British were particularly desirous of entering into the city of Canton, while the Ch'ing officials refused to allow them to do so (the English and Chinese versions of the treaty diverged on this point). Popular antiforeignism at Canton put the Manchu officials in a ticklish position. Friction continued until 1858, when the French and British occupied Canton, shipped the governor-general off to India, and sent a powerful force north to Tientsin (on the coast near Peking). Giving in to this show of force, the Manchus signed a treaty that allowed for diplomats to take up residence in Peking—a major concession. The Manchus did not honor this commitment, and when the European ministers arrived in the following year, the shore batteries opened up on them, sinking several English vessels. The British and French responded in 1860 by landing a large force on the coast, which marched inland and entered Peking. The emperor was obliged to flee to Manchuria. Thus, at the peak of domestic uprisings, the Manchus found their capital invaded by a foreign army and their ruler put to flight.

By all rights, the Ch'ing empire should have come to an end when it lost its capital. Instead, it survived for another half century. After looting and burning the summer palace, the Western powers negotiated highly favorable agreements with the emperor's brother, Prince Kung (1833-98). They then decided to support the Ch'ing against its internal enemies as the best guarantee of stable conditions favorable to their commercial interests. Modern Chinese patriots have seen this accommodation as a Manchu betrayal of the Chinese people. The Manchus were willing to surrender some of their sovereignty in order to retain their rule over China. The Western powers were willing to lend support in the suppression of the Taipings. In this manner was the Manchu-Chinese dyarchy of the early Ch'ing converted into a Manchu-Chinese-Western synarchy in the late Ch'ing.

The T'ung-chih reign period (1862-74) was known as a time of "restoration," when a conscious effort was made to revive the essential traditional values of the imperial system. Although capable of limited innovation, leaders of the restoration, like Prince Kung and Tseng Kuo-fan, were simply trying to preserve a system that was recognized to be in decline. Most of their attention was directed toward suppressing rebellion, cleaning up governmental corruption, and promoting education. Their efforts preserved Ch'ing rule for a time but in doing so deferred accommodation to some of the new processes that were at work. European expansion had changed for good the defense situation in China, yet Tso Tsung-t'ang was sent west to push Ch'ing frontiers out into Central Asia. International economic pressure in the form of capitalist expansion meant that no state could survive which supported itself entirely on a traditional agricultural base. The technological changes in military practice alone made the traditional organization of the imperial government untenable. Finally, the growth of population cast doubt on the viability of Chinese social organization. In the last quarter of the nineteenth century famines struck with increasing severity and frequency. The old order was in crisis.

5. DECLINE OF THE TOKUGAWA IN JAPAN

The early modern state created at the turn of the seventeenth century by the military might of the Tokugawa house and its allies was to last over 250 years. Under Tokugawa hegemony, the struggles between the rival warlords of the previous period were brought to an end and the Japanese experienced an unprecedented era of peace and order. In the early decades of the Tokugawa period, down to the middle of the seventeenth century, the leaders of the military elite that had asserted dominance over Japanese society demonstrated considerable flexibility in adapting to peace and creating a new political system. Their major preoccupation was with mechanisms of control in an effort to bring about social stability. By the end of the seventeenth century the Tokugawa shogunate and the governments of the warlords' domains, which taken together constituted the new political regime, had become rigid in their orientations. As the eighteenth century brought new challenges, the political structure ran out of elasticity, and institutions and procedures adequate to earlier needs were no longer easily adaptable to new socioeconomic pressures. The regime, despite sporadic attempts at recapturing the initiative, was on the defensive.

By the 1830s there were increasing signs that only fundamental reordering of key institutions might have arrested the long-term decline. Before any such basic modifications in the system were achieved, however, Japan was to face a concerted threat from outside in the form of European and American demands for trade and diplomatic contact. It was this challenge that precipitated the political crisis that toppled the Tokugawa structure in 1868.

In Japan, even more clearly than in China, the origins of the most crucial of the processes of decline in the early modern state were internal rather than external. Outside pressure, or foreign "impact," was not a critical factor until at least 1830, and even then its significance can be accurately understood only in the context of internal pressures for reform. In Japan, moreover, the loss of stability was clearly due more to a steady and often rapid pace of economic growth and social change than to economic stagnation, population growth, or the political processes most central to dynastic decline elsewhere.

Degeneration of Hereditary Rule

Political power in the Tokugawa system tended to be quite diffuse because of the existence of the semiautonomous daimyo domains with their separate jurisdictions, which dated back to the more clearly feudal institutions of the sixteenth century. The traditional Japanese practice of delegating authority nominally held by superiors to individuals or groups lower in the hierarchy made political power even more diffuse. As a result, the personal abilities of the Tokugawa shogun or of the daimyo lords were not in normal times crucial. When Yoshimune (r. 1716-45), the last of the truly forceful personalities to hold the position of shogun, left the scene in the mid-eighteenth century, real power within the central government fell to men who dominated the various councils and higher offices within the increasingly bureaucratic structure of administration. The same process took place in the various domains in similar situations.

This was not a novel solution to the problem of maintaining capable leadership in a hereditary system. There were ample precedents in the latter half of the seventeenth century as well as earlier in Japanese history, and the transition from active shoguns to passive figureheads was smooth enough not to have caused by itself a major loss in administrative efficiency. A passive shogun, however, did contribute to the ever-present danger of factional strife. The major source of friction within the shogunate in the eighteenth century was the rivalry between the chief *fudai,* or "inner lords," who viewed leadership in the absence of a strong shogun as their hereditary prerogative, and the lower-ranked retainers of the Tokugawa house, who, on occasions, used such positions as chamberlain to wield considerable influence. In a manner familiar to bureaucratic systems elsewhere, the chamberlains—a post that originally entailed waiting upon the shogun's immediate needs within the household (in this respect comparable to eunuchs in China)—came to be used by strong shoguns seeking informal channels of information and detours around the unwieldy formal structures of government. Since the chamberlains were normally men of little independent power, their loyalty to the shogun was often more easily obtained than that of the entrenched *fudai* "inner" lords and others within the regular bureaucracy. When the shogun himself was not vigorous, however, this arrangement sometimes permitted chamberlains to manipulate policy in his name. Tanuma Okitsugu, who held the post of grand chamberlain in the period 1764-86, was the outstanding example of this; and the friction between the upstart Tanuma and the more powerful of the *fudai* councillors severely complicated the issue of how the Tokugawa should respond to the internal difficulties it faced in this period.

After Tanuma's tenure, the question was largely resolved in favor of the dominance of *fudai* lords, and on the whole the absence of vigorous leadership was perhaps less a factor in the decline of the regime than was the inappropriateness of the approaches taken toward new problems. Eventually, however, the larger issue of ability versus heredity was raised in connection with the overall system of allocating rank within the samurai class by inheritance rather than merit.

The growing ineffectiveness of Tokugawa government machinery to maintain social and economic control does not appear to have been primarily due to bureaucratic corruption as such. Factionalism, graft, favoritism, and other instances of bureaucratic corruption do not seem to have increased dramatically over time within either the shogunate or the domain governments. Rather, the loss of effectiveness evident in the late eighteenth and early nineteenth centuries stemmed primarily from the inadequacy of governmental structures designed for the very different social and economic conditions of an earlier period. For example, the prohibitions against geographical or occupational mobility aimed at a static, stable equilibrium proved impossible to enforce in the long run because the government machinery had never been designed to cope with the long-range consequences of growth of urban centers or the conditions in the countryside that made migration to towns and cities attractive. Nevertheless, there are two major areas in which Tokugawa failure can be attributed to a deterioration of administrative vitality: military preparedness, which will be discussed later, and tax collection.

Recent studies of taxation in the Tokugawa period have tended to discredit the view long held by most historians that the overall tax burden on the common man became heavier as the period progressed. On the contrary, there is evidence of a marked decline in administrative efficiency in collecting revenue. The land surveys essential for accurate tax assessment were too sporadic and too incomplete to enable tax collectors to keep pace with the growth of agricultural production. All too often, increased yields on old fields and the creation of new ones escaped official notice. Since taxes were calculated on the basis of outdated estimates of total crops, even the trend toward increasing the official percentage of the harvest to be paid as taxes (from 40 percent in the beginning of the Tokugawa to 50 percent and ultimately in some cases to 60 percent) did not adequately serve the purpose. Many of the gains in agriculture in the seventeenth and eighteenth centuries thus remained in the hands of peasant cultivators or village landlords, to be sold for profit in the urban markets. Why the task of keeping tax assessments abreast of change—a task basic to the support of the regime and the samurai class as a whole—was handled so badly is unclear, but the result was a critical loss of control over the agrarian sector upon which government revenue largely depended.

This shrinking, percentagewise, of the government's share of agricultural production, however, was only one aspect of the larger economic problem. The ability of the regime to maintain control over the economy as a whole was increasingly undermined by the growth of urban commerce and nonagricultural production. There had taken place in the seventeenth and eighteenth centuries a rapid rise in urban population—ironically, touched off initially in large part by the political decision to remove samurai from the land—and this in turn had proved a tremendous stimulus to the Japanese economy. A national market system took form, centering on the two metropolises of Tokyo (Edo) and Osaka; sophisticated financial institutions were developed by urban merchants to meet the needs of an increasingly monetized system of exchange; and commercial farming and rural handicraft industry spread into the hinterland to supply the demands for a wide diversity of consumer goods. It was this transformation of the economic sphere to which the Tokugawa political elite failed to adapt.

The reasons behind the negative consequences suffered by the regime are complex but can be summarized under three headings. In the first place, both the shogunate and the daimyo domains continued to rely on an agricultural tax-in-kind as their primary source of revenue. Quite apart from the question of the efficiency of tax collection, the agrarian sector was growing less rapidly than the economy as a whole. Yet the Tokugawa and most of the domains never developed means of systematically tapping commercial activity as a source of revenue. Moreover, the collection of taxes-in-kind placed the government at a disadvantage, for it was forced to market these tax goods in order to realize cash for expenditures. Since prices rose and fell according to supply and demand, bumper harvests often meant low prices, while high prices came when the government had the least to market.

A second, related factor was a long-term rise in the standards of living and changes in the patterns of consumption in Tokugawa cities. Both the ruling elite and the samurai class as a whole were urban based, which meant that they faced a situation in which their income remained steady while that of others—notably the merchant elite—rose. The attempt to keep abreast of the rising standards of consumption put a heavy strain on government as well as samurai family expenditures. As early as the turn of the eighteenth century the shogunate found itself in financial difficulties. The huge treasury reserve bequeathed by the founder Tokugawa, Ieyasu, had been eaten away by such special projects as the ostentatious mausoleum for Ieyasu built at Nikko, such emergency expenditures as the rebuilding of the city of Edo after the fire of 1657, and by the extravagant life-style pursued by later shoguns. The samurai, in the process of being transformed from a warrior class into a civic and cultural elite, also sought material symbols to express their social and political status. Despite sporadic exhortations to be frugal and return to the spartan life-styles of their warrior forefathers, the average samurai found it difficult to resist the temptations of conspicuous consumption. The problem was that his purchasing power did not grow apace with his economic expectations.

The third factor, one that underlies both of the above, was the failure of the Tokugawa to establish direct control over the commercial system, thus leaving it largely in the hands of a combination of urban merchants and rural suppliers, who manipulated the market for their own profit. Much of the actual process of translating agricultural goods collected as taxes into ready cash was to be handled by privileged merchants, and it was not uncommon for a considerable proportion of that revenue to remain in their hands in the form of commissions and other costs. In addition, the government's share of the total was further reduced by interest payments on its loans from merchant financiers, for, lacking reserves for major projects or tiding over lean years, the shogunate and the lords ran up large debts.

Tokugawa leaders, while not fully comprehending the causes of the ailment, were not indifferent to the painful symptoms. It was particularly apparent that the purchasing power of the samurai class was being eroded. At various times, beginning in the early eighteenth and extending into the nineteenth century, attempts were made at reforms. For the most part these were limited to efforts at reducing government expenses and preventing merchants from manipulating urban prices. The latter failed to bring any lasting relief from inflation, while the former could be achieved only by cutting the largest single government expense, the stipends of the samurai class. During the 1770s and 1780s, Tanuma Okitsugu—the chamberlain mentioned above—did propose a number of novel expediencies in an attempt to generate more revenue. These included a plan to stimulate exports and a policy of selling monopolies in order to effectively tax internal commerce. Tanuma fell from power before his schemes could bear any real fruit, and his conservative opponents among the *fudai* lords condemned such positive approaches to commerce as economic heresy. The 1830s and 1840s witnessed further attempts at reform, but the only substantial measure of real success was achieved in some of the outer domains of the *tozama* lords, which thus grew stronger as the shogunate weakened.

The indebtedness of the Tokugawa and domain governments was not in itself sufficient to bankrupt the regime. Their creditors were their subjects and had neither the political nor military power to force the issue; nor is there any real evidence that any significant portion of the urban merchant elite found the situation unsatisfactory. The real threat posed to the regime lay in the broader ramifications these economic changes had for the social system as a whole. They contributed directly to class conflict and outbursts of rebellion, which in turn proved fatal to the regime once foreign pressure and the growing independence of powerful lords revealed how seriously Tokugawa military strength had declined.

Social Change and Class Conflict

Economic growth of the sort experienced in Tokugawa Japan affected different classes in varying degrees, thus upsetting the social balance achieved in the early seventeenth century. Inflation and the practice of cutting stipends to meet government deficits meant that economic conditions for the samurai class were no longer consistent with its status as a political and social elite. Indeed, large numbers of those at the lowest ranks were actually threatened with impoverishment as their purchasing power fell. Adding insult to injury was the contrast—all too apparent to the contemporary eye—between the plight of the samurai and the rise of the two strata most benefitted by economic development: the urban merchant and the village landlord. Both tended increasingly to live a style of life more affluent than that afforded the lower samurai, thus inciting resentment and alienation. Middling and lower samurai also grew alienated from their lords and superiors over the issue of talent as a criteria for promotion in bureaucratic careers. More and more asked what justified a hereditary system of allocating political positions when their superiors were failing so clearly to cope with their problems. Lower samurai, thwarted in their individual ambitions at a time when their status as an elite was being eroded, were prominent actors in the anti-Tokugawa movements of the 1860s.

The long-term effects of the growth of a market economy in village Japan also contributed to social instability and class strife. The changes that took place within many villages can be summarized under two headings: increased vulnerability and increased polarization. The shift to commercial or quasi-commercial farming made peasants more vulnerable to natural disasters to the extent that they were no longer self-sufficient in the food crops necessary to subsist. They were also vulnerable to new disasters in the form of fluctuations in the marketplace. Over time, the differences in the degree of success in taking advantages of the opportunities within the new market system also led to increased social tensions within many villages. Tenancy, with the accompanying changes in the relationship between landowners and the landless within the village, also became increasingly common. Thus the gap between the more successful peasants and those at the opposite extreme widened, creating new tensions. By the turn of the nineteenth century there was ample evidence of stress and strain in the form of sporadic, yet large-scale, eruptions of violence against the samurai officials and against peasant landlords.

The rebellions among the peasantry and the isolated actions of dissident samurai did not in themselves constitute a mortal threat to the regime in the period prior to 1860. Although the samurai that made up the coercive force of the government were less and less cut from the pattern of their warrior forefathers, neither the shogunate nor the domains had real difficulty in mustering sufficient arms to suppress such outbursts so long as they were limited to the peasantry or small numbers of samurai acting outside the system. The more important trend was the decline of Tokugawa military power versus that of the outside lords and the emergence to leadership, within important domains, of samurai cliques bent on altering the political balance within the Tokugawa system. Regionalism and independent power groupings were a latent factor in the Tokugawa political system from the beginning. The equilibrium between central authority and local autonomy had been sustained by a combination of Tokugawa military superiority and the acceptance of a national govern-

10.5 Taken from an eighteenth century woodblock print depicting samurai brawling in the streets of Edo, this scene was a common sight in the entertainment district of urban centers and a cause of concern for the declining morale of this elite class.
Source: G. B. Sansom, *Japan: A Short Cultural History*, rev. ed., Prentice-Hall, Inc., 1962, p. 497.

ment when it contributed to social stability and the well-being of the various regions. The erosion of the former and the inability to maintain the latter undercut the bases of the Tokugawa hegemony.

The Tokugawa house lands and those of the inner lords upon which the shogunate was most dependent for military support were among the areas most heavily affected by the economic and social changes described above. The Tokugawa samurai retainers were thus most subject to the demoralizing effects of these changes. Over time, the once mighty military alliance that Tokugawa Ieyasu had forged at the turn of the seventeenth century had suffered serious losses in military preparedness and overall strength. By comparison, such outside domains as Choshu and Satsuma had maintained a higher relative potential for military action. In the case of Satsuma, which was situated in southern Kyushu far from the economic center, the primary reason may be the fact that the waves of socioeconomic change had yet to erode the foundations of domain cohesiveness and samurai morale. Satsuma was thus more successful in controlling and mobilizing domain resources in the struggles of the 1860s. The evidence in Choshu is that the domain took advantage of its strategic location on the key coastal shipping routes to profit from commercial activity, thus moderating the impact of change and preserving a greater level of political strength. It was these domains that took the lead in the 1860s when several decades of political maneuvering between the shogunate and the more important domains failed to resolve the internal problems and the immediate threat of foreign encroachment added an external crisis to the growing turmoil of domestic politics.

External Pressures and Cultural Change

The details of the impact of European and American expansion on mid-nineteenth century Japan will be dealt with in Chapters 11 and 12. Here it is important to note the effect of that impact on the political equilibrium. By the 1830s, almost a quarter of a century before the first significant display of force by the West (Commodore Perry's arrival with an American fleet in 1853), the threat of potential foreign encroachment became a factor in domestic politics. Those important domains whose leaders were excluded from the inner councils of the Tokugawa government linked the need for stronger defenses to their call for internal reforms. The foreign menace, even in this early stage of Western pressure, served as a key justification in these critics' eyes for at least a partial break with past precedents and an alteration of some of the most fundamental of Tokugawa traditions—e.g., the limitations on military strength in the outside domains and the veiled hostage system requiring alternate attendance by the lords at the shogun's castle. Whether the shogunate could have long maintained its hegemony had it yielded to such demands for internal change is a moot point; but its inability to cope with the foreign menace was a central factor in the rapidly accelerating rate of decline in the 1850s.

Again, the history of the shifts in cultural values and political ideas that culminated in the ultimate loss of legitimacy for the old regime is best treated in Chapters 12 and 13. But here it needs to be pointed out that the Tokugawa period witnessed major new developments in the realm of political and social thought. Some of these were the result of heterodox attempts to resolve dilemmas inherent from the beginning in the poor fit of Chinese neo-Confucian principles and the Tokugawa reality. Others can be correlated with the socioeconomic changes and the stress generated by them. The overall result by the nineteenth century, while not yet revolutionary, was intellectual ferment and an increasing willingness on the part of disgruntled thinkers to question the status quo. In this, Western ideas, imported through the Dutch trading post at Nagasaki, were to play a significant, although not necessarily the only, role, for Japanese critics of the regime also proved quite resourceful in drawing upon their own past for alternatives to the present.

CONCLUDING REMARKS

One of the central problems that needs to be addressed in a study of modern history is the question of the imbalance of power among the civilizations of Eurasia that led by the nineteenth century to the domination of the globe by the nations of Western Europe. How is one to account for the fact that the once powerful early modern empires of Asia were subjected to the intrusion and domination of Westerners? To explain this change entirely in terms of the capabilities and innovations of the Europeans would have the effect of making the Asians passive objects of Western initiative and would invite the assumption that the people of Western Europe were somehow more innately capable than the people of West Asia, South Asia, or East Asia. It would also overlook the fact that Europeans in previous centuries had dealt with Asian civilizations from a position of relative weakness. One corrective to common misconceptions is to see the shifting balance among civilizations in terms of the internal changes taking place within Asian societies themselves, specifically in the loss of vigor of the early modern empires. The decline of these empires is considered here in anticipation of the following chapter on Western European domination precisely because what might appear from a Western perspective as the ascendancy of Europe can be seen from another vantage point as, in part at least, a function of changes within Asian societies.

What was the nature of decline, and how did decline processes manifest themselves in the various empires described in Chapter 9? One set of decline processes affected the state apparatus of the empires, inviting comparisons along the lines of state organization. How, for example, did the differing arrangements for selection of rulers affect the quality of rule in the Ottoman, Mughul, or Ch'ing empires? How did the organization of ministries and court councils contribute to or detract from effective executive decision making in the Ottoman, the Chinese, or the Japanese cases? What kind of a military system supported each regime and what kinds of strains appeared with the passage of time to make those systems less reliable?

Another set of questions can be formulated to see how the tensions within the society affected the stability and strength of the political order. How, for example, was the Ottoman empire affected by the tensions among different ethnic, linguistic, and religious groups, and how did this diversity influence the military and administrative problems of maintaining control over northern Africa, Arabia, and parts of eastern Europe? What problems were posed for the Ottomans and the Manchus in China by reliance on tribal military forces ethnically distinct from the indigenous populations of the areas they ruled? How did the Mughuls and the Tokugawa shogunate manage to balance the forces of the military lords pledged to their support, and how did the assignments of lands and revenues restrict or inhibit the power of the central rulers? How did changes in social structure and ideological values affect the loyalties of subjects and the revenues restrict or inhibit the power of the central rulers? How did changes in social structure and ideological values affect the loyalties of subjects and the revenues of the state?

External factors, too, could contribute to the decline of empires. Military threats or adventures along the periphery of the empire could impose strains on state revenue and, in extreme cases, the loyalty of subjects. Commercial relations also affected the economic well-being of the early modern empires. One question that might be raised here and considered again in connection with the next chapter is the impact of maritime trade and Western contacts in the period prior to the establishment of Western hegemony in the eighteenth and nineteenth centuries. In anticipation of Chapter 12 it might be asked what changes in the course of decline constituted vital threats to the survival of early modern empires requiring radical alterations, and which were merely weaknesses, susceptible to correction or restoration within the existing framework of institutions and values?

BIBLIOGRAPHY

10.P DECLINE OF EARLY MODERN EMPIRES: PROCESSES

Eisenstadt, Shmuel N., *Social Differentiation and Stratification* (Scott, Foresman paperback, 1971), 248 pp. Chapter 6 outlines stratification in traditional empires with sections on India and China.

———, ed., *The Decline of Empires* (Prentice-Hall paperback, 1967), 180 pp. Selections dealing with many aspects of the topic drawn from the literature on many empires with very brief but useful remarks by the editor.

Hobsbawm, E. J., *Primitive Rebels: Studies in Archaic Forms of Social Movement in the Nineteenth and Twentieth Centuries* (Norton paperback, 1959), 202 pp. Generalizations about social banditry and millennarianism based on Western examples.

Ibn Khaldun, *The Muqaddimah*, abridged edition from the translation of Franz Rosenthal (Princeton University Press paperback, 1967), pp. 123-295. Wide-ranging remarks on the fortunes of dynasties and cities by a brilliant Arab historian and thinker of the fourteenth century.

Weber, Max, *From Max Weber: Essays in Sociology* (Longon, 1947), pp. 196-264. A classic discussion of bureaucracy by one of the great sociological thinkers.

10.1 DECLINE OF THE OTTOMANS IN WEST ASIA

Coles, Paul, *The Ottoman Impact on Europe* (New York, 1968), 216 pp. A brief account of Ottoman relations with the Christian powers, illustrated.

Gibb, Hamilton A. L., and Harold Bowen, *Islamic Society and the West*, 2 vols. (London, 1950), Vol. 1, pp. 173-199. An in-depth analysis of the causes of Ottoman decline.

Holt, Peter M., *Egypt and the Fertile Crescent, 1516-1922: A Political History* (Cornell University Press paperback, 1966), pp. 61-163. The impact of Ottoman rule on the Fertile Crescent.

Inalcik, Halil, "The Heyday and Decline of the Ottoman Empire," *Cambridge History of Islam*, Vol. 1 (Cambridge, 1970), pp. 324-53. A reliable narrative, by one of the leading authorities.

Lewis, Benard, *The Emergence of Modern Turkey* (Oxford University Press paperback, 1968), pp. 1-39. A brilliant summary of the causes of Ottoman decline.

Pallis, Alexander, *In the Days of the Janissaries* (London, 1951), 224 pp. A colorful selection of extracts from the travelbook of the Ottoman writer Evliya Chelebi, describing life in seventeenth century Istanbul.

10.2 DECLINE OF THE SAFAVIDS IN IRAN

Algar, Hamid, *Religion and State in Iran, 1785-1906* (Berkeley, 1969), pp. 1-44. A discussion concerning the relationship of the Iranian *ulama* with the state, centering upon the late eighteenth century.

Keddie, Nikki R., "The Roots of the Ulama's Power in Modern Iran," *Scholars, Saints and Sufis* (Berkeley, 1972), pp. 211-29. Examines the peculiar relationship of the Iranian *ulama* to the state, beginning in the late Safavid period.

Lambton, Ann K.S., "Persia: The Breakdown of Society," *The Cambridge History of Islam*, 2 vols. (Cambridge, 1970), Vol. 1, pp. 430-67. Describes the decay of Iran in the eighteenth century and the course of events under the Qajar dynasty during the nineteenth century.

Lockhart, Lawrence, *The Fall of the Safavi Dynasty and the Afghan Occupation of Persia* (Cambridge, 1958), pp. 1-34. Analyzes the causes of Safavid decline.

Spuler, Bertold, "Central Asia from the Sixteenth Century to the Russian Conquests," *The Cambridge History of Islam*, 2 vols. (Cambridge, 1970), Vol. 1, pp. 468-94. Describes the course of events on Iran's northeast frontier.

10.3   DECLINE OF THE MUGHULS IN SOUTH ASIA

Chandra, Satis, *Parties and Politics at the Mughul Court, 1707-1740* (New Delhi, 1972), pp. xv-1 and 257-68. A valuable discussion of the causes of Mughul decline.

Habib, Irfan, *The Agrarian System of Mughul India, 1556-1707* (London, 1963), pp. 317-51. A work of the greatest importance, which postulates the theory of a financial crisis besetting the Mughul empire during the second half of the seventeenth century.

Ikram, Sheikh Mohamad, *Muslim Civilization in India* (New York, 1964), pp. 254-76. A brief account of Mughul decline during the eighteenth century.

Russell, Ralph, *Three Mughul Poets* (Cambridge, Mass., 1968), pp. 1-36. An account of late Mughul culture, seen from the perspective of eighteenth century Delhi.

Spear, Percival, *Twilight of the Mughuls: Studies in Late Mughul Delhi* (Cambridge, 1951), pp. 1-83. Mughul decay, seen from the perspective of late eighteenth and early nineteenth century Delhi.

————, *The Oxford History of Modern India, 1740-1947* (Oxford, 1965), pp. 37-56. Examines some of the extraneous factors that contributed to the disintegration of the empire.

10.4   DECLINE OF THE CH'ING EMPIRE IN CHINA

Elvin, Mark, "The High-Level Equilibrium Trap: The Causes of the Decline of Invention in the Traditional Chinese Textile Industries," in W. E. Willmott, ed., *Economic Organization in Chinese Society* (Stanford, 1972), pp. 137-72. A daring hypothesis about the factors inhibiting economic development in late imperial China.

Fairbank, John K., Edwin O. Reischauer, and Albert M. Craig, *East Asia: Tradition and Transformation* (Boston, 1973), 969 pp. Chapters 9 and 16 deal with the peak and decline of the Manchu dynasty in China.

Ho, Ping-ti, *Studies on the Population of China, 1368-1953* (Cambridge, Mass., 1959), 341 pp. Describes the takeoff of the Chinese population in modern times with analysis of the factors and discussion of the nature of Chinese population data.

Hsu, Immanuel C. Y., *The Rise of Modern China* (New York, 1970), 830 pp. Chapter 6 presents an authoritative account of the downturn in dynastic fortunes, and Chapter 10 covers the great rebellions.

Kuhn, Philip A., *Rebellion and Its Enemies in Late Imperial China* (Cambridge, Mass., 1970), 254 pp. The militarization of the Chinese countryside in the course of the rebellions of the nineteenth century changed the nature of the elite and of Ch'ing power.

Michael, Franz, and Chung-li Chang, *The Taiping Rebellion: History* (University of Washington Press paperback, 1966), 244 pp. Succinct and authoritative account of the greatest insurrection of the nineteenth century.

10.5   DECLINE OF THE TOKUGAWA IN JAPAN

Beasley, W. G., *The Meiji Restoration* (Stanford, 1972), 513 pp. Chapters 1 and 2 provide a concise summary of recent scholarship on the causes of Tokugawa difficulties.

Bolitho, Harold, *Treasures Among Men: The Fudai Daimyo in Tokugawa Japan* (New Haven, 1974), 278 pp. The Introduction offers a very succinct discussion of the cumulative erosion of central control over the daimyo domains, an erosion the author attributes primarily to the ambiguous role of the fudai lords.

Hall, John W., *Tanuma Okitsugu, 1719-1788: Forerunner of Modern Japan* (Cambridge, Mass., 1955), 208 pp. Analyzes the failure of an innovative attempt to respond to the problems faced by the shogunate.

Hanley, Susan B., and Kozo Yamamura, "A Quiet Transformation in Tokugawa Economic History," *Journal of Asian Studies* 30.2:373-84 (1971). A very brief summary of revisionist research on the question of Tokugawa economic trends.

Sansom, George B., *A History of Japan, 1615-1867* (Stanford University Press paperback, 1960), 462 pp. Standard if somewhat dated reference on the weakening of the Tokugawa regime.

Totman, Conrad D., *Politics in the Tokugawa Bakufu, 1600-1843* (Cambridge, Mass., 1967), 346 pp. Detailed but clear account of long-term changes within the decision-making structures of the shogunate; see especially Chapter 10.

GLOSSARY

Amir. Generally, a military commander or governor; occasionally a sovereign title, as in the case of the amir of Bukhara.

Ashikaga. A family of military aristocrats who held an increasingly tenuous hegemony over Japan and gave their name to the period 1333-1573.

Banners. Military-political units into which Manchu society was divided as it mobilized for the conquest of China; additional banners were added, including Mongols and Chinese; after the conquest the banners became hereditary garrison units.

Ch'ien-lung (1736-95). Reign title of the Manchu emperor under whom the Ch'ing dynasty reached its greatest prosperity and began to decline.

Choshu. A large *tozama*, or "outer domain," at the southern end of the island of Honshu, which was among the leaders in the anti-Tokugawa movements in the 1860s.

Deccan. The great tableland of central India. The Narbada River was traditionally regarded as constituting the dividing line between northern India and the Deccan plateau.

Dere-bey. A feudal landholder in Ottoman Anatolia (Turkey).

Devshirme. The system whereby the Ottoman empire recruited slaves for the administration and the army by levying a child tribute upon the Christian provinces in the Balkans (Rumelia).

Diwan. The principal revenue official of the Mughul empire (equivalent to *vazir*); there were also *diwans* appointed to each province. The *diwani* granted by the Mughul emperor Shah Alam to the British East India Company in 1765 authorized the company to collect the revenue of Bengal, Bihar, and Orissa on behalf of the emperor.

Edo (Tokyo). The castle city that was built as headquarters for the Tokugawa at the end of the sixteenth century and grew into the world's largest city. Renamed Tokyo ("Eastern Capital") in 1868 when the imperial court took possession of the Tokugawa castle.

Fars. The homeland of the Achaemenid and Sasanid dynasties; a province in southwestern Iran, with its present capital at Shiraz.

Fudai daimyo. Trusted vassals of the Tokugawa who in addition to governing their own domains served within the Tokugawa central government; hence referred to here as "inner lords" to distinguish them from the *tozama*, or "outer lords" (q.v.).

Ghazi. A warrior living in the frontier areas of the Muslim world and engaged in holy warfare (*jihad*) against non-Muslims.

Hijaz. The central and northern coastal region of western Arabia, in which the Muslim pilgrim cities of Mecca and Medina are located. The ancient overland trade route linking southern Arabia to the Mediterranean world passed through the Hijaz.

Jagirdar. The holder of a *jagir*, or revenue assignment, in Mughul India.

Janissaries (from Turkish, *yenicheri*, "new troops"). Technically slaves, recruited by means of the *devshirme*, or child tribute levied upon the Christian population of the Balkans. The Janissaries were the best disciplined and most feared troops of the Ottoman sultans, especially during the centuries of imperial expansion.

Kapikulus. The personal slaves of the Ottoman sultans.

Khutba. The sermon given in the congregational mosque on a Friday, in which are included prayers for the well-being of the ruler. The usual proof of sovereignty in Islam is to have one's name read in the *khutba* and impressed upon the coinage.

Lin Tse-hsu (1785-1850). Chinese official sent to suppress the opium trade at Canton; representative of enlightened Chinese scholar-officials loyal to the throne.

Mamluk. A slave-soldier, generally although not exclusively a Turk, a Georgian, or a Circassian.

Mansabdar. The holder of a *mansab*, a salaried rank in the administrative hierarchy of the Mughul empire.

Mujtahid. An acknowledged authority on the Islamic "sciences" among the Shiis.

Nawab. A Mughul provincial governor, or *subahdar*. It was the title used by the representatives of the European trading companies in eighteenth century India when referring to the de facto independent rulers of Bengal, Awadh, and the Carnatic. Hence the English word nabob.

Nizam al-Mulk. An honorary title in Persian meaning "regulator of the state." The most famous holder of this title was the *vazir* of the eleventh century Seljuk sultan, Malik-Shah. The Nizams of Hyderabad derive their title from the fact that the eighteenth century founder of the dynasty was given the title Nizam al-Mulk by the Mughul emperor, Muhammad Shah.

Opium War (1839-42). First defeat of the Ch'ing by Western military power, resulted in imposition of unequal treaties.

Özbegs (also, **Uzbeks**). A Turkish people who, since the second half of the fifteenth century, have occupied the area between the Syr Darya and Amu Darya rivers (formerly Russian Turkistan and now divided between the various Central Asian republics of the U.S.S.R.).

Qizilbash (Turkish, "red head"). A confederacy of nine Turcoman tribes assembled by Shah Ismail Safavi and thereafter forming the dominant military class of the Safavid empire. Among the Qizilbash tribes were the Afshars and the Qajars, who provided the dynasties that succeeded the Safavids. The nickname Qizilbash refers to the peculiar red headdress (with twelve points in honor of the twelve Shii imams) worn by the followers of Shah Ismail.

Samurai. Originally a term used of various types of retainers and servants, it came to refer exclusively to the military vassals and, hence, the hereditary elite of the Tokugawa period.

Shiis. Those who follow the *shia* (or "party") of Ali, Muhammad's son-in-law and the fourth caliph of the Muslims. The Shiis, although subdivided into a number of sects, constitute the largest minority group (as opposed to the Sunni majority) within Islam and are today chiefly to be found in Iran and Iraq.

Sipahi (Persian, "soldier"; hence the Anglo-Indian term sepoy). In the Ottoman empire the *sipahi* was a cavalryman who maintained himself, his horse and arms, and in some cases mounted retainers out of a revenue assignment known as a *timar*.

Shogun. The hereditary title of the leader of the Tokugawa signifying their national hegemony; although originally a title given by the emperor to his commander in chief, it came to imply civil as well as military supremacy.

Subahdar (also **nawab**). A Mughul provincial governor; the officer in charge of a *subah*, the largest unit of administration in the Mughul empire.

Sultan. A ruler, "one who exercises power"; the title adopted by territorial rulers in the Muslim world from the eleventh century onwards.

Sunnis. Those who follow the *sunna*, or "practice," of the Prophet Muhammad; the majority community in the Islamic world.

Taiping Rebellion (1850-64). The greatest mass movement in nineteenth century China, it almost ended Ch'ing rule; notable for radical social doctrines and Christian influences.

Timar. A revenue assignment in the Ottoman empire for the maintenance of a *sipahi*, or calvaryman.

Tokugawa Ieyasu (1542-1616). The founder of the Tokugawa shogunate who was apotheosized as embodying the tradition of military leadership.

Tozama daimyo. Regional leaders who were confirmed as lords over semiautonomous domains after agreeing to accept the Tokugawa hegemony at the turn of the seventeenth century but were largely excluded from the inner councils of the central government; hence the translation "outer lords."

Tseng Kuo-fan (1811-72). Chinese official and general loyal to the Manchus who led suppression of Taiping Rebellion; archetypical counterinsurgency theorist.

T'ung-chih reign period (1862-74). A period of conservative revival or "restoration," when Ch'ing officials tried to meet new challenges with traditional techniques.

Turcoman. A term of unknown origin. One explanation of its derivation links it to the Persian *Turk manand*, meaning "Turk-like." Although appearing at different times in different areas, the Turcomans generally spoke a West Turkish language, retained memories of a pastoral nomadic background, and displayed a life-style of a kind associated with Turkish peoples over an extensive area of West and Central Asia.

Ulama. The Arabic plural of *alim*, meaning a scholar trained in the Islamic "sciences." Collectively, the *ulama* enforced the Sharia and determined the social norms that governed the life of the Muslim community as a whole.

Vazir. The minister of a Muslim ruler. In fact, a ruler might appoint concurrently two or more *vazirs* to have charge over different areas of administration, but the term is usually applied in the sense of a chief minister, as with the Ottoman "grand vizier."

Maritime Integration Under Western European Domination

1500 to 1920

Maritime contacts between the societies of Western Europe and Asia began in the early sixteenth century. For the most part the power and stability of the early modern empires were too great to be affected by the initially modest scale of European trade and evangelism. The European presence was important first upon the open seas, limited coastal regions, and weakly integrated islands of Southeast Asia. Western economic and military power did not surpass that of the great empires until the late eighteenth and early nineteenth centuries. Three broad stages in the development of Western European domination may be distinguished. The first was a factory-fort stage, characterized by the establishment of commercial outposts in coastal locations accessible to products and markets. A second stage, from 1750 to 1850, was an era of commercial colonialism when monopoly companies rationalized the control of production and trade, expanding their power and influence upon Asian conditions. In the second half of the nineteenth century rivalry among European nations and the cumulative effects of the industrial revolution led to an aggressive increase of Western power over Asian societies, leading frequently to the annexation of Asian territory as colonies. European dominance was asserted earliest over the islands of Southeast Asia, when the Portuguese and then the Dutch competed to control the lucrative spice trade. The Spanish, extending their empire westward across the Pacific, occupied the Philippines. Manila served as a base for trade with China in which galleons exchanged American silver for Chinese silks. In West and Central Asia, expansion of the Russian empire through the extension of land frontiers brought the Russians into conflict with the Ottomans, the Manchu-Ch'ing, and eventually the Japanese. Because it involved annexation of contiguous land areas, the growth of the Russian empire resembled that of the Asian empires as much as it did those of Western Europe. By the nineteenth century France and England challenged the supremacy of the Iberian powers. As European rivalries unfolded, England displaced France to gain control of South Asia, divided island Southeast Asia with the Dutch, and dominated the trade and politics of the China coast. Late in the nineteenth century two new imperialist powers emerged in the Pacific which may be contrasted with the Western European powers: Japan and the United States. The fate of Asian societies varied widely in the age of imperialism. In West Asia many areas remained under French and British domination, while the forms of the Ottoman empire were preserved until the First World War. South Asia and all of Southeast Asia except Thailand experienced colonial domination until World War II. In East Asia Japan made colonies of Korea and Taiwan and brought China itself under its hegemony. For the duration of World War II Japan also displaced Europeans and Americans in Southeast Asia.

528

11

PROCESSES

The Foundation of European Domination through Seapower

a. Maritime innovations and exploration
b. The establishment of enclaves: the factory-fort stage
c. Economic penetration and political intervention: commercial colonialism

The Culmination of Western European Dominance in Imperialism

d. Imperialist technology
e. Colonial administration
f. Economic imperialism
g. Cultural imperialism

PATTERNS

1. European Domination in West Asia

2. Western European Domination in South Asia

3. Western European Domination in Southeast Asia

4. Maritime Integration in China

5. Maritime Integration in Japan

11. MARITIME INTEGRATION

	1 WEST ASIA	2 SOUTH ASIA	3 SOUTHEAST ASIA	4 CHINA	5 JAPAN
1450		Vasco da Gama reaches Calicut 1498 Portuguese establish base at Goa 1510	Treaty of Tordesillas 1494 Albuquerque establishes Portuguese factory-fort at Malacca 1511 Magellan crosses Pacific for Spanish		Portuguese arrive in Japan 1542 Jesuits arrive 1549
	Russian conquest of Kazan 1552 Russian conquest of Astrakhan 1554 Battle of Lepanto 1571 Expedition of Yermak the Cossack crosses the Urals 1583	Defeat of Spanish Armada 1588	Portuguese dominate Spice Island trade Spanish take Manila 1571	Portuguese establish base at Macao 1557	Factory-fort at Nagasaki; arrival of Spanish
1550		English East India Company factories established on Indian coast	Dutch encroach on Portuguese holdings Dutch establish factory-fort at Batavia 1619	Jesuits gain access to court in Peking	Tokugawa hegemony 1600 Limitation of foreign trade, ban on Christianity 1616 British withdraw, Spanish expelled 1624 Dutch have only remaining factory 1639
1650	Ottoman Turks besiege Vienna 1683 Treaty of Carlowitz 1699	Dutch gain foothold in Colombo and on Malabar coast English E.I. Company rents Bombay 1668 English E.I. Company given zamindari rights for Calcutta 1698	Extension of Dutch control over Java and other islands		

Central Asia / Middle East	India	Southeast Asia	China — Volume of trade in tea and silk grows	Japan — Ban on foreign books eased 1720
Treaty of Passarowitz 1718 Kazakh Little Horde submits to Russia 1731 Kazakh Middle Horde submits to Russia 1740 Part of Kazakh Great Horde submits to Russia 1742	Carnatic Wars, British displace French interests in India, 1744-63 Battle of Plassey, British E.I. Company extends power in Bengal, 1757			
1750			Western trade restricted to Canton 1760	
Treaty of Küchük Kaynarja 1774 Russian annexation of Crimea 1783 Napolean invades Egypt 1798 Russo-Iranian War 1805-13	Parliamentary acts regulate East India Company, 1773, 1781, 1784	British take Penang 1786 British encroach on Dutch holdings	British Macartney embassy 1793 Volume of opium smuggling rises	Russian pressure begins 1792 British probes begin 1808 Foreign translation bureau 1811 Order to fire on foreign ships 1825
Suppression of Kazakh Khanates 1822-48 Second Russo-Iranian War 1826-28		British and Dutch divide spheres 1824 Dutch institute culture system in Java Gradual extension of British control in Burma, Malay peninsula and Borneo	Ch'ing attempt to suppress smuggling Opium War 1839-42, Ch'ing forced to sign unequal treaties, open ports	Importation of modern arms begins 1848 U.S. demands 1853 Ports opened 1858 Attacks on Kagoshima, Choshu 1863-64 Meiji Restoration 1868
Alma-Ata founded 1854 Russians invade Kokand and Bukhara 1865-66 Khanate of Khiva a Russian protectorate 1873 Battle of Plevna 1877	Indian Mutiny 1857 British government replaces East India Company as ruling power 1858 Victoria proclaimed Empress of India 1877	French establish protectorates in Indochina	Anglo-French invasion of Peking 1860	
1850				
McMahon Declaration 1915 Balfour Declaration 1917; British enter Jerusalem and Baghdad Treaty of Sèvres 1920		United States takes Philippines from Spain	Defeat by Japan 1895; Powers move to partition China Open Door notes, partition averted	Sino-Japanese War 1895 Extraterritoriality ends 1899 Anglo-Japanese treaty 1902 Russo-Japanese War 1905
		Japanese occupation of Western colonies	Japanese invasion 1937	War in China 1937; in Pacific 1941-45 Defeat and occupation
1950		United States opposes national liberation movements in Indochina	Korean War	Korean War

531

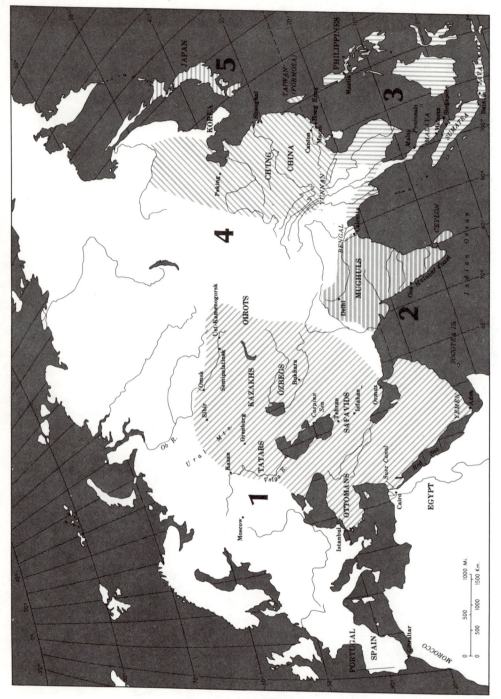

Map 45 Maritime integration under Western European domination

PROCESSES

Two kinds of forces transformed the nature and the conditions of the civilizations of Asia in modern times. One of those forces was the expansion of Western European power to a world scale—a development so influential that much of the modern period may be characterized as an era of maritime integration under Western domination. The other great force, at once more elusive and more concrete, was an ever-accelerating change in the nature and volume of human knowledge. This breakthrough in the ability to understand and manipulate the human environment, natural and social, constituted as fundamental a mutation in human society as the agricultural revolution that accompanied the birth of civilization. These forces and their manifestations in the context of Asian societies will be the subject of this and subsequent chapters.

EUROPEAN EXPANSION IN THE CONTEXT OF EURASIAN INTERACTION

An overriding concern in the study of modern Asian history is the question of how much weight should be attributed to the force of Western impact or influence. The preceding chapter, by focusing on the decline of early modern empires in Asia, has already underscored the point that indigenous developments within Asia continued unabated and indeed conditioned the nature of European contact and penetration. The Asian civilizations were by no means blank surfaces upon which dynamic Europeans were free to make their impress. Still, the ascendancy of the Western powers in the nineteenth and early twentieth centuries was global in scope and so vigorous that it challenged the integrity and continuity of all the great civilizations of Asia. So recent were these events and so strong is their persisting influence that our vision of history tends to be colored, if not obscured, by them. This is perhaps doubly so for Americans, since our society is at once a product of European expansion and recently a central actor in the continuing extension of Western influence.

While the degree of global dominance the Western powers attained in the late nineteenth century was unprecedented, the ascendancy of peoples from one area of Eurasia over the peoples of other areas was something that had happened before. The most notable instance was the Mongol conquest empire, discussed in Chapter 8 of Volume 1. Whereas the Mongols based their strength on horsemanship, expanding outward along land lines from Central Asia to the nearest centers of civilization, the extension of Western European power was based on seafaring and spread first along the coastline of Eurasia, working its way inland. Two contrasts between the Westerners and the Mongols serve to complicate the comparison. The first is that while the Mongols were pastoral nomads who lacked a literate tradition and urban culture of their own, the Europeans were themselves the bearers of a Graeco-Roman Christian civilization. As a consequence of this fact, the potential for cultural conflict was greater in European expansion than it had been in Mongol expansion if only because the Europeans saw fit to rationalize their actions in cultural terms, in patronizing formulations such as "the white man's burden." The second contrast is that the period of European ascendancy coincided with the industrial revolution, which transformed technology and economic organization in ways the Europeans were able first to turn to their own advantage. Neither of these contrasts with the Mongol case should be construed as indicators of some innate superiority in Western civilization. An investigation of the stages of European interaction with the civilizations of Asia reveals that in the initial centuries of contact the Europeans were often actually awed by the cultural refinements of the great Asian cities, while the Asians found little to admire on the European side. Western cultural influence, and notions of superiority, came to fruition only in the nineteenth century and tended more often to follow than to precede military supremacy.

If one looks for internal factors in the European social milieu which can explain the maritime expansion of the Atlantic seaboard nations, one must conclude that a central factor was the chronic political instability in Europe itself. This continuous rivalry of small states, which fueled the rivalry for control of the seas and lands beyond the seas, was in marked contrast to the political unity and relative social stability of the early modern empires in Asia. While expansion and conquest brought enormous wealth to Europe in modern times, the competition that expansion entailed caused as much warfare and bloodshed in Europe itself as anywhere else on the globe. The notion that technological superiority is a permanent or inherent characteristic of Western civilization is easily dismissed. The technological dominance of the West was a new phenomenon in the early modern period. Moreover, by the early twentieth century Japan had demonstrated that an Asian society was fully as capable of industrialization and imperialist expansion as any other state, making it necessary to speak of imperialism in terms of the "industrialized powers" without reference to geographical region or cultural heritage.

THE PERIOD

Understanding of the integration of Eurasia under the domination of Western European seapower can be greatly facilitated by distinguishing three broad stages of development. These are: *the factory-fort stage* (ca. 1500-ca. 1750), *the stage of commercial colonialism* (ca. 1750-ca. 1850), and *imperialism* (ca. 1850 to World War I). Each stage was characterized by certain typical features of European-Asian interaction, shaped in each case by the relative vigor of the two sides and their particular cultural patterns. The transition from one stage to the next was largely determined by economic and technological factors that altered drastically the temporal and spatial rhythms of human interaction. Rather than review the chronology of these stages, which varied in each part of Asia, it will suit our purposes here to consider briefly the sequence of expansion of the various European powers.

The Portuguese. When the Europeans first made the breakthrough in navigation that allowed them to open a sea route to Asia, it was the Iberians who took the lead. Several factors contributed to making this so. The Italian city-states, which were wealthier and more commercially developed than those of the Iberians, dominated the spice trade from Asia by concentrating their sea power on the Mediterranean. Venice, which came to terms with the Ottoman Turks in the latter half of the fifteenth century, profited from a carrying trade between Ottoman ports and Europe and had little motive for venturing out on the Atlantic. The Portuguese, facing the Atlantic and adjacent to the coast of Africa, were in a natural position to explore that coast. Furthermore, the Iberian peninsula had had direct experience of Muslim occupation so that the crusader's hostility to Islam lived on there, but more important, perhaps, there were openings to Arabic science and scholarship. Portuguese advances in seafaring were due in large part to royal patronage of Prince Henry the Navigator, who in the middle decades of the fifteenth century encouraged the study of cartography and naval architecture. The Portuguese advance was gradual: first a fortress was seized in Morocco and then a string of small settlements for cultivation, trade, and fishing was extended down the Atlantic coast of North Africa. In 1498 Vasco da Gama sailed around Africa and crossed over to Calicut on the southwestern (Malabar) coast of India, thereby establishing a route for trade with the Indies which bypassed the Mediterranean and the Ottoman territories in West Asia. In the next four decades the Portuguese moved aggressively into the Asian trade routes, establishing outposts at Goa in western India, Malacca on the Malay peninsula, and Macao in southern China.

The Spanish. The second Iberian power to expand by sea was Spain, which rapidly created an overseas conquest empire, the largest components of which were in the Americas. As early as 1494 a Line of Demarcation was established to distinguish the Spanish from the Portuguese spheres of expansion. Most of the Americas were under Spanish jurisdiction, except for the easternmost portions of South America, which fell into the Portuguese zone. Consequently, Asian trade was less important than the extraction of precious metals from the Americas, which soon made Spain enormously wealthy. The one Spanish hold in Asia developed in conjunction with these interests. Extending their power westward across the Pacific, the Spanish took control of a group of islands in Southeast Asia which they named the Philippines. Manila, taken by the Spanish in 1571, became the base of their trade operations in the western Pacific. The economic importance of Spanish trade stemmed from the silver they mined and minted in Mexico and Peru, and the Spanish "pieces of eight" became the medium for expanding world trade by the 1560s. Shipped across the Pacific, much of the silver found its way to China, where it paid for the silk and other products that stuffed the famous Manila galleons.

The Dutch. Prior to the Protestant Reformation and the Dutch war of independence against Spain, the merchants and sailors of the Netherlands were restricted to a carrying trade between Iberian ports and points north on the coast of Europe. By the 1590s the Dutch obtained the independence and knowledge of navigation they needed to enter into the world trade competition. Their target was the Portuguese-dominated spice trade in Southeast Asia. Within half a century they displaced the Portuguese and consolidated their holdings across a vast sweep of islands from Ceylon in the west, through Malacca and Java, where they established an administrative center at Batavia, to the Moluccas on the east. Their advantage over the Portuguese stemmed from superior ships, arms, equipment, and organization, as well as the fact that the Dutch were far better merchants than were their Iberian predecessors, who mixed piracy and missionary activities with their trade. In 1602 a unified trading monopoly, the Dutch East India Company, was formed under state charter. The Dutch moved profitably into regional Asian trade, facing, at most, fragmented opposition from local rulers, and moved ever deeper into the manipulation and administration of the economy of the Indonesian archipelago, displacing Asian competitors by force.

The English. Having only modest economic resources and being relatively isolated, the English were late entrants in the European competition for global enterprise. Under Elizabeth I (r. 1558-1603) rivalry with Spain prompted the growth of a strong navy, leading to the defeat of the Spanish Armada in 1588. By 1600 the East India Company was formed under crown charter. The English were still relatively weak, however, and the Dutch with five times the number of ships were able to expel them from early footholds in Southeast Asia. Consequently, English energies were diverted elsewhere, especially toward South Asia, where the East India Company was to make major inroads in the eighteenth century. From India they developed a subsidiary trade with China, which was to grow to tremendous proportions by the beginning of the nineteenth century. In contrast to Spain, which reaped its wealth from the New World, and Holland, which exploited the Spice Islands, the British expansion led to India and China, the heartlands of two of the major Eurasian civilizations, although British ascendancy in those regions came only in the nineteenth century as England became the first nation to undergo industrialization.

The French. France, last of the Atlantic seaboard nations to build an oversea empire, was inhibited by the conflicting demands of Continental concerns and a revolution. A French Compagnie des Indes Orientales was formed in 1664 and competed vigorously with the British for a foothold in India but was eventually forced out. Later the French were to develop a major interest in peninsular Southeast Asia—French Indochina—and in West Asia, but in neither area did their commercial interests or military power reach the scale attained by the British in India.

The Russians. By way of contrast to the maritime expansion of Western Europe it is instructive to consider the contemporary growth of the Russian empire extending outward from eastern Europe. A continental empire with an autocratic hereditary ruler and a state-supported religious orthodoxy, Russia resembled in all major respects the early modern empires of Asia. Common ties of classical heritage, religion, race, and royalty, however, encouraged intimate communication with Western Europe, which enabled the Russian elite to apply the latest advances in technology and organization in their uneven struggle with the tribal peoples of Central Asia. The growth of the Russian empire was accomplished by the annexation of contiguous territories—a development that had nothing to do with sea power. By 1600 the rulers of Moscow had pushed their control eastward beyond the Urals into the lower basin of the Ob River and southward down the Volga River to the Caspian Sea. By 1650 eastward expansion had reached the Pacific, and by the early nineteenth century a Russian presence had been extended across the Aleutian chain to Alaska and southward on the eastern Pacific coast as far as northern California. Along the southern borders of the growing Russian empires there was constant probing and conflict with the major Asian empires and, in the nineteenth century, with the other imperialist powers, particularly England and Japan.

The Americans. A settlement colony of predominantly European peoples, the United States was barely established as a nation by the time three centuries of Iberian-Asian sea trade had elapsed. Factors of both geography and culture influenced the early development of American contacts with Asia, which consisted largely of trade at Canton in south China under the umbrella of a dominant British presence. When, in the latter half of the nineteenth century, the United States began to play an active role in Asia, it did so as a Pacific power, a natural consequence of its expansion across the continent, and the nearest Asian states, Japan and Korea, felt the pressure first. American commercial and industrial expansion, fostered by the revolutionary institutions of a new democratic and secular state, were paralleled by a powerful sense of cultural mission, which helped to rationalize the displacement, subjugation, and destruction of indigenous peoples as conquest of the new continent proceeded. An extension of American cultural values, perhaps in part to prove their universal validity, led to the development of an extensive missionary movement, much of which was directed toward Asia, particularly China. At the end of the nineteenth century the United States joined the older nations as a full-fledged imperialist power by taking the Philippines from a weakened Spain in 1898, thereby acquiring for the first time an Asian colony.

THE FOUNDATION OF EUROPEAN DOMINATION THROUGH SEAPOWER

a. Maritime Innovations and Exploration
Fundamental to the expansion of Western European states was the development of improved vessels, sailing techniques, and naval gunnery, which made possible the circumnavigation of Africa and the subsequent destruction of rival Islamic naval forces in the Indian Ocean. Innovations in the fifteenth century which adapted Asian elements, such as the Arab sail, to European ships produced vessels that were at once seaworthy and easily maneuverable. Advances in science and nautical experience, which again owed much to the Arabs, enhanced European understanding of geography, improved cartography, and made it possible to observe and record the position—or at least the latitude—of a point on an unknown coast. Construction of high superstructures and the placement of heavy cannons on the decks enabled small numbers of vessels to deliver superior firepower to Asian waters. Exploration, which progressed rapidly from the discovery in the 1490s of America and a route around Africa, was urged on by mixed motives—the desire for personal glory, commercial greed, religious zeal, and curiosity about the contours of an undertermined earth. By the 1520s an expedition commenced by Magellan completed the first voyage around the world, and rapid changes took place in the European world view.

b. The Establishment of Enclaves: The Factory-Fort Stage
The form of interaction that commenced shortly after the first Iberian voyages around the coast of Africa was characterized by the establishment of small trading posts, called fac-

tories (from factor, the agent in charge of trade), which were usually fortified for protection. Consequently, this period may be referred to as the factory-fort stage. In this initial phase the Westerners came largely as traders to purchase spices and manufactured goods unobtainable in Europe. Despite an interest in promoting the Christian faith, these early Western visitors had little perceptible influence on the early modern empires, which were far richer and more powerful than their own. This was in marked contrast to their experience in Africa and the Americas, where relatively small forces of Europeans were able to overpower, exploit, and even enslave substantial populations. By virtue of the firepower of their ships the Portuguese could dominate Asian coastal waters, but they lacked the means to extend their power very far inland. There ensued during the seventeenth and the first half of the eighteenth century an era in which the Europeans traded on the periphery of Asia, all the while adding to their knowledge of world conditions and developing rapidly in commerce, technological skill, and military technique.

c. Economic Penetration and Political Intervention: Commercial Colonialism

European rivalries, national and religious, which intensified from the sixteenth century onward, were accompanied by a steady rationalization of economic policy. Concepts of mercantilism which stressed the importance of wealth in the form of money led governments to pursue policies that promoted industry, commerce, and sea power with the aim of obtaining a favorable balance of trade. The chartered companies, which grew out of sixteenth century English and Dutch experience, involved the extension by the state of broad monopoly powers to merchant interests for overseas expansion, including powers to establish fortifications, annex territory, conduct warfare and diplomacy. As the volume of Asian trade increased, substantial interest groups developed huge capital investments that needed to be secured by regularization of the conditions of trade. In the home country this was accomplished by securing favorable legislation that would guarantee profit to both the private sector and the state by maintaining a monopoly and keeping taxes at nominal rates. The British East India Company's cornering of the tea trade in the eighteenth century is a classic instance of such policies. Between the home country and Asia security was obtained by improving the size, speed, and reliability of sailing craft and eliminating rivalry. By the early nineteenth century the British had established virtual world hegemony on the seas, and they soon completed acquisition of a string of strategic points at Gibraltar, Capetown on the southern tip of Africa, along the Suez Canal, Aden, Ceylon, Singapore, and Hong Kong. International law and treaty arrangements were used to stabilize competition among the powers. In Asia the desire to regularize trade led the rather autonomous agents of the chartered companies to extend their activities beyond the coastal trading enclaves. A need for quality control and the desire to get around middlemen led to more direct dealing with local producers and to efforts to specify the types of materials to be used or the crops to be planted. Economic stabilization was sought by the extension of credit and insurance and intervention to influence local tax policy. Since civil unrest and political disturbances could interfere with trade, the European merchants found it useful to develop their own police and military forces. These actions, over time, led in many places to the development of virtual colonies within Asian territory in which European commercial representatives came to exercise governmental powers over a subject Asian populace. Such a system evolved first in Southeast Asia, where the Dutch developed a plantation economy.

THE CULMINATION OF WESTERN EUROPEAN DOMINANCE IN IMPERIALISM

The British ascendancy in Europe and domination of the seas following the defeat of Napoleon in 1815 resulted in a period of relative stability among the Western powers in the middle of the nineteenth century. Often identified with the reign of Queen Victoria (r. 1837-1901), this period saw a change in economic policy and attitudes toward overseas colonies. The chartered monopolies were replaced by economic competition among private companies as mercantilism gave way to the conception of free trade, and management of colonies was taken over directly by the home government. By the latter half of the century, however, industrial development and a rising tide of nationalism set off a new era of intense rivalry in Europe, which after about 1870 developed into a global scramble for colonies and possessions, reaching a fever pitch in the 1890s. This age of imperialism was a competition among new industrialized states, Japan and the United States included. Although explanations of imperialism vary widely, it is clear that the mass psychology of nationalism was an important spur in the race to claim the last independent areas of the world and that the scale of capital investments overseas increased dramatically.

d. Imperialist Technology

Industrial and technological advances by the latter half of the nineteenth century made possible increasingly large and rapid steamships, the construction of the Suez Canal, and the laying of telegraphy cables, which in effect brought the imperialist powers and the Asian colonies closer together. Construction of railways made possible the commercial exploitation of the interior of the Asian continent from the centers of imperialist commerce in the major port cities. Associated also with industrialization was the development in the home countries of a mass society with growing classes of literate, urban citizens concerned and vocal about the overseas affairs of their nation. Newspapers, relaying overnight to a mass readership the news of an obscure missionary in some far-off corner of Asia, could bring the force of public opinion to bear with devastating effect on the legislators and executives of a representative government.

e. Colonial Administration

A consequence of improved communication and transportation was that decision making in colonial empires became centralized in the home country. Whereas early colonial administrators in Asia had enjoyed wide latitude in making decisions and setting policies, by the end of the nineteenth century even minor decisions could be made centrally on the basis of a constant flow of reports and cables from overseas. Tighter control over colonies brought with it an elaboration of administration entailing the imposition of alien concepts of law, government, property, and public services by a body of colonial administrators who, as agents of the imperialist power, constituted the effective government of the colony.

f. Economic Imperialism

Economic exploitation, which was at the center of colonialism from the start, changed in form as industrialization took place. Under mercantilism colonies were developed as sources of goods and raw materials for the controlling country, to whose markets its exports were largely confined, and the growth of industry in the colony was seldom encouraged. By the 1850s industrial capacity had developed to the point where colonies could provide a significant factor in demand, and Asian markets were developed, usually through the forced manipulation of tariffs, for the consumption of European manufactured goods. By 1900 a new level of capital accumulation had been achieved in which major banking interests, frequently internationally organized, sought opportunities in preindustrial economies to finance large-scale projects such as armament industries and railroad construction. Part of a global integration of finance and industry, this type of investment derived its profit from the long-term return of interest at favorable rates. Consequently, the governments of the industrial powers became involved in guaranteeing stability in the developing economy by advancing further into the control of the country's affairs, whether in a colonial or semicolonial situation.

g. Cultural Imperialism

The global domination that industrialized Westerners came to enjoy in the nineteenth century inevitably produced a need for explanation of so unprecedented a turn of historical events. One set of perceptions, which had firm roots in Western civilization and some echoes of the Crusades, was the notion of a Christianizing mission. For those who took this kind of view, all of mankind was of one family but Westerners had a duty to save their wayward cousins. Such assumptions led to massive missionary and humanitarian efforts to change religious beliefs and social practices in Asia. Another line of reasoning, which sought a sanction in supposedly scientific principles, tried to explain Western dominance in racial terms, as the result of an innate superiority of the whites over nonwhites. This explanation seemed to fit the facts fairly well except that Japan, which rapidly indus- trialized by the early twentieth century, confused the picture greatly. Even today the Japanese are accommodatingly classified as honorary whites in South Africa. Still another set of explanations made analogous use of the theory of evolution and survival of the fittest—social Darwinism—to bolster the view that Western societies had developed superior institutions. As a consequence of a complacency about Western dominance and the assumption that Western political and social institutions represented the eventual pat- tern for all of mankind, colonial administrations undertook to impose many of their own forms on subject Asians. A parallel development in history and the social sciences was the view that other societies would necessarily from that time on develop in the direction of European models. Westernization was identified with modernization, and the comparabil- ity of Eurasian civilizations was lost sight of in Europocentric views of history. The de- velopment of this cultural imbalance under imperialism is noted here; its impact on Asian civilizations will be considered in Chapters 12 and 13.

In considering the patterns that follow, the reader should bear in mind that the subject matter of this chapter overlaps with those that precede and follow it. Asian history is examined here from the perspective of interaction with European civilization. The span of time involved coincides with primarily indigenous processes at work within Asian civiliza- tions described first in terms of decline of early modern empires and subsequently in terms of cultural disintegration. The sequel to this chapter, in the sense of a continuation of the study of interaction between Asia and the West, is Chapter 13, which will deal with the subject of cultural renaissance and nationalism.

PATTERNS

1. EUROPEAN DOMINATION IN WEST ASIA

At first sight no paradox could be more striking than the fact that West Asia, which had been in uninterrupted communication with the Christian lands bordering the Mediterra- nean and the Black Sea throughout the entire period of European maritime expansion across the globe, was the last area in Asia to feel the full weight of European colonial ambitions. Although the implacable advance of Russia into the Muslim world began as early as the sixteenth century and reached its culmination in the nineteenth century, elsewhere in West Asia the intrusion of the maritime powers was mainly a nineteenth century phenomenon. Russia apart, formal colonial domination did not come about until after the First World War, with the establishment of British mandates in Iraq and Palestine and French mandates in Syria and the Lebanon. The reasons for this paradox are to be sought partly in the balance of military power between Islam and Christendom in the early modern period and partly in the psychological attitudes that underlay Muslim-Christian relations. But, whatever the causes, there is no mistaking the contrast between the situation in South Asia and Southeast Asia, where the Europeans were the aggressors, and in West Asia, where throughout the sixteenth and most of the seventeenth century the Ottoman empire was the agressor and the states of southern and southeastern Europe its potential victims.

The Retarded Establishment of European Domination

To take the military aspect first, it will be recalled that when the Portuguese embarked on the exploration of the West African coastline, leading to the circumnavigation of the continent and the discovery of the route to India, one of the principal motives for these voyages of discovery was to find out what lay beyond the Muslim world. In other words, it was the barrier to eastward expansion set up by the belligerent Muslim regimes of West Asia during the fifteenth and sixteenth centuries that provided the catalyst for the European discovery of the Indian Ocean.

It cannot be stressed too emphatically that the greatest military power known to the Europeans of the early modern period was the Ottoman empire, a power that bestraddled the Balkans, the Levant, and much of North Africa and whose warships dominated the Mediterranean, the Black Sea, the Red Sea and even the Persian Gulf. From a European point of view, this empire, seemingly organized in such a way as to be permanently ready to engage in aggression, constituted a perpetual threat to the very survival of Christendom, a view that continued to be held as late as 1683, when an Ottoman army besieged Vienna for the last time. Throughout the sixteenth and seventeenth centuries, and for long after, there extended across southeastern Europe a no-man's land between the Ottomans and their Christian neighbors, which, except during periods when temporary truces were negotiated, formed both a military frontier and an "iron curtain" separating the Muslim and Christian worlds. The same was true at sea. Ottoman galleys or the galleys of their clients, the Corsairs of Algiers, Tunis, and Tripoli, scoured the Mediterranean shores of Italy, France, and Spain in quest of slaves and plunder, while, whenever they were able to take the initiative, the galleys of Spain, Venice, and the Knights of Malta endeavored to turn the tables on their ancient foes. In the Mediterranean the era of the Crusades continued down to the lifetime of Napoleon, its victims gracing alike the slave markets of Algiers and Istanbul, Legnano and Valetta.

European historians have habitually placed great emphasis on the decline of the Ottoman empire, the so-called Sick Man of Europe, and on the related "Eastern Question," but they have tended to overlook the resilience of the Ottomans, even in their darkest days. As late as 1877 Europe was astonished by the dogged courage with which an Ottoman army, badly equipped and inadequately serviced, resisted the might of czarist Russia in the trenches of Plevna, as were the Allied commanders at Gallipoli in 1915, confronted with the same phenomenon. Under these circumstances, and because of their mutual rivalries, the European powers remained relatively cautious in their dealings with the Ottoman empire until late in the eighteenth century and, in fact, greatly overestimated the military potentiality of the Muslim states of West Asia. Even as late as the Napoleonic period the British authorities in Calcutta, anticipating an overland invasion of India by combined French and Russian forces, reckoned the Ottoman sultan, the Qajar shah of Iran, and other Muslim rulers west of the Indus allies capable of assisting in repelling the invaders.

Unlike some other parts of Asia, the terrain of much of West Asia consists of desert and arid mountain ranges, thus posing formidable logistical problems to European armies, especially to those of the maritime powers, as the British discovered to their cost during the course of campaigning in nineteenth century Afghanistan. It was, for example, a terrain favorable to guerrilla warfare which enabled the Circassian chieftain Shamil to hold the

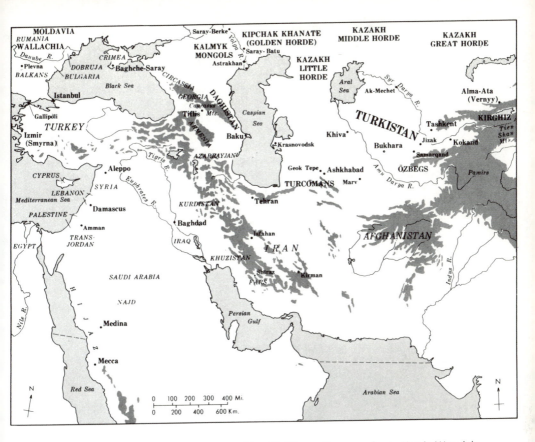

Map 46 Western European domination in West Asia

Russians at bay in the Caucasus between 1834 and 1859. When, in 1873, General Kauf-mann advanced against Khiva with three separate columns approaching from three direc-tions, it was because he knew the history of earlier Russian expeditions against the khanate, of three unsuccessful Cossack attempts during the seventeenth century and two abortive expeditions in 1717 and 1839, all forced to retire on account of the deserts encircling the oasis.

Delayed European penetration of West Asia was also connected with the long and bitter history of mutual antagonism between Christian and Muslim. In some other cultures, European intrusion might be viewed as a disaster, a humiliation, a curiosity, and even, for some groups, an opportunity for self-advancement, but for the Muslim of West Asia the European Christian was generally seen as a despised and hated unbeliever whom, in some place or in some form, his ancestors had been fighting almost since the lifetime of the Prophet. Everything that emanated from Europe—dress, diet, manners, scientific knowl-edge, or technology—smacked of infidelity and had therefore to be rejected. Even the very presence of Europeans in the heartlands of Islam was defiling. Down to the nineteenth century relatively few Europeans, apart from slaves, were permitted to acquire first-hand experience of the interior of West Asia, and those who did were mainly diplomats and eccentric explorers. Even commercial transactions were, if possible, conducted through the mediation of local non-Muslims—Jews, Greeks, or Armenians. At all times it was danger-ous for a European, even an accredited ambassador, to move freely in a Muslim city, even the capital of the Ottoman empire. Even today it is forbidden for non-Muslims to approach

541

Mecca and Medina. In the seventeenth century, at a time when European states were gradually evolving a common "law of nations," envoys to the Sublime Porte were literally dragged into the sultan's presence and, notwithstanding their alleged immunity, were promptly imprisoned if the government they represented and the Ottoman empire went to war.

Thus, at a time when most of Asia had been forced to come to terms with European military and technological superiority, Muslim psychology obstinately refused to regard Europeans with anything but hatred and contempt. And when a Muslim ruler allowed himself to be bribed or overawed by a demonstration of European military power, ordinary Muslims, their prejudices reinforced by the local *ulama,* did not necessarily follow his example, regarding it as outrageous that infidels, other than *dhimmis,* should freely walk the streets of Muslim cities. In 1829 an infuriated mob, *ulama*-inspired, massacred the entire staff of the Russian mission in Tehran, and down to the twentieth century, even at the height of European imperialism, there were sporadic assaults upon Europeans who approached shrines closed to non-Muslims or who outraged Muslim feelings of propriety. Such incidents may have counted for nothing in the long run, or resulted in punitive responses by the European powers, but they demonstrated, long after the Islamic world had ceased to be able to confront the Christian world on equal terms, the Muslim's relentless animosity towards the unbeliever.

Early West European Contacts and Confrontations
The earliest contacts in the early modern period between the maritime powers of Europe and the Muslim regimes of West Asia occurred in the Arabian Sea, where Portuguese expansion coincided with a strenuous Ottoman attempt to assert its naval supremacy in those remote waters. Off the Horn of Africa, the south Arabian coast, and in the Persian Gulf the Portuguese steadily gained the edge over their Ottoman opponents, and when they themselves were finally displaced it was by their Dutch and British rivals. Thereafter, and throughout the eighteenth century, there was a modest amount of European commercial activity in the Persian Gulf, although the tribal anarchy in post-Safavid Iran and the piratical activities of the sheikhdoms on the southern shores of the Gulf offered little incentive for expansion. It was Napoleon's projected invasion of India, followed by the advance of Russia in the direction of Iran and Afghanistan, that led the British, thoroughly alarmed for the safety of their Indian possessions, to seek a predominant position in the affairs of Qajar Iran. Here, however, they found themselves at a disadvantage *vis-à-vis* their Russian rivals. British determination to maintain the territorial integrity of Afghanistan as a barrier to Russian encroachments compelled them to oppose Qajar designs for the reconquest of Herat, leading to a brief Anglo-Iranian conflict in 1856 and thereby strengthening the standing of the pro-Russian party among the shah's advisers. More significant in the long run was the fact that the Iranian capital, Tehran, and the fertile province of Azarbayjan were in easy striking distance of Russia's Caucasian frontier, whereas the regions most susceptible to British military pressure were the arid and then underpopulated provinces of Kirman, Fars, and Khuzistan. It would be in Khuzistan, however, that oil would be struck in 1908, leading to the foundation of the Anglo-Persian Oil Company in the following year and of the industry that is the key to Iran's present-day development.

Iran avoided colonial status on account of the mutual rivalry between Britain and Russia, but in 1907, as part of an attempt to reduce mutual differences, the two powers agreed to divide that country into spheres of influence. During the First World War, Iran, although neutral, was occupied by British and Russian troops on the pretext that an Ottoman invasion was imminent and that German agents were at work among the tribes. After the war and the temporary Russian withdrawal from the area following the 1917 revolution, Britain attempted, unsuccessfully, to impose upon Iran a treaty that would have converted that country into a virtual protectorate. Both before and after the war, extraterritorial privileges and foreign concessions were as much a feature of Iran as of other Asian countries that did not have formal colonial status, and this state of affairs was only gradually rectified after the coup d'état of 1921, which ousted the Qajar dynasty and brought to power the modernizing Riza Shah Pahlavi (r. 1925-41). During the Second World War, Iranian neutrality was once again disregarded by the Allies, and following the withdrawal of British and American troops in 1946 the Soviet Union made a concerted although unsuccessful attempt to use Azarbayjani and Kurdish separatist movements to establish Soviet satellite regimes in the northwest.

In the Mediterranean the first maritime power to challenge Ottoman naval ascendancy was Habsburg Spain. The victory that the combined fleets of Spain, Venice, and the Papacy achieved at Lepanto in 1571 did not, as has been so often claimed, mark the end of Ottoman seapower, but it did dispel the illusion that the Mediterranean had become an Ottoman lake. It was the Habsburgs and Venetians, hitherto the major victims of Ottoman aggression, who most felt the reduction in pressure and it was they who now headed the counterattack. By way of contrast, France, Britain, and Holland, all of whom were preoccupied with the dangers of Habsburg hegemony in Europe, entered into commercial relations with the Ottoman empire, including the provision of firearms and metal to be used by the Ottomans in the struggle with Spain. European merchants now established themselves in small numbers in such major centers as Istanbul, Smyrna (now Izmir), and Aleppo. Some of these newcomers, often trading in collaboration with indigenous Christian merchants, acquired considerable leverage over the economic life of the city or region in which they resided, but their political significance was negligible. Culturally, they made available for some Muslims "a window on the West," but it was the indigenous Christian communities that benefitted most, assiduously wooed as they were by Catholic missionaries who sought to reunite the Eastern Churches with Rome. Throughout the Levant the French king assumed the role of protector of his fellow Catholics and claimed access on their behalf to the Holy Places of Christendom, a role later adopted even more vigorously by the czar on behalf of Orthodox Christians.

Later European Imperialism in West Asia: The Maritime Powers

It was Napoleon's expedition to Egypt in 1798 that was the catalyst for increased British and French involvement in West Asia. The strategic and commercial potentialities of the area were thereafter seen as incalculable, and the two powers relentlessly jostled each other for the dominant position, especially in Istanbul and in Egypt, independent of Ottoman control from around 1806, where the British eventually ousted the French by establishing a virtual protectorate in 1882. Notwithstanding this intense rivalry, which extended throughout the nineteenth century, there was one issue upon which both powers were more or less in agreement. This was to prevent at all costs Russian dismemberment of the Ottoman empire, a resolve that took Britain and France into the Crimean War of 1853-56 against Russia and very close to yet another clash in 1877-78. Unfortunately, all external attempts to shore up the crumbling institutional framework of the empire proved unsuccessful in consequence of the failure of all Ottoman efforts at internal reform and in the face of nationalist movements—Greek, Serbian, Rumanian, Bulgarian, and even Armenian—which were utterly incompatible with the multinational traditions of Ottoman rule.

Surveying the preceding century of territorial losses, Ottoman statesmen on the eve of the First World War were bound to conclude that Anglo-French "protection" had brought few tangible gains: Egypt was lost, the Balkans were all but lost, and Russia continued to advance its Caucasian frontier. The North African *beyliks* were gone: Algiers and Tunis to France in 1830 and 1881 respectively; Tripoli, with the Dodecanese Islands, to Italy in 1912. Britain had acquired Cyprus in 1878. It is not altogether surprising, therefore, that in

1914 the Ottoman empire preferred the Central Powers, especially as Britain and France were now in alliance with Russia. But although it had been stripped of its African and European provinces (apart from eastern Thrace) and still suffered the abuses of the hated Capitulations, extraterritorial privileges, and foreign concession hunting, the Ottoman empire remained intact in Asia. It was the decision to join the alliance with Germany and Austria-Hungary that led directly to the loss of the Asian provinces—and, incidentally, to the birth of modern Turkey. The victors of 1918 were determined not only to take possession of what was left of the empire but even to partition a substantial part of the Anatolian heartland, to be divided into French, Italian, and Greek "spheres of influence." The Straits were to be internationalized and in eastern Anatolia the Armenians and the Kurds were to be granted self-determination. These punitive measures, incorporated into the Treaty of Sèvres (August 1920), were never implemented, due to the achievement of Mustafa Kemal (Ataturk) in drawing the Turks out of their postwar mood of defeat and despair, in arousing a new spirit of pragmatic nationalism, and in driving the invading Greeks back across the Aegean (1922).

The Ottoman provinces in Asia fell to Britain and France, Russia being conveniently preoccupied since 1917 with revolution and counterrevolution. It was the British who had fought their way to Baghdad and Jerusalem in 1917, but they knew that they would have to share the spoils with the French, as already envisaged in the secretly negotiated Sykes-Picot Agreement of May 1916. As a result, the Fertile Crescent passed under infidel rule for the first time since the Crusades. The form adopted was that of the mandate, a novel concept of imperial trusteeship which placed an area regarded as unprepared for assuming the full responsibilities of statehood under the temporary tutelage of a European power responsible to the League of Nations for that area's welfare. Although subsequently regarded as a device for extending the imperial possessions of Britain and France, this was not how it was seen by the idealists of the time. It was assumed, for example, that the United States would assume mandatory responsibilities for the fledgling Armenian republic (subsequently incorporated into the Soviet Union). Elsewhere, mandates were awarded to Australia, New Zealand, and South Africa.

In the course of expelling Ottoman forces from the Fertile Crescent, the British had enlisted the assistance of the sultan's Arab subjects and, in particular, the Hashemite ruler of Mecca, Sharif Husayn, hereditary guardian of the Holy Cities of Arabia, whom the British wrongly viewed as a counterweight among Muslims to the Ottoman sultan-caliph. In the McMahon Declaration of October 1915, the British had committed themselves to the establishment of a Hashemite kingdom consisting of the Arab heartlands of Palestine, Syria, Iraq, and the Hijaz, while in the Balfour Declaration of November 1917 the Allies, partly in order to make a favorable impression in the United States, had committed themselves to the idea of a Jewish homeland. Two incontrovertible statements can safely be made about these various arrangements: the McMahon Declaration of 1915, the Sykes-Picot Agreement of 1916, and the Balfour Declaration of 1917 were clearly incompatible with each other; and they no more took cognizance of the views of the actual inhabitants of the region than had the "Partition of Africa" in the 1880s.

In the period following the First World War, Turkey and Iran, guided by purposeful dictators, in some important respects turned their backs on the past and acquired some of the trappings of the contemporary European nation-state, regarded as the model to be emulated by the Western-educated elite in both countries. Elsewhere, France demanded and obtained the mandates of Syria and the Lebanon, thereby dashing the hope of Amir Faysal, Sharif Husayn's son, that he would become the ruler of an Arab kingdom with its capital at Damascus. The British compensated him by creating for him the mandatory kingdom of Iraq, but that was little consolation for the loss of a united Arab state, carved out of the lands that had once been the core of the Umayyad caliphate. At the other end of the

Fertile Crescent, the British established two further mandates, that of Palestine, shortly to become the setting for the inexorable struggle between the Palestinian Arabs and Jewish immigrants, and that of Transjordan, where King Faysal's brother, Abd Allah, became amir and, in 1946, king. Hashemites now ruled in Baghdad and Amman but in 1924 Sharif Husayn himself was unexpectedly driven out of the Hijaz by the Wahhabi ruler of Najd, Ibn Saud (c. 1880-1953), who thereafter established the kingdom of Saudi Arabia, dominating the greater part of the Arabian peninsula. British rule continued, however, in Aden and the Aden Protectorate while Oman and the littoral sheikhdoms of the Persian Gulf remained no less firmly under British tutelage. Only the Shii imamate of the Yemen remained largely sealed off from external pressures until the coup d'état of 1962, followed by the intervention of Egypt and Saudi Arabia.

Between the world wars the British were the dominant external influence in West Asia, plagued by the forces of Egyptian and Arab nationalism and by the intractable problem of the Palestine mandate. The outbreak of war in 1939, the unexpected collapse of France and the emergence of the Vichy regime, the strategic importance of the area to both sides, and the direct impact of the war on every aspect of daily life ensured that West Asia after 1945 would be very different from what it had been in 1939, although many Frenchmen and Englishmen were unwilling to face the fact. Syria and the Lebanon became independent in 1946, Britain and the United States declining to assist France in regaining her former dominant position in those countries. In 1946, Britain partitioned the former Palestine mandate, leaving behind the two successor states of Jordan and Israel. In Iraq the mandate had formally ended in 1932, but that kingdom remained essentially a British client state until the monarchy, the old ruling elite, and the special relationship with Britain were all simultaneously swept aside in the bloody coup d'état of 1958. In the Arabian peninsula change came more gradually, but with the withdrawal of the British from Aden (now the People's Democratic Republic of Yemen) in 1967 and from the Trucial States of the Persian Gulf in 1971, where Iranian hegemony is now replacing that of Britain, old-style European imperialism disappeared from West Asia, to be replaced by new patterns of great power rivalry provided by the United States and the Soviet Union.

European Imperialism in West Asia: Russia

Russian expansion into West and Central Asia necessarily differed in character from expansion by the maritime nations of Western Europe, both because the process took place across land frontiers and because the incorporation of contiguous territories into the Russian empire was to prove more permanent than the ephemeral conquest of overseas colonies. The Russian penetration of the Muslim world was an extension of the medieval struggle betwen Christian Slav and Muslim Tatar, a struggle that included ideological elements of holy warfare against the unbeliever but also important processes of acculturation between the two societies. In some ways this struggle resembled that between Christian and Muslim in the Iberian peninsula and left behind it a somewhat similar legacy. From the Russian point of view, the conflict with the Tatars was seen as a crusade to purify the soil of Holy Russia. As in Spain, so also in Russia, the clergy became the spearhead of popular resentment against the remnants of Tatar domination, and it was at the hands of the clergy that the Muslims of the region of the middle Volga suffered ferocious persecution during the late sixteenth and seventeenth centuries, notwithstanding the fact that many leading Muscovite families had Tatar ancestry, just as many nobles in Castile had Muslim or Jewish forebears. Much later, during the nineteenth century, when Russian expansion had passed far beyond the limits of what was traditionally regarded as European Russia, the advance resembled not so much that of medieval Spain as that of the contemporary United States, with a similar belief in manifest destiny. The spearhead for penetration eastward and southward was now the Russian army, using the most lethal weapons of the age against scattered and poorly armed tribal groups. Behind them came peasant colonists, their advance facilitated by the railroad, who expropriated the nomads' grazing lands, driving the dispossessed tribesmen into hopeless revolts, which in turn led to predictable massacres by the army.

During the thirteenth and fourteenth centuries the Chingizkhanid Mongols, who had conquered the western extension of the Eurasian steppe zone under the leadership of Batu and the other descendants of Chingiz Khan's son Jochi, had become assimilated to the indigenous Turkish peoples inhabiting the steppes north of the Black Sea and the Caspian, from whom they also acquired the external trappings of Islam. Thereafter there evolved in this area a distinct Tatar Muslim culture of which the most enduring legacy was to be the Tatar language, the vehicle by means of which the Tatars retained their cultural identity under Russian rule and which was to be of crucial importance in the Tatar renaissance of the nineteenth century. With regard to the conquered Christian inhabitants of the forest zone north of the steppes, the Mongols established a system of indirect rule whereby those Russian princes who were prepared to serve as their tax gatherers were permitted to retain their former authority, now reinforced by that of the Mongol khan in his headquarters at Saray-Batu or Saray-Berke on the Volga. Unwisely, the Mongols interfered hardly at all with the Russian clergy, which, during a period when the traditional rulers had either been extinguished or had become agents of the "Tatar yoke," assumed the role of leaders of the people in much the same way as the Greek clergy were later to do in Greece under Ottoman rule. One consequence of this growth in the prestige of the clergy was to restrict the spread of Islam under Tatar rule and to provide a barrier to Russian assimilation of Tatar culture other than among those, mainly the ruling elite, who had dealings with the khan and his entourage.

By the middle of the sixteenth century the once-dreaded Mongol khanate of Kipchak, which the Russians called the Golden Horde, had disintegrated, not so much in consequence of external pressures as from those intertribal rivalries to which Turco-Mongol confederacies were so susceptible. In place of a single khanate there had emerged several successor states of which the most important were the khanates of Kazan and Astrakhan on the Volga, the khanate of the Crimea, and the khanate of Sibir, east of the Urals on the upper Tobol River. Of these khanates, Kazan and the Crimea had become the chief repositories of that Tatar culture that the Russians were so soon to attempt to stamp out. Ivan the Terrible annexed the khanate of Kazan in 1552 and Astrakhan in 1554. In 1583 the Cossack leader Yermak crossed the Urals and captured the town of Sibir in the opening phase of that eastward expansion that was to extend the Russian empire as far as the Pacific Ocean and that was the Russian equivalent of the opening of the American West. In the first stages of the conquest of Siberia it was the pelt of the sable that drew desperate men to those desolate regions in much the same way as men were later drawn to the west coast of Africa in the quest for slaves, to California for gold, and to the Rand for diamonds.

The khanate of Sibir had disappeared by the first decade of the seventeenth century. The khanate of the Crimea proved altogether more resilient. The khan maintained a formidable army of well-mounted irregular cavalry, and after 1475 he enjoyed the protection of the Ottoman sultan, whose nominal vassal he became in that year. A detachment of Crimean Tatar cavalry almost invariably accompanied Ottoman armies on campaign in the Balkans, where their predatory habits of warfare made them much feared. As late as 1571 the Crimean Tatars entered and plundered Moscow and it was not until 1783 that Catherine the Great formally annexed the khanate.

The Russian advance against the Tatars drew them inexorably towards the Black Sea and the Caspian and into contact with much more formidable Muslim powers—the Ottoman and Safavid empires and the Kazakh Hordes, beyond which lay the Özbeg khanates of Khiva, Bukhara, and Kokand. For two centuries, beginning with the reign of Peter the Great

(1682-1725), Russia exerted a constant pressure on the Islamic world in three different directions—southwest against the Balkan provinces of the Ottoman empire, south into the Caucasus and against Iran, and southeast into the Kazakh steppe—and in all three areas the intervention was to prove crucial and long lasting.

The Russian advance into the Balkans during the eighteenth and nineteenth centuries was not an isolated phenomenon but part of a broad pattern of Christian reconquest involving not only Russia but also the kingdom of Poland and the Habsburg empire. This meant that Russia's advance into Ottoman territory necessarily touched on the interests and aroused the hostility of other European powers. What mattered in this complicated situation was not simply the extent of territory gained but the timing and the method used. If, for example, the weight of Russian pressure on the Ottoman frontier led the Sublime Porte to throw all its resources against the Russian aggressors, the consequence of this action might well be a further accretion of exposed territory to the Habsburgs farther west. Such an outcome was, from the Russian point of view, highly undesirable, since the czar was at war with the Ottoman empire in the interests of Russia and not Christendom as a whole, in exactly the same way as the Habsburgs were solely intent upon their own territorial aggrandizement. A further complication was the various Christian peoples who were being "liberated" from Ottoman rule. Diverse in race, language, and even the form of Christianity they professed, each community enjoyed a distinctive culture, a unique historical experience, and a tradition of turbulent and bitter rivalry against its neighbors. If, for example, the Habsburgs found it difficult to absorb into the imperial system those Magyars who had lived for nearly two centuries under Ottoman rule, the Russians found the local politics of Wallachia and Moldavia (now Rumania) no less baffling. What counted in the long run, however, was that the various peoples of the Balkans had assimilated comparatively little of Ottoman civilization and, most important of all, Islam had made little headway except in certain rather isolated areas (Albania, Bosnia, Herzogovina, and the Dobruja). They might resent and resist Habsburg or Russian domination but they were determined to free themselves from Ottoman rule. But for the intervention of Britain and France during the course of the nineteenth century it seems certain that the Ottomans would have been swept out of the Balkans and the Russians would have become masters of the Straits long before the outbreak of the First World War.

Russian penetration of the Caucasus followed a pattern different from the advance into the Balkans. Here the population was composed mainly of Circassian Muslim tribesmen, some of whom occupied a mountainous terrain ideally suited for resisting an invader. In addition, the region also sheltered the Georgians and the Armenians, both of whom had maintained during many centuries of Muslim overlordship their distinctive Christian cultures and who now openly welcomed the substitution of Russian for Ottoman or Iranian rule. Russia's advance into the Caucasus region began during the eighteenth century (as early as Peter the Great's reign there had been a brief incursion into Safavid territory as far as the province of Gilan on the southwest shores of the Caspian), and by the end of the century Russia was beginning to put pressure on the Muslim khanates in what is now Soviet Azarbayjan, regarded by the Qajar shah of Iran as his vassals. The formal annexation of Georgia (another traditional Iranian vassal state) to the Russian empire in 1800 was only one of several causes that led to war between Russia and Iran from 1805 to 1813 and again from 1826 to 1828, as a result of which the Iranian northwest frontier was drawn at the Aras River and Russia acquired most of the territory that now comprises the Soviet Socialist Republics of Georgia, Armenia, and Azarbayjan, including the great oil fields of Baku. Although the construction of a military highway across the mountains to Tiflis, the capital of Georgia, ensured control over the southern Caucasus region, the northeastern territory of Daghistan remained unsubdued until 1859, when the guerrilla chieftain Shamil finally surrendered. It is is interesting to note that the Caucasian stories of Lermontov, Tolstoy, and

11.1 Miniature celebrating the triumph of the shah over the infidel Russians in the war of 1804-13. Fath Ali Shah Qajar (1797-1834) is shown unseating the Russian commander while the latter's troops prepare to flee. Severed Russian heads lie at the feet of the Iranian horses. In reality, the Qajar army proved no match for Russian discipline and firepower. Courtesy: The British Library.

other much-read nineteenth-century novelists indicate that this frontier region possessed for stay-at-home Russian readers an escapist fascination comparable, at a later date, to British romances set on the Indian northwest frontier or to French tales of the Foreign Legion.

The Kazakhs and Özbegs first appear in history during the fifteenth century, when the latter migrated from the steppes north of the Syr Darya into Turkistan, where they gradually assimilated with the Turco-Iranian inhabitants of the oases and completed the Turkicization of the region. Meanwhile, the Kazakhs remained on the steppes to the north of the Aral Sea, the Syr Darya, and the Tien Shan Mountains, where throughout the sixteenth century they formed a great nomad empire much feared by their neighbors and also began what was to prove a rather slow process of Islamicization. By the early years of the seventeenth century, however, their great days had passed and the empire had disintegrated into three separate tribal confederacies known (from west to east) as the Little Horde, the Middle Horde, and the Great Horde. All three hordes suffered constant decimation and the loss of livestock in consequence of merciless expeditions mounted against them by the Oirot Mongols to the east of them and also by the Kalmyk Mongols of the lower Volga, against whom the Kazakhs proved incapable of offering any effective resistance. This century and a half of persecution, still remembered in Kazakh folklore, ended with the Manchu (Ch'ing dynasty) subjugation of the Oirots in 1758. Thereafter, however, the Manchus claimed the Kazakhs, especially the tribes of the Great Horde, as tributaries of the Ch'ing empire. This is why the Kazakhs of the eighteenth century regarded the coming of the Russians as the lesser of two evils.

The Russians entered the Kazakh steppe from the north, advancing along a line of forts extending from Orenburg to Omsk (1716) and then on to Semipalatinsk (1718) and Ust-Kamenogorsk (1719). This line of forts was then moved southward, deeper and deeper into the steppe, until by 1847 the mouth of the Syr Darya had been reached and in 1853 Russian troops had seized the fort of Ak-Mechet in the Özbeg khanate of Kokand. In 1854, Alma-Ata (then known as Vernyy), capital of the present-day Kazakh Soviet Socialist Republic, was founded. Fearful of further Oirot and Kalmyk raids, the Kazakhs had long since submitted to Russian overlordship: the Little Horde in 1731; the Middle Horde in 1740; and part of the Great Horde in 1742. For a century or more the Kazakhs (to whom Russians in the czarist period gave the name of Kirghiz while referring to the true Kirghiz of the Tien Shan region as Kara-Kirghiz) were left under the rule of their own khans. This, however, was only a temporary measure until such time as the Russians were ready to suppress the khanates: that of the Middle Horde in 1822; the Little Horde in 1824; and the Great Horde in 1848.

The pattern of colonial administration on the Kazakh steppe took shape during the 1850s, when this vast region (almost four times the area of Texas) was organized into the three provinces (*oblasts*) of the Orenburg Kirghiz, the Siberian Kirghiz (with its headquarters at Omsk), and of Semipalatinsk. At first, Russian rule did not appear particularly oppressive. The Kazakhs were allowed to retain their own customary laws, they were exempted from military service, and for administrative purposes the Russians employed Volga Tatars as intermediaries. The consequences of this policy, which was officially halted in 1860, proved far reaching: the Tatars acquired both economic and political leverage with the Kazakhs, while not only Islam itself but also Pan-Islamic and Pan-Turkish ideas began to be disseminated on the steppes by Tatar missionaries and teachers. In the 1870s the Russians, fearful of the influence the Tatars now exercised over the Kazakhs, established Russo-Kazakh schools to accelerate the Russification of the latter, while at the same time taking measures to end instruction in Tatar. In consequence, there emerged by the end of the century a Kazakh intelligentsia which accepted that further progress for the Kazakhs necessarily meant close cooperation with Russia. This intelligentsia, from among which would emerge, after 1917, the leadership of the liberal nationalist Alash Orda, was the product both of Russian education and of a cultural nationalism derived from Tatar advocates of Pan-Turkism.

There was, however, another aspect of Russian rule which, even before the formal abolition of the khanates, had provoked sporadic and occasionally persistent revolts led generally by members of the lesser tribal nobility (*batyrs*). In the second half of the eighteenth century Cossack settlements had begun to impinge on tribal grazing lands and this was followed in the first half of the nineteenth century by more intensive agricultural settlement. It was during the 1890s, however, that there began a massive colonization by Russian and Ukrainian peasants of the misnamed "virgin lands" of the northern steppe zone—for centuries, the Kazakhs' finest pastures. Inexorably, the nomads were driven back onto more arid land and when they resisted, the colonists either took the law into their own hands and slaughtered them, or else called in the army. Kazakh uprisings were brutally suppressed and the climax came in 1916, when the government ordered the mobilization of the Kazakhs not for military service but for conscript labor service. This final injustice, the climax to two decades of oppression, provoked a massive revolt in which the Kazakhs rose up and massacred the settlers, only to be massacred in their turn with even greater savagery and thoroughness. Many fled into Chinese territory.

The Bolshevik Revolution of 1917 brought them no respite, for they were soon caught between Red and White armies, both of which harried their remaining flocks and took punitive reprisals for their alleged betrayal of one or other cause. After the civil war, the failure of the moderate Alash Orda party to obtain favorable consideration for the Kazakhs in the new Soviet order was the prologue to the liquidation of the "bourgeois nationalist" leadership, followed by further colonization, the enforced collectivization of livestock, and devastating famine. The Kazakh Soviet Socialist Republic was established in 1936, but today the proportion of Kazakhs to non-Kazakhs in the republic falls considerably short of 30 percent. There are now little more than 3.5 million surviving Kazakhs, of whom about 500,000 live in China or the Mongolian People's Republic, to which they fled in 1917.

In contrast to the Kazakhs, the Özbegs fared somewhat better under czarist rule, primarily because, unlike the fertile steppe of Kazakhstan, Turkistan is a relatively arid desert region of oasis and riverine settlements, with a climate unsuitable for European colonization. Having reached the Syr Darya at Ak-Mechet in 1853, the Russians thereafter advanced cautiously against the three Özbeg khanates of Kokand, Bukhara, and Khiva. The motives for this advance have been argued at length by historians and, among them, the official czarist justification on the grounds of the impossibility of maintaining a settled frontier between a "civilized" European power and an "uncivilized" tribal population is one that will be familiar to students of European expansion in other parts of the world. There was also that peculiarly Russian sense of a continental manifest destiny, reinforced by the army's thirst for military glory, beside which commercial incentives took distinctly secondary place. In addition, there was a genuine fear of British penetration into what was regarded as a natural sphere of influence for Russia. The movement of British agents in the remote khanates of Central Asia (the "great game" in Rudyard Kipling's *Kim*), British campaigns in Afghanistan and, following the revolution, British intervention in both Baku and Ashkhabad could all be instanced as proof of British ambitions in the area. At the same time, the Russians themselves were not averse to playing the same game and, by putting pressure on Afghanistan, making the British more amenable in the Balkans or elsewhere.

During 1865-66 Russia invaded the khanate of Kokand and forced its ruler to accept the status of a Russian vassal, just as the British had done with various Indian rulers. There followed in 1866 an attack on Bukhara in which Russian losses were remarkably low. At the battle of Jizak (1866) the Bukharans lost six thousand men as compared to six Russians killed, indicating that future conquests should be relatively easy and therefore acceptable to the government in St. Petersburg. In the following year the governor-generalship of Turkistan was set up, comprising all the territory acquired since the advance to the Syr Darya in 1847. Its headquarters were at Tashkent, soon to develop as a typical colonial city with its strictly segregated "old" or "native" quarter and its "new" or "European" one, symmetrically laid out like the cantonment area and "civil lines" of an Anglo-Indian city. The first governor-general, General K. P. von Kaufman (1867-82), was the indubitable architect of Russia's Central Asian empire. It was Kaufman who attacked the amir of Bukhara in 1868, compelling him to accept the status of a Russian vassal, to cede extensive tracts in the Samarqand region, and to pay an indemnity of 500,000 rubles. It was he too who masterminded the attack on Khiva, thus compelling the khan to become, like his rival in Bukhara, a Russian vassal. Finally, in 1875-76, a clerical-led insurrection in Kokand resulted in the expulsion of the ruler, regarded by his subjects as a cat's-paw of the Russians, and the proclamation of *jihad* against the unbelievers. This gave Kaufman the pretext he needed and he swiftly occupied the khanate, which was abolished in favor of direct rule by Russia. None of the three khanates had been able to offer much resistance to the invaders. Far more spirited was that of the Turcoman tribes in the desert country that divided Khiva and Bukhara from the Iranian frontier. Some of these actually defeated a Russian expeditionary force at Geok Tepe in 1879 and submitted only after their bloody defeat and massacre at the same fortress in 1881. In 1884 the Marv oasis was occupied and in 1885 Russian troops clashed with Afghan troops on the northwest frontier of Afghanistan, thereby almost provoking war with Great Britain. The frontier with Afghanistan was subsequently settled by the Russo-Afghan Boundary Convention of 1887, as was the Pamir frontier by the Anglo-Russian Convention of 1895.

Under czarist rule the governor-generalship of Turkistan comprised the modern Uzbek, Turkmen, and Tadzhik Soviet Socialist Republics and the Kara-Kalpak Autonomous Soviet Socialist Republic (an area totaling more than three times the size of California), together with Kirghizia and the southern region of Kazakhstan. It consisted of four *oblasts* (of which Transcaspia, with Ashkhabad as its capital, enjoyed a considerable degree of autonomy) as well as the two protectorates of Khiva and Bukhara, where Özbeg institutions were little effected by Russian proximity. The governor-general of Turkistan was a serving army officer whose immediate superior was the minister of war in St. Petersburg, and Russian rule in the area retained down to 1917 a distinctly military character very different from British rule in India or Dutch rule in Java. In general, Kaufman and his disciples regarded "native" culture as thoroughly barbarous and greatly deprecated the too favorable impression that some visiting Turkistani rulers and notables made at the czar's court. On the other hand, he was determined for reasons of expediency to interfere with Islamic law and customs as little as possible and not to antagonize the *ulama* more than was absolutely necessary. Slavery, however, was outlawed, although it continued to survive in various forms longer than most Russian administrators cared to admit. Most important of all, the Russians were resolved not to build up a "sepoy army" of native troops such as had given the British in India such cause for alarm in 1857, but in any case their own manpower was more than adequate to meet their needs.

The impact of Russian rule on the cultural life and nationalist aspirations of the Turkish peoples of Central Asia will be discussed in Chapter 13. Among the material consequences of that rule, three aspects deserve emphasis: railroads, cotton, and irrigation. The Trans-Caspian railroad reached Samarqand from Krasnovodsk on the Caspian as early as 1888 and in addition to strengthening Russia's military hold over the area provided the means for exporting a high-grade cotton, of a kind introduced from the United States in 1883, at a price that compared favorably with prices on the world market. Cotton production thereafter increased rapidly but, as in the case of other colonial societies, the transition to a one-crop economy in some areas had an unfavorable effect on traditional agrarian and landholding patterns. It also made the area dependent on the importation of Ukrainian and

Siberian wheat, for which the Orenburg-Tashkent railroad was built between 1899 and 1906 and the Turkistan-Siberia railroad was begun just before the First World War, although not completed until 1930. Mainly to increase the production of cotton, some ambitious hydraulic projects were undertaken although in general these proved less effective than their advocates had anticipated. In irrigation, as in mining, the most striking achievements postdated the revolution, although both coal and copper mining in Kazakhstan go back to the 1850s.

The colonial experience of the Muslim subjects of the czars diverged fundamentally from that of all other colonial peoples in consequence of the Bolshevik Revolution of 1917. Had czardom survived the First World War or been replaced by a liberal parliamentary regime, it seems probable that the nationalist movements that were stirring among the empire's Muslims prior to 1914 would have eventually exploded in an irresistible demand for independence such as was to occur in India, Egypt, or Java. In fact, such demands were expressed very plainly after 1917 but were everywhere forcibly suppressed, the new Soviet government being utterly determined to prevent the dismemberment of the Soviet Union, whether by forces from within or without. Often, it was the European workers in such cities as Tashkent and Ashkhabad who crushed dissident movements among the "natives," displaying a determination and brutality the czarist regime had rarely exceeded.

To write of Soviet "colonialism" in Central Asia, as some American and European authors do, is somewhat misleading, and it goes without saying that no present-day Soviet citizen would permit such an assertion by a Westerner to pass unchallenged. In so controversial an issue, what appears to be beyond dispute is that the Muslims of Central Asia were forcibly incorporated into the Russian empire during the nineteenth century and that the Soviet Union cannot and will not now permit them to secede. It does not follow, however, that they would wish to do so. It is perhaps of some significance that since the purge of "bourgeois nationalists" in the 1930s the leadership in the Central Asian republics has been under far less pressure to liberalize its ways than has the leadership in the European republics of the Soviet Union. It must be stressed that the establishment of the Central Asian republics, whatever the motives for bringing them into being, has given their citizens a strong sense of cultural identity and also a considerable amount of administrative autonomy. They probably have greater certainty of employment, better health and educational facilities, and more opportunities for advancement than any other peoples on the mainland of Asia. Islam is officially frowned upon but Islamic customs relating to birth, circumcision, marriage, and burial are extensively observed, even in families in which the men have served in the Red Army and been stationed for long periods in European Russia. For those who tenaciously retain the faith of their ancestors there is the consolation that time may be on their side, since the birthrate of the Muslims far exceeds that of any other group of Soviet citizens.

2. WESTERN EUROPEAN DOMINATION IN SOUTH ASIA

When Vasco da Gama arrived at Calicut in 1498 he proclaimed Portuguese sovereignty over the Indian seas, but he soon found himself in conflict with local Muslim powers that contested his claim. In the naval wars that followed between Portuguese fleets and those of Calicut, Gujarat, and Mamluk Egypt, the Portuguese had triumphed by 1509. In 1510, Alfonso d'Albuquerque was sent from Portugal to India to establish on the rimland of southern Asia a network of strategic bases that were to be coordinated and controlled from a common center. By 1516 he had secured strong points around the Indian Ocean from the east coast of Africa to Southeast Asia by the conquest of the island of Socotra off the Horn of

Africa; by the occupation of the island of Ormuz, which controlled entry to the Persian Gulf; and by the capture of Malacca, which dominated the straits of the same name between Malaya and Sumatra. Goa, on the west coast of India, was captured by Albuquerque in 1510 and was converted into an impregnable base and the capital of the first Western European commercial empire in Asia.

Throughout the sixteenth century the Portuguese were primarily interested in policing the seas and monopolizing as much trade as possible at the base settlements, while at the same time they sought to maintain their technological superiority and to increase the number of their bases in the coastal areas of the Indian peninsula. Thus the successors of Albuquerque established additional settlements on the west coast at Diu, Daman, Salsette, Bassein, Chaul, and Bombay; on the east coast at San Thomé, near Madras; and in Bengal at Hugli, near the mouth of the Hugli River.

The Factory-Fort Stage

The Portuguese did not concern themselves with territorial empire building. Their goal, first formulated by Albuquerque, was to secure effective military, cultural, and political control over their coastal bases. Goa became the model for what they hoped all their bases would be like. Goa began as a fortress and developed into a large city with its own laws and governmental institutions. The cultural impact of the Iberian presence was felt mainly through the conversion of the indigenous population to Roman Catholicism and through intermarriage between Portuguese men and Indian women, which was encouraged in order to create a community that would be Portuguese in identity and loyal to the Portuguese crown. At the same time, the Portuguese allied themselves with the local enemies of neighboring Muslim regimes. Since the Hindu state of Vijayanagar, for example, had engaged in frequent conflicts with its Muslim neighbors over the past century and a half, it was viewed as a natural ally by the Portuguese.

In the sixteenth century the Portuguese succeeded in diverting much of the maritime trade of the Indian Ocean from Muslim ships, both Arab and Indian, to their own, at the expense of indigenous ports like Calicut, Surat, and Cambay, which lost some of their wealth to the new Portuguese bases. The trade in cotton goods (notably calico, which took its name from the port of Calicut) and in pepper (which had been a monopoly of Malabar), and much of the Red Sea trade, including that in coral and pearls, gradually changed hands. Although the Portuguese trading monopoly largely benefited Europeans, it also had the effect of providing a world market for Indian goods, especially spice and muslins, on a scale hitherto unknown. Furthermore, European and Chinese goods now reached India more directly than before. For example, trade in chinaware became a significant commercial venture of the Portuguese.

Until the rise of Dutch power in the seventeenth century, the Portuguese were the undisputed masters of the Indian Ocean. Any ship sailing without their authorization was treated as a pirate vessel and was liable to seizure and confiscation. Though the Portuguese were able to retain Goa until the twentieth century, their power and influence in the Indian seas declined rapidly after the sixteenth century, when the Dutch and English combined superior naval power with greater commercial strength to surpass the Iberians.

The shift in the balance of power among the Europeans trading in South Asia was in part a reflection of the course of events in Europe. Following the defeat of the Spanish Armada in 1588, the Dutch and English saw clearly that Iberian control in the Indian Ocean could be challenged. A Dutch fleet, consisting of four ships, sailed for Southeast Asia in 1595 and accomplished its mission by establishing Dutch influence in Indonesia in spite of Portuguese opposition. It was the Dutch capture of Malacca from the Portuguese in 1641 that opened the way for a Dutch attack on Portuguese Ceylon. Colombo fell in 1654, and the smaller bases and settlements on the Malabar coast had passed into Dutch hands by 1663.

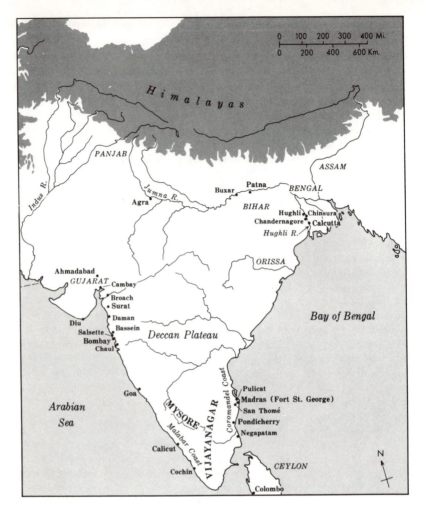

Map 47 Western European domination in South Asia

Just as the sixteenth century was dominated by the Portuguese, so the seventeenth century was dominated by the Dutch. The more important Dutch factories (i.e., trading posts) in India were at Pulicat, Surat, Chinsura, Cassimbazar, Baranagore, Patna, Balasore, Negapatam, and Cochin. By displacing the Portuguese the Dutch gained a virtual monopoly over the spice trade of South and Southeast Asia, which they maintained throughout the seventeenth century. They also engaged in the carrying trade between India and Southeast Asia. From India, the Dutch exported indigo, raw silk, textiles, saltpeter, rice, and opium.

The first voyages of the English East India Company were to Southeast Asia in an effort to capture a share of the spice trade, but by 1608 their attention was turning towards India and a company agent was sent to deal directly with Jahangir at the Mughul capital of Agra. Negotiations over the years resulted in the establishment of the company's first factory in Surat. In 1619, after another round of negotiations to obtain commercial privileges from the Mughuls, the English were permitted to establish factories in Agra, Ahmadabad, and Broach as well. Agra, the Mughul capital, did not fall into the pattern of coastal bases, since this factory was established primarily to sell broadcloth to the officers of the imperial court and to buy high quality indigo. In 1668 Bombay was rented to the East India Company at an annual rent of £10 by Charles II, who had received it from the Portuguese as part of the dowry of his wife, Catherine of Braganza. Insulated from disturbances on the mainland, Bombay steadily prospered and by the late seventeenth century had taken the place of Surat as the leading English settlement on the west coast.

In the southeast, on the Coromandel coast, the English rented the town of Madras from a descendant of a local governor of the defunct Vijayanagar empire and constructed there a fortified factory known as Fort St. George. In Bengal, the English were slower in finding a central location for their trade in silk, cotton piece-goods, saltpeter, and sugar. The foundation of Calcutta dates from 1690, when an agent of the company, Job Charnock, secured permission to establish a factory at Sutanuti on the Hugli River. The settlement grew in the 1690s when the factory was fortified, and in 1698 the British were granted *zamindari* status, that is, the status of superior landholder, including the right to collect the revenue, in relation to the three villages of Sutanuti, Kalikata (Calcutta), and Govindapur.

The French were the last of the European powers to compete for commercial gains in the Indian Ocean. Just as the English company was founded at a time of political consolidation under Elizabeth, so the French company was founded in 1644 during political consolidation under Louis XIV, on the advice of his able minister, Colbert. After a fruitless attempt to colonize Madagascar, the French turned to India and by 1700 had established factories in Pondicherry, a village south of Madras, and in Chandernagore in Bengal.

The Spread of Commercial Colonialism

In Southeast Asia, where indigenous power was weak, European colonialism, primarily Dutch, escalated rapidly in its military, political, and economic aspects. In India, however, the English and the Dutch were obliged to acknowledge the superior authority of the Mughul government, even while they were fighting one another. It is also important to bear in mind that commercial rivalry in the Indian Ocean depended in large part on the course of events occurring in Europe. European alliances, wars, and treaties determined the extent and often the very nature of conflict in South and Southeast Asia. Even in this early period of European contact, policy matters were ultimately decided in the Hague and in London, although the difficulties in communication allowed for considerable autonomy on the part of company officials in Asia.

Only when the Mughul empire began to disintegrate did European colonialism develop in South Asia. By the end of the seventeenth century the Dutch had been largely restricted to the Indonesian archipelago, leaving the French and English as arch-competitors for South Asian trade. Anglo-French rivalry became a global conflict in the eighteenth century as both countries struggled for world dominion. The three Carnatic wars fought between the French and the British in South India between 1744 and 1763 were in fact an extension of the contemporary Anglo-French conflicts in Europe and North America. Whereas the Anglo-Dutch wars of the seventeenth century had had little impact on Indian politics, in the eighteenth century the breakdown of Mughul centralized authority and the emergence of a number of successor states that had formerly been Mughul viceroyalties encouraged the French and the English to interfere in the internal affairs of Indian states as well as to engage one another in combat.

Internal interference was first exercised in the succession struggles of these states in much the same way as the Dutch were to do in Java. The earliest case of such interference occurred in 1749, when the French governor of Pondicherry installed his own candidates on the vacant thrones of the Carnatic and Hyderabad. The British in Madras realized that the success of pro-French claimants to the thrones of these newly formed kingdoms would ultimately jeopardize their own position. They therefore supported the rival candidates as a defensive action against the French.

The British defeated the French in India as they did elsewhere in the world, although the French had shown them the way to capture political power when such power was in dispute. Their opportunity came with the death in 1756 of the nawab of Bengal, Alivardi Khan, the ruler since 1740 of the former Mughul province that had now become an independent state. The British intervened in this case not to stop the French but to support one faction against another. The details of this intervention, fascinating as they are, are not necessary to an understanding of the dynamics that led to the Battle of Plassey in 1757. At Plassey an army under Robert Clive, a company clerk turned soldier, defeated the indigenous ruler, replaced him with another, and thereby established British power in eastern India. As a result of this intervention the company received the right to collect the revenue for an area of over nine hundred square miles of territory to the south of Calcutta while enjoying de facto power as kingmaker of Bengal.

Behind Britain's subsequent conquest of all India lay the superiority of her sea power and her ability to utilize her bases on the coasts of the subcontinent to her best advantage. From their base in Bengal, the company's troops moved on to Bihar, where they encountered and defeated Mughul troops at Buxar in 1764. As a result, the company was given the right to administer the revenues of Bengal, Bihar, and Orissa by the Mughul padshah, Shah Alam, who, in effect, thereby gave the East India Company a legitimate standing among the various powers on the mainland of India.

Thereafter, British control gradually expanded northwestward from Bengal until, with the annexation of the Panjab in the 1840s, the British frontier reached the river Indus. There was a parallel movement of expansion from Madras and Bombay: Tipu Sultan of Mysore (r. 1782-99) was ultimately crushed by armies operating from Madras, which was continually reinforced from the sea; in western India, the Marathas were finally defeated in 1818 by armies converging from Madras and Bombay. The base settlements of Calcutta, Madras, and Bombay thus became the nuclei of the vast territorial empire known as British India. Not all of India, however, was directly incorporated into the empire, since many principalities were allowed to retain a semi-autonomous status under the supervision of a British Resident and were known as the Princely States.

Until 1858 British India was ruled by the East India Company and not by the British government. Parliamentary acts of 1773, 1781, and 1784 established some degree of supervision over the company's affairs in civil, military, and revenue matters, in particular by the creation of a Board of Control in London and by Parliament scrutinizing the company's administration prior to the renewal of its charter every twenty years. Beginning with the Regulating Act of 1773, the British government superimposed upon the company's administration in India a formal institutional structure that was to evolve over the next century and a half into the constitutional and legal framework of the British Government of India, which was to survive down to 1947. The first governor-general, Warren Hastings (1774-85), held the title of governor-general of Fort William in Bengal but was granted a de jure authority extending over all three presidencies (the term used for the three separate governments of Bengal, Madras, and Bombay). Calcutta thereby became the capital of British India and the real center of political and military power, although the minor presidencies of Bombay and Madras fought tooth and nail to retain their de facto independence.

Several significant points need to be made regarding the political aspects of the company's rule in South Asia. First, considerations of trade and seapower naturally favored Calcutta, Madras, and Bombay in the newly evolving political system as against the traditional inland administrative centers such as Delhi or Hyderabad. Second, considerations of trade and profit were paramount in formulating political and cultural policy. For this reason, for example, the company discouraged Christian missionary activity in India, while at the same time it trained its civil servants in a way that would make them proficient in Indian languages and informed about Indian religion, society, and history. This was the function of the College of Fort William, established in Calcutta by the governor-general, Lord Wellesley, in 1800. Third, in this period company officials generally sought to maintain the continuity of Mughul political institutions because monopoly of trade, and not transformation of the Indian polity, was their objective. And finally, trade profits earned through control of the manufacture and export of India's finished goods allowed the company to settle for moderate assessments of the land revenue.

Given the fact that India was conquered and ruled by a company of merchant stockholders, it is not surprising that the commercial aspect of the colonialist process was perhaps the most significant of all. In the coalition of forces behind the plot to depose the ruler of Bengal in 1757, for example, one finds an alliance of commercial interests in which company officials combined with Jagat Seth and Ami Chand, two Marwari millionaires who had accumulated much of their wealth through profitable dealings with the Europeans. From 1757 to 1772, a period of fifteen years, Bengal was subjected to organized profiteering by the company and its servants (often working at cross-purposes with their employers in England to enrich themselves at the expense of the company), assisted and encouraged by the Hindu commercial classes that shared the vast profits with them. Only when the chaotic situation became so bad that a famine resulted in 1770 did Parliament act to compel the company to assume direct responsibility for administration and justice. In understanding the company's commercial success it is important to note that although the fear of French intervention in India continued to be acute until Napoleon's defeat in 1815, actual French power in India had been virtually eliminated by the end of the third Carnatic war in 1763. No European commercial rivals could challenge British power after that time.

The British company elite did not seek to destroy indigenous industries but to profit from the role of being the sole agent for their distribution in Europe. Resulting profits were used in a variety of ways, including the purchase of Chinese tea. Throughout the eighteenth century the most important articles of export from Bengal were cotton and silk piece-goods, raw silk, sugar, salt, jute, saltpeter, and opium. Fine cotton cloths, especially muslins, were in great demand all over the world. So long as Bengal remained independent, her middle classes profited from European trade and the province enjoyed a favorable balance of trade (exports exceeded imports, balanced by a large influx of bullion). But because commercial colonialism meant rule by a foreign company for the profit of an alien people thousands of miles away, it eventually proved a disaster for Bengal and ultimately for all of India. Most of India's previous intruders had settled permanently in India and, as a ruling elite, had sought to retain its capital resources within the subcontinent. Now India was ruled by remote control with the result that valuable wealth was drained from the country to enrich another country. It is estimated that between 1757 and 1780, 38 million pounds sterling was drained out of Bengal alone, either in the form of bullion or in articles of export in exchange for which Bengal received little, if anything. It was wealth such as this, derived from overseas colonies, that provided Britain with the capital to launch the world's first industrial revolution.

The Culmination of Western Dominance in Imperialism

The industrial revolution in England changed the nature of British interest and rule in India at the same time that it brought about profound economic and social changes in England itself. Long before the official demise of the company in 1858, the older mercantile elite within England had already lost much of its power in Parliament and elsewhere to new industrial capitalists. India was important to these new capitalists as a source for raw materials and as a dumping ground for her cheap manufactured goods. Even without political pressure in Parliament, technology itself destroyed the *raison d'etre* of company mercantilism and, with it, Indian arts and crafts. The application of power spinning and power weaving to the production of cotton goods was sufficient in itself to ruin the Indian

Resaidar
Sheik Jumnah Hoossein.

Resaidar
Gholam Hossein.

Summed Khan,
(Sillahu Burdar.)

Jemadar
Abdul Rahman.

Jemadar
Mirza Behtomoy Beg

11.2 Muslim officers of Skinner's Horse, an East India Company regiment of irregular cavalry, early nineteenth century. The establishment of British rule in India was made possible by the willingness of Indian troops to serve in the company's army. Courtesy: The British Library.

manufacture of cotton goods. Later in the century, tariff policies only accelerated economic decay in India by inhibiting the developing of new Indian industries using the latest technology.

In India, the period between the demise of company rule in 1858 and the First World War has been called the golden age of the British raj. British India (but not in a strictly constitutional sense the Princely States) became part of the far-flung British empire, and in 1877 Benjamin Disraeli, Tory prime minister, proclaimed Queen Victoria empress of India, one year before the term imperialism was first defined. Responsibility for Indian affairs was now vested in the secretary of state for India, a member of the British cabinet in London, whose instructions were communicated by telegraph to the governor-general in Calcutta. The governor-general, who now had the additional title of viceroy, became very much an agent of a foreign government ruling the Indian empire by remote control. Sea power had reached its ultimate achievement in that a foreign nation could control the destiny of another society and culture thousands of miles away by means of naval superiority backed by advanced technology and bureaucratic management.

The development of communications within India was the result of efforts to tighten up and integrate imperial rule rather than benefit the peoples of South Asia. The innovations in communications—railways, steamships, canals, telegraphs, and cables—which greatly benefited the operations of British capitalists, occurred mainly after 1858. By 1871 an extensive system of railways linked the different provinces and also the hinterland of each province with its ports. The construction of telegraphs was begun in 1851 and an efficient postal system with cheap rates was introduced in 1854. As for road and canal building, the establishment of the public works department in 1854-55 initiated a vigorous program of ambitious projects. Finally, it was in 1865 that the first telegraphic connection was established between India and Europe.

The most important achievement of all, which not only brought India close to Europe for purposes of imperial integration but made the exploitation of China easier for Europeans, was the opening of the Suez Canal in 1869, which led to an enormous increase in the volume of trade. In 1855-60 the average annual value of Indian trade was about 520,000 rupees, but for the five years starting in 1869 the average annual value of exports and imports amounted to 9 million rupees. In the early twentieth century it exceeded 20 million rupees, reaching the 60 million level before 1930. By means of the railways, whose terminal points were strategically located in the great port cities, India exported jute from Bengal, wheat from the Panjab, cotton from Gujarat, tea from Assam, and coffee from Mysore, while importing goods of European manufacture, which traveled into the interior on the same railways.

The invention of steel in 1856 by means of the Bessemer process resulted in the development of modern armaments industries and more lethal wars. The entire range of the new military technology, from steel-clad warships to new firearms with greater long-range precision, could now be employed to ensure British hegemony in South Asia and beyond. During the period of company rule the military establishment in India, consisting overwhelmingly of Indian troops (sepoys), had been divided between the three presidencies, with sepoys of the higher castes being recruited in such numbers that, by the time of the so-called Indian Mutiny of 1857 (an uprising centering on the area of what is now Uttar Pradesh and in which the sepoys played a leading part), they far outnumbered Europeans in the army. After the mutiny the army was reorganized according to imperial needs and former company regiments of European troops were merged into royal regiments, incidentally provoking a "white mutiny" in 1858 among 10,000 European troops. Thereafter, the proportion of European troops was raised and that of Indian troops reduced. In 1863 there were 65,000 European troops as against 140,000 Indians and the same ratio was maintained till the outbreak of the First World War. Artillery was now exclusively in the hands of the European troops. Another important change was in the ethnic composition of the Indian troops. No longer trusting the high-caste brahman sepoys of Uttar Pradesh, where the mutiny had occurred, the British recruited "martial races" to do their fighting and so turned increasingly to Gurkhas from Nepal, Sikhs and Muslims from the Panjab, and Muslim Pathans from the northwest frontier area.

One of the more striking characteristics of the new imperialism, aside from the growth of a highly efficient and technologically superior military machine, was the evolution of a civil administration in India which was linked to Britain by the most elaborate communication system yet known. The British in India built one of the most impressive bureaucratic machines of any universal state or empire hitherto discussed, which was responsible for the centralized administration of millions of people. British India was divided into provinces and these provinces had a British governor. The basic unit of administration was the district, and during the height of imperial rule in the 1890s there were 250 of these, averaging four thousand square miles each, with an average population of 875,000 people. India was ruled by a virtual caste of about one thousand elite Englishmen who guided the destiny of 221 million persons directly in British India and 67 million indirectly in Princely India by means of Residents at the courts of the maharajas. Efficiency, impersonality, and *esprit de corps* were the mark of this elite, which took enormous pride in its work. From 1861 onwards, the introduction of codes of law and court procedures modeled on those of England enabled imperial propagandists to proclaim that under the Pax Britannica Indians had achieved equality before the law for the first time in their history.

An important aspect of the economic system operated by the British in India was the transportation by rail of raw materials and cash crops from the interior to the port cities for export abroad. In the late nineteenth century, a complementary aspect of this system was the concerted and largely successful effort by British manufacturers to dump their finished goods onto the Indian market without any appreciable competition from Indian producers or Western rivals. Thus, in effect, Indians became dependent solely on the British for such commodities as silks, woolens, leather goods, clocks, china, glassware, paper, cardboard, and stationery. Until well after independence in 1947 Indians were to remain dependent on foreigners for bicycles, automobiles, trucks, tractors, sewing machines, umbrellas, soap, pens, flashlights, and other necessities.

It was perhaps inevitable that the British, who controlled the major sea-lanes of the world and the greatest empire in history, should develop a belief in the innate superiority of themselves and their culture. The company's cultural policy until the 1830s has been characterized as Orientalist, meaning that it was relatively sympathetic to Indian attitudes, beliefs, and culture patterns. Civil servants were encouraged to learn Indian languages, even to read Indian literature and study Indian history. The College of Fort William in Calcutta actually trained them in such a way as to acculturate them to Indian values. Cultivation of an intellectual interest in Indian culture was normative among at least some company officials from the time of Warren Hastings, who in 1784 established the Asiatic Society of Bengal, where civil servants met regularly to exchange their findings on Indian archaeology, numismatics, languages, and religion. Their scholarship and their enthusiasm led to vital discoveries about the Indian past.

In the 1830s this cultural policy began to change. With the defeat of Napoleon in 1815 the British were acquiring a new and aggressive self-confidence. In terms of the intellectual life of Britain itself, both the philosophical assumptions of the Utilitarians and the religious revivalism of the Evangelical Movement tended to make young Englishmen newly arrived in India feel remote from and contemptuous towards almost everything Indian. Virtually all aspects of India, both past and present, came to be regarded as decadent and worthless in the new "progressive" era. The Westernizers, like Lord Macaulay (appointed president of the Committee of Public Instruction in 1834), asserted that the acquisition of English culture was the only way to attain the goal of modernity: only if Asian peoples would disown their traditional heritage and assimilate English culture by speaking like Englishmen, eating like Englishmen, dressing like Englishmen, and perhaps dreaming like Englishmen could they ever hope to improve their lot and enter the modern world. Paradoxically, the seeds of late nineteenth century imperialist attitudes were implanted by thinkers such as Macaulay who were themselves sincere and dedicated reformers who saw the world in terms of material improvement and moral uplift. Unfortunately, their moral certitude and lack of a sense of relativity engendered a fierce intolerance for everything different from what they took for granted.

This imperialist mentality reached its culmination in the years between 1880 and 1910, a period of supreme self-confidence among the British ruling elite. Unquestioning in their sense of their own supremacy and little troubled by thoughts of external threats to their empire, they shared a common faith in the virtues of English civilization and the English way of life. Gone apparently were even the liberal sentiments of a Macaulay, who at least held out hope that Indians could improve their mental condition and join the mainstream of progressive nations. Instead, the British ruling elite acquiesced in the stereotype of the British official in India as the epitome of integrity, courage, and dedication to duty, while the Indian he ruled was viewed as devious, cowardly, and timid. It was thought essential for the Englishman to protect himself against being corrupted by Indian customs or attitudes, and intermarriage with Indians, which had been far from rare in the late eighteenth century, became unthinkable. Yet there was also a growing undercurrent of doubt and of disillusion, well expressed in Rudyard Kipling's poem "The White Man's Burden," which is far from being, as it is generally supposed to be, a hymn to imperialism. In any case, notwithstanding a diminution of self-confidence and the loss of a sense of mission, diagnosed, for example, in E. M. Forster's *A Passage to India* (1924), the blatant assertion of European superiority, no less than the loss of political sovereignty and economic exploitation, was to stir Indian resentments and eventually contribute to the rise of nationalism in South Asia.

3. WESTERN EUROPEAN DOMINATION IN SOUTHEAST ASIA

The first area of Asia to be significantly affected by the expanding maritime activities of the Western Europeans was Southeast Asia. For that reason, this section will give more consideration to the early stages of European domination than is the case elsewhere in this chapter. There are at least three obvious reasons why European encroachment advanced most rapidly in Southeast Asia. First, the spice trade originated there, and the high value and light weight of these exotic goods made spices profitable to trade even in the face of long and dangerous voyages in ships of small capacity. Second, the islands of Southeast Asia, where the first European inroads in Asia were made, were more accessible by sea than was the Asian mainland. Third, and partially as a result of the insular fragmentation of the terrain, the indigenous political regimes were of smaller size than the great empires of mainland Asia and hence were less formidable obstacles to the extension of European power. It should not be inferred from these remarks, however, that Western domination over the peoples of Southeast Asia was easy or unopposed or that it penetrated very deeply in its initial phases.

The events of European domination in Southeast Asia can be fit comfortably into the three-stage chronology adopted for this chapter. The factory-fort stage began in the early sixteenth century with the arrival of the first Portuguese ships. The spice trade and missionary activities were the chief concerns of the Europeans during this earliest period. The Portuguese, Spanish, and Dutch were the principal Western actors, although the English

11.3 American bombing on the Plain of Jars in Laos. This recent perception of Western aggression, seen here in a drawing by one of the victims, illustrates the point that processes of imperialist domination continue in new forms down to the present time. Courtesy: Harper & Row, from Fred Branfman, *Voices from the Plain of Jars* (New York, 1972).

and French played minor parts. The Malay peninsula, Java, the Spice Islands (i.e., Moluccas), and the Philippines were the areas that felt the greatest impact of the European presence. The era of commercial colonialism corresponded roughly with the nineteenth century. In this second stage of the European encroachment Britain, France, and Holland were the most important nations as trading monopolies gave way to more elaborate forms of economic exploitation under the protection of colonial administrations. The expansion of the China trade prompted a heightened concern about sea lanes and access routes to East Asia. The imperialist era, which began in the late nineteenth century, saw the Spanish displaced by the Americans in the Philippines and a consolidation of the French and British positions on the Southeast Asian mainland and of the Dutch control over their island empire as well. The imposition of Western institutions of government and education hastened the definition and political development of what were to become the modern nation-states of Southeast Asia.

Early Trade and Missions: The Factory-Fort Stage
The patterns of European contact with Southeast Asia were shaped both by the motives and capabilities of the Westerners and by the existing conditions among the indigenous societies at the time of their arrival. Another factor, which accounts for many significant changes over the long duration of European presence in the area, was the rivalries and confrontations among these outsiders, rivalries that often had their origin in the regional conflicts of far-off Europe. The Portuguese and the Spanish were the first arrivals. They came from opposite directions, they encountered different conditions, and they followed policies that had markedly different results.

The Portuguese came to Southeast Asia via India, where they had established an outpost at Goa in 1510 on the Malabar coast of India. In 1511, Alfonso d'Albuquerque erected a factory-fort at Malacca on the western coast of the Malay peninsula. Albuquerque's aim was to extend a policy of seizing and fortifying key points along the trade routes from East Asia to West Asia. In the Indian Ocean the Portuguese were consciously trying to destroy the Arab domination of the sea trade in a struggle in which religion often provided justification for the killing of Muslims. In Malacca they were vigorously resisted by the sultan, who was a Muslim, but Hindus and Chinese in the trading community were quick to do business with the Europeans once it became clear who was the dominant power.

The Portuguese entered the island world just at the time when Islam was spreading rapidly among the Malays. When the Portuguese sailed on from Malacca to the Moluccas they found the spice islands divided between the two rising sultanates of Ternate and Tidore. The Iberians exploited the conflicts between these two regimes in making alliances and attempting to extract agreements from the rulers which would give them a monopoly over spices such as cloves. They also established themselves in Flores and Timor and built an outpost at Ambon (Amboina), where they conducted a lucrative trade and carried on missionary activities. Despite agreements made with the Portuguese, the sultans continued to carry on trade with others, frustrating all efforts to secure a monopoly that would make the spice trade more profitable for the Portuguese. The high-handed manner in which the Portuguese dealt with the sultans and conflict over religious matters often led to bloodshed. In Ternate, for example, missionary activities and a dispute over the division of the clove monopoly in the 1560s prompted the Portuguese to murder the sultan, with the result that their garrison was massacred and the trade shifted to Tidore.

It was in ways such as these that the European traders affected the economic and political life of Southeast Asia. One result of the Portuguese presence was the displacement of much of the commercial activity of Arabs, Chinese, Malays and others to new locations. The seizure of Malacca forced many traders, particularly Muslims, to shift their activities to the state of Acheh in northern Sumatra. Another outcome was the stimulation of those states

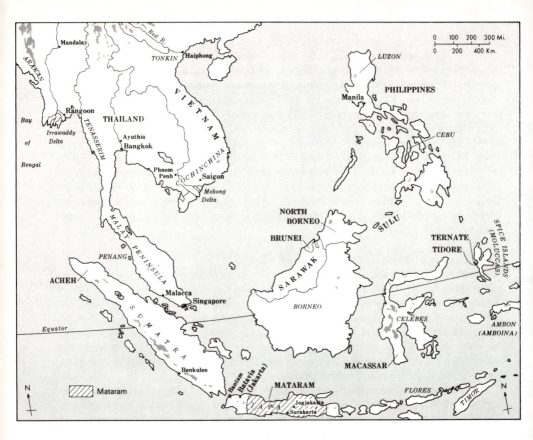

Map 48 Western European domination in Southeast Asia

placed in position to benefit from shifting trends in coastal trade and the spread of Islam. Acheh, Tidore, and Ternate are examples, as are the sultanates of Sulu (near the Philippines), Brunei (northwestern Borneo), and Macassar (on the Celebes). Macassar profited from the fact that the traditional trade between Java and the eastern end of the Indonesian archipelago was constricted in the seventeenth century. This was due in part to the intervention of Europeans, notably the Dutch, who established a factory-fort at Batavia (Jakarta) in 1619, but mostly to the fact that the great Javanese state of Mataram, extending its power outward to the northern sea ports, pursued policies that inhibited commerce. Macassar benefitted by supplying staples such as rice to the spice islands, which had previously relied on Java. Macassar also became a major center of Islamic activity.

The Spanish entry into Southeast Asia was accomplished by crossing the Pacific from Mexico and staking a claim to the Philippines. Papal bulls and agreements legally barred the Spanish from the area. The Treaty of Tordesillas (1494) divided Spanish and Portuguese spheres to the west and east of a line 370 leagues west of Cape Verde Islands (in the Atlantic), and the clarifying Treaty of Zaragoza (1529) formalized a Spanish renunciation of all claims in the Moluccas, which would have placed all of the Philippines in the Portuguese sphere. Nevertheless, the Spanish were determined to gain a share of the lucrative Asian trade. Ferdinand Magellan, whose expedition for the Spanish crown (1519-21) accomplished the first circumnavigation of the globe, met death in the Philippines while interposing Spanish power in a dispute between local leaders. Subsequent expeditions across the Pacific failed until 1565, when Miguel Lopez de Legazpi established a fort on the island of Cebu, near where Magellan had been killed. By 1571, however, Legazpi took Manila, on the northern island of Luzon, and made it the center of government for the new Spanish colony. Attacks by the Portuguese failed to dislodge the newcomers.

Because of their physical location, the islands of the Philippine archipelago were isolated from many of the cultural and economic influences that were so important in the societies of the islands to the south and west. Buddhism and Hinduism had no impact in the Philippines, and Islam was just establishing a foothold in the southernmost islands when the Spanish arrived. Likewise, the islands were too remote from the shore of China to be included in the sphere of that civilization, although Chinese trade and immigration played an important part in Philippine history. There were no indigenous states or empires to provide a unifying vehicle for the islands as a whole; the largest political unit was the *barangay*, a kinship unit of up to one hundred families. These negative factors—weak ties to other civilizations and a minimum level of political organization—help explain the receptivity (or ineffectual resistance) of the region to Spanish influence. On the positive side, the Spanish were prepared to take advantage of their opportunities. Legazpi came as governor-general, ready to apply the lessons the Spanish had learned in the Americas. Catholic missionaries were an important constituent of the Spanish administration from the outset. Twenty years after the founding of Spanish capital at Manila there were 140 missionaries in the islands. Eventually, six different orders participated in the Christianizing mission, founding towns, churches, and educational institutions. To avoid rivalry, each order was allocated a specific sector of the archipelago. So successful were the Spaniards in their religious and educational work that Spanish became the *lingua franca* throughout the islands and Christianity the dominant religion.

The chief goals of the Spanish administration, in addition to the propagation of Christianity, were to gain entry into the spice trade and to develop commercial ties with China and Japan. The jealousy of the Portuguese and later the Dutch shut the Spanish out of the Spice Islands. Religious hostility toward the Muslims of the south—the Spanish called them Moros, i.e.; Moors—led the Iberians to carry on a holy warfare against these Southeast Asian extensions of their old Islamic foe which lasted until the nineteenth century. Trade with China, however, thrived as Spanish silver from Mexico attracted Chinese merchants to sell their goods in Manila. The galleon trade was regulated by the Spanish crown, the limited space on each year's sailing being allocated by a committee drawn from the social elite of Manila. The prosperity of the Philippine capital was dependent on the Chinese community, which supplied the silks for the galleons and many other essential goods and services. The rapid growth of the Chinese population of Manila, to thirty thousand by the 1630s, fed anxieties in the smaller Spanish ruling group and led to many conflicts and restrictive measures. Nevertheless, external factors—the constriction of trade at the Chinese source or interdiction by the Dutch, the English, or by pirates—were the most serious causes for concern.

Around the year 1600 the Dutch, a newly independent Protestant sea power, began to move into the islands, where in a matter of decades they displaced the long-established Portuguese and frustrated the efforts of the less heavily capitalized English. It was the Portuguese who pioneered in the spice trade by establishing a chain of factory-forts, investing European capital (largely German and Italian), concluding purchasing arrangements with local rulers, and even licensing indigenous trading vessels. But the Dutch went far beyond them in the scale of their investment, in the elaboration of a corporate mechanism to manage their trade, and in the systematic way they broke down competition and resistance. Furthermore, the Hollanders concentrated their efforts on business to the exclusion of missionary activities. The Dutch aimed at a complete monopoly in nutmeg, mace and cloves. Initially, the Dutch were welcomed by the islanders as allies against the hated Portuguese, and at times they cooperated as fellow Protestants with the English against the

Catholics, but the merchants from the Netherlands were quick to dispose of these allies. Ambon was their first target. Arriving there in the late 1590s they bested the Portuguese by 1605 and executed a surviving party of English and Japanese in 1623. In the seventeenth century, the power of the sultans in the Spice Islands was broken by the military suppression of revolts, reducing those rulers to the status of Dutch protectorates, and the Dutch resorted to the forced destruction of trees to prevent overproduction of spices, which could undermine the value of their trade. Although their monopoly was never complete, an important element in the Dutch success was their ability to displace both the Malay states and the other Europeans in the sea trade. In 1619 a base was established at Batavia, forcing out the English, and in 1641 Malacca was taken from the Portuguese, leaving Bantam in northern Java as the last free pepper port. To the west the Dutch forced the Portuguese out of Ceylon and took over the lucrative cinnamon production there. In the east, nine major attacks on the Philippines in the first half of the seventeenth century and one against Macao (1622) all failed, but the Dutch did take Taiwan (Formosa), which they held from 1624 to 1661, profiting from the China trade and the exchange of bullion between China and Japan.

In this early period of contact, the European traders and missionaries found their way to the courts of rulers in mainland Southeast Asia, but with little impact on local conditions. French missionaries had brief success in the seventeenth century in gaining preferential treatment from the Thai court at Ayuthia, but these advantages proved short lived when their faction lost favor at court and they were expelled. In Vietnam French missionaries sought favor with both the Trinh rulers of the north and the Nguyen rulers of the central region, but the fall of the French monarchy in the late eighteenth century prevented them from taking advantage of opportunities created by the Tayson Rebellion in 1773. A Spanish venture to intervene in the affairs of the Cambodian court at Phmon Penh in the 1590s amounted to little more than the intrigues of adventurers which had no lasting impact on local affairs.

The deepest inroads into Southeast Asian society in the factory-fort stage were those made by the Spanish and the Dutch. The Spanish, because they created a unified rule in the Philippines for the first time, defined that region as a distinct political entity and imposed the institutions that would rule it. The highest level of government was modeled after the government of Mexico, with a governor-general and a court that represented the Spanish crown. At the local level royal fiefs (encomiendas) encompassed a number of barangays for the purposes of rent, taxation, and administration, but these units were frequently unprofitable. Dutch attacks in the early 1600s forced the Spanish to make heavy exactions for labor service and foodstuffs. Subsequently, these demands evolved into government purchases under conditions that amounted to a taxation in kind. A conservative element of the Spanish administration was the co-option of the local elite as village headmen and local administrators. From this group there evolved a local landholding class, the caciques, a Filipino elite that dominated and exploited the peasantry. Under quite different circumstances, Dutch administration in the Indonesia archipelago also made extensive use of the local elite. Early Dutch commerce continued the indigenous Malay pattern in which trade was dominated by the local ruler. The Dutch simply imposed trading agreements upon local sultans, which allowed the purchase and export of spices under profitable conditions. In this system of indirect rule the Dutch East India Company avoided many administrative duties, which were still carried out by the local ruler, and although the indigenous sultans lost much of their independence under European domination, their positions were made more secure by the interdiction of Dutch power in local rivalries. The effect of Dutch rule, particularly in the spice islands, was not to impose a new set of political institutions as the Spanish did in the Philippines but, through outside intervention, to preserve the islands at the stage they had reached in the late seventeenth century.

Commercial Colonialism

Changing trends in world trade and in European politics altered the interaction of the maritime powers with the societies of Southeast Asia in ways that tended to increase the influence of the Westerners over the area. One factor was the industrial revolution and the growth of commerce, which led to more complex patterns of trade. A second factor was the rise of British power, a development related both to industrialization and to the disruptions of the French Revolution, which led to a prolonged British supremacy on the seas. A third change was the demise of old crown-chartered trading companies and their replacement in Southeast Asia by private commercial enterprise and European colonial administration. A few examples will serve to illustrate these points.

By the middle of the eighteenth century the age-old spice trade was surpassed by volume trade in more basic commodities. Sugar and coffee were two crops that could be efficiently produced on large plantations. Rice was grown in the river deltas of Burma, Thailand, and Vietnam, making mainland Southeast Asia a food-surplus area by the late nineteenth century. Tin, mined in Malaya, was to be joined in the twentieth century by rubber as an exportable industrial raw material. It was the Dutch East India Company on the island of Java which first became a territorial state regulating an agricultural society. The company, with its bureaucratic organization, was more stable than the hereditary states it confronted on the island. From the late 1600s on, the Dutch intervened in the political affairs of Bantam on the western end of the island and the great state of Mataram in central Java in a series of actions they referred to as wars of Javanese succession. The last independent principalities were reduced to puppet status in the so-called Java War of 1825-30. Liberal efforts in the early 1800s to support the government of the colony through moderate taxation while leaving agriculture in private hands failed to produce adequate revenues. Consequently, in the 1830s the culture system was introduced whereby native cultivators were obligated to make delivery of a fixed quota of goods or the land and labor to produce them for export by the Netherlands Trading Company. As a result of this system the sugar industry boomed, transforming the Javanese countryside while preserving the old forms of exploitation through crop delivery and corvée labor. Within a decade exports were quadrupled, and the Dutch used the profits from Java to pay off the debts of their home government. In Java itself the increased exports brought greater wealth to the peasantry, a development that was accompanied by an explosive growth in population. Despite the wealth the export economy brought, the concentration on sugar, at the expense of other crops, led at times to serious food shortages in Java. Batavia, as the center of the Dutch administration and the principal port, soon surpassed Jogjakarta and Surakarta, the older political centers inland. In a similar manner Rangoon eclipsed Mandalay in Burma, while in Vietnam Haiphong and Saigon developed at the expense of the old imperial capital at Hue. The court of Thailand, although retaining its independence from foreign rule, responded to the opportunities and dangers of Western trade by locating itself in the port city of Bangkok instead of the older island capital of Ayuthia.

British power expanded significantly in the second half of the eighteenth century at a time when the Dutch were undergoing a decline in vigor. In South Asia the English won their competition with the French for domination in the subcontinent, while in China the British East India Company dominated the tea trade at Canton, where they overcame Dutch competition to establish a monopoly in the Atlantic market. The carrying trade in Indian opium, which linked South Asia with China and allowed the British to pay for Chinese goods in something other than cash, passed through Southeast Asia. The British had long been interested in the spice trade of the islands, but now developments in India and China created a greater desire to dominate the sea lanes and a need to shelter ships coming from the Bay of Bengal during the monsoon season, both of which factors drew them to Southeast Asia. The British occupied Manila briefly in the 1760s, and in 1786 a British settlement was founded on the island of Penang on the western side of the Malay peninsula. It was the French Revolution and the subsequent activities of Napoleon that provided an opportunity for the takeover of Dutch holdings in Malacca and the Indonesian islands. After these areas were returned to Holland in 1816, Thomas Stamford Raffles, the British administrator who had headed the occupation of Java, undertook to establish a British trading port on the island of Singapore. The British thus gained a strategic naval base and introduced a center of free trade at the heart of the Dutch colonies. By a treaty of 1824 the Dutch and British agreed to divide their spheres in Southeast Asia along the Straits of Malacca, the Dutch relinquishing Malacca in exchange for the British pepper port of Benkulen on Sumatra. No mention was made of Borneo but the two powers eventually divided that island as well. In the 1840s James Brooke was sent to Borneo to deal with the sultan of Brunei and run a British coaling station. He subsequently established himself as the raja of Sarawak, founding a hereditary line of white rulers. In the 1880s the North Borneo Company took control of the northern tip of the island, countering claims of the sultanate of Sulu.

The end of the old East India companies brought many peoples of Southeast Asia under the jurisdiction of colonial administrators, who often interfered in local affairs in a much more energetic fashion than had the earlier spice traders. Corruption and debt ended the Dutch company in 1800. A short-lived Spanish company was formed with royal patronage in the late eighteenth century, and although it succeeded in establishing direct commercial relations between the Philippines and Spain, it lost money, so that Manila was thrown open to free trade in 1834. The British East India Company lost its monopoly over trade with China and Southeast Asia in 1833. In part, this change was due to the climate of opinion, which favored free trade and unrestricted enterprise. When they had the opportunity to do so, British administrators tried to impose land ownership and tax structures in Java during their brief tenure there and in Burma which resembled those in force in parts of India. Such practices, however well intentioned, disregarded local practice and downgraded the position of the indigenous elite, causing confusion and demoralization while seldom producing the desired revenues. A more important motive in the "forward movement" of Western colonial government in the nineteenth century was the concern for the security of their territories. The British, for example, acquired Burma piecemeal, taking Arakan and Tenasserim in the 1820s to insulate the border of India and adding upper Burma in the 1880s so as to safeguard interests in the Irrawaddy delta region.

The Forward Movement: Imperialism

It was competition among the Western powers that spurred the forward movement of colonial administrations in the late nineteenth century. The British consolidated their hold over Burma partly in response to the activities of the French in Vietnam. Both powers were interested in access routes to western China. When the French discovered that no easy access to China was offered through the Mekong delta, they turned their attention northward to the Red River and explored the possibilities of a link with Yunnan through Hanoi. Thailand, caught between these competing forces, was in danger of being partitioned. Skillful Thai diplomacy and the mutual interests of Britain and and France, however, led to the preservation of an independent Thai kingdom, which served as a buffer between British Burma and French Indochina. The French settled their border dispute with Thailand on the east in the 1890s and the British did the same in the west a decade later.

Changing technology, particularly faster steamships, telegraph, and the Suez Canal, all enabled Western powers to exercise closer administrative control over their colonies. In general, a distinction may be made between areas under direct and indirect control. After 1900, Western-style governmental forms were imposed on areas under direct control. The French maintained a colonial bureaucracy in Tonkin (North Vietnam) and Cochinchina

(South Vietnam), as did the Dutch in Java and the Americans in Luzon. In Burma the British ruled the colony as an extension of India with a tendency to impose Indian administrative forms in a manner that disrupted the local social and political order. Burma was not separated from India until 1935, by which time a bicameral legislature was created. In the Malay peninsula the British ruled indirectly through a system of Residents attached to the courts of the local sultans with broad powers to dictate policies over matters of economics and external affairs.

One of the marked effects of imperialism on the economies of Southeast Asia was the tendency to orient activities toward the export of raw materials. Prior to the Second World War Southeast Asia produced 90 percent of the world market's rubber and rice and more than half of its copra, palm oil, and tin. The Western investment that made these exports possible distorted the indigenous economies in a number of ways. For one thing, economic development was concentrated near or linked to the seaports, while inland areas were often allowed to decline into a stagnant subsistence agriculture. Traditional patterns of regional trade were interrupted by colonial divisions and regulations that favored the purchase of manufactured goods from the home industries of the imperialist powers. The concentration of Western presence and capital in limited areas tended to split the countryside off from the cities and to undermine traditional handicraft industries.

The cultural impact of imperialism can be seen in overt attempts to promote new values and institutions among the peoples of the colonies. This was nowhere more obvious than in the effort to impose the Christian religion. France, in particular, became active on behalf of Catholic missionary interests in the nineteenth century. In 1839 the Portuguese lost their right of patronage in Southeast Asia and six vicariates of Indochina were assigned to the French missionary society. A cultural influence perhaps more subversive than religion was the example set by Western residents and civil servants in the directly administered areas after the turn of the century. These self-confident and powerful proponents of Western methods were far less willing to accommodate to local practice than earlier generations of Europeans had been. They were not disposed to intermarry with Asians, to mix with the local elite, or to serve indigenous rulers; in fact, they tended to live in isolated communities for whites only. The example of their life-style and the ascendancy of their power in the era of imperialism served to undermine respect for the indigenous elite. In the centers of Western trade and administration there grew up a new class of Asians who accommodated themselves to Western values and institutions. This group included not only natives of Southeast Asia but also Chinese and Indians who entered the colonies to take advantage of economic opportunities created by Western domination. The implications of this ethnically stratified pluralism and Western cultural influences upon the societies of Southeast Asia will be examined in Chapters 13 and 14.

4. MARITIME INTEGRATION IN CHINA

In East Asia, European maritime expansion and domination took a different course than it did elsewhere on the continent. A principal reason for this difference was the fact that the Chinese and Japanese empires displayed great cohesiveness and vigor and were not seriously influenced by Western incursions until well into the nineteenth century. Neither China nor Japan experienced colonial control as did most areas in South and Southeast Asia. Another difference in East Asia was the fact that external pressures came from three directions: by sea from Western Europe, by land in northern Eurasia from Russia, and later across the Pacific from the Americas. Another element in the Chinese pattern was the role Japan played in the late nineteenth and early twentieth century as an Asian imperialist power performing in China many of the same functions that European powers carried out in other culture areas. Despite these differences in timing and geography, the historical experience of China in recent centuries offers clear illustrations of all the essential processes of maritime domination in variations patterned by Chinese conditions.

The Chinese Tributary System and Early European Contact

One reason that the confrontation between Western European nations and the Manchu Ch'ing regime in China reached the intensity it did was that the conflict was sharply focused around specific issues where practice in the two cultures was incompatible. The most celebrated of these issues related to the constellation of ideas and institutions called the tributary system. These forms constituted an established and widely recognized set of conventions for the regulation of interactions of peoples in East Asia. When Western Europeans first reached Ming and Ch'ing China by sea they had no choice but to conform to the established modes of behavior which the Chinese enforced. This situation prevailed for the sixteenth, seventeenth, and eighteenth centuries. Trouble arose, however, in the nineteenth century when European nations became strong enough to challenge the power of the Ch'ing state and to impose a Western system of international law upon the trade and diplomatic relations of East Asia. Since these institutions embodied some of the core values of Western and Chinese civilizations, the conflict between them was understood at the time to involve a profound test of strength.

The tributary system grew out of a long historical experience in which the Chinese came to view themselves as the most culturally advanced of peoples and therefore as the center of civilization. The term for China, Chung-kuo ("Central States," "Middle Kingdom"), very early embodied this notion. In later times, Confucian statecraft elaborated upon the role of the emperor, who occupied a central position, pivotal between the affairs of earth, mankind, and heaven. In hierarchic terms this ruler was necessarily superior to all others, one inference being that other states could not deal with China on a basis of equality. The tributary system formalized, in theory at least, a set of guidelines for the recognition of Chinese cultural superiority. States, tribes, and peoples beyond the boundaries of Chinese settlement were allowed to pay court on the Chinese emperor. Rulers or their representatives sent items of local produce to the Chinese court at specified intervals following prescribed routes. Detailed regulations on the Chinese side stipulated what was to be sent and how many persons might come, while a body of trained Chinese interpreters accompanied them and instructed them in the proper method of obeisance before the emperor, which was called the *kowtow*, meaning literally to "strike the head" (on the ground) and consisted of the "three kneelings and nine prostrations."

The primary function of the tributary system was to enhance the position of the emperor of China and to provide a framework for the regulation of activities on China's frontiers. In practice there was considerable flexibility. Trade, for instance, was often worked into the scheme of tributary activities, despite the fact that most commercial contact was restricted to remote border sites. It should be stressed, however, that the theory of tributary submission to China was an idealization of the way things ought to be, not a description of what actually happened. In the extreme cases, as under the Sung, China was forced to pay tribute to more powerful states or even to submit to foreign rule.

The first Europeans to come to China by sea were the Portuguese at the beginning of the sixteenth century. They were followed by the Spanish, the Dutch, and later the English and Americans. By the 1550s the Portuguese had established a base for residence and trade at Macao, a tiny peninsula southeast of Canton. Although they dealt only with local officials, they were allowed to regularize their position there and a permanent settlement grew up. Heavily fortified, with a harbor, a church, commercial and government buildings, Macao resembled in its essentials early factory-forts elsewhere in Asia.

During the first centuries of maritime contact the Portuguese and Dutch engaged in commerce and piracy along the south China coast—activities of little value or importance to the rulers of the great land-bound empire. The one group that did manage to enter the interior of China, to reach the capital, and to take up residence there was Jesuit missionaries working under the patronage of the Portuguese crown to spread their faith among the "heathen." The great Jesuit breakthrough in China was accomplished by Matteo Ricci (1552-1610), who first devised a strategy for reaching Peking. Since China was a tightly controlled centralized empire, the Jesuit aim was to convert the ruler and the ruling class first in the hopes that the rest of the population would then follow. In order to gain acceptance they consciously took on the manners and dress of the Chinese scholar-official class. This entailed learning to read and write Chinese, mastering the Chinese classics, and the being able to discourse in Mandarin about academic subjects. The idea was to use their learning as a tool to win the respect and confidence of the Chinese before exposing them to Christian doctrine. Sciences, particularly astronomy, mathematics, and cartography, proved to be the most useful subjects.

The early Jesuits were an exceptional group of men by any standard. Ricci had a photographic memory and was well schooled in the most advanced European science of his day. After two decades of cultivating contacts among the faction-ridden Chinese officialdom of the late Ming, he was allowed by the emperor to reside in Peking from 1601. By the 1620s the superiority of Jesuit astronomical calculations was recognized and the Jesuits were charged with revising the Chinese calendar. From that time on they held posts in the Chinese capital and maintained contacts with influential figures in the court, adroitly weathering the change of rule from Ming to Ch'ing by agreeing to serve the Manchus. Hundreds of Western books were translated into Chinese and several thousand Chinese were converted to Catholicism, but the dream of converting the largest empire on earth was never realized. Chinese and Manchu emperors tolerated the Jesuits' residence in the capital but took a dim view of missionary activity in the provinces. Attacks by rival Catholic orders, the Dominicans and Franciscans, and conflicts among the sponsoring nations, Spain, Portugal, and France, tarnished the Jesuit image in Chinese eyes. A controversy over the spiritual authority of the emperor and the Pope led eventually to a hardening of positions on both sides by the 1740s. The delicate balancing between Confucian practice and Catholic dogma which the Jesuits had developed was undone.

The primary impact of the Jesuit effort was not on China but on Europe. There, the glowing reports the Jesuits sent home of the tranquility, order, and prosperity of the Chinese empire caught the imagination of Westerners, whose own civilization was fragmented by incessant warfare. The imperial government in which the sovereign recruited learned men into government service through examinations presented a model worthy of emulation. For Enlightenment thinkers the Confucian moral order provided an example of a state and society which achieved harmony without the aid of religion.

The Canton Trade: A Variant of the Factory-Fort

The focal point for Western trade in China was the southern port city of Canton, where the Ch'ing government permitted the "barbarian" merchants to obtain desired Chinese goods under strict supervision. On the Chinese side, trade was regulated by a superintendent of Maritime Customs, who enforced the regulations, collected customs duties, and acted informally as a conduit of "tribute" to the imperial household. This official designated a group of Chinese merchants, the cohong, who enjoyed a monopoly over trade with the Europeans. Attached to these monopoly merchants were specialized interpreters, security merchants, and purchasing agents licensed to deal with foreigners. The merchants on the Western side were mostly representatives of crown-chartered monopolies like the British

East India Company which came to dominate the Canton trade in the eighteenth century. These "foreign devils," as the Cantonese called them, were allowed to come to Canton only during a fixed trading season and while there were compelled to live in the thirteen factories. The latter were a collection of commercial buildings on a small tract of river frontage outside the city walls. Foreigners were not allowed to enter the Chinese city or to have contact with the local populace. They were most explicitly forbidden to deal directly with Chinese officials. They could, however, exercise on a nearby island and visit the ladies on the "flower boats" in the river. Such were the conditions of early Sino-Western trade.

Despite the restrictions on the agents of the "Honorable Company," trade thrived. As Europeans developed a taste for tea, that item took the lead in exports. The British, who shipped a few thousand pounds of tea annually in the early 1700s, were shipping more than 20 million pounds per year at the end of the century and their ships outnumbered all the rest at Canton.

Two problems contributed to British discontent. The first was the rising cost of the exactions and miscellaneous fees that were levied on ships seeking to trade at Canton. These fees, which amounted to several thousand ounces of silver per vessel, were needed by the Chinese merchants and officials to satisfy the demands of their superiors in a chain of tribute and customary fees which led ultimately to Ho-shen and the emperor in Peking. The British first tried, in the 1750s, to open trade at another port farther north. James Flint, a Chinese-speaking agent of the East India Company, even traveled north to Tientsin to petition the throne for relief from the avarice of what was believed to be a local Canton interest group. The imperial reaction was to punish Flint with prison and banishment, to permanently limit trade to the single port of Canton, and to strengthen the restrictions on foreigners. Having failed in an informal petition, the British were left with the unappealing option of a representation to the throne through the forms of the tributary system. Two formal embassies were sent to China to seek improved trading conditions. Lord Macartney, who was sent to China in 1793, was treated with great courtesy by the Ch'ing government and was allowed to present gifts to the emperor. Macartney refused to perform the kowtow and was allowed to bend on one knee before the emperor as he might have done before his own sovereign. This the Chinese recorded as a kowtow. Macartney was sent away without any of the trade concessions requested. A second embassy under Lord Amherst in 1816 was denied audience with the emperor because of the ambassador's refusal to perform the kowtow.

The second cause for British discontent with the Canton trade in the eighteenth century was the fact that they bought more in China than they sold and so experienced an annual imbalance of payments. The principal British import at Canton was cotton from Bengal which was carried from India to China by English and Indian merchants, called country traders, acting on their own behalf. This was still insufficient in volume to make up for the amount of bullion the East India Company shipped into Canton at a net loss of about a million ounces of silver per year in the 1780s and 1790s. The source of the trade deficit was the fact that the British had no goods the Chinese needed; British manufactures were of little interest to the Chinese, who viewed their own economy as completely self-sufficient. The solution lay in the discovery of a product the Chinese were willing to buy in quantity and for silver: opium. Why the use of this drug should have become widespread in Chinese society at this time is a question that has not been satisfactorily answered. In any case, opium was a boon to British trade. The East India Company soon cornered the market. Grown and sold under a company monopoly in Bengal, the opium was not carried in company ships because the drug was prohibited in China. It was shipped to China by the country traders, who fed it into a vast smuggling network along the coast. By the 1830s opium led cotton as the chief British empire export to China and reversed the balance of trade. The Ch'ing government, alarmed by the outflow of silver, smuggling, and the spread

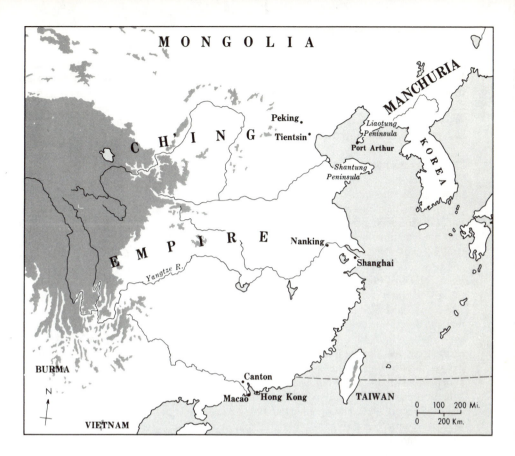

Map 49 Maritime integration in China

of drug addiction, took action to stop the trade. The result was a test of strength that ruined the Canton system.

The Canton system, which typified the first phase of Western maritime contact with China, was an institution that allowed for limited commercial exchange under conditions controlled by and profitable to the Chinese. The Europeans were obliged to accept the system because they needed Chinese products and they were not strong enough to challenge Chinese power. In practice, the system worked much like the factory-fort except that military security was provided by the Chinese, the guns pointing at the visitors instead of the natives. By the nineteenth century conditions had changed. European economies were being transformed by industrialization and the volume of commercial activity grew accordingly. Old crown charters gave way to private trading firms and the idea of monopoly was superseded by the call for free trade and competition. Perhaps most important was the development of military power and the emergence of a British hegemony over the seas. Under these circumstances the Ch'ing effort to suppress opium and reaffirm the Canton system was doomed to failure.

Under the Canton system there was no contact between governments. On the Chinese side the cohong were designated as the only persons with whom the foreigners might deal, while on the Western side symmetry was preserved by chartered trading companies. When the East India Company monopoly came to an end at Canton in the 1830s the bulk of British trade was already handled by country traders and their agency houses. Regulation of their activities was provided for by a superintendent of trade who represented the British crown. Thus, when Commissioner Lin was sent to Canton to deal with the opium problem, the stage was set for a confrontation between governments. It was a form of confrontation for which China, with no foreign office and no diplomatic service, was ill prepared. In the showdown that followed the Canton system was ended and the tributary system struck a mortal blow.

The Treaty Port System: A Variant of Commercial Colonialism

The fighting that the opium question precipitated demonstrated the superiority of British firepower and the vulnerability of the Chinese coast to mobile naval forces. A threat to the city of Nanking obliged the Manchus to sue for peace. Imperial clansmen were sent as imperial commissioners to do the negotiating, since important concessions were required from the emperor. In the early 1840s treaties were signed with Britain, France, and the United States. These were the first of the "unequal treaties" that regularized the forms of European domination in China. As agreements between technically sovereign governments, couched in terms of Western international law, the treaties violated the spirit of the Chinese tributary system by compelling the emperor to recognize and deal with foreign rulers on a basis of equality. The actual content of the treaties was worse since China was really in an inferior position, in effect granting as rights to the Westerners special concessions made at gunpoint. In the first round of treaties the British were given the island of Hong Kong, five coastal ports were opened to Western residence and trade, the Chinese were prohibited from funneling trade through merchant monopolies, and tariffs were set at a low rate favorable to the foreigners. Opium smuggling was not dealt with.

In retrospect the unequal treaties mark the beginning of China's "open century," which was to last until 1950. The opening of China effected by Western military force should not be viewed simply in the context of economic exploitation; it was of great importance in terms of Chinese culture and politics. On the Ch'ing side there was grave concern about the admission of foreigners into China, and resistance to full implementation of the treaties continued for two decades. Although trade developed rapidly at the new treaty ports, particularly Shanghai, conflicts continued to exist, and there was no diplomatic channel through which to clear them up. Official resistance and popular hostility prevented the British from taking up reisdence in Canton. Mounting frustrations led the British and French to seize the city of Canton in 1858 and conduct military operations up and down the coast, which forced the Manchus to negotiate a treaty at Tientsin. One feature of the agreement was the provision for diplomatic representatives to reside in Peking. The Manchus did not intend to honor this agreement and opened fire on the British and French ministers when they arrived off Tientsin in 1859. The response of the European powers was to send a joint military expedition to Peking in 1860. A treaty was signed by Prince Kung, who subsequently led the way in setting up the Tsungli Yamen, an office for dealing with foreign policy questions relating to the Western powers. Gradually the Ch'ing regime began to accommodate to the realities of European power. Western representatives took up residence in Peking, but it was not until 1873 that they were granted an audience with the emperor and not until 1877 that a Ch'ing embassy was established in London.

The treaty ports that sprang up along the China coast from the 1840s on constituted multiple bases for Western commercial and missionary enterprise. Socially and politically they formed a single extended foreign community, which tended to remain sealed off from the deeper currents of Chinese society. Despite great power, the treaty-port establishments never extended their influence to the direct administration of the hinterland or the development of colonies, as was the case in India. In numerous ways they resembled the old Canton factories or the self-governing Arab communities that had been tolerated in Chinese sea ports as far back as T'ang times. Typically the Western merchants in the treaty ports situated themselves along the waterfront outside the Chinese city. The core facilities included a consulate, commercial buildings, warehouses, residences, churches, a club, a race course, and a burying ground. Commercial values set the tone of treaty-port life. Adventurous and ambitious men pursued wealth through the uncertainties of trade. They worked hard, drank heavily, and died young. A mixed population of Chinese driven by hardship from the countryside or attracted by the lure of commerce found employment as servants, prostitutes, laborers, peddlers, clerks, or commercial agents, and the cities grew with explosive speed.

The dominant figure in the treaty port was the consul, who wielded power for the home government, regulated the life of the community, and dealt with the Chinese officials. The contemptuous treatment of the Chinese by the consuls, exploiting the military supremacy of the Western naval forces, has been characterized as gunboat diplomacy. Consuls could, and did, compel cooperation from recalcitrant provincial officials by the simple expedient of ordering their naval forces to bombard them. From the middle of the nineteenth century onward Western powers took it upon themselves to patrol Chinese waters, including the Yangtze River, with their own gunboats to safeguard commerce. This military intrusion into China was seen as part of a civilizing mission to control piracy and impose order where Ch'ing authority was inadequate. The "law" being upheld was embodied in the treaties.

One feature of the treaties particularly galling to the Chinese was extraterritoriality—the exemption of Westerners from the jurisdiction of Chinese law. This meant that Chinese officials were powerless to punish offenses by sailors, merchants, or missionaries, who were answerable only to their own consuls. Sometimes this immunity was extended to protect Chinese in Western employ or converts of Christian missions, in effect denying the Manchu government jurisdiction over its own subjects. Another feature was the most-favored-nation clause, whereby concessions extended to one nation were automatically shared by others. Where the treaties failed to provide adequate basis, rights could simply be asserted. In this manner the treaty ports developed into self-governing communities with their own police, municipal governments, taxes, chambers of commerce, and even courts of law. The foreign settlements in the treaty ports evolved eventually into "concessions" under the exclusive control of foreign governments. These were in effect urban colonies concentrating on commerce and the exploitation of cheap labor in light industries rather than the collection of taxes or the development of plantations as was the case in South and Southeast Asia.

The most subversive group of Westerners who gained access to China during the open century was the missionaries, particularly the Protestants. They were aggressive agents of cultural imperialism, learning Chinese, distributing tract literature, moving among the people in the countryside, setting up schools, and preaching a foreign gospel. The missionary intrusion among the Chinese populace, their criticism of many traditional social practices, and their advocacy of Christian values aroused widespread concern and hostility. Among a credulous population, unused to contact with foreigners, a rich demonology grew up about missionaries, who were said to cast spells and eat babies. These stereotypes were often propagated by Confucian literati jealous of missionary usurpation of gentry functions such as education, moral leadership, and social service. Many practices strange to Chinese experience gave plausibility to lurid rumors—the mystical sacrament of communion, the Catholic concern with the last rites before death, the payment of money by orphanages to discourage infanticide and increase baptisms, the passionate singing and emotionalism of fundamentalist services, and the intimate association between priests and nuns were examples. The fact that the Taiping rebels professed to believe in Christianity did nothing to encourage tolerance among orthodox Confucians. Attacks on missionaries and their converts were frequent occurrences. Serious outbreaks, like the massacre of French Catholics at Tientsin in 1870, led to harsh reprisals by the European powers, punishment of Chinese officials, payment of indemnities, and additional political concessions.

Imperialism

After the fiasco of 1860 China enjoyed a decade of relatively positive relations with the Western powers, who chose to lend support to the Manchu ruling house with the calculation that a continuation of Ch'ing authority would be more conducive to stable trading conditions than a change of government in China. Support included military aid in suppression of domestic rebels like the Taiping and the Nien and even assistance in the collection of customs revenues. Frederick T. Ward, an adventurer from Salem, Massachusetts, organized a mercenary force with Western arms called the Ever-Victorious Army. After Ward was killed, this force was taken over by an English officer, Charles C. "Chinese" Gordon. In the 1850s, when rebel activity drove the Ch'ing officials from Shanghai, the foreign consuls undertook to collect the tariff on behalf of the Manchu government. This innovation was motivated by a fear that failure to uphold the low treaty tariff would result in higher exactions on goods inland. Subsequently there evolved a Maritime Customs Service, which was an agency of the Ch'ing government staffed by Western officers. By 1875 the service employed more than four hundred Westerners from seventeen nations under the direction of an Irishman, Robert Hart. Thus it was that one of the major sources of Manchu revenue was in the hands of foreign administrators.

After 1870 relations with the imperialist powers deteriorated. A particularly stunning blow was an 1895 defeat by Japan in rivalry over Korea, which demonstrated that China had failed to master the weapons and techniques of modern warfare and had been surpassed by an Asian nation the Chinese considered their cultural inferior. As the tide of imperialist competition mounted, China's tributaries were stripped away. Burma was annexed to the British holdings in India, Indochina came under French control, Korea and Taiwan became colonies of Japan, while the Russian empire nibbled at China's northern border and competed with Japan for control of Manchuria. In 1900, attacks by the antiforeign Boxer movement in north China against Chinese Christian converts, missionaries, and diplomatic representatives in the legation quarter in Peking prompted a joint invasion of the Chinese capital by the imperialist powers, including Japan. The ruling Empress Dowager Tz'u Hsi was forced to escape in disguise and severe penalties were imposed on the weakened empire. It appeared at this point that China might be dismembered and turned into colonies. Each power controlled its own sphere of influence—the French penetrated into the southwest from Vietnam, the British dominated the Yangtze valley, the Germans developed a hold on the Shantung peninsula, while the Japanese concentrated on the Liaotung peninsula and Manchuria. Division of China was avoided by an uneasy balance among the powers. The American "Open Door" diplomatic notes of 1899 and 1900 expressed the concern over the possible division of China. The notes to the great powers provided for continued commercial access of all powers to China and the preservation of China as an administrative and territorial entity.

The preservation of a Chinese state facilitated rather than inhibited the economic exploitation of China. Indemnities imposed on the Ch'ing empire following the Sino-Japanese war and the Boxer conflict forced the government to float huge loans through foreign banks at high interest rates. The Boxer indemnity, for example, amounted to a third of a billion dollars, but long-term financing, to be paid off by 1940, would have more than doubled the figure. As penalties for losing wars, the indemnities made no contribution to China's economic welfare. In the first decade of the twentieth century a point was reached where China owed the international bankers more than forty million ounces of silver per year—a sum that exceeded the entire government revenue a hundred years before. The pattern of

11.4 An alleged Boxer poster depicting foreigners in a hostile light. The Boxer movement of 1899-1900 began as a manifestation of popular discontent in north China but was later turned against Chinese Christians and their Western protectors. Source: Arthur H. Smith, *China in Convulsion* (New York, 1901).

large loans at unfavorable rates was continued after the Manchu fall in 1911. Revenues from the maritime customs and even provincial taxes had to be diverted to paying foreign debts. To secure their loans, foreign administrators moved in to reorganize and manage the traditional salt monopoly. In this manner, the nominally independent government of China became in effect a collection agency for imperialist banks.

The major theme of this section has been the domination in China of Western European nations extending their power by sea. This was the pattern in the nineteenth century. But we must consider also two divergences from the pattern—the roles of Russia and Japan—which come to dominate the picture in the twentieth century. The Russian empire expanded eastward by land and was thus viewed from China in the perspective of traditional threats to the northern border. By the seventeenth century the Russians had begun establishing outposts along the Amur River. Vigorous efforts by the early Manchu rulers to deal with tribal peoples in the north included agreements in the 1680s and 1720s with the Russians which confirmed Ch'ing control of the Amur, Manchuria, and Mongolia. These early treaties, written in Latin by Jesuits, had the effect of extending equal recognition to the Russian ruler. The Russians were allowed to maintain a religious mission at Peking and to send trading missions at regular intervals. By the nineteenth century the Russians were able to take advantage of Ch'ing defeats by the other powers to gain concessions. In 1860, for example, they obtained the eastern seacoast of Manchuria and in 1901 they were the leading beneficiaries of the Boxer indemnity. They would have taken over Manchuria, too, had they not been frustrated by the Japanese. Unlike the European maritime pressure, the threat of Russian land expansion to the Chinese frontier has remained to the present day a continuing source of tension.

Japan's imperialist career in China proceeded out of phase with that of the European powers. While the Western powers were preoccupied with the First World War, the Japanese moved in on German holdings in Shantung and in 1915 pressed the Twenty-one Demands on the new Republic of China. These demands, if granted, would have given Japan extensive economic rights in China and virtual control over the Chinese government. When Japanese aims were frustrated by a rising Chinese nationalism, Japan turned in the 1930s to outright conquest. In 1931 Manchuria was invaded and the following year a puppet state of Manchukuo ("Manchu-land") was created using the last emperor of the Ch'ing as a ruler. In 1935 an equally artificial "North China-land" was created to control the provinces around Peking. Full-scale invasion came in 1937, when the government of the Republic of China was driven from its capital at Nanking and the coastal and central provinces were occupied by Japanese forces. When the Chinese Nationalists refused to surrender, the Japanese were obliged to form more puppet governments at Nanking in 1938 and 1940. Thus, when China approached colonial status, it was decades later than other parts of Asia, at the hands of an Asian and not a Western power, and in the form of puppet states rather than an outright colony.

5. MARITIME INTEGRATION IN JAPAN

The Japanese archipelago lies off the extreme eastern rim of the Eurasian continent—the "Far East" from the perspective of an expanding Europe. This geographical fact, coupled with the relative (in comparison to India or China) lack of economic appeal for Europeans, had much to do with the timing and character of Western pressure on the Japanese in the modern era. The Portuguese did not reach Japan until the mid-sixteenth century, some fifty years after the voyage of Vasco da Gama. Although there was initially great enthusiasm among Portuguese and Spanish over the prospects of trade as well as converting the

Japanese populace to Christianity, within a little over a half century the Western sea powers lost interest and all but the Dutch had either withdrawn voluntarily or been driven away. Between the early seventeenth and the turn of the nineteenth century there was no direct challenge to the seclusion policy of the Tokugawa regime. While the Dutch trading post at Nagasaki served as a porthole through which the Japanese and the Europeans were to peer at one another from time to time, with the exception of small numbers of Japanese intellectuals there was little sustained curiosity on either side.

This attitude of mutual disregard was to undergo dramatic change at the turn of the nineteenth century as the expansion of the West brought about a fundamental shift in the geographical context. Whereas Japan had previously been on the extreme eastern limits on the map of Eurasian interaction, barely within the periphery of Western vision, it was now moving steadily closer to the central focus of Russian, British, and American attention in the eastern hemisphere. As the Russians extended themselves across the Urals into Siberia and the North Pacific they found Japan their neighbor. Japan's proximity to China brought it to British attention as the latter concentrated more and more energy on the attempt to open up the Chinese empire. As the Americans discovered they had a Pacific coast and that Japan lay along the shortest route to China and the rest of Asia, Japan ceased to be the "Far East" and became from the perspective of the new United States the "Near West". The result of this new and unwelcome attention was a relentless diplomatic and military pressure on Japan to give up its seclusion and be swept into the new international order.

The Abortive Attempt to Establish Enclaves: 1542-87

The first Europeans in the modern era to "discover" a route to the Japanese islands were the Portuguese, who arrived off the coast of southern Kyushu in 1542. In actuality, these Europeans were following a well-worn sea route that extended down past the coast of China as far as Indonesia in Southeast Asia. Although relatively isolated, the Japanese were by no means secluded at this time in their history. The old Ashikaga overlords, who had maintained a loose hegemony in the fourteenth and fifteenth centuries, had stimulated overseas contact with the outside world by sponsoring official trade with Ming China. With the decline of the Ashikaga, other types of interaction with Japan's Asian neighbors became more important. The most common was an indiscriminate combination of trade, smuggling, and piracy as Japanese seamen mixed with Koreans, Okinawans, Chinese, and other privateers in quest of profits in the China seas. Groups of Japanese adventurers are recorded as far away as Southeast Asia, where some acted as mercenaries selling their services to both sides in the clashes between Europeans and local rulers.

At home during the sixteenth century the political scene was chaotic. Warlords, locked in what was the final phase of several centuries of struggle for political hegemony, were too preoccupied with civil war to divert much attention to matters beyond the borders. On the other hand, the Portuguese were received with considerable interest in Japan in this initial stage. By the 1580s, the Westerners had established trade at several points on the southern island of Kyushu, the most important being Nagasaki, where they had even begun the process of fortifying their position with onshore artillery to supplement their naval firepower. Force of arms, however, was not at this time a significant factor. During these initial decades relations with leading political figures were not only peaceful but friendly. The Catholic priests who played a central role in this early interaction had remarkably good rapport with Japanese lords and their samurai retainers. Both Oda Nobunaga (who emerged as the most powerful of the contending leaders in the 1570s) and Hideyoshi (who was to establish a new national hegemony by 1590) were very favorably impressed by the European churchmen. A number of the more prominent political figures, primarily in Kyushu, actually converted to Christianity, bringing thousands of their subjects over to the new faith The overall picture by the mid-1580s was one of extraordinary success. Jesuit sources claimed over 150,000 converts by 1582 with the number still growing daily (the estimate eventually was to reach 500,000 in a population of approximately 25 million). The Portuguese sea captains had come to dominate the carrying trade between Japan and China, and the Europeans seemed to have a firm foothold as a base for further growth.

The reasons behind this extraordinary success are complex, but several generalizations can be made. The most obvious factor of importance was the political and intellectual climate of Japan at this point. Japan was in a very fluid state, divided politically and very open in its attitude toward the outside world. Trade and especially the firearms that the Westerners could supply offered potential advantages in the domestic struggles of the moment. Moreover, the very pluralism of political power meant that the Europeans could play one leader off against another in their drive to gain opportunities to trade and to proselytize. The fluid state of Japanese politics was paralleled by an openness of mind toward foreign ideas. The Christian missionaries were not confronted with an entrenched orthodoxy, for the Buddhist sects that had once dominated the intellectual and religious life of the country had lost much of their spiritual vigor, with the most important ones concentrating their energies on maintaining a secular base. Because of this, they were looked on by the military elite as local rivals for political authority and economic resources, and the more successful of the warlords—Oda and Hideyoshi in particular—were ruthless in their efforts to crush Buddhist secular power. Such leaders saw little reason to protect the Buddist faith against a new creed. Furthermore, the Catholic fathers had information about distant lands and world events that interested the Japanese elite. Hideyoshi was especially concerned about events in the Philippines. Nor should we ignore the personal appeal of the Europeans with whom Hideyoshi and others came into contact. Francis Xavier and his fellow Jesuits were, for the most part, extraordinarily dedicated men, loyal to their faith, spartan in their daily lives, and willing to sacrifice all for their cause. These were virtues highly valued in the personal code of the Japanese samurai. It has even been suggested that the aristocratic backgrounds of the missionaries and the many coincidental similarities between Iberian and Japanese society at this juncture in history helped to establish rapport and facilitate communication between the samurai warrior and the Jesuit soldier of God. The new religion they preached itself bore enough superficial similarities to some aspects of Buddhism to allow for common discourse.

As time passed, however, the negative side of European presence loomed larger in Japanese eyes. There were clear signs of a growing reaction as early as 1587. In that year Hideyoshi, apparently alarmed by the Portuguese attempt to further secure their foothold on the Kyushu coast and perhaps angered by the arrogant attitude taken by an individual priest, suddenly ordered the foreigners deported. Whatever his motivation, he did not immediately enforce this first exclusion order. Commercial and missionary activity actually increased with the arrival of the Spanish in the 1590s and the British and Dutch shortly thereafter. But friction also increased. Rivalry between the Europeans was intense and each was eager to warn the Japanese of the conquests elsewhere in Asia and the evil intentions toward Japan of the other. Despite warnings the Europeans also became more blatantly involved in domestic intrigue and were increasingly arrogant in their campaigns to convert the populace. Catholicism, insofar as it appeared to demand loyalty to a foreign pope and insofar as it offered a potential tie for binding together dissident warlords, came to be seen as a political threat by the new central regime taking shape in Japan. In the 1600s Tokugawa Ieyasu, who inherited Hideyoshi's position and was determined to create a stable base for lasting central power, adopted a stern policy of suppression of missionaries and monopoly control over foreign trade. Foreign priests were deported or martyred alongside Japanese Christians who refused to recant. Western ships were restricted to Nagasaki and one other Kyushu port in 1616. By 1624 the British had found the terms of Tokugawa trade too unprofitable to continue, while the Spanish were officially excluded because of

Map 50 Maritime integration in Japan

Japanese awareness of their conduct in the Philippines. By 1641 the Portuguese had also been driven off, leaving the Protestant Dutch, who agreed to refrain from preaching religion to carry on a restricted trade from the single port of Nagasaki. In order to complete the severing of ties with the outside world, Japanese were prohibited from traveling abroad.

For the rest of the seventeenth and down through the eighteenth centuries, the Japanese remained outside and largely unaware of the global drama of European expansion. It would be inaccurate to say that the transformation that Europe and areas under European domination were passing through had no effect at all on Japan. The Dutch were a very real, if tiny, conduit for some types of information, and even the Tokugawa authorities who sought most fervently to prevent change did not oppose the importation of knowledge of subjects such as medicine or astronomy. By the nineteenth century the cumulative effects of "Dutch studies" can be seen working as an erosive force—if by no means the primary one—on the cultural base of Tokugawa rule. This is a topic we will return to in subsequent chapters. What needs stressing here is the fact that on the whole contact with the world through Nagasaki had no great immediate significance for Tokugawa society in the seventeenth and eighteenth centuries. The early tide of Western expansion had been turned back by the dikes of the Tokugawa seclusion policy.

Western Imperialism in the Nineteenth Century

The first waves of what was to become a new floodtide of Western expansion began to reach Japanese shores at the very end of the eighteenth century. The Russians, having gradually extended their land empire eastward from their European base, crossed through Siberia to their Pacific frontier. By the 1790s they were probing for weak points in Japanese control over Hokkaido and the northern islands while simultaneously seeking diplomatic and commercial contact with the Tokugawa. The Japanese response was firm, although the Tokugawa leaders did not yet recognize the severity of the storm that was gathering. Russian emissaries were turned away, and when Russian seamen raided northern settlements the Japanese retaliated by imprisoning the crew of a Russian vessel. Distance prevented the Russians from escalating the confrontation despite the fact that by contemporary Western standards the Japanese military defenses were sadly outdated. Nor did the Tokugawa take significant steps to improve them, although somewhat more attention was now given to Hokkaido as an integral part of Japan.

During the Napoleonic wars the vanguard of renewed Western presence in northeast Asia changed as the Russians gave way to the British, who were to continue the policy of threatening military force if diplomatic overtures were repulsed. The incentive for this renewal of British interest in Japan was threefold. As a direct result of their struggles with the French, the British now sought to transfer Dutch bases in Asia to their own control as they did, for example, in Singapore. Thus at one point in 1808 a British warship forced its way into Nagasaki harbor searching for a Dutch prize. Second, and more important, the upsurge of interest in Chinese trade to complement their colonial operations in India naturally brought Japan closer to the focus of their attention in East Asia. Finally during the 1820s and 1830s, whaling in the northern Pacific had become a very profitable enterprise and Japan loomed as a place to provision and shelter maritime hunters.

The other Western nation increasingly present in the North Pacific was the United States; and as the British became preoccupied with the Anglo-Chinese wars of the 1840s and 1850s, it was the Americans who stepped into the forefront of the Western campaign to integrate Japan into the new international order. The Americans, like the British, were concerned about the Japanese treatment of shipwrecked sailors, whom the Tokugawa viewed as trespassers and subject to imprisonment. But Western objectives were much broader than merely securing navigation rights. Japanese ports were to the Americans an essential link in a new passage to the Orient, as way stations and coaling depots for American shipping. The acquisition of California from Mexico and the plans for a transcontinental railroad had given the Americans a vision of a much larger role to play in Asia as a whole. If the China trade was a primary focus, potential profits from commerce with Japan were not to be ignored. Moreover, international trade was often in this American view only one aspect of the overall mission of bringing "civilization" to the non-Christian world. In return for Asian raw materials and exotic products, Americans, like their European counterparts, were intent on exporting the less tangible "goods" of Western religious values, social and political institutions, and even elements of its aesthetic culture.

Thus in 1853 an American naval force under the command of Commodore Matthew Perry—who was intent on success in order to redeem his failure to be promoted to an Atlantic fleet command—was dispatched with orders to open the Japanese islands to navigation, commerce, and diplomatic relations. Having had time to ponder the news of the Opium War in China and confronted with a very immediate threat of American naval attack as well as the possibility of joint action by the British and French fleets operating off the China coast, the Tokugawa agreed reluctantly to negotiate. Beginning with the first American treaty in 1854 and extending through a series of other treaties with Western powers in the 1850s and 1860s, the Tokugawa negotiators steadily gave ground. Although the Tokugawa offered no armed resistance, there were uncoordinated attempts by local domains and individuals to repel the barbarians by force. These brought forth dramatic demonstrations of Western superiority in firepower. In 1863, after an Englishman had been killed by a Satsuma swordsman for an insulting act against the lord of that domain, the British destroyed much of the city of Kagoshima by naval bombardment. The following year a joint Western expedition captured the coastal defenses of the Choshu at the tip of the main island in order to destroy cannon that had been used by that domain to block passage through the Straits of Shimonoseki.

The results of this gunboat diplomacy were fatal to the old regime in Japan. Each of the unequal treaties signed under duress saddled the Tokugawa with heavier burdens and further limited its options. In the first place each included the most-favored-nation clause that prevented the Tokugawa from granting privileges to one power in order to ally with it against the others, as the Tokugawa attempted at one point to do with France. Diplomatically, the West usually presented a united front. Second, this united front was used to deny Japanese markets any real protection against Western goods. Tariffs and other forms of control over imports were carefully restricted, thus dictating to the Japanese a foreign-trade policy designed to benefit the West. Third, although travel in the Japanese hinterlands was limited in the early decades, foreigners were given what amounted to practical sovereignty within their treaty-port settlements, much as was done in China. This included the humiliating and much denounced practice of consular jurisdiction—that form of extraterritoriality that placed foreigners accused of criminal or civil wrongs outside of the control of Japanese courts and into the charge of foreign settlements. The Tokugawa regime, undermined by decades of domestic difficulties, did not long endure the internal reaction against the consequences of these treaties. The acquiescence to foreign settlements, the violent shocks to the economy dealt by the influx of Western goods and the outflow of specie, and their loss of initiative and bankruptcy of policy in foreign affairs precipitated a united opposition among its domestic enemies and brought the regime down in 1868.

The Meiji Restoration of 1868, which established a new set of leaders in Tokyo, will be discussed at greater length in subsequent chapters (see Chapters 12 and 13). In terms of foreign affairs, however, the creation of a new government brought no immediate solutions to the problems confronting Japan. In 1871 approximately half of the central figures in the new Meiji government traveled to America and Europe in an intensive quest for first-hand information that might help in coping with foreign pressure. Then and in subsequent diplomatic encounters the Japanese leaders quickly learned two inescapable truths about the Western posture in global affairs. First, there was no viable alternative for a country as vulnerable as Japan to full integration into the new international order. The Western version of international law and the world view that underlay its basic principles for regulating relations between nation-states would not accommodate East Asian or Japanese traditions of diplomacy any more than the Western theories and mechanisms for international commerce would permit a closed Japanese economy. Second, survival within this new international order as structured by the American and European powers was dependent on gaining acceptance as a full-fledged member of the "community of nations" if one was to have any hope of results at the negotiating table.

The lessons to be drawn from these two generalizations seemed unambiguous to the Japanese leaders. Thus in the decades that were to follow they pursued for the most part a consistent policy aimed at increasing Japanese military and economic power while attempting to persuade the Western treaty signatories that the more humiliating clauses were unnecessary in contracts between civilized nations. Both objectives entailed large-scale importation of elements of Western culture. Matching military firepower and entering into economic competition with the West meant adopting Western technology in weaponry, shipbuilding, textile machinery, and railroad transportation. The demands of a successful foreign policy were also among the more powerful stimuli to importing foreign culture, because "civilized" in the eyes of Western policymakers was defined by Western criteria. Thus, for example, critics of the new civil and criminal laws who complained that they were modeled too closely after European legal codes were met with the argument that, quite apart from the question of the relative merits of traditional Japanese justice, the reforms were necessary if the negotiations to remove the humiliation of consular jurisdiction were to be successful. Foreign values and ideas were also spread as a result of the opening of the country to Christian missionaries, a concession granted in order to gain a better bargaining position on other issues in the treaty negotiations. As we will note later, on the one hand there were other forces at work in facilitating the diffusion of Western culture to Japan, and on the other hand, much of the modernization of Japanese society was not due directly to Westernization in the literal sense. Nevertheless, in order to avoid the fate of India, China, or Southeast Asia, the Japanese accepted much of the impact of Western cultural imperialism.

Japan among the Imperialist Powers, 1868-1911

While being "civilized" was a prerequisite for acceptance at the Western negotiating table, it by no means ensured success. From the Meiji Japanese perspective, success in an age of gunboat diplomacy required gunboats. As Japanese advocates of military preparedness and expansionism have been quick to point out, breaches in the Western united front and the abolition of the unequal treaties were to come only after the Japanese demonstrated proficiency in the new military as well as diplomatic style. In the half century between 1868 and 1918 the Japanese became increasingly involved, sometimes reluctantly but more often eagerly, in the imperialist rivalry for spheres of influence in China, Manchuria, and Korea. Here the familiar combination of motives—economic gain, national and individual glory, and a sincere if self-serving sense of mission—were at work among various individuals and groups as well as the government in Japan. In the case of Korea, in the initial stages there was also the question of national defense, since in the minds of Japanese military planners that peninsula was of special strategic concern.

Japan began to exert its influence beyond its own borders in 1875. Although the majority of Meiji leaders had vetoed a proposal in 1873 to go to war with their Korean neighbors in an attempt to open new diplomatic and commercial relations, they did sanction a modified version of Perry's tactics to pressure the Korean government into allowing Japan to open trade. In 1895, after two frustrating decades of rivalry with China—which viewed Korea as a traditional tributary state—in the turbulence of Korean politics, the Japanese startled the West by defeating the larger and presumably more powerful Chinese military. Although Russia, backed by France and Germany, denied the Japanese some of the fruits of that victory—notably a naval base at what was to become Port Arthur on the Liaotung peninsula—the Japanese were grudgingly allowed into the privileged ranks of foreigners in Shanghai, and Taiwan became Japan's first colonial possession in the modern era.

The question of Korea, however, was not settled in the Sino-Japanese War of 1895. Indeed, the question became more heated as the Russians aggressively moved into the vacuum left by the defeated Chinese. It was to be settled only after the Japanese found an opportunity to break through the heretofore united diplomatic and military front of the Western powers. The opportunity came as a result of British-Russian rivalries. Russian activity along the entire shared border with British Asian colonies and spheres, ranging from Turkey to China (where the Russians had violated informal agreements regarding Manchuria), had moved the British to seek allies. The rapid modernization of the Japanese military and the manner in which it had performed in the antiforeign Boxer Rebellion of 1900 led the British to sign the Anglo-Japanese alliance of 1902, trading recognition of Japanese interests in Korea for potential aid in securing the British empire against a European enemy. Thus accepted as a full partner and assured of British aid if Russia's allies should join in any hostilities, the Japanese were in a position to gamble when in 1904 negotiations with the Russians over Korea broke down. The ensuing Russo-Japanese War of 1904-05 marked a crucial turning point in Japanese foreign affairs. The series of land and sea victories against a major Western power astounded much of the world and led directly to a series of bilateral agreements with Russia, the United States, England, and other powers recognizing Japan's exclusive influence over Korea and special interests in southern Manchuria, in return for which Japan guaranteed them that it would not seek to upset the status quo of Western imperialism in South, Southeast, or East Asia. By 1910 Korea had become a formal colony and Japan began to play to the fullest the second of its dual roles in the modern era—namely, as a vehicle for penetrating Asian societies and further opening them to the spread of modernization.

Japan's Dual Role in the Twentieth Century

The phenomena of individuals and groups of Asians serving as cultural brokers or agents for Western penetration is a familiar one in the modern era. Japan as a nation-state was to play an analogous role as both recipient and transmitter of Western impact. As recipient, Japan was caught up in the international forces we have described and suffered some of the same cultural crises that affected other Asian societies. The climax of this role as recipient was to come in 1945, when the country was occupied by American troops for six years and thereafter remained in the position of a quasi-satellite within the American military, economic, and political sphere through the 1950s and the 1960s. This American occupation, however, came after the failure of Japanese imperialist ventures in the 1930s and 1940s. From the point of view of global history, the defeat in the Pacific War was the consequence of Japan overreaching itself in its contest with Western imperial powers in China and Southeast Asia. But there were other consequences. On the one hand, the use of modern, Western-style military technology and industrial economic power in the Japanese attempt to dominate China opened parts of the Chinese hinterland that had previously not yet felt the full impact of Western expansion. As in the colonies of Taiwan and Korea, Japan was the vehicle for the importation of modern institutions and ideas that, although first filtered and adapted in the Japanese context, were largely Western in origin. On the other hand, as a result of the new crisis created by the Japanese invasion, Chinese in ever larger numbers were activated and joined political movements aimed at driving out both Western and Japanese imperialism. This consequence was even clearer in Southeast Asia, where Japanese victories in the early 1940s destroyed the bases for British, Dutch, and French rule. Thus, in the immediate postwar period the Europeans were forced to relinquish their political hold on Burma, Malaya, Indonesia, and parts of Indochina, while the United States finally granted formal independence to the Philippines.

The innumerable twists and turns of the course that led Japan to war with the United States in 1941 are not our concern here, although some of the ideological forces at work in the 1920s and 1930s will be discussed in a later section on Japanese nationalism. Some general propositions can be offered, however, as an introduction to the complex question of why the Japanese leadership, so cautious and successful in the early stages of Japan's expansion, should have become so rash as to commit the nation to a war that in retrospect seems to have held so little prospect of victory. One popular interpretation has been that there were different types of leaders in the 1930s—xenophobes and militarists too intent upon conquest to rationally weigh the dangers, much less the morality, of their policies. The issue of morality aside, this is a gross simplification that has distorted objective study of prewar Japan. While the nature of the internal political crisis of the 1930s is essential to understanding Japanese foreign policy, it is also necessary to consider changes in the international order and their effect on Japan's position within it in the period 1911-41. In 1911 Japan's new-found ability to deal with the West from a position of strength depended

11.5 The triumphant return to Tokyo of Admiral Togo after the capture of Port Arthur in 1905. The victory over the land-based Russian empire (the first reversal for a Western nation at the hands of Asians) marked the beginning of Japan's emergence as an imperialist power. Source: *The Russo-Japanese War*, III, 7 (March, 1905).

on certain fundamental economic conditions: (1) China must remain a source of raw materials and markets; (2) other materials and manufactured goods produced in the West or in Western colonies must be available for continued military security and industrial growth; and (3) there must be favorable trade conditions in Western markets in order to earn foreign exchange to pay for imports. These economic considerations were in turn combined with specific military and diplomatic prerequisites: (1) maintenance of the internal political status quo in China and Manchuria; (2) continuation of the bilateral agreements with the West to ensure no encroachment on Japanese spheres of influence; (3) the existence of the Anglo-Japanese alliance as protection against a Western united front in the event of friction. Each of these conditions for security and affluence underwent a direct challenge in the decades that were to follow.

The Chinese Revolution of 1911 destroyed the status quo and by the late 1920s produced antiforeign movements that challenged Japan's exploitation of China proper and threatened its hold on southern Manchuria. The 1917 Bolshevik Revolution destroyed the detente with Russia and opened the way for Russian encouragement of anti-Japanese activities in China and eventually border skirmishes in Manchuria. The series of post-World War I conferences that began in Versailles and extended through the 1930 London Naval Treaty promised a new era in international relations without specifying the substance or creating mechanisms for regulating it. While the Japanese accepted arms limitations and guidelines for cooperative economic policies in China, they became increasingly aware of the loss of their alliance with England as Anglo-American cooperation grew. With the onset of the depression in the late 1920s Japanese access to Western markets was increasingly frustrated by the drop in demand and the erection of protective tariff barriers. In 1937, after having previously seized all of Manchuria, the Japanese dispatched troops to China to prevent the Kuomintang from asserting control over the northern Chinese provinces and to coerce the Nanking government into suppressing anti-Japanese activities. As Chinese resistance continued despite steady escalation on the part of Japan, the Japanese found themselves vulnerable to Western economic retaliation. The United States threatened to cut off critical supplies such as oil and aviation parts as well as other materials upon which Japanese military and industry depended. Simultaneously, the European powers refused to guarantee uninterrupted supplies from Southeast Asia. By 1940 a major crisis had been created.

It was at this point that the Japanese leaders decided on what they themselves recognized as a fateful gamble to bring about a breakthrough and end the stalemate in China. Counting on German victories in Europe to prevent Russian, British, or French action in Asia, the Japanese executed a rapid series of military strikes aimed at crippling the American fleet and seizing control of critical areas in Southeast Asia. The underlying assumption, as much a hope as a firm conviction, was that the United States, unable to bring its full might to bear, would accept Japanese hegemony over an East Asian Co-Prosperity Sphere, and agree to negotiate an early end to the war. Instead, Japan, the first Asian nation to seriously challenge Western dominance in the contemporary era, suffered total defeat and was stripped of both its military power and its foreign possessions.

CONCLUDING REMARKS

In this chapter we have considered the extension of European maritime activities to a global scale, the resulting patterns of contact between Westerners and the civilizations of Asia, and the gradual emergence of Western European domination in Asia. In view of the fact that the Atlantic seaboard lagged behind many areas of Asia in terms of wealth, resources, technology, and military power at the beginning of the sixteenth century, the comparative historian is challenged to explain why and how the Europeans achieved a dominant position in Eurasia by the nineteenth century. First of all, what factors account for the nature of European maritime expansion? Arabs had traded for centuries along the coastline from eastern Africa to the western Pacific without militarizing their trading stations or seizing adjacent territory. The Chinese had sent powerful naval expeditions as far as Africa in the early fifteenth century, but these had not resulted in colonization or even sustained commercial contact. On land, the expansion of the Russian empire eastward to the Pacific was undertaken in an aggressive drive that was no less vigorous than those of the early periods of Ottoman or Manchu Ch'ing rule, but the Russians consolidated their holdings to a greater degree than did their southern and eastern neighbors.

A perplexing set of problems center around the role of wealth and commercial activity in the transformation of Europe. Why, if European trade with India and China was generally more profitable to the Asians in its initial stages, did the greatest commercial transformation take place in Europe? What values and institutions inhibited Asian entrepreneurs from competing successfully with Westerners? Why in the Asian empires was maritime development and the spread of knowledge about Europe and the rest of the world limited? To what extent can this be attributed to the very stability and affluence that these empires enjoyed in early modern times?

It is clear that the attainment of European domination and the nature of the exploitation that the imperialist powers were able to carry out in each area of Asia depended as much on indigenous conditions as on Western capabilities. Geography can account for some of the differences. The insular sultanates of Southeast Asia were easier to assault in small ships than were the landmasses of the Ottoman or Ch'ing empires. But what explains the fact that India became a colony and Japan did not, or that Europeans made inroads earlier in South Asia than in either West Asia or East Asia? To answer these sorts of questions one must go back to the subject matter of Chapters 9 and 10 and ask how the cultural orientations and the internal decline processes of the early modern empires affected their foreign relations. How did Islamic or Confucian cultural values influence receptivity to Western thought? Or how did the flexible governmental arrangements of the pluralistic Mughul and Ch'ing regimes facilitate the participation of foreigners as technicians, tax collectors, or mercenaries within the imperial system so long as they did not threaten the interests of the ruling group? Again, to what extent did Western power, when exerted through various kinds of indirect rule, act to perpetuate weak or declining Asian governments and thus retard the pace of social change and cultural innovation?

Throughout this chapter it is important to keep chronology firmly in mind to see the attainment of Western hegemony as a relatively brief, if extraordinary, historical era and to avoid the assumption that the transient phase of imbalance when Western power dominated the globe was the result of some innate superiority of people of European stock.

BIBLIOGRAPHY

11.P MARITIME INTEGRATION UNDER WESTERN EUROPEAN DOMINATION: PROCESSES

Boxer, Charles R., *Four Centuries of Portuguese Expansion, 1415-1825* (University of California Press paperback, 1969), 102 pp. Observations on the first maritime empire on a world scale.

Levenson, Joseph R., ed., *European Expansion and the Counter-Example of Asia* (Prentice-Hall paperback, 1967), 141 pp. A brief reader of selections with useful remarks by the editor stressing the problems of comparability and perspective in the study of civilizations.

McNeill, William, *The Rise of the West* (University of Chicago Press paperback, 1963), 828 pp. Part 3 considers the period from 1500 to the present as an era of Western dominance.

Nadel, George H., and Perry Curtis, *Imperialism and Colonialism* (Macmillan paperback, 1964), 154 pp. Selections from academic authorities and historical actors with a useful introductory essay and bibliography.

Parry, J. H., *The Establishment of the European Hegemony, 1415-1715* (Harper Torchbook paperback, 1961), 202 pp. A succinct account of the first phases of Western European domination.

Winks, Robin, ed., *British Imperialism: Gold, God, Glory* (Holt, Rinehart and Winston paperback, 1963), 122 pp. Selected excerpts from important interpretations of imperialism with concise introduction and good bibliography.

11.1   EUROPEAN DOMINATION IN WEST ASIA

Daniel, Norman, *Islam, Europe and Empire* (Edinburgh, 1966), 619 pp. A far-ranging examination of the way in which Europe has impinged upon the Islamic world during the past two centuries.

Lewis, Bernard, *The Emergence of Modern Turkey,* second edition (Oxford University Press paperback, 1968), pp. 40-72. An account of the buildup of European pressure on the Ottoman empire.

————, *The Middle East and the West* (Harper Torchbook paperback, 1964), 140 pp. A brilliant overview by a leading Islamicist.

Pierce, Richard A., *Russian Central Asia, 1867-1917: A Study in Colonial Rule* (Berkeley, 1960), 359 pp. A fine piece of scholarship which is indispensable for the student of Russian rule in Central Asia.

Rustow, Dankwart A., "The Political Impact of the West," *The Cambridge History of Islam,* 2 vols. (Cambridge, 1970), Vol. 1, pp. 673-97. A brief introduction to a subject of great complexity.

Wheeler, Geoffrey, *The Modern History of Soviet Central Asia* (London, 1964), 272 pp. A good introduction to developments since 1917.

11.2   WESTERN EUROPEAN DOMINATION IN SOUTH ASIA

Furber, Holden, *John Company at Work* (Cambridge, Mass., 1948), 407 pp. A readable study of the extension of the British East India Company's trade and administration in eighteenth century India.

Majumdar, Ramesh C., H. C. Raychaudhuri, and Kalikinkar Datta, *An Advanced History of India,* third edition (New York, 1960), pp. 631-771. A standard textbook treatment.

Panikkar, Kavalam M., *Asia and Western Dominance* (Collier paperback, 1969), 364 pp. Western domination viewed by an Indian historian and diplomat; a counterbalance to Europocentric views.

Philips, C. H., *The East India Company, 1784-1834* (Oxford University Press paperback, 1961), 374 pp. British scholarship on the company's history.

Spear, Percival, *A History of India* (Pelican paperback, 1965), pp. 61-157. Accessible account by a leading British authority.

————, *The Nabobs: A Study of the Social Life of the English in Eighteenth Century India* (Oxford University Press paperback, 1963), 213 pp. A lively account of the dominant European elite in South Asia.

11.3   WESTERN EUROPEAN DOMINATION IN SOUTHEAST ASIA

Bastin, John, ed., *The Emergence of Modern Southeast Asia: 1511-1957* (Prentice-Hall paperback, 1967), pp. 1-117. Well-selected readings dealing with the themes of this chapter.

Bastin, John, and Harry J. Benda, *A History of Modern Southeast Asia* (Prentice-Hall paperback, 1968), pp. 1-65. A lucid short essay by two authorities in the field.

Benda, Harry J., "The Structure of Southeast Asian History: Some Preliminary Observations," *Journal of Southeast Asian History* 3.1:106-38 (March, 1962). Offers a framework for viewing Southeast Asian history from within rather than from a European perspective.

Cady, John F., *Southeast Asia: Its Historical Development* (New York, 1964), 657 pp. A standard textbook.

Hall, D. G. E., *A History of South-East Asia* (London, 1955; second edition, 1964), 955 pp. An early overview by a leading authority; delightful to read.

11.4   MARITIME INTEGRATION IN CHINA

Fairbank, John K., *Trade and Diplomacy on the China Coast* (Stanford University Press paperback, 1963), 489 pp. The classic account of the traditional Chinese tributary system and its replacement following the Opium War by a Western-imposed treaty system.

Franke, Wolfgang, *China and the West* (Harper Torchbook paperback, 1967), 165 pp. A brief survey of Sino-Western relations by a leading German sinologist.

Hsu, Immanuel C. Y., *The Rise of Modern China* (New York, 1970), 840 pp. Chapters 7, 8, and 9 describe the traditional system of foreign relations and the encroachment of the West; chapters 12, 13, and 14 take the story through the turn of the century.

Hu Sheng, *Imperialism and Chinese Politics* (Peking, 1955), 308 pp. A Chinese Marxist analysis of modern Sino-Western relations; informed by a strong sense of grievance but still a good corrective to Western accounts.

Spence, Jonathan, *To Change China: Western Advisers in China, 1620-1960* (Little, Brown paperback 1968), 335 pp. Brilliant cameos of representative Westerners, focusing on what they tried to do in China and how the Chinese made use of them.

Waley, Arthur, *The Opium War Through Chinese Eyes* (Stanford University Press paperback, 1958), 256 pp. Translations from Chinese documents arranged to present the Asian perspective on the first great Sino-Western confrontation.

11.5   MARITIME INTEGRATION IN JAPAN

Beasley, W. C., *The Meiji Restoration* (Stanford, 1972), 513 pp. Chapters 3, 7, 8, 9, and 12 treat the impact of the Western threat on Japanese politics in the mid-nineteenth century.

Crowley, James B., *Japan's Quest for Autonomy: National Security and Foreign Policy, 1930-1938* (Princeton, 1966), 428 pp. A revisionist interpretation of the formulation and implementation of Japanese foreign policy in the crucial years to World War II.

Iriye, Akira, *After Imperialism: The Search for a New Order in the Far East, 1921-1931* (Atheneum paperback, 1969), 375 pp. A brilliant overview of the failure to achieve a stable solution to the "China problem" in the aftermath of the First World War.

Mayo, Marlene J., ed.; *The Emergence of Imperial Japan: Self-Defense or Calculated Aggression?* (D. C. Heath paperback, 1970), 105 pp. Well annotated excerpts selected to illustrate the differing interpretations of early Meiji foreign policy, with good bibliography.

Okamoto, Shumpei, *The Japanese Oligarchy and the Russo-Japanese War* (New York, 1970), 355 pp. An analysis of the processes of decision making and the role of public opinion in the late Meiji period.

Passin, Herbert, ed., *The United States and Japan* (Prentice-Hall paperback, 1966), 174 pp. A collection of interesting essays dealing primarily with the postwar period.

GLOSSARY

Alfonso d'Albuquerque. Viceroy of Portuguese India (1509-1515), who established a string of bases from Africa to Southeast Asia in the early sixteenth century.

Barangay. A kinship unit of up to one hundred families, the form of local organization in the Philippines prior to the Spanish conquest.

Battle of Plassey (1757). British intervention into South Asian politics which resulted in the East India Company collecting the land revenue in large area of Bengal.

Boxer movement (1900). A popular uprising in north China that was eventually directed against Christians and foreigners, leading to a joint invasion of Peking by the imperialist powers.

Caciques. An indigenous elite of landholders and administrators who developed under Spanish rule in the Philippines.

Caliph (Arabic, **khalifa**). Originating with the title of the Prophet Muhammad's successor, Abu Bakr, Khalifat Rasul Allah, "Successor of the Messenger of God." The caliph was the head of the Islamic *umma,* "the community of believers," and was referred to as *amir al-muminin,* "commander of the faithful."

Canton system. The complex of institutions by which the Ch'ing government controlled and regulated Western trade with China through officially designated monopoly merchants.

Carnatic wars (1740-65). Power struggle in South Asia between France and England, an extension of their global conflict.

Culture system. Forced delivery of quotas of goods or the equivalent in land and labor imposed in Java by the Dutch East India Company in the 1830s.

Twenty-one Demands. Unilateral demands secretly forced on the Chinese Republic in 1915; would have given Japan extensive power over China.

Dhimmi. A member of a non-Muslim religious community (e.g., a Christian or a Jew) living under the protection of a Muslim ruler in accordance with the requirements prescribed by the Sharia.

Extraterritoriality. The exemption by treaty of Westerners from the jurisdiction of Asian laws.

Hijaz. The central and northern coastal region of western Arabia, in which the Muslim pilgrim cities of Mecca and Medina are located. The ancient overland trade route linking southern Arabia to the Mediterranean world passed through the Hijaz.

Jihad. The holy warfare that Muslims were enjoined to wage against non-Muslims.

Kazakhs. A Turkish people who, since the middle decades of the fifteenth century, have practiced pastoral nomadism in the Central Asian steppe region north of the Aral Sea and the Syr Darya River.

Khan. A title widely used among the Turkish and Mongolian peoples of Central Asia; frequently but not invariably denoting a sovereign authority; also, a military commander, as in Muslim India.

Kipchak. The name given by the Arabs to the steppe region north of the Caspian and the Black seas, and inhabited by predominantly Turkish tribes. The Mongol khanate of Kipchak, known to the Russians as the Golden Horde, was the appanage of the descendants of Chingiz Khan's eldest son, Jochi. Acculturation between the Kipchak Turks and the Turco-Mongol armies of the Chingizkhanids produced the ethnic stock known in later Central Asian history as Tatars.

Magellan's Voyage (1519-21). Expedition for the Spanish crown which opened the way to trans-Pacific penetration of Asia.

Matteo Ricci (1552-1610). Italian Jesuit who devised first successful strategy for gaining residence in China; Jesuits subsequently held minor posts in Peking.

Moluccas. The spice islands, important targets for European traders from the sixteenth century.

Open Door. American diplomatic notes of 1899 and 1900 which advocated keeping China open to exploitation of all the powers instead of dividing it into exclusive colonies.

Opium. A narcotic derived from opium poppy pods, it was smuggled into China by independent merchants under license to the British East India Company, which controlled production of the drug in South Asia.

Özbegs (also, **Uzbeks**). A Turkish people who, since the second half of the fifteenth century, have occupied the area between the Syr Darya and Amu Darya rivers (formerly Russian Turkistan and now divided between various Central Asian republics of the U.S.S.R).

Sino-Japanese War (1895). Japan's defeat of China in Korea; led to a sense of heightened distress in China and the rise of Japanese prestige.

Spanish Armada. Destroyed 1588, a reference date for the tilt of maritime supremacy away from Spain and Portugal, and toward the Dutch and English.

Suez Canal. Opened 1869; marked an intensification of European activity in Asia, facilitated deeper penetration into Asian societies.

Treaty of Tordesillas (1494). Division of the Asian world into Spanish and Portuguese spheres; supplemented by Treaty of Zaragoza (1529).

Tributary system. The traditional Chinese view that they were the center of human civilization, and the institutions that obliged other rulers to submit tribute to the Chinese emperor because he had no moral equals.

Turkistan (literally, "the land of the Turks"). A term sometimes used to describe all those areas of Central Asia inhabited by Turkish peoples. During the nineteenth century, the term Russian Turkistan was applied to the area between the Amu Darya and Syr Darya rivers, together with the steppe region beyond the Syr Darya. The term Chinese Turkistan was used to describe the Tarim basin, modern Sinkiang.

Ulama. The Arabic plural of *alim*, meaning a scholar trained in the Islamic "sciences." Collectively, the *ulama* enforced the Sharia and determined the social norms that governed the life of the Muslim community as a whole.

Unequal treaties. Treaties granting Western powers favorable conditions of residence and trade in China imposed upon the Ch'ing government by force of arms during the nineteenth century.

Vasco da Gama. Circumnavigated the coast of Africa and reached Calicut in southwestern India in 1498; this opened the way for a sea trade between Europe and Asia.

12

The Crisis of Social and Cultural Disintegration

The Crisis of Social and Cultural Disintegration

1700 to 1950

The combination of political decline within and Western penetration from without produced crises of great import throughout most of Asia in the nineteenth and twentieth centuries. Politically, the results became clear as the unity imposed by the large land empires of the Ottomans, Mughuls, and Manchus crumpled. The Islamic world of West Asia was fragmented into a number of kingdoms, sheikhdoms, and small nation-states, most of which became client states of one or another of the Western colonial powers, generally Britain or France. South Asia passed under British control, while Southeast Asia was divided among the Dutch, French, British, Portuguese, and Americans. The Chinese heartland of the Ch'ing empire escaped formal colonial rule, but its satellites were stripped away and foreign domination was established over the coastal areas. In Japan, as in a few other countries, foreign domination was fended off but only after the old regime had been replaced by a new political system.

In the process of the collapse of the traditional empires and their smaller counterparts, the civilizations of Asia entered into a new era of accelerated change. Old elites in the social and economic spheres as well as in active politics found their positions becoming seriously threatened or even untenable. The general populace, whether under colonial rule or that of indigenous governments, experienced various forms of disruption to the preexisting patterns of daily life. Innovations in agriculture and commerce undoubtedly benefitted some segments of society while causing suffering in others, but in either case the older patterns were modified as new trade routes developed, markets shifted or expanded, and the range of commodities available created new demands. New forms of production and trade affected demographic conditions as populations grew in the new urban centers. Wherever such phenomena occurred they had ramifications for the social structure and relations among individuals, classes, and communities.

Dislocations of the political, social, and economic systems of Asian societies tended to erode and undermine cultural self-confidence. Intellectual and artistic integrity was weakened by new values, and the religious consensus of each community became strained as beliefs about the sanctity and efficacy of tradition were challenged.

PROCESSES

a. Commercialization and proletarianization
b. Population change and colonial urbanization
c. Social demoralization and cultural imperialism
d. Displacement of old elites and formation of new counterelites
e. Challenge to cultural symbols and world view

PATTERNS

1. **Social and Cultural Disintegration in West Asia**

2. **Social and Cultural Disintegration in South Asia**

3. **Social and Cultural Disintegration in China**

4. **Social and Cultural Disintegration in Japan**

12. DISINTEGRATION

	1 WEST ASIA	2 SOUTH ASIA	3 CHINA	4 JAPAN
1780				Increased unrest in rural and urban areas
1790	Sultan Selim III, r. 1789-1807			
1800	Qajar dynasty under Aqa Muhammad Khan, 1796	Gradual extension of British administrative institutions from urban centers		
1810	Egypt under Muhammad Ali Pasha, r. 1805-48 Sultan Mahmud II, r. 1808-39 Muhammad Ali Pasha massacres Mamluks, 1811	Growth of comprador class of Indians in British employment		
1820				
1830	Mahmud II suppresses Janissaries, 1826 Death of Abbas Mirza (1833), Iranian crown prince and military reformer	Emergence of Western-educated intelligentsia Calcutta Medical College 1835		Osaka riots, 1837
1840	Tanzimat period 1839-78		Opium War; unequal treaties open ports to foreign residence	

596

		Domestic rebellion		
1850	Importation of modern arms begins 1848 Admiral Perry arrives 1853	Growth of foreign-dominated trade and industry in treaty ports Development of Chinese comprador class	Anti-British uprisings 1857	Dar al-Funun Academy, Tehran 1851
1860	Ports opened 1858 Serious inflation begins 1861 Meiji Restoration 1868		Indigo rebellion 1859-62	Robert College, Istanbul 1863 Galata Saray lycee, Istanbul 1868
1870	First railroad 1872 Military conscription, land reform 1873 Commutation of samurai stipends 1876 Satsuma rebellion 1877	Missionary penetration of countryside		Alburz College, Tehran 1873
1880	Matsukata deflation 1881-85	Limited adoption of Western technology and education	Increased rural unrest and hardship	
1890	Parliament opens 1890; revised civil codes	Defeat by Japan 1895 Chinese-led reform movement fails 1898		Sayyid Ahmad Khan 1817-98, Indian Muslim educationalist
1900		Boxer movement 1900; foreign invasion Manchu reform; constitutionalism End of examination system		Ismail Gaspirali 1851-1914, Crimean Tatar educationalist
1910		Revolution, fall of Ch'ing dynasty 1911 Language reform; shift to vernacular May Fourth Movement; criticism of traditional society and culture 1919		

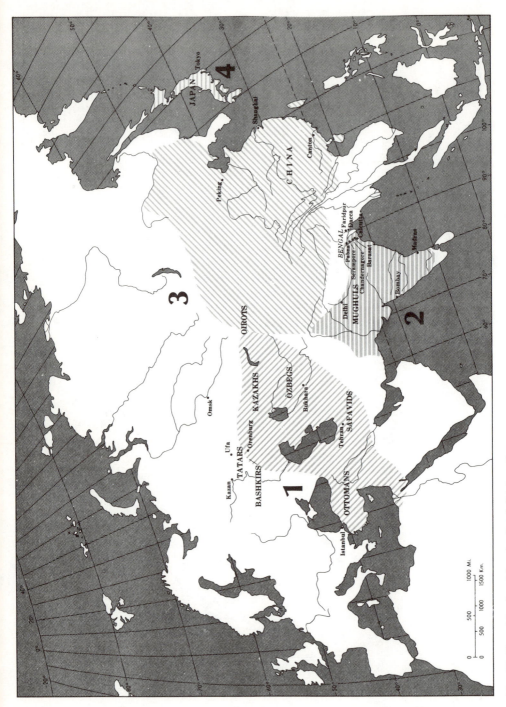

Map 51 The crisis of social and cultural disintegration

PROCESSES

Chapter 10 was devoted to an analysis of the historical developments that sapped the political vitality of the early modern empires in East, South, and West Asia. The present chapter is concerned with a stage beyond that of decline; namely, the disintegration of the old order within Asian civilizations. The distinction between decline and disintegration is a crucial one, for periods of dynastic decline and the fall of political regimes have been recurring phenomena in the history of all civilizations. The decline and fall of empires need not involve fundamental, long-term change in the institutional structure of the society as a whole or alteration of the network of social norms and human attitudes that constitute the cultural system. New political dynasties can be established even by foreign invaders with only marginal disturbance to the underlying continuity of social and cultural life. In the late nineteenth and early twentieth centuries, however, the breakdown of the early modern empires was followed in most areas of Asia by a radical alteration in the basic patterns of these civilizations. The social structure, warped by internal and external pressures and pierced through by foreign influences, began to buckle, the rhythms of daily life were distorted, and the old cultural order began to disintegrate.

The concern here is not so much with the fate of a given political regime or the substitution of foreign for native rulers as it is with the more fundamental question of what ultimately rendered it impossible to reconstruct a stable social and cultural system by merely reassembling the old constituent parts or reestablishing a new political order on the basis of old political principles. What was brought into question by the twentieth century was the very integrity and viability of the civilization itself. The crisis challenged the core of the cultural tradition. Old symbols lost their meaning, fundamental beliefs lost their credibility, and the basic institutions ceased to work. When the early modern empires, which were at once the embodiment and the patrons of tradition, collapsed, they could not be reconstituted. In less visible ways other cultural elements became as untenable as the early modern political institutions became unworkable. In the confusion and humiliation of Western domination it gradually became apparent that the whole civilization was threatened.

Continuities, of course, existed. The rate and scope of change was not uniform and some traditions could be and often were maintained. Yet it is clear that in the late nineteenth and early twentieth centuries most Asian societies were entering an era in which the cumulative effects of new roles in the family, new forces within the marketplace, new perspectives on religion and the meaning of history, and new expectations regarding political power were bringing about a transformation in the shape of the civilization. In retrospect, these changes can be viewed as the first stages of the "modernization" of Asian societies and as such will be discussed once again in Chapter 14; but here the focus is on the disruption and destruction of the old rather than on the creation of a new order. The distinction, like all analytical distinctions of this sort, may seem somewhat artificial, particularly since the passing of the old order and the formation of a new one occurred simultaneously in time; yet it was by no means an abstraction from the point of view of those Asians caught up in the experience of wrenching change and demoralization that marked this initial stage of the modern transformation. Later, when nationalist leaders offered salvation in a future that would transcend the past, the participant's perspective was altered and change took on a more positive aspect. That crucial shift in perspective, however, belongs to the set of processes to be discussed in the next two chapters. In the initial phase change was perceived as the creator of crises.

The most easily identifiable of the many causal factors in the disintegration of the old order within Asian civilizations in the modern era is Western penetration. Thus it is not surprising that much of the writing in Asian as well as Western languages on the history of the last two centuries has been couched in terms of "Western impact" and "Asian response" (or in rhetoric of nationalism and anticolonialism—"imperialist agression" versus "the struggle for freedom"). Without denying the substantial validity of such views, we would modify them by stressing two considerations. First, "Western impact" must not be construed in such a way as to perpetuate the tired cliches about the "dynamic" West and the "stagnant" East. The actors in this drama were Asians as well as Europeans or Americans, and it is necessary to stress the interplay and interaction between them rather than consigning the Asian to the passive role of merely being acted upon or at best reacting to the lead of Western performers. Second, and more to the central issue, the metaphors of impact and response have often led to an oversimplification of the multifaceted character of the Western presence in Asia and hindered the historian's understanding of what it was specifically that Asians were in fact responding to. Economic impact, for example, has too often been characterized in general terms of net loss of precious specie or the unfairness of the tariff provisions in the unequal treaties without asking the further question of what were the actual ramifications of such economic facts for the daily life of Asians involved. Again, in the mid-twentieth century, when political independence from alien rule and the thirst for political freedom have come to be viewed as a natural motivation for all peoples, we are in danger of forgetting that in fact not all people at all times in all civilizations have concerned themselves with such abstractions as national sovereignty, and, indeed, the contemporary meaning of such terms as nation would have been differently understood by most Asians in the early nineteenth century (as would also be the case in earlier periods of European history). The mere replacement of Mughul princes (themselves originally foreigners) by British viceroys or the addition of Europeans to the already-existing dual system of Manchu-Chinese tax collectors was not necessarily viewed at the time as an aberration in the preordained polity or a violation of natural political rights. Moreover, the subjective perspective of the Chinese retailer, the Bengali brahman, the Japanese samurai, or the Syrian peasant was not normally that of a spectator to a global drama of East-West struggle, much less that of a participant in a historical saga involving a dialectical move from feudalism to capitalism to socialism. Such terms could become meaningful only after previous ways of conceiving of one's universe were no longer satisfactory. The central task of this chapter, therefore, is to examine the concrete effects of Western penetration on political, social, economic, and cultural life and to explore how, for example, the influx of French products, the application of Anglo-Saxon real estate law, or Christian proselytizing in an American missionary school might have led to a crisis in these civilizations.

a. Commercialization and Proletarianization

The most thoroughly documented aspects of Western penetration into the life of Asian societies in the modern era are the economic. The ongoing revolution in the techniques of economic organization and industrial production taking place in Europe and North America reversed the comparative economic positions of previous centuries to give the West a clear competitive superiority that it still retains today. The shift of the major East-West trade routes from overland routes to the new highways of the seas disrupted or at least reduced drastically the relative importance of older patterns of international trade. Western dominance over maritime transportation, combined with accumulated organizational experience in investment banking and joint stock companies, which permitted greater concentration of capital and increased efficiency in its systematic utilization, gave the Western European and North American a decided advantage even in the early stages prior to the industrial revolution and full-blown imperialism. Industrialization in the West had by the end of the nineteenth century multiplied that advantage many times. In cotton textiles, for example, the Asian weaver could no longer match the speed of production, the uniformity of quality, or the low costs (even with transportation costs added) of the Manchester mills. Moreover, Western technology continued to give birth to new products—for example, kerosene as a substitute for lamp oil—that often cut deeply into the demand for traditional products produced locally. Gradually many Asian handicrafts that had once outsold their counterparts on world markets sank to the level of exotic curios for the knickknack shelves of Victorian sitting rooms. True, world demand for some items, such as Asian tea and silk, actually increased, and certainly Asian agricultural and mineral production was stimulated by the growth of international trade. But the tight grip of the Westerner on this trade prevented the benefits of this growth from being fully felt in Asia. Even outside those colonial areas where Europeans and Americans had effective political control, the lack of tariffs against excessive imports, the pull of Western demand for raw materials, and the complexities of adjusting to the new international monetary system had numerous and often very grave consequences for the old order.

The influx of cheaper and/or superior manufactured goods had a most direct effect on Asian economic life. This was true not only among urban artisans but in the rural hinterland as well. In many instances, the labor force in Asian handicraft industries was made up of marginal peasants who could remain part-time agriculturalists despite inadequate land holdings only so long as they could earn income in by-employments such as cotton weaving. If that supplemental income dropped because of competition with foreign imports, a peasant cultivator might well be forced off his land to become part of the proletariat dependent entirely upon the sale of his labor. On the other hand, the increase in demand for exportable agricultural commodities—coffee, tea, jute, cotton, or silk—was by no means an unmixed blessing, even where the profits were not completely siphoned off by middlemen and Western shippers. The commercialization of agriculture—that is, the growth of cash crops—upset the existing economic equilibrium in many regions of Asia. Agricultural land and labor were diverted from foodstuffs for local consumption to commercial crops destined for distant consumers.

Not only did the diversion of resources render the conditions favoring famine more likely, it also placed the agriculturalist at the mercy of market fluctuations and phalanxes of middlemen over which he had virtually no control. The linking of domestic economies to international trade meant that the exchange of goods was increasingly dependent upon a monetary system that made the peasant cultivator more vulnerable than ever to those who specialized in the manipulation of coinage, the changers and lenders of money. Where the advantages of larger-scale farming and the need for large amounts of capital were greatest, peasants on small holdings found themselves unable to cope with altered circumstances and lost their land, either to drop to the status of tenant farmers or to join the ranks of rural and urban wage laborers, thus accelerating the process here termed proletarianization.

b. Population Change and Colonial Urbanization

Economic change in Asian societies was accompanied by important alterations in their demographic character in the modern era. With the exception of Japan, Asian populations grew dramatically prior to industrialization, a fact that often meant disastrous pressures on available resources. Standards of consumption, the ecological balance, and the overall quality of human life clearly suffered. The primary causes of this population pressure seem to vary from one area to another and are not in every instance attributable to Western influence. Yet one type of problem was that Western medical techniques modified the mortality rates in Asian societies well before any dramatic increases in the population of foodstuffs became evident. Whereas in the mid-twentieth century the production of foodstuffs and the spread of attitudes conducive to lower fertility have begun slowly to outstrip the rate of population growth, in the early stages overall mortality rates dropped more quickly than did birthrates. The disruptive effects of such demographic changes were great, especially where they were not accompanied by parallel economic development.

Another important demographic change was the growth of new cities. One of the most visually apparent aspects of Western presence in Asia was the port city. Beginning often as a small factory-fort or foreign enclaves in treaty ports, by the end of the nineteenth century such cities as Bombay, Calcutta, Madras, Singapore, Hong Kong, and Shanghai were among the world's largest metropolises. Cities as such were, of course, not new phenomena; indeed, they had always provided centers for important religious, intellectual, and political functions within Asian civilizations. But in the modern era the number of urban Asians swelled enormously (even if this was not always reflected in percentage figures because of the simultaneous growth of total population). These new cities were primarily administrative centers for Western power, entrepots for transshipping commodities, and bases for Western economic penetration into the hinterland. Thus, they were dominated by a European and American presence. The social and political, as well as the economic, life of the members of this foreign elite and their native middlemen or brokers (translators, suppliers, native officials, journalists) constituted a marked departure from the cultural style of older cities. The patterns of economic opportunity, social mobility, family solidarity, voluntary association, education of youth, and the general psychology of the urban populace in these new metropolises came to differ greatly from that of their counterparts in the preexisting urban centers or rural villages. A cultural gap was thus created between those coastal sectors locked into a new international order and the hinterland, where change differed in both pace and direction. It would be a mistake, however, to simply view the new cities as spearheads of progress leading the lagging countryside toward greater prosperity and a better life. In this early stage of the modern transformation, the Western-dominated coastal cities were yet to become centers of industrial manufacturing capable of competing with Western centers of production. Lacking an adequate economic base, these Western-built "gateways to the East" and "jewels of the Orient" typically consisted of densely packed slums in the native quarters segregated from, and in the sharpest contrast with, the spacious parks and wide boulevards of the foreign settlements and cantonments.

c. Social Demoralization and Cultural Imperialism

The social dislocations in both urban and rural areas that were effected by the change we have been discussing were often very severe and were frequently accompanied by widespread disorientation. Family ties were strained as old roles became inappropriate, former expectations were frustrated by new circumstances in the work place, community relations underwent stress as their functions were altered, and traditional truths were no longer confirmed by everyday experience. These tensions and frustrations, especially when combined with economic deprivation and political instability, led to a breakdown of the normative order, to social demoralization. One form this took was increased social violence, such as banditry. A more passive form was self-destructive behavior: the increased incidence of opium addiction in southern China and alcoholism in India. Not only did the Western impact contribute to the root causes of such phenomena, but in these two examples European merchants and colonial governments actually encouraged drug addiction and alcoholism because of the profits and revenues generated from supplying such commodities.

It is one of the great ironies of this period that the agents of Western cultural penetration included large numbers of Christian and secular reformers bent upon uplifting the Asian heathen and cleansing Asian societies of such social evils as opium addiction. Leaving aside the question of motivation and long-run contributions, it is clear that in the short run, missionary support of social welfare provisions, medical services, and educational facilities contributed in substantial ways to the disintegration of the old cultural order. Missionary activity constituted one form of the cultural imperialism that challenged Asian culture with alien views of history and religion, foreign political values and social norms, different methods and standards for ascertaining truth.

Yet another form of cultural imperialism which had demoralizing effects on Asians under Western colonial rule stemmed from the methods of Western bureaucracy. The quest for increased efficiency in colonial bureaucracies often led to the standardization along Western lines of such crucial governmental operations as tax collection and legal codes. Where these involved questions of community relations, religious practices, and other mores and customs, they had ramifications beyond the problems of economic oppression or issues of political freedom. Asians, like their counterparts in Africa, Latin America, and elsewhere, were being challenged on the broader front of the integrity of their own culture.

d. Displacement of Old Elites and Formation of New Counterelites

To this point attention has been focused on the processes of disintegration affecting all levels of Asian societies. As real and significant as these effects of Western dominance often were upon the everyday life of the general populace, they were surpassed in both scope and depth by the direct impact on the old elites within these societies. In colonial areas the former political elite was in some instances simply stripped of its decision-making power. In other colonies and in regions where full colonialism was not established—for example, China—power over certain spheres of public affairs might be retained by indigenous rulers and their officials but were circumscribed by definite limitations or subject to foreign veto. Where Westerners did not themselves fill the positions of the former political elites and political functions did continue to be performed by Asians, there were often changes in the recruitment, training, and style of what were in essence new native elites. Older political roles were modified by Western dominance, and Asian political functionaries served as political brokers between the West and the indigenous populace. Nor was politics the only sphere in which older elites were being displaced. Western presence, by greatly altering the economic circumstances, also served to create a new type of business elite. Older merchants often lost their former preeminence to entrepreneurs specializing in foreign trade and new forms of industry and purveying to the needs of the foreign settlement. In a similar fashion, competition from Christian missionaries, Western-style medicine, foreign educational systems, and Western military science reduced the functions of many types of traditional specialists, thereby eroding their prestige as well as their economic position. Moreover, new professions were generated by the expansion of colonial administration and the growth of Western-dominated cities. Journalists, lawyers, translators, and other types performed the role of cultural (as distinct from economic or political) broker and vied with older professions for social standing in a social hierarchy made more complex by the coexistence of the new with the old. As cultural brokers or intermediaries, they possessed special knowledge of the West and of Western institutions which they interpreted to their countrymen. As both exploiters and part of the exploited, their loyalties were torn. They were a class of marginal men, caught between two parent cultures, neither of which fully accepted them. Although they profited from their roles in the colonial situation, they were never completely assimilated into Western circles by reason of factors such as skin color, religion, and nationality. Yet their countrymen, over whom they wielded considerable influence, often regarded them as agents of an alien civilization.

As might be expected this displacement of old elites supplied the leadership for many types of reaction against foreign dominance. Potentially of greater significance for the twentieth century, however, was the growth of dissatisfaction among members of the new elites. Although these individuals were often the most Westernized of Asians and frequently enjoyed very real advantages as brokers between East and West, many suffered from the frustration of being locked into roles that were both humiliating and in contradiction to the very same political principles (e.g., national self-determination) or social values (e.g., egalitarianism) they had come to internalize during their Western education. Thus, in addition to frustration of political ambitions and resentment at economic deprivation, one may speak of the intellectual alienation of a new native intelligentsia—a phenomenon of central importance in the rise of Asian nationalism.

e. Challenge to Cultural Symbols and World View

In addition to disruptive social processes, the traditional order of Asian civilizations was subjected to attack on the abstract level of symbols of value and truth. The very conception of the universe was challenged by new "scientific" paradigms. Astronomy and cartography changed the shape of the world and altered the human's place in it. The power of scientific models of explanation resides in their ability to predict results and to withstand repeated demonstrations. The utility of a predictive model in a practical field like navigation greatly aided in the adoption of new paradigms. Where the new paradigm conflicted with a traditional belief—for example, that the world is flat—a severe cultural conflict could result. Core values in each civilization, be they religious or ideological, could be contradicted at various points by new modes of scientific thought. Where such challenges were perceived, it was necessary to resolve them by denying the new mode of explanation, by circumscribing its significance (thereby minimizing the conflict), or by adjusting the previously held body of beliefs (changing values).

It should be noted that the development of scientific thought, with its increasingly explicit rules of evidence, testing, and inference, threatened all cultures alike. Science may have posed a challenge to Asian cultural values, but it played no less havoc with European values. Pragmatic Chinese were ready to accept Jesuit astronomers in order to improve their calendar because eclipses could be predicted more accurately; they were unimpressed with other Jesuit lore that rested on faith and authority, such as tales of miracles and salvation. In Europe itself scientific thinking, be it astronomy or the theory of evolution, posed a direct challenge to Christian doctrines central to the Western cultural heritage. So, too, in Asia, the development of a new view of reality undermined the traditional assumptions. Once scientific theories intruded into areas of classical or customary orthodoxy, the intellectual rational for the civilization was threatened.

The crisis of cultural disintegration which we will consider in this chapter marks the culmination of the processes of decline which undermined the early modern empires. In large part, it was Western dominance and the intrusion of European values and institutions into Asian settings which precipitated the crisis of the indigenous order. The resulting destruction, displacement, or discrediting of traditional elements presented Asians with what amounted to a crisis of identity. The more articulate efforts to resolve that crisis led to a series of redefinitions of culture and of civilizations. In the next chapter we will discuss the most outstanding of these revival efforts as cultural renaissance movements that culminated in nationalism and the establishment of independent states throughout Asia.

PATTERNS
1. SOCIAL AND CULTURAL DISINTEGRATION IN WEST ASIA

In the preceding chapter it was stressed that European pressure on West Asia was a relatively late phenomenon, gathering momentum during the eighteenth century but not, except for Russian territorial expansion, taking the form of direct political control before the twentieth century. European expansion as such was not, therefore, the sole cause of cultural disintegration in the Islamic world. That disintegration had begun much earlier but intensified in consequence of European intrusion. This is a problem that has long perplexed Islamicists: Why did Islamic civilization, which in the tenth or eleventh century seemed, materially and intellectually, so far in advance of medieval Christendom, turn in upon itself and assume a torpor from which nothing short of infidel aggression and exploitation could arouse it? It is not possible to explore this fascinating theme here, but certain aspects of the problem must be stressed in order to give perspective to the process of cultural disintegration.

First of all, it should be noted that in the period of the decline of the early modern empires Islamic societies almost everywhere were dominated by military elites, generally of Turkish descent. This process did not begin in the eighteenth century. It had been steadily gaining momentum since the period of Seljuk and Il-khanid rule in Iran, Iraq, and Anatolia and of Mamluk rule in Syria and Egypt, and it had been further intensified under the rule of the Ottomans, the Safavids, and the Özbegs. Closely linked with the militarization of society was a resurgence of tribalism. Wherever tribal chieftains, whether bedouin Arabs, Turcomans, Afghans, or Kurds, could muster a sufficient following, they won the day over the forces of more sophisticated but, from a military point of view, less effectively organized nontribal societies. In the early eighteenth century, for example, Afghan tribalism destroyed in the Safavid regime in Isfahan and then provoked a reaction of Turcoman tribalism which, in the person of Nadir Shah, drew together the two forces and led them into India to destroy the Mughul regime in Delhi. In the tangled knot of mountain ranges where modern Turkey, Iraq, and Iran now share common frontiers, Kurdish tribalism reasserted itself, to remain a potent force down to the second half of the twentieth century and a perpetual thorn in the side of the present-day government of Iraq. In Iran, cultivators and townsfolk alike were held to ransom by powerful tribes such as the Persian-speaking Bakhtiyari and the Turkish-speaking Qashqai. One great merchant family in nineteenth century Shiraz actually accelerated the formation of a new tribal grouping, that of the Khamseh, as a counterweight to the Qashqai, in order to ensure security for the internal trade of the province of Fars. Tribal elites generally proved tenacious of their tribal language, culture and life-style, even when outwardly urbanized and sedentary. Not surprisingly, they tended to be regarded by those who lived under their yoke as ferocious, irreligious, and unpredictable. In the case of nineteenth century Iran, for example, the *ulama,* as leaders of the urban population, came to regard the Turcoman Qajar dynasty as a usurping and illegitimate authority.

The rule of these military and tribal elites placed a great strain on the governing institutions of the traditional Islamic state, which inevitably acquired increasingly military and tribal overtones. Legitimate authority, when pitted against naked force, everywhere lost ground, and the coup d'état became a standard way of bringing about political or social change. One long-standing institutional weakness in Islam had been the failure to develop a law of primogeniture for regulating the succession to the throne, a failure made more serious by the existence of the harem with its unavoidable rivalries among wives and half-brothers. During the period of the early modern empires this weakness became more obvious than ever before. In the great days of the Ottoman empire the successful contender for the throne had arranged for his surviving brothers to be strangled, although in a more humane age this practice gave way to incarceration in cages in the Topkapi Sarayi in Istanbul. In Iran mutilation—blinding or castration—was used as a way of disqualifying rivals from ruling, and in Mughul India recurring wars of succession supplied the epithet *takht ya takhta* (literally "throne or coffin"). The growing ineffectiveness of the civil administration made dynasties increasingly subservient to turbulent and often mutinous praetorians, and whether these consisted of tribal levies like the Qizilbash, or converted slaves like the Janissaries, they enjoyed a free hand to pillage and oppress the very people they were supposed to protect. Prior to Sultan Mahmud II's suppression of the Janissary corps in 1826, the latter had terrorized Istanbul and the other cities of the empire for a century or more, as had the Mamluks in Ottoman Egypt prior to their massacre by Muhammad Ali in 1811.

Nowhere was there any evidence of the emergence of a European-type nation-state, yet loyalty to the traditional rule of sultan or shah was proving difficult to maintain in this age of usurpation and unchecked violence. For the average Muslim there still survived the feeling of belonging to the *umma*, the "community of believers," and with it the concept of the *Dar al-Islam* ("the World of Islam") pitted against the *Dar al-Harb* ("the World of Infidelity"), but in practice his horizons were narrow and parochial and hardly extended beyond his city quarter, his village, or his tribal encampment. Conceivably, he knew less of the outside world than his ancestors prior to the eighteenth century had known, since neither men, nor commodities, nor ideas moved as easily across the Islamic world as they had once done. As for the menace of European intervention, he remained largely unaware of it, while for the most part his rulers pretended not to notice it.

If it is correct to regard the *Dar al-Islam* in the classical period of Islamic civilization as a single *ecumene*, bound together by one faith, one law, and one sacred language, by the eighteenth century regional differences had become almost as apparent as the evidence of a common heritage. The homogeneous character of that civilization had been lessening steadily ever since the Arab element had become diluted in late Abbasid times, and the process had been further accelerated under the Turco-Mongol dynasties of the fourteenth and fifteenth centuries and even more during the period of the early modern empires. Thus, to take the case of the arts, while dome and minaret are universal features of Islamic architecture, the difference between the architectural styles of Ottoman Turkey, Mamluk Egypt, and Safavid Iran is one measure of the growth of regional cultural diversity. Much the same is true in the case of the literature of mysticism, a literature common to virtually all Islamic societies in the early modern period. Once, this literature would have been written exclusively in Arabic. Later, Persian took its place beside Arabic as a language not only for courtiers and bureaucrats but also for Sufi mystics. Throughout the sixteenth, seventeenth, and eighteenth centuries, however, both languages lost ground to new vernaculars. Sufi poetry was now being composed in Ottoman, Chaghatay, and Azari (Azarbayjani) Turkish, while farther afield Urdu, Sindhi, and Bengali in the Indian subcontinent, Malay in Southeast Asia, Swahili in East Africa, and a number of other regional languages became the vehicles for the diffusion of ideas and sentiments once expressed exclusively in Arabic or Persian.

The trend away from universalism and towards cultural parochialism found clearest expression in the spread of the Sufi brotherhoods, which were both the pivotal and representative institutions of the age and without reference to which traditional Islamic society in its last centuries must remain largely incomprehensible. The Sufi brotherhood was no new phenomenon, but it now became ubiquitous, impinging upon almost every aspect of Islamic social life. In an urban setting there were generally close links between the brotherhoods and the artisans, the petty traders, and the guilds. Tombs of individual Sufi saints became shrines, and whether they were located within or near a town or village or in some remote rural setting, they became pilgrimage centers for townsfolk, villagers, and tribespeople alike. The supernatural claims of mendicant dervishes were admitted by all classes of the population, and among the pastoral and mountain tribes (as in the case of the Daghistanis of the Caucasus or the Kirghiz of the Tien Shan) they proved the most effective disseminators of the Muslim faith. Sometimes the dervish convents became centers of political intrigue, linked with antisocial elements such as urban street gangs or rural bandits, and prudent rulers were inclined to placate them, especially in such regions as

Anatolia and Turkistan, where the dervishes enjoyed almost universal support. In the Ottoman empire the head of the Mevlevi order girded the sultan at his accession with the sword of Ayyub, martyr-companion of the Prophet, and the Bektashi dervishes were the spiritual chaplains of the Janissaries, with whom they maintained a turbulent alliance until the suppression of the latter in 1826.

The widespread popularity of Sufi mysticism, institutionalized in the dervish brotherhoods, was a natural response to a period of acute social unrest, physical violence, and spiritual pessimism, the last manifesting itself in attitudes ranging from personal quietism to messianic activism. Normative religious values had failed to meet the emotional needs of the times, which were now answered by the dervishes, with their ecstatic poetry, their esoteric teachings, and their allegedly miraculous and magical powers. No matter that they were ignorant of theology, were often disreputable or immoral, and were sometimes unscrupulous social dropouts who had chosen the holy poverty and idleness of the open road. They carried an appealing message and they were listened to in perhaps much the same way as the mendicant friars of thirteenth century Christendom had been listened to. Inevitably, they reinforced the prevailing intellectual torpor of an age in which, in contrast to earlier centuries, the scientific spirit of inquiry had totally disappeared, genuine learning was rare, such scholarship as there was seemed stunted and pedantic, and the best literature was court literature, the flattering dynastic chronicle and the laudatory ode. In contrast, the visual arts flourished during the sixteenth and seventeenth centuries, benefitting from the immense resources at the disposal of the early modern empires, as can be seen by any visitor to Istanbul, Isfahan, or Delhi. Art historians tend to regard as decadent subsequent eighteenth century developments in the various styles, but the prime cause of this so-called decadence was a drying up of funds, resulting in shoddy or tasteless workmanship and the use of substitute materials.

Commercialization and Proletarianization

Prior to the Portuguese circumnavigation of Africa at the close of the fifteenth century, West Asia had served as the crossroads and marketplace of the known world. Here the commerce carried along the caravan routes and sea-lanes of three continents converged. But with the discovery of the sea route from Europe to India, which was later extended to China and Japan, the economic importance of West Asia declined. This was due in large measure to the fact that although the merchants of West Asia had performed the service of middlemen and purveyors of luxury goods between the markets of China, India, Africa, and Europe, almost from the beginning of recorded history West Asia itself had been the prime source of very few of those commodities. Later, from the sixteenth century onwards, as European merchants and adventurers scoured the non-European world for tropical produce, cash crops, and minerals, they discovered that West Asia, unlike India, Indonesia, or Latin America, had relatively little to offer them. This realization, coupled with an erroneous belief in the military capacity of the Muslim powers and especially of the Ottoman empire, accounts in large measure for delayed European penetration of the area. Not until the opening of the Suez Canal in 1869, the development of commercial cotton growing in Russian Turkistan in the last decades of the nineteenth century, and the shift to an oil-burning economy on the part of the industrialized nations did West Asia resume its former economic significance.

Not that European economic relations with West Asia were of no importance. On the contrary, the importation of precious metals from European possessions in South America had catastrophic effects on market conditions throughout the Ottoman empire from the late sixteenth century onwards. Moreover, during the same period that the rest of Asia was being exposed to European commercial penetration, European manufactured goods and especially textiles were finding expanding markets in West Asia. If the consequences in West Asia were somewhat less severe than in South or Southeast Asia, it was because the European trader in West Asia lacked the coercive support of a colonial regime to assist him in controlling the economic organization of the area. In general, the flooding of the local markets with European goods was less obvious than elsewhere in Asia, partly because it was unaccompanied by steady political pressure and partly because the local agents of European commercial expansion were comprador groups—Muslim, Jewish, and Christian (Greek, Armenian, Maronite, etc.)—who were already the traditional middlemen of the region, and especially of the coastal areas of the eastern Mediterranean seaboard, where there was most European involvement. Because European economic penetration came late and tended to be concentrated in the ports, the traditional economic life of the Islamic city, centering upon the bazaar, survived intact into the twentieth century. It is only in the last decades, and less in consequence of direct European pressure than of a galloping indige- nous consumerism, that the traditional rug merchant has become an importer of wallpapers and bathroom fittings, the erstwhile coppersmith has stocked his booth with transistor radios, and the seller of exotic perfumes has replaced his wares with Parisian cosmetics. Even the physical relocation of the retail trades has been a slow process. In Tehran, which, with Beirut, is the richest and most consumer-conscious metropolis in West Asia, the nineteenth century bazaar long survived as the commercial hub of the city for much of the population, notwithstanding the proliferation of European-style stores, cafés, and boutiques in the newer suburbs.

The discovery of the sea route between Europe and the Far East in 1498 dealt a perma- nent blow to the ancient caravan trade of Central Asia. From very early times, the nomadic tribes of the steppe zone had found it more profitable to protect the caravans passing through their territory (they obtained income both from levying tolls and supplying pro- visions, guards, and guides) than to plunder them, which would have resulted in the merchants seeking alternative routes. It appears, however, that as soon as the overland trade began to diminish in consequence of the opening of the oceanic routes, the Central Asian tribes that had hitherto protected the caravan trade found that source of income drying up and felt tempted to recoup their losses by plundering their erstwhile clients, who consequently felt less inclined to risk their lives and property if it could be avoided. The process is impossible to document but it seems safe to assert that between the sixteenth and the eighteenth centuries the overland routes became increasingly perilous and therefore less used, and by the end of the eighteenth century there can be no mistaking the evidence. The total volume of the caravan trade had shrunk beyond recognition. Enfeebled central governments, suffering from loss of revenue as a result of the contraction of trade, had been compelled to acquiesce in the local predominance of tribal groups, which supplemented their livelihood as pastoralists by brigandage on the roads and blackmail against the towns. Those towns and cities that had been important primarily as a result of their location on the caravan routes, such as Marv, Balkh, Nishapur, Herat, Bukhara, and Kashgar, now became picturesque ruins or survived largely as local marketing centers. The once-renowned prov- ince of Khurasan, stretching from the shores of the Caspian Sea to the Hindu Kush, had become by the beginning of the nineteenth century an undercultivated, underpopulated no-man's land, divided up among rapacious local leaders and exposed to the constant depredations of Turcoman slave raiders from the north and Baluchi slave raiders from the southeast. The story is much the same for the area lying between the Amu Darya and the Syr Darya, and for the steppe zone. The disintegration of the Kazakh empire during the seventeenth century as a result of Oirot and Kalmyk raids, coinciding as it did with the steady advance of Russian outposts along the northern fringes of the steppe zone, resulted in a shift northward in alignment of the east-west caravan routes, seeking Russian protection.

Population Pressure and Urbanization

Accurate demographic statistics for West Asia during the eighteenth and nineteenth centuries are lacking, but prior to the First World War it appears that the region did not experience a population growth comparable to the enormous increase in population that occurred in the Ottoman empire during the sixteenth and seventeenth centuries. In the case of Iran, for example, the population in 1867 was estimated at between 4 and 5 million, in 1913 at 10 million, and in 1968 at 27.3 million. In fact, nineteenth century European travelers in much of West Asia, observing abandoned or shrunken urban settlements and an apparent lack of population, even in relatively fertile tracts, supposed the existing population to be far below what it must have been in the distant past. That the population of West Asia during the eighteenth and nineteenth centuries probably remained fairly static is hardly surprising, since virtually no new external factors were introduced to modify the prevailing life-style. Much of the area was extremely arid and had never sustained more than a small population, consisting mainly of pastoral nomads. Where irrigation was practicable the soil could be extremely productive, but the limited potentialities of preindustrial hydraulic agriculture had been discovered and exploited centuries before. During this period no new crops were introduced, there were no major dietary improvements, and the diseases that had ravaged the area for so long—cholera, plague, smallpox, influenza, trachoma—continued to do so. Since it was only after the First World War that parts of West Asia experienced direct colonial rule, European medical knowledge was restricted to the larger metropolitan centers, and even there it was confined to the occasional missionary hospital or consulate dispensary. In any case, European medicine was eyed with suspicion by the *ulama* and with positive hostility by indigenous medical practitioners. Down to the end of the nineteenth century devastating epidemics continued to take a heavy toll, as did famine. Most famines were fairly local in extent, due to drought and crop failure over a limited area, but mortality could be high because of the lack of means for transporting large quantities of grain from areas where there was a surplus.

If population growth was not characteristic of this period, neither was there a spectacular increase in the size of most cities. Nineteenth century European observers were better placed to note increases in urban than in rural population, but their figures, although rough estimates, seem to imply only a gradual recovery following a period of stagnation and a slow return to the prosperity of earlier times. In contrast to China or India, thriving European treaty ports and colonial settlements were not characteristic of West Asia. The historic metropolitan centers of the Islamic world were generally located inland, away from the sea, and prior to the twentieth century such cities as Damascus and Aleppo in Syria, Mosul and Baghdad in Iraq, Konya, Kayseri, and Erzurum in Turkey, and Tehran, Tabriz, and Isfahan in Iran remained traditional Islamic cities. On the other hand, there were a few coastal cities where the European impact paralleled that in other parts of Asia. Istanbul played host to a large and influential population of European residents, located in their own quarter of Galata, and Alexandria and Beirut also had sizeable European communities. Port Said and Suez came into existence as a result of the building of the Suez Canal. Abadan, with its European residential suburb, developed after 1912 to service the Anglo-Iranian Oil Company's refinery. In areas under Russian rule there were a few European-type cities such as Ashkhabad and Alma-Ata, although Tashkent, despite the Russian appearance of its nineteenth century suburbs, continued to maintain the dual character of a colonial administrative headquarters and a traditional Central Asian caravan city.

Down to the Second World War most West Asian cities retained an appearance that European visitors described as "picturesque." Public buildings in a European sense were rarely to be found, thoroughfares were narrow and tortuous, and most dwellings were single-storied and without external windows, conveying an impression of seclusion and mystery. The skyline was framed by the domes and minarets of mosques and colleges, and often the whole ensemble was still enclosed within massive walls and gateways, encircled by gardens and burial grounds. The nerve center of the city remained the bazaar, while its social organization continued to be shaped by the needs of the extended family. When large-scale developments were eventually introduced these generally left the core of the old city untouched, taking the form of a suburban sprawl beyond the walls. Here, concrete and glass frequently replaced the traditional mudbrick, but the home of the modern businessman, lawyer, or government servant retained its age-old privacy, notwithstanding the imported gadgets and status symbols of bourgeois Europe or America. Only farsighted leaders who understood the link between the physical environment in which Muslims lived and the prevailing conservative temper of society attempted to impose new patterns of living. Thus Mustafa Kemal Ataturk, rejecting Ottoman Istanbul, converted the provincial Anatolian town of Ankara into a new capital laid out in the contemporary architecture of Germany and the Balkans between the world wars. In a similar spirit, Riza Shah Pahlavi imposed a grid pattern upon the labyrinth of streets that had been nineteenth century Tehran and drove wide boulevards through the heart of the ancient cities of Iran, to meet in a central square, adorned with rotary traffic circle, fountain, or statue. In cities far from the sea the presence of Europeans provided an exotic element that barely impinged upon the consciousness of the local populace. In nineteenth century Tehran, for example, the spacious British and Russian legation compounds were enclaves of Europe in the midst of a traditional Islamic city, in no way influencing the life-style of the surrounding population, apart from a handful of servants, tradesmen, and hangers-on. The same could be said of the British and Russian consulates in Tabriz and Mashhad or the British consulates in Shiraz or Kirman. They were centers of imperial power and intrigue rather than of economic or cultural domination. Only in the Mediterranean ports such as Istanbul, Alexandria, and Beirut was there a genuine social response to the European presence, or any genuine process of acculturation.

Social Demoralization and Cultural Imperialism

Social demoralization as a factor in the social disintegration of West Asia was not a process derived exclusively from European intervention but was due also to internal factors already noted—the military and tribal character of later Islamic dynastic history, the debilitating influence of the Sufi brotherhoods, and a loss of intellectual vigor extending back over several centuries. This is not to underestimate, however, the direct consequences of those European pressures, which prior to 1798 were still remote from the heartlands of Islam but which grew steadily in intensity throughout the nineteenth century, reaching their culmination in the first five decades of the twentieth century. Those pressures included territorial aggrandizement in the Balkans, Central Asia, India, and North Africa, resulting in an acute awareness of European military and technological superiority; commercial adventurism, including the granting of loans to rulers in return for favorable concessions and monopolies; diplomatic intervention in the form of the imposition of extraterritorial privileges and of consular courts administering the hated Capitulations; and missionary activity, which, while rarely gaining a convert, furthered the spread of infidel ideas that were already creeping in as a result of personal contacts between educated Muslims and Europeans, often in such forms as religious relativism, positivism, and Free Masonry.

Islamic society responded in a number of characteristic and often atavistic ways to the various pressures that were threatening the established social order. One phenomenon of the period, hitherto little studied, was a rise in the level of urban factionalism and violence. One of the few studies as yet undertaken, of Aleppo between 1760 and 1828, reveals a city torn apart by rivalry between the Ottoman bureaucracy, the *ayan*, or prominent landholders, the Janissary corps, and the *ashraf*, or persons claiming descent from the

Prophet. At the same time, law and order in the surrounding countryside were threatened by the depredations of bedouin Arabs, Kurds, and Turcomans. Much the same kind of situation seems to have prevailed in Damascus, while the history of Baghdad between 1704 and 1831, a period when the city was ruled by virtually autonomous Mamluk governors, was punctuated by manifestations of social unrest, rioting, and coups d'état. Likewise, the sources for the history of Isfahan under the early Qajars illustrate a similar situation, with prominent figures among the *ulama,* supported by gangs of local youths organized in loosely knit fraternities, competing with the shah's officers for control of the city. As always when central governments appeared flabby and ineffective, tribal chieftains levied blackmail upon the villages and towns, sometimes with the cooperation of dissident factions within the walls. In the Ottoman pashalik of Baghdad the threat came from bedouin Arabs and the Kurds, in central and western Iran from the Bakhtiyari, the Qashqai, and the Lurs, and in Khurasan from the Turcomans. Social banditry, highway robbery, and slave raiding became endemic over vast tracts of territory converging upon the modern frontiers of Iran, the Soviet Union, Afghanistan, and Pakistan.

Another apparent characteristic of this period was a rise in the level of the persecution of religious minorities, which rulers were no longer able to or could afford to prevent. Outbursts of mob fanaticism aimed at these minorities tended to be especially common in periods of extreme social tension and unrest. In early Qajar Iran, for example, the level of tolerance for the minorities (Armenian Christians, Jews, and Zoroastrians) seems to have undergone a sharp drop from Safavid times, resulting in well-documented cases of lynching, the seizure of women and property, and enforced conversion. As the nineteenth century wore on, the tendency for minorities to seek outside support from Christian missionary societies, European Jewish and Bombay Parsi welfare associations, and foreign legations increased a popular resentment already fueled by the minorities' long-standing commercial and social contacts with Europeans. For centuries, the Ottoman empire had been a plural society in which the minorities had contributed enormously both to the material welfare and the day-to-day administration of the regime. With the buildup of European pressure on the frontiers of the empire and with the European powers utilizing the grievances of the Christian minorities as an excuse for further intervention, the level of tension between the Muslim majority and the non-Muslim minorities surfaced in increasingly ferocious encounters, of which the Armenian massacres during the First World War were to be the horrific climax.

The Challenge to the Islamic World View

The traditional Islamic world view regarded the Muslims alone as true believers while infidels, unless they accepted conversion to Islam, were condemned to everlasting damnation. Fortuitously for Muslims, this reassuring vision of the afterlife had been confirmed in a practical way during the first Islamic centuries as a result of the visible domination of Muslims over non-Muslims. Thus not only were Muslims, presupposing that they lived godly lives, assured of future bliss, but they also seemed to have within their grasp the good things of this world as well. This favorable historical scenario had been threatened from time to time by such unlooked-for reverses as the Christian reconquest of the Iberian peninsula, the ravages of the heathen Mongols, and the loss of the Balkan provinces of the Ottoman empire, but prior to the nineteenth century such reverses had scarcely impinged upon the awareness of Muslims living in the heartlands of the Islamic world. How then, as the nineteenth century wore on, were Muslims to account for their increasing oppression, humiliation, and exploitation at the hands of unbelievers?

The *ulama,* confronted by this dilemma, reacted in much the same way as the Hebrew prophets had reacted to the woes of Judah, justifying the shame and misery of the present age as divine retribution for a generation of sinners. It is thus no accident that some Islamic reform movements during this period insisted upon a return to the puritanical simplicity and spiritual rigor of a golden age when all Muslims were good Muslims, combined with intensified hostility towards the unbeliever, wherever the latter was encountered. Such movements were frequently spearheaded by the Sufi brotherhoods: Shamil, the Daghistani guerrilla whose protracted resistance to the Russian advance into the Caucasus was noted in the previous chapter, was both a tribal leader and a Naqshbandiyya dervish. The combination of religious reformism or messianic zeal with tribal grievances or unrest could provide one of the most potent forms of resistance to European domination, and Shamil's struggle in the Caucasus had its counterpart in Abd al-Qadir's resistance to the French advance into Algeria in the 1840s, the revolt of the Mahdi in the Anglo-Egyptian Sudan in the last decade of the nineteenth century, the Sanusi struggle against the Italians in Libya, the guerrilla campaigns of Abd al-Karim's Berbers against the Spanish in Morocco, and the conspiracies of numerous "mad mullas" among the Pathans of the northwest frontier of British India.

At a very different level, there was the problem of absorbing modern European science and technology into the traditional Islamic intellectual framework. Muhammad had told his followers to search for knowledge, even as far as China, but nineteenth century European learning clearly involved intellectual criteria wholly at variance with the orthodox Muslim world view. For a long time, therefore, Muslims endeavored to acquire the formulas that seemed to bestow superior power upon their European foes while ignoring the social and educational framework within which the European system operated. Where military skills were involved, would-be innovators such as the Ottoman reforming sultans, Selim III (r. 1789-1807) and Mahmud II (r. 1808-39), Egypt's Muhammad Ali Pasha (r. 1805-48), and Iran's crown prince, Abbas Mirza (d. 1833), introduced European instructors, weapons, uniforms, and drill into their military establishments but failed to perceive that this was not enough. Throughout the nineteenth century only a few farsighted reformers, such as the Crimean Tatar educationalist Ismail Gasprali (1851-1914) and the Indian Muslim leader Sayyid Ahmad Khan (1817-98), realized that it was not enough to acquire European know-how but that it was imperative to come to terms with what lay behind that know-how by acquiring a thorough knowledge of contemporary European higher education, and especially science. Such thinkers continued, however, to advocate the integration of European learning into an essentially conservative pedagogical framework, thereby countering reactionary opposition by arguing that what appeared to be a dangerous infidel innovation was, in reality, a return to what had formerly been a part of Islamic culture but had subsequently become perverted and forgotten by later obscurantist generations. This was the way Abbas Mirza, for example, justified his European-trained troops in the face of criticism from the Iranian *ulama*. Later, in India, Sayyid Amir Ali (r. 1849-1928) defended the Islamic position on slavery and the status of women in his *Spirit of Islam* (1891) by using a similar line of argument.

Displacement of Former Elites and the Alienation of the Intelligentsia

Perhaps because of the innate conservatism of the Islamic social order, it was not until the twentieth century that there was much displacement of incumbent old-style elites by new Westernized elites. Certain powerful groups steadily lost ground during the nineteenth century, such as the *ulama* and the dervishes in Ottoman Anatolia and the tribal khans in Iran, although this became apparent only in retrospect. The gainers, however, were not the numerically small and uninfluential European-educated intelligentsia but the high-level government officials and military officers who half-heartedly adapted European techniques of control and coercion to strengthen their traditional grip on society, a process still to be found in parts of West Asia. Most innovators of the nineteenth century—whether hereditary rulers such as Sultan Mahmud II, talented adventurers such as Muhammad Ali Pasha, or

12.1 Dervishes of the Mevlevi Order of Jalal al-Din Rumi performing their mystical dance at their convent in Istanbul. The decline in the intellectual vigor of Islamic society in the early modern period has been ascribed by some historians to the influence of the dervish orders. Courtesy: Sir Thomas Arnold, *Painting in Islam,* (Oxford, 1928), Plate 42.

reforming administrators such as the leaders of the Ottoman Tanzimat movement between 1839 and 1878—were social conservatives whose main concerns were to renovate or replace decayed institutions, to stabilize and strengthen their own position, and to hold the European imperialists at arms' length. They did not seek to bring about radical changes in the societies they governed. Much the same was true, *mutatis mutandis,* of the more influential commercial and intellectual groups: in order to make any appreciable impact, they had to work within the system. Almost everywhere the authority of the *ulama* was pervasive, even if it was gradually being eroded among those Muslims in close contact with European society. The *ulama* continued to retain their hold over traditional judicial and educational institutions and could still apply the ultimate sanction of the lynching mob. Only very slowly did new occupations develop for the Western-educated elite, as journalists, teachers, doctors, lawyers, agents for European commercial houses, and dragomans (from the Turkish *tercüman,* meaning "interpreter") of the European legations. Training for these new occupations was occasionally obtained by residence abroad—in Paris or St. Petersburg, for example. Sometimes it was acquired in local European schools such as Robert College in Istanbul (founded in 1863) or Alburz College in Tehran (founded in 1873), both of which were established by American Protestant missionaries, or in the Russo-Kazakh schools set up by the colonial administration in Kazakhstan. Of no less importance was the emergence of indigenous schools providing a European-type education such as the Dar al-Funun in Tehran (founded in 1851), the Galata Saray *lycée* in Istanbul (founded in 1868), and the even more influential *usul-i jadid* ("new method") schools, set up by Ismail Gasprali in the Crimea, which were later transplanted by Kazan Tatar educationalists into Turkistan and Kazakhstan.

The spread of such schools was of great significance for the future, but the process was a gradual one and it is important to realize that the acquisition of a formal European-type education or the application of European skills or methods to earning a livelihood rarely impinged deeply upon the private world of family, marriage, religion, and personal philosophy. Naturally there might be some degree of alienation, but before 1914 it was muted: the strength of family ties, loyalties, and obligations, the conservatism of the female members of the household, and the prevailing social milieu all operated in the direction of compromise between conflicting world views. The real challenge, when it came, was not so much the ideas of the West, derived, as all Muslims knew, from a civilization spiritually inferior to their own, but its material prosperity. It is the consumerism of the West, seen at its most aggressive in present-day Beirut or Tehran, that has done more to weaken the structure of traditional Islamic society than any other European challenge, imperialist or intellectual.

2. SOCIAL AND CULTURAL DISINTEGRATION IN SOUTH ASIA

In Chapter 10 the decline of the Mughuls was portrayed as the decline of an early modern bureaucratic empire. Although originally aliens when they invaded the Delhi sultanate, the Mughuls established themselves permanently in the subcontinent, adjusted to the prevailing Indo-Islamic culture and life-style, and contributed to a further synthesis of Hindu and Muslim elements, which constituted a new phase in Indian civilization. The decline of Mughul military power, institutional vitality, and culture was largely an internal affair defined in terms of the prevailing economic, political, and social conditions of the late seventeenth and early eighteenth centuries. Only the most reactionary Hindu nationalist would today argue that Mughul rule, like British rule, was a form of foreign colonial domination. Only if one believes that Hinduism and the Sanskritic great tradition alone characterize the true India can one argue that the Islamic faith and the Iranian cultural heritage of the Mughuls categorize them as alien intruders.

The British impact was another matter, since the pattern of British domination was altogether different from that of the Mughuls. Foreign rule by remote control from London was the crucial factor differentiating the colonial period from the Mughul period, since India under the British was a colony being exploited for the advantage of another country. British economic, administrative, and strategic priorities led to the imposition of alien institutions upon an indigenous culture in order to control and exploit it more effectively.

Commercialization and Proletarianization

The most striking factor in the disintegration of traditional Indian society and culture was the process whereby India was converted into a supplier of raw materials for the factories of Great Britain and into an involuntary market for the finished products from those same factories. Under pressure from the newly emerging British industrial-entrepreneurial elite, India's economy was transformed to meet a new set of economic imperatives. The British developed a technology that made it possible for the interior of India to produce raw materials for the world market on terms highly advantageous to Britain, but Indian society and culture rested on an agricultural order that was to be profoundly shaken by the new economic measures initiated from the 1850s onwards. As commercial agriculture spread, peasants tended to turn to the cultivation of nonfood crops, such as cotton, very often to the point where they had to buy their foodstuffs from local dealers. The commercialization of agriculture made peasants less able to survive poor harvests in periods when the monsoon rains were inadequate. Thus, years of successive drought in the 1870s and 1890s led to widespread famines and much agrarian unrest. It has been estimated that between 1875 and 1900, 15 million people in India died of famine.

Pressure to produce crops for a commercial market resulted in the undue prominence of the moneylender. The moneylender had existed in pre-British India but had played only a subordinate role in the rural economy. But British rule provided highly favorable conditions for expanding the role of the moneylender, who not only provided local credit but also fulfilled the essential role of enabling the cultivator to convert the value of his crop into cash to meet the land revenue demand. If, as often happened, the cultivator defaulted on his debt, the moneylender could use the new British-imposed legal system to gain a hold over the land and possessions of the indebted peasant. This happened not only in India proper but in outlying areas of the British Raj such as Burma, where Indian moneylenders bought up considerable tracts of land from defaulting Burmese peasants.

Local handicrafts and the village artisan class also suffered new competition as the railroads that carried away the commercial crops brought back machine-made industrial products. It has been estimated that in the years between 1850 and 1890, millions of village artisans were compelled to find other ways of earning a living and in most cases the only avenue open to them was agriculture, which, in turn placed further pressure on the available supply of land. The picture is equally grim for the period between 1890 and 1947, since agricultural output rose too slowly to alleviate the problem.

Studies of the province of Bengal under the British suggest that the impact was most devastating in eastern India. This was because in this region the British imposed a land system and a land-revenue collection procedure that not only favored a class of rich landholders (known as zamindars), who were for the most part absentee landlords resident in Calcutta, but completely failed to provide any legal rights for the cultivators until 1859, when for the first time their occupancy right was defined by law. Moreover, in parts of Bengal and Assam the British established a plantation system for the cultivation of indigo and tea, respectively, which in many ways resembled the system imposed on a much grander scale by the Dutch in Indonesia. The indigo disturbances of 1859-62 in Bengal were symptomatic of a number of agrarian disturbances that erupted periodically in the countryside against harsh and oppressive conditions.

Population Change and Colonial Urbanization

By some estimates, India's population increased by over 500 percent in the three centuries between 1650 and 1950—from about 100 million to 532 million. Unlike areas in Europe that experienced demographic changes of similar magnitude, however, most of this increase in India had to be absorbed into the agrarian economy, since industrial growth lagged far behind population growth. The British, it is true, built cities such as Calcutta, Bombay, and Madras, but until the turn of the twentieth century these served purely as administrative headquarters and commercial entrepots, not as industrial centers. As cities, they offered opportunities to the regional elites but not to the masses, and were therefore much less densely populated than they have more recently become. Greater Bombay, which since independence in 1947 has become an enormous city of over 6 million people, had only around 750,000 inhabitants a hundred years ago. Greater Calcutta, which today services the most important industrial area in all of India, has roughly 7 million residents. At the turn of the twentieth century, Calcutta, then the capital of British India and the only large city in all of the eastern Gangetic region, had a population of only 1.25 million.

The opportunities for new kinds of employment that the British provided for Indians consisted largely of administrative and clerical positions in newly established institutions located almost invariably in the cities of their own making. Calcutta is perhaps the best illustration of this because it was the most important city in British India. Here lived the major comprador families and the great absentee landholding elite in eclectically ugly mansions; here were located the best Western-style institutions of higher learning that equipped the indigenous elite to take advantage of the colonialist system; and here were to be had the jobs in agency houses, in the bureaucracy, in the courts, in missionary establishments, in colleges, schools, newspapers, and in the mushrooming voluntary associations. In the nineteenth century there was a large exodus of upper-caste young Bengalis from the rural areas to Calcutta. There they learned English, became socialized to the system, achieved fame and fortune in colonialist-related professions, and almost always invested in land. Productive investment was simply not possible, since industry, when it did finally come late in the nineteenth century (mainly in the form of jute factories), was owned by Europeans. It would be difficult if not impossible to find one family among the three upper castes of Hindu Bengal that was not deeply affected by Calcutta's urbanization process.

These three Bengali upper castes—Brahman, Baidya, Kayastha—so monopolized elitist positions under the British that they constituted Calcutta's most privileged class, known as the bhadralok ("the people of quality"). So successful were they in learning how to manipulate the colonialist system as a "native elite" that throughout most of the nineteenth century they monopolized the best professional positions not only in Calcutta, but elsewhere in South Asia as well. By 1900, for example, in Bengal, the three upper castes of the bhadralok held 80.2 percent of all high government appointments alloted to "natives," though they constituted only 5.2 percent of the total population of the region. Lower-caste Hindus, who constituted 41.8 percent of the population, held only 9.5 percent of high government appointments. Bengali Muslims, who were in the majority with 51.2 percent of the population, held only 10.3 percent of high government appointments.

The point is that cities like Calcutta, which functioned to facilitate British imperial colonialism, did not serve as industrial catalysts for urbanizing the Bengal countryside. The bhadralok gravitated to Calcutta and not only succeeded there but quite often became modernized in the process. But the mass of the people, lower-caste Hindus and Muslims, remained in the countryside, which underwent no comparable change. In fact, the destruction of indigenous "cottage industry" as a result of the importation of mass-produced British goods so agrarianized Bengal that in 1900 half the total urban population of 2.5 million lived in Calcutta. This meant that out of a total Bengal population of 43 million, 95 percent of the people lived in the countryside. Dacca was the only other city in Bengal with more than 35,000 people. Before the rise of Calcutta, Dacca was the most affluent city of Bengal, with an estimated population in 1800 of 300,000, engaged mainly in weaving. But the impact of the industrial revolution in Britain destroyed its textile industry, reducing the population by 1867 to approximately 51,000. Its reemergence dates from the first partition of Bengal in 1905, when it gradually became Calcutta's archcompetitor and a cultural metropolis for Bengali Muslims.

To appreciate fully the impact of colonialism in these terms, one has only to set Indian urban development against that of industrializing Europe. In 1600, 1.6 percent of the estimated population of Europe was urban; in 1700, 1.9 percent; and in 1800, 2.2 percent. Thus, on the eve of England's industrial revolution, Europe, like India, was an overwhelmingly agrarian society. By 1801 about 10 percent of the people of England and Wales lived in cities of 100,000 or larger. This proportion doubled in forty years and doubled again in another sixty years. By 1900, at a time when Bengal was still overwhelmingly agrarian, Britain had become thoroughly urbanized.

Displacement of the Old Elite and Formation of New Counterelites
As British rule supplanted the old Mughul order, many of the old elite roles and functions also changed hands. New administrative offices, new courts, new schools, new services and institutions were created, to be staffed by new men recruited from the indigenous populace and trained by the British.

The British trained and socialized Indians into modern life because they needed native participation in their system. For example, in the period between the 1770s and the 1830s, British institutional innovations in and around Calcutta closely reflected the company's administrative, judicial, and commercial needs. The Asiatic Society of Bengal, which was to prove extremely important for its pioneering work in reinterpreting the Indian tradition, was established not only to encourage scholarly research but also to assist in the intellectual acculturation of British officials in South Asia. Bengalis associated with it not only benefitted professionally by becoming India's first trained archaeologists, ancient historians, philologists and the like, but created a new historic consciousness among the native intelligentsia by zealously pursuing their own pre-Muslim heritage. The College of Fort William, which helped professionalize the interests of the Hindu literati in Calcutta and played a major role in modernizing the Bengali language, was founded as a training center for British civil servants in India. Similarly, the Baptist Mission in Serampore, the earliest Protestant mission in Bengal, accomplished much in the training of Hindus as modern educators, printers, publishers, journalists, and prose stylists, despite its obvious strategic intent of converting Bengalis to Christianity.

This pattern continued throughout the British period. The growth of the legal profession, which was extremely lucrative for many middle-class Bengalis, stemmed partly from the immense amount of litigation over property ownership, a consequence of the Permanent Settlement of 1793, which had established the Bengali *zamindars* as British-style landlords. The need for native doctors to take care of native troops in the army led to the establishment of the Calcutta Medical College in 1835. The later proliferation of institutions dedicated to medical research in Calcutta was a consequence of the strides made in Europe for the prevention and cure of disease.

Although cities like Calcutta provided the institutional setting for the new intelligentsia, it was colonialism and imperialism that moulded the intelligentsia's attitudes, aspirations, and life-style. Calcutta had excellent schools at every level, one of the largest universities in Asia, and the largest number of Western-educated graduates of any Indian city. But the average graduate rarely achieved more than a clerical position in the bureaucracy because the British monopolized the upper echelons, although they willingly hired natives for the thousands of subordinate positions. The British reliance on an indigenous bureaucracy is exemplified by the administrative offices in Calcutta known as the Writer's Buildings, which occupy twelve massive blocks of the city—one of the largest administrative districts in the world.

Another major role assumed by South Asians under British rule was that of comprador. As early as the seventeenth century, when Europeans first settled in the coastal regions of India, the indigenous inhabitants discovered that the newcomers—the masters of ships and guns, of organizational techniques and the domineering manner—were also men of business. The traditional commercial, banking, and clerical castes not only willingly associated with this new kind of merchant but imbibed his values and learned the tricks of his trade. In fact, so pervasive was the commercial role of the indigenous broker in relation to the company agent that, in Calcutta, most of the great families of the nineteenth century owed their wealth and class status to the advantageous associations established by their ancestors with Europeans in the eighteenth century during the vacuum created by the disintegration of Mughul authority which preceded British territorial expansion.

The Tagores, the most famous family of the Bengal cultural renaissance, first accumulated riches in the eighteenth century from profitable relations with the French in Chandernagore and then with the English in Calcutta. Dwarkanath Tagore (d. 1846), sometimes known as the earliest modern Indian entrepreneur and perhaps the most successful of all compradors, also pioneered in such quasi-industrial enterprises as sugar refining, coal mining, and steam shipping. Nabakrishna Dob, who founded the Sabhabajar Raj family, was powerful and wealthy as a result of his close contacts with Clive and Hastings. Gobindaram Mitra made his money as a collector in Calcutta and promptly bought land with it—much to the advantage of his descendants. During the Napoleonic wars Ramdulal Dey built his fortune largely on the American shipping trade, which flourished at the expense of East Indian Company shipping.

The golden age of the comprador was during company rule. From 1750 to 1850 the Bengali compradors steadily rose to prominence in the economic life of the region. By the end of that period they constituted the link between the British trading firms and the indigenous bazaar, and they also provided a significant portion of the capital that British entrepreneurs invested in commercial and plantation enterprises. Unfortunately for India, however, the rise of capitalism in Britain and the rise of imperial colonialism in South Asia inhibited the comprador from productive investment leading to the industrialization of society. Instead, government policy and the desire for social (i.e., *zamindar*) status drove the prominent families to invest in land, leaving the collection of goods from up-country markets to non-Bengalis such as the Marwaris and industrial development to the British themselves. Moreover, after the middle of the nineteenth century, the dimensions of international business under imperialism expanded to a level of organization beyond the comprador's experience and required an access to overseas credits and markets beyond his reach. More and more, comprador families withdrew from commerce, investing their wealth in land while sending their sons into the professions.

Within the comprador class were a number of professional intellectuals whose crucial roles in India and elsewhere were those of broker, mediator, and interpreter, functioning between alien and indigenous cultures. The earliest grouping of this kind in India, and the most important throughout the British period, was the Bengali intelligentsia, drawn from the native elite known as the *bhadralok*, who originated among the three upper castes of Bengal. The intelligentsia came from the villages and towns of rural Bengal to the metropolis in search of opportunity in three distinct phases: first, during the eighteenth century, when the compradors came from near Calcutta and settled in the city; second, during the early nineteenth century, which was the time of the exodus of the literati from the districts of West Bengal into Calcutta; and third, during the late nineteenth century, which saw the arrival in Calcutta of the Hindu elite from East Bengal.

Many of the intelligentsia came to Calcutta as boys and received all their education in the new kinds of educational institutions in the metropolis. More often than not, their earliest exposure to the new learning of the West took place on an elementary level in missionary schools, in Eurasian academies, in the modernized *pathsalas* (indigenous schools) of the Calcutta School Society, or in schools founded by the intelligentsia themselves. On the college level, by 1860 Calcutta had what was probably the most diverse set of institutions of higher learning to be found anywhere within the British empire. Learning English was the key to achieving success within the colonial system, although some members of the intelligentsia achieved the same success through the medium of a modernized Bengali, which was acquiring an expanded and enriched vocabulary as a result of contact with English language and literature.

The pattern of professionalism followed British colonial needs. A sketch of the professional development of some early members of the intelligentsia suggests how the new elite was established in India. Rusomoy Dutt, born into the respectable Rambagan Dutt family of Calcutta in 1780, began his career as a clerk in an English comprador firm at sixteen rupees per week and developed rapidly into what today would be called an efficiency expert. He started his private fortune with a ten thousand rupee bonus awarded him for recommending ways and means of saving the company several times that amount. The British used him later in various administrative capacities. The immense amount of litigation over property ownership, which was partly a consequence of the Permanent Settlement of 1793, made law one of the most lucrative professions for the native elite. Perhaps the earliest of a long line of successful Indian lawyers who fully mastered the intricacies of the foreign-imposed system was Prasana Kumar Tagore (b. 1800), who earned approximately 150,000 rupees a year from legal practice.

The more scholarly intellectuals were recruited in educational institutions such as the College of Fort William and Sanskrit College or apprenticed themselves in occupations and professions related to education and the transmission of knowledge. In return for the specialized assistance of the learned scholar, the government or missionary establishments offered him training as a teacher, prose stylist, philologist or linguist, compositor, printer, publisher, or librarian. A good case in point was Ram Camul Sen, whose intellectual entrepreneurship earned him a rags-to-riches reputation among the Bengali intelligentsia. He found his first job in 1803 as a subordinate clerk's assistant in the Calcutta chief magistrate's office. A year later he got a job in the Hindoostanee Press as a compositor, earning eight rupees a month. Despite his low salary, Ram Camul always performed far more than was required of him, profited from his knowledge of English, and extended his range of contacts. Under the sponsorship of an eminent Orientalist, and utilizing the skills and techniques acquired during his employment at the Hindoostanee Press, Sen began his extraordinary rise as an intellectual entrepreneur. By 1814 he had been appointed the "native" manager of the Hindoostanee Press. During the years that followed, he became the most influential Indian in institutions as diverse as the Asiatic Society of Bengal and the Calcutta Mint. When Sen died in 1844, he left an estate of one million rupees.

Of course, not all members of the intelligentsia were rich and successful under the colonial system. In fact, during the late nineteenth century, the ranks of unemployed or underemployed journalists, lawyers, educators, and other professionals swelled to alarming proportions. Though a medical practitioner such as Durga Bannerji could still make 100,000 rupees in ten years of work, and a civil servant such as Dord Sinha could earn a

12.2 A Hindu husband assaulting his wife with a chopper. The artist intends the couple to represent the new Westernized generation, plagued by the curses of alcohol and adultery. The umbrella and handbag indicate their alienation from the traditional life-style. Bazaar painting (Kalighat style), Calcutta, about 1880. Courtesy: Board of Trustees of the Victoria and Albert Museum, London.

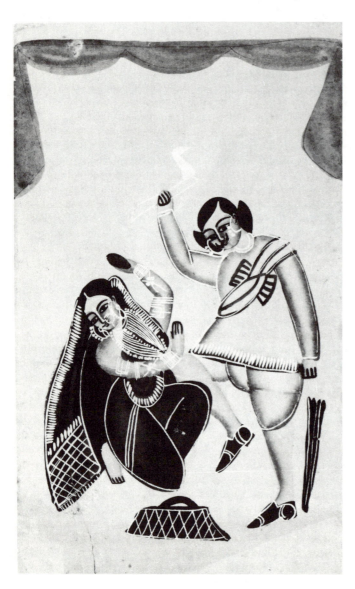

considerable fortune and a title in the bureaucratic structure, the majority of professionals experienced the grim consequences of living in a society that had changed but had not industrialized.

Challenge to Cultural Symbols and World View

Just as rationalism, positivism, and the spread of scientific knowledge challenged and undermined traditional concepts and beliefs in the West, so also in India did these same forces gradually affect the thinking of the more sophisticated strata of the intelligentsia. At Hindu College, established in 1816 in Calcutta, advanced Western learning was first transmitted to Indian students. This institution of higher learning, later known as Presidency College, and staffed for the most part by highly competent British professors from Cambridge and Oxford, exposed thousands of young Indians to such subjects as modern science, mathematics, history, comparative philology and literature, philosophy and the history of Western philosophy. Gradually, through the efforts of missionaries, voluntary associations, and the government, similar colleges were established in Calcutta and elsewhere. Meanwhile, public and private libraries of printed materials increased, as did publishing houses and bookstores. It was not literacy that accounted for the intellectual awakening of Calcutta, since the intelligentsia were largely of the upper castes, who already knew how to read Bengali, Sanskrit, and/or Persian. It was the impact of books and newspapers containing revolutionary new ideas about the physical sciences, society, government, human relations, and history that opened new mental horizons and gave rise to a new conscience and consciousness.

As early as 1830, an entire generation had emerged from Hindu College. Known as Young Bengal, they were influenced by empiricism, utilitarianism, and radical social thought. The early tenets of Comtean positivism, with its stress on atheism, humanism, and the perfectability of mankind through an understanding of sociology, were widely held in Calcutta circles by the 1850s. Meanwhile, young Bengalis were being trained in modern medicine (some went to England and Scotland to study), while other well-educated Bengalis were being recruited into those areas of government service where scientific knowledge was required. It was one such Bengali, Radhanath Sikdar, the head computer of the Trigonometrical Survey, who in 1845 determined by mathematical calculation that an obscure-looking peak in the Himalayas was actually the highest mountain in the world. Although the peak was named after Col. Everest, who was at that time surveyor-general, the real credit for the discovery is due to the Indian mathematician.

The new rational spirit remained under the British artificial and isolated in a society that was not undergoing appreciable socioeconomic and technological change in the direction of industrialization. Thus, P. C. Ray, an eminent chemist, could justify his work in the name of national liberation and ultimately become a disciple of Gandhi. Thousands of Indians had, through the new education and exposure to Western attitudes, lost their faith in the sacred myths, symbols, and values of the Hindu cosmological order, but so long as India and the Indian masses remained backward and underdeveloped, their new enlightenment, although professionally rewarding, culturally alienated them from their own society. The problem of cultural identity became a serious and agonizing problem among the intelligentsia. One solution to the problem was compartmentalization—separating their modernizing attitudes from their day-to-day socioreligious links with the mass of their superstitious countrymen; another was to justify culture in terms of a nationalist ideology. Still others converted to Christianity or to secularism, finding a new life in communities of like-minded Westernized Indians. Another group, to be discussed in the next chapter, sought a middle way between Westernism and militant nationalism, while psychologically averting the pitfalls of compartmentalization. Rather than perceiving innovations from the West as an integral part of Western culture, this group reinterpreted them to conform to

Hindu patterns of meaning while retaining the essence of their original function. This was the path of indigenous modernization that enabled an Indian to be Hindu and modern at the same time. This "Brahmo" path was the prototype for the more progressive sections of the Hindu middle class today.

Social Demoralization and Cultural Imperialism

While the countryside stagnated for lack of economic development, the mass of Indians suffered as their traditional social order disintegrated. Commercialization of agriculture and the moneylender reached beyond the rural areas into the hills and jungles, where tribal peoples hitherto beyond the pale of the Hindu great tradition were swept into the orbit of colonialism. After 1813, India was opened to Christian missionaries who promised salvation from the miseries of earthly existence and equality after death—provided the heathen would convert to the worship of an alien god. Long before and long after the rebellious outbreaks that swept much of northern India in 1857, there occurred in various parts of the country outbreaks of violence among the cultivators, among the coolies in the plantations, among the tribal peoples, and even among the traditional aristocratic elites, who increasingly found themselves deprived of the sources for their wealth and privilege.

There were tensions resulting from social dysfunction in Western countries such as England and Germany too, but these were in a state of transition from an agrarian to an industrial society, whereas India's economy remained for the most part stagnant, first under the East India Company and then under the crown. In colonies like India, the dislocation resulting from modern change was not accompanied by the beneficial aspects of industrial development. Among the intelligentsia of a city like Calcutta, cultural alienation and unemployment and underemployment (which increased dramatically in the late nineteenth century) created enormous tension among many young men, driving some to alcoholism and suicide. Identity crises were created by the tension between traditional responsibilities to family and caste and the requirements of a new commitment to rationalism, reinforced by stirrings of social conscience. Sometimes these identity crises were resolved by an individual's joining a modernizing community such as the Brahmo Samaj or by becoming successful in the British colonial system as a professional. But in many elite families there were instances of failures who sought oblivion in alcohol. The evil was evidently so pervasive among the urbanized middle class that Bands of Hope were organized in Calcutta late in the nineteenth century to combat it, although down to the beginning of the twentieth century the British administration continued to derive a sizeable yield of revenue from the sale of whisky and opium.

For some Indians, the solution to economic stagnation and social dislocation was to seek out opportunities abroad by emigrating to some other part of the British empire. It has been calculated that between 1834 and 1937 about 30 million Indians emigrated overseas. Of these, 23.5 million subsequently returned to India, leaving 6.5 million as a permanent diaspora. Yet the latter figure is far too low, since the emigration statistics are themselves misleading and do not distinguish between Indians overseas who returned permanently to India and those who returned for short visits on family business, to marry, and so forth. Moreover, with the passing of time, the overseas Indian communities grew in size not so much as a result of a continuous flow of newcomers as by natural increase.

Some of these emigrants went to Southeast Asia, to Fiji and Mauritius, and to the Caribbean. Others followed the British flag into the interior of Africa. By the early 1940s there were 2 million in Ceylon, 1 million in Burma, 766,000 in Malaya, and 102,000 in Fiji. By the early 1960s there were 500,000 in Mauritius, 340,000 in British East Africa, 25,000 in British Central Africa, and 480,000 in South Africa. There were 270,000 in British Guiana and 135,000 in Trinidad. The emigrants included both Muslims and Hindus, laborers, merchants, and moneylenders. Some eventually rose to positions of economic power and political leverage, thereby generating bitter resentment among the indigenous Burmese, Malays, or Africans. This movement of people was, in sheer numbers, impressive by any standard, but, set against the vast population reserves of the subcontinent, it did little to relieve the demographic pressure.

Within India itself more violent solutions were sometimes sought, and local uprisings occurred from time to time. The pretexts for these disturbances were frequently expressed in religious terms, but in most cases it appears that they were spontaneous protests against oppressive conditions in which the objects of popular resentment were either the property of the local landholders and moneylenders or the offices and institutions of government. The peasant uprising in Barasat in 1831 fits this description, as do the Faridpur uprisings in 1838-47 and the 1873 agrarian revolt in Pabna, all of which occurred in Bengal. The indigo disturbances of 1859-62 in lower Bengal eventually involved tens of thousands of cultivator-coolies and constituted one of the most widespread protest movements in that region.

Also significant were the predominantly tribal uprisings frequently referred to as "revitalization movements," in which anthropologists have perceived examples of traditional societies and cultures in the process of disintegration fighting desperately for survival. "Revitalization" here refers to the cultural response to severe external intrusion, which was often the direct outcome of the colonial presence, involving administrative encroachment, missionary interference, land alienation, and other causes of agrarian discontent. British power in nineteenth century India was too deeply entrenched and the indigenous resistance far too weak for such uprisings to have any real success. In the twentieth century, however, popular discontent was to be effectively harnessed to the cause of nationalism, the subject of the following chapter.

3. SOCIAL AND CULTURAL DISINTEGRATION IN CHINA

It was clear in 1911 when the Ch'ing dynasty collapsed that an era in the history of Chinese civilization had come to an end. Not only was the Manchu ruling house gone, but gone with it was the imperial system, which was not to be revived. The founding of a republic was more than a change of political institutions; Chinese culture and society were also transformed. Along with the Son of Heaven went the Confucian state philosophy and the social order that it rationalized. The imperial system had been the embodiment of the core values of the traditional high culture, the great tradition. When the imperial era ended that set of cultural symbols lost its cohesion and its utility. The traditional order was a highly refined complex of institutions and values evolved for the management of a society based on agriculture, artisan manufacture, and limited commercial organization. What made the traditional order untenable and led to its disintegration was the onset of a radical transformation of the society resulting from the emergence of an industrial sector that could not be contained within the old arrangements.

Sectors: Coastal and Rural China
The disintegration of traditional Chinese society and culture took a long time, the century from the 1830s to the 1930s being the period in which the essential transformation took place. Causal factors are to be found both within and outside of Chinese society, but the most prominent impulses for change came from the external sources discussed in the preceding chapter. One effect of imperialist encroachment was to divide China into two sectors. It was in the treaty ports along the coast and waterways that Western commerce and industry first began to make inroads into Chinese society. The development of these trading posts into urban centers with Western political, financial, and educational institu-

tions created a new sector of Chinese society distinct from the interior. One cause of the disintegration of traditional Chinese culture was its irreconcilability with the social and cultural forms of this new urbanized, commercialized, Westernized coastal sector. Another cause was the disruptive effect of efforts on the part of the traditional sector, particularly the imperial government, to transform itself in response to the challenges of industrialized intruders. The timing of China's modernization is to be understood in terms of the relationship between this new, rapidly evolving coastal sector and the more slowly changing society of the interior. The sheer immensity of rural China in both area and population meant that the economic and social forces emanating from the urban areas penetrated only slowly. The first stage of disruption of the traditional order was intensified by the imperial government itself, which initiated reforms in response to the challenges of foreign powers. As will be seen in Chapter 13, the second wave of change took the form of national mobilization under the leadership of the modern urban elite. A third stage, to be considered in Chapter 14, saw the emergence of a social revolution in the Chinese countryside.

Development in the Coastal Sector

The processes of commercialization and proletarianization were most fully manifested in nineteenth century China in the treaty ports. Traditional China had commerce and laborers, of course, but mercantile activities were generally well integrated into the dominant complex of agriculture and bureaucracy which linked the countryside and the government. The most lucrative forms of trade, like salt or the export of tea, tended to be organized under officially regulated monopolies, while merchant and craft guilds provided a noncompetitive regulation for the rest. When the treaty ports developed in the 1850s and 1860s, the surrounding countryside, torn by civil unrest, brought forth merchants, craftsmen, and laborers in unlimited numbers to populate the commercial enclaves safe from the imperial government and rebel alike. At the mercy of foreign investors and international trade conditions, they were ruthlessly exploited in a pocket of capitalism beyond the protection of either law or custom as these were known in Chinese society.

The treaty ports and foreign concessions served as centers for the dissemination of European culture in China. Under foreign military domination they were open to a variety of influences. Architecture, commercial practice, dress, and law were some of the areas in which European influences were most obvious. Newspapers were published both in Chinese and Western languages and foreign currencies circulated. Missionaries established churches in the treaty ports as bases from which to fan out into the Chinese countryside. Toward the end of the century the social gospel was emphasized and medical programs and schools eclipsed purely evangelical activities. By the 1920s a string of Christian colleges accounted for a sizeable percentage of the Chinese students receiving a higher education.

The primary economic activity of the treaty ports was interregional and overseas trade. Initially, this was an export trade involving the purchase, storage, and shipment of Chinese agricultural products like tea, hog bristles, and tung oil and handicraft manufactures like silk and porcelain. Under favorable treaty conditions foreign industrial goods came in to challenge domestic products. Western merchants were also in a position to compete with traditional institutions. Steamers, for example, soon surpassed sailing junks in the coastal carrying trade from port to port. Not only were Western ships faster and cheaper, but the Western firms had more convenient credit arrangements, more reliable insurance practices, and superior banking facilities. Light industries were established to take advantage of abundant Chinese labor to process agricultural raw materials using Western equipment. For the most part, this industrial sector was limited to consumer goods that could find a market among those elements of the Chinese population who had money to spend on manufactured goods. Items like matches, cotton textiles, cigarettes, and housewares were produced for local consumption. Vigorous efforts were made to extend the market inland. Oil companies, for example, gave away free lamps to promote demand for petroleum products.

Inevitably, these commercial and industrial centers did have an economic impact upon their hinterlands. Not only did manufactured products compete with handicraft products, but the demand for raw materials, land, and labor modified the patterns of agricultural production. As cities expanded land was consumed for residences and manufacturing sites. Close to the city truck farming was more profitable than subsistence farming, and farther out cash crops like cotton and tobacco often displaced food crops on a greater scale than ever before. Grain had to be brought in to feed the urban population, thereby stimulating the development of a transportation network and demand in rural markets. Some attempt was made to extend rail and road networks out from the new urban centers, but these remained extremely limited by the middle of the twentieth century.

The impact of the coastal cities on the Chinese economy should not be overestimated, however. Even though commerce and industry developed rapidly, the volume was small. The trade from China's ports was only about 1 percent of the world trade volume. By 1933 the output of modern industry amounted to no more than 3.4 percent of the net domestic product. The influence of the urban centers was as much political and cultural as it was economic. Strikes and boycotts of foreign goods by the infant labor movement in the 1920s reverberated throughout China. The business class played an important role in financing and helping to organize the Nationalist government after 1928. The Nationalists were able to form a centralized banking complex and issue a national currency. The reservoir of commercial and industrial expertise which accumulated in this modern sector was later to play an important role in China's industrialization.

Rural China

Despite considerable urbanization and commercial development along the coast and waterways, China failed for a time to undergo a general economic transformation of the sort that turned Japan into an advanced industrial power. Many factors can be cited to account for the inertia of China, but none is more fundamental than the nature of rural Chinese society. China was, and is today, a country in which most of the population is at least partly engaged in agriculture. Of a population that approached half a billion around 1933, 80 percent of the work force, or more than 200 million adults, were in farming households. Traditionally there existed within China a network of cities and trading centers concentrated along internal waterways and meshed with the tax and rice-tribute system that fed the imperial government, the capital, and the military establishment. Too weak in capital resources to accomplish the transformation of the economy, the Ch'ing government lost substantial resources due to domestic rebellion, and the imperialists used indemnities and loans to siphon off whatever could be accumulated at the top. Likewise, the new coastal sector was too small to have much effect upon rural China. Agriculture accounted for 65 percent of the domestic product in 1933, while industry, much of which was still handicraft, and trade amounted to 10 percent each. Nor was foreign investment much of a stimulus. On a per capita basis China in the 1930s attracted only the equivalent of U.S. $3.75 compared with $20.00 for India and $86.00 for Latin America.

Two features of rural China which help explain its slow response to commercial and industrial stimuli are the systems of transportation and marketing which linked the farming regions to the cities and ports. With the exception of waterways, traditional China lacked a transportation network that could move goods efficiently over long distances. The old imperial system of hostels and message depots was designed to move official communications and people on official business with their households and their possessions, but it was not designed to move commercial goods. In areas not served by roads, overland transport moved along paths, carried on the backs of pack animals and sometimes on wheelbarrows, but most often by men either on their backs or by using a variety of arrangements with bamboo poles. Heavy items with a low value per unit of weight, like coal, ore, or even grain, simply could not be profitably moved by such means. There were some flat areas in north China where ox carts were used traditionally, but motorized transport was very slow to develop in the twentieth century. Before 1949 roads tended to be restricted to the immediate vicinity of major urban areas or links between them. Moreover, railroad construction was utterly inadequate. China, which covers an area larger than the United States (including Alaska), by 1945 had only about sixteen thousand miles of track, less than the state of Maine, and nearly 50 percent of that was in the Japanese colonies of Taiwan and Manchuria.

Studies of agricultural development in the Ming and Ch'ing period have shown that Chinese peasants were alert to changing market conditions, new crops, and new techniques—fully as rational in their economic calculations as their counterparts elsewhere. Their options were restricted, however, by the conditions under which they operated. Agricultural China has been portrayed as a cellular structure of peasant villages nucleated about local markets. The positioning of the markets and the areas they serviced was determined by the distance that surrounding farmers could afford to transport their goods—usually a day's walk. Peasants were obliged to do both their buying and selling at this local market, which remained a nearly self-sufficient unit. Some wealth flowed out of the area in the form of taxes and rent (if there were absentee landlords), but little flowed back in. Earnings might be brought in if the villages produced special agricultural products light enough to repay the costs of porterage (like tea or silk), or special handicraft products, or perhaps the export of manpower (as servants, soldiers, or urban workers who might remit some meager earnings). The near self-sufficiency and the poor earning power of these rural units meant that the agricultural sector of China lacked buying power, which in turn meant that there was very weak demand to stimulate production of the industrial sector.

Conditions for the peasantry were generally very bad and did not improve in the first half of the twentieth century. Whole provinces lived closed to the subsistence level with poor diets, bad hygienic practices, and self-denial contributing the undernourishment of the population. Agriculture was labor intensive with only the bare minimum of equipment. Population growth meant that there was an enormous labor reserve, much underemployment, and little incentive to mechanization. It also meant that the most labor-consuming local products were preferable to the cheapest manufactured product. Farms were small, around three acres in the south and five acres in the north, and fragmented into an average of six parcels. Houses were often clustered close together in the dense village settlements the Chinese have historically preferred, but the land was scattered about in tiny plots in a way that inhibited both rational management and efficient assessment. Ownership of farms by the farmers ran around 50 percent, and partial ownership added another 30 percent, with a variety of tenant and sharecropping arrangements accounting for the rest. Tenancy ran highest near urban areas, where city people sought to safeguard their wealth by investment in land.

The small size of farming units meant that they could barely support their operators, leaving little surplus for marketing. An equally serious circumstance was the fact that the bulk of farm produce was in subsistence food crops led by rice and wheat, which were the staples of south and north China, respectively. Low productivity and a large population meant frequent shortages of food. Faced with high rents and high taxes many, perhaps a half of the peasants had to borrow money each year to feed their families between harvests. Credit patterns reveal social structure at the local level. Peasants typically borrowed money at rates that ranged from 20 to 40 percent on an annual basis. Since the borrowing was usually for food it did not constitute a capital investment and made no contribution to production. Over 80 percent of the loans came from merchants, wealthy farmers, land-lords, and village shops. The result was an economic dependency in which the local elite profited from the peasant's deprivation. Wealth extracted from the countryside in this way was often invested in land, contributing to increased tenancy.

Weakening of the Traditional Elite and Social Demoralization

By the twentieth century, numerous forces were at work in the rural areas to break down the existing relationship between the peasantry and the rural gentry. The end of the exam-ination system and the subsequent collapse of the imperial government removed the mechanisms that had legitimized gentry authority. Their privileged position in doubt, land-lords resorted increasingly to organized force to keep the peasantry in line. The militariza-tion of the countryside by both rebel and reformist elements was well underway by the middle of the nineteenth century. The collapse of political authority early in the twentieth century led to warlord rivalries and the countryside suffered the ravages of innumerable rag-tag armies. Partly for security, but also to benefit from the advantages of urban life, many landlords moved to the cities. This broke the reciprocal bonds that had once given strength to the local community. A new class of rent collectors, often armed thugs, acted as middlemen between the absentee landowners and the peasants. Changes in the family system and new attitudes on the part of the younger generation after 1911 led to a weaken-ing of the clan system and a further abdication of responsibility by the elite vis-à-vis their poor relations in the villages.

Failure to provide for the security and well-being of the peasantry led to serious disrup-tions. The reaction of a hostile populace to the subversive influence of missionaries has already been noted. Failure to maintain irrigation systems, control floods, and stock re-serves of grain led to an increase in the frequency and severity of famines after 1870. In a famine situation peasants were forced to sell all their possessions, abandon their land, sell their children, and even at times to resort to cannibalism. Millions died in the biggest famines, many more became refugees. The inadequacy of traditional institutions to handle these emergencies and the activism of foreign missionaries in famine relief and health activities gave additional evidence that the gentry class was not performing its task. The Japanese invasion proved finally that the upper classes were incapable of protecting the mass of the peasantry from the depredations of foreign troops, and stimulated the peasantry to action.

Reform and Disintegration of the Imperial System

It has already been noted in the preceding chapters that in the 1850s the Manchu regime faced potentially mortal challenges from domestic rebels internally and European aggres-sors externally. Instead of collapsing, the Ch'ing empire responded vigorously to both kinds of challenges and lasted another fifty years. When the end finally came in 1911, it was due less to organized opposition, which was not very strong, than to a lack of cohesion. The apparent contradiction between the strength the empire displayed in its earlier response and the weakness that was revealed at the end can be explained in terms of a gradual disintegration that was underway after 1850. To a significant extent, disintegration of the political order was self-initiated. It was precisely the reforms of the late Ch'ing period which undermined the integrity of the traditional order.

Reform was seen by the Chinese and Manchus alike as a necessary evil required to ward off destruction. The banner under which the reformers marched was that of self-strengthening (*tzu-ch'iang*). The idea was to borrow a limited amount of Western learning in order to defend China against further encroachment. In the 1890s this philosophy came to be embodied in the formula of the reformer-official Chang Chih-tung (1837-1909):

"Chinese studies for the base, Western studies for practical application." Unfortunately for China, the compartmentalization of knowledge proposed in this formula was to prove untenable. Limited adjustments, intended to offer short-term relief from pressures for change, accumulated over time until the internal coherence of the old institutions was broken down. Let us consider some examples.

Foreign relations was one of the areas in which the Manchu regime was forced to modify and finally abandon traditional practice. Opening the empire to foreign travel and residence and relaxing the requirements of the tributary system were failures of the most serious sort, for they showed that the emperor could not maintain the integrity of the frontiers, but they were also realistic adjustments that allowed the Ch'ing to coexist with the foreign powers and even to derive some support from them. Acceptance of the treaty system, however, involved institutional changes. Foresighted scholars and officials like Lin Tse-hsu (1785-1850) and Wei Yuan (1794-1856) realized by the 1840s that it was necessary to learn about the Western barbarians in order to deal with them. Western works on international law were translated into Chinese and a number of interpreters and Western affairs specialists were recruited, mostly from the merchant community in Canton. By the 1860s the Tsungli Yamen was created at the capital to deal with coastal defense and the affairs of the Western powers. As a new and unprecedented organization, it marked the beginning of the abandonment of the belief that the basic institutions of the empire were perfect and not subject to modification. In practice, however, the Tsungli Yamen wielded little power. Its influence derived from the membership of influential persons like Prince Kung, who was concurrently a member of the Grand Council. It was a transitional institution that helped to legitimize new forms of organization. Attached to it were the foreign-staffed customs inspectorate and a language school (the T'ung-wen kuan). This latter organization was for years headed by an American missionary, W.A.P. Martin, who introduced Western sciences into the curriculum, in addition to languages. Many of China's early diplomats were trained there. Around 1900 this college for interpreters became part of the new Imperial University, later Peking University, China's most prestigious educational institution.

The first and most clearly focused programs of reform through innovation were those concerned with modernization of the military establishment. We have already seen how the hereditary banner forces lost their effectiveness and how regional forces were created under the command of Chinese officials like Tseng Kuo-fan and Li Hung-chang to suppress the great rebellions of the mid-nineteenth century. It was not long until the need for modern weapons became widely accepted in Ch'ing ruling circles. At first it was assumed that ships and guns and a minimal knowledge of foreign conditions were all that were needed to make China's armed forces the equal of the West. But as new weapons were acquired, as naval vessels were purchased or manufactured, it became clear that only Western-style units could make use of them. There followed the establishment of military schools with foreign instructors to produce a new generation of officers who could replace the Confucian soldier-officials like Tseng Kuo-fan who commanded what were essentially conglomerations of militia units. Yuan Shih-k'ai (1859-1916), a subordinate of Li Hung-chang, was the outstanding example of this new militarist type. In the 1890s he was charged with training a new military force in north China. After 1900 Yuan emerged as the most powerful commander in China. In 1911 he was able to use his modern forces to cause the abdication of the Manchu ruler and to take the presidency of the new republic away from Sun Yat-sen. Many of Yuan's proteges became military governors of provinces and some followed him as presidents.

The most challenging problem involved in adopting Western military technology was the financing and management of a modern industrial base sufficient to supply modern armed forces. The Ch'ing bureaucracy was designed to regulate and collect taxes from a preindustrial grain economy. Chinese officials had little expertise in matters related to science, technology, industry, or capital investment. Therefore, when it was decided to build a modern arms industry the government was obliged to turn to outsiders for help. Capital was provided by the government or raised through subscription, and merchants were recruited to operate the enterprises. Following the precedent of government—commercial enterprises like the salt monopoly, these institutions were referred by the phrase "official supervision and merchant management." Under the patronage of powerful Chinese officials like Li Hung-chang, a variety of enterprises were organized including arsenals, coal mines, a steamship company, a telegraph service, and cotton textile mills. Government participation was necessary to provide the initiative, protection, and influence needed, but it also involved liabilities. Officials might choose to squeeze money out of the enterprises rather than to reinvest it, or they might try to take the enterprise with them by physically taking the machinery when transferred to a new post. A notorious example of governmental interference was initiated by the Empress Dowager Tz'u Hsi (in power from 1862 to 1908), who used funds intended for a modern navy to build a marble pavillion (in the shape of a boat) on a lake at the summer palace.

Merchants who participated in these new "mandarin enterprises" found themselves torn between two worlds and two social systems. Many of the most successful merchant managers gained their early experience working for Western firms in the treaty ports. Once they joined government enterprises they found themselves under the jurisdiction of officials who enjoyed social status and influence by virtue of their examination degrees and official titles. It was only natural, then, for merchants to try to improve their social standing by purchasing degrees and official titles. The sale of degrees to raise emergency revenues was an expedient increasingly resorted to after 1850. The effect of this practice in the short run may have been a stabilizing one since it enabled the government to tap commercial wealth and brought influential merchants into the political arena. In the long run, however, the sale of degrees debased the standards of government service and demoralized those who followed the orthodox academic route. In terms of economic development, the effect was to draw talented individuals away from commerce and industry, thereby discouraging capital investment and entrepreneurship.

Similar cultural conflicts awaited those who acquired expertise in Western technology. Yung Wing (1828-1912), who graduated from Yale in 1854, found it difficult to fit into Chinese society when he returned. His knowledge of English was useful and he was employed in buying American machinery for one of the new arsenals. He was unfit for an official post because of his education, so he served as an adviser to one of the Chinese regional commanders, fitting into a traditional role as a kind of private secretary possessing technical competence but lacking an official position. The need for technical expertise was such that by the 1870s groups of students were sent abroad for training at government expense. The largest program (120 students) included groups that went to Connecticut under the guidance of Yung Wing. Conservatives in the bureaucracy were hostile to such projects for fear that foreign-educated students would have a subversive influence on Confucian values. Upon returning to China these students often found themselves at a disadvantage in competition with regular degree holders. They were usually assigned to technical duties relating to such matters as weapons, shipping, railroads, telegraphy, or mining.

Schooling in Western subject matter involved more than just a threat to the traditional degree holders. Schools established in conjunction with the self-strengthening program stressed technical subjects ranging from basic sciences such as chemistry and physics to applied sciences such as engineering and medicine. Inevitably, however, as students gained proficiency in Western languages, they pursued an understanding of politics, literature, philosophy, and other subjects across the gamut of Western culture. Yen Fu, for example, was trained in an arsenal school to handle technical subject matter, but he went on to become one of China's greatest translators of literature in humanities and social sciences, providing Chinese with a window on the world of English thought. The cultural consequences of the flood of Western ideas into Chinese discourse will be considered in the next chapter. The point here is that pursuit of military modernization had unintended consequences in subverting the very system it was designed to protect.

After the defeat by the Japanese in 1895, Chinese confidence was severely shaken. Reform efforts now entered a new phase. Radical intellectuals such as K'ang Yu-wei (1858-1927) and Liang Ch'i-ch'ao (1873-1929) advocated sweeping changes in the imperial government. Gaining the confidence of the young Kuang-hsu emperor they succeeded in having a shower of reform decrees issued during the "hundred days" of 1898. These measures would have transformed the educational system, reorganized the government, encouraged economic modernization, and generally moved China along the road that Japan had pursued since the Meiji Restoration some thirty years before. Conservative opposition to the reforms led to Kuang-hsu's imprisonment within the palace and a resumption of rule by the Empress Dowager. Here Yuan Shih-k'ai supplied her with the necessary military backing she needed to make her move. The reformers were forced to take refuge abroad as conservative Manchus reasserted their power at court. The division between Chinese and Manchus was now widened and, in growing numbers, young Chinese intellectuals went to Japan for training, and there the first revolutionary organizations took form.

The precarious state of Ch'ing independence following the Boxer fiasco of 1900 compelled the Manchus to undertake their own program of reform. From 1901 to 1905 superficial reforms were carried out which changed the names of many offices, eliminated a number of useless posts, reorganized the military, and established a foreign ministry (under pressure from the powers). The most substantial reforms were those that created a national school system and by 1905 ended the examination system.

Japan's defeat of Russia in that year greatly strengthened the popularity of the idea of constitutional monarchy. Under heavy Chinese pressure, and in part to forestall a growing revolutionary movement, the Ch'ing court endorsed the idea of a constitutional government while seeking to minimize concessions. The old boards were converted to ministries, and provincial assemblies and a national assembly were created. In practice the Manchus actually increased their representation in the top posts while trying to undermine the power of the Chinese governors-general in the provinces. Intending to stall as long as possible, the Empress Dowager in 1908 promised implementation of the constitution in nine years. As it turned out the old woman died within the year and the regents who succeeded her were obliged by pressure from the new provincial assemblies to establish a national assembly in Peking in 1910 and agree to convene a parliament and move to constitutional government by 1913. In this manner did the Chinese capitalize on moderate reforms to demand more extensive change. Although the Manchu regime collapsed in 1911 the expectation of constitutional government was to remain a piece of unfinished business all through the republic period and even after 1949.

Displacement of the Old Elite

The cumulative effect of the changes in both the governmental apparatus and the developing urban areas was to destroy the cohesion of the old social order that had given China stability in the early modern period. The main elements in the Ch'ing ruling structure, the Manchus, the scholar-officials, and the local gentry were all challenged or displaced by new leadership. Those individuals who survived the transition in leadership positions did so by changing roles.

In the early Ch'ing period the Manchus constituted a hereditary ruling group that monopolized the throne and maintained military supremacy throughout the empire. We

12.3 Examination hall in Peking. The Ch'ing abandonment of the traditional civil service competitions marked the end of the era in which Confucian literary training provided the key to power and influence in Chinese society, opening the way to the emergence of new elites. Source: S. Yamamoto, pub., *Peking* (Peking, 1909), Plate 20.

have seen already how the crises of the nineteenth century forced them to defer to the military superiority of the imperialist powers externally while allowing a new class of Chinese military commanders to develop internally. Transition to a republic ended the possibility of hereditary rule and swept away the remnants of the Manchu regime. There emerged after 1911 regional warlords who exercised a purely military power without any basis of legitimacy. In the 1920s the Nationalist and Communist parties emerged as mass political movements with programs for national unification. They competed regionally at first with the warlords, then with the invading Japanese, and finally with each other to end both the foreign intervention and the domestic division that had grown out of Manchu weakness. The leaders who accomplished this reintegration were a new type in China: they were armed with ideologies of broad appeal, headed tightly disciplined mass parties, and commanded modern armies under the control of the party leadership.

The scholar-official class that had dominated Chinese government for centuries lost its position once classical studies ceased to be an adequate preparation for managerial careers. First the intrusion of the West and then the demand for military and industrial technology created needs in government that the traditional elite could not satisfy. Recruitment of foreigners, merchants, and foreign-trained Chinese broke the cultural and political monopoly of the Confucian scholar class. Creation of a modern school system and the abandonment of the traditional examinations severed the tie between education and indigenous culture. Moreover, the schools no longer provided a political orthodoxy.

In the years after 1911 a reform movement modified the nature of the Chinese written language, substituting for the ancient classical language a new popular language (pai-hua, literally "plain talk"). For two reasons, this was a momentous step, as significant for China as the shift from Latin to the modern national languages had been in Europe some centuries before. First, classical Chinese was an archaic language full of literary allusions accumulated since the time of Confucius. Moreover, it corresponded to no spoken form and thus existed only as a means of written communication for those who were initiated into its use. This had the effect of barring all but a favored minority from literacy and, consequently, from government. The creation of vernacular written language made widespread literacy possible for the first time in Chinese history and by so doing broadened the base of political participation. Second, the classical language had enjoyed universality in East Asia. Educated Japanese, Korean, and Vietnamese could use it with the same clarity as could the Chinese. The creation of a Chinese national language, based on the Peking dialect (Mandarin), broke the strongest remaining linguistic and literary link within the East Asian or Chinese culture area.

The gentry class, which had traditionally provided leadership at the local level, losts its legitimacy with the passing of the examination system. Missionaries in the nineteenth century and political cadres after 1920 invaded the countryside to challenge the gentry role. The education of women and the infusion of Western values through new popular magazines and newspapers led to conscious criticism of the family and clan system. Weakening of the traditional bonds that held the peasants and gentry together led eventually to the mobilization of the peasantry, the displacement of the gentry, and a new form of political organization that allowed the peasantry an active role.

4. SOCIAL AND CULTURAL DISINTEGRATION IN JAPAN

The Tokugawa regime was not successful in dealing with the difficulties it faced at home in the eighteenth and nineteenth centuries. The cause of its failure stemmed from its attempt to apply conservative reforms to problems created by major departures from the traditional patterns of economic and social life. Eventually Japan was to face much the same type of cultural disintegration that threatened other societies in Asia. In the Japanese case, however, there were two major differences. First, these disruptive changes were well underway by 1825, more than a quarter of a century before Perry and the opening of Japan to Western penetration. Although the threat of foreign military aggression, the shock of being linked into an international economic system, and the challenge from the influx of alien culture vastly accelerated these processes of disintegration and brought Japan closer to the point of crisis, the crisis had its roots in prior developments within the Japanese society. Secondly, new leadership, willing to make radical alterations in the old forms, seized power in the 1870s. This modernizing elite responded with sufficient speed and flexibility to avert a full-scale crisis such as that in China or in South and West Asia.

Pre-Western Challenges to the Traditional Order

Unlike China, preindustrial Japan did not experience any great upsurge in population (which leveled off around the 30 million figure in the early eighteenth century). The most dramatic social change in the Tokugawa period had to do with where the population lived—that is, the emergence of numerous large urban centers. Urbanization on the scale reached in the eighteenth century was unprecedented in Japanese history, and as a consequence by the early nineteenth century the traditional social structure, with its peasant base supporting a small aristocratic elite, had undergone substantial transformation. This transformation was to have different ramifications for each of the separate strata affected, but everywhere it tended to be disruptive of the traditional framework of institutions and values.

The cities and castle towns were the residences of two very distinct classes—the samurai and the townsmen. Although each of these was further divided on scales of prestige, wealth, and power, they had been segregated into two major categories by a complex system of legal and customary regulations. The uppermost strata of the urban commercial class, however, had developed a close symbiotic relationship with the ruling elite by providing essential economic services in return for a considerable measure of financial power and personal wealth. Within the urban context, this merchant elite also enjoyed a high degree of social prestige. Yet, on the whole, it was content to forego political power in exchange for its privileged position in the economy. Nor did it seek to challenge the amalgam of neo-Confucian and feudal cultural assumptions that underlay the orthodox view of Tokugawa society.

On the other hand, the urban subculture of this commercial class, with its acceptance of material gain, conspicuous consumption, and gratification of the senses, eventually proved a corrosive influence on the life-style of the military aristocracy. The drama, novel, and the wood-block print of this wealthy urban class contrasted markedly with the literature and art forms that constituted the heritage of the aristocratic elite. From the late seventeenth century on, the contemporary literature was increasingly filled with the jeremiads of samurai moralists warning that the values of family honor, civic duty, military valor, and feudal loyalty were being undermined by the appeal of the Gay Quarters, where Kabuki stage plays, geisha entertainers, prostitutes and other diversions beckoned. Moreover, such urban pastimes were an expensive drain on samurai income, especially when it was cut further by the government's practice of attempting to balance its budget by withholding a portion of the stipends paid to samurai. Thus the samurai class as a whole tended to fall into chronic debt to its merchant inferiors.

Lower samurai, who were the most plagued by economic impoverishment and the relative loss of social prestige, were particularly demoralized by the anomalies of a high nominal status that carried less and less real weight in the urban world in which they found themselves. It was also these samurai in the lower ranks whose functions in an era of peace were of the least obvious importance (men whose fathers once wielded the warrior's sword now handled account books as minor clerks) and whose access to offices of real significance was blocked by the system of hereditary rank. Thus it is understandable why contemporary social critics bemoaned the loss of morale among this strata of the traditional elite. Vigorous samurai reaction against the disintegration of the traditional social structure, however, came only late in the Tokugawa period, and then it was largely harnessed to the anti-Tokugawa political movements led by the feudal domains themselves.

The other stratum of Tokugawa urban society that suffered from the dislocations brought about by urbanization was the new urban proletariat. Politically oppressed by the combination of merchant elite and samurai authorities and economically vulnerable to the fluctuations of the business cycle and high consumer prices, this lower class was on occasion driven to violent demonstrations against city officials, rice retailers, and pawnbrokers. The most spectacular urban riots took place in 1837, when a low ranking samurai official in the Oska city administration—Oshio Heihachiro—led an attempt at taking over the city to protest the plight of the urban poor. Like other such "smashings," as they were referred to, this outburst of violence neither represented any lasting political movement nor could seriously threaten the military power of the regime. It was, however, an indication of the deeper problem created by the shifting structure of Tokugawa society.

Violent outbursts also grew more frequent and more serious in the rural countryside, where the bulk of the Tokugawa populace continued to live. In the early part of the nineteenth century some four hundred "incidents" were recorded. Here also the effects of urbanization were felt since the growth of cities had been accompanied by the development of an intricate network of supply in order to meet the urban demand for foodstuffs and other rural products. As large numbers of villages were drawn into this network of production and transportation, because of their proximity to urban centers or the existence of special local products, traditional social relationships underwent change and new attitudes toward work, authority, and village solidarity slowly began to spread.

Agriculture in the typical village of the seventeenth century, prior to the greater spread of cash crops and the growth of commercialization, had been organized around a small number of cooperative groups. The members of these groups worked the fields and shared the harvest collectively (if by no means equally). The landless peasant or small holder pooled his labor with that of relatives or of one of the several larger landholders who headed these groups. Although serving the obvious economic function of exchanging surplus labor for surplus land, the interaction between the members of this cooperative group was not limited to economic exchange. The economy was only part of the larger web of social, religious, and political ties that bound them together. These were stable relationships structured on the model of kinship, with even the lowest in the hierarchy (while not actually related by blood) being assimilated on a permanent basis into the collectivity; and all members interacted as a group along the whole range of village life, much in the manner of an extended family.

The growth of commercialized farming and rural industries brought about important changes in this manner of organizing work and society in many Japanese villages. In the first place, landless peasants or marginal holders had new options for selling their labor. The new cities and towns offered jobs and, despite the Tokugawa restrictions against leaving the village, peasants were attracted in large numbers. Since the demand for labor in agriculture was also increasing, this often forced larger landholders to restructure their work operations. For the lower-strata peasants who remained in the village, there were also new opportunities for work in nonagricultural production—for example, brewing, textile spinning and weaving, and handicraft work. Even where these were only by-employments for slack seasons, they introduced into the village new concepts concerning specific cash payments. Thus these trends meant not only competing alternatives to the cooperative group but also new criteria for evaluating the economic profitability of older patterns of human relationships. Time and work could now be measured in hard monetary terms. New opportunities could also mean new ambitions and expectations about enhancing one's economic situation.

In this way the commercialization of agriculture led to important social and economic shifts in those villages most affected. The demand for greater efficiency and the need to hold labor were powerful incentives to replace the older cooperative organization with tenancy. Instead of directly overseeing the labor of the group on common fields, larger landholders in many villages parceled out much of their land to individual families in a system of sharecropping. The landlord usually remained in the village as a cultivator himself and the new tenant relationship retained much of the older, highly personal and diffuse character. Nevertheless, the tenant's opportunity for independent success or failure was greatly increased.

Since the landlord was often also the initial purchasing agent in the network of supply that linked the village producer and the urban consumer, the narrowly defined economic aspect of the relation became more salient both in bargaining over what proportion of the crops should be paid as rent and in the arranging of the sale of crops on the commercial market. The landlord was also the only major source of loans in villages increasingly being drawn into a monetized economy. In these and numerous other ways relations between the upper and lower strata of villagers became colored by monetized exchange in a market economy. The corrosive effect on vertical ties within the village is indicated by the increasing incidence of tenants grouping together to protest landlord exploitation in the later Tokugawa period. More often, however, the village elite turned economic frustration into demonstrations against the local authorities, maintaining village solidarity by placing the blame on tax collectors or government attempts to create official monopolies on rural commercial products.

There is also evidence in some villages of a different type of disharmony resulting from the slow erosion of the older social system. Petitions to samurai officials regarding appointments to key village offices indicate rivalry among the affluent peasants over political power. Contemporary documents also reveal other forms of this strife: for example, disputes over financial assessments or seating arrangements for the seasonal festivals at local shrines. These strains in village solidarity were caused by the increasing instability within the upper strata of the peasantry. Opportunities for greater failure as well as success in commercialized farming and other rural entreprises meant greater fluctuations in family fortunes over time. Often the established order of power and prestige within a village was threatened by the rapid rise of a family formerly below the top echelon of the social pyramid. Older families, whose positions as village head and whose seat in the front at community religious affairs had been secure for generations, were not always able to maintain the economic stature that originally had buttressed their political and social status. In a social system in which a close correlation between status and hereditary family lineage was the ideal, the problem of the *nouveau riche* was a critical one, which could be highly subversive of the traditional social fabric in the village, just as it was in the merchant-samurai context of the cities.

These cultural, social and, economic challenges to the traditional Tokugawa order, fraught with potential danger as they were, had yet to reach the level of a full-scale crisis by the early nineteenth century. The newly emergent commercial classes in both the city and the villages still largely accepted the legitimacy of the old order, as did also the displaced samurai and the oppressed tenant farmers. The latter couched their complaints in predominantly conservative terms, and the authorities put down the outbursts of violent protest without major effort. The new factors that were to threaten to precipitate a crisis situation were introduced by the intrusion of the Western powers.

The Initial Shock of Maritime Integration under Western Dominance

The Tokugawa social order was exceedingly vulnerable to foreign impact in the mid-nineteenth century because of the preexisting cracks in the internal structure. Moreover, the economic shock of that impact was transmitted all the more rapidly and directly because of the prior existence of a national market system. The network of interdependency that spread outward from the two centers, Tokyo (Edo) and Osaka, proved highly sensitive to external interference.

Japan's vulnerability to Western naval pressure was dramatically illustrated when the mere presence of Perry's flotilla in Tokyo harbor caused an immediate disruption of coastal shipping and forced prices in the Tokugawa capital sharply upward. Once the trading ports at Yokohama and elsewhere were opened, the Japanese monetary system was thrown into a panic. While highly developed and reasonably adequate for domestic needs, the Japanese monetary system functioned on quite different exchange ratios than those current in world money markets. Gold and silver coinage had different buying power in relation both to each other and to goods in the marketplace. One striking illustration of the problems involved in integrating Japan's economy into the international economic order was the extraordinary profit realized by Western money speculators in the late 1850s. Westerners began to buy Japanese gold with Mexican silver dollars (the standard medium for international trade in East Asia at this time). Fifty ounces of silver in Mexican coin could be exchanged in Yokohama for 30 full ounces of Japanese gold—a sum worth 150 ounces of silver in the international system. The gross profit on one trip for Westerners dealing in specie was thus a handsome 300 percent. Eventually the Japanese were able to stem the outward tide of precious specie caused by this type of manipulation, but it was only one of a whole set of monetary problems that confronted the Tokugawa once foreign trade became a fact of economic life. A combination of government money manipulations, domestic turmoil, and foreign trade set off a chain of events. The incompatible elements interjected into the bloodstream triggered an inflationary fever that sent the price of rice and foodstuffs spiraling upward in 1861. In 1865 rice on the market doubled in price. In 1866 it tripled.

One of the many factors serving to drive prices up and down was Western demand for Japanese goods. Here can be seen clearly one of the dilemmas facing an economy in this stage of confrontation with the international system. Although an unfavorable balance of trade causes an outflow of gold and silver, a favorable balance of trade is not in itself necessarily a happy state of affairs. Excessive exports can be as disruptive as excessive imports. In the 1860s Western merchants competed vigorously in the Japanese market for available supplies of raw silk and cotton. Despite substantial increases in the production, the demand outstripped the supply, driving prices beyond the reach of urban artisans and rural entrepreneurs who were often unable to obtain raw materials at prices that permitted an adequate return on their labor. For example, silk weaving in Kyoto, one of the major industries of that city for centuries, suffered a severe depression as a result of the spiraling price of raw silk due to Western demand.

Simultaneously, the more common problem of foreign imports was to be faced. Imports of large quantities of cotton cloth, for example, cut deeply into the market for domestic textiles. The efficiency of the English mills, cheap shipping and low tariffs (assured by the treaties forced upon the Japanese) combined to make it possible for British merchants to deliver superior finished cottons at prices equal to or lower than Japanese products. Peasants who had become dependent on such by-employments to supplement their otherwise inadequate incomes from cultivation now found their livelihood threatened by outside forces.

The Overthrow of the Tokugawa

Economic dislocation, although the most tangible and easily measured, was by no means the only or even the most important shock dealt to the traditional order by the Western intrusion. The weakness and indecision that the Tokugawa regime revealed in signing the treaties set off political tremors that in 1868, culminated in the overthrow of the government and the collapse of the traditional political structure.

When Western pressure became evident in the 1830s, critics of the prevailing social conditions within Japan were quick to see the relationship between internal stability and external strength. Various lords outside of the Tokugawa inner councils petitioned the central government for reforms that might permit them to put their domains in a stronger position to help drive the barbarian away from Japanese shores. While the lords within the councils of the Tokugawa shared the goal of maintaining seclusion, these two segments of the ruling elite became pitted against each other over the domestic consequences of foreign policy. For the Tokugawa leaders the reforms suggested by the outside lords were threatening in at least three ways. First, in order to pay for local efforts at strengthening coastal defenses, the outside lords requested a lightening of the burden imposed by alternate attendance—the requirement that all maintain expensive residences in Edo (Tokyo). Both the expense and the element of hostage involved in alternate attendance had been explicitly intended as crucial mechanisms for regulating the powerful outside lords and thereby preserving Tokugawa hegemony. To drop these was to eliminate an important safeguard in the political system. Second, permission to carry out armament programs to increase the military potential of the local domains, albeit designed for defense against the outside threat, might also destroy the internal military balance. Despite over two hundred years of peace between the Tokugawa and its old foes, many leaders within the central government viewed any such growth of the strength of the local domains as a potential threat to Tokugawa hegemony. Ultimately these suspicions were to be borne out. Third, the hereditary allies of the Tokugawa house, who, in the absence of a vigorous shogun, actually controlled Tokugawa policy, were extremely jealous of that role. To allow the larger outside domains to take part in policymaking was to threaten their own control and thereby the delicate political balance that had kept domestic peace and a large measure of order throughout the previous two and a half centuries.

In the late 1840s the Tokugawa leaders were persuaded to compromise on the first and second points, removing some of the restrictions on local lords in order to permit some attempts at building up Japan's coastal defenses, but they did not give substantial ground on the third issue. The sudden arrival of Perry and the Tokugawa unilateral decision to give the Western representatives much of what they demanded destroyed the working arrangement with the outside lords. A full political crisis developed as long smoldering grievances came to the surface and new elements emerged to the fore. One of the more powerful domains, Choshu, formed a compact with ambitious xenophobes among the imperial court, so long dormant in the political scene, to defy Tokugawa foreign policy and expel the barbarians in the name of the higher authority of the throne. The Tokugawa responded with a show of force in the attempt to bring this dissident domain back into line and keep others from breaking ranks. The result was the opposite. Expeditions against Choshu shocked other outside lords into considering the consequences of remaining divided in the face of Tokugawa willingness to resort to force. At the same time the expeditions revealed the degree to which the Tokugawa military machine had been weakened over the generations. No longer was it capable of enforcing its will through sheer might. For the outside lords—the most important of whom included the southwest domains of Satsuma, Tosa, and Hizen as well as Choshu—the foreign issue of how to handle the Western threat was transformed into a domestic question of how to coerce the Tokugawa into accepting their new claims to a full partnership in central decision making. By 1867 an alliance had been formed among these lords, ambitious court nobles, xenophobic samurai, and other elements alienated from the status quo. In a fierce, if brief, civil war the Tokugawa regime was destroyed and a Restoration under the reign of the Emperor Meiji (a youth of seventeen) was proclaimed in January 1868.

Continued Disintegration in the Early Meiji Period

In the process of destroying the old regime many of the value assumptions and traditional institutions that constituted Tokugawa political culture were called into question. Was a hereditary system of rank compatible with the need for talent in office? Was a decentralized structure of government capable of dealing with the need for internal reforms and the threat of external aggression? How could resources, human and natural, be mobilized to meet the crisis? What was the role of the throne in politics? In the Meiji period (1868-1912) the new leadership attempted to resolve these issues in the course of promoting economic development and seeking international equality. Some of the details of their programs of modernization and the nationalist ideology behind them will be given elsewhere. In the initial period of transition, however, it should be stressed that nation building required a good deal of ground clearing. Thus, the new Meiji regime, sometimes consciously, sometimes unwittingly, pursued policies that further accelerated the processes of disintegration at the same time that they aimed at eventually reintegrating Japanese society within a new cultural configuration. As a result the first two decades of the Meiji period were characterized by considerable turbulence and marked by outbursts of reaction against the dislocations accompanying continued social change. The frequency of peasant demonstrations actually increased in the first decade after the overthrow of the Tokugawa, while disgruntled samurai were quick to take up the arms that they had laid down after the Tokugawa civil war in rebellion against the new regime. Others, bewildered by wrenching change, turned to swell the ranks of the followers in the new millennarian religions that had mushroomed in the mid-nineteenth century.

The economic plight of the lower classes and the necessity of alleviating it to prevent further political instability was quite apparent to the new Meiji leaders. Indeed, this was one of the specific reasons for their decision to divert scarce capital and expertise to a crash program for creating an industrial base. But it was to require decades before Japan's infant industries expanded sufficiently to absorb the large and growing reservoir of labor, and wages were to remain low well into the mid-twentieth century. Nor did other government measures taken to stabilize the economy produce immediate benefits for rural and urban workers. The land reform of 1873 and the drastic, if successful, deflationary policies adopted in the 1880s further served to swell the ranks of tenant farmers. In some aspects the Meiji land reform resembled the policies of Western colonial administrations, for it was aimed primarily at systematizing tax collection and thereby providing larger revenues for the government. In the Japanese case the adoption of a fixed annual tax payable in cash had two adverse effects for marginal cultivators. First, since the annual rate was based on a fixed assessment of the value of the land rather than on the actual harvest, there was no provision for adjusting for years of bad crops. Second, as described in Chapter 11, the Tokugawa land tax had been collected in most cases in kind without regard for the prevailing market price of the crops. The new tax system shifted the burden of exchanging crops for sufficient cash to meet the tax onto the producer. A bumper crop might actually result in an increased tax burden (if an oversupply of farm products had lowered the market price) and drive the peasant into the arms of the moneylender with his exorbitant interest fees.

The ballooning debt of the national government incurred in large part because of expenditures in armaments and importation of technology needed to meet the Western challenge led, in 1881, to the stringent reforms known as the Matsukata deflation. Finance Minister Matsukata retrenched government spending, manipulated the currency system, and increased taxes. Prices throughout the country dropped sharply. Forced to sell in the prevailing market, the peasant found it correspondingly difficult to meet fixed tax assessments. Where cultivators were without savings and had already mortgaged their land, they faced foreclosure to pay interest and tax arrears. In all, tens of thousands are reported to have lost title to their fields in the 1881-85 period. The majority remained on the land to cultivate it as tenants, surrendering as much as half or more of the harvests to landlords. Others drifted to the cities to become urban proletarians and a small number even contracted to go abroad to Hawaii or the west coast of America.

Displacement of Old Elites

The ranks of the dispossessed and uprooted were not limited to those on the lower margins of late nineteenth century Japanese society. Large numbers of the old military aristocracy also found themselves cut loose from positions of security. Indeed, there was considerable irony—not lost on contemporary observers—in the fact that the "Restoration" borne in large part on the shoulders of disgruntled samuari seeking to control the forces at work in the 1860s was to culminate in a social revolution that destroyed many of their legal privileges, military functions, and economic prerogatives. True, in Meiji and even later periods, the new elite showed clear continuities with the old as the government bureaucracy, political-party leadership, military officer corps, corporate directorships, and academic hierarchies were filled by men with samurai lineages in numbers disproportionate to their percentage of the total population. Nevertheless, the degree of continuity between the old and the new elites was far less than would appear from that statement. The emphasis was now on different types of qualifications, particularly those involving Western expertise or political connections resulting from participation in the anti-Tokugawa struggles. In the competition for influence and rewards in a changing society, high rank in the old aristocracy was no longer sufficient to guarantee either. A surprising percentage of those former samuari who were successful in the new environment were younger men originally from middle or lower echelons of the samurai class—in some instances the equivalent of foot soldiers or supply clerks. Ito Hirobumi (the chief architect of the 1889 Constitution), Yamagata Aritomo (prime mover in shaping the modern military establishment), Iwasaki Yataro (creator of the vast Mitsubishi enterprises), and Fukuzawa Yukichi (founder of Keio University) are examples of individuals who did not have the ascribed social status to have risen to comparable heights in the previous system. Moreover, these members of the new elites were joined by men of commoner origins: for example, Yasuda Zenjiro and Shibusawa Eichi in the business world.

The point here is not the question of the degree of openness or opportunity for social mobility, but rather the displacement of the former elites. Although the Meiji leaders were careful to make generous economic settlements where possible and treated defeated Tokugawa opponents with a magnanimity calculated to reduce political hostilities, still the overwhelming majority of daimyo lords and their highest retainers lost their political influence. Ordinary samuari turned out of their stipended posts were staked to a new life with government bonds in lieu of pensions—but these bonds rapidly lost purchasing power in

12.4 This group of Japanese business leaders includes men drawn from the former samurai as well as the old merchant and peasant classes. By the turn of the twentieth century they had emerged as the nation's new economic elite. Source: Joseph I. C. Clarke, *Japan at First Hand* (New York: Dodd, Mead and Company, 1918).

the inflation of the 1870s. Hereditary commanders of military units lost their posts to men of lesser families better qualified to handle Western artillery or close-order drill of peasant conscripts.

Former political and military elites were not the only groups to feel personally the consequences of change. The Osaka and Edo merchant houses that had handled the financial affairs of the samurai class and dominated the national market were now confronted with a new era. Some contented themselves with traditional activities despite their shrinking role in an expanded economy. Others collapsed under the new pressures or made the transition only after radical reorganization. The most successful example of the latter is the House of Mitsui, which rapidly shifted its attention to modern manufacturing industries and enterprises directly relevant to international trade. Mitsui accomplished this, however, only after thrusting family members and hereditary managers into the background and replacing them with new managerial talent drawn largely from ex-samurai like Nakamigawa Hikojiro and Dan Takuma, both of whom had been educated in Western techniques. Even where they survived, the former mercantile and financial elite were now in direct competition with business rivals who rose to prominence in the decades immediately following 1860.

Among the most painful adjustments was that forced upon the intellectuals who had once performed important roles as political advisers, cultural arbiters, educational leaders, and moral apologists for the Tokugawa system. In the first burst of enthusiasm for the new order in the 1870s, this former cultural elite was abruptly rejected as belonging to bygone age. Buddhist temples were pillaged to satisfy Western collectors of exotica; neo-Confucian scholarship was scorned by many as responsble for the stagnation of Japan in the Tokugawa period; traditional painting, literary forms, and music were neglected for a time. In 1870, the newly created national university in the court city of Kyoto was suddenly closed and plans for a higher education system centering on Western knowledge and employing foreign teachers were drawn up. Even those national scholars, the disciples of Motoori Norinaga and Hirata Atsutane (see Chapter 13), who claimed to have provided the intellectual inspiration for the resurgence of loyalty to the imperial throne seemed to have been thrust aside along with their neo-Confucian and Buddhist rivals.

Eventually traditional arts and ethics were restored to a position of some respect, yet Japanese society nevertheless suffered from much the same kind of cultural disintegration that other Asian societies experienced in the same stage. There were, however, very important differences. One of the most important was the fact the foreign control over the leading sectors of change was avoided. The majority of present-day metropolitan areas—Kyoto, Edo (Tokyo), Osaka, Nagoya, etc.—were well established in Tokugawa times as the residences of elites and centers for domestic commerce. These indigenous cities survived the transition to a twentieth century industrial economy and successfully absorbed much of the migration that took place from rural areas. The two notable exceptions to this pattern of continuity were Kobe (on the Inland Sea south of the Osaka-Kyoto area) and Yokohama (down the bay from Tokyo), selected as sites for treaty ports in the 1850s partially to keep foreigners at a distance from the politically sensitive seats of the shogunate and the imperial court. Physically and functionally, these ports resembled the Western-dominated Calcutta or Shanghai, but the Meiji government had inherited the policy of retaining as much control as diplomatic pressure and the threat of military force permitted. Western import-export houses lined the waterfront, foreign settlement areas pulsed to the rhythms of colonial life-styles, and international courts exercised jurisdiction over citizens of the treaty powers within these ports. Yet the sites of the more significant economic activity, social trends, and political developments were the urban centers of Osaka and Tokyo, both Japanese in origin and under indigenous leadership.

A second aspect in which the Japanese case differs from other Asian areas was the speed with which the Japanese moved through this transitional period and succeeded in the task of creating a new modern order to replace the old one lost in the nineteenth century. This will be our focus in the next two chapters.

CONCLUDING REMARKS

The central focus of this chapter has been the crises of Asian civilizations in the nineteenth and twentieth centuries. These crises were viewed as the combined consequences of internal decline in the early modern empires of Ottoman West Asia, Mughul South Asia, Ch'ing China, and Tokugawa Japan and the impact of European and American expansion. As such, these crises should be seen as stemming from a complex of factors that combined in patterns unique to each individual cultural area and time period yet sharing certain features in common.

One of the most obvious differences between areas had been in the timing and pace of the change that resulted in a sense of crisis. The economic impact of Western maritime expansion was felt sooner and more directly in areas immediately surrounding such foreign dominated cities as Calcutta and Shanghai; while in West Asia, although the initial consequences for the overland trading system were important, the importation of Western goods and the demand for raw materials or handicraft products were late in developing. Perhaps paradoxically it was Japan, where such foreign trade was soon brought under the control of Japanese rather than foreigners, which felt some of the greatest shocks from being linked with the international markets.

Politically, South Asia, which was largely under direct colonial rule by the latter half of the nineteenth century, would seem to have undergone the earliest changes. But there were also major political changes in Japan, which remained outside of colonial rule, and in China, where at most the situation might be described as semicolonial, as hereditary lords and Confucian bureaucrats gave way to new elites. Here, as in South Asia, new specialists gained positions of influence—for example, English-trained lawyers in India, military commanders in China, business managers in Japan. Often, as in the case of the Tagore family in Bengal, these new men were drawn from the compradors who served as cultural intermediaries as well as commercial agents in Asian-Western interactions. Others as in China were recruited from the ranks of returned students who had received schooling abroad. These changes, however, were much slower and less drastic in West Asia despite the fact that the great Islamic empires had come apart considerably earlier than had the empires elsewhere in Asia. Military and other technology in West Asia had been more successfully compartmentalized or controlled by older elite groups.

In all cases the pace of change was felt more slowly in the rural hinterland than in the capitals and the coastal cities. In Japan, the smallest and most economically centralized of the Asian states, the difference between rural and urban areas was far less than in China. In South and West Asia the vast majority of villagers, remote from major cities with less contact with the outside world, were much less aware of crisis, and the traditional images and values have continued to have reality.

But differences in timing and pace of change do not in themselves explain the contrasts between different areas. Indeed they themselves require explanation. Why were some societies more vulnerable to these disintegrating processes than others? Why did some perceive and respond with such alacrity to the challenges and why did those responses take different forms? Why were Chinese peasants more easily stirred to violent rebellion in the nineteenth century than were Japanese peasants; or why did discontent and demoralization lead to passivity or banditry in one place but religious fervor or revolutionary behavior in another? The central question raised in this chapter is precisely the question of why some Asians would turn to new institutions and values in organizing their lives while others remained immobilized in the face of crises. The next chapter will focus more tightly on the various types of solutions to crisis proposed by indigenous intellectuals and political activists and the means they used to rally people behind efforts to realize their aims.

BIBLIOGRAPHY

12.P THE CRISIS OF SOCIAL AND CULTURAL DISINTEGRATION: PROCESSES

Bottomore, T. B., *Elites and Society* (Penguin paperback, 1966), 160 pp. A concise summary of the relationship between elites and their societies; Chapters 3-5 are particularly relevant here.

Eisenstadt, Shmuel N., *Modernization: Protest and Change* (Prentice-Hall paperback, 1966), 166 pp. Discusses tensions arising out of change in the modern era.

More, Wilbert E., *The Impact of Industry* (Prentice-Hall paperback, 1965), 117 pp. A succinct statement of one of the more prevalent views of the changes in social organization and values that accompany commercialization and industrialization.

Stone, Lawrence, "Theories of Revolution," *World Politics* 18.2:159-76 (1966). Analysis of various types of approaches to the study of conditions that lead to social upheaval.

Wallace, Anthony F. C., *Culture and Personality* (Random House paperback, 1966), 213 pp. Chapter 4, "The Psychology by Culture Change," discusses the impact of social disorganization.

Wolf, Eric, "Peasant Rebellion and Revolution," in Norman Miller and Roderick Aya, eds., *National Liberation, Revolution in the Third World* (Free Press paperback, 1971), pp. 48-67. Examines link between urban leadership and rural masses necessary to create a revolutionary force.

12.1 SOCIAL AND CULTURAL DISINTEGRATION IN WEST ASIA

Birge, John K., *The Bektashi Order of Dervishes* (London, 1937), 291 pp. An in-depth study of one of the most influential of all the dervish orders and one that played a prominent social role in the period of Ottoman decline.

Heyd, Uriel, "The Later Ottoman Empire in Rumelia and Anatolia," *The Cambridge History of Islam*, 2 vols. (Cambridge, 1970), Vol. 1, pp. 354-73. Describes the period of Ottoman decline, as it affected the two regions of the empire closest to the capital.

Holt, Peter M., "The Later Ottoman Empire in Egypt and the Fertile Crescent," *The Cambridge History of Islam*, 2 vols. (Cambridge, 1970), Vol. 1, pp. 374-93. Describes the period of Ottoman decline, as it affected Iraq, Syria, and Palestine.

Hourani, Albert, "The Fertile Crescent in the Eighteenth Century," *A Vision of History: Near Eastern and Other Essays* (Beirut, 1961), pp. 35-70. A brilliant essay postulating new ways of looking at the Fertile Crescent in the period of Ottoman imperial contraction.

Lunt, James D., *Bokhara Burnes* (London, 1969), 220 pp. An account of the travels of Sir Alexander Burnes through Afghanistan, Turkistan, and Iran during the early nineteenth century, giving an eyewitness description of the decay of cities that had formerly been centers of Islamic learning and culture.

Polk, William R., and Richard L. Chambers, *Beginnings of Modernization in the Middle East: The Nineteenth Century* (Chicago, 1968), 415 pp. A wide-ranging anthology of essays, touching on many aspects of Islamic society in a period of painful transition.

12.2 SOCIAL AND CULTURAL DISINTEGRATION IN SOUTH ASIA

Broomfield, John H., *Elite Conflict in a Plural Society: Twentieth Century Bengal* (Berkeley, 1968), 349 pp. Study of the formation of *bhadralok* in Bengal; an example of a new emerging elite.

Fuchs, Stephen, *Rebellious Prophets: A Study of Messianic Movements in Indian Religions* (Bombay, 1865), 304 pp. An anthropological approach to popular movements.

Kling, Blair B., *The Blue Mutiny: The Indigo Disturbances in Bengal, 1859-1862* (Philadelphia, 1966), 243 pp. A socioeconomic analysis of one of the great uprisings.

Kopf, David, *British Orientalism and the Bengal Renaissance: The Dynamics of Indian Modernization, 1773-1835* (Berkeley, 1969), 324 pp. Examines the emergence of an Indian intelligentsia and their changing perceptions of the Indian cultural heritage.

12.3 SOCIAL AND CULTURAL DISINTEGRATION IN CHINA

Fairbank, John K., and Ssu-yu Teng, *China's Response to the West* (Atheneum paperback, 1963), 296 pp. Translations of carefully selected documents from the period 1839 to 1923 showing the change in Chinese perceptions of the world and China's place in it; excellent commentary to each document.

Hao Yen-p'ing, *The Comprador in Nineteenth Century China: Bridge between East and West* (Cambridge, Mass., 1970), 315 pp. The most authoritative study of the new comprador element in Chinese society; Chapters 8 and 9 look beyond the narrow economic setting of the comprador to examine his significance for China's relations with the West.

Hsu, Immanuel C. Y., *The Rise of Modern China* (New York, 1970), 830 pp. Chapters 15 through 21 describe the disintegration of the imperial order and the intellectual and social ferment at the end of the nineteenth century.

Pruitt, Ida, *A Daughter of Han: The Autobiography of a Chinese Working Woman* (Stanford University Press paperback, 1967), 254 pp. The opium problem, footbinding, the breakdown to the traditional family system, the Manchus, Japanese encroachment, and Western missionaries, all seen through the eyes of a lower class Chinese.

Schwartz, Benjamin I., *In Search of Wealth and Power: Yen Fu and the West* (Harper Torchbook paperback, 1964), 298 pp. Intellectual biography of a Chinese thinker and translator who searched for the sources of Western strength.

Wakeman, Frederic, Jr., *Strangers at the Gate: Social Disorder in South China, 1839-1861* (University of California Press paperback, 1967), 276 pp. Local history that looks into the social dislocations behind rebellion in nineteenth century China.

12.4 SOCIAL AND CULTURAL DISINTEGRATION IN JAPAN

Beasley, W. G., *The Meiji Restoration* (Stanford, 1972), 513 pp. The most comprehensive treatment in English of the events leading up to and immediately following the overthrow of the Tokugawa regime.

Jansen, Marius B., *Sakamoto Ryoma and the Meiji Restoration* (Stanford University Press paperback, 1961), 423 pp. A lengthy but often lively account of the collapse of the old order as seen through the life of one of the important participants.

Pyle, Kenneth B., *The New Generation in Meiji Japan: Problems of Cultural Identity, 1885-1895* (Stanford, 1969), 248 pp. A provocative analysis of the cultural tensions faced by Meiji intellectuals in a period of rapid change.

Smith, Thomas C., *Political Change and Industrial Development in Japan* (Stanford University Press paperback, 1955), 126 pp. A clear, concise account of the critical problems that motivated early Meiji leaders to attempt to restructure their society.

————, *The Agrarian Origins of Modern Japan* (Atheneum paperback, 1966), 250 pp. An excellent analysis and very readable account of the changes in Tokugawa village life and their significance for the modern era.

Scheiner, Irwin, *Christian Converts and Social Protest in Meiji Japan* (Berkeley, 1970), 268 pp. An objective treatment of late nineteenth century Japanese Christianity as both a cause and effect of cultural disintegration.

GLOSSARY

Bhadralok. Literally, "people of quality"; three upper castes in Bengal which profitted from monopolizing posts under the British in Calcutta.

Chaghatay (d. 1241). Second son of Chingiz Khan and founder of the Chaghatay khanate in Central Asia; also, Chaghatay Turkish, the language spoken in that khanate and the precursor of present-day Özbeg.

Choshu. A large *tozama*, or "outer domain," at the southern tip of the island of Honshu, which was among the leaders of the anti-Tokugawa movements of the 1860s.

Dar al-Harb. "The abode of war"; that is, those regions not under the sovereignty of a Muslim ruler.

Dar al-Islam. "The abode of Islam"; that is, those regions under the sovereignty of a Muslim ruler and where the Sharia was enforced.

Dervish. A Sufi; either a religious mendicant or a member of a Sufi brotherhood *(tariqa)* attached to a dervish convent *(khanqah)*.

Fars. The homeland of the Achaemenid and Sasanid dynasties; a province in southwestern Iran, with its present capital at Shiraz.

Fudai daimyo. Trusted vassals of the Tokugawa who in addition to governing their own regional domains also served within the Tokugawa central administration; hence referred to here as "inner lords" to distinguish them from the *tozama*, or "outer lords" (q.v.).

Hizen. Also known as Saga, a *tozama*, or "outer domain," in Kyushu (east of the city of Nagasaki) which supplied such modern leaders as Okuma Shigenobu.

Hundred days of 1898. Abortive effort by the Ch'ing emperor Kuang-hsu to impose reforms from above; led to his imprisonment in the palace and the radicalization of Chinese reformers.

Il-khan. The title assumed by the Chingizkhanid Mongol rulers of Iran (1256-1353), originally implying subordination to the supreme *khaqan* in Mongolia. In recent centuries some tribal chieftains in Iran, such as the chieftains of the Qashqai, have assumed the title.

Janissaries (from Turkish, *yenicheri*, "new troops"). Technically slaves, recruited by means of the *devshirme*, or child tribute levied upon the Christian population of the Balkans, the Janissaries were the best disciplined and most feared troops of the Ottoman Sultans, especially during the centuries of imperial expansion.

Kazakhs. A Turkish people who, since the middle decades of the fifteenth century, have practised pastoral nomadism in the Central Asian steppe region north of the Aral Sea and the Syr Darya River.

Khurasan. Formerly a vast area extending northeastward from the central Iranian desert to the Amu Darya River, with its metropolitan centers located at Nishapur, Marv, Herat, and Balkh. Today Khurasan consists of a province in northeastern Iran, bordering the U.S.S.R. and Afghanistan, and with its capital at Mashhad.

Madrasa. A theological college where the *ulama* were trained in the Islamic "sciences."

Motoori Norinaga (1730-1801). An influential writer and teacher whose ideas about ancient Japanese culture contributed greatly to imperial loyalism and modern Japanese nationalism.

Mulla. A member of the *ulama*.

Özbegs (also, **Uzbeks**). A Turkish people who, since the second half of the fifteenth century, have occupied the area between the Syr Darya and Amu Darya rivers (formerly Russian Turkistan and now divided between various Central Asian republics of the U.S.S.R.).

Pai-hua. Colloquial Chinese, adopted as a written language following establishment of the Republic in 1912.

Samurai. Members of the hereditary class of military retainers who under the Tokugawa served as the political elite.

Sharia. The Law of Islam, derived from the Quran, the *Hadith,* or *Sayings of the Prophet,* and the analogical interpretations of the jurists.

Tosa. A large *tozama,* or "outer domain," on the Pacific coast of the island of Shikoku (with its castle town at Kochi) which was among the leaders in the anti-Tokugawa movement of the 1860s.

Tozama daimyo. Regional lords over semiautonomous domains who, although among the most powerful of Tokugawa domains, were largely excluded from the inner councils of the central government.

Tsungli Yamen. Office created by the Ch'ing government in 1860 for dealing with the Western countries, forerunner of a modern foreign office.

Turcoman. A term of unknown origin. One explanation of its derivation links it to the Persian *Turk manand,* meaning "Turk-like." Although appearing at different times in different areas, the Turcomans generally spoke a West Turkish language, retained memories of a pastoral-nomadic background, and displayed a life-style of a kind associated with Turkish peoples over an extensive area of West and Central Asia.

Ulama. The Arabic plural of *alim,* meaning a scholar trained in the Islamic "sciences." Collectively, the *ulama* enforced the Sharia and determined the social norms that governed the life of the Muslim community as a whole.

Umma. The Islamic "community of believers."

Yuan Shih-k'ai (1859-1916). As organizer of China's first Western style military forces he was able to capture the presidency of the Republic in 1912, setting a model for subsequent warlords.

13

The Emergence of Nationalism in Modern Asia

The Emergence of Nationalism in Modern Asia

1800 to 1950

The crises described in the preceding sections eventually provoked individuals and communities throughout much of Asia to endeavor to stem the tide of social and cultural disintegration. These reactions ranged from stubborn defense of the traditional status quo to open acceptance of Western models. The most prevalent and successful of these reactions took a form familiar in modern Western history—that of nationalism.

Nationalism in Asia embraced, although sometimes ambivalently, both the conservative's concern for protecting the cultural traditions of the past and the reformer's conviction that fundamental changes were essential for survival. This seemingly paradoxical position was made viable by redefining both the unit of political loyalty and the cultural traditions to be defended. While Pan–Arabism, Pan–East Asianism, or notions of a Greater India can be seen as attempts to preserve the integrity of a whole civilization, usually such ideologies were less successful than were appeals to more narrowly defined nationalism. Nevertheless, such appeals historically owed much to cultural renaissance movements originating within the older empires and gave way only slowly to the narrower focus on nation-states. The resulting nationalist movements were usually committed to economic and social reforms, entailing dramatic changes within the existing patterns in the civilization. However, the most successful nationalist leaders placed great stress also upon the positive aspects of their cultural heritage, emphasizing the need to revive traditional virtues in the face of foreign vices.

Thus in Asia, as elsewhere, nationalism was most clearly perceived as a reaction to foreign domination. But both the steps by which nationalism emerged and the forms that it took were heavily influenced by the particular conditions of the crisis occurring in each separate area, and the way that crisis was perceived.

PROCESSES

a. Nativist reaction
b. The dilemma of the Westernizer
c. The quest for cultural renaissance
d. The appeal of Marxism
e. Nationalism as a salvation ideology
f. The emergence of revolutionary
   nationalist movements

PATTERNS

1. **Cultural Renaissance and Nationalism in West Asia**

2A. **Cultural Renaissance and Nationalism among Hindus in South Asia**

2B. **Cultural Renaissance and Nationalism among Muslims in South Asia**

3. **Cultural Renaissance and Nationalism in Southeast Asia**

4. **Cultural Renaissance and Nationalism in China**

5. **Cultural Renaissance and Nationalism in Japan**

13. NATIONALISM

	1 WEST ASIA	2 SOUTH ASIA	3 SOUTHEAST ASIA	4 CHINA	5 JAPAN
1700		Shah Wali-Allah of Delhi, 1703-62, Muslim theologian			Ogyu Sorai, 1666-1728
					Motoori Norinaga 1730-1801
					Spread of Mito writings
1750		Battle of Plassey 1757, British de facto rulers of Bengal		Han Learning: search for early source of classical authority by Confucian scholars	
		Orientalist era; Hindu professional elite emerges under British; new intelligentsia reappraise Indian past			
		Brahmo Samaj movement led by Rammohun Roy, 1772-1833			
1800	Sultan Mahmud II, r. 1808-39				

1850 / 1900 / 1950				
Midhat Pasha, 1822-83, Ottoman reformer	Death of Sayyid Ahmad Barelwi, 1831, leader of "Indian Wahhabis"	Javan resistance to Dutch 1825-30	Wei Yuan 1794-1856, statecraft advocate	Perry's demands 1853
Tanzimat period 1839-78				Rise of *sonno-joi* thought
Sayyid Jamal al-Din Afghani, 1839-97, Pan-Islamic propagandist	Anti-British uprisings in north 1857; British capture of Delhi; Bahadur Shah II deposed and exiled		Tseng Kuo-fan, conservative Confucian revival and counterinsurgency	
Ismail Gaspirali 1851-1914, Crimean Tatar educationalist	Theological seminary, Deoband 1867	Suez Canal 1869, closer control of colonies by home country	Self-Strengthening movement	Meiji Restoration 1868
Beginning of Young Ottoman movement 1867	Gandhi 1869-1948			*Meirokusha* formed 1873
Ottoman constitution promulgated 1876	Muslim Anglo-Oriental college at Aligarh 1875	Ethical Policy, tighter Dutch control		Okuma Shigenobu leaves government 1881
Khartoum captured by the Mahdi 1885	Indian National Congress 1885	Anti-Spanish independence movement in Philippines	K'ang Yu-wei, 1858-1927, radical Confucian reform	Sino-Japanese War 1895
	Ramkrishna Mission founded by Vivekananda 1863-1902			
Constitutional movement begins in Iran 1905	Muslim League founded 1906		Tsou Jung writes anti-Manchu Revolutionary Army 1903	Russo-Japanese War 1904-05
First Iranian parliament (*majlis*) 1906		Sarekat Islam founded in Indonesia 1912	T'ung-meng hui founded in Tokyo 1905	
Young Turk Movement 1908	Khilafat movement 1919-24	Growth of intelligentsia fostered by Western education	Fall of Manchu dynasty 1911	
Crimean Tatar *Milli Firka*, Kazakh *Alash Orda* formed 1917		Nahdatul Ulama in Java 1926	Republic founded 1912	
Turkey proclaimed a republic 1923		Philippine Commonwealth 1935	May Fourth Movement 1919	
			Sun Yat-sen, 1866-1925, organizes Kuomintang	Manchurian Incident 1931
			Nanking government established 1927	War in China 1937
		Japanese occupation 1942-45, displacement of Western colonial powers	Japanese invasion 1937	Defeat and occupation by U.S. 1945
	Partition of British India 1947, formation of India and Pakistan	Trend toward national independence after World War II	People's Republic founded 1949	
			Great Proletarian Cultural Revolution 1966	

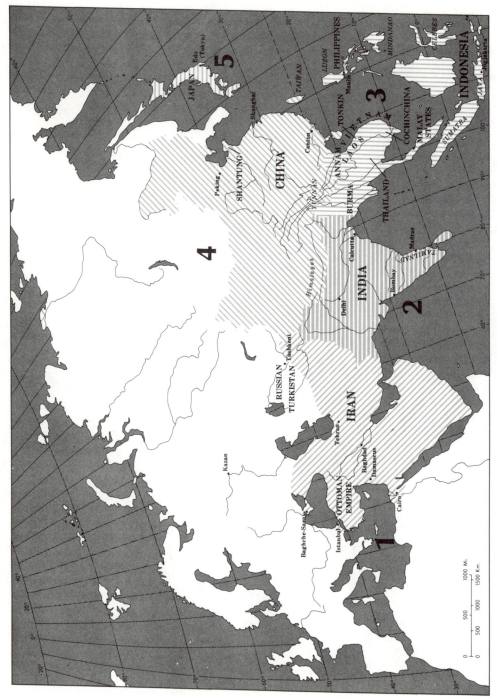

Map 52 The emergence of nationalism in modern Asia

PROCESSES

The establishment of Western dominance and its consequences for Asian societies made the nineteenth and early twentieth centuries a period of extreme imbalance among the civilizations of Eurasia. By the middle decades of the twentieth century, however, there had appeared clear trends in the direction of restoring that balance as many Asian societies responded in dynamic ways to the crises of foreign encroachment and internal disintegration. In most cases this response took the form of a nationalist movement for independence from Western dominance and entailed fundamental changes in key institutions and core values. This chapter will focus on the emergence of Asian nationalist movements and, in particular, the processes by which new leaders, alienated from the old order, searched for new social, political, and moral principles that might serve as formulae for national salvation. The following chapter will then treat changes in life within Asian societies which resulted from the attempts to translate nationalist formulae into a new reality—a reality colored by the cumulative effects of many decades of Western domination. Whereas in this chapter primary emphasis will be placed on a relatively narrow strata of intellectuals and political activists whose writings and careers constitute the clearest articulation of Asian reaction to the crises of the modern era, it should be remembered that the events most Asians experienced were the actual tides of social and political revolution as change impinged on their daily lives. The careers of spokesmen and leaders, then, are convenient tokens of the movements they led, but by no means do they constitute descriptions of those movements.

THE PERIOD

The processes associated with the gradual development of a nationalist response can be traced back into the late eighteenth and early nineteenth centuries. Although various strata and groups within separate Asian societies differed in both the character and timing of their reaction, it is possible to suggest a periodization. In the earlier phases concerned Asians reacted not as innovators but as defenders of core values and central institutions within the indigenous cultural traditions. As the crisis became more evident in the middle and late nineteenth century, sensitive Asians came to the conclusion that only a thorough revitalization of those traditions, a cultural renaissance, would save their civilizations. For others, by the late nineteenth century the old institutions and traditional norms had become too discredited to be relevant to the problems that beset them. Western models and intellectual orientations had great attraction for many such alienated intelligentsia and they turned to Westernization in their quest for national salvation.

The turn of the twentieth century, however, ushered in an extended period of intense conflict among imperialist powers, and the image of Western superiority was badly tarnished as a result of three influential wars. In 1905 the Japanese succeeded in debunking the racist myth of Western military invincibility by destroying the Russian fleet, capturing Russian bases in Manchuria, and forcing the Czarist regime to conclude a humiliating peace. Many Asians, including Chinese who had suffered from Japanese aggression, were given a new perspective as they observed Japan's rise to the status of an international power in a white man's world. The spectacle of World War I, when the Western nations became locked in fratricidal combat that lacked any apparent meaning, cast a great shadow on the notion that Western civilization held any key to rational progress in human values. While the myth of Western superiority lingered on, it was dealt another massive blow in the World War II period when one after another the British, Dutch, Americans, and French were forced to flee in abject defeat before the Japanese thrust into China and Southeastern Asia. The eventual defeat of Japan and the reestablishment of some forms of Western dominance after the war were largely offset by the successful resistance to United States' military power first by the Chinese in Korea and more recently by the North Vietnamese in Indochina. The Western ideology that remained most influential in late twentieth century Asia was Marxism-Leninism, which often appealed precisely because it did repudiate the tenets of earlier Western imperialism, although here, too, Asian socialists continue to seek ideological as well as political independence from the West. The overall impact of these events was to help strengthen those Asian nationalist movements that eschewed both the extreme conservative defense of tradition and the wholesale adoption of Western culture.

THE EMERGENCE OF ASIAN NATIONALISM

a. Nativist Reaction

The earliest reaction to the crisis resulting from internal decline and foreign encroachment was that of individuals and groups that can be labeled *nativists*—cultural conservatives who clung tenaciously to the old order. This was the natural reaction of elites and subelites in the early modern empires of Asia. Their view of the crisis that beset them was that the problem was one of temporary decline in government efficiency and social morality. Thus, these nativists advocated only those reforms aimed at readjusting the status quo and correcting deviation from the orthodox principles of good government. While many among the Chinese gentry, Islamic *ulama,* Mughul princes, and other traditional leaders were to remain unreconciled to the need for more far-reaching changes, their influence was to wane as nativist policies failed to stem the tide of disaster and it became evident that the old order, whatever its merits, was too vulnerable to survive in the new era.

Some among the old elite were willing to attempt a minimum of selective borrowing from Western technology in order to defend existing institutions and orthodox values. The eventual fate of such compromises is best illustrated by the self-defeating results of the so-called Self-Strengtheners in China. Western military techniques could not be grafted onto the old order without altering the economic structure, interjecting alien concepts into education, distorting the system by which individuals were recruited into positions of power, and undermining the whole framework that supported the status of the traditional elite and the legitimacy of orthodox values. Eventually, nativist solutions were discredited and new salvation ideologies were proposed.

b. The Dilemma of the Westernizer

At the opposite extreme from the conservative nativist were those Westernized intellectuals and comprador types who enthusiastically embraced the coming of the West as opening the door to a new cultural era. Typically alienated from their own traditions, these would-be reformers were greatly attracted by the material affluence, military power, and cultural achievements of Western civilization and advocated massive importation of foreign culture in order to thoroughly Westernize their countries. The fundamental issue for proponents of Westernization, however, was the dilemma of cultural identity. Complete Westernization meant the explicit acceptance of the claims to superiority of an alien civilization. The blanket repudiation of one's own heritage meant conceding the inferiority of one's own cultural origins—admitting in effect that the history of the civilization had led to bankruptcy—and thus accepting the blame for impotency and degradation. Moreover, if all that was to be valued in the modern era originated in the West, what was the role to be played for someone outside of the West beyond that of slavish imitator? The psychological burden of the Asian Westernizer was thus enormous.

This was more than a psychological dilemma, however, for on the one side Westernizers were vehemently attacked by their fellow countrymen, while on the other they were snubbed by representatives of the very civilization they admired. Europeans and Americans, flushed with the arrogance of power and prone to racist explanations of Western domination, were seldom prepared to fully accept even the most Westernized of Asians as true equals or to apply the ideals of Western political and social morality to non-Western societies. Within Asian societies the attraction of the Western model proved too limited to rally sufficient segments of the nation behind the wholesale eradication of indigenous traditions. Thus the Westernizers remained a minority often vilified in their own country as agents of foreign powers. Many such Westernizers themselves eventually became disillusioned with the desirability as well as the possibility of transplanting whole cultural systems from abroad as the West proved itself vulnerable to violent internecine strife and serious class conflict in the years immediately preceding and following World War I.

c. The Quest for Cultural Renaissance

Faced with the tremendous power of the West and their own society's impotence, Asians who rejected the extremes of both nativism and Westernization were impelled to search for a new formulation that would allow them to retain their sense of identity and self-respect as Asians. Such a formulation would have to reconcile a sense of history with a recognition of the essential changes taking place in the modern era. The concept of *cultural renaissance* was central to one such ideological orientation. It retained a commitment to the past yet utilized elements of that heritage to sanction change within tradition. Typically, the quest for a cultural renaissance entailed an attempt to revitalize society by appealing to elements drawn from the classical tradition, often claiming to have rediscovered some past stage in history which could be viewed as a golden age embodying the authentic genius of the civilization. The present was seen as a corruption of the original tradition, a product of excrescences and distortions. One prevalent explanation of why such values had been eclipsed was to identify foreign influence as a scapegoat—if it was not the West that was to blame then it was earlier alien elements interjected by, for example, the Mughul conquest of a Hindu India or the importation of Chinese Confucianism into a Shinto Japan. What needed to be done, therefore, was to purify the culture in order to return to what was essential and good.

Advocates of such revitalization movements tended to portray the main problem in moral rather than economic or political terms. Associations were created to reform religious practices and improve educational facilities in order to promote such virtues as hard work, thrift, cleanliness, loyalty to family, and civic concern. Religion, perceived as an integral element in the identity of the civilization, was often central to these movements, which contained a strong strain of puritanical self-restraint and self-discipline. In the effort to cleanse indigenous religious practices and beliefs of what were seen as impurities, a determined historical search was sometimes made to substantiate and document the original teachings of the great ethical reformers of the past. This stress on religious and ethical values and the attempt to rally a defense against Western influence led to such stereotyped perceptions as the notion that the West was characterized by materialism while the essential nature of Asia (or the "East" or the "Orient") was spiritual. Such formulations often included the concept of Pan-Asianism—the assertion of a common identity for all Asians. Despite the fact that Asian civilizations did not share a common historical heritage and that there was little substance to this Asian identity beyond the common experience of Western oppression, Pan-Asianism was to remain a persistent minor theme.

Appeals to the heritage of a distant past faced limits. For one, they entailed considerable reinterpretation of the orthodox view of tradition. Attempts at reinterpretation led to bitter controversy and divided opinions about the definition of the cultural tradition as familiar doctrines were stretched further and further from their commonly assumed meanings. Another problem was the fact that, no matter how construed, classical texts and historical legends simply could not be made to yield up sufficient precedents to sanction every reform or counter every challenge from the West. Fragments could be found that suggested primitive forms of democracy or a theory of evolution or a notion of atomic structure, but there was no way to match, refute, or dismiss the potency, for example, of modern science as it had been developed in the West. Advocates of cultural renaissance who claimed that everything of real value and utility could be found within the true indigenous tradition were thus constantly put on the defensive by the European, American, or native Westernizer who loudly proclaimed the opposite. A third difficulty derived from the social origins of these traditional doctrines. The classical heritage was usually the expression of a literate elite and consequently it reflected a view of society that favored the position of particular castes or classes—the established priesthood, the warrior-aristocrat, the scholar-official. For the reforming intellectual such traditional doctrines seldom provided adequate justification for new roles or social relationships and, moreover, accentuated his distance from the populace as a whole.

d. The Appeal of Marxism

Marxism was yet another and very different alternative that presented itself to the twentieth century Asian who found himself disaffected with his own culture yet disenchanted with Western models. Marxist ideology in effect allowed him to reject simultaneously both the discredited values of Western imperialism and the fossil of the indigenous orthodoxy. The degradation of the contemporary period in his country's history was due, in this formulation, not to some inherent weakness in its cultural character but rather to the workings of immutable laws that were universal to all human societies. Asia was caught up in a dialectical process—the transition from feudalism with its inevitable contradictions to yet a new stage in history. Western societies, while more advanced in one sense, were not necessarily superior, since, enmeshed as they were in the conflicts of capitalism, they too had yet to reach the higher stages of historical progress. As reformulated by Lenin, Marxism promised the Asian both a model for revolutionary change within his or her society and a dynamic role to play on the world stage. The initial success of the Bolshevik Revolution, with its small vanguard acting on behalf of the masses, seemed to mean that positive action to bring about immediate social change was possible. Moreover, by taking action against the forces of imperialism, the Asian could cease to be a passive spectator and take part in the destruction of the international system of colonial exploitation, which, in the Marxist-Leninist analysis, was the last remaining prop for capitalism in a decadent West.

Thus, in theory, Marxist-Leninist converts could escape the issue of the superiority of the West, transcend the dilemma of cultural identity, and devote their attention to national liberation and social revolution in the quest for universal salvation through socialism. In practice, however, the Marxist-Leninist, like the Westernizer, faced serious resistance from within to the wholesale rejection of tradition and, like other reformers, the danger of continued domination from without by foreign (albeit socialist) powers upon whom he or she depended for aid. It is not surprising, therefore, that the most successful movements led by Marxists-Leninists in Asia have been those that combined the call for a social revolution (to be defined by universal standards) with a strong appeal to a nationalist identity shaped by an indigenous heritage.

e. Nationalism as a Salvation Ideology

Examples of all the above responses to the crises of the modern era can be found even in late twentieth century Asia; but the type of reaction that was to have the most profound impact was that of nationalism. Part of the reason for the appeal of nationalism as a salvation ideology has been the fact that it is sufficiently broad in scope to encompass many of the diverse themes in the responses already discussed. Nationalism was less a defense of a past culture than an assertion of a present identity as an Asian in the face of threat and oppression. The essential elements, however, included the notion that a people were one because they shared a common history and that their identity was bound up with their language, customs, and institutions. But these were elements that needed to be revived, reinterpreted if not fashioned anew, and consciously embraced as a means of rejecting alien values. Also present was an emphasis on a sense of pride as a member of a national group—the idea that fellow nationals should cherish and esteem one another regardless of social class and that the group as a whole must work together to actualize its union in the building of a nation-state. This in turn entailed the belief that a certain defineable territory belonged to the national community and that the community should establish its own national political power and consolidate its independent rule over that territory.

Ironically, it was the Europeans and Americans themselves who offered the Asians the most clearly defined blueprint for nationalism as a salvation ideology. Imperialism in Asia had developed out of national rivalry in the West, and concepts regarding the right of peoples to national independence and the organization of a nation-state were part of the cultural baggage that Westerners brought with them on their trip east. The lessons of the French and American revolutions and the history of nationalism in the West were not lost on Asian students attending colonial or missionary schools. Often it was those individuals most deeply imbued with Western values who emerged as the leaders of nationalist movements. Some asserted their nationalism as vehemently as they did precisely because they were so attuned to a foreign culture and so estranged from their own. Nationalism was one cultural element that could be borrowed from the West precisely because it promised delivery from the West.

Nationalism also owed much to indigenous cultural renaissance movements, but three essential differences should be noted. First, the concept of cultural renaissance was much wider in scope, embracing often a whole civilization, while nationalism appealed to a single ethnic or linguistic community, often fragmenting a civilizational area. Second, the advocates of cultural renaissance frequently made a claim for cultural superiority in universal terms, while nationalists were typically more defensive. Nationalists did not claim general validity for their culture, only the right of their national community to exist independently and exercise its own standards. Of course, there did appear (notably in Japan) a type of chauvinistic, aggressive nationalism that then developed into an imperialism similar to that of the West, but this was not typical of nationalism elsewhere in Asia. Third, advocates of cultural renaissance were usually so committed to the integrity of their traditions that they found themselves unable to compromise with alien influences on core values and central institutions. Nationalists displayed a greater flexibility. Using the nation as their sanction, they were relatively freer to borrow from foreign models and to modify traditional practices where the result promised to strengthen the nation.

f. The Emergence of Revolutionary Nationalist Movements

By the turn of the twentieth century nationalism had become the sanction for revolutionary movements of two sorts in Asia. One type aimed primarily at national liberation, the overthrow of the old political order, the ouster of foreign oppressors, and the establishment of an independent state. These were often quite elitist movements, stressing social reform as a means of national strength rather than as an end in itself. Even here, however, the appeal for mass support and the call for national unity were to have significant ramifications for relations between the classes. A second type aimed more directly at social revolution, the displacement of elites and ruling classes and the achievement of political freedom and economic justice for all strata.

By the second decade of the twentieth century revolutionary nationalist movements had brought down the last of the great early modern empires in Asia—the Ottoman, the Manchu, and the Czarist regimes were swept away. The aftermath of World War I provided yet a greater stimulus for the formation of independence movements. Indians and Chinese had participated in the war in Europe yet had reaped no rewards in the peace settlement at Versailles. The rise of the Soviet Union also provided a model and a source of aid for some independence movements as agents of the Comintern helped organize in areas as diverse as Indonesia, India, and China. The period since World War II has been the great era of national liberation in Asia. The effective break in colonial administration caused by German and Japanese conquests made the reassertion of Western control extremely difficult. Where it was attemped, in Indonesia and Vietnam for instance, fierce resistance by independence movements obliged the colonial powers to retreat. As the weakness of the West became evident and the international climate more favorable to self-rule, peoples throughout Asia regained political sovereignty. In some places, Japan briefly, Korea and Vietnam for longer periods, colonial rule was followed by political sovereignty under foreign military and economic domination—what has been called neocolonialism. This in turn has given a new spur to nationalism.

From our perspective of the comparative study of civilizations in Asia, the emergence of modern nation-states raises a number of interesting questions. First, we may note that different strands in the civilized tradition have influenced the type of states that have emerged. In China, for instance, the People's Republic follows the general contours of the early modern empire, even where this involved annexing peoples like the Tibetans who were not Chinese in the strictest sense. In South Asia, British India divided along religious lines as separate Hindu and Muslim states were formed. In West Asia the Ottoman empire divided along ethnic and linguistic lines as Turks, Arabs, and others went their separate ways. Second, where the early modern empire involved the subjugation of one Asian people by another, nationalism in the sense of anti-imperialism could develop only after the collapse of the traditional empire. This was the case for both the Arabs and the Chinese, who had been ruled by the Turks and the Manchus, respectively. Third, where the new states included diverse ethnic and linguistic elements they were not nations in the narrow sense. The development of nationalism could still pull them apart. The fragmentation of Pakistan and the formation of Bangladesh is an example of this. A fully developed Bengali nationalism could conceivably seek inclusion of West Bengal, now a part of India.

Thus, in the earlier phases of European encroachment sensitive Asians reacted to the perception of a crisis by appealing to core values within their own indigenous cultural tradition, by seeking a cultural renaissance. Later, when traditional values and institutions had been discredited and the disruption of old norms had progressed to the point of cultural disintegration, it was the sense of a nationality that provided a sanction for resistance to external pressure or control. The reader should note that in the case of a cultural renaissance the unit that is being defended—often in the form of an early modern empire—is a civilization, while in the case of nationalism it is a smaller, more parochial entity. In making the shift, as we do in this chapter and the next, from the empire to the nation we may well be seeing the end of the civilization as a meaningful level of Asian social organization. Certainly there is a tendency to reduce the scale of the units of our comparison. Be that as it may, in both the cultural renaissance and nationalism phases there was a persisting search for identity and cohesion in the face of European domination and as a sanction for social change, development, and adaptation to modern conditions.

Cultural renaissance, as a response to the experience of foreign domination and the absorption of alien values, was not something new in the historical experience of Eurasian civilizations. Indeed, the familiar Renaissance in Western Europe involved a revival of Greek and Roman cultural elements after a long ingestion of Christian influences. In China in the twelfth century the Sung neo-Confucian synthesis was marked by a similar conscious return to elements of the classical heritage following a period of Buddhist ascendancy.

Chapter 8 described the domination of Central Asian peoples over the centers of Asian civilizations, and the following chapter portrayed the formation of early modern empires as involving to varying degrees a response to Mongol domination and an adaptation of Mongol organization. But the contrasts between Central Asian and Western European domination are worthy of repetition. Nomadic peoples, few in number, without powerful literary traditions, and possessing relatively simple economic institutions, tended to settle among their wealthier civilized subjects and to become acculturated to the values of sedentary society. That superior military power was insufficient to overwhelm or displace the traditional civilizations is at least partially illustrated by the failure of Timur and his descendants to shift the locus of dominant power to a capital in Central Asia. European domination, by contrast, was the accomplishment of societies that possessed dynamic cultural traditions of their own and that by the nineteenth century easily outmatched Asians in wealth, technology, and economic development. Furthermore, the Europeans never settled in Asia in appreciable numbers and so remained largely immune to the possibility of acculturation.

Contrasts in the cultural levels of Central Asia and Western Europe, however, are not sufficient to explain the profound impact of the more recent domination upon Asian societies. Europeans came to Asia bearing their own cultures, but they also came as the agents and conduits of new forces of change—industrialization is an example—which respected no culture. The force of European aggression reached its highest level precisely as the core institutions of Western civilization—the church, kingship, social class, and property—were in turmoil and Europe was fragmented into parochial nation-states that competed furiously for world hegemony. Disruptive as these changes in the old order were for the Europeans, they sprang from indigenous causes; for the Asian, modernization was perceived as being at once antitraditional and foreign. This helps to account for the complexity of the Asian responses. Cultural renaissance and nationalist movements were responses not simply to an alien threat but to an alien threat plus the disintegration of the traditional order. Facing the dual challenges of Westernization and modernization, the Asian identity crisis was not easily resolved. The conflicting demands of these two challenges clouded all values with ambiguity. The West was regarded both hostilely as the cause of Asian humiliation and positively as a model of nationhood and development. Likewise, traditional values were cited as an explanation for the weakness of Asians in the face of European aggression and embraced as a sanction for resistance to the West. The irreconcilable demands of cultural identity and social change underlie much of the confusion and distress that has characterized modern Asian nationalism.

It remains to be noted that although nationalism has proved to be a viable tool for mobilizing people and organizing economic development, it cannot supplant older cultural traditions. Nationalism is inherently parochial and it necessarily involves competition and rivalry. Such fragmentation must raise serious questions about the fate of the enduring shared values that characterized the civilizations of Eurasia.

PATTERNS

1. CULTURAL RENAISSANCE AND NATIONALISM IN WEST ASIA

It has been stressed in an earlier chapter that the full impact of European expansion was not felt in West Asia until long after it had been felt in other parts of Asia. In consequence, that impact was only one factor among several that contributed to the quest for a redefinition of cultural identity that preoccupied almost all Muslim communities at some stage of the nineteenth or twentieth centuries. Hardly less significant than the impact of European imperialism was the ongoing upsurge of reformist movements founded on the supposition that the solutions to Islam's ills were to be sought in the revocation of the distant past—the recurring preoccupation with a golden age expressed in theological terms. Very frequently these reformist ideologies contained, whether explicitly or implicitly, a strong undercurrent of dissatisfaction with the political status quo, to be seen most clearly in the Wahhabi movement. Such undercurrents of dissatisfaction, however, went far beyond the rather restricted circle of religious reformers and their followers. In the case of the Ottoman empire, the fact that the sultan-caliph was clearly unable to protect his Muslim subjects from oppression at the hands of infidel Christians greatly diminished his authority in the eyes of very many Muslims, while others, like the Wahhabis, deplored the exercise by the Ottoman dynasty of lawmaking functions such as no early Muslim rulers had dared to assume.

Within the Ottoman empire, the discontent of the sultan's Arab subjects mounted as Turkish rule became increasingly inept. The Arabs saw themselves as the people who had given form and direction to the whole Islamic historical experience, yet now they were subject to an oppressive colonial regime that exploited them in the interests of far-away Istanbul and of a grasping Turkish ruling elite. Thus, their resentment at the continuation of Ottoman Turkish rule—notwithstanding the impeccable credentials of past generations of Ottoman rulers as *ghazis* in the service of Islam—may be compared to Chinese resentment during the same period at the prolongation of Manchu dominance. In the case of Iran, the Shii clergy had grown accustomed since the early eighteenth century to regarding the authority of the shah as being in some sense a usurpative and illegitimate authority, and this attitude was reinforced during the second half of the nineteenth century when the later Qajars, under pressure from the diplomatic representatives of the European powers, recklessly squandered the limited resources of the country by admitting foreign speculators and concession hunters. Even in remote Bukhara, where the reigning dynasty was celebrated for its obscurantist religiosity, the fact that the amir had become, after 1868, a vassal of the White Czar raised doubts as to the extent to which the regime could be regarded as truly Islamic. If, almost everywhere in the nineteenth century, ineffective and incompetent Muslim rulers prompted some of the shrewdest as well as some of the most pious among their subjects to question their fitness to exercise dominion over their fellow Muslims, contemporary research and writing by European scholars in the field of Islamic studies contributed towards an increased awareness on the part of educated Muslims of their past heritage of political grandeur and intellectual achievement, a development that had its counterpart in other Asian societies where European Orientalism contributed to nostalgia for some golden age or other. Thus the study of comparative Turkish languages and dialects by European Turcologists increased Ottoman Turkish awareness of a Turkish racial and cultural heritage extending over vast regions of the Eurasian heartland, thereby providing the substance that would later sustain Pan-Turkish and Pan-Turanian ideologies. Similarly, in Iran, although at a rather later date, European archaeological concern for pre-Islamic Iranian civilizations, deriving from a European preoccupation with Biblical and Classical studies, further stimulated Iranian awareness of their most ancient past and thereby gave a new, pre-Islamic dimension to Iranian nationalism.

These processes necessarily varied in their timing, in their intensity, and in their impact from one part of West Asia to another, but almost everywhere there was one question that, sooner or later, and in one form or another, came to be asked: how to reconcile traditional Islamic universalism with redefined concepts of cultural identity and, as an extension of that process of redefinition, of particularist nationalist aspirations. For the Iranians the question proved less difficult than it did for the Ottoman Turks and the Arabs, but in all instances the answer was conditioned by external factors—European interference in the affairs of the Muslim world, the impact of the introduction of European technology and economic imperialism, the growth of communal tensions, and so forth. In the following survey of Muslim renaissance and nationalist movements, the four major cultural groups—the Turks of the Ottoman empire, the Turks under Russian rule, the Iranians, and the Arabs—will, for the sake of clarity, be treated under separate headings.

The Turks of the Ottoman Empire

Like the Austro-Hungarian empire of the Habsburgs, the Ottoman empire was neither a state nor a nation, but an idea embodied in the person of the ruler, the sultan-caliph, descendant of the *ghazi* sultans who had once been the invincible sword-arm of Islamic expansionism. Loyalty and patriotism could be felt only towards the dynasty; no other cement held the fabric together, certainly not the ideal of Islamic universalism, which meant nothing or less than nothing to the numerous non-Muslim peoples of the empire. For this reason, perceptive Ottoman statesmen understood only too well that there was no possibility of evolving a truly Ottoman nationalism since, as in the case of Austria-Hungary, the spread of the idea of nationalism (as it was currently conceived among the nation-states of Western Europe) among the subject peoples would lead inevitably to the emergence of new or long submerged nationalist ideologies that would bring about the ultimate disintegration of the empire. Thus, as a substitute for the ideology of nationalism, which they could never hope to mould to the empire's needs, Ottoman politicians, publicists, and intellectuals toyed with a succession of substitute ideologies, which, at their most rudimentary, were substitute loyalties—Ottomanism, Islamism and Pan-Islamism, Turkism and Pan-Turkism. Although there is no clearcut chronological framework within which the rich intellectual ferment of the Ottoman empire in the last century of its existence can be set, it is useful to relate major developments in Ottoman political thought to the various contemporary modifications that were being made to the institutional structure of the empire. Thus Ottomanism may be regarded as the intellectual counterpart of the Tanzimat reforms between 1839 and 1878, Pan-Islamism coincided with the reign of the reactionary sultan Abd al-Hamid II (1876-1909), and Turkism and its various offshoots flourished with the coming to power of the "Young Turks" in 1908.

It was the function of the reforming sultan Mahmud II (1808-39) to undertake the role of a belated Peter the Great, striving in the best traditions of enlightened despotism to renovate the decrepit institutions of the empire. Upon his death his two colorless successors allowed his reforms to be continued by a handful of farsighted leaders of the bureaucracy, who were intent on dragging the empire into the nineteenth century and imposing upon it an institutional superstructure resembling that of the European powers. This innovative period, known as the Tanzimat, was initiated in 1839 by an imperial rescript that guaranteed certain fundamental rights to the sultan's subjects, Muslim and non-Muslim alike, and these were reinforced by the rescript of 1856, which guaranteed non-Muslims religious equality with Muslims. The climax to the Tanzimat reforms came with the promulgation of a constitution for the empire in 1876. This and much else that had been achieved in the preceding decades was then undone during the repressive reign of Abd al-Hamid II, who was intent upon altogether different objectives.

There has been a tendency to denigrate the achievements of the Tanzimat reformers and their facile concern with imitating European models. It is also fashionable to decry their attempts to implant in the unprepared soil of the empire concepts such as religious toleration and equality between Muslims and non-Muslims, seen now as token gestures of "Westernization" designed to placate the European powers and to prevent them from interfering further in the affairs of the empire. In fact, the achievements of the Tanzimat period were far from negligible. The traditional framework of Ottoman government, based on the Ruling Institution, was replaced by departments of state under a council of ministers; the central bureaucracy and the provincial administration were made both more effective and more responsive to the needs of the times; and strenuous efforts were made to introduce a legal system based on the French model, although the Sharia remained supreme in matters of family life and inheritance. The Tanzimat period also witnessed the establishment of a number of schools and colleges—including a military academy and a faculty of medicine—which laid the foundations for the expansion of higher education in the decades preceding the First World War. Along with the appearance of novel European-style educational institutions, there emerged an equally novel Europeanized intelligentsia who exchanged ideas among themselves and sought to win supporters for the cause of Westernization through the agency of the press and a small number of literary societies and social clubs such as the reformers had encountered on their travels in France, England and, less commonly, Russia. The spread of ideas, however, depended upon ease of communication, and the leading writers of the Tanzimat period—Ibrahim Shinasi (1826-71), Ziya Pasha (1825-80), and Namik Kemal (1840-88)—were therefore deeply committed to spreading a simplified Turkish language stripped of the elaborate Arabic-Persian accretions that had long since made the written word scarcely intelligible to the average Turk. In Istanbul itself the life-style of the ruling elite, senior members of the bureaucracy, and many professional men was now beginning to conform more closely to that of their European counterparts than to the traditional life-style prevailing in most other parts of the Islamic world. But it is significant that anticlericalism was not a feature of the Tanzimat period: even the most enthusiastic Westernizers chose to ignore Islam rather than risk a head-on confrontation.

For all that, the Tanzimat reformers were not without enemies. Conservatives, especially among the *ulama,* mistrusted them. The European powers did nothing to ease the path of reform by refraining from intervention. The Christian minorities, who should have welcomed the reforms, perceived that a renovated empire was a more serious obstacle to their nationalist aspirations than a decrepit one, and did little or nothing to further their success. There were also some among the new intelligentsia who were dissatisfied by the pace and direction of the reforms, directed as they were by men with bureaucratic experience and, for the most part, bureaucratic objectives. These latter had always been prone to think in terms of mechanistic solutions and they tended to underestimate the intractable problems ever present in the plural composition of Ottoman society. A younger generation, which included some of the finest minds of the time, among them Namik Kemal, was growing increasingly dissatisfied with what the Tanzimat reformers had achieved so far. Its leaders were idealistic and impatient, and in 1865 they formed a kind of secret society modeled on the Carbonari of contemporary Italy. In 1867 the government, detecting a revolutionary flavor in the movement, sent its leaders into exile while others fled abroad. In that same year the Turkish press gave the movement the name of *Yeni Osmanlilar,* "New" or "Young Ottomans," and the name stuck.

Two aspects of the Young Ottoman movement are of particular significance. First, it sought to combat the centrifugal forces of ethnic nationalism spreading among the subject peoples of the empire, and thereby endangering its intricate structure, by offering an alternative form of nationalism—Ottomanism—which was love for the Ottoman fatherland, a concept that was, however, virtually meaningless to the Christian *millets* of the empire and meant little more to the non-Turkish Muslims of the Asian provinces. Second, the Young Ottomans tried to accelerate the process of change already set in motion by the Tanzimat reformers, and they were intent on reducing the still formidable power wielded by the traditional landowning, administrative, and clerical classes, power that sooner or later could be used to undermine what had been achieved so far. It was this fear that was the basis of the Young Ottoman demand for a constitutional monarchy of the British type.

13.1 A session of the first Ottoman Parliament, Istanbul, April 1877. As in their institutions, so also in culture and life-style, the Ottoman Turkish reformers of the Tanzimat period (1839-77) sought an accommodation with the West which foreshadowed Ataturk's vigorous assertion of Western values between the world wars. Courtesy: S. T. Rosenthal, from *Illustrated London News*, 14 April 1877.

Vaguely liberal and progressive, the Young Ottomans endeavored to present the empire with a patriotic alternative to the suicidal quest for self-determination for the various minorities. They sought to ensure that there could be no return to the evils of the past and, perhaps incongruously, they thought in terms of Islamic revitalization. Unfortunately for their program, their leaders were intellectually inconsistent and divided by bitter personal rivalries. Vain and quarrelsome, their indiscretions led to frequent spells of exile while their personal ambitions made them all too susceptible to the temptations of office. By 1876, however, their hopes seemed to be coming close to fulfillment. The greatest living Ottoman statesman and reformer was Midhat Pasha (1822-83), who had held a succession of important appointments in both Istanbul and the provinces, including that of grand *vazir* for a short time in 1872. In 1876 he had engineered the deposition of two sultans, the first a capricious despot and the second a lunatic, and had brought to the throne the latter's younger brother, Abd al-Hamid II, and with him a constitution of which the new ruler appeared to approve. Midhat Pasha was again appointed grand *vazir* and it appeared that a turning point had been reached in the protracted story of Ottoman decline and recovery. But the reformers had misjudged their new master.

In his later years Abd al-Hamid manifested clear signs of paranoia bordering upon insanity. In his early years, however, he was neither inactive nor unintelligent. He was not opposed to an extension of the reforms in the narrow sense of further improvement in the administration, but he was unswervingly hostile to the constitutional aims of the Young Ottomans and had set his heart upon restoring the traditional authority of the sultan-caliph. He had accepted the constitution, largely to deflect the hostility of the European powers, and an Ottoman parliament met for the first time in March 1877, but in the following February he dissolved the chamber. Midhat Pasha had already been dismissed and sent into exile in 1877. He returned in 1881 at the insistence of the British, but was then put on trial for the alleged murder of a former sultan. Since foreign intervention prevented his execution then and there, he was sent as a prisoner to the Hijaz, where he was murdered in 1883. Meanwhile, Abd al-Hamid determined to establish a personal and authoritarian rule, supported by the entire paraphernalia of despotism including informers, *agents provocateurs*, and secret police. Without turning his back on Westernization as a *tool* for strengthening the empire, he rejected the more progressive elements of the Tanzimat and Young Ottoman periods and sought to strengthen the traditional Islamic components of the regime and at the same time to restore the diminished prestige of the throne. He mistrusted the Ottoman bureaucracy for its involvement in the Tanzimat reforms, while he regarded his Christian subjects as irredeemably disloyal. Manifestations of restlessness were punished with savage repression, earning the sultan the soubriquet of Abdul the Damned in Victorian England, and it was during this reign that the Armenians of Anatolia, hitherto regarded as being among the sultan's most loyal subjects, first became the objects of political persecution. Concern for reviving the Islamic universalist foundations of the empire did, however, result in Abd al-Hamid showing a greater degree of concern for the welfare of his Arab subjects than any sultan had shown before. His personal entourage included Arab advisers and divines; some attempts were made to develop the neglected Asian provinces; and, partly in response to religious sentiment, the construction of the Hijaz railway was begun.

Abd al-Hamid endeavored with some success to link the fortunes of the empire with the ideology of Pan-Islamism, then widely believed to offer a remedy for the humiliations that Muslims everywhere were experiencing at the hands of the European powers. The driving force behind the Pan-Islamic movement was Sayyid Jamal al-Din Afghani (1839-97), a mysterious conspiratorial figure who flitted from one Muslim court to another on secret missions and who, despite his denunciation of European imperialism and especially of the British, may have acted on occasion as a secret agent of at least one European power. Although claiming to be an Afghan and a Sunni by birth, he was probably born an Iranian

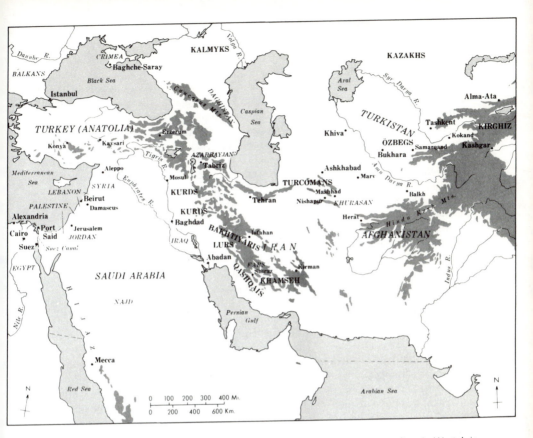

Map 53 Nationalism in West Asia

and a Shii. With regard to the latter fact, it may be significant that while he occupies an important place in the history of Islamic revitalization in the nineteenth century, his concern with orthodox theology fell considerably short of his fascination for philosophy, especially its more esoteric and hermetic aspects. His political activism and his hostility to European imperialism seemed to link him with movements such as those of the Wahhabis in Arabia and the Sanusis in Libya, but he was far from being a fundamentalist. His dream was to give Islam a political cohesion and a unity that would enable it to confront the challenge of European expansionism, and it was in the role of supreme leader of a Pan-Islamic movement that he cast Abd al-Hamid, the only Muslim ruler of the age who could possibly serve the purpose. Afghani seems to have felt no special predilection for the Ottoman empire other than as the obvious political structure upon which he could build a greater Islamic unity. Abd al-Hamid, however, clearly recognized that no one was more likely than Afghani to promote his own aspirations as politico-spiritual leader of the entire Muslim *umma*, "the community of believers," a concept that was rooted in the Ottoman dynasty's claim to have succeeded to the defunct Abbasid caliphate and that in the last years of the nineteenth century was given a new lease of life, especially among those Muslims living on the fringes of the *Dar al-Islam* in India and Indonesia.

Pan-Islamism, however, further alienated the non-Muslim subjects of the empire, did little to reconcile the Arab masses to Ottoman rule, and provided no obvious solutions for the Turks themselves in their pursuit of their own identity. Indeed, some of the most dynamic elements in Turkish society now recognized the need for a more radical approach.

For such as these, the Young Ottoman movement was seen as irrelevant and in its place they established the Ottoman Committee of Union and Progress, founded in 1889, a secret society of a kind long familiar in Italy and the Balkans and whose members were later to become known as the Young Turks. Initially its membership was not exclusively Turkish, but the majority came from the middle strata of Ottoman society, including a sizeable element of army officers. In 1896 an unsuccessful coup d'état leading to imprisonment and exile temporarily weakened the movement, but it revived in the first decade of the new century and was now dominated by members of the officer corps. Its headquarters were transferred to Salonika, a city with a significantly large population of Jews and Free Masons, and here in 1908 a group of officers initiated an uprising against the government, resulting in the deposition of Abd al-Hamid and the accession of his brother as Mehmed V (1909-18). The constitution of 1876 was restored and the Young Turks seemed about to establish a parliamentary and secular regime far beyond anything envisaged by even the most progressive among the Young Ottomans.

Certainly the Young Turks made a substantial contribution to the modernization of Turkey, but unavoidably their rule coincided with the Balkan Wars of 1912-13, further uprisings among the Christian population of the empire and, finally, involvement in the First World War as an ally of Germany and Austria-Hungary. Conscious of the implacable hostility of the Christian *millets* to further integration within the empire, the Young Turks embarked upon a harsh program of Turkification, of which the Christian Armenians were to become the most conspicuous victims although not even the Muslim Arabs were exempt from pressure. This preoccupation with Turkification was the logical outcome of the ideological sterility of both Ottomanism and Pan-Islamism, and for a while Turkism for the Turks of the Ottoman empire acquired a romantic extension in the form of Pan-Turkism, the political and cultural unification of all the Turkish peoples, including those under Russian and Chinese rule. For the Turks of the Russian empire Pan-Turkism and Pan-Turanism (the unification of the Turkish peoples of Inner Asia) proved an intoxicating dream which was soon to threaten the new Soviet regime no less than it had threatened its czarist predecessor. For the Turks of Anatolia, however, the defeat of the Ottoman empire in the First World War, foreign occupation and partition by the vindictive Allies, and the direction taken by the Turkish revolution of Mustafa Kemal (later to assume the title of Ataturk) necessitated the rejection of this impracticable ideology as much as of its nineteenth century predecessors. Ataturk's goal was a secular Turkish republic resting securely upon Anatolian Turkish nationalism and Westernization. Under his inspired leadership the Turks of Anatolia at last evolved a new identity, but one in which the components of Kemalist nationalism and the Islamic traditions of the Ottoman past remained necessarily most uncomfortable bedfellows.

The Turks under Russian Rule

Within the frontiers of the Russian empire lived some of the most tradition-bound communities in the entire Muslim world, subjects of the khan of Khiva and the amir of Bukhara, but also some of the most enlightened, the Tatars of Kazan and the Crimea. By the second half of the nineteenth century some Tatars had endured European colonial domination for almost three hundred years and their familiarity with European ways far exceeded that of any other group of Muslims. Compared to the Turks of the Ottoman empire, their situation was less ambiguous but also less promising. It was less ambiguous because the problem of identity was less complicated. Whereas the Ottoman Turks had to come to terms with what it meant to be a Turk and a Muslim in an empire that was a plural society with regard to both its Muslim and its non-Muslim components, for the Turkish peoples of Central Asia the question of identity was, at least in a superficial sense, much more straightforward: they were Muslim "hewers of wood and drawers of water," enduring a heavy Christian yoke.

Inevitably, regional and tribal distinctions among them were important, but there was also a special kind of affinity based on a common religion and culture, reinforced by the fact that the various Turkish languages of the area were, in the main, closely related to each other. But the long-term prospects for these peoples were less promising. Subjects of an autocratic and militaristic European empire in which they were deeply embedded by geography as well as history, their only hope of seeing the fulfillment of their communal aspirations was by means of a thoroughgoing liberalization of the entire regime. The Russian empire, however, was not to be liberalized but overthrown, and considerations of ideology, national security, and economic self-interest ensured the rejection of secessionist solutions by its Soviet successor.

The cultural renaissance of the Muslims of Russia went hand in hand with both the extension of the empire and the tardy efforts of nineteenth century Russian society to catch up with the rest of Europe. Thus it was that the winds of change blowing through the Russia of Alexander II and Alexander III touched the Crimean and Kazan Tatars at the very time when, as fellow Muslims, they were most affected by the plight of the Kazakhs, Özbegs, and Turcomans newly absorbed into the empire. It was in Baghche-Saray, the old capital of the Crimean Tatar khanate, that there occurred during the second half of the nineteenth century that movement known as the Tatar Renaissance, which was to be both an inspiration and an example to Muslim reformers and modernizers far beyond the frontiers of Russia. The central figure in that movement was Ismail Gasprali (1851-1914), also known as Ismail Bey Gasprinsky, one of the most influential of Muslim educational pioneers. He did not, however, emerge from an untilled soil. The ground had been well prepared in advance.

For the first two centuries after Ivan the Terrible's conquests, the Volga Tatars had been harried by the Russian state and persecuted by the Orthodox church, although they had, for the most part, resisted conversion and had frequently revolted against their oppressors. Then, in 1773, Catherine the Great had granted religious toleration to her Muslim subjects and, following the suppression of Pugachev's rebellion of 1773-74, in which many lower-class Tatars had participated, she removed the commercial disabilities formally imposed on the Tatar bourgeoisie and went some way to restoring the social standing of the Tatar landholding class. Finally, in 1788, she granted the Muslims of the empire a Spiritual Assembly, headed by a Mufti, with its headquarters at Orenburg, later transferred to Ufa in Bashkiria. These developments were to be of crucial importance in the evolution of the Muslim peoples of the empire. The removal of former economic and social disabilities enabled the Volga Tatars to emerge during the nineteenth century as an enterprising and relatively prosperous bourgeoisie serving as intermediaries between the Russians and the isolated Muslims of Central Asia, to whom they imparted an awareness of the common experience of the Turkish peoples of Eurasia, thereby strengthening their cultural identity in the face of Russian domination. Moreover, since they were both physically and intellectually closer to the heartlands of the *Dar al-Islam,* the Tatars conveyed to the Turks of Central Asia a sense of belonging to a greater Islamic community, of which hitherto the Kazakhs and the Kirghiz, in particular, had scarcely been aware. From Ufa the Spiritual Assembly supervised a growing network of traditional Muslim schools, largely staffed by Volga Tatars, while the printing press of Kazan published, in addition to the Quran, religious commentaries in Tatar, which circulated far into Central Asia.

These developments did not pass unnoticed by the Russians at a time when their exploitation of the newly conquered territories in the east was displacing the Tatar bourgeoisie, which had hitherto enjoyed a virtual monopoly of the overland commerce with Central Asia. The Russians rightly feared the intellectual ascendancy of the Tatars and of the Tatar schools over their new and by no means submissive subjects, and in the case of the Kazakhs they endeavored to circumvent Tatar influence by the establishment of Russo-

Kazakh schools, where Russian, and not Tatar, was the medium of instruction. In this they enjoyed the unqualified support of the pioneer Kazakh modernizer, Chokan Valikhanov (1835-65), a member of the tribal nobility who, for a time, served as a cadet at the military academy at Omsk and became the friend of Dostoevski. Prior to his early death, Valikhanov laid the foundations for the future development of Kazakh studies. A somewhat analogous figure to Raja Rammohun Roy in Bengal, he fought off the obscurantist clerical influences emanating from Bukhara, believing that the future advancement of the Kazakhs was dependent on close and willing cooperation with Russia. Predictably, it was from the Russo-Kazakh schools that there emerged the first and most idealistic generation of Kazakh disseminators of Russian culture among the steppe peoples.

The Tatar contribution to Islamic modernism is most fully exemplified in the career of Ismail Gasprali. Educated in Baghche-Saray and Moscow, he was influenced both by the writings of the Pan-Slavists and by Russian liberals such as Alexander Herzen, while visits to Paris and Istanbul reinforced his early enthusiasm for nationalism and liberalism. Towards the Ottoman empire he felt a deep and abiding affection, and he supported both the aims of the Tanzimat reformers and the ideas of the Young Ottomans. Later he was attracted by the Pan-Islamic ideology of Jamal al-Din Afghani, sympathizing with the goal of freeing Muslims everywhere from Christian domination while at the same time seeking to eliminate the prevailing ignorance and superstition that characterized most Muslim societies in his day. In 1883 he began to publish in Baghche-Saray the newspaper *Terjuman (The Interpreter),* which thereafter exercised an immense and unrivaled influence over the Muslims of Russia (and to some extent also, those of Istanbul) for nearly a quarter of a century. In it he stressed the need for the renovation of religion, social reform (including an improved status for women), self-help and self-reliance, and the unity of all Muslims, which in practice came to mean all Turks. One of Ismail Gasprali's dearest wishes was to see the emergence of a common language for the Turkish peoples. In view of his sentiments towards the Ottoman empire, the language he hoped would serve this function, and the language in which *Terjuman* was written, was the simplified Ottoman Turkish of the Tanzimat period and not Tatar or the elaborate Chaghatay Turkish of Central Asia. Despite his liberalism and his nationalism Ismail Gasprali could not visualize the passing of the Ottoman or the Czarist empire, and with regard to the latter—whether from conviction or prudence—he seems to have assumed, as did many other influential Muslim intellectuals, that the destinies of the Russians and the Turks who shared the great expanses of Eurasia were inextricably bound together. Partnership, however, depended upon several uncertain factors that deeply concerned him. One of these, very obviously, was the relations between Russia and the Ottoman empire and, to a lesser extent, Iran. Another was raising the level of the Turkish peoples of Russia, and especially the Tatars, so that in the future they could participate with the Russians on roughly equal terms. This, he believed, could be achieved only through modern education. His conviction may be compared with that of Sayyid Ahmad Khan in India, who was concerned that Indian Muslims should catch up with the Hindus in the race to acquire Western knowledge.

In Baghche-Saray he established a model school in which the medium of instruction was Tatar and in which European subjects such as mathematics and geography were included in the curriculum, as well as Arabic, Quranic studies, and the principles of the Sharia. This new pattern of education was known as *usul-i jadid* ("new method") and it was soon being introduced among the Volga Tatars and even among the Kazakhs and the Özbegs by devoted followers of Ismail Gasprali, mainly Tatars, who were nicknamed Jadids, or "innovators," by their reactionary opponents, who denounced the new method for smacking of infidelity. Nevertheless, it has been estimated that on the eve of the First World War there were over five thousand such schools, and a proportionate rise in Muslim literacy.

Ismail Gasprali had never been a lone figure but a leader closely associated with co-workers and disciples. In 1893 he made a personal visit to Russian Turkistan, where his journal *Terjuman* was already known to progressive Özbegs. This visit and a decade of preparation bore fruit in 1901, when the first new-method school was opened in Tashkent. Two years later another was opened in Samarqand. The influence of the Jadids grew steadily but slowly, opposed not only by the ultraconservative *ulama* but also by the Russian administration. The establishment of Özbeg printing presses with a creditable range of publications and, above all, the founding by the Jadids of several periodicals written in Özbeg were indicative of a changing mood, but in the protectorates of Khiva and Bukhara the power of the clergy was an almost insurmountable barrier to the spread of the new ideas prior to the revolution.

The Jadid movement was the principal agency for the spread of both Islamic modernism and European science among the Muslims of Russia. It provided the intellectual backbone of a highly talented intelligentsia, parallel in certain respects to that of Russia itself, but beyond the Tatar bourgeoisie of the Crimea and the Volga-Ural region its impact was limited. While the bourgeoisie of the latter area had come to resemble in their outward appearance and life-style their Russian counterparts, the Tatar peasantry remained much as it had always been, and this was even more true in Central Asia, where tribal and clerical elites set the prevailing tone of society. Paradoxically, however, Islam, although overwhelmingly influential as a spiritual and moral force, did not exclusively mould the perceived historical identity of these peoples, perhaps because they themselves had played no great part in the affairs of the *Dar al-Islam* before the coming of the Mongols and Timur, and also because their social values, especially in the case of the nomadic Kazakhs, Kirghiz, and Turcomans, reflected a folk culture in which Islamic and pre-Islamic elements were inextricably interwoven.

The growth of nationalist movements among the Turkish peoples of Central Asia followed a broadly parallel course down to the revolution. In the case of the Tatars and the Azarbayjani Turks of the southern Caucasus region, the early years of the twentieth century brought great changes. A new generation emerged impatient with Ismail Gasprali's political conservatism. Socialism and the abortive revolution of 1905 encouraged the growth of more radical attitudes, and Pan-Islamism gave way to a Pan-Turkish ideology such as the Young Turks were espousing in the Ottoman empire. In 1905 a group of nearly a hundred prominent Tatars met in Kazan and resolved to petition the government regarding their grievances. Although rebuffed by the government, partly in consequence of the undisguised hostility of Muslim conservatives towards their liberalizing aspirations, they proceeded to hold in semisecrecy an All-Russian Muslim Congress in Nizhni Novgorod, followed a year later by a second congress in St. Petersburg. From the latter emerged the Union of Russian Muslims, popularly known as *Ittifak*, which embodied a bourgeois middle-of-the-road position unacceptable to conservatives and radicals alike. Although in theory *Ittifak* was supposed to represent the views of the broad spectrum of Russian Muslims, it was in fact dominated by Crimean and Volga Tatars and by Azarbayjanis. Only a few Kazakhs participated and no Central Asians attended. The ethnic and geographic imbalance of its membership, its moderate stance on almost all issues (it rejected both nationalist and Pan-Islamic solutions and declared unswerving loyalty to the czar), and the fact that its program displeased both the conservatives and the radicals provided obvious parallels with the Indian National Congress in the first two decades after its founding in 1885. Significantly, however, a third congress, held in 1906, expressed the demand for cultural autonomy with novel insistency, setting the mood for the next decade. Leadership now passed to a new generation of Young Tatars, who in February 1917 founded the *Milli Firka*, or "Nationalist Party," with the convocation of an assembly at Simferopol in the

Crimea. In retrospect, their aspirations can be seen to have been totally unrealistic. In the Crimea itself the Tatars were greatly outnumbered by European colonists and when, following the end of destructive civil war in the region, a Soviet Republic of the Crimea was established in 1921, the Communist Party enjoyed a monopoly of power, although former members of the *Milli Firka* who cooperated with the new regime at first enjoyed some fruits of official patronage, and Tatar, along with Russian, was given the status of an official language. This phase ended in 1928 when Moscow initiated a purge of the Crimean Tatar "bourgeois nationalists" and when, in 1944, the Red Army reentered the peninsula, following a brief German occupation and the Crimean Tatars were condemned as Nazi collaborationists and were exiled to Siberia or to the Central Asian republics.

The concern for cultural autonomy manifested by the Crimean Tatars in the years preceding the revolution was also felt among the Volga Tatars and the Bashkirs, who, at the Moscow Pan-Russian Muslim Congress held in 1917, sought an autonomous Volga-Ural homeland within a federal Russian state. These dreams faded with the coming of revolution and civil war, but a number of prominent Tatars joined the Communist Party and participated in the formation of a Tatar Socialist Republic in 1920, without, however, abandoning their earlier commitment to a Tatar national identity. Thereafter, dissatisfied with a situation in which real power lay with the Communist Party leadership and apprehensive regarding Tatar numerical weakness in the new republic (a bare 50 percent of the population), they began to advocate the foundation of an entirely new component within the Soviet state, Turan, which would include not only the Volga-Ural region but also Kazakhstan and Turkistan and would contain within its boundaries the great majority of Tatar and Turkish-speaking Soviet citizens. This dream of bringing together all the Tatar and Turkish peoples of Eurasia into a single entity, which was particularly associated with Mir Sayyid Sultan Galiev (1896-1930), one of those Tatar leaders who had made the (nominal) transition from nationalism to communism, raised yet again a specter that had long troubled Russia's rulers—the power of Islam to unite her Asian subject peoples, whether under the slogan of Pan-Islamism, Pan-Turkism, Pan-Tatarism, or Pan-Turanism. The deviation known as Sultangalievism, condemned as early as 1923, was finally extirpated in the purges of the Volga Tatar intelligentsia which began in 1929.

The Kazakh experience was similar to that of the Tatars. Originally, Kazakh nationalism had been less obviously anti-Russian because the Kazakh sense of solidarity with the rest of the Muslim world had been far weaker than that of the Tatars or the Özbegs and because their outlook was more parochial. They were far removed from the centers of Islamic modernism, and the influence of Jadidism was somewhat neutralized by the more positive aspects of the Russian-Kazakh school system. They did not share Ismail Gasprali's enthusiasm for Ottoman Turkish and they were reluctant to accept Tatar intellectual leadership. On the other hand, from the late nineteenth century onwards they were being increasingly exposed to the expropriation of their ancestral grazing lands by Russian and Ukrainian colonists. As in the case of the Tatar press in Kazan and Baghche-Saray, it was the Kazakh press, dating from 1899, that contributed so much to the shaping of Kazakh cultural identity. In 1913 A.B. Baitursunov (1872-1928) and other leading Kazakh intellectuals began to publish in Orenburg the newspaper *Kazakh*, which rapidly became the principal mouthpiece of Kazakh nationalist aspirations in a period when Kazakh emotions were reaching a new intensity of bitterness and fury at the heedless pace of European settlement. The climax came in the bloody uprising of 1916 and its even bloodier suppression, already described in Chapter 11, which naturally predisposed the Kazakhs to welcome any change of masters. In 1917 the leading Kazakh intellectuals formed the liberal nationalist *Alash Orda* party and, hoping to win for themselves some measure of autonomy, adopted an anti-Bolshevik stance vis-à-vis the counterrevolutionary armies then operating on the Kazakh steppes. The implacable hostility of the latter towards their modest aspirations for autonomy compelled them in 1919 to take the side of the Soviets, and they obtained an autonomous Kazakh Republic, elevated in 1936 to a Kazakh Soviet Republic, but with the Kazakhs remaining a minority of some 30 percent of the total population. At first, the leaders of the *Alash Orda,* as in the case of the intellectual elite among the Crimean and Volga-Ural Tatars, participated in the new order, but from 1928 onwards the old-style Kazakh intelligentsia was systematically liquidated for being "bourgeois nationalist."

The course of events in Turkistan followed a somewhat different pattern, but here the old ways had proved exceptionally resilient; the *ulama* was more than usually influential and obscurantist, and Islamic modernist movements had made little headway. Moreover, traditional social attitudes tended to be reinforced by the proximity of the ramshackle regimes of the amir of Bukhara and the khan of Khiva. At the same time, there was a small but strategically well-placed minority of Russian immigrants—mainly artisans and railway workers—who constituted, along with the military garrisons, a dominant and assertive European element in such centers as Tashkent, Samarqand, and Ashkhabad. Prior to the revolution the impact of Jadidism had resulted in the emergence of an Özbeg intelligentsia that, although numerically inconsiderable, possessed a considerable distinction. So pervasive was its influence that even in the protectorates, where political activity of almost any kind was liable to savage repression, there appeared Young Bukharan and Young Khivan movements. At the outbreak of the Bolshevik Revolution a Muslim Congress convened in Tashkent and an autonomous Muslim government was formed in Kokand. Russian workers in Tashkent, however, had no intention of permitting the region to fall into the hands of the former subject population, and the newly formed Workers' Soviet dispatched a military force against Kokand, which occupied the city and imposed punitive measures. For the next two years Turkistan, in virtual isolation as a consequence of the civil war raging in the steppe zone to the north, remained under the control of the Tashkent Soviet, but at the end of 1919 the region was once more brought under direct control from Moscow with the arrival in Tashkent of Red Army units. These latter shortly afterwards occupied the two protectorates, setting up the short-lived Peoples' Republics of Bukhara and Khorezm. For the most part, the Muslim population of Turkistan, especially in the more remote areas, remained resentful and disaffected, and the Basmachi guerrilla movement constituted a serious threat to law and order until as late as 1925, surviving in the mountainous country east of Bukhara down to 1936. Some nomadic groups, mainly Kazakh and Kirghiz tribesmen, fled into Afghanistan or Chinese Sinkiang. As in the case of the Tatar and Kazakh intelligentsia, a number of Özbeg intellectuals became members of local Communist parties while continuing to pursue "bourgeois nationalist" goals until they were eliminated between 1930 and 1938. By then, however, the formation of the various Central Asian soviet socialist republics provided the major ethnic groups with an institutional framework within which they were able to attain at least some of their goals of separate cultural identity.

The Iranians

The position of the Iranians throughout the nineteenth century and during the first quarter of the twentieth century was strikingly different from that of the Turks, whether subjects of the Ottoman sultan or the Russian czar. On the one hand, the Iranians possessed a more precise sense of national identity derived from the historical continuities of the past. On the other hand, Iranian society prior to the First World War remained more tradition bound and impervious to external influences than almost any other part of West Asia outside of the Arabian peninsula.

Iranian nationalism, as it developed in this period under stress of European diplomatic pressure and economic exploitation, was characterized by several distinctive elements. First, there was the Persian language. Although Iran was a plural society sheltering long-established ethnic, linguistic, and religious minorities, the most obvious definition of an Iranian was a person who spoke Persian. Second, there was religion. Since the early sixteenth century the overwhelming majority of Iranians had been Shii Muslims, clearly differentiated from and traditionally hostile to their Arab, Turkish, Turcoman, and Afghan neighbors, who were Sunnis. Third, there was a perception of a historic homeland which, notwithstanding territorial losses suffered during the nineteenth century, corresponded (and still corresponds) to the core provinces of Safavid and even Sasanid times. Fourth, there was that sense of cultural continuity which characterized Iranian society through many centuries of domestic upheaval, barbarian invasion, and foreign domination, providing an unbroken link stretching from the pre-Islamic Iranian empires, through the Islamic centuries of alien Arab, Turkish, and Mongol rule, down to the present day. Fifth, there was the specific Iranian response to imperialist pressures, which took the form of constant interference by Britain and Russia, beginning in the Napoleonic period and continuing down to the Second World War; the imposition of unequal treaties and the hated Capitulations; and various forms of commercial exploitation, especially with regard to the oil industry. This response gave Iranian nationalism both a strongly xenophobic content and also a certain element of unreality as Iranians came increasingly to blame every misfortune on the machinations of their foreign oppressors.

Yet, notwithstanding pressure from Britain and Russia in its internal affairs, Iran prior to the First World War was still very remote from the main flow of European influences spreading into Asia and Africa, and throughout the nineteenth century Tehran was far less exposed to the intellectual impact of the West than was Istanbul or Cairo. There was no Western-educated intelligentsia comparable to that of Istanbul or Baghche-Saray, apart from a handful of Iranians who had acquired some knowledge of European ways either on the staff of diplomatic missions abroad or as a result of personal acquaintance with foreigners resident in the country. The rule of the Qajars and of their supporters, generally related by blood or marriage to the dynasty or to members of the Qajar tribe, followed traditional lines but was marked by exceptional venality and rapacity. Away from the capital, however, the authority of the central government was severely curtailed by the local power of the tribal chieftains and the larger landholders (often one and the same person) and by the pervasive influence exercised by the ulama, and especially the mujtahids, over the urban population.

Iranian society under the Qajars was profoundly conservative and immobile, yet, as the nineteenth century advanced, there was a steady rise in the level of popular discontent due to the greed and corruption of the local representatives of the government, the ineptitude of the court in the conduct of foreign relations, the indebtedness of the shah to foreign governments, and the granting of valuable concessions to European companies or individual speculators. Following an age-old Iranian tradition this discontent generally expressed itself in a religious form, and even the highly localized revolts of the Babis, which began in 1848, may be regarded, in part at least, as manifestations of social grievances expressed in a sectarian and messianic guise. The Shii ulama, although they played a leading role in the brutal suppression of the Babis, were no less dissatisfied with the state of the country, having developed since the demise of the Safavid dynasty, and especially during the Qajar period, a strong tradition of antagonism towards the throne and its agents. Thus, in 1892, when Nasir al-Din Shah was compelled to cancel a tobacco concession, granted to a British company only two years earlier, in consequence of popular indignation, it was the Shii mujtahids who headed the opposition. During the next decade and a half political activism took the form of secret societies, many of whose members were traders and artisans in the bazaars, and these secret societies have been compared to those conspiratorial Shii associations that had once endeavored to undermine Seljuk rule and to those that later had contributed to the rise of the Safavids. Significantly, the man who assassinated Nasir al-Din Shah in 1896 was said to have been a disciple of Jamal al-Din Afghani.

This groundswell of resentment and frustration reached a climax in what is generally referred to as the Constitutional Movement, which began in 1905 with the demand for a "house of justice" and was followed in 1906 by the convocation of a national assembly and by the promulgation of a constitution. Paradoxically, however, these developments were the achievement not so much of a Western-educated intelligentsia or a modernizing bureaucracy such as had been instrumental in initiating the Tanzimat reforms in the Ottoman empire as of a number of prominent *mujtahids* and *mullas*, supported by the bazaar merchants and the craft guilds, a small number of Western-educated intellectuals, and some tribal elements, especially the great Bakhtiyari tribe from the Isfahan region, which had its own quarrels with the regime and which could provide much needed muscle power. Thus, although later generations of educated Iranians were to regard the Constitution of 1906 as the cornerstone of personal freedom and parliamentary democracy for their country, the fact remains that the principal goal of many of the constitutionalist leaders was not so much a parliamentary system of government as justice for all, that age-old quest for a renewed "right ordering" of society in an age of tyranny and ungodliness. Thus it was not only the reactionary opposition of the Qajar ruling elite and the selfish ambitions of Britain and Russia which ensured the failure of constitutionalism in Iran. No less important were the basic contradictions in the movement, the divisive ambitions and confused aims of those who participated in it, and in particular the differing and conflicting goals of the conservative *ulama* and the highly unrepresentative Westernizers.

By the outbreak of the First World War the achievements of the constitutionalists were very modest indeed. There followed invasion, the Allied occupation, dislocation of food supplies, famine, and a postwar British attempt to establish a virtual protectorate over the country while Russia was in the throes of revolution. New patterns of political activism in Azarbayjan and Gilan, carrying an implicit threat of secession, and tribal unrest over vast tracts of country seemed to presage imminent disintegration. In these circumstances, the coup d'état of 1921, which enabled Riza Khan first to obtain formidable power as a reforming war minister and then, in 1925, to mount the throne as Riza Shah Pahlavi, marked a decisive turning point in modern Iranian history. The contribution of the Pahlavi dynasty to the process of Iranian modernization will be dealt with in the following chapter. Here, it is appropriate to stress its contribution to the development of Iranian nationalism. There can be no doubt that in ridding the country of the Qajar dynasty, under which Iranians had suffered so many humiliations at the hands of foreigners; in curbing the high-handedness of that state-within-a-state, the Anglo-Persian Oil Company; and in asserting national self-respect after decades of abject subservience to Britain and Russia, Riza Shah personified the new mood of which he was both cause and effect. He ordained that, henceforward, the country would be known as Iran and not Persia, Iran being the name by which the Iranians had called their country for well over two thousand years while Persia was a term of European origin, derived from the Greek name for the province of Fars.

It was in the period between the world wars under Riza Shah that Iranian nationalists came to see pre-Islamic Iran, and especially the Achaemenid and Sasanid periods, as embodying the quintessential greatness of the Iranian spirit. There was a corresponding tendency to downgrade the achievements of the more recent Islamic centuries, perhaps even (although this was rarely expressed) to regard Islam as an alien accretion brought in by the despised Arabs. Certainly some intellectuals regarded Islam as having contributed to the backwardness of Iran in the nineteenth century and hence to her powerlessness in the face of European aggression. Meanwhile, European scholarship, especially in the disciplines of archaeology and linguistics, was making great strides in the reconstruction of the ancient

Iranian past. In Iran itself Iranian writers, some with more enthusiasm than learning, were helping to popularize these discoveries and in so doing to disseminate the achievements of successive golden ages in the Iranian past. Several public buildings were erected in the style of Achaemenid Persepolis or Sasanid Ctesiphon, and attempts were made to purge the Persian language of foreign (i.e., Arabic) accretions. Even today Iranian nationalism cannot be understood without taking account of this historical dimension. Significantly, the 1971 celebrations of the two-thousand-five-hundredth anniversary of the Iranian monarchy were inaugurated by the shah in a ceremony of national reaffirmation held in front of the tomb of Cyrus the Great.

The Arabs

Among the various responses to the problem of cultural identity manifested among the peoples of West Asia, Arab nationalism emerged only belatedly, at a time when the demise of the Ottoman empire was clearly approaching. If elsewhere in Asia nationalism was primarily the consequence of European imperialism impinging upon a subject population, in West Asia the role of oppressor was filled by the Ottoman Turks, and this notwithstanding the fact that they shared a common Islamic heritage with their Arab subjects. Arab nationalism evolved in the last half century of Ottoman rule partly in response to the growth of Turkish nationalism, took shape between the world wars under stress of the impact of intensified European domination over West Asia, and continues its search for an appropriate balance between the conflicting pressures of Islamic universalism, Pan-Arabism, and the diverse interests of the various sovereign states among which the Arab world is currently divided.

What is an Arab? To pose the question is at least one way of approaching the complex nature of nationalism in the Arab world but it is worth remembering that, to the world in general, the term has undergone considerable modification in recent years—in fact, in line with the changing nature of Arab nationalism itself. Thus, a century ago an Arab meant for most Europeans an inhabitant of the Arabian peninsula and, in most instances, a bedouin. Today the term describes anyone who speaks Arabic, and in the final analysis it is probably true to say that the most straightforward description of an Arab is a person whose first language is Arabic. Alternatively, an Arab is a person who feels himself or herself to be an Arab. Clearly, narrow ethnic definitions are misleading since, apart from the bedouin of the more remote areas of Arabia, the original Arab invaders of Egypt and the Fertile Crescent long ago intermarried with the subject population of the conquered provinces, while in the Maghrib they mingled with the indigenous Berber stock. Nor is it possible to equate being an Arab with being a Muslim, since there are some Arabs (the Christian Arabs of Lebanon and Palestine, for example) who are not Muslims, while the majority of Muslims are not Arabs. Nevertheless, it is obvious that, for most Arabs, Islam is a part of their perceived self-identity. Then again, the course of the history of the Muslim world, and especially the Fertile Crescent, during the last two centuries has contributed to a sense of split identity, of being both an Arab and at the same time being, for example, a Syrian or an Iraqi. Finally, it is worth stressing that a sense of Arab identity is not the consequence of the recent emergence of Arab nationalism. Rather, it is an element to be found in the self-awareness of the Arabs throughout the recorded centuries of their history, even before the coming of Islam.

It was stressed in Chapter 12 that Muslims during the eighteenth and nineteenth centuries experienced feelings of profound frustration and bewilderment that they, the People of God, should have been subjected to humiliation and exploitation at the hands of infidel Europeans. It was an experience that challenged their whole perception of the course of human history and of the meaning of Islam. These feelings of frustration and bewilderment, however, were seen in a somewhat different perspective by the Arabs than by other Muslims. The Arabs saw themselves as the prime movers in that great revolutionary upheaval in human history, the dissemination of Islam; as the people who were the architects of Islamic civilization, its institutions, its social patterns, and its intellectual achievements. Yet very early in the history of Islam—within a period of less than three centuries—actual leadership had passed out of Arab hands: in Spain and the Maghrib to the Berbers and in the east first to the Iranians and then to the Turks. Since that time the Arabs had never regained their former ascendancy and had remained a subject people everywhere outside the Arabian peninsula. To take the single case of Egypt, from the ninth century onwards that country had been ruled by a succession of alien military elites—Turkish, Kurdish, Circassian, and even Albanian—never by Arabs.

The eighteenth and nineteenth century decline of the Ottoman empire, with its resultant social disintegration, violence, factionalism, and European commercial penetration, severely weakened Arab identification with and sense of commitment to Ottoman Islamism, and this alienation was intensified during the centralizing Tanzimat period (1839-78), the reign of Abd al-Hamid II (1876-1909), and the rule of the Young Turks, with their rigorous policy of enforced Turcification. Even so, prior to the twentieth century the process was very gradual and scarcely perceived by most foreigners, since some of the most significant developments in the Arab world of the late nineteenth century, such as the Pan-Islamism of Jamal al-Din Afghani (1839-97) and the reformism of Muhammad Abduh (1849-1905), were far from being opposed to Ottoman rule and to some extent required the maintenance of the imperial fabric for the effective fulfillment of their objectives. Moreover, the Egyptians, who would eventually contribute so much to the shape of Arab nationalism, had been compelled to drift somewhat outside of the mainstream of developments in the Fertile Crescent by virtue of the fact that, although Egypt remained a nominal province of the Ottoman empire down to 1914, it had undergone intensive (although competing) Anglo-French economic penetration throughout the middle decades of the century under the formal administration of the Khedives, successors of Muhammad Ali Pasha, who were generally manipulated by European financial interests. Finally, in 1882, the British occupied the country and transformed it into a *de facto* protectorate. In consequence, the emerging Egyptian intelligentsia, living under a quasi-colonial regime, was inevitably more preoccupied with ameliorating and bringing an end to British rule than with developments in the Ottoman empire proper. Prior to the end of the First World War, Western-educated Egyptians were proponents of Egyptian nationalism rather than Arab nationalism, and in some respects their struggle against the British more closely resembled the course of the Indian nationalist movement than contemporary developments in Damascus, Beirut, or Baghdad. Not that Arab intellectuals in the Fertile Crescent were unaware or unconcerned with events in Egypt—the abortive uprising of Ahmad Urubi against the British in 1882 and also the career of the Sudanese Mahdi, who captured Khartoum in 1885, were followed with keen interest—but perspectives in the Ottoman provinces were very different.

In centers like Damascus and Beirut there was to be found from the 1880s onwards a growing mood of disenchantment with the status quo, although it remained for the most part restricted to the numerically tiny Western-educated elite. As was the case in other parts of Asia, European scholarly research into the Arab achievement in the early Islamic centuries, exposure to European learning in missionary and other schools and colleges, and humiliating European intervention in the affairs of the empire all provoked the new elite to question their present status as Arabs both in the light of their glorious past and in view of their actual relationship to the disintegrating imperial superstructure. During the reign of Abd al-Hamid political activism, institutionalized in secret societies, was necessarily conspiratorial, revolutionary and, ultimately, violent, but the transition from Abd al-Hamid's despotism to the rule of the Young Turks only further accentuated this trend, since the Young Turk policy of intensive Turcification invoked a no less intensive Arabism as an inevitable response.

The outbreak of war in 1914 brought all these undercurrents to the surface. The Allies, and especially the British from their base in Egypt, assiduously wooed the Arabs with promises of support for their aspirations, not least because they dreaded the consequences of the sultan-caliph proclaiming a *jihad* ("holy war") that would unsettle the millions of Muslims living under British and French rule in the Maghrib, Egypt, the Sudan, and even distant India. In particular, the British threw their influence behind the Hashemite sharif of Mecca, who, they believed, as guardian of the Holy Cities of Islam and as a lineal descendant of the Prophet, could be used as a prestigious counterweight to the Ottoman sultan. In exchanges between the British high commissioner in Egypt, Sir Henry MacMahon, and Sharif Husayn, the British agreed to the establishment of a Hashemite Arab kingdom incorporating the greater part of the Fertile Crescent with the Hijaz, but under strict British tutelage. French interests in the area had been disregarded in the MacMahon Declaration (October 1915), but with scant regard for the latter, the Sykes-Picot Agreement of May 1916 between Britain and France recognized French claims to a sphere of influence, resulting in 1920 in the establishment of the two French mandates of Syria and the Lebanon, in addition to the British mandates of Iraq and Palestine. Finally, the Balfour Declaration of November 1917, with its promise of a Jewish homeland, also conflicted with the MacMahon Declaration. Meanwhile, the Arab Revolt, which began in June 1916, and the British advance against Jerusalem and Baghdad brought an end to Ottoman rule in West Asia outside Anatolia, and this was confirmed by the punitive treaty of Sèvres (August 1920), which resulted in the fragmentation of West Asia into British and French client states. The French had no sympathy with Hashemite aspirations for uniting the Fertile Crescent in a single Arab kingdom, but the British, although their ambiguous agreements had greatly contributed to the betrayal of the Arab dream of political unification, endeavored to offer half a loaf in compensation for loss of the whole. In Palestine, Transjordan was separated from the British mandated territory and established as an amirate (elevated in 1946 to a kingdom) for a younger son of Sharif Husayn, Abd Allah, grandfather of the present ruler of Jordan, while Sharif Husayn's eldest son, Faysal, driven from Damascus by the French in 1920, was made king of Iraq, a British mandate until 1932. Apart from these events, Hashemite ambitions suffered an irrevocable setback when the formidable Ibn Saud, descendant of the Wahhabi amirs of Najd in central Arabia, expelled Sharif Husayn from the Hijaz in 1924 and subsequently established the modern kingdom of Saudi Arabia.

These developments contributed to the growth of Arab nationalism but at the same time inhibited or distorted the political evolution of the area. As elsewhere in Asia in the late nineteenth and early twentieth centuries, nationalism among the Arabs was compounded by a subtle interplay of forces—the pressure of European imperialism, revised perceptions of older historic roles and identities, and the rise of a Western-educated intelligentsia. The events that followed the First World War, at first apparently so favorable to Arab aspirations, effectively partitioned West Asia between the British and the French, apart from those more remote parts of the Arabian peninsula where traditional Islamic regimes survived relatively free from external pressure. The British, demonstrating a deep-rooted attachment to operating through traditional ruling elites within a colonial framework and also a romantic attachment on the part of their local "experts" to the traditional Arab (i.e., bedouin) social order, brought all their considerable influence to bear in favor of dynasticism and autocracy—on behalf of the Hashemites in the Fertile Crescent and on behalf of various local sheikhs in the Persian Gulf region and south Arabia. This policy contributed directly to the ongoing dichotomy between the so-called traditional and progressive (i.e., monarchical and nonmonarchical) Arab states, which remains a major obstacle to their close cooperation and to Pan-Arab aspirations of political unity.

Between the world wars, Arab nationalists perceived that they had exchanged one master (the moribund Ottoman empire) for others—British or French imperialism and the lengthening shadow of Zionism. A few forward-looking nationalists took comfort from the course of events in Turkey, where Ataturk, having overturned the iniquitous settlement of Sèvres by expelling the Greek invaders and playing the Allied governments off against each other, had undertaken a revolutionary restructuring of Turkish society. Yet, then and afterwards, most Arab nationalists, even when they admired specific aspects of the Kemalist revolution, felt unable to accept the full implications of secularism for Arab society. Under the mandates, Pan-Arab ideology, while remaining a potent and immensely appealing ideal for the increasingly politicized masses, was necessarily overshadowed by the immediate objectives of confronting and expelling the new rulers of the Fertile Crescent. This diversion, in turn, reinforced regional identities—Syrian, Lebanese, Palestinian, and Iraqi. By the outbreak of the Second World War the problem of the split personality of Arab nationalism had thus been further intensified, embodying the two conflicting concepts of Islamic universalism, now expressed in terms of Pan-Arabism, and of regional identities, perhaps even predating Islam itself.

2A. CULTURAL RENAISSANCE AND NATIONALISM AMONG HINDUS IN SOUTH ASIA

There was no unified Indian response among Hindus and Muslims to the disintegration of their societies and cultures in the era of British imperialism. From the thirteenth century onwards, South Asia accommodated two major communities, two major universal religions. Sometimes, as in the fifteenth century or under the early Mughul emperors, the two cultures interacted fairly closely, influencing one another and even inspiring the formation of syncretic movements such as neo-Vaishnavism in Bengal and Sikhism in the Panjab. But from the late seventeenth century onwards Mughul policy drifted back to its Islamic heritage, alienating non-Muslims and precipitating militancy and rebellion among the Hindu Marathas and the Panjabi Sikhs. When the British took over India, it appears that Hindus and Muslims had completely lost the syncretic ideal of Akbar, and though they shared many common cultural practices, they looked upon one another as separate communities. Thus the rise of an intelligentsia, the emergence of a renaissance ideology, and nationalism itself in South Asia were truly never Indian but followed divergent Hindu and Muslim lines. This is crucial, for it helps to explain why South Asia is now divided between India, Pakistan, and Bangladesh. Here the Hindu response will be considered, while the Muslim response will be taken up in the following section. The primary focus will be on Bengal, where the processes of cultural renaissance were most manifest.

The Urban Intelligentsia and Cultural Renaissance
The earliest response to the British impact came in the new metropolitan centers on the coasts rather than in the older indigenous centers of administration, commerce, and pilgrimage. The British East India Company chose Bombay as the administrative capital of western India; Madras served the same function for southern India; and Calcutta became the administrative and commercial center for the eastern Gangetic region, but also the capital of British India. Given these advantages, Calcutta became the earliest, and for some time, the most significant location for the development of a cultural renaissance, nationalism,

and modernization among Indian Hindus. As we have already seen, it was primarily the Hindu elite of Bengal who left their villages and towns to seek fame and fortune in Calcutta.

The Bengali Hindu compradors and intelligentsia owed their existence to the needs of the British in Calcutta. Their genesis can be traced back to the period between 1772 and 1830 (the "Orientalist" era), when numerous Indians acquired a working knowledge of English, new professional skills, and a fresh mental outlook through contact with Englishmen, generally within an institutional setting. This new indigenous elite consisted largely of entrepreneurial brokers. The Hindus far more than the Muslims at this formative period were quick to grasp the intricacies of the colonialist system and to succeed within it.

The rise of an intelligentsia was of crucial importance because it brought into being a cadre of modern sophisticated professionals who were ultimately to pose a great danger to the survival of European rule. As their ideas, attitudes, and style of life changed, they became progressively alienated from their own people. Bengal presents a clear illustration of the process, in that the more these professionals were exposed to new schools, the more proficient they became in their new occupations, and the more sophisticated they became regarding the sources of Western vitality and power, the more they understood the causes of their own culture's inferior position. Also, the more they learned about the West and bemoaned their own culture's deplorable condition, the more disenchanted they became with the orthodox leadership and ideology within their own Hindu tradition and yearned for something more appropriate to their own rationalized mentality and to their strong desire for a new identity in the modern world.

Rammohun Roy (1772–1833), considered by some to be the "father of modern India," was probably the earliest member of the intelligentsia of Bengal to decry openly the abuses and shortcomings of contemporary Hindu society from the standpoint of contemporary Western values (e.g., rationalism, humanism, humanitarianism). His image is derived largely from his legacy, the Brahmo Samaj movement, which throughout the British period sought to reform Hinduism socially and spiritually. His genius lay in conceiving a middle path between the conservative nativists who defended the status quo against the intrusion of foreign ideas and practices, and the Westernizers who completely repudiated their Hindu heritage. Rammohun did not succumb to the lure of alien cultural imports but devoted much of his time and energy to reinterpreting his own socioreligious tradition. While resisting the missionaries and other Europeans on the one hand, on the other he fought a long drawn-out battle for the cultural purification of Hinduism. As a result he alienated Europeans as well as members of his own elitist class, whom he condemned for rationalizing away the existence of moral and social evils.

In his *Abridgement of the Vedanta* (1815), Rammohun penned his first public denunciation of contemporary Hinduism, a work that contained the ideological seeds of Indian regeneration. He argued that image worship as then practiced in India was an aberration from the authentic monotheistic tradition, wherein worship of "the true and eternal God" left no room for "idolatry." "Hindoo idolatry," with its "innumerable gods, goddesses and temples," was the curse of India and had destroyed the "texture of society." Although Rammohun was himself a member of the highest caste of Kulin brahmans, he seems to have identified more with his role as a member of the intelligentsia who had learned English in the service of the company. He attacked traditional brahmans, whom he blamed for the miserable state of affairs in India, since they had preferred to conceal the wisdom of the authentic Hindu tradition "within the dark curtain of the Sanskrit language," rather than transmit the truth to the people in their own languages. For this reason, he himself translated the ancient scriptures into Bengali to awaken his countrymen from what he saw as false Hinduism. This included such practices as *sati* (the burning of widows), the selling of female children under the pretense of marriage, Kulinism and its nefarious polygamous practice designed merely "to gratify brutal inclination," and caste rigidity, which he saw as a major cause of the decline of Hindu civilization. He wrote that "whenever respectability is confined to birth only, acquisition of knowledge and practice of morality in that country must surely decline."

Sociologically, Rammohun and the hundreds of charismatic leaders of Hindu reform that followed him in all parts of India represented a new type of intelligentsia and a distinctively new social elite. The renaissance stood for social change. The critics of contemporary Hindu practices were spokesmen of a class that was urban, literate, and sophisticated, and their social status owed more to wealth than to caste. They were a professional group, receptive to new knowledge, ideas, and values, and the intellectuals among them created a syncretic cultural tradition. Perhaps more important, they mentally transcended kin and caste, and thought in broader social terms.

British Orientalist scholarship and the development of an historical consciousness among the intelligentsia led to a reevaluation of the Indian past (which for Hindus meant the pre-Muslim past) and the longing for an Indian renaissance. Thus it was the European antiquarian interest in ancient India that prompted Hindus to acquire a new awareness of their own past—an awareness that enhanced their sense of self-respect vis-à-vis both the Muslims and the English and that fed directly into a newly felt nationalism.

In an English translation of one of the *Upanishads,* made in 1816, Rammohun Roy was probably the first of the intelligentsia to divide Indian history into an age of god (the age of the *Upanishads,* 900-600 B.C.), an age of darkness (600 B.C. to 1800 A.D.), and an age of future expectations, when India could again flow in the mainstream of world progress. His charismatic image as progenitor of modern India has been attributed to the fact that he steered a middle course between Hindu conservatism and estranged Westernism. His path of vitalism through the Brahmo Samaj proved far more satisfying to the modernizing intelligentsia than did Westernization. Rammohun's genius or vision enabled him to probe deeply into the rediscovered pre-Muslim golden age of the Hindus and to find there what appeared to be modern values. When Rammohun looked back to the beginning of classical India, he found monotheism not idols, philosopher-reformers in pursuit of reason and truth rather than priestly domination in temples that degraded the spirit, social egalitarianism rather than caste *dharma,* women with a status equal to men in place of *sati,* child marriage, and the polygamous exploitation of women, and tribal republics rather than despotism.

In the decades that followed Rammohun's death in 1833, the Bengali intelligentsia who reinterpreted their past were far from agreement as to which golden age contained the proper source of inspiration for contemporary Bengali Hindus. Likewise, there was no unanimity as to where and when Hindu civilization went wrong or who was responsible. If some actually saw classical Indian history as a golden age followed by a dark age, others emphasized the steady decline of Hindu institutions in the wake of the Muslim invasions. Vivekananda (1863-1902), for example, a former Brahmo who started his own Ramkrishna Mission, argued in defense of postclassical institutions, including caste distinctions, which in his mind were refinements of and not extraneous additions to the authentic tradition. These institutions were good ones when they functioned properly, and it would be a costly mistake to throw out the institutions merely because they were functioning poorly. Rather, one should revitalize and update them by infusing them with modern values, such as egalitarianism. Thus Vivekananda defended caste because it expressed the natural and necessary grouping of men, but he opposed special privileges for some castes.

Rammohun and Vivekananda represented two distinct patterns of reevaluation among the intelligentsia. When Vivekananda defended caste he was arguing that Hindu traditions might be altered to fit modern functions, just as European traditions had been adapted to meet contemporary needs in the West. In debates with Christians he could argue from this vantage point that just as there had been a Protestant reformation in Christendom, so there could and would be a modern ethical and religious reformation of Hinduism. Rammohun, equally critical of the West's complacent assumption of its own superiority, chose a different method, searching out parallels in the Indian heritage to demonstrate that it was not necessary to adopt the Western model. Another example of this process of reevaluation was that of Bankim Chandra Chatterji (1838-94), India's first great modern novelist and philosopher of neo-Hinduism. At the very time when Christian scholars in Europe sought to historicize Christ through exegesis, Chatterji sought to do the same for Krishna.

These approaches, which by no means exhaust the variations on the theme of renaissance in Bengal, were mostly dynamic attempts to change India and to ease her transition into the modern world. It cannot be stressed enough that the use of apologetics should not be equated with a defense of privilege and tradition. Quite the contrary, by inventing golden ages and transmitting them as myths to justify change, the Bengali intelligentsia subverted the true forces of conservatism and helped to undermine the position of those with a vested interest in the status quo.

The intelligentsia, although dissatisfied with their own social order, were unwilling to renounce their heritage and become Westernizers. Instead, they formed organizations designed to change the existing order—to modernize it. From Rammohun Roy came the Brahmo Samaj, from Vivekananda came the Ramkrishna Mission, both of which were Bengali; from Dayanand Saraswati (1824-83) came the Arya Samaj, largely a Panjabi phenomenon. Branches of each one of these movements proliferated throughout India or gave birth to other organizations dedicated to reform and rejuvenation. Thus by the beginning of the twentieth century the Brahmo Samaj had approximately 250 branches throughout the subcontinent from the Himalayas to Tamilnad and from the northwest frontier to Burma.

After Rammohun's death in 1833, Debendranath Tagore (1817-1905) assumed leadership of the Brahmo Samaj. Debendranath's outstanding contributions to reform were in the fields of religion and ethics. His *Brahmo Dharma* (1849) was a popular reinterpretation of the Hindu faith based on Rammohun Roy's view of the classical tradition and represented the first major effort at developing by means of Hindu sources a practical, puritanical ethic that aimed at totally transforming the character of the movement. Stress was placed on the virtues of hard work, rational behavior, self-sacrifice, thrift, cleanliness, and efficiency.

Two other Brahmos, Vidyasagar (1820-91), an atheist, and Keshub Chandra Sen (1838-84), a theist, were the most radical leaders of social reform between 1855 and 1875. Vidyasagar's efforts led to the passage of legislation allowing widow remarriage in 1856. Though he was less successful in getting the government to legislate against Kulin polygamy, continual Brahmo protest against the practice contributed to its ultimate disappearance by the twentieth century. Vidyasagar helped establish the first girls' school in India imparting nonsectarian and secular education. The Bethune School of Calcutta opened in 1849 and Vidyasagar was its first secretary. He also opened Calcutta's Sanskrit College to all castes and broadened the curriculum. He was also instrumental in getting the government to establish a number of secondary schools in various districts to make available a modern Western-style education, taught in Bengali.

Keshub Sen, who established his own Brahmo Samaj in 1866 because Debendranath Tagore was not moving fast enough, also accomplished much as a reformer. His efforts led to the passage in 1872 of the Brahmo Marriage Act, which was important not only for the rights the government granted to the Brahmo community but also because it served as a prototype for the Indian Constitution of 1949, which extended these same rights to all Indian citizens. Both documents guaranteed freedom of conscience and worship, while repudiating discrimination on grounds of caste or sex. After 1872, Brahmos of every caste intermarried, widows remarried, child marriage was abolished, monogamy was rigorously imposed, and all girls and boys were given some education. Keshub and his followers also championed the rights of the peasants against *zamindar* oppression and brought out the first journal, priced at one penny a copy, designed to reach peasants and workers (*Sulabh Samachar*, 1870).

The zeal to expose social abuses within Hinduism and then enlist support to reform them continued for at least another generation until the forces of conservative Hinduism and militant nationalism coalesced against the West. A new radical grouping known as the Sadharan Brahmo Samaj pushed reformation as far as it could between 1878 and 1905, when nationalism was growing rapidly. Brahmos championed the first degree-awarding college for women, which was founded as Bethune College in 1878, and were among the first to work among the new industrial proletariat in the jute factories, to establish charitable hospitals and schools for the poor, to rehabilitate prostitutes and educate their children. In the first decade of the twentieth century, they finally sought out the outcastes, or untouchables, in an effort to spread education among them.

The Origins of Indian Nationalism

Vidyasagar and Keshub Sen had tried to persuade the British government in India to use legislation as a means of bringing about social reforms. The British, however, did not support the more radical proposals for the modernization of Indian society, partly perhaps because they tended to be costly. Keshub succeeded with his Brahmo Marriage Act, but in that same year of 1872 he failed to win government support for an ambitious program of free compulsory education. Gradually it dawned on the intelligentsia that they had to politicize their efforts at reform, learn to manipulate the British political system and use political means to achieve social ends. Moreover, an increasing number of young Bengalis were going abroad to study in British universities or to compete with Englishmen in examinations for the higher echelons of the administration in India. While abroad they often imbibed the quasi-religious notion of nationalism which had been sweeping Europe throughout the nineteenth century.

Some scholars argue that the renaissance ended when politics and the concept of nation captured the imagination of the younger generation of Bengalis during the 1890s. In no other figure among the intelligentsia is this tension between cultural revitalization and political militancy more clearly illustrated than in the life and career of Asia's first Nobel Prize winner in literature (1913), the great Bengali poet, Rabindranath Tagore (1861-1941). Born the son of Debendranath Tagore, the socioreligious reformation of Hinduism was firmly implanted in his mind from childhood. He also grew up during the confrontation between imperialism and nationalism, with the result that he experienced a continual identity crisis in which he alternated between adherence to his Brahmo legacy and rage at the destructive impact of European economic exploitation and racial discrimination. In his Brahmo phases he was open to Western influences and acutely conscious of India's cultural sterility, but in his nationalist phases he sought to stem the demoralizing influences from the West by erecting a dam at India's frontier.

Then, between 1898 and 1906, during a period of extreme reaction in Bengal against the British, Tagore turned political and supported the boycott and burning of foreign goods, and other nationalist acts. In 1901 he wrote *What Is A Nation?*, reducing the concept to an equation: glorious heritage plus political determination through the collective will of the people. But in 1907 he had shaken himself free of nationalism, returning for the last time to Brahmo reformism and universalism. In his greatest novel, *Gora*, serialized in Bengali, Tagore declared in the conclusion that:

Today I am really an Indian! In me there is no longer any opposition between Hindu, Muslim or Christian. Today every caste in India is my caste, the food of all is my food![1]

1. Rabindranath Tagore, *Gora* (Macmillan, 1924), by permission of the Trustees of the Tagore Estate and Macmillan, London and Basingstoke.

Political nationalism in India has been associated closely with the institution known as the Indian National Congress, which was first organized in 1885. At first it was made up of Brahmo-type moderates from all over India who represented the intelligentsia and other segments of the urban elite. These moderates did not advocate independence from Britain but used political weapons to air their grievances and to win British popular support for their recommended social and economic reforms. They realized that no full-scale modernization of India was possible without political support from the British government. What they wanted was equality with British citizens and an end of their status as subjects. Thus they petitioned for equality of opportunity in the civil service, greater representation in the Legislative Councils, the encouragement of indigenous industries, and free compulsory education.

What the idea of the nation meant to moderates is perhaps best illustrated in the writings and speeches of Surendranath Bannerji (1848-1926), who, in his lifetime, moved from the position outlined above to advocacy of self-determination by constitutional means. Bannerji did not start out as a nationalist leader but as a brilliant young Bengali who got himself admitted to the British bureaucracy in India. His nationalism began when he was dismissed from the civil service on account of a minor misdemeanor, which, had it been committed by an Englishman, would have involved no more than a departmental reprimand. Gradually he harnessed his energy and intellect to the service of India, moving across the subcontinent stirring up his compatriots to join in a united effort to organize politically against British imperialism. The generation of nationalists that Bannerji represented always expressed faith in England's sense of justice and fair play, even going so far as to argue that British rule in India was providential. "England is our political guide and our moral preceptor in the exalted sphere of political duty," Bannerji wrote. "From England must come the crowning mandate which will enfranchise our peoples," he added, for "we have been fed upon the strong food of English constitutional freedom" and have been "brought face to face with the struggles and triumphs of the English people in their stately march towards constitutional freedom." Bannerji was a secularist, as were many moderates who urged Hindus and Muslims to bury religious differences and identify totally with the Indian nation. A related idea was the belief that there was no contradiction between nationalism and the path of sociocultural reform. Bannerji's closest friends were Brahmos, and he openly accepted the ideas of Rammohun Roy and Keshub Sen. He believed that Hindus, Muslims, Christians, and Parsees could join together in fraternal goodwill to work for their motherland under British auspices.

Unfortunately for the moderates, the British bureaucratic structure of government seems to have become increasingly rigid during the last decades of the nineteenth century, and except for some inconsequential constitutional reforms, the British surrendered nothing essential to the demands of the moderates. Quite the contrary, the British retaliated against the moderate demands of the nationalists by partitioning Bengal in 1905, apparently with a view to weakening the movement and perhaps dividing the Bengali Muslims from the Hindu intelligentsia. The British insisted on retaining a virtual monopoly of posts in the civil service, did little to accelerate Indian representation in local government, made little effort to industrialize India, and rejected all demands for free compulsory education. The consequence of their reluctance to act was a radicalization of the Indian National Congress, in which swaraj ("independence") become the aim of a new generation of freedom fighters. Moreover, terrorism and other forms of violence now became accepted weapons in the struggle against British rule.

Indian nationalism as an independence movement began with this generation of militants. An attempt was made to enlist mass support among the peasantry in the freedom struggle as more and more of the intelligentsia realized the importance of reaching the depressed agrarian sector to win mass support for national liberation. In the process the

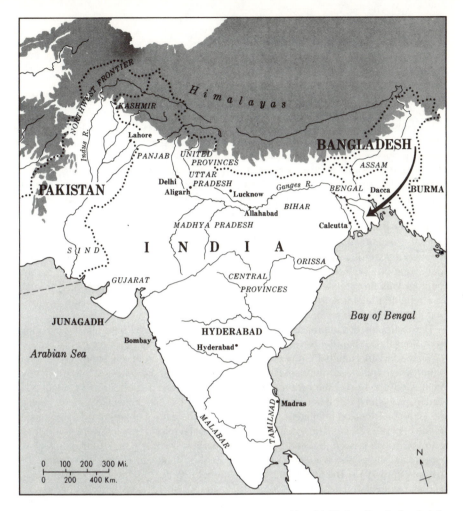

Map 54 Nationalism in South Asia

English language, used by the intelligentsia from different parts of the country to communicate with one another, was increasingly disavowed as the common spoken language for the Indian people. A concept of nation developed which stressed a common history, a common literary and religious tradition, and a common cultural heritage. Unfortunately, however, no common cultural heritage united the mutually antagonistic Hindu and Muslim communities. Crucial to this process of reaching the mass of the people was the need to identify nationalism with the world view of the ordinary man. This led to a marriage of politics and religion, which divided Hindus from Muslims and both from other religions. Thus, in the twentieth century, the moderate secular appeal for a united India which had been formerly so effective among the urban intelligentsia gave way to pluralistic nationalism based largely on the narrow religious loyalties of the common man.

The other critical aspect of the new concept of nation was *swadeshi* ("economic self-sufficiency"), which was the older renaissance ideal now politicized as a weapon against British imperialism. It meant that at the same time that one fought for *swaraj* ("independence"), one sought to build up one's nation from within. This was to be accomplished by boycotting foreign goods—sometimes actually burning them—and stimulating the production and sale of Indian-produced goods such as textiles, metalware, cigarettes, and other finished articles. In Bengal, where the movement erupted into a revolutionary episode following the partition of the province in 1905, *swadeshi* also meant promoting an indigenous system of education which included the establishment of a National Council of Education and the founding of Jadavpur University, with a technical and scientific curriculum and classes conducted in Bengali.

Extremist nationalist ideology was exemplified by younger Brahmo defectors in Bengal who had become thoroughly disenchanted with the West and thoroughly defensive about exposing the social abuses in contemporary Hinduism. Their objective was to unite all classes and castes of Hindus under the banner of nationalism. Such a perspective was expressed by Aurobindo Ghose (1872-1950). Aurobindo was a Bengali with a Brahmo background (his grandfather was Rajnarian Bose, president of the Adi Brahmo Samaj), who had been deliberately Anglicized by his father, who kept the boy abroad in England as a student for the first twenty years of his life. When Aurobindo returned to India he found himself "denationalized," and he turned against Westernization with a vengeance. His ideological contribution came in the way he idealized his native land and its religion, identifying one with the other as no previous thinker had done. The resulting nationalist ideology was strongly stated in a speech given in 1907, in which he identified nationalism as a religion that came from God and that required its adherents to struggle against their opponents with faith in the immortality of nationalism.

The examples of cultural renaissance and nationalism cited here are drawn primarily from Bengal, but parallel developments were taking place in other regions as well. After 1885 the Indian National Congress provided for leaders from the entire subcontinent a forum where Indians could increasingly seek to challenge the power of the British government. Until the turn of the century the Congress remained a cautious and genteel body of leaders, but after 1900 it became the embodiment of the nationalist movement. Inevitably, the Western-educated intelligentsia who made up the early Congress leadership tended to divide over priorities and tactics. Those who put social reform first and were willing to work with the British toward that end became "moderates" on the issue of independence. The Moderates, under the leadership of Gopal Krishna Gokhale (1866-1915), were in the majority until 1915. The Extremists, those who put *swaraj* ("independence") first, were led by Bal Gangadhar Tilak (1856-1920). Tilak and Gokhale were both Western-educated brahmans from Poona in western India, but their politics contrasted sharply. Whereas Gokhale favored gradualism and cooperation with the British, Tilak took a hard line towards both the British and the Muslims. Identifying with local Maharashtrian tradition, Tilak idealized the figure of Shivaji, who in the seventeenth century had led the Marathas against the Mughuls. Useful as this example of an indigenous guerrilla tradition may have been as a source of inspiration to militant nationalists, the glorification of Shivaji was insulting to Indian Muslims, many of whom glorified the Mughul past. Tilak was jailed for six years in 1909 on the charge that he had incited a wave of anti-British terrorism. The effect of this imprisonment was to make Tilak a hero, and following his release in 1915 the Extremist position prevailed in the Congress. Tilak's own leadership potential, however, proved limited. His stress on a Hindu identity for India alienated Muslims and gave impetus to the division of Indian nationalism along the lines of religion—that is, communalism. With his death in 1920, the kind of regional leadership he represented was overshadowed in the 1920s by the all-India leadership provided by the charismatic figure of Gandhi, a disciple of Gokhale.

Gandhi and Indian Independence
The greatest prophet of the new national salvation ideology was Mohandas K. Gandhi (1869-1948), who led India to independence in 1947. No other Indian leader was so effective in transforming the legacy of renaissance movements and regional nationalisms

into a truly mass-supported and all-embracing Hindu nationalism. The Bengali intelligentsia had failed to enlist mass support in the freedom struggle since their political activism tended to reflect their elitist status and assumptions, tempered only by an occasional outburst of terrorism, and hence made no appreciable impact on the rural masses. But with the emergence of Gandhi as an Indian nationalist after World War I, ideology and action were so closely interwoven and so effectively communicated to the everyday understanding of the Indian peasant, that by the late 1920s millions of Indians had become participants in the struggle for national liberation. Like Mao in China, Gandhi understood the crippling effects of European colonialism and imperialism on the agrarian sector, and it was there, not in the city, that he sought India's revitalization and reconstruction. He believed that imitating Western industrial capitalism would not save India but would only intensify her agony. The needs of Western capitalism had made rural India so poverty-stricken by destroying craft industries and by creating a demographic imbalance that the only path to salvation was to be rid of the British and then launch a great crusade to rehabilitate the Indian villages.

Though Gandhi was himself a member of the intelligentsia and had lived in England for three years, where he prepared himself for a barrister's career, he repudiated the bankruptcy of the comprador and intelligentsia classes, which had been nurtured and sustained by British imperialism. His revolutionary techniques such as *satyagraha* ("truth force") and *ahimsa* ("nonviolence") were less effective against the British authorities than they were in uniting the Hindu population behind him and in developing his extraordinary charisma. Gandhi sanctified the political struggle not only through his ideology but by the austerity of his life-style, by asceticism, and by his religious and moral teachings. In the eyes of millions, Gandhi was no mere politician, but second only to Buddha as the greatest of Indians.

Unlike Mao in China, however, Gandhi repudiated modern civilization. His desire to revitalize the countryside was in fact a desire to keep traditional preindustrial civilization alive. This was the cornerstone of his nationalism. Gandhi saw no panacea in tractors or collective farms or industrialization but aimed at revitalizing the old values, urging a return to small villages, which would be organized democratically, with people reciprocally helping one another while being guided by Hindu religious principles. "We hold the civilization that you Westerners support as civilization to be the reverse of civilization," he once wrote. "We consider our civilization far superior to yours." He went on to say that "we consider your schools and law courts to be useless; we want our own ancient schools and courts to be restored." He rejected the idea of spending money on such things as railways and defense establishments, and above all he renounced the need for European-made cloth. Instead of advocating that Indian factories should produce cloth on a mass-production basis, he urged that every villager's home have its own spinning wheel to produce all the cloth it needed. For Gandhi, traditional (i.e., preindustrial) civilization in both India and Europe had been based on morality and religion, with tolerably fair justice for all and with the mass of the population living in virtually self-sufficient and relatively prosperous village communities.

Although insufficient time has passed to allow a detached assessment of Gandhi's success or failure, it would seem that his salvation ideology and revolutionary methods proved inappropriate and unacceptable either for achieving independence or providing India with realistic goals to survive in the modern world. The British were not driven out by nonviolence or truth force: once a consensus had developed in Britain that the forcible retention of their Indian empire was likely to prove impracticable and unprofitable, they began the process of gradual devolution of power until, in 1947, they finally granted full independence. Ironically, Gandhi was assassinated in 1948 by a fanatic devotee of the same idealized Hindu civilization that he himself had so ardently defended. Gandhi's identifica-

The leaders of South Asian resistance to European domination were all subjected to heavy Western cultural influences in their early careers.

13.2 Gandhi, with the Agha Khan and the poetess Sarojini Naidu outside the Ritz Hotel, London, at the time of the Round Table Conference, 1931. The photograph captures the diverse life-styles of Indians who were all, in their very different ways, the products of the European impact upon the subcontinent. Courtesy: The Bettmann Archive.

13.3 Jawaharlal Nehru (1899-1964) and Muhammad Ali Jinnah (1876-1948), the Bombay-born lawyer who abandoned a lucrative practice in London to become the charismatic leader of a mass movement for the creation of an Islamic state within the Indian subcontinent. **Courtesy: The British Library.**

tion of nationalism with religion, while it did win mass support, made Indian nationalism essentially Hindu in character, thus ending the earlier trend toward pluralistic nationalism and contributing to the further division of religious communities which led to the partition of the subcontinent in 1947 and the creation of Pakistan as a separate Muslim state. Moreover, the leadership of India after independence was rooted in the urbanized intelligentsia, and no sooner had Gandhi disappeared from the scene than it returned to the Brahmo legacy of modernizing Indian society and culture. The new middle class elite turned its back on Gandhi's vision of a mythical rural paradise guided by ancient Hindu precepts and embarked instead (if the Constitution of 1949 is to be taken seriously) on the goal of creating an industrialized society and a secular nation-state, thereby diverting attention from the Herculean problem of the stagnant Indian countryside, glutted with a poverty-stricken, illiterate mass of people.

2B. CULTURAL RENAISSANCE AND NATIONALISM AMONG MUSLIMS IN SOUTH ASIA

Although manifestations of cultural renaissance and nationalist sentiment among Indian Muslims emerged partly in direct response to the threat of European encroachments during the nineteenth and twentieth centuries, they were also due to developments that were taking place within Indian Muslim society itself and that were present as early as the eighteenth century. These developments included the erosion of Muslim political supremacy and consequent political fragmentation, tensions deriving from the unresolved conflict between Sunni orthodoxy and Sufi heterodoxy, a perceived lack of moral leadership on the part of the traditional Muslim ruling elite, and the psychological effects of subjugation to infidel Hindu and Christian rule. On the positive side, however, was the resilience of Indian Muslim culture in its late Mughul phase, exemplified by the vitality of Urdu as a vehicle for literary expression.

Both before and during the period of European domination a handful of Indian Muslims had endeavored to revitalize their torpid community in ways that were essentially traditional and backward looking but reflected somewhat similar attempts in the Muslim heartlands of West Asia. Shah Wali Allah of Delhi (1703-62), for example, sought to reform the religious life of his community, to narrow the gap that divided the Sufi mystic from the orthodox Sunni Muslim (a long-standing preoccupation of sensitive Muslim thinkers), and also to rally the Muslim leaders of northern India behind the Afghan chieftain, Ahmad Shah Durrani (1747-73), against the Marathas. He also took the momentous step of rendering the Quran into Persian, while in the next generation his sons translated it into Urdu. Among the students who sat at the feet of Shah Wali Allah's sons was Sayyid Ahmad Barelwi (1786-1831), a former freebooter whose occupation had come to an abrupt end as a result of the British pacification of central India in 1817-19. Sayyid Ahmad Barelwi took the theme of communal revitalization a stage further by transforming it into an activist program of *jihad* ("holy warfare") against the unbelievers, perhaps partly in consequence of a pilgrimage to Mecca and contact with the Arabian Wahhabis. Having acquired a following of like-minded Muslims, he made his way to the trans-Indus country where, in alliance with local Pathan tribesmen, he harried the frontiers of the Sikh kingdom of the Panjab until his death in battle in 1831. Thereafter, his followers managed to survive for many years in a relatively inaccessible tract of the northwestern frontier region where, as late as 1863, the British were compelled to send a major expedition against them.

The uprising of 1857 in Uttar Pradesh included distinctive Muslim elements. These took the form of support not only for the restoration of the last Mughul emperor and of the *nawabi* court at Lucknow, but also for local religious leaders. Following the suppression of the uprising, manifestations of Muslim dissatisfaction with British rule remained fairly unobtrusive although the occasional conspiracy and assassination, attributed by the British to what they termed the Wahhabi movement of Sayyid Ahmad Barelwi, indicated profound undercurrents of frustration. Frustration and concern for the future of Indian Islam provided the thematic link between the career of Shah Wali Allah of Delhi, the movement of Sayyid Ahmad Barelwi and his followers, Muslim participation in the rebellion of 1857, and the various "Wahhabi conspiracies" that surfaced in the 1860s and 1870s. All, in some sense, sought to turn the clock back, and all to a very large extent were failures. They did, however, underscore the narrow and parochial horizons of the Muslims of India and demonstrated the need for change. That change of outlook began for Indian Muslims, as for other Asians, with a cultural renaissance and a search for a renewed identity.

The cultural renaissance of Indian Muslims centered on their sharpened perception of their former role in history, that splendid past of conquest and empire still embodied in the crumbling monuments of past dynasties, still personified in the descendants of great figures from the Mughul past such as the Nizam of Hyderabad, and still preserved in the late Mughul heritage of Urdu language and literature. As in other parts of Asia during the period of European domination, the British themselves through their antiquarian interest in the Indian Muslim past also stimulated Muslim perceptions of what that past had been and how far they had fallen during the preceding century and a half. In general, the British were more aware of the Muslim cultural heritage in northern India than they were of the Hindu, due partly to the fact that, at the time of the initial British conquests, Mughul rule was still a very recent memory and also because, as they moved "up country," they were confronted by the impressive architectural remains and the abiding folk memory of celebrated Muslim rulers such as Firuz Shah Tughluq, Akbar, and Shah Jahan. Furthermore, they adapted much of the old Mughul administrative system to their own use and in a certain mood saw themselves as the historic heirs of their Mughul predecessors. As historians, the British often represented the rule of former Muslim dynasties as having been tyrannical and repressive, in contrast to the mildness and justice of their own rule, but even when they wrote history with a conscious bias, the effect for Indian Muslims of the nineteenth and twentieth centuries was still an intoxicating brew of long-forgotten glories. Among the educated there came to be felt acute nostalgia for that past as well as a sense of the present decadence and ineffectiveness of their community.

Communalism and Renaissance

The Muslim question, as it came to be called by British writers, was not simply the problem of European domination, although that was a part of it. There was also the problem of Muslim relations with the Hindus, the majority community. In effect, this meant that during the first half of the twentieth century the Indian subcontinent contained two quite distinct nationalist movements: an Indian nationalist movement, predominantly Hindu in inception and composition, directed against the continuation of European domination, and an Indian Muslim nationalist movement, which was opposed to the continuation of European domination also but was even more preoccupied with the threat of Hindu majority domination after British withdrawal.

Communalism is the term used to describe the deep-seated antagonism between Hindus and Muslims in the Indian subcontinent, an antagonism that in certain areas and at certain times has been (and remains) very pervasive and very bitter. The historical antecedents of present-day communalism have yet to be studied objectively and no general study of the phenomenon has been published so far. It can, however, be stated that Hindu-Muslim communal tensions and outbursts long preceded the establishment of British rule but that certain factors in the colonial situation further exacerbated them. Those writers who assume either an inherent and ongoing Hindu-Muslim confrontation or, on the contrary, a continuing and beneficent symbiosis, invariably find appropriate chapter and verse to fit their arguments, but these in turn generally reflect their own personal prejudices. Briefly, the debate centers on two main propositions. First, there is the proposition that Islam and Hinduism are naturally antipathetic, oil and water, which can never mingle. This view, shared by both Muslim and Hindu communalists, represents Islam as an alien intrusion into India and emphasizes its non-Indian and West Asian origin and character. It was this view that led to the definition of Muslims and Hindus as two distinct nationalities and that led inexorably to the bloody partition of 1947. The other proposition, shared by those Hindus and Muslims who once believed in the practicability of a united subcontinent evolving towards secularism and parliamentary self-government, is that Hindus and Muslims are alike Indians and that Islam in India is not the same as Islam in Egypt or Turkey but has assumed over many centuries a peculiarly Indian character.

Unfortunately for the advocates of the latter proposition, it is a historical fact that throughout the nineteenth century the Muslims of India, even when they came into contact with the British regime, as they did in Bengal and Uttar Pradesh, did not (with a few notable exceptions) participate in the educational system that evolved under the British and thereby denied themselves the professional training necessary for that comprador status acquired by so many high-caste Hindus, especially in and around the Presidency cities. One reason for this lack of participation, termed backwardness by the British, was undoubtedly religious prejudice—the traditional Muslim contempt for the non-Muslim and all his works. Perhaps no less important, although largely unrecognized by the contemporary British, was the resilience of late Mughul elite culture, exemplified in the literary traditions of such Urdu writers as Ghalib (1796-1869) or in the life-style portrayed in Mirza Muhammad Ruswa's picturesque novel of pre-British Lucknow, Umrao Jan Ada (1899). Another reason for Muslim lack of participation in English education was British hostility towards the Muslim community in the years immediately following the 1857 rebellion when government officials questioned whether Muslims could ever be loyal subjects of a non-Muslim state. Subsequently, British attitudes towards the Muslims changed, partly at the prompting of enlightened and pro-British Muslim spokesmen such as Sayyid Ahmad Khan (1817-98) and partly out of apprehension as to the political aspirations of the emerging Hindu intelligentsia. But the Muslims were never able to catch up with the Hindus in the field of English education, which in turn meant that they could never catch up with them in any aspect of public life. In British India there were always too few Muslim lawyers, journalists, teachers, officials, and businessmen.

The man who was most conspicuous in trying to remedy this situation was Sayyid Ahmad Khan, the descendant of a family that had come to Delhi from Herat during the sixteenth century and had served the Mughul court for generations. Sayyid Ahmad Khan, who himself felt a deep attachment to that Mughul past, wrote a detailed account in Urdu of the historical monuments of Delhi and also edited a Persian historical chronicle relating to the sultans of Delhi. Acquiring a fluency in English unusual for a Muslim of his day, he entered the British service, remained steadfastly loyal during the crisis of 1857, and thereafter enjoyed the warm support of British officials in the Northwestern Provinces (now Uttar Pradesh). He totally rejected the British assumption of inherent disloyalty on the part of Indian Muslims, but he also believed that British hostility and indifference, coupled with the innate conservatism of his community, had enabled the Hindus to get ahead of the Muslims in the sphere of education and comprador activities. He therefore devoted his very considerable energies to the cause of Muslim education. His crowning achievement, which enjoyed the support of both the British and a number of prominent Muslim leaders, was the founding of the Mohammedan Anglo-Oriental College at Aligarh in 1875, now Aligarh Muslim University. Recognizing that most elite Muslims were reluctant to allow their sons to be educated in institutions where they would be exposed to deleterious Hindu and European influences (e.g., idolatry, Christianity, rationalism, atheism, alcohol, and moral permissiveness), he conceived Aligarh as a center where Muslim youth could obtain a European education within a Muslim religious and moral environment.

It is undoubtedly true that Sayyid Ahmad Khan was an elitist in educational matters, protesting most vehemently, for example, against the admission of the children of dancing girls and prostitutes to schools where they would contaminate the children of "respectable families." Some Indians, even in his own lifetime, saw him as an archcommunalist because he believed that the Muslims, as a community, had nothing to gain and plenty to lose by throwing in their lot with the Hindu-dominated nationalist movement. With regard to the Hindus, it would perhaps be more accurate to see him as an exponent of coexistence and separate development. He saw himself less as an Indian than as an Indian Muslim, and he believed that his community was less threatened by the continuation of the conservative British regime than by the political aspirations of the Hindu intelligentsia, coupled with the growing economic stranglehold of the caste Hindus over his undereducated coreligionists. Probably his most positive role was to persuade at least some Indian Muslims that a knowledge of European science and technology was not incompatible with Islamic values and the Muslim way of life, although here he was strongly opposed by Muslim traditionalists trained in the seminary of Deoband, founded in 1867. In future years the products of Deoband would exercise a most potent influence on the Indian Muslim community, denouncing Sayyid Ahmad Khan's brand of modernism and reformism, rejecting contemporary flirtations with European positivism and relativity, and vigorously meeting the challenge presented by Christian and Arya Samaj missionaries.

By the opening years of the twentieth century Muslim leaders in India were beginning to diagnose the plight of their community and with it to recognize the paradox that the Indian nationalist movement, dominated by Hindus and institutionalized in the Indian National Congress, had little or nothing to offer the Indian Muslims unless they acquiesced in the status of a minority community in an independent but Hindu-controlled India. This was something that apparently most Muslims could not accept and it is important to ask why they felt this way. Some Hindu writers have attributed the Muslim insistence upon special treatment, and eventually partition, to a Machiavellian British policy of divide and rule, to the vested interests and sectional selfishness of the conservative Muslim elite, and to the insatiable ambition of Muhammad Ali Jinnah (1876-1948), the architect of Pakistan, but the situation was more complicated than that. First, it should be noted that it proved exceedingly difficult for Indian Muslims to subordinate their religious identity as Muslims to a national identity as Indians. Elsewhere in the Islamic world, where the historical experience and the arithmetic of minorities has been different, it has sometimes proved possible to achieve some degree of noncommunal identity—as in the case of the Palestinian Arabs, whether Muslim or Christian—but in general most Muslims in the twentieth century still find the age-old distinction between Muslim and non-Muslim hard to forget.

Among the factors that contributed both to a renaissance of Hinduism during the nineteenth century and to the emergence of Indian nationalist sentiment were pressures for the reform and renovation of Hindu traditions and values, the widespread belief in the existence of various golden ages in the past history of India, and the complacent assumption of the superiority of ancient Hindu civilization over all other civilizations (sanatva). In consequence, manifestations of xenophobia were by no means directed exclusively against the British but were aimed, sometimes with even greater venom, against the Muslims. For example, one Hindu writer with a marked communal bias has declared that:

. . . the courts of all medieval alien rulers in India reeked with sodomy, drinking orgies, sexual revelry, eunuchs, plotting and counter-plotting, murders and massacres, and destructive and demolition fury. . . . The entire alien rule in India for over a millenium until the British took over was a harrowing nightmarish period in which rape, rapine, levy of cruel and despotic taxes, manslaughter and rounding up of Indians to be sold as slaves abroad were very common occurrences.[2]

Thus, Islam as a religion and a way of life came to be identified with the subjugation of Hindu India at the hands of invading Turkish barbarians, a process sometimes seen as no different in kind but far more violent in its consequences than the later conquests of the British, and this view continued to be propagated, notwithstanding the fact that most Indian Muslims were of indigenous Indian descent and only a minority were the descendants of Turkish or Iranian immigrants. Pursuing this line further, communal historians maintained that if there was something to be said in favor of at least some aspects of British rule (e.g., that they had made an end of Muslim tyranny in Hindu Mysore) there was little that could be said on behalf of their Muslim predecessors. Certainly the glorification of Maratha history and in particular of the Maratha struggle against the Mughuls, which was part of the political style of some prominent nationalist leaders such as Tilak (1856-1920), was interpreted both by their own followers and by apprehensive Muslim observers as being essentially communal and anti-Muslim in spirit, as were the activities of the Arya Samaj missionaries in the Panjab.

In retrospect, it appears that with so much to lose from a further deterioration of communal relations and with so much to gain from their amelioration, it was incumbent upon the leadership of the Indian National Congress to lean over backwards in attempting to win the confidence of the Muslims. In fact, they did little or nothing of the kind. Even when an attempt was made it was done ineptly, as when Gandhi and some other Congress leaders supported the Khilafat movement between 1919 and 1924. In this instance, Indian Muslim public opinion was deeply concerned regarding Allied intentions towards the defeated Ottoman empire and especially towards the institution of the caliphate, long vested in the Ottoman dynasty and shortly to be abolished by Ataturk in 1924. For a while, Congress support for the Khilafat movement seemed to herald the opening of a new phase in Hindu-Muslim cooperation, but the realities of communal politics soon came to the fore again. In any case, as Hindu communalists were quick to point out, it was preposterous for Hindus to be supporting an issue that only underscored the Indian Muslim sense of a split personality divided in allegiance between India and the Muslim heartlands to the west.

Pakistan: The Problem of Muslim Nationalism
In reality, Indian Muslims had only a limited choice of options open to them. One way was to trust the credentials of the more forward-looking and secular-minded Congress leaders and to work for the common goal of independence, reiterating that Muslims were as much Indians as Hindus and both were victims of a common colonial experience. Muslims of this persuasion were always to be found within the Congress ranks in small numbers, and after 1947 they remained in India in order to show that the new republic could be as much a homeland for Indian Muslims as for Hindus. Other Muslims, apprehensive of the future, adopted a conservative position of waiting upon events, concluding that perhaps the safest barrier against Hindu majority domination was the continuation of a British presence, which in turn depended on Muslim goodwill for recruiting a large part of the British-Indian army. Most Muslims, however, looking ahead to an eventual British withdrawal in some form or another, saw the solution to the problem in persuading the British to accept the principle of a special status for the Muslims in any future devolution of imperial authority. It was with just such an eventuality in mind that the Muslim League was formed in 1906 and

2. P.N. Oak, *Some Blunders of Indian Historical Research* (New Delhi, 1966), pp. 140, 151.

that Muslims began to pin their hopes upon communal electorates in the various elective councils through which the British were beginning the slow process of decolonization. Thereafter, every ingenious device known to the constitutional lawyer was enlisted as a means of securing for the Muslims some kind of guaranteed status vis-a-vis the Hindu majority, although all such attempts more or less foundered in the face of the bickering, bad faith, personal ambition, and lack of vision among the spokesmen of both communities. These failures of statesmanship in the years between the world wars, which also witnessed the transformation of the Muslim League into a mass movement, probably ensured that the partition of British India in 1947 into two mutually hostile successor states was the only viable solution possible at the time.

In so far as the creation of Pakistan answered the political aspirations of the great majority of politically conscious Muslims, it may be regarded as the fulfillment of the Indian Muslim quest for national identity. But to go beyond that statement and to attempt to define more precisely that Indian Muslim sense of national identity only underscores the basic problems that have beset Pakistan since independence. First, that search for identity could never be expressed solely in geographical terms. Apart from East Bengal and the lands watered by the Indus and its tributaries, Indian Muslims were almost everywhere a minority deeply embedded within the numerically much larger framework of Hindu society, so that most Muslims, whether urban or rural, lived side by side with Hindu neighbors. Even in the great days of Mughul rule it may be doubted whether such metropolitan centers as Agra, Delhi or, later, Lucknow ever contained a majority of Muslims, and it was this physical proximity of the two communities that was to make the rioting and massacres of 1946-47 so horrific. But if, prior to the creation of Pakistan, Indian Muslims looked to no clearly defined homeland, it was no less true that neither race nor language provided a common denominator for establishing their identity. The racial origin of Indian Muslims was both highly diverse and a matter for largely subjective speculation. The traditional elite habitually claimed a foreign origin, Iranian or Central Asian, and set great store upon its Irano-Mughul cultural heritage, but, by way of contrast, the racial antecedents of the Muslim masses of Bengal, Bihar, and Malabar were overwhelmingly indigenous. Similarly with language, Urdu, the literary vehicle of late Mughul culture, was the *lingua franca* of the Muslims of the upper Gangetic plain, but the majority of Muslims elsewhere spoke regional vernaculars—such as Sindhi, Panjabi, Pashtu, or Bengali.

Since the cultural pattern of Indian Islam was one of such extreme diversity it may be wondered what common bond linked the Bohra or Ismaili merchant of Gujarat or Bombay with the Bengali cultivator, or the Pathan tribesman with the nobleman of Hyderabad or the *sayyid* of Delhi. The answer was only Islam itself, but it was the conviction of the men who worked for the creation of Pakistan that Islam alone was enough. Pakistan means the "Land of the Pure" (i.e., of those pure in faith), and it was their aim to establish a homeland where Indian Muslims would be free to build for themselves a truly Islamic society. This concept of an Islamic nation-state, a state that had a religious goal as its *raison d'etre,* carried with it from its first inception profound inconsistencies. Some of these, viewed now in retrospect, can be seen to have been virtually unavoidable, such as the conflict between the interests of West Pakistan and East Pakistan, resulting in the secession of Bangladesh, and the increasing dissatisfaction of the Pathans and the Baluchis with a regime that continues, in their view, to be dominated by Panjabis and Sindhis. Perhaps most threatening in the long run is the paradox of a nation-state dedicated to the preservation of specifically Islamic values endeavoring to achieve goals of modernization which necessarily involve a modification of traditional values and the adoption of new forms of social and economic organization, and which thereby pose a continuous challenge to the basic concept of Pakistan.

3. CULTURAL RENAISSANCE AND NATIONALISM IN SOUTHEAST ASIA

The varied patterns of cultural and national development which are characteristic of Southeast Asia in modern times reflect the great diversity of the region and also the different colonial experience of each society. Not only is Southeast Asia, like West Asia, divided among many states, it lacks unifying historical experiences and religious institutions that might serve to typify it as a cultural sphere. For this reason generalization about Southeast Asia as a whole is extremely difficult, and no attempt will be made here to deal with all of the region. Instead, the processes will be discussed first in the context of an overview of the region and then with reference to individual countries. The cases to be given special attention here are Indonesia, the Philippines, and Vietnam. Thailand, the only state in the region to escape foreign rule, will be discussed in the next chapter.

Perhaps more than in other regions of Asia, the tempo and rhythm of nationalism in Southeast Asia were affected by the conditions of colonial domination. Four stages stand out clearly: 1) The first was the period from the early contacts in the sixteenth century until the middle of the nineteenth century, when European encroachment penetrated primarily into Java and the island of Luzon in the Philippines. Trade was concerned for the most part with agricultural products and beyond these limited Western outposts most of the rural society and the traditional ruling elite remained undisturbed by external events. 2) The second stage was provoked by intensified rivalry of the industrialized countries which led in the late nineteenth century to the annexation of all of Southeast Asia, except Tahailand, by the West European powers and the United States. This period, which lasted until the Second World War, saw the extension of direct control over colonies by home governments, which sent out bureaucrats and professional specialists to reshape the traditional social order, displace native rulers, and encourage economic development. Subjugation by rival Western powers exposed Southeast Asians to global rivalries and, increasingly, to the forces of the world market. The traditional Chinese model of interstate relations, based on the Confucian conception of a moral hierarchy of rulers centered about the Chinese throne, which had provided a framework for interaction in much of Southeast Asia, was swept away because China, in decline, could extend little or no protection to her former tributaries. One lasting effect of the imposition of European notions of international law and the discrete demarcation of boundaries was to divide and combine peoples in arbitrary ways for the convenience of colonial administration and without consideration for traditional political or linguistic boundaries. Laos, for example, was created by the French. 3) The Japanese occupation, in most areas from 1942 to 1945, was the third period. Brief as it was, this experience of rule by a single Asian power brought a decisive change to most of the region. It dealt a lethal blow to European colonialism and set in motion many of the forces of national independence. 4) The postwar era is the fourth phase. Characteristic of these years has been the termination of colonial controls, the establishment of new nation-states, conflict within the region, and the intervention of new external forces, particularly the competition of China, the Soviet Union, and the United States.

Nativist reaction to Western domination tended to be pronounced in those areas that experienced the most direct colonial control. Here, one must distinguish between two tendencies in Western administration, between direct administration by Europeans on the one hand, and indirect rule through indigenous leaders on the other. Where indirect rule was practiced, as by the British in the Malay states or the Dutch in the outer islands of Indonesia, traditional social and cultural forms were preserved under indigenous leaders who came to terms with the colonial power. In directly administered areas like Java, where the native rulers were displaced, alienation was often severe. Frequently the religious community—Islamic or Buddhist (including Confucian gentry in Vietnam)—played an im-

13.4 Chulalongkorn, the Thai king in 1903. Although Thailand maintained its independence from Western rule, the royal family, which served as a symbol of national unity and provided direction to the country's development, consciously adopted many of the forms of European royalty. Source: A. Cecil Carter, ed., *The Kingdom of Siam* (New York, 1904).

portant role in defining the traditional values being defended. In Java, for example, a royal prince of the house of Jogjakarta led a five-year resistance struggle (1825-30) in defense of both the Javanese royalty and Islamic orthodoxy. One reason why religious leaders were important in areas under direct administration was because they were the only remaining potential leadership group. Popular uprisings among the peasantry were also not uncommon occurrences. These disturbances tended to be guided by traditional utopian or messianic folk beliefs and directed against either unbelievers or outsiders, like the Chinese and Indians who poured into Southeast Asia during the colonial period.

In the second stage of colonial administration, as the powers attempted to partially make over Southeast Asian societies, increasing numbers of "natives" were exposed to Western education, either abroad in Europe, the United States, and Japan or in new colonial universities in Rangoon, Hanoi, and Batavia. Again depending on the circumstances, these new recipients of Western education could be either part of a co-opted native elite, such as the sons of Malay sultans, and therefore conservative in their politics, or part of a rising new urban intelligentsia with no vested interest in the old order. This last group, which became numerically significant from the 1920s on, tended to be hostile to the colonial order and consequently attracted to radical social programs, notably Marxism-Leninism. Because they had no base of wealth or fixed social position, the new intelligentsia tended to view the state as the proper vehicle for social action and to advocate developmental change that would place themselves in positions of leadership.

The cultural renaissance and revival movements in Southeast Asia took many forms, among which religious movements stood out, particularly in Malaya and Indonesia, where Islam was the principal faith. Syncretic combinations of European and indigenous elements were also attempted. No single pattern characterized the whole region. Where Marxism gained adherents, it was not always among similar groups. In Malaya the communist movement was strongest among the Chinese minority in opposition to both the British and a system of government that favored the old Malay elite. In Indonesia the Communist Party attempted to attack Dutch control through urban strikes, while the communist movement in the Philippines was primarily a rural action force that attacked an indigenous landowning class. In Vietnam the communists were influenced heavily by the Chinese example and succeeded in gaining leadership of the nationalist movement and establishing state power.

A nationalist independence movement matured first in the Philippines in the 1890s. By the 1920s demands for independence were being voiced in other areas. Often it was a colonial governing body that provided the vehicle for these expressions. Organized political movements were usually suppressed and their leaders jailed, exiled, or executed. So effective was colonial repression that prior to 1942 there was no colony moving toward nationhood with the exception of the Philippines, which had been promised complete independence by 1946. It was the Japanese invasion that gave the greatest stimulus to nationalism. Initially the Japanese were welcomed throughout Southeast Asia and proclaimed their Greater East Asian Co-Prosperity Sphere, which had considerably more appeal to Asian pride than did European white supremacy. Despite the often very harsh conditions that existed under Japanese rule, the new order provided great opportunities for nationalist movements to develop. Not only did the Japanese allow Southeast Asians to assume more active leadership roles, toward the close of the war they encouraged the formation of political movements and armed forces and even proclaimed independent governments. The Japanese, of course, were motivated by a desire to forward their own war aims, while Southeast Asian collaboration was based in large part on calculations of self-interest. This can be illustrated by an example that involved South Asia as well. In Burma, Subhas Chandra Bose, an Indian Nationalist who had spent some years in Germany, cooperated in 1943 with the Japanese who had formed an Indian National Army and in the following year proclaimed a government of Free India (Azad Hind), preparatory to an

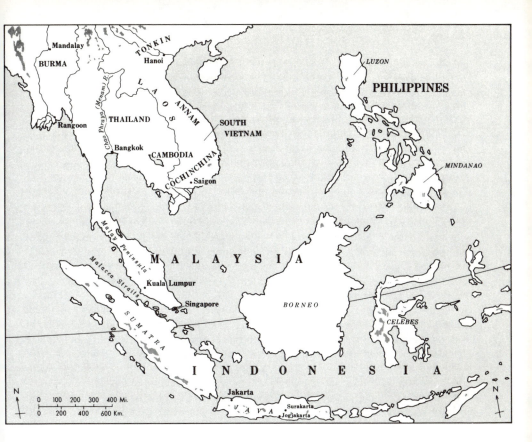

Map 55 Nationalism in Southeast Asia

unsuccessful Japanese attack on the British colony. The Japanese were particularly success-ful in mobilizing young people who were impressed by the efficiency of Japanese organiza-tion and whose radicalism put heavy pressure on older leaders in the postwar era. Also, movements of resistance to Japanese rule, which were organized late in the war, provided a training ground for many who were to participate in the struggle for independence after the war.

Indonesia

The Dutch governor-general and the Council of the Indies reported to a colonial minister in the home country, who in turn was responsible to the Dutch Parliament. Over the course of a complicated evolution of administrative arrangements there emerged a distinction in the colony between government lands subject to direct Dutch rule and native states where indigenous rule persisted. Worsening conditions in Java in the 1890s prompted the Dutch to institute administrative reforms, referred to collectively as the Ethical Policy, which had the effect of tightening Dutch control over local affairs, particularly in Java, which was the heartland of the colony. An influx of Dutch administrators after 1900 tilted the balance in the "European" colonial elite in favor of those who were oriented toward the life-style and values of the Dutch homeland. The older style of accommodation to Indonesian conditions gave way to a less compromising Dutch style of life and a more strident advocacy of the superiority of Western ways. Eurasian, Chinese, and other segments of the colonial elite found themselves compelled to adhere to Dutch practice in their public life. This tendency had the effect of creating a gap between the colonial elite and the common people. Dutch-language schools increased in number after the turn of the century and there was a gradual trend toward the creation of a common legal system and a structure of Dutch-style political institutions. A Volksraad ("People's Council") was established in 1918, and in 1936 provincial governorships were introduced on the model of the Netherlands.

The impetus toward cultural revival was manifested most clearly in the Muslim community. The opening of the Suez Canal in 1869 enhanced contact with West Asia, exposing Indonesian Muslims to the Islamic reform movements there. Whereas the conservative Wahhabi movement had spurred reform sentiment in the early nineteenth century, by 1900 Indonesian and Malay students were returning from al-Azhar University in Cairo, where the modernization of Islam was being advocated. In 1912 the Muhammadiyah, a reformist organization, was founded in Java and soon had hundreds of branches. The vigor of Muslim activity was shown by the number of the faithful making the pilgrimage to Mecca. In 1926, two years after the holy city came under Saudi Arabian control, more than fifty thousand Indonesians made the journey. In opposition to the modernizing trend in Islam, conservatives formed their own organization, Nahdatul Ulama ("Awakening of the Ulama"), in 1926, which was strongest in rural Java.

Increased educational opportunities, particularly in schools with a Dutch curriculum, created after 1900 an ever larger intelligentsia racked by questions of cultural identity. In the years before 1914 the native primary school system was converted into a network of Dutch native schools with instruction in the European tongue. By 1915 the system had twenty thousand students, and by 1940, forty-five thousand. Institutions of higher education, notably a school for native doctors which began instruction in Dutch in 1875, provided many who were to assume top leadership positions in the twentieth century. One effect of Western education was to create a class of modernized professionals who vied with remnants of the native elite for position and status, thereby hastening the breakdown of the traditional social order. Recognizing the decline of the old order, educated members of the nobility sought new identities, compatible with modern conditions, which would allow them to retain a sense of their own culture. One such movement was Budi Utomo, founded in Java in 1908 by students in the above-mentioned medical school. Many other groups, including young Javans, young Sumatrans, young Celebes, and young Islam, were formed as the new Dutch-educated generation sought its way. Another effort to reconcile the heritage with modern change was the creation by a member of the Javanese court nobility of the Taman Siswo school system, which combined Western curriculum and instructional methods with inculcation in traditional values, much as Muslims in India had sought to do with the creation of an Anglo-Oriental college at Aligarh.

Signs of a shift from cultural renaissance to the beginnings of nationalism or at least protonationalism can be detected in the Sarekat Islam ("Islamic Union") movement founded in 1912. Despite its ostensible Muslim form, Sarekat Islam originated among Javanese merchants facing increased competition from Chinese. The movement soon attracted a wide following, particularly among the intelligentsia, who soon took over its leadership. Its charismatic personality was Umar Said Tjokroaminoto, a Dutch-educated member of the Javanese nobility, a brilliant orator who could appeal alike to the educated city dweller and the unlettered villager. Tjokroaminoto's name was that of a traditional Javanese savior, and the appeal he made to the masses drew heavily on folk religion, while other elements in the organization were engaged in the advocacy of socialism and agitation among workers. The movement, which linked for the first time in Indonesian history urban leadership with the rural populace, had a membership of two million by 1919, but it reached a far wider audience. The Dutch, alarmed by outbreaks of unrest in that year, abandoned both tolerance and their Ethical Policy and repressed the movement. At this juncture the movement split, some of the socialists forming an Indies Communist Party (PKI, Perserikatan Komunis di India), while the Muslims responded to the pan-Islamic Khalifat (Califate) movement of the early 1920s. The Khalifat movement soon lost its momentum, and a revolt led by PKI members in 1926 resulted in a repression that devastated the infant communist movement.

Indonesian nationalism took a long step forward in 1927 with the formation of the Indonesian Nationalist Party (PNI, Partai Nasional Indonesia). Its leader, Sukarno, was a young Dutch-trained engineer who had spent some of his formative years in the house of Tjokroaminoto. The message of the PNI was nationalism that transcended the group and the locality—an Indonesian identity, which encompassed a single nation, a single language, and a single people. As the idea of Indonesia gained acceptance among the varied population of the Dutch colony, the Malay language, already a *lingua franca* for administrative and commercial purposes, was rechristened "Indonesian" and popularized as a national language. During the decade of the 1930s vigilant Dutch suppression of the PNI, which included the exiling of Sukarno to Sumatra, dashed hopes of an effective independence movement and forced many educated Indonesians into collaboration within the framework of the legitimate legislative organs.

It was the Japanese occupation of the Indies that brought latent nationalism to fruition in the form of a successful independence movement. The Japanese were warmly greeted when they occupied Java and their takeover was actively assisted in Sumatra. A division of Japanese administrative spheres between the army and the navy, however, divided rather than unified the Indonesian territories. The Japanese-sponsored organization Puerta (an acronym for a title that meant "Center of the People's Strength"), deemphasized "Indonesia" as a unit, while Masjumi (short for "Consultative Council of Indonesian Muslims") stressed a religious rather than a national identity. Nevertheless, intelligentsia leaders such as Sukarno were returned from exile and given an unprecedented opportunity in voicing support for the Japanese to reestablish a following through such organs as the Djawa Kokokai ("Java Service Association"). As the war drew on the Japanese established paramilitary organizations such as Hizbullah ("Allah's Army") and conventional forces such as PETA, a Javanese defense force of sixty-five thousand men, which enabled the Indonesians to prepare for their own defense against the returning Dutch. At war's end an independent Indonesian state was proclaimed with Sukarno as president and Mohammed Hatta as vice-president. The collapse of Japanese power sparked a pervasive and violent national uprising in which pent-up discontent was expressed in attacks on the Japanese, newly arrived British forces, minority groups, and many political leaders. The infant republic adopted a policy of *diplomasi,* "negotiation," toward the returning Dutch, who gradually built up their military strength and in two "police actions" in 1947 and 1948 recaptured most of their lost territory. Just as the Dutch succeeded militarily, however, the international side of the *diplomasi* triumphed by turning world opinion decisively against the colonial power, which was forced in 1949 to recognize a sovereign state, subsequently designated the Republic of Indonesia.

The Philippines

The pattern of nationalism in the Philippines contrasted considerably with that in other parts of Southeast Asia. In some respects the Philippine case resembles Latin America as much as Asia. Since there was no strong centralized state or dominant high culture in the Philippines prior to the colonial era, cultural revival and renaissance forces were less important than was the demand for national independence. The cultural conflict with the colonial powers was moderated by the fact that large numbers of Filipinos embraced Christianity. Relatively easy access to education under Spanish rule meant that Filipino political consciousness developed early and helps to account for the fact that the Philippines had the first anticolonial movement and were the first to gain independence among the Southeast Asian colonies.

The Spanish population of the Philippines was never large, and the elite that evolved there in colonial times was a mixed group of Europeans, Filipino *caciques* ("native elite"), Chinese, and Chinese mestizos. The Europeans played a limited role in this class, controlling the governmental and clerical positions. In the latter half of the nineteenth century ethnic Chinese began to displace the older Chinese mestizos as the dominant commercial class in the urban areas, while the Filipino *caciques* solidified their position as a landowning class at the expense of the peasantry. Western education created a literate elite known as *ilustrados*, who, resentful of Spanish overlordship, especially of the church hierarchy, led the movement for independence.

The first stirrings of Philippine nationalism date from 1872, when Spanish repression of a mutiny prompted many *ilustrados* to go abroad, usually to Spain, for the purposes of higher education. It was in the Iberian mother country that these Filipinos organized the Propaganda Movement, which demanded political representation, civil rights, and access to clerical positions in the church hierarchy, which were monopolized by Spanish friars. Although the goals of this movement were reformist in nature, the concerns of these young intellectuals encompassed the search for a national identity, an awareness of a distinct history, and an interest in Tagalog literature. *La Solidaridad,* a newspaper that started publication in Spain in 1889, was the mouthpiece of the movement. Jose Rizal, a medical doctor who had once considered joining the church before he was radicalized by Spanish actions, became the leading figure in the movement, popularizing his ideas by writing novels. The Filipinos were influenced in their anticlericalism by the Freemasonry movement then in vogue in Spain, and they organized lodges in both Spain and the Philippines. In 1892 Rizal returned to the Philippines and organized a moderate organization called La Liga Filipina. The Spanish, unwilling to tolerate such an initiative, deported Rizal to Mindanao.

Meanwhile, among a lower stratum of Philippine society, a revolutionary movement was developing. A clerk from Manila named Andres Bonifacio started a secret organization of the Masonic type called Katipunan, in which the Tagalog language was used. In 1896 Bonifacio initiated a rebellion in the area around Manila. Inept Spanish policies, which included the trial and execution of Rizal, forced the whole class of *ilustrados* closer to opposition and thus created a solidarity among the Filipinos which had not existed previously. Bonifacio was replaced at the head of the movement by a Chinese mestizo official named Emilio Aguinaldo, but the struggle for power considerably weakened the rebel movement. Aguinaldo agreed to go into exile in exchange for amnesty and a large sum of cash. The revolution got a new lease on life when the United States invaded the Philippines and Aguinaldo was returned to the islands by the Americans,, who wanted him to create a second front against the Spanish. *Ilustrados* now joined Aguinaldo's movement in such numbers that they were able to moderate its tone, stressing nationalism but recognizing the sanctity of private property and social privilege. Aguinaldo declared the independence of a Philippine Republic in June 1898, and a moderate constitution dictated by an *ilustrado*-dominated legislature was promulgated the following January. The United States, which had defeated the Spanish and decided to annex the Philippines as a colony, commenced hostilities with the republican forces in February 1899.

American suppression of the insurgent independence movement succeeded through the exercise of superior military force and by offering conditions that split the *ilustrados* from the more radical elements in the movement. From as early as 1900 the policy of the United States contained the implication that the Philippines would some day become independent and that American administration was transitional. In practice this meant that conservative *ilustrados* were allowed to fill governmental positions left by the Spanish and to control internal social policy through American-style legislative organs. The one solid nationalist gain from the republican revolution was the creation of an Independent Philippine church, which subsequently forced the Catholic church to name Filipino priests and to dispose of some of its estate lands. In 1935 a Philippine Commonwealth was created, which allowed a substantial degree of self-rule, with the United States retaining control of foreign affairs, immigration, the military, and finances. Manuel Quezon, a willing collaborator in the gradual evolution toward independence, dominated Philippine politics through his Nacionalista Party. Thus it was that the Westernized, landed elite of the islands came to terms with American colonial occupation and deferred independence in exchange for domestic power and a secure social position. An end to American rule was scheduled to occur in 1946.

Although the Philippines saw more fighting than did any other part of Southeast Asia, the Japanese invasion did little to alter the course of Philippine nationalism. Manuel Quezon, the president of the Commonwealth, fled the islands with General Douglas MacArthur in 1942 and sat out the war in Washington, D.C., as the head of a government in exile until his death in 1944. Most members of the Filipino elite collaborated with the Japanese, who made strenuous efforts to win over the *ilustrados* and to pursuade Filipinos that their real interests lay with their fellow Asians and not with a white colonial power. In 1943, considerably ahead of the American schedule, a Japanese-sponsored republic was established under a former member of Quezon's cabinet. Many Filipinos, however, refused to cooperate with the Japanese. These included the Commonwealth Filipino Army, which fought together with the Americans in the first days of the war, and a guerrilla resistance movement that grew in size during the war. Because the Japanese could not occupy much of the territory beyond Manila and other important centers, large areas were held by partisan forces. This circumstance gave an opportunity to communist-led revolutionary forces to play a substantial role in the resistance. The conditions of peasants had worsened during the 1930s, when substantial uprisings occurred. Under an abrasive Japanese rule many more people were pushed into resistance until the countryside neared the brink of social revolution. The Hukbalahap (short for the Tagalog version of "People's Anti-Japanese Army") movement attacked the rural social order by distributing land to those who worked it, the landlords, often as not, having taken refuge in Manila. After the war ended the United States granted the Philippines independence on July 4, 1946, and the core of the Nacionalista Party, both collaborators and resistance leaders, continued on in power. The Huks now converted their movement to electoral politics, but despite the fact that they won seats they were barred from office by the conservative elite. The Hukbalahap (redesignated "People's Liberation Army") returned to the countryside, where it led an armed insurrection. In the early 1950s the able policies of the charismatic Ramon Magsaysay, himself a wartime guerrilla leader, succeeded in decimating the Huk movement by a combination of suppression and reform. Magsaysay was elected president in 1953 but died in a plane crash in 1957, after which time the conservative Filipino elite returned to politics as usual, emulating a life-style based on American stereotypes while the conditions in the rural areas worsened.

Vietnam

Under French colonial administration Vietnam was divided into three regions, or "countries:" Tonkin in the north, Annam in the middle, and Cochinchina in the south. Cochinchina, which had come under Vietnamese settlement and rule only in the eighteenth century, was relatively thinly populated and less culturally cohesive than were the two northern areas. French administration and water-control projects turned Cochinchina into a rich rice-producing region, and there evolved there a landowning class, many of whose members acquired French educations under colonial rule. In the two northern regions there existed an older Chinese-style gentry class, which derived its position from both land and Confucian education. Political movements tended to develop in the north, while the culturally less assimilated south was the locus of religious movements like the syncretic Cao Dai religion and Hoa Hao Buddhism, which functioned on a regional basis. In Annam a protectorate extended loose French control over the remnants of a Vietnamese monarchy at Hue until the 1890s when administrative consolidation tightened colonial control throughout Vietnam.

Nativist reaction to foreign cultural influence was manifested first in Vietnam by resistance to French Catholicism. French missionaries, who were active in Vietnam as early as the sixteenth century, were opposed by the Confucian Vietnamese elite, which saw in the European faith a challenge to its own privileged position in society, which derived from its monopoly on ideological leadership. Nevertheless, Christianity gained adherents until there were seventy thousand Vietnamese converts by the middle of the nineteenth century, at which time attacks on the clergy and their followers led to French intervention and the establishment after 1862 of the colony of Cochinchina. Catholicism became a factor in the factional rivalries of the Nguyen court, and while some Vietnamese advocated exterminating Christians, there were some Catholics among the elite who tried to act as a bridge between East and West. Nguyen Truong To (1827-71), for example, was a Vietnamese provincial official who advocated that the emperor introduce Western-style reforms, much as progressive Chinese scholars were to do in the last decades of the century.

The development of nationalism in Vietnam was strongly influenced by Vietnam's cultural tie to China as a tributary state within a common Confucian universe. Resistance to Catholicism was based on a defense of the integrity of a Confucian social model. Likewise, when the French defeated the Chinese in 1885 and imposed protectorates over Tonkin and Annam, the resistance movements that harrassed them were inspired by a Confucian notion of loyalty to the throne and not by a modern conception of the nation. Pham Boi Chau (1867-1940), one of the leading figures of Vietnamese nationalism, was inspired by the ideas of the Chinese reformer Liang Ch'i-ch'ao to advocate a monarchical model of modernization. Chau traveled to Japan in 1905, where he had contact with Liang and a variety of Chinese revolutionaries. He later went to south China, where the Vietnamese organized a revolutionary organization like that of Sun Yat-sen with the intention of liberating their homeland. In 1927, after the success of the Kuomintang in China, a Vietnamese Nationalist Party (Viet Nam Quoc Dan Dang), modeling itself on the Chinese party, was created in Hanoi. Weak in manpower and resources, this revolutionary force was decimated by the French when it attempted armed insurrection in 1930. The subsequent development of Vietnamese nationalism was left largely to the communists.

The Indochina Community Party was formed in South China in 1930 as part of the international communist movement. Ho Chi Minh (1890-1969, born Nguyen That Thanh), the party's founder, was an experienced agent of the Communist International. As a young man Ho drifted through a number of jobs and traveled to France before the First World War. In France he discovered Marxism, joined the Communist Party, and in 1923 went to the Soviet Union to begin a career as a revolutionary organizer. The genius of the Vietnamese party lay in organization. Exploitation of peasant discontent through the formation of rural soviets in the north and a brief period of open agitation while a leftist government was in power in France in the late 1930s extended the party's infrastructure in Vietnamese society but failed to threaten French rule. It was the Second World War that provided Ho Chi Minh with an opportunity to build state power. Ho was a captive of the

Chinese Nationalists until 1944, when the Chinese and their Western allies freed Ho for the purpose of creating a resistance movement in Vietnam. Ho formed a communist-controlled front group, the Viet Minh (short for "Revolutionary League for the Independence of Vietnam"), which quickly linked up with revolutionaries throughout Vietnam. When the Japanese surrendered in 1945 the Vietnamese emperor Bao Dai at Hue declared the country independent. A few months later he abdicated in favor of the Viet Minh, who briefly controlled Saigon and more firmly controlled Hanoi, where Ho Chi Minh proclaimed the Democratic Republic of Vietnam. French efforts to regain control of their former colony led to prolonged fighting, which was terminated by the French defeat at Dien Bien Phu in 1954. Subsequently Vietnam was divided at the seventeenth parallel, with the Democratic Republic of Vietnam occupying the north and the Republic of Vietnam set up in the south as an American client state.

4. CULTURAL RENAISSANCE AND NATIONALISM IN CHINA

There can be no doubt that China has developed in the twentieth century a nationalism as virulent as that of any country in Asia. Yet there are a number of factors that set Chinese nationalism apart from the patterns elsewhere. First of all, China did not undergo a total loss of national sovereignty. China experienced only a semicolonial exploitation at the hands of the Western powers; and Japan failed to complete the military pacification of the China mainland. Second, the fact that the Ch'ing empire was a foreign conquest dynasty distorted the development of both a cultural renaissance and of nationalism in China. One result of this circumstance was that Chinese nationalism, when it did emerge, developed in two distinct stages. The first stage was anti-Manchu and focused on the overthrow of the imperial order. The second stage was directed against imperialism, particularly the encroachments of the European powers and Japan. A third factor in the Chinese case has to do with the role of culture in the definition of what is Chinese. In scale China far exceeds any other nation-state. Traditionally China was a cultural area in itself—as much a civilization as a state. Today, too, as part of the socialist world, China has a cultural identity as a center of Marxism-Leninism in addition to her identity as a nation.

Late Ch'ing Quest for Cultural Revival
It was noted in Chapter 9 that scholarship in early Ch'ing period turned inward and backward in a search for greater authenticity within the classical sources of the Confucian tradition. The result was a bookish textual scholarship, which has been characterized as Ch'ing empiricism. In exploring their literary heritage the eighteenth century scholars tended to bypass the relatively recent authorities of the Sung period (Sung Learning) in favor of the more ancient authors of the Han period (Han Learning). Scrupulous study of the Han sources served to heighten awareness of discrepancies between two versions of the classical texts known as the New Text and Ancient Text. These versions dated from the Han period (206 B.C.-220 A.D.) following the first unification of China by the state of Ch'in in 221 B.C. The Ch'in ruler had attempted to bolster the influence of his own state ideology by outlawing all other schools of thought, burning their books, and executing scholars who advocated them. Subsequently in the Han, survivors of the great Ch'in purge reconstituted the teachings of Confucius from memory. These writings, set down in the Han script of that day, came to be known as the New Text versions of the classics. Some two centuries later a second version of the Confucian texts emerged, claimed to have been discovered in the wall of a house belonging to a descendant of Confucius. Written in an ancient style of

characters, these were known as the Ancient Text versions of the classics. In the attempted usurpation of the period 9-23 A.D. the ancient texts were used to justify ideological innovations. Eventually the Ancient Texts came to be accepted as authoritative. In the eighteenth and early nineteenth centuries these Ancient Texts were shown to have been forgeries. Consequently, a movement developed among Chinese scholars to reinterpret Confucianism in light of a new understanding of the classics. Thus classical studies in the nineteenth century were able to supply a sanction for criticism of the official orthodoxy and eventually, as we shall see, for the advocacy of radical change.

It is important to bear in mind that the Confucian tradition was not a monolithic structure but a complex fabric of many strands. When in the middle of the nineteenth century thoughtful Chinese became aware of the need to counter Western power, there were a variety of ideological sanctions for action. Wei Yuan (1794-1856), for example, was an advocate of the school of statecraft. His interest was directed primarily toward governmental affairs. It was from such an outlook that he pursued the study of geography and tried to collect information about the Europeans. Conservative restorationists like Tseng Kuo-fan, bolstering their counterinsurgency warfare against the Taipings and other rebels with ideological instruction, made use of an entirely different element in Confucianism. They appealed to some of the doctrines of Wang Yang-ming, who in the sixteenth century had distinguished himself in suppression of insurrections and rebuilding of community leadership. When outright borrowing from the West was advocated, it was justified through the use of classical sanctions. An early formula was that of "self-strengthening," based on a phrase from one of the classics. The self-strengthening formula and the distinction between Chinese learning as a base or core to which Western learning could be added were notions that gained great popularity among officials and scholars by the 1890s. In essence, these were rationalizations for change through which Chinese intellectuals tried to persuade themselves that they could defend their cultural tradition by limited borrowing. The effect of both restorationist and reformist uses of classical sanctions was to shift emphasis gradually from the *belief* in Confucian doctrines as the embodiment of the truth to the *use* of Confucianism as an embodiment of Chinese cultural identity. This shift, slight as it first seemed, led eventually to the rejection of the core values in the Confucian tradition.

In China the processes of cultural renaissance were manifested in the reform movement of 1898. Throughout the nineteenth century Chinese intellectuals had continued to subscribe to Confucian values and to see the imperial institution as the proper vehicle for China's salvation. The fact that the ruler was a Manchu was irrelevant so long as the throne was the legitimate locus of authority. The leading reformers, K'ang Yu-wei (1858-1927) and his young protégé Liang Ch'i-ch'ao (1873-1929), were both from the Canton area, which was to produce much of the leadership of the Chinese revolution. Impressed with the West, particularly with what he saw in Shanghai and Hong Kong, K'ang became convinced of the need for reform. To bolster his advocacy of reform he turned to the New Text school of Confucian learning. K'ang wrote two books in the 1890s in which he argued that the Ancient Text versions of the classics were really forgeries of the Han period and that Confucius had really been a reformer. By casting doubt on the Ancient Texts K'ang threw into question the authenticity of existing Confucian thought, thus opening the way to a reassessment of the Chinese past. Confucius, said K'ang, had been a reformer in his own time, not advocating a return to the past as was often thought, but portraying the past in utopian terms as a model for society. K'ang Yu-wei himself had written in 1887 a utopian work, the *Book of the Great Unity (Ta-t'ung shu)*, which pictured a society with no fixed family units, with dormitories and dining halls for all, universal education, health and welfare agencies, a single world government, local elections, government management of the economy, and rewards for invention and discovery. The full contents of this work K'ang prudently revealed only to his students and confidants.

Blocked from high office by conservative elements at court and thus barred from direct communication with the throne, K'ang Yu-wei took bold action in organizing students at the metropolitan examinations of 1895 and 1898. The Japanese defeat of Chinese forces in 1895 had created a sense of crisis, and the German leasing of territory in Shantung in 1897 raised the specter of an imperialist division of all of China. In 1895 the students sent a joint memorial to the throne calling for continued resistance to Japan and political reforms. This event marked the politicization of the scholar class and its first group action. In the same year a Society for the Study of Self-Strengthening was formed including students, scholars, progressive officials, and sympathetic Westerners. The purpose of the short-lived organization was to promote new ideas from Japan and the West and to advocate reform for national salvation. Significantly, the first publication of the society dated itself in terms of years since Confucius rather than the reign of the current emperor. Conservatives saw in this an indication of loyalty to the Confucian tradition displacing loyalty to the ruling house. Many study groups, newspapers, and magazines concerned with reforms of various kinds appeared throughout China at this time. In 1898 K'ang Yu-wei organized a National Protection Society, which was devoted to the preservation of Chinese sovereignty, the independence of the Chinese as a people, and the religions of China, as well as the advocacy of reform.

K'ang Yu-wei's conception of reform was quite consciously modeled after Peter the Great of Russia and the Meiji program in Japan. K'ang did finally get access to the sympathetic young Kuang-hsu Emperor in 1898, and a brief series of reform edicts was issued before Manchu reactionaries led by the empress dowager, Tz'u-hsi, took the young ruler into custody and expelled the reformers. For all practical purposes this marked the end of a viable effort at a Confucian renaissance. Confucianism was above all an imperial ideology. When the Confucian classics were reinterpreted as a sanction for change it was necessary that the emperor act as the instrumentality for change. Under circumstances in which the throne was in Manchu hands and the Manchus saw Chinese reform as a threat to their power, the Chinese intellectuals met disappointment. This fact was appreciated at the time. T'an Ssu-t'ung, a brilliant youthful reformer, willingly remained in Peking to be executed as the first martyr to the revolution.

Early Chinese Nationalism: The Republican Revolution of 1911

Manchu suppression of the 1898 reform effort left little hope that Confucian loyalism, no matter how radical, could salvage the imperial system and transform China. Increasingly, frustrated Chinese intellectuals were driven to the conclusion that Confucianism and the imperial system to which it was bound would have to be sacrificed if the integrity of China was to be preserved. This shift of loyalties from the high culture or elite values of the Confucian tradition to a belief in the organic unity of the Chinese people, their race, and their territory marked the transition from cultural renaissance to nationalism. A multitude of factors encouraged the trend. The very radicalism of the Confucian reformers served to undermine confidence in the adequacy of classical learning. New occupations, training abroad, and missionary schools all contributed to the ranks of alienated Chinese intellectuals who felt themselves caught between the conflicting value systems of China and Europe. Belated Manchu reforms, when they did come after 1900, only served to further erode Confucian scholarship by ending the examination system and establishing modern schools.

In the first decade of the twentieth century Chinese nationalism took the form of a revolutionary movement to overthrow the Ch'ing dynasty. In their drive to establish a new and strong Chinese state these nationalists identified the Manchus as one of the sources of Chinese weakness. This was nowhere more strongly stated than by Tsou Jung, who in 1903, at the age of eighteen, wrote a tract called *The Revolutionary Army*. Appealing to a sense of Chinese racial pride, he called for the destruction of the Ch'ing:

The autocracy of the last few thousand years must be swept away, the slavery of thousands of years abolished. The 5,000,000 barbarian Manchus adorned in their furs, lances, and horns must be destroyed, and the great shame they have inflicted in their 260 years of cruel and harsh treatment expunged, that the Chinese mainland may be purified.[3]

The most prominent of the early Chinese revolutionaries was Sun Yat-sen (1866-1925), known subsequently to a generation of schoolchildren as the "father of the nation." Sun Yat-sen's life is illustrative of the cultural alienation that plagued many Westernized Asians and drove them eventually to embrace nationalism. From a poor family in south China, Sun was exposed in earliest childhood to tales of the great Taiping rebellion, only recently suppressed, in which Cantonese leaders had challenged the ruling dynasty. Unlike K'ang Yu-wei and Liang Ch'i-ch'ao, Sun received no classical education. While still a child he was sent to Hawaii to reside with an elder brother. It was there that he received his first training in a missionary school and Oahu College during the formative years from thirteen to seventeen. At least nominally a Christian and more literate in English than in Chinese, he reacted violently against the backwardness of his native village when he returned to China. In the British colony of Hong Kong he studied Western medicine at an English school. Prolonged contact with Westerners served to make Sun Yat-sen conscious of his identity as a Chinese. Humiliated by China's weakness, as it was revealed in events like the defeat by France in 1885, he became an ardent nationalist dedicated to strengthening his country. He began the practice of medicine in Macao in 1892, but within a year be abandoned medicine for political activism. He became a revolutionary.

As a would-be savior of China, Sun Yat-sen spent most of his revolutionary career in the pursuit of power. As early as 1885 he tried to communicate with China's most powerful official, Li Hung-chang, to advocate reform. By the 1890s he sought to use the strength of secret societies and the wealth of overseas Chinese communities to support his activities. His first revolutionary organization, the Revive China Society (founded 1894), failed in a plot to seize power in Canton in 1895. Now famous as a revolutionary, Sun was obliged to remain abroad for years, traveling around the world from one Chinese community to another to promote his cause. After 1900 the revolutionary tempo increased rapidly. In 1905 Sun was named leader of the T'ung-meng hui ("United League," or "Revolutionary Alliance"), formed in Tokyo from a spectrum of revolutionary groups including many students and intellectuals. Sun Yat-sen was chosen for the leadership because of his age, his reputation, and his experience in dealing with foreigners. It was symptomatic of a sense of racial solidarity in the new Chinese nationalism that a lower-class Cantonese with a foreign education could be looked upon as a leader by Chinese students. When the dynasty fell in 1911, Sun was chosen as the first president of the Republic of China, an office he held for less than two months before being replaced by the general Yuan Shih-k'ai. Once again Sun Yat-sen was obliged to go into exile as competing warlords divided the republic.

The May Fourth Movement
Once the imperial system came to an end, the Chinese intellectual world erupted in a brilliant burst of creativity which has been called the Chinese renaissance. This movement shared some elements with the process we have called cultural renaissance, but it also differed from it in important respects. The Chinese renaissance was not a period of revival within tradition, as the reform movement of the nineteenth century had been. It was more of an appraisal of the tradition. Freed from the weight of Confucian orthodoxy and government control, Chinese intellectuals subjected their entire cultural heritage to the closest scrutiny. Language reform, popular education, Western science, political revolution, and

3. Quoted from Chun-tu Hsueh, *Revolutionary Leaders of Modern China* (New York: Oxford University Press, 1971), p. 164.

13.5 Sun Yat-sen returning from a ceremony at the tomb of the Ming founder, Nanking, 1912. The Chinese revolutionaries paid homage to the Ming ruler, who nearly six centuries before drove the Mongols from China, to symbolize their own rejection of Manchu-Ch'ing rule. Source: Frederick McCormick, *The Flowery Republic* (London, 1913).

the emancipation of women all contributed to the critique of the tradition and the search for new values. China underwent, in a very short span of time, a cultural rebirth in which there was a conscious search for new values and new institutions. In this search, the returned students from Japan, Europe, and the United States played a leading role. Some undertook an attack on the past. Confucianism was subjected to withering criticism, as was the old family system, religion, and the traditional political order. A "doubt antiquity" movement set about the debunking of old beliefs about the past. Historians like Ku Chieh-kang studied the distortion of the historical record by the Manchu state. Others sought to salvage cultural valuables from the past. Hu Shih elevated the study of the vernacular novels of the Ming and Ch'ing periods by claiming for them the status of great literature. This was part of a search for a popular Chinese tradition untainted with the unhappy political associations of the elite culture. Every conceivable foreign doctrine and school of thought was auditioned at this time. Ancient Greek philosophers, Bergson, Kant, and Marx were all studied carefully for possible adoption in China. Famous authorities such as John Dewey, Bertrand Russell, and Rabindranath Tagore visited China and spoke to avid audiences.

In the decade after 1911 many Chinese were disposed to look to the West for models that might be applied to the development of China. After the First World War, however, attitudes toward the West changed, the atmosphere in China was transformed by a rising Chinese nationalism, and the cultural movement became politicized. The irrationality and brutality of the European war were sufficient to raise doubts in Chinese minds about the superiority of Western civilization. Still worse were the advantage Japan took of the war to seize Germany's holdings in Shantung and the acquiescence in that seizure by the Allied powers during the war settlement at Versailles in 1919. Stung by this betrayal, students in Peking staged a demonstration on May 4 to protest their country's humiliation. Inept suppression of the Peking students by the warlord police roused sympathy nationwide and the movement spread among all strata of society drawing students, workers, and merchants together in the cause of the nation. Chinese nationalism now reached a second stage. The target now was imperialism and the goal the formation of a state strong enough to unify China and regain her independence.

In the broadest terms the intellectuals of the May Fourth Movement may be classified under two headings: those who stressed individualistic standards of truth and value and those who put the nation first. It was the latter orientation that prevailed. Westernized scholars like Hu Shih, who advocated a Deweyan pragmatism, had no quick solutions to the problem of national salvation. Marxism, on the other hand, did offer a comprehensive plan for revolution and social transformation. It was scientific and universal in its pretensions. Moreover, despite its Western origins, the Leninist form of Marxism linked imperialism to European capitalism and thus provided a sanction for resistance to European domination. Intellectual leaders at Peking University like Ch'en Tu-hsiu (1879-1942) and Li Ta-chao (1889-1927) had begun an exploratory study of Marxism by 1918. The success of the Bolshevik Revolution presented an inspiring example to the Chinese. The leadership role of the tightly disciplined Leninist party also offered the Chinese intellectuals the prospect of a crucial role in the revolutionary process in keeping with their own elite tradition.

Anti-Imperialism and the Emergence of Nationalist China

After 1919, patriotic Chinese turned to practical political organization. Two new parties were formed: the Kuomintang (Nationalist Party) and the Chinese Communist Party. Both were organized on the model of the Communist Party of the Soviet Union, which sent aid and advisers to China through the vehicle of the Comintern (Communist International). Up until 1945, at least, it was the Kuomintang that played the dominant role in Chinese politics.

Sun Yat-sen, out of power since 1912, continued to seek support for his revolutionary activities. In 1923 he concluded an agreement with Soviet agents which provided for substantial aid to the Kuomintang. Sun explicitly rejected communism as inappropriate to China. It was a marriage of convenience: the Soviets viewed Sun as the strongest national leader in China; Sun needed aid if he was to seize power. Very rapidly a Kuomintang base was built up at Canton. More than a thousand Russians were sent to equip and train an army, establish a military school, and reorganize the party, while like numbers of Chinese were sent to the Soviet Union for training. Meanwhile, the members of the smaller Chinese Communist Party, which had been formed in 1921, were obliged to join the Kuomintang as individuals. This swallowing of the Communist Party by the Nationalists, arranged to satisfy Sun Yat-sen's desire that all revolutionary elements be subject to his discipline, was forced upon the Chinese comrades by the Comintern authorities. The merger was rationalized in theory as a united front on the supposition that China was not yet ready for a social revolution because it had still to carry out a bourgeois-democratic revolution and free itself from imperialism and the remnants of feudalism (i.e., the warlords).

The nationalist movement made rapid strides in the decade of the 1920s, and it looked to many observers as if China was about to erupt in revolution. Incidents in Shanghai and Canton in 1925, in which Chinese were killed by foreign-controlled concession police, led to massive boycotts and strikes directed primarily against British commercial interests. Agents of the young Communist Party, the Comintern, and the Kuomintang were active in organizing strike activity in great ports of Hong Kong and Shanghai, bringing trade to a standstill and terrifying the foreign merchants and missionaries. Sun Yat-sen's plan had been to mount a northern expedition that would crush the power of the various warlords and unify China. Although Sun died in 1925, the northern expedition was eventually carried out by his successors two years later. The dominant figure who emerged in the struggle for control of the Kuomintang movement was the director of the military academy, General Chiang Kai-shek (1887-1975). Hostile to the communist elements in the Kuomintang, Chiang disarmed and underminded the leftist labor movement in the Canton area in 1926. During the northern expedition in 1927, Chiang veered toward the coast with his forces and suppressed the strikers in Shanghai. Having secured support from commercial elements in that city, Chiang proceeded to purge communists from the Kuomintang ranks throughout the lower Yangtze valley. The Kuomintang government apparatus, which had moved to the middle Yangtze city of Wuhan, was thrown into confusion by these moves. Borodin, the principal Comintern representative, Madame Sun Yat-sen, the Russian advisers, and many leading leftists were obliged to flee to the Soviet Union. The members of the Chinese Communist Party took refuge in the countryside and the foreign concessions. With right-wing support, Chiang established his own government at Nanking. Moderate elements at Wuhan and numerous warlords were incorporated into the new Nationalist regime. In 1928 a second phase of the northern expedition brought north China under nominal Kuomintang control.

Sun Yat-sen's nationalism was eclectic in character. His writings expressed with great force the frustration of the Westernized Asian caught between cultures. He was concerned for the dignity of the Chinese race and integrity of the Chinese homeland. His dream was to make the Chinese, whom he characterized as a "plate of loose sand," realize their potential strength through political unification. Sun's plans for China's development were concerned with railways, harbors, and land reform and had little to say about cultural forms. The great heritage of Chinese high culture was remote from Sun's own experience and he was open to borrowing from the West. In Chiang Kai-shek, however, one finds a concern for cultural forms that is much more firmly committed to preservation of a national essence. Chiang Kai-shek, despite brief military schooling in Japan and a tour in the Soviet Union in 1923,

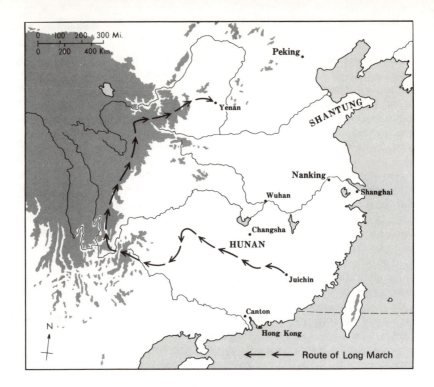

Map 56 Nationalism in China

did not share the cosmopolitan outlook of Sun Yat-sen. In his book *China's Destiny* (1943), Chiang characterized the whole spectrum of foreign ideas as a threat to Chinese self-respect:

After May 4th, two types of thought—individualistic Liberalism and class-war Communism—were suddenly introduced among the educated classes and spread throughout the whole country. . . . As a result, the educated classes and scholars generally adopted the superficial husks of Western culture and lost their own respect and self-confidence—lost their confidence in Chinese culture. Wherever the influence of these ideas prevailed, the people regarded everything foreign as good and everything Chinese as bad.[4]

Under Chiang's leadership the Nationalist government carried out a selective revival of Confucianism. Some Confucian ceremonies were performed, Confucian values were stressed in schooling, and traditional forms of art and literature were promoted as part of the national essence. In the 1930s a New Life Movement was launched, which aimed at the improvement of national morality through the practice of a number of Confucian virtues. The virtues stressed were those like loyalty, obedience, and shame, calculated to make model citizens out of Chinese youths. This appeal to traditional forms was an encouragement to the most reactionary elements in Chinese society and something of an obstacle to those Westernized Chinese who provided the talent for many of the most constructive programs under the Nationalist administration.

4. Chiang Kai-shek, *China's Destiny* (Roy Publishers, 1947) p. 98. By permission of Roy Publishers.

National Independence: The People's Republic of China

The final phase of the development of Chinese nationalism took place under the guidance of the Chinese Communist Party. After 1927, when the survivors of Chiang's terror were forced into the countryside, the Communist Party gradually slipped away from the control of the Soviet Union. By 1935 a distinctly Chinese leadership emerged in the person of Mao Tse-tung (1893-1976). The son of a peasant in the central province of Hunan, Mao went to school in the provincial center of Changsha just as the 1911 Revolution swept away the imperial government. In 1918 he traveled to Peking and worked in the library at Peking University in the eye of the intellectual storm that was brewing. Mao took part in the Marxist study group organized by Li Ta-chao, the librarian and intellectual leader. With this brief exposure to the ferment in Peking Mao returned to his native Hunan, where he engaged in teaching and eventually revolutionary activity. A founding member of the Chinese Communist Party, Mao worked on peasant organization during the first united front with the Kuomintang. After the split between the parties in 1927 he headed a partisan force in the mountains of south China. His peasant background and his long experience in rural revolutionary work well suited Mao to make a practical and theoretical adaptation of Marxism-Leninism to Chinese conditions.

For the first ten years of its existence the Communisty Party in China was controlled by the Soviet Union and presided over by leaders who stressed the primacy of the working class in the revolution and who consequently concentrated their energies on seizing control of cities. By 1934 the increasing Nationalist control over urban areas and the massive encirclement campaign to destroy the Communist base areas in the countryside forced the red forces to abandon south China and flee on the "Long March." During the course of that epic six-thousand-mile migration, the last of the Soviet-trained leaders were removed and Mao took control of the party. By 1936 the party headquarters was reestablished in Yenan, in northwestern China, and not long thereafter Japanese invasion forced an end to the fighting between the Communists and the Nationalists and a second united front was formed, which was to last until the Japanese surrender in 1945. It was during this period of resistance to foreign invasion that the Chinese Communist Party experienced its most rapid growth. This success was due in large part to the fact that the Communist movement embodied the cause of nationalism. Many patriotic and uprooted Chinese joined the guerrilla movement because it was an effective means of opposing the Japanese. In Marxism the Communists possessed an ideology more rigorous and more relevant to the needs of a developing nation than anything the Kuomintang had to offer. But the appeal of Marxism was further enhanced by Mao's insistence that the universal truth of Marxism had to be combined with the concrete conditions in China to produce a Chinese national form of Marxism.

In a pronouncement written just prior to the establishment of the People's Republic of China in 1949 Mao Tse-tung reviewed the course of the revolution from K'ang Yu-wei onward with an eye to the problems of cultural identity and nationalism. The government of the People's Republic has accomplished in large part the tasks of national independence. China has gained a respected position among the great powers, regained much lost territory, and stood up to the Soviet Union and the United States. China's conflict with the Soviet Union, which became overt in the 1960s, marks the maturation of Chinese nationalism in the sense that rejection of the Soviet model entailed the conscious rejection of even an indirect Westernization in favor of a Chinese style of communism. The Maoist form of Marxism, a secular state ideology, has been the dominant guiding force in the radical transformation of Chinese society. As an ideology, Marxism plays many of the roles for contemporary China that Confucianism formerly played for imperial China. Confucianism, discussed in connection with the early modern empire in Chapter 9, was "modern" in the sense that it provided a rational, secular blueprint for society and gave to the political authorities (the imperial apparatus) a central role in executing the blueprint. While Marxism differs widely from Confucianism in specific values, it generally shares with it the view that personal and social activities are the proper subject matter for analysis and manipulation by political authorities. Thus, the central role of the Communist Party and its state in directing change, while it may contrast with the patterns in other Asian societies, echoes a condition long prevalent in China.

By providing a perspective on Chinese society which is at once historical and materialist (or scientific), Marxism has enabled the leadership of the Communist movement to analyze conditions in terms that are both descriptive and prescriptive. The traditional order of the early modern empires was classified as feudal, while the more recent exploitation by imperialist powers was part of the international spread of capitalism. In the Marxian view these terms designate a sequence of historical stages from an ancient slave economy through the feudal economy built on serfs and the industrialized capitalist society, to be followed eventually by socialism and communism. The inevitable evolution of human society through these stages is energized by the conflict of classes in the economic order. In ancient society there was a built-in conflict between the slaves and the slave owners, in feudal society between the serfs and the landed aristocracy, and in modern capitalist society between the bourgeoisie and the workers (proletariat). The nature of this conflict is described figuratively in terms borrowed from the argumentation of classical logic. Thus, the conflict of social classes progresses like a dispute, from thesis through antithesis to synthesis. In this dialectic of social forces, the clash of classes is referred to as contradiction. The term dialectical materialism aptly describes this perspective, which attributes a logical structure to the development of concrete historical forces.

Merely describing or classifying the elements of Chinese society in Marxist terms entails passing value judgments. Since oppressed classes attempt to overthrow exploiting classes, they tend to push historical development forward and are therefore progressive. A view more at odds with the spirit of traditional Confucian orthodoxy would be hard to imagine. The Confucian emphasis on order and subservience to the elite is turned upside down in an idealization of the progressive character of rebellion and a condemnation of the reactionary quality of the oppressive forces of order. Another characteristic of dialectical materialism which had profound implications for Chinese society was the notion that the more abstract cultural forms like literature, art, philosophy, and religion are rooted in the concrete base of a given historical stage. The content of these higher or ideological forms is determined by the nature of the social context from which they spring, and their validity is restricted to that historical era. It follows that a system of thought like Confucianism or a religion like Buddhism, which grew out of a feudal stage in Chinese history, has no relevance for the China of the future. They are historical artifacts scarcely more appropriate to the present than arrowheads or pottery shards in a museum. This relegation of cultural elements to stages of history had great appeal for Chinese intellectuals in the 1920s who wished to break with the past and embrace the universal and scientific truth of Marxism. As the Chinese Communists later moved in the direction of nationalism in the 1930s, a conscious effort was made to appeal to elements of the tradition.

Despite the independence and vigor of the new nation, the policies of the Chinese Communist Party and the People's Republic have remained uncertain with regard to the status of the Chinese cultural tradition. Some forms of folk art, cleansed of any trace of superstition and religion, have continued in vogue with the communists. In the early 1950s Western values were openly attacked, while Soviet forms in the arts and literature enjoyed a brief popularity. Vigorous efforts were undertaken to evaluate the Chinese tradition from a Marxist materialist standpoint. Despite the fact that many progressive or proto-materialist elements were identified, the problem of "inheritance" of this rich "cultural legacy" was unresolved. The problem was that traditional cultural forms were the products of feudal ruling groups and carried with them the social values of the old society. In the 1960s it became clear that the communists had been unable to completely replace the old feudal and bourgeois values with a new proletarian culture. During the Great Proletarian Cultural Revolution (1966-69), new campaigns were launched against Western values as well as against old habits, thoughts, and customs. Publication in literature and the humanities came to a virtual standstill. It was apparent that a stable reconciliation between the progressive values of the revolution and the reactionary values of the old society had not yet come about. By 1973 a major ideological campaign was underway which linked as its targets Mao's former designated successor and would-be assassin, Lin Piao (1907-1971), and the ancient sage Confucius. On the positive side the criticism of Confucianism was accompanied by a popular movement to study the progressive qualities of the Legalists, ancient rivals of the Confucians, and to reinterpret Chinese history in light of the struggle between these two schools.

5. CULTURAL RENAISSANCE AND NATIONALISM IN JAPAN

Nationalism, as Japanese came to embrace it in the twentieth century, would have had only limited meaning or emotional appeal to their seventeenth century ancestors. Although early Tokugawa Japan already possessed many of the characteristics of a modern nation-state—an ethnically homogeneous populace with a common history and political sovereignty over a distinct geographical area—the notion of nationhood was not then a meaningful reference for identity, much less a sanction for behavior. The main foci for identity were, for the commoner, a village community or the extended family group and, for the elite, a feudal domain. Loyalty was a duty a samurai owed his feudal lord, who, in turn, owed allegiance to the Tokugawa house as a hereditary dynasty. But neither the Tokugawa shogun as national hegemon nor the shadowy figure of the emperor as national sovereign can be thought of as commanding the type of transcendental authority of a national monarch in early modern Europe. Sanctioning political authority and underlying the norms of political behavior was a set of ethical assumptions stemming largely from a neo-Confucian reading of human history and the natural principles that govern the larger world. It was this originally Chinese view of the moral order of the universe, intermixed with Buddhist and Shinto precepts and adapted to the traditions of the Japanese samurai class, that formed the focus of a cultural loyalty. Cultural identity resided in an identification with the devotion to an ethical conception of what it meant to be civilized in general rather than what it meant to be a Japanese in particular.

By the end of the Tokugawa period, however, these foci for loyalty—the cultural traditions, the Tokugawa regime, the feudal domain, the village community—were being rapidly replaced by a new identification that transcended them and demanded ultimate devotion to Japan as a nation. Articulated in the decades following the Meiji Restoration of 1868, this modern nationalism spread during the early twentieth century outward from the political center and downward from the elite until it came to constitute a type of secular religion. Instilled in the populace by mass media and the newly restructured institutions of central government and public education, this ideology was to serve as justification for patriotic sacrifice in the expansion of the empire and the war against the United States; and as such it came to be termed "ultranationalism" in the aftermath of humiliating defeat. More significant from our viewpoint, however, is how this nationalism functioned as a salvation ideology to justify abandoning the traditional past and undertaking the restructuring of Japanese society to meet the crisis of cultural disintegration.

As elsewhere in Asia many of the ideas that became central to modern Japanese nationalism can be traced back to a small number of intellectuals searching for a means to cope with the general cultural malaise they perceived in their society. Once again, however, the timing of Japanese history presents a contrast with its Asian counterparts. In Japan the initial call for a cultural renaissance was sounded well before the West attempted to assert domination in the mid-nineteenth century. Although the foreign threat was a major stimulus to the formulation of Japanese nationalism, the institutional setting was rather different from that of colonial South Asia or the Chinese treaty ports.

Cultural Renaissance in Tokugawa Japan

The beginnings of alienation from cultural orthodoxy in the Tokugawa period can be seen clearly in the eighteenth century, when groups of dissident intellectuals first called into question the adequacy of neo-Confucianism as a means of comprehending and responding to the socioeconomic changes of their times. One current of this criticism, as heard in the voice of Ogyu Sorai (1666-1728), originated from within the traditions of Chinese scholarship itself. Ogyu, himself a Japanese Confucian scholar, was disturbed at the failure of Tokugawa leaders and their Confucian advisers to formulate policies appropriate to the present. He viewed their preoccupation with fixed precedents as a distortion of Confucianism. Ogyu insisted that while historical inquiry was indeed the path to understanding the present—a key tenet in neo-Confucianism—the true message to be learned was that great leaders made history. The significance of this approach to history for later Tokugawa thought was the concept that reform was not a matter of readjusting society to bring it into accord with timeless principles of a traditional order but rather a matter of making creative responses to the conditions of the particular times in which men found themselves.

The hold of the orthodoxy on the minds of Japanese Confucians proved extremely resistant against such attempts at reinterpretation during the eighteenth century. But this Confucian stress on the relevance of historical inquiry as a source of understanding basic truths about social life had ramifications in the Japanese context which were to render the Chinese intellectual framework vulnerable by the turn of the nineteenth century, when a small but vigorous reaction had developed in the form of what came to be known as National Learning. The point of departure for the thinkers who led this intellectual movement was the realization that Japan had a history of its own—a past distinct and different from that of China. Was Japanese history not as valid a subject matter as the Chinese history studied in the Confucian academies? Were not the ancient Shinto religious texts and the early chronicles concerning the origins of the Japanese imperial house important sources of historical information?

Motoori Norinaga (1730-1801), who won considerable reputation during his lifetime for his mastery of these ancient texts and the billiance of his commentaries on classical poetry and prose, utilized this Japanese past to launch a biting attack on Chinese Confucianism. In his hands and those of others associated with this movement, the ancient period prior to the importation of Chinese learning emerged as a Japanese golden age, a time when men's hearts were naturally sincere and, as a consequence, society was both harmonious and prosperous. The obvious question, then, was why were present conditions in the land so different. The answer they gave was that Chinese culture—the borrowing of institutions and values foreign to Japan—had corrupted the purity of the Japanese soul and formed a layer of corrosion that obscured the essential genius of Japanese culture. These men were not, however, calling for a reorganization of contemporary society or a restructuring of the political system. What they thought necessary was a revitalization of native culture and thereby a restoration of morality. Nevertheless, two of their basic arguments were to have radical political implications: (1) Japanese culture had an origin and an historical life separate from that of Chinese civilization, and (2) the historical manifestation of the uniqueness of Japan as a cultural entity was the uninterrupted reign of the imperial family.

This emphasis on a Japanese past glory that might be recaptured and the unique position of the imperial institution in Japanese political culture was to become increasingly more salient as the threat of Western encroachment created a new sense of crisis in the nineteenth century.

Responses to the Western Threat

The first careful consideration of the meaning of Western expansion for Japanese society came from a group of intellectuals employed by Mito, a small domain to the north of Edo (Tokyo) whose lord was a close relative of the Tokugawa House. The Mito school was orthodox both in its support of the Tokugawa regime and in its adherence to neo-Confucian principles as the ultimate source of truth. Barbarian intrusion, which began to concern Mito advisers as early as the 1820s, was viewed as clear evidence that the internal crisis had reached serious proportions. The solution was a revitalization along traditional lines—that is, a restoration of the ideal order as understood within the neo-Confucian paradigm. This would assure that the barbarians would be turned back and Japan defended. In their analysis of what had gone wrong within the country and what it was that needed defending, however, Mito thinkers produced a description of Japan as a nation that incorporated key elements from the nativism of the National Scholars. A very heavy emphasis was placed on the Japanese as a historical community and the imperial throne as a rallying point in the struggle against the outside threat. Their slogan was "revere the emperor and expel the barbarian" (sonno-joi), catchwords widely used in the 1850s and 1860s to exhort Japanese to patriotic effort.

The lord of Mito, Nariaki, was also in the forefront of a group of influential domain leaders from various parts of the country who sought to persuade the Tokugawa to reorganize Japan's military defenses. By the 1850s many voices within the country were calling for extraordinary measures to drive off the Western barbarian, including the adoption of Western military technology in an attempt to fight fire with fire. Here was an inherent dilemma for the Tokugawa. If it carried out radical reforms of its military and political organization it might undermine its claim to authority based on two centuries of tradition; but if it should fail to strengthen itself it would lose credibility. Eventually the Tokugawa did purchase foreign arms and began to build the potential for producing up-to-date weapons within Japan. The Tokugawa also allowed other domains to begin importing foreign military technology. The sanction for this break with the past was an argument similar to that expounded in contemporary China. The borrowing of foreign weapons or military techniques did not constitute a betrayal of traditional culture so long as the existing values and institutions were not jeopardized. For the traditionalist this was to be merely a grafting on of a useful branch, not a break with the cultural roots.

For others, however, the recognition of Western superiority in military science led to consideration of the question of whether the West did not have other things to offer. If Western astronomy, medicine, metallurgy, and ballistics were demonstrably superior to what existed in Japan, could it be that the foreigner understood some underlying principles within the natural world not comprehended by the neo-Confucian orthodoxy? By the end of the 1860s the number of activists and thinkers who had lost faith in the ability of the traditional order to cope with the crises of internal decline and external pressure had greatly swollen and many of them were prepared to look outside for new solutions.

The Meiji Restoration

By the mid-1860s political activists and thinkers of a great variety of persuasions found common cause against the Tokugawa house. The regime became the scapegoat for national disaster and was blamed for obstructing the national unity necessary if Japan was to survive the foreign threat. This was a critical juncture for the development of Japanese

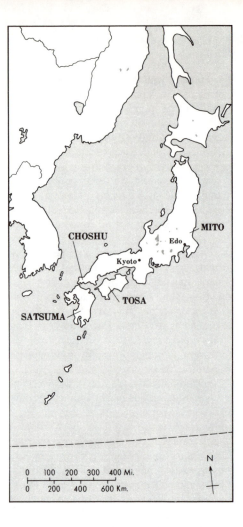

Map 57 Nationalism in Japan

nationalism, for it was here that the imperial throne moved to the center of political thought. The concept of the imperial will, which took precedent over and was the only legitimate authority for government policy, was used to justify anti-Tokugawa acts. Anti-Tokugawa forces moved to battle as "loyalists" protecting the throne against Tokugawa "rebels." The throne as an overriding focus for ultimate loyalty also justified the insubordination of those samurai activists whose domain leaders were slow in acting or who supported the status quo. True, domain loyalties were quite strong and were to remain so through the early years of the new era after 1868. Moreover, it was the domains that served as the primary vehicles for the movement against the Tokugawa regime. But the ideological sanction for this radical break with the political tradition was neither individual nor domain rights. It was an appeal to patriotic devotion to the nation as a whole and to the imperial throne, which symbolized that unity.

The major commitment of the new men who were ushered into power by the events of the 1860s is most easily couched in negative terms. They were against the status quo. They shared a view that Japanese society had to be reformed wherever necessary to bring about an end to the military weakness, diplomatic humiliation, economic dislocation, social unrest, political disunity, and intellectual uncertainty—the evils that had come to afflict the nation in the late Tokugawa period. Beyond this broad consensus on the need for some type of change there was little clear agreement on what precisely should be done or how to go about it. Thus the first three decades after the overthrow of the Tokugawa were a period of groping toward workable solutions and acceptable justifications for the wrenching changes that such solutions demanded.

Clearly, the most urgent questions involved the external threat. Here those reformers who advocated Westernization as a means of equality in the international realm came to the forefront. Already by the end of the Tokugawa their argument that Western firepower could be matched only through the acquisition of Western technology had been accepted. In the early years after 1868 the economic problems facing the new government stimulated a similar consensus concerning the need to import Western industrial methods for the production of nonmilitary goods as well. In this way exports could be increased, imports cut through competition from domestic production, and jobs made available to peasants agitating because of the destruction of traditional handicraft industries.

Proponents of Westernization often went far beyond the technological, however. Fukuzawa Yukichi (1835-1901) and other members of an active intellectual association known as the Meirokusha (the "Meiji Six Society") advocated the wholesale adoption of European and American values and institutions in order to transform Japanese society in its entirety. Western child-rearing practices, educational curriculum, business organization, parliamentary politics, Christianity, and even the English language were held up as models for revolutionary change. The underlying assumption of such proponents of Westernization was that Europe and America represented Japan's future. They stood higher on the evolutionary or developmental staircase up which all human societies progressed as they moved through time from man's primitive past. The Western societies were ahead and leading the way along a path away from superstitious tradition toward an enlightened future. This faith in progress became central to the conceptual framework within which the most significant intellectual and political debates took place in Meiji Japan. But inherent in this paradigm of social evolution were three crucial questions that continually plagued Japanese reformers.

The first was one that troubled even the most ardent of the Westernizers as they became more sophisticated about the range of variation among the Western models: Which model was the most suitable for a latecomer such as Japan? Or, as this was phrased in some of the more heated debates, How fast could Japan attempt to move up the staircase toward the future? It was this question that became important, for example, in the debates over what type of constitutional system Japan would adopt to supplant the old Tokugawa structure. Okuma Shigenobu (1838-1922), a leading official who later founded an opposition party as well as a prestigious private university, and others within and without the government in the late 1870s believed the British parliamentary system with its limited constitutional monarchy to be the furthest advanced government in the world and called for Japan to leap forward into modernity by adopting it as a model. Some of Okuma's opponents accepted his premises and characterization of the English system but argued that Japan should adopt a less advanced form of constitution more in keeping with its own level of development. A similar argument was articulated by spokesmen for the new business community who admired Anglo-American capitalism but rejected aspects of laissez-faire economics on the grounds that in the early stages infant industries required government support to develop.

A second question of concrete significance concerned the issue of whether Japan had to pass through the same stages of development as Western societies had. This became a practical concern as Japanese became aware of the shortcomings of modern industrial societies abroad. Would industrialization lead to the type of labor strife and class warfare that threatened social harmony and national unity in the more advanced societies? In the 1900s, although Japanese industrialization was still only very limited, a fierce debate raged among government bureaucrats, factory owners, academic intellectuals, and socialist organizers. While one side argued that the solution lay in early enactment of social legislation aimed at meeting the problem before widespread social unrest occurred, the business elite and the more powerful factions within government followed a policy of paternalism aimed at strengthening traditional attitudes of submissiveness to authority and loyalty to the group. In the latter's view the Japanese cultural heritage could be used to make the nation immune to the social diseases that infected Western modernization.

Reaction to overreliance on Western models, of course, was not new in the 1900s. From the outset the proposals of the radical Westernizers had been criticized by those who challenged the position that Japan as a nation could be made strong by the mere imitation of the West. Rather, they argued, modern institutions and technology must be adapted to fit the special conditions of Japan. To do otherwise would be to abandon the very values and customs that made Japan a distinct nation and thereby destroy the cultural identity of the Japanese as a people. Even Japanese Christians found comfort in the belief that it was possible to be dedicated, as Uchimura Kanzo insisted, to both Jesus and Japan. It was this third challenge of Westernization that had the most fundamental impact on intellectuals and political leaders, for the appeal for a Japanese style of modernization was both psychological and practical. In order to rally diverse sectors of society and mobilize human energies for a national effort to achieve greater equality with the West, leaders sought symbols meaningful to the great mass of Japanese as well as to the old samurai elite. The insistence on the distinction between Western civilization and Japanese culture also served as a defense against the arrogance and racism of Europeans and Americans.

By the end of the Meiji period (1912), although there remained a wide spectrum of conflicting ideologies in Japan, it was possible to speak of a new orthodoxy having been established to supplant the old Tokugawa world view. Some of its major tenets had been laid down as early as the 1880s, when the curriculum of the new public education system had undergone changes aimed at shifting the emphasis away from individualism as preached in Western textbooks toward the obligations owed by the individual to society and government. In the 1890s the civil codes that had been borrowed from continental Europe were revised to strengthen the legal position of the family vis-à-vis its individual members. In these and other ways new guidelines for political and social behavior were established. The key premises and values in this new orthodoxy can be summed up as follows: (1) The institution of the imperial throne was the embodiment of all that made the Japanese a distinct and unique people. To be a Japanese was to owe devotion to the throne and obedience to the imperial ministers to whom political power had been delegated. (2) This devotion was of the same sort as the loyalty, respect, and love felt by a filial child toward his or her parents. The role of the emperor was that of a benevolent patriarch. (3) Since the emperor was above partisan politics, however, the realization of imperial benevolence toward his subjects was entrusted to the imperial ministries of government, and the emperor's role was to legitimate policy rather than participate actively in its formulation. (4) Politics therefore was not the process of reconciling conflict between individual, sectional, or class interests. The selfish pursuit of such narrow interests would only endanger national progress and was counter to the spirit of Japanese civilization. Relations between individuals and classes should be patterned after that of the extended family, with each member striving to contribute to the total good within a context of warm sentiments and cooperative feelings. Ambition on the part of the individual was sanctioned insofar as it aspired to further the good of the national community, the family state.

These values of harmony, solidarity, loyalty, and submissiveness to the collectivity and the authority of its leaders were held up as the core of a distinctly Japanese cultural heritage. The essence of the Japanese nation, it was argued, lay not in the organization of human institutions or the technological means by which national ends were pursued but in the spirit or soul that made for a unique national character. Thus those institutions that had existed in the previous era could be cast aside—many of them, after all, were Chinese and thereby alien in any case—and the Japanese could borrow selectively from abroad without endangering this inner spirit or jeopardizing the cultural identity as a separate people. In this way Japanese leaders hoped to combine the best of Eastern tradition and Western progress.

The 1920s and 1930s

Meiji nationalism gave Japanese leaders a powerful sanction and rationale for radical social, economic, political, and cultural changes, some of which will be discussed in the next chapter. During the years following World War I, however, the rapid tempo of internal change and the growing complexity of international trends combined to bring about new dissension as Japanese society underwent yet another series of crises.

Industrialization, which was greatly spurred by the First World War, created marked gaps between the work force and managers and between the developing urban sector and the stagnating rural sector of the economy. Large-scale class strife between labor and management as well as between tenant farmers and landlords seemed imminent in the 1920s. Wider dissemination of Western ideas concerning liberalism and socialism posed more questions regarding the core values of Meiji nationalism, especially the principles of hierarchical authority and self-sacrifice. A social democratic movement led by academics, student groups, labor organizers, and others called for the greater liberalization of politics and reform programs to equalize wealth and power. The two major parliamentary parties, which had fallen heir to the political power once held in the hands of a small circle of Meiji leaders, were attacked as overly conservative and responsive only to the interests of the large business firms.

During the same period Japan's position as an imperialist power in East Asia deteriorated. Chinese nationalism, with the support of Russia, threatened Japan's hold on Manchuria and its economic position in the coastal cities. The policy of cooperation with England and with the United States was severely strained by a combination of Anglo-American diplomatic maneuvering aimed at curtailing further growth of Japanese power in East Asia and by the closing off of European and American markets to Japanese goods because of the onset of the world depression.

These domestic and international trends triggered a strong reaction in the Japanese political and intellectual climate. In the view of many military officers, civil bureaucrats, conservative politicians, and intellectuals, the chief cause of both sets of problems was that Westernization had gone too far. They believed that the parliamentary parties, modeling their approach to politics on that of the West, had degenerated into representatives of special interest groups pursuing selfish concerns through corrupt practices. The system of private capitalism borrowed from the West had led to a stress on profit and materialism which was considered subversive to the spirit of harmony and cooperation. Academic institutions were preaching alien doctrines, including Marxism, that were thought disruptive to national unity. Infatuation with Western cultural fads and fashions were blamed for undermining the family and the morality of youth. The cutting of military expenditures and the joining of international disarmament pacts were seen as overt signs of an inner weakness that only encouraged the Western powers to treat Japan with scorn and mock its attempts to imitate foreign cultures. In this view, the only possible solution was a revitalization of the spirit of the Meiji Restoration, a return to the core values of Japan's own cultural heritage, and a reaffirmation of the willingness to sacrifice for the national good.

During the 1930s men of this persuasion, particularly those drawn from the military and civil bureaucracies, gained control of Japanese government. In its basic tenets their ideology cannot be said to have differed fundamentally from the nationalism of the earlier Meiji period, but the tone was far more fervent. The historical myths concerning the divine origin of the imperial line as descendant from the sun goddess was given greater emphasis in the schools, and the metaphor of the nation as a single family took on a more literal meaning. The largest differences between the climate of opinion in the two periods, however, lay in the virulence of the anti-Western feelings and the further reduction of tolerance for dissent within Japan. In important ways both were the products of the increasingly tense international situation. The seizure of Manchuria in 1931, precipitated by a plot within the overseas army to force the hand of their superiors at home, sharpened the conflict with Chinese nationalism and turned world opinion against Japan. When Japanese attempts to influence affairs in the northern provinces around Peking led to an armed clash in 1937 that quickly escalated into an undeclared war between Japan and the Nanking government, the Western powers retaliated diplomatically and economically. These frustrations brought about a state of national mobilization as the threat of a wider war loomed.

The ideas by which spokesmen for the Japanese elite attempted to justify Japanese aggression in the 1930s were also drawn largely from the cluster of ideas that constituted Meiji nationalism. The Western powers, it was argued, had already seized control of most of the world's economic resources. In order to survive economically as an industrial society, Japan depended upon access to the raw materials of East Asia, just as the United States could draw upon those of Latin America, Britain upon India, the other European powers upon Africa and Southeast Asia. To this argument from national interests was added a call for Pan-Asianism. Japanese interests in Asia were said to differ from those of the Western powers in that Japan proposed to provide the leadership necessary to protect the Orient from the exploitive penetration of Occidental culture. In the Meiji period this "yellow man's burden" argument had been widely shared by liberals, who attacked the *real politik* geopolitical strategies of the Meiji government, as well as by some of the Meiji leaders themselves. The primary focus at that time had been China, and many Japanese intellectuals as well as political activists had sympathy for and close ties with such Chinese nationalists as Sun Yat-sen. Late into the 1930s some Japanese leaders still clung to the hope that a *modus vivendi* could be worked out with the Kuomintang on the basis of anticommunism and mutual cooperation against the Russians. Once war broke out in Europe, the Japanese broadened their appeal to include the Southeast Asian colonies and succeeded in the early years of the Pacific War in gaining cooperation from some nationalist leaders there and even in India.

Defeat and the New Japan
The devastating defeat and subsequent occupation of Japan in 1945 discredited the policies of the government and shattered faith in prewar nationalist ideology. Patriotic sacrifice had led to disaster. The imperial throne had proven so vulnerable to manipulation by a political elite as to seriously undercut its symbolic appeal. The West had once again decisively demonstrated its superiority, and during the Occupation, Western political and social ideas were systematically inculcated through the new school system and the mass media. Western concepts of political democracy, social justice, and individual freedoms were embodied in the new institutions created under American rule. The military was destroyed and many civilian leaders most closely associated with prewar nationalism were purged.

This renewed respect and enthusiasm for Western institutions and cultural values, as real as it has been in the postwar period, did pose the familiar dilemma of cultural identity for many Japanese. By the 1960s, as Japan recovered its political equilibrium and regained economic momentum, there was widespread concern about how to evaluate the cultural heritage and the Meiji Restoration in the light of the disaster of the 1940s. One form it took was a heated national debate over the teaching of morality in public education. While tradition and prewar nationalism continued to be suspect, the need for a set of values that would justify pride in being Japanese, promote love of country, and stimulate a sense of civic duty was strongly felt.

For some Japanese the answer has been faith in internationalism as embodied in such organizations as the United Nations or in movements for world peace through disarmament. This has also been manifested in support for the socialist parties, which claimed to follow a universal path to progress by eschewing both the Japanese past and the Western version of the future. Something similar to this can be seen in the appeal of the most significant mass religious movement in the postwar period, the neo-Buddhist Soka Gakkai, which through its political offspring, the Komeito, became an important minority force in the parliament of the 1960s. Yet another popular variation of how Japanese should conceive of their role in the postwar world has been the older view that Japan is uniquely qualified to serve as a bridge between East and West, combining the best of both. This has been an argument often heard among supporters of the Liberal Democratic Party, which has been in the majority in government since the end of the Occupation. In foreign policy, however, pro-Americanism has remained the central premise of the Liberal Democrats and the business elite, despite frustrations over the delayed return of Okinawa and American-imposed limitations on relations with China and to a lesser extent the Soviet Union.

Ironically, the sudden and unexpected reversal of American policy toward Peking has been one of the primary stimuli to recent reconsideration of whether Japan should not take a more independent stand in foreign affairs. Other stimuli have been the threat of being economically isolated from American and European markets by new tariff and monetary policies and the world oil crisis of the 1970s. Some observers in the early 1970s expressed considerable anxiety about a resurgence of nationalist sentiment vis-à-vis the outside world. Many would agree that there is still an unresolved problem for Japanese of how to maintain a sense of national identity while seeking equality and acceptance within a framework of cooperation with the American and European powers.

CONCLUDING REMARKS

Nativist reaction to crisis—that is, the attempt to find solutions within existing indigenous institutional and value patterns—was apparently much stronger in West Asia than in Japan, with India and China falling in between in comparative as well as geographical terms. Ironically, the ability of older elites to remain in positions of influence in parts of Southeast and West Asia as well as for a shorter time in China often seems to have been closely correlated with Western imperialist policies—old elites were prolonged in power in part, at least, because European and American policymakers saw it in their own interests not to further undermine them. This was one of the obstacles that faced would-be modernizers or other nationalist leaders seeking political independence and social reforms. Although the main targets of nationalist movements have been foreign influences, the struggle for independence has been different for an Okubo Toshiaki seeking to block further Western economic penetration in Japan than for a Gandhi aiming at the ouster of an entrenched colonial regime. It was different too for a Mao engaged in military campaigns simultaneously against the armies of Japan and the Kuomintang, or a Sukarno or a Ho Chi Min fighting to prevent the return of a Dutch or French administration after they had been dislodged by the Japanese in World War II, or a Nasser determined to regain Arab hegemony over parts of Palestine from the Israeli nation.

Foreign ideas have been another outside factor in the shaping of Asian nationalism, and here again timing could play an important part in determining what kinds of Western ideologies were available for Asian reformers to draw upon. After the Bolshevik Revolution, Marxism-Leninism had tremendous appeal as a model for the future, particularly in China and Southeast Asia, where political ideas, social values, and economic principles borrowed from British, French, or American sources failed to meet the crisis. In Japan, some intellectuals even turned to German fascism for inspiration, although here too those who identified too closely with Western models were faced with difficulties in reconciling nationalism with foreign cultural values.

The shift from cultural renaissance to nationalism has been complicated in many cases by the fact that the early modern empires and modern nation-states are often quite different in scope. What are the implications for the new nations of West Asia of the fact that the Arab peoples were once joined within greater Ottoman empire under Islamic leadership and the fact that they are now divided among nations whose boundaries were set by European powers? In a like manner, What problems have been created by the formation in India of a single nation from what was a linguistically and administratively fragmented British colony, and in Southeast Asia of several nations from a Malay-speaking population that was divided in colonial times?

BIBLIOGRAPHY

13.P   THE EMERGENCE OF NATIONALISM IN MODERN ASIA: PROCESSES

Deutsch, Karl W., *Nationalism and Social Communication* (Cambridge, Mass., 1966), 345 pp. An influential approach that attempts to analyze the conditions conducive to growth of national loyalties.

Emerson, Rupert, *From Empire to Nation: The Rise of Self-Assertion of Asian and African Peoples* (Cambridge, Mass., 1960), 366 pp.

Kohn, Hans, *Nationalism: Its Meaning and History* (Van Nostrand paperback, 1955), 191 pp. A standard view, concisely stated, of the rise of nationalist ideas in Europe with brief references to similarities in Asia and elsewhere.

Shafer, Boyd C., *Nationalism: Myth and Reality* (Harcourt, Brace and World paperback, 1955), 319 pp. Chapter 1 offers a brief but useful definition of nationalism.

Stone, Lawrence, "Theories of Revolution," reprinted in Bruce Mazlish, Arthur D. Kaledin, and David B. Ralston, eds., *Revolution: A Reader* (Macmillan paperback, 1971), pp. 44-57. Summarizes typologies of political movements aimed at reorganization of societies.

Wallace, Anthony F. C., "Revitalization Movements," *American Anthropology* 53.2:264-81 (1956). A brief typology of a class of movements; available in Bobbs-Merrill reprint series.

13.1   CULTURAL RENAISSANCE AND NATIONALISM IN WEST ASIA

Cottam, Richard W., *Nationalism in Iran* (Pittsburgh, 1964), 319 pp. Examines various facets of Iranian nationalism during the past hundred years.

Hourani, Albert, *Arabic Thought in the Liberal Age, 1798-1939* (Oxford University Press paperback, 1970), 373 pp. A perceptive and full-bodied piece of scholarship.

Karpat, Kemal H., "Turkish Nationalism"; Zeine, Zeine H., "Arab Nationalism"; and Savory, R. M., "Persian Nationalism," *The Cambridge History of Islam*, 2 vols. (Cambridge, 1970), Vol. 1, pp. 551-65, 584-94, and 617-26. Three important statements regarding the nature of nationalism in West Asia.

Keddie, Nikki R., *An Islamic Response to Imperialism: Political and Religious Writings of Sayyid Jamal al-Din "al-Afghani"* (Berkeley, 1968), 212 pp. An important study of a controversial and elusive figure.

Lewis, Bernard, *The Emergence of Modern Turkey*, second edition (Oxford University Press paperback, 1968), pp. 73-487. A first-rate piece of analysis by a leading scholar in the field of Turkish history.

Zenkowsky, Serge A., *Pan-Turkism and Islam in Russia* (Cambridge, Mass., 1960), 282 pp. An exhaustive study of the greatest importance for the recent history of the Muslims of Central Asia.

13.2A CULTURAL RENAISSANCE AND NATIONALISM AMONG HINDUS IN SOUTH ASIA

Chaudhuri, Nirod C., *The Autobiography of An Unknown Indian* (London, 1951), 515 pp. The dilemma of cultural identity as perceived by a leading intellectual.

Fisher, Louis, *Gandhi, His Life and Message for the World* (Mentor paperback, 1964), 189 pp. The most accessible brief biography.

Kopf, David, *British Orientalism and the Bengal Renaissance: The Dynamics of Indian Modernization, 1773-1835* (Berkeley, 1969), 324 pp. The first phase of the renaissance in which Indians altered their perceptions of their cultural heritage.

Nehru, Jawaharlal, *Toward Freedom* (Beacon Press paperback, 1958), 440 pp. An autobiography tracing his changing perceptions.

————, *The Discovery of India* (Doubleday paperback, 1960), 426 pp. Nehru's view of Indian history, written while imprisoned by the British.

Wolpert, Stanley A., *Tilak and Gokhale: Revolution and Reform in the Making of Modern India* (Berkeley, 1962), 370 pp. Two western Indian leaders who represent the opposing forces in the Indian National Congress at the turn of the century.

13.2B CULTURAL RENAISSANCE AND NATIONALISM AMONG MUSLIMS IN SOUTH ASIA

Ahmad, Aziz, *Islamic Modernism in India and Pakistan, 1857-1964* (London, 1967), 294 pp. An important contribution to the study of modernist movements in Islam.

Hardy, Peter, *The Muslims of British India* (Cambridge University Press paperback, 1972), 255 pp. An outstanding work of synthesis.

Ikram, Sheikh Mohamad, *Muslim Civilization in India* (New York, 1964), pp. 277-96. A brief summary of events following the collapse of Mughul rule.

Mujeeb, Mohammed, *The Indian Muslims* (London, 1967), pp. 389-562. A leisurely narrative by a scholar of great learning and perception.

Sayeed, Khalid B., *Pakistan, The Formative Phase, 1857-1948* (London, 1968), 341 pp. Essential reading for understanding the genesis of Pakistan.

Stephens, Ian, *Pakistan,* third edition (New York, 1967), 304 pp. A description of the making of Pakistan and of the first years of the new nation by a British journalist with first-hand knowledge of that country.

13.3 CULTURAL RENAISSANCE AND NATIONALISM IN SOUTHEAST ASIA

Bastin, John, and Harry J. Benda, *A History of Modern Southeast Asia* (Prentice-Hall paperback, 1968), Part 2, "The Southeast Asian Response." An authoritative but concise summary of Southeast Asian responses to Western domination with stress on the Japanese interregnum.

Kahin, George McT., *Nationalism and Revolution in Indonesia* (Ithaca, 1952), 490 pp. Survey by an authority in the field.

Lacouture, Jean, *Ho Chi Minh, A Political Biography* (Vintage paperback, 1968), 313 pp. A readable account translated from French.

Marr, David G., *Vietnamese Anticolonialism, 1885-1925* (Berkeley, 1971), 322 pp. A scholarly study of the precommunist phases of cultural renaissance and nationalism in Vietnam.

McVey, Ruth, *The Rise of Indonesian Communism* (Ithaca, 1965), 510 pp. Focuses on the early decades of the twentieth century.

Steinberg, David J., ed., *In Search of Southeast Asia: A Modern History* (Praeger paperback, 1971), 522 pp. An integrated overview of the modern period by seven authors. Excellent annotated bibliography, pp. 439-98.

13.4   CULTURAL RENAISSANCE AND NATIONALISM IN CHINA

Fairbank, John K., Edwin O. Reischauer, and Albert M. Craig, *East Asia: Tradition and Transformation* (Boston, 1973), 969 pp. Chapters 19, 20, 24, and 25 cover late nineteenth and early twentieth century changes in intellectual perceptions and political programs.

Fairbank, John K., and Ssu-yu Teng, eds., *China's Response to the West* (Atheneum paperback, 1968), 296 pp. The best collection of documents showing the shifting positions of Chinese intellectuals from late nineteenth to the early twentieth century, with valuable commentary.

Hu Shih, *The Chinese Renaissance* (Chicago, 1934), 110 pp. A classic account by a leading Western-educated Chinese intellectual who was himself a major figure in the May Fourth Movement.

Levenson, Joseph R., *Confucian China and Its Modern Fate: A Trilogy* (University of California Press paperback, 1968), pp. 49-145. A brilliant analysis of the cultural choices facing Chinese at the end of the imperial system and positions taken at various stages in the transition from culturism to nationalism.

Pa Chin, *Family* (Doubleday Anchor paperback, 1972), 329 pp. Translation of a famous novel depicting the generation gap of the early twentieth century when Chinese youth put their nation ahead of family, clan, and class.

Treadgold, Donald W., *The West in Russia and China*, Vol. 2, *China 1582-1949* (Cambridge University Press paperback, 1973), 251 pp. A concise account of the introduction of Western thought into China made doubly valuable by the companion volume on *Russia, 1472-1917*.

13.5   CULTURAL RENAISSANCE AND NATIONALISM IN JAPAN

Marshall, Byron K., *Capitalism and Nationalism in Prewar Japan: The Ideology of the Business Elite, 1868-1941* (Stanford, 1967), 163 pp. An attempt to show how the tenets of Japanese nationalism, often in sharp contrast to the Anglo-American capitalist creed, were reconciled with the values of Japanese business leaders.

Matsumoto, Shigeru, *Motoori Norinaga, 1730-1801* (Cambridge, Mass., 1970), 261 pp. A monograph on the life and thought of a central figure in the late eighteenth century renaissance whose writings have had continued influence in the twentieth century.

Morris, Ivan, ed., *Japan 1931-1945: Militarism, Fascism, Japanism?* (D. C. Heath paperback, 1963), 77pp. A mixture of excerpts from contemporary sources and later analyses of the "ultranationalism" of the 1930s exemplifying different views.

Passin, Herbert, *Society and Education in Japan* (Columbia University Press paperback, 1965), 347 pp. This historical overview, especially Chapter 7, with its appended translations from selected documents, clarifies much about how the school system was used to propagate nationalist values.

Pyle, Kenneth B., *The New Generation in Meiji Japan: Problems of Cultural Identity 1885-1895* (Stanford, 1969), 248 pp. An attempt to show how nationalism provided a resolution to the tensions of cultural disorientation for Meiji intellectuals.

————, "Some Recent Approaches to Japanese Nationalism," *Journal of Asian Studies* 31.1:5-16 (1971). A clear summary of the variety of ways in which Japanese nationalism has been studied, with valuable bibliographical notes.

GLOSSARY

Ancient Text. Refers to versions of the Confucian classics purported to have been "discovered" about the time of Christ, and since they were written in an ancient style of characters the claim was made that they were older and more authoritative than the New Text versions, which had been written down from memory following the burning of the books in the third century; different schools of scholarly interpretation were based upon the two versions.

Brahmo Samaj. A movement aimed at the social and spiritual reform of Hinduism led by Western-educated members of the intelligentsia.

Caliph (Arabic, **khalifa**). Originating with the title of the Prophet Muhammad's successor, Abu Bakr, Khalifat Rasul Allah, "Successor of the Messenger of God." The caliph was the head of the Islamic *umma,* "the community of believers," and was referred to as *amir al-muminin,* "commander of the faithful."

Chiang Kai-shek (1887-1975). Military officer in Sun Yat-sen's Kuomintang, first commandant of Whampoa Military Academy, seized power in Northern Expedition of 1927-28, established Nationalist government at Nanking, frequently held office of president of Republic of China in Nanking, Chungking, and Taiwan (after 1949), heading a regime that never actually controlled all of China.

Chinese Communist Party. Formed by a handful of revolutionaries in 1921 under guidance of Comintern agents, who forced it into alliance with stronger Kuomintang, persecuted by Chiang Kai-shek from 1927, hampered by Moscow-controlled leadership until the emergence of an independent Chinese leadership headed by Mao Tse-tung in the mid-1930s.

Chinese revolution (1911). Overthrew the Manchu Ch'ing rule, ending the imperial phase of Chinese history, leading to the establishment of the Republic in January 1912, the event from which Chinese Nationalists still date their calendar.

Comintern. Short for Communist International, Moscow controlled organization for spreading world revolution, increasingly used for Soviet purpose in the Stalin period, disbanded by World War II.

Communalism. The division of Indian society along the lines of religion, that is, between Hindus and Muslims.

Dar al-Islam. "The abode of Islam"; that is, those regions under the sovereignty of a Muslim ruler and where the Sharia was enforced.

1895. Japanese defeat of China, created sense of crisis among Chinese intellectuals, heightened the threat of partition of China by the powers.

Emilio Aguinaldo. Leader of the independence movement that founded a Philippine Republic in 1898.

Ghazi. A warrior living in the frontier areas of the Muslim world and engaged in holy warfare *(Jihad)* against non-Muslims.

Ho Chi Minh (1890-1969). Born Nguyen That Thanh, joined the Communist Party in France, became agent of Communist International, later founded Indochina Communist Party, played leading role in Vietnamese revolution through long career.

Hukbalahap, or **Huk.** This was a short form of the Tagalog name for the People's Anti-Japanese Army in the Philippines during World War II and later the same short form was used for the Philippine People's Liberation Army.

Ilustrados. Educated Philippine elite under Spanish rule who became dissatisfied with the church and Iberian control in the nineteenth century.

Intelligentsia. An intellectual or political vanguard, here the class of Western educated intellectuals who found themselves caught between Asian and Western cultures.

Jihad. The holy warfare that Muslims were enjoined to wage against non-Muslims.

Jose Rizal. Filipino medical doctor who wrote influential novels critical of Spanish control in the late nineteenth century.

K'ang Yu-wei (1858-1927). Chinese intellectual leader and reformer in late nineteenth and early twentieth century; reinterpreted Confucian tradition in response to the challenge of the West.

Kazakhs. A Turkish people who, since the middle decades of the fifteenth century, have practiced pastoral nomadism in the Central Asian steppe region north of the Aral Sea and the Syr Darya River.

Khalifat movement, or Califate movement. A pan-Islamic movement of the early twentieth century which provided an important vehicle for mobilizing Muslims in South and Southeast Asia.

Kuomintang. Nationalist Party, reorganized by Sun Yat-sen on the model of the Communist Party of the Soviet Union with aid from the Communist International in the 1920s; under leadership of Chiang Kai-shek various segments of the party formed the Nationalist government at Nanking in 1928.

Malay. A language widely spoken in the islands of Southeast Asia and the Malay peninsula, now referred to separately as Malay and Indonesian.

Mao Tse-tung (1893-1976). Peasant from Hunan who gained education, participated in May Fourth Movement, helped found Communist Party in 1921, became party leader in 1930s when party was driven to forming guerrilla bases in mountains, emerged as Marxist theoretician in 1940s, dominant figure in People's Republic since 1949, often taking a revolutionary line at odds with substantial segments of the leadership.

May Fourth Movement. General term for Chinese renaissance of the decade after 1911 revolution implying shift to vernacular written language, criticism of traditional society, search for new values, and birth of Chinese nationalism; the movement takes its name from student demonstration in Peking May 4, 1919, protesting betrayal of China at Versailles peace conference in which Japan kept control of former German holdings in Shantung.

Mestizo. Spanish term for a person of "mixed blood."

Millet. A non-Muslim religious community living under the protection of a Muslim state (especially the Ottoman empire) and maintaining a considerable degree of internal autonomy under its own religious leaders.

Mohandas K. Gandhi (1869-1948). The first Indian nationalist leader to succeed in mobilizing Indians from all sectors of society. A British-educated lawyer, Gandhi endorsed an antiindustrial self-help approach based on the promotion of handicrafts.

Mujtahid. An acknowledged authority on the Islamic "sciences" among the Shiis.

Mulla. A member of the *ulama*.

Nawab. A Mughul provincial governor, or *subahdar*. It was the title used by the representatives of the European trading companies in eighteenth century India when referring to the de facto independent rulers of Bengal, Awadh, and the Carnatic. Hence the English word nabob.

New Text. Refers to versions of the Confucian classics written from memory following the book burning of the third century B.C., so called because they were written in the new script of that time, in contrast to Ancient Text versions, purported to have been "discovered" two centuries later written in an older style; differing schools of scholarship based themselves upon these two versions.

Nizam al-Mulk. An honorary title in Persian meaning "regulator of the state." The most famous holder of this title was the *vazir* of the eleventh century Seljuk sultan, Malik-Shah. The Nizams of Hyderabad derive their title from the fact that the eighteenth century founder of the dynasty was given the title Nizam al-Mulk by the Mughul emperor, Muhammad Shah.

Özbegs (also, **Uzbeks**). A Turkish people who, since the second half of the fifteenth century, have occupied the area between the Syr Darya and Amu Darya rivers (formerly Russian Turkistan and now divided between various Central Asian republics of the U.S.S.R.).

Propaganda movement. Movement for political representation, civil rights, and equality of opportunity in the church hierarchy led by Spanish-educated Filipinos in the nineteenth century.

Quran. The Muslim "Holy Book," which is held to be the Word of God, transmitted to the Prophet Muhammad by the Angel Gabriel.

Rabindranath Tagore (1861-1941). Nobel Prize-winning Bengali author whose works represent the tensions in the Indian intelligentsia between cultural revivalism and nationalism.

Rammohun Roy (1772-1833). One of the first Bengali intellectuals to criticize traditional Hindu values from the perspective of Western culture, he sought a moderate course that would reform Hinduism.

Samurai. Members of the hereditary class of military retainers who under the Tokugawa served as the political elite.

Sayyid. A descendant of the Prophet Muhammad through his daughter, Fatima, and his son-in-law (and cousin), Ali.

Sharia. The Law of Islam, derived from the Quran, the *Hadith,* or *Sayings of the Prophet,* and the analogical interpretations of the jurists.

Shiis. Those who follow the *shia* (or "party") of Ali, Muhammad's son-in-law and the fourth caliph of the Muslims. The Shiis, although subdivided into a number of sects, constitute the largest minority group (as opposed to the Sunni majority) within Islam, and are today chiefly to be found in Iran and Iraq.

Suez Canal. Opened 1869; intensified European penetration into Asian societies.

Sufi. A dervish or mystic. Hence, Sufism, Islamic mysticism.

Sukarno (1901-70). Dutch-trained engineer who played a central role in forming a national identity among the Malay-speaking people of the Indonesian archipelago, later president following independence.

Sunnis. Those who follow the *sunna,* or "practice," of the Prophet Muhammad; the majority community in the Islamic world.

Sun Yat-sen (1866-1925). English-trained doctor from poor family in south China, one of the earliest Chinese revolutionaries, briefly president of the Republic in 1912, later built Kuomintang (Nationalist Party) into effective militarized party with help from Communist International.

Swadeshi. Literally, "of our own country"; the Indian term for boycotting foreign-manufactured goods in the early twentieth century struggle against British rule.

Swaraj. Independence, one of the goals of the Indian National Congress in its radical phase after 1900.

Tanzimat (Turkish, "reforms," "reorganization"). The term applies to the political reforms introduced into the Ottoman empire between 1839 and 1878.

T'ung-meng hui. United League or Revolutionary Alliance; formed by Sun Yat-sen and others in Tokyo, 1905, this was China's first political party, combining intellectuals, merchants, and other elements from all parts of China in a revolutionary conspiracy to overthrow the Manchu Ch'ing government; forerunner of the Kuomintang.

Turcoman. A term of unknown origin. One explanation of its derivation links it to the Persian *Turk manand,* meaning "Turk-like." Although appearing at different times in different areas, the Turcomans generally spoke a West Turkish language, retained memories of a pastoral-nomadic background, and displayed a life-style of a kind associated with Turkish peoples over an extensive area of West and Central Asia.

Ulama. The Arabic plural of *alim*, meaning a scholar trained in the Islamic "sciences." Collectively, the *ulama* enforced the Sharia and determined the social norms that governed the life of the Muslim community as a whole.

Umma. The Islamic "community of believers."

Vazir. The minister of a Muslim ruler. In fact, a ruler might appoint concurrently two or more *vazirs* to have charge over different areas of administration but the term is usually applied in the sense of a chief minister, as with the Ottoman "grand vizier."

Viet Minh. Short for "Revolutionary League for the Independence of Vietnam," a Communist-lead alliance formed by Ho Chi Minh which fought against the Japanese in World War II and subsequently formed the core of the armed resistance against the French.

Yuan Shih-k'ai (1859-1916). General who organized China's first Western style military force, he emerged in the 1911 revolution as the most powerful figure, forcing the revolutionaries to name him president of the Republic; tried to bypass new legislative organs and make himself emperor, a model for subsequent warlords.

14

Cumulative Forces for Change in Modern Asia

Cumulative Forces for Change in Modern Asia

1850 to present

The emergence of a European-dominated international economic system, the collapse of the old regimes, the rise of nationalist movements—these are key aspects of what is often termed the modern transformation or simply the modernization of Asia. These developments, however, constituted only the initial phases of a longer and more complex set of historical changes. In the colonial areas the imperial powers imposed a wide variety of new institutions that tended to undermine indigenous cultural patterns. Where Asians retained, or when they regained, their independence, the nationalist regimes themselves turned to new political forms as well as to novel technological means in order to mobilize their people so that they could cope with internal problems while strengthening their nations in the face of external pressures. Such political and economic innovations opened the way for changes in the social structures and cultural attitudes of the formally independent countries as well as in the colonial territories. The cumulative result was to alter these civilizations, in some instances quite dramatically, in others more subtly.

The timing of these changes, however, has been by no means uniform. Nor can it be assumed—as terms like modernization, industrialization, political development, or Westernization sometimes imply—that the direction of these changes is, in the final analysis, the same. Two factors are at work against such a course: the divergent character of the existing traditions and the strength of the nationalist determination to preserve cultural as well as political independence. Thus this chapter focuses in part on one of the most interesting and important of all issues for the comparative historian—whether "modernization" has an internal logic that will eventually produce everywhere the same type of cultural change.

PROCESSES

a. The trend toward secularization
b. Economic development through industrialization
c. Political consolidation in the nation-state
d. The mobilization of society

PATTERNS

1. Cumulative Forces for Change in Modern West Asia

2. Cumulative Forces for Change in Modern South Asia

3. Cumulative Forces for Change in Modern Southeast Asia

4. Cumulative Forces for Change in Modern China

5. Cumulative Forces for Change in Modern Japan

14. MODERN ASIA

	1	2	3	4	5
	WEST ASIA	INDIA	SOUTHEAST ASIA	CHINA	JAPAN
1840					
1850			Mongkut takes Thai throne 1851, Western advisers brought in		
1860				Growth of urban commercial and industrial sector in treaty ports	Treaty ports opened 1858
1870		Beginnings of significant industrial development under British rule	Trend toward tighter colonial control	Students sent abroad to learn Western science and technology; Western advisers brought in to create new military apparatus	Meiji Restoration 1868 Land reform and conscription 1873
1880			Chulalongkorn r. 1868-1910, modernization of Thai administration		Satsuma rebellion 1877
1890		Jawaharlal Nehru 1889–1964	Rapid increase in numbers of European-educated Asians		Meiji Constitution 1889
1900					

Decade	Middle East / Iran	India	Southeast Asia	China	Japan
1910	Iranian constitution 1906; Young Turk Movement 1908; Arab revolt begins 1916			Manchu reforms; Shift to vernacular literature	Beginning of Taisho reign 1912; World War I, rapid industrial growth
1920	Treaty of Sèvres 1920; Sultanate abolished in Turkey 1922; Turkey proclaimed a republic 1923; Caliphate abolished 1924			Formation of mass parties; Nanking government established, limited administrative modernization	Universal male suffrage 1925; Beginning of Showa reign 1926
1930	Iraq independent 1932		Vietnamese Buddhists organize to meet challenge of Christianity	Communist guerrilla war strategy evolved	Manchurian Incident 1931
1940	Death of Ataturk 1938; Abdication of Riza Shah Pahlavi 1941; accession of Muhammed Riza Shah Pahlavi; Syria and Lebanon independent 1946	Partition of India 1947		Communists refine political study methods	February rebellion 1936; War with China 1937; Pacific War 1941-45; U.S. Occupation 1945-52
1950	Musaddiq prime minister of Iran 1951-53; Anglo-Iranian Oil Co. nationalized	First five-year plan 1951; State guided economic development	Communist insurgency in Malaya	People's Republic 1949, first strong central government; Land reform, rapid industrial growth	Rapid economic development
1960	Iraq becomes a republic 1958; Iranian land reforms 1962-70		Mobilization of Vietnamese society through continuous warfare	Great Leap Forward; Great Proletarian Cultural Revolution	
1970			Constitutional authoritarianism in the Philippines 1972		

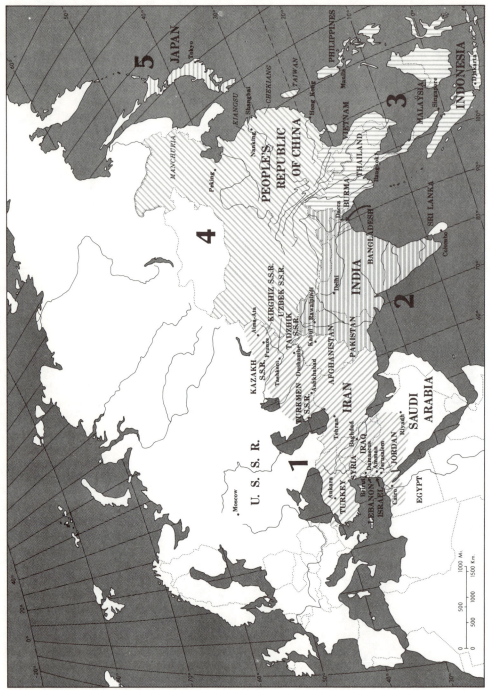

Map 58 Change in modern Asia

PROCESSES

THE CONCEPT OF MODERNITY

For many Asians the solution to the crises facing their civilizations lay in "modernizing" their societies to meet the threat of social disintegration and political impotence. In one place after another over the last one hundred years new elites have acquired power and attempted reforms aimed at "modernization." In some cases this has been consciously equated in the minds of these elites—as well as in the minds of their opposition—with "Westernization," "Europeanization," or even "Americanization." This has also been the view taken by many Western observers. Such a view, it is argued here, is misleading, for it assumes, often with more than a little arrogance, that the Western pattern of modernity is the only pattern, deviation from which is a perversion to be lamented or ridiculed. True, the processes that will be included under "modernization" cumulated and brought about a transformation in Western Europe and North America earlier in time than elsewhere in the world. Moreover, the West has served both as a stimulus and as a model for modernizers in Asia. Nevertheless, it is clear that many of these processes have long been at work within civilizations in Asia, often prior to and separate from contact with the West. It is the combination of these forces and the changes they produced in Asian civilizations that should be our focus rather than the fact of cultural borrowing. Clearly, also, some of the institutions and values in the pattern of contemporary Western civilization are not, strictly speaking, "modern" at all, being rather themselves part of a particular cultural tradition that continues to coexist with the modern. Thus it is possible to ask such questions as when and how did the West itself become modernized—questions that would present logical as well as semantical puzzles if we merely equate Westernization with modernization (e.g., when did the West become Westernized?).

What is needed to understand the modern transformation of Asian civilizations is a set of analytical criteria—categories, rubrics, definitions—broad enough to aid in identifying essential characteristics of modern societies wherever they may be located. This is not necessarily to say that there will be no differences among contemporary civilizations in Asia, Africa, Latin America, or the West. On the contrary, as has been noted throughout this historical survey, the individual patterns of civilizations and the manner in which civilizations underwent change are indeed in some sense unique. The inertia or momentum of tradition, geographical factors, or historical accident have meant that processes can combine in very different ways to produce important dissimilarities. Nevertheless, there are common aspects of modernization as a set of processes and it is these that make comparison both possible and of interest.

Another difficulty with the concept of modernity that frequently appears in discussion of the subject is the tendency to equate modernization with progress. The result often is a debate only partially relevant to the task of understanding the modern era in Asia. It is definitely the case that one of the key attitudes shared by people in the modern era has been the belief that human history is a unilinear development toward some higher perfection—that life is getting better and better every day in every way. Again, this is an important question: Is the modern era an advancement from previous eras in the sense of being preferable? Whatever our value judgments, however, we should certainly not beg the question of whether progress has actually taken place by defining modernization as progress at the outset. Nor is it fruitful to make metahistorical assumptions about the inevitability of progress. We should be able to characterize modernity and distinguish it from past eras without necessarily committing ourselves to historical evolution as an iron law. In other words, we seek a set of defining criteria broad enough to include such diverse political systems as modern fascism and parliamentary democracy, economic institutions as conflicting as state socialism and private capitalism, or ethical views as varied as social Darwinism and Christian existentialism. All of these have features that are clearly modern, whether or not they are to be considered either inevitable or desirable.

Having identified some of the more common pitfalls in conceptualizing modernization, it is still no easy matter to describe in concise terms what is meant by modern. There is only a loose consensus among historians or social scientists and many issues are often hotly debated. One of the broadest and most useful approaches, however, involves the concept of increased adaptive capacity of modern societies, the development of greater rational control over their environments. This has been stated very succinctly by Benjamin Schwartz:

Modernization involves the systematic, sustained and purposeful application of human energies to the "rational" control of man's physical and social environment for various human purposes.

I use the adjectives purposeful, systematic and sustained because it is quite obvious that the process of rationalization as such began long before the "modern age" and is almost coextensive with human history.[1]

The rationality here is a rationality of means and it should be pointed out that it leaves aside the question of whether the ends, or goals and purposes, are themselves rational. Modernization is thus conceived as a set of processes that have so altered social, political, and economic institutions as to bring about a great leap in the direction of coordinating human energies and controlling the human as well as the natural world. The usefulness of this approach is perhaps most clear when attempting to characterize the ideas and attitudes underlying or resulting from modernization.

a. The Trend toward Secularization

Common to many major changes in values and attitudes within Western societies as they modernized—the Enlightenment, the Protestant Ethic, the Scientific Revolution, Pragmatism—has been a pervasive trend toward secularization. Although older religious views continue to coexist, more and more of the environment, both human and natural, has been desanctified or removed from the realm of the sacred, that mysterious or divine sphere where human control is by definition limited. The realm of the secular, those aspects of the world believed amenable to human control, has thus been extended. In the mid-twentieth century this has culminated in such remarkable biochemical and medical miracles as the resurrection from death through heart transplants or the artificial creation of life in the laboratory. Although it is usually the wonderous advances in technology that receive attention, the point here is the popular acceptance that such activities belong within human purview. This acceptance has not always been immediate by any means, as can be seen in the strong reactions in the past and indeed in the present against extending human control over mental and emotional phenomena through psychotherapy, "brainwashing," and other forms of systematic behavior modification.

Faith in progress and man's capacity for creating his own future have been the hallmark of the modern era—a faith in salvation through the conscious manipulation of the ultimate conditions for social life. As was noted in the preceding chapter, this faith was most powerful when linked with other salvation ideologies such as nationalism, for the revolutionary aspect of the modern era in Asia has been the steady desanctification of the status quo of tradition. History is now to be actively made, not passively received. Secular views of nature and history are not without precedents in previous eras of Asian civilizations.

1. Benjamin Schwartz, quoted in Marius B. Jansen, ed., *Changing Japanese Attitudes toward Modernization* (Princeton University Press, 1965), pp. 23-24. By permission of the author.

Individuals and groups in earlier periods have held views that contrasted markedly from the often-heard generalization that Asians are tradition bound or spiritual. What is striking about the modern era in Asia as in the West is the permeation of society at all levels by secular views and the modification of popular religious beliefs where necessary to accommodate to a new emphasis on the ethical righteousness of this-worldly efforts in the cause of progress.

Finally, it should be noted that progress has been increasingly defined in terms of material affluence to be achieved through the acquisition of the particular method of scientific research and the application of its results to technology. The fact that the modern West developed science and technology to a level far beyond anything known in premodern Asia is one of the key arguments offered by those who would equate the spread of scientific attitudes with Westernization. Yet, while it is true that these processes of secularization and rationalization were accelerated by borrowing from the West, it is also true that the other processes of modernization taking place within the economic, political, and social life of Asian civilizations constitute indigenous forces influencing ideas and values.

b. Economic Development through Industrialization

The sphere of human activity most clearly affected by these new attitudes and advances in technology has been the economic. Indeed, for some, industrialization is the primary factor and all other aspects of modernity are seen as flowing from the transformation of the economic base. This is perhaps too simplistic a view for our purposes, but there is no question that the changes wrought by economic development, even in those Asian societies that have been the slowest in modernizing their economies, have been enormous.

Central to the modern economic transformation has been the integration of natural and human resources into extended networks of production and distribution of goods, systematizing economic exchange and shifting the main focus from local areas to regional and national markets. These in turn have been linked to an international system of trade, global in scope. In Chapter 12 we saw the disruptive aspects of the commercialization of agriculture and the impact of foreign trade. Here we need to consider economic systematization as part of the effort to meet the crisis of disintegration of the old order. Increased systematization of production and distribution—whether under private capitalism, state socialism, or some combination of the two—not only permits a more efficient use of resources through the division of labor and specialization of products but also makes possible the concentration of surplus for capital reinvestment in industrialization. Much of the faith in progress that marks the modern era has been a faith that the systematic application of technological innovations and the mechanization of production would solve society's material problem. Typically, Asian governments in the twentieth century have been greatly concerned with rational economic planning and the promotion of industry. The actual degree of success as measured by growth in income per capita, however, has varied greatly, Japan being the only outstanding example of unquestioned success. Moreover, even in cases where the per capita income has soared—such as in oil-rich Kuwait—the problems of distribution of wealth have remained serious. In order to understand more fully the underlying reasons for the relative economic success or failure of different Asian countries, it is necessary to consider both the level of development in the preindustrial stage and also the social conditions and political history in each case.

c. Political Consolidation in the Nation-State

Parallel to the desanctification of the natural environment and the systematic attempt to make more efficient use of natural resources has been a trend toward centralization of government and politicization of the society. Autonomy and authority within regional, local, or communal political units have been reduced in favor of greater consolidation of power and concentration of decision making in national governments. The result has been a reduction of the sphere of social life outside of the effective control of government. These are trends that have their roots in earlier centuries, as has been described in Chapter 10 on early modern states. But now, more rapid communications, refinements in bureaucratic control techniques, and such ideologies as nationalism, socialism, and welfare statism have enabled governments to extend the scope of decision making further into religious, intellectual, and social, as well as economic, life. Thus the health, education, and welfare of the populace as a whole have come to be considered matters for direct central government intervention. The attempt to mobilize or harness human energies has involved the "plugging in" of individuals to an extent far beyond that of previous eras. One of the best examples is the modern educational system. The growth of public, or mass, education has meant that the preparation of individuals for social roles (i.e., the socialization, acculturation, or conditioning) becomes the direct concern of the nation-state.

On the other hand, modern societies are also characterized by politicization in the sense of greater participation in the political process by individuals and groups from all classes, including the lower strata. This is most evident in cases where representative parliaments or mass electoral systems have been instituted. It would be a mistake, however, to measure political modernity merely by the extent to which Asian nations have borrowed the representative institutions of the British parliamentary or American congressional systems. In much of Asia (as in Latin America, Africa, and parts of Europe itself), political life is tightly controlled by authoritarian regimes. Whether such regimes will eventually give way to Western-style representative government is a moot question. Yet two points should be made. In many cases such regimes are themselves dependent on the support of military organizations or party structures that differ in important ways from traditional armies or elite groupings. Second, and of greater significance, is the fact that even in the cases where decision making is highly centralized, nationalist movements have had to seek popular support and elitist regimes have often sought to increase their mass base, thus politicizing segments of the populace previously on the outer fringes of normal political life.

d. The Mobilization of Society
The modern society is not only an industrial and bureaucratic society, it is also an urban-centered, mobile, achievement-oriented, mass society. Let us look at each of these facets in turn.

The consolidation of political power and the concentration of production in industrial centers have greatly enhanced the role of the city. We saw in Chapter 12 that the process of modern urbanization began in many cases with the establishment of Western colonial power in the treaty ports and coastal cities of Asia. With the growth of mechanized industry and communications networks, the process is accelerated; metropolitan areas become the nerve centers and leading sectors in the modern transformation. As the society modernizes and industrial production increases, the agricultural sector diminishes inversely and the agrarian village community gradually loses its former place as the primary setting for life as lived by the great mass of the populace. Where this process is furthest advanced, as in Japan, the majority now lives in urban environments. Even where the majority is still situated in the rural hinterland, there is marked migration from the village into the cities, especially where the pursuit of economic opportunity has been legitimized and overbalances the pull of traditional ties to the native locality.

This physical or geographical mobility is one aspect of the fluidity of modern societies. Another is increased occupational mobility as new economic roles are generated. Industrialization, like bureaucratization, institutionalizes greater specialization of function and division of labor at the same time that it expands the scale of economic organization. This fact, together with the accelerated rate of overall change, reduces drastically the likelihood of a new generation following in the occupational footsteps of its parents. Here enters yet another form of mobility—vertical mobility within the social hierarchy. The functional requirements of new factories, modern armies, and more elaborate bureaucracies have tended to place heavier emphasis on individual achievement as opposed to hereditary ascription. In other words, the demand for new skills or attitudes that are best acquired through on-the-job training or new educational institutions tends to reduce (although by no means eliminate) the relevance of such attributes as geographical origins, blood relationships, or even class membership in order to permit the more efficient mobilization of human resources. Even where the ideologies of democracy and egalitarianism have had only partial acceptance, the trend has been toward more universalistic criteria for recruitment and the opening of opportunities for movement up (and down) the social pyramid.

Vertical mobility may or may not be accompanied by a flattening of the pyramid itself—that is, a reduction in the disparity of power, wealth, and prestige between those above and those below, although the tendency certainly seems to be toward less social distance between elites and nonelites. Elites may continue to dominate decision-making power and economic resources but the social cleavages that characterize aristocratic societies have lessened. Moreover, the monopoly on what is thought of as high culture—the set of ideas and symbols only partially accessible to the commoner—has given ground to new mass cultures, as traditional cultural forms are eroded by new values more readily shared by the populace as a whole. Here there may be an analogy with the fate of cultural and religious elites in era of universal religions (see Chapter 6), when the sanctified traditions of the classical period were popularized and salvation became possible—in theory at least—for all. Such aspects of the modern salvation ideologies as scientism and nationalism also proclaim a universal path for all. By the same token, the most valued forms of art, theater, music, and literature are accessible at least in theory to all strata of society through mass communication and subsidized cultural institutions. Whether the analogy holds and the subsequent development of new religious and cultural elites with monopolies over new esoteric forms in later ages is to be paralleled by a reversal of this modern trend toward popularization and mass culture is an interesting issue for speculation.

The concept of mass society implies the absorption or assimilation of the individual into a relatively undifferentiated whole. The individual is disconnected from older molecular structures to become a free-moving atom. This is the process by which primary and intermediary groupings such as the family, the community, the geographic region, economic occupation, religious sects, and the like lose many of their functions and thereby their importance as referents for self-identification and orientation for behavior. In part, this is the result of political elites attempting to promote loyalty to the nation-state and transfer the function of socializing people for new roles away from traditional institutions. In part, it is the consequence, intended or unintended, of greater mobility and the dissemination of information through mass communications. Individual horizons are extended and the ability to empathize with others over time and space is enhanced.

Many observers have stressed the positive aspects of this last process, pointing to the increased freedom of choice and spread of the values of individualism. Others, however, have pointed on the negative side to the loss of community, which can produce personal disorientation and pervasive anomie. Indeed, it can be argued that many of the negative aspects suggested in the discussion of cultural disintegration in Chapter 12 have been intensified rather than lessened by the processes of modernization. Universal criteria for achievement are impersonal, as are the bureaucratic procedures associated with the efficiency of modern administration. Relationships in the economic marketplace tend to be highly specific, focusing on contractual dealings that encompass at any given time only a limited range of human concerns. Roles in modern organizations are narrowly specialized and give little rein to the complex potential for human activity. Reaction against these features of modernity, it has been argued, are at the root of the continued social violence and disorder experienced by societies as they move along the path of modernization.

By way of conclusion to this section, it is important to stress again that we are not suggesting that there is only one path toward modernization. The order in which the processes have been discussed is not meant to imply either a temporal or a logical sequence. Different societies may experience different processes to different degrees and at different stages. Moreover, these processes have interacted with one another as well as with preexisting conditions within the various regions of Asia to produce very distinct patterns. Hence, only some of the variations among modernizing societies in Asia and between Asia and the West in the modern era can be ascribed to "backwardness" or the failure to achieve a given level of modernity. Often what looks to be a deviation due to the inertia of tradition may actually be a case in which an older institution or normative view has been revitalized to accommodate to the new. In such cases the issue of what is modern and what is traditional is as complex as it is in similar cases in Western Europe or North America.

PATTERNS

1. CUMULATIVE FORCES FOR CHANGE IN MODERN WEST ASIA

Excluding those Muslim regions that were incorporated into the Czarist empire and are now an integral part of the Soviet Union, the history of the Muslim peoples of West Asia in the twentieth century is the divergent story of more than a dozen sovereign states, all of which are committed to achieving the declared goal of "modernization," although the sense in which they apply the term and their priorities in attaining that goal are widely disparate. In the section that follows it is neither practicable nor desirable to review the efforts of each state in turn. Instead, the factors stressed in the preceding section will be examined in the light of the experience of one country, Iran, treated as a case study, while, where appropriate, comparisons will be made with other West Asian countries. Iran, rather than an Arab state, has been chosen to exemplify the processes of modernization in West Asia because Iran constitutes the most striking "success story" in the area.

It is worth bearing in mind that nation building among the Arab states of West Asia is made more difficult by the problem of evolving genuine "national" identities against an intellectual background that includes powerful undercurrents of Pan-Arab sentiment. Iraq, Syria, Lebanon, and Jordan were all, in a sense, artificial creations, brought into existence in the wake of the peace settlements following the First World War. Their frontiers are colonial-type frontiers in the sense that they were originally demarcated primarily to suit British and French imperial interests, and thus they are comparable to the no-less-artificial frontiers of many African states that gained independence after the Second World War. On the other hand, countries like Iraq and Jordan have acquired a political identity that has been developing for more than half a century, a period in which their peoples have experienced changes more profound than any their forefathers experienced in the preceding two or three millennia. As modern nation-states, they have developed and will continue to develop distinct national personalities and interests that are often at variance with Pan-Arab aspirations. It is a measure of the extent of their regional particularism that all attempts at mergers among them have, so far, proved abortive.

It might be supposed that Turkey, even more than Iran, should have been chosen as a model for the rest of West Asia. The area of what is now modern Turkey was for many centuries the heartland of the most powerful and extensive Muslim regime in history, and no Muslims have been more continuously exposed to the influences of Westernization than the Turks. Yet the events that followed the demise of the Ottoman empire set Turkey somewhat apart from the other countries of West Asia. The fact is that while other Asian peoples in the early twentieth century struggled to emulate Europeans, the Turks, guided by that remarkable revolutionary, Mustafa Kemal Ataturk (1881-1938), sought to *become* Europeans. That the able and devoted men who made, with Ataturk, the Kemalist revolution were willing to reject so much of their Islamic and Asian past (although not, it should be noted, what they felt to be their specifically Turkish past) may seem surprising, if compared with the attitude of nationalists in, say, India or Indonesia. This can be viewed partly as a measure of how close the symbiotic relationship between the Ottoman Turks and their European neighbors has always been. The nineteenth century awakening in Turkey had been profoundly influenced by contemporary European culture (even Turkish racial theories, which at their most extreme made Turkish the first language in the world and the first human being a Turk, owed much to the influence of the racial philosophies of nineteenth century Europe), and it could be argued that intellectuals and reformers in the Ottoman empire were thereby able to make a more balanced assessment of the nature of European civilization than were their equivalents in Calcutta or Batavia, who saw the West through the distorting mirror of their own colonial situation.

As a former ruling group the Turks in their postimperial phase continued to regard their erstwhile subjects, including the Arabs, with some degree of contempt. Europe, and Europe alone, was seen as the model for the future, and the men who brought into being the new Turkish republic intended to be a part of it. By Europe, however, they meant *Western* Europe. With the peoples of the Balkans, their former subjects, they shared only a common past of antipathy and violence. Towards Russia, which was regarded as the historic foe who had done most to rob them of their imperial possessions and which was, in addition, the enslaver of the Turkish peoples of Central Asia, they felt the deepest hostility, which was scarcely lessened by the fall of czardom. Thus, when the Turks of the early twentieth century looked to Europe, they looked to Paris, London, and Berlin—to Paris for culture and ideas, to London for parliamentary government, and to Berlin for technology, higher education, and military organization. This attitude survived the disasters of the First World War and the humiliations of the Allied peacemaking. With the inauguration of the republic in 1923, Europeanization became the proclaimed goal for modern Turkey. Today, nearly four decades since the death of Ataturk in 1938, the fact that Turkey is a full and active member of the North Atlantic Treaty Organization is indicative of an ongoing determination to assert Turkey's Europeanness.

In fact, the history of Turkey since the end of the First World War diverges totally from the rest of the Islamic world. In 1919 the triumphant Allies had not only seized the remaining provinces of the Ottoman empire but were bent upon the partition of Turkey itself into British, French, and Italian spheres of influence, with, worst of all, a Greek occupation of part of western Anatolia. The Allied *diktat* was meekly accepted by the sultan's government in Istanbul, reeling under the disasters of the last months of the war and in no position to offer much resistance, but it was uncompromisingly rejected by a handful of younger army officers and dedicated patriots, headed by Mustafa Kemal, one of the few Turkish commanders to emerge from the war with an enhanced reputation as a result of his part in the Gallipoli campaign. Mustafa Kemal and his supporters withdrew into the rugged hinterland of Anatolia, and from Ankara, soon to become the capital of the new republic, he denounced the settlement imposed by the Allies and also, by implication, he challenged the legitimacy of the moribund and discredited Ottoman regime. Slowly, and against all odds, he gained ground internationally. He placated his new Soviet neighbors, wooed first the Italians and then the French, expelled the Greek invaders after a fierce and exhausting struggle (1922), and then forced the British to accept the *fait accompli*. There followed the abolition of the sultanate (1922) and of the caliphate (1924), the inauguration of the republic at the new capital, and the beginnings of a dedicated, ruthless program of modernization, which is still without parallel in the history of West Asia. Essentially a man of moderation, Ataturk (the honorary name meaning "Father Turk," which was given to Mustafa Kemal by the National Assembly in 1934), unlike the other dictators of the period between the world wars, set his face against any kind of Turkish irredentism such as appealed to advocates of Pan-Turkism and to traditionalists nostalgic for past imperial glories. What Ataturk sought for his people was a true Turkish homeland for a relatively homogeneous population living within stable, internationally recognized frontiers. This has remained ever since a consistent feature of Turkish foreign policy, and the dispute over Cyprus bears this out. Originally, Turkey never sought to annex the island but only to prevent its annexation by Greece, both in the interests of Turkey's own national security (Cyprus is little more than forty miles from the Turkish mainland) and on behalf of the Turkish Cypriot community, which makes up around 18 percent of the population. Turkey's decision in the summer of 1974 to carve out a Turkish Cypriot enclave on the northern part of the island was the consequence of a conviction that the Turkish Cypriot minority could never expect fair play from the dominant Greek Cypriot majority.

Ataturk ruled as a dictator in an age of dictators, yet his ultimate goal for Turkey was never dictatorship. Convinced that parliamentary institutions were an intrinsic part of that European civilization of which he was determined that the Turks should be a part, he endeavored to introduce parliamentary political parties that would function in the Westminster style, and it was hardly his fault if the experiment was not an unqualified success. Since his death in 1938 the central theme of Turkish history has been the struggle to evolve an effective two-party system of government in a country in which the absence of any democratic institutions in the past, the prevalence of rural poverty and illiteracy, and persistent loyalty to those Islamic values that Ataturk sought to eliminate continue to set a formidable distance between the overwhelming mass of the enfranchised voters and that minority of officials, army officers, intellectuals, and professional people which remains dedicated to the preservation and extension of Ataturk's lifework. Thus, to have chosen Turkey as a model for the development of West Asia would have meant choosing a Muslim country that is, so far, unique in having rejected the Islamic value system as the basis for its social order, and also one in which the course of events has tended to be shaped by parliamentary struggles of a kind that have no parallel elsewhere in the area.

The Turks have endeavored to evolve a secular and democratic society (a process Ataturk would have regarded as the quintessence of Westernization and even Europeanization) in a relatively poor country possessing few natural resources. Iran, on the contrary, is a country that, at the beginning of the twentieth century, was far behind Turkey in the extent to which it had been exposed to modernization but that today has outstripped every other nation-state in West Asia in terms of its economic growth—due primarily to an ever-increasing oil revenue. Unlike Turkey, Iran has come far along the path towards modernization and industrialization without adopting in their entirety the political structures of Western Europe, remaining a monarchy in which the decision-making processes are the preserve of a small elite of professional administrators, senior army officers, technocrats, and members of influential families answerable directly to the shah, whose ultimate power rests on the maintenance of a large and well-equipped army. No Arab country has so far attempted a sociopolitical revolution comparable to that of Kemalist Turkey or a socioeconomic revolution comparable to that of Pahlavi Iran, although Saudi Arabia may one day evolve along lines similar to the latter. In fact, it is no accident that Turkey and Iran should be, in their different ways, pacesetters for the area. No country in West Asia has been more exposed to external influences than Turkey, while Iran has long possessed a sense of cultural identity and a feeling of apartness from its neighbors, which has provided the psychological infrastructure for the emergence of a dynamic nationalism of a type not unfamiliar to nineteenth and twentieth century Europe.

Political Consolidation in the Nation-State

Among the factors that are virtual prerequisites for successful modernization are access to advanced technology, access to capital, distinctive groups or classes able and willing to seize the opportunities presented by a developing economy, and political stability. In the case of Iran, a major factor contributing to the process of modernization has been the role of the ruling Pahlavi dynasty, first under Riza Shah (1925-41) and then under his son, Muhammad Riza Shah (1941-), which established and maintained a strong centralized administration capable of initiating far-reaching changes and of curbing traditional divisive elements. Since the death of Mustafa Kemal in 1938 such leadership and drive have been missing in Turkey.

By 1921 the Iranian experiment in constitutional government, begun in 1906, could be seen to have been a failure, partly on account of foreign intervention in the country's affairs but also because the necessary political leadership was lacking. During those fifteen years Iran had a constitution and a parliament, which assembled irregularly, but day-to-day government remained corrupt and ineffective. The exercise of political power continued to be the monopoly of traditional ruling groups, now functioning through the forms of a European-style parliamentary monarchy, while away from Tehran the perspective was very different, local authority continuing to be the preserve of tribal khans, great landowners, members of the *ulama,* and even the consular representatives of Great Britain and Russia. In these circumstances, the coup d'état of 1921, which brought Riza Shah to power, must be regarded as a positive reaction to a situation bordering upon the hopeless. Born in 1878, Riza Khan (his title until he mounted the throne) was forty-three at the time of the coup and a colonel in the Qajar shah's Cossack Brigade, which had formerly been trained and officered by the Russians. In striking contrast to Mustafa Kemal, with whom he is often compared, he had received no formal education and had no knowledge of the world beyond the frontiers of Iran. Characteristic of an endemic Iranian suspicion of the motives for political action of any kind, his rise was at first attributed to the machinations of the British. Immediately following the coup, the new government was headed by a liberal journalist, Sayyid Ziya al-Din Tabatabai, who had been a fellow conspirator with Riza Khan. He was soon superseded by the latter, who had become minister of war, and when, in 1925, Parliament voted the deposition of the last Qajar ruler, Riza Khan, now prime minister, was proclaimed shah. Until that moment, it might have been predicted that a republic would have been established, with Riza Khan as president, as had recently occurred in Turkey. Instead, by mounting the Peacock Throne himself, Riza Shah linked the future development of Iran to the fortunes of a renovated monarchy. That decision has been of incalculable significance in shaping the subsequent history of the country, and even today, half a century later, its consequences are still being felt. Whether the motive behind the decision was, as some have claimed, personal ambition, apprehension of clerical opposition to republican institutions, or a conviction that Iranian society was politically too backward for republicanism and retained a traditional residue of loyalty to the throne, the fact remains that in twentieth century Iran modernization and monarchy have been inextricably linked, an example that has not escaped the notice of the oil-rich potentates of the Arabian peninsula.

Riza Shah ruled in the classic manner of the dictators of the early twentieth century. He maintained his hold over the country by means of the army, the *gendarmerie,* and the security forces, all of which he modernized in terms of organization, equipment, and discipline. He brooked no rivalry from able or aspiring men below him, or any opposition from the dissident intelligentsia, which nevertheless grew in number in consequence of his establishment of Tehran University in 1934 and of an increasing number of young Iranians going abroad to study. He retained parliamentary institutions from the constitutional period, but he used them primarily to rubber stamp the government's policies. In consequence, Parliament atrophied as an element in the political life of the country, while continuing to provide an alternative ideal of government for those, especially among the intelligentsia, who were disenchanted with the Pahlavi regime. In practice, however, politics in the lifetime of Riza Shah meant court politics—how to win and retain the confidence of this dynamic but also narrow and suspicious leader.

Notwithstanding all this, Riza Shah's achievements were impressive. With the support of the reorganized armed forces he imposed upon the country an effective, if somewhat brutal, policy of centralization, forcibly coercing dissident elements such as the tribes and the more reactionary clergy and making it plain to the world at large, and especially to the British, that the old days of concessions and Capitulations were gone forever. There followed the building of an infrastructure of communications, the establishment of state industries and monopolies, the introduction of a legal system based on European models, modernization of the bureaucracy, and the creation of a French-type educational system. These developments followed a course somewhat similar to events in contemporary Turkey, but in Iran the substitution of a ruthless, if effective, authoritarian regime for rule by a devious and ineffectual oligarchy had the side effect of somewhat cramping the intellectual development of the Western-educated classes, since the prevailing atmosphere was definitely not congenial to independent or critical thought.

When Riza Shah was compelled by the Allies to abdicate in 1941, in consequence of his allegedly pro-German attitude, his son and successor, Muhammad Riza Shah, was only twenty-one and had hitherto had little experience of public affairs. While the occupying forces of the Allies concerned themselves primarily with the war effort, there was a resurgence of political life in the country, although irresponsible factionalism, intense personal rivalries among members of the ruling elite, and a willingness to serve the interests of the foreigners were as prevalent in this period as they had been in the period immediately preceding the rise of Riza Shah. Below the level of the rancorous bickering of "establishment" politicians, however, some sections of society, especially the urban bourgeoisie and the younger generation, which had been exposed to new educational values and social goals, were becoming highly politicized. Much had happened between 1921 and 1941—there had been some modification of the traditional class structure and there had been a dissemination of new attitudes and expectations—and those who participated, however marginally, in the political life of the country were now more numerous than ever before. Characteristic of this period was the rapid growth of the press in the form of a great many newspapers, most of them short lived and with very small circulations, but which nonetheless intensely stimulated political awareness.

In the 1940s and early 1950s political attitudes in Iran could be divided into four main categories. First, there were the traditionalists, who feared that the pace of change set by Riza Shah and later by his son would undermine fundamental Islamic values. This was the position of many (although not all) of the *ulama* and included within a broad spectrum of conservative attitudes extremist religious organizations such as the *Fidaiyan-i Islam*, or "Devotees of Islam," who advocated violence and even assassination to gain their objectives. Second, there were those who welcomed the achievements of Riza Shah, who accepted leadership from the throne, and who believed in the need to retain an authoritarian and army-backed regime to maintain and extend what had been achieved so far. People in this group, then and now, were devoted monarchists in that they believed that the economic development of the nation and also the national revival taking place in their time were a direct consequence of the leadership provided by the Pahlavi dynasty. Third, there were those, especially among the intelligentsia, who shared with the monarchists a commitment to the economic development of the country and to a nationalist ideology but who rejected the central role of the throne, regarding the Pahlavi "revolution," with its inevitable downgrading of parliamentary institutions, as a retrogressive and unnecessary stage in the nation's evolution. This was the position of many of those who made up the National Front, formed in October 1949 around the pivotal figure of Dr. Muhammad Musaddiq (prime minister, 1951-53), and remains the position o many who, to this day, continue to resent the prevailing patterns of government in Iran. Finally, there was the Tudeh Party, comprising both recruits from former communist parties and also radicals who, while generally sympathetic to the Soviet Union, sought to evolve a distinctly Iranian brand of communism. Much of the strength of the Tudeh Party, outside Tehran, came from Turkish-speaking Azarbayjan, and there political radicalism tended to feed on separatist aspirations.

The factional infighting of the period 1941-53 is a confused and unedifying story, but certain distinctive trends are apparent. First, there was the concern during the war years to be rid of the Allied occupying powers as soon as possible and without an accompanying loss of territory, notwithstanding a heavy-handed attempt by the Soviet Union to create secessionist regimes in the northwest (the Autonomous Republic of Azarbayjan and the Kurdish Republic of Mahabad) during 1945-46. Second, there was the oil question, centering primarily but not exclusively on the status of the Anglo-Iranian Oil Company and the terms of the concession by which it extracted crude oil mainly from the Masjid-i Sulayman area, terms universally regarded in Iran as unfair and exploitive. Third, there was the question of the future relationship of the palace to the post–Riza Shah political setup now that the young Muhammad Riza Shah was gaining in experience and support, especially among the army and conservatives generally. Finally, although less apparent because the issues of foreign occupation, oil, and the monarchy tended to obscure all else, there was the question of the long-term development of the country and especially the question of land reform.

The dominant political emotion in Iran in the postwar years was bitter resentment towards the Anglo-Iranian Oil Company, a resentment then to be found in other underdeveloped countries where oil was the principal or the only economic asset and where the process of extraction was exclusively in foreign hands. In Iran, the AIOC, with its headquarters at Abadan in Khuzistan, was regarded as a state within a state. It was felt by Iranians that in the areas where the company operated, the writ of the central government hardly ran. It was well known that the company made private agreements with local sheikhs and tribal chieftains without consulting the Iranian government. The company employed few Iranians in managerial posts, while Indians and Pakistanis were generally preferred in the middle and lower echelons of administration. With few exceptions, the European employees of the company behaved as if they were part of a colonial society. Worst of all, Iranians felt that they were receiving totally inadequate compensation for the extraction of what was seen as a diminishing resource. By the early 1950s the AIOC had become as much a symbol of quasi-colonial status for the Iranians as the Capitulations once were for the Turks or the treaty ports for the Chinese. Thus, when Dr. Musaddiq threw down the gauntlet to the AIOC there was hardly an Iranian, even among his opponents, who did not rejoice at the prospect that this seemingly impregnable bastion of European colonial domination was about to be assailed.

In retrospect, it seems obvious that in launching a simultaneous attack on the AIOC and the Pahlavi dynasty, Musaddiq took on more than he could handle, but Musaddiq's antipathy towards the Pahlavi regime was as longstanding as was his hatred for the British. Born in 1880 or 1881 into a traditional landowning family descended from the former Qajar dynasty, Musaddiq had held a succession of important governmental posts in the last years of Qajar rule. His had been one of the three dissenting voices when Parliament, in

1925, had elevated Riza Khan to the throne, and thereafter he withdrew from public life until 1944, presumably in protest against the new regime. It seems that during his premier-ship between 1951 and 1953 he was moving quite deliberately in the direction of a republic. In fact, his protracted feud with the court reached its climax with the royalist coup d'état of August 1953 and his own subsequent trial for treason. This resulted in a prison sentence that lasted until 1956, followed by enforced retirement on one of his estates until his death in 1967. His closest supporters in the National Front and also the leading mem-bers of the Tudeh Party were imprisoned or executed, including the former foreign minister, Husayn Fatimi. Others escaped or went into voluntary exile. In the shah's words, Musad-diq's "negative nationalism" was replaced by his own "positive nationalism." Henceforth, the shah abandoned the ineffective role of merely "holding the ring" and set out to rule as well as to reign. In this new role he could count on encouragement from the United States and Western Europe, the loyalty of the armed forces, and support from the monied classes and the great mass of the urban bourgeoisie, although in time some of the *ulama* and the old-style landowning class would come to have second thoughts about him.

Massive foreign aid, including long-term loans, the Point Four Program, and military equipment and training, was provided by the United States, fearful at the height of the Cold War lest Iran, so long threatened from the north, would drift helplessly into the Soviet sphere of influence. The oil controversy was settled by the establishment in Iran of a National Iranian Oil Company, which functioned through an international consortium of companies, Dutch, British, and American. In 1955 Iran joined Great Britain, Pakistan, Turkey, and Iraq in the Baghdad Pact, a military defense agreement directed against the Soviet Union, which, following the defection of Iraq in 1958, became known as CENTO. Following the overthrow of Musaddiq, the activities of the security forces (SAVAK) created an atmosphere of fear and suspicion that permeated most levels of Iranian society but pressed most heavily on the professional classes and intellectuals generally. This phase of counterrevolutionary heavy-handedness proved so effective that it eliminated all overt opposition to the regime, which was indeed its prime purpose. Those who could not reconcile themselves to the new order and were able to leave went abroad. The remainder kept their thoughts to themselves and outwardly conformed. Unfortunately, the ensuing atmosphere of political repression and intellectual conformity among a people traditionally noted for their individualism and the satiric barb of their wit had an especially depressing effect upon intellectual life, upon higher education, and also perhaps upon the innovative potential of the bureaucracy.

The effect of the post-Musaddiq exclusion of Iranians from the kind of febrile political life in which they participated between 1941 and 1953 has been to divert the energies of this shrewd, sardonic, and brilliant people to new goals and, in particular, to the pursuit of affluence. While the age-old goals of position, prestige, and power have remained constant, the means of attaining them have changed. For the past twenty years a common feature of the upper echelons of Iranian society and also of the rapidly expanding urban bourgeoisie—whether businessmen, industrialists, contractors, bankers, speculators in real estate, officers in the armed forces, lawyers, engineers, etc.—has been preoccupation with the acquisition of wealth and with the ostentatious adoption of what is perceived to be a European or American life-style. The consequence is the emergence of a ruthless, "go-getting" society, in which acquisitive instincts are restrained only by the pervasive strength of family ties and traditional patron-client relationships, which has nevertheless provided much of the incentive for successful modernization. The long-term effects can be seen by contrasting the Iran of today with the state of the country twenty years ago.

These impressive achievements have been carried through under the guidance of a regime that is overtly and impenitently paternalistic. Most major decisions, whether in foreign policy, economic development, or social innovation, emanate directly from the

14.1 The ''White Revolution'' in action. The shahanshah of Iran granting title deeds to the representative of the peasants of villages near Qazvin during the second phase of the Land Reform movement, 1965. Courtesy: Iranian Embassy, Washington, D.C.

shah himself. In general, however, while the interests of the military and of the monied classes have been well served, the shah's government has developed a high degree of pragmatism. Thus, in foreign relations, although the shah brought Iran into the unpopular Baghdad Pact (later renamed CENTO), leaned heavily for military and financial support on the United States, and pursued a distinctly pro-Western line, he prudently took advantage of the contraction of the Cold War to repair the broken bridges between Iran and the Soviet Union and to embark on a policy of economic cooperation with the latter which has been highly beneficial to both countries. To the south, Iran's well-trained armed forces, with their highly sophisticated weaponry, ensure strategic domination of the waters of the Persian Gulf, in response both to the withdrawal of the long-standing British military presence in the area and to the potential threat of a hostile Arab regime establishing a foothold on the opposite shore.

In his internal policies the shah sees himself as a unique phenomenon, a royal revolutionary who, especially between 1962 and 1970, carried out a largely successful redistribution of the land for the benefit of the actual cultivator which has perhaps few parallels outside the communist world. This aspect of the shah's leadership was exemplified in 1963 by a national referendum endorsing far-reaching reforms, which in addition to land redistribution included the nationalization of forests, profit sharing by industrial workers, amendment of outdated electoral laws, and the creation of a literacy corps intended to eliminate widespread illiteracy in the countryside. Further reforms have included the granting of the vote and the provision of increased educational and employment opportunities to women.

In certain respects, politics in Iran have remained court politics. The forms of the Constitution are maintained by politicians who nevertheless exercise authority by virtue of the royal will and not by popular mandate. Traditionally, Iranian cabinets have been composed mainly of courtier-politicians familiar with well-tried patterns of compromise, articulate ambivalence, and the sophisticated balancing of diverse interests. More recently, a new type has emerged, the technocrat trained in a European or American university and possessing proven professional competence, generally in the field of engineering. Government is conducted through various clearly perceived hierarchies—the ministries and their staffs, the armed services, the security forces, the National Iranian Oil Company, and other state industries—but the decision-making processes function behind closed doors, with a minimum of public discussion. The media—radio, television, and the press—are either government controlled or, as in the case of the press and the publishing industry, exercise a self-imposed restraint in order to forestall anticipated censorship.

Despite all this, government in Iran—authoritarian, highly centralized, and largely immune from public criticism—has still proved capable of initiating and carrying through complex schemes of modernization and industrialization which are undoubtedly having far-reaching consequences on the quality of life of the Iranian people as a whole. At the same time, the bureaucracy in general still lacks a sense of institutional integrity, while at the lower levels there is much inefficiency and subservience to superiors. Nor are these defects counterbalanced by rigorous public debate regarding the great changes currently occurring at almost every level of Iranian society.

Secularization and Social Mobility

The concept of secularism must be regarded as one of the basic problems facing the would-be modernizer in a traditional Islamic society, and indeed there are some who would argue that the secular assumptions and scientific temper of twentieth century Europe or America are hardly to be reconciled with the fundamental principles of Islam, notwithstanding the strenuous endeavors of reformers to render them compatible. In practice, most Muslims living in a modernizing society draw back from the ultimate confrontation.

They accept increasing material affluence, the advance of the technological frontier, and man's increasing ability to manipulate both human and natural resources while seeking to prevent external pressures from impinging too sharply upon the intimate world of personal life-styles and family loyalties, the relations between husband and wife or between parent and child, and the traditional patterns of behavior that accompany the cycle of marriage, birth, and death. It is in education, and especially in higher education, where an incompatibility of aims and a failure to comprehend ultimate goals most often manifest themselves, and this tends to be more marked in the social sciences and humanities than in the pure or applied sciences. Intellectual qualities such as critical relativity, situational responses in ethics and politics, the weighing of intangibles, and a skeptical temper are very alien to the traditional systems of Islamic learning.

In Turkey, Mustafa Kemal, who exemplified a century of Ottoman exposure to alien European values, had not long embarked on his revolutionary reconstruction of Turkish society before he became convinced that traditional Islamic values were utterly at variance with his goal of Europeanization, and hence his determined and well-publicized attacks upon the Islamic way of life in the name of his new creed of secularism. These attacks included the abolition of the caliphate (1924) as the logical outcome of his earlier abolition of the sultanate (1922), the substitution of European-type legal codes for the Sharia, the abolition of the Muslim calendar and the introduction of the European working week, the use of the Latin in place of the Arabic script, the abolition of titles and the adoption of European-style family names, the wearing of European dress and the prohibition of the veil, the extension of voting rights to women, the outlawing of polygamy, and the suppression of the dervish orders. These measures were carried out vigorously and with a remarkable degree of success, notwithstanding predictable opposition on the part of social conservatives. Yet, paradoxically, post-Kemalist Turkey continues to be, as postrevolutionary France was, a society divided against itself, divided between those who are committed to the Kemalist revolution or who are its beneficiaries and those who are, for whatever reason, still unreconciled to it.

In Iran, although Riza Shah manifested a ferocious anticlericalism when confronted by opposition from members of the *ulama*, whom he identified, as did Mustafa Kemal in Turkey, with the forces of reaction, the growth of secular attitudes among Western-educated Iranians has been much more gradual than in Turkey. There has been, for example, no change in the script, the calendar, or the working week, although former titles have been abolished, European-style family names have been adopted, European dress is ubiquitous in the cities, and a beginning has been made with regard to equalizing the status of women. In retrospect it seems that the spread of secular attitudes has been due less to any overt manifestation of anticlericalism than to the fact that the material preoccupations of so many Iranians have resulted in the diminution of the social role of the Shii *ulama*. When individual clerics, as has happened in the past decade, have challenged the government with regard to such issues as the land distribution program, the status of women and, in foreign policy, excessive dependence on the United States, the government's rejoinder has been a denunciation of corrupt reactionaries representative of no one but themselves. By way of contrast, the regime is careful to placate moderate *ulama*, recognizing that they still exercise great influence among the lower middle class and the poor. In general it may be said that a certain latitudinarian and even skeptical facet of the Iranian temperament has contributed more than any ideology to the increasingly secular tone of Iranian society, and this is particularly true of the bourgeoisie, especially the new and influential managerial and technocratic elite. This is an obvious area where the temper of contemporary Iranian and Turkish society differs greatly from that of Arab society almost everywhere in West Asia, and it seems clear that Arab reformers in, say, Iraq or Syria will meet with formidable obstacles in trying to follow in the footsteps either of the Iranians or the Turks.

This statement is not intended to imply that Iranians and Turks possess an inherently greater capacity for adapting themselves to the process of modernization than do Arabs. Rather, the intention is to stress that the process is made more difficult for Arabs on account of their unique relationship to Islam and the depth of their commitment to Islamic values and the Islamic faith. This can be seen at its most striking in the case of Saudi Arabia. There, enormous oil revenues have enabled the Saudis to acquire some of the most advanced aircraft in the world in order to provide an up-to-date air defense system. This in turn involves the training of pilots, navigators, ground staff, and maintenance engineers to operate machines that embody the latest in Western technology. Similarly, the Saudi Arabian government is initiating extraordinarily ambitous projects to provide that kingdom with an adequate infrastructure in communications, education, and basic industrial needs. Yet the same government that is enlisting for the development of the country highly sophisticated examples of Western technology and organizational methods insists that its subjects live in strict accordance with the Sharia, the law of Islam. Nor is there any evidence to suggest that many Saudis, even among those who have been educated or trained abroad, disagree with what seems to the European observer to be a basic inconsistency. The point is that the Arabs far more than the Iranians or the Turks see themselves as especially bound to observe and uphold the unique spiritual heritage that became theirs in a very special sense when God chose Muhammad, an Arab, to be the messenger of his revelation.

So far as Iran is concerned, the unobtrusive advance of secular attitudes is only one aspect of profound changes in the traditional social system which are now taking place and which may, in time, provide a model for other would-be modernizing societies in the Islamic world. One obvious factor in the situation is the rapid and relentless growth of the towns and cities, especially Tehran, now approaching a population of three million. This is due not solely to an increasing urban birthrate—Iran, with a population of just over thirty million, is far from facing a population explosion—but to a spontaneous and almost ubiquitous flight from the country to the towns and especially to the capital. The phenomenon is not, of course, unique to Iran but is a feature of virtually all developing economies. Life in the city may be less secure and in some respects even more deprived than life in the village, but it is perceived to be a more exciting life that offers chances of self-improvement, in most cases never to be fulfilled. Hence, whether for good or evil, the city is proving to be an irresistible magnet, especially for the young. Geographical mobility finds its counterpart in other kinds of mobility. There is now very extensive occupational mobility in the sense that many people, even among the distinctly underprivileged, no longer work at the same craft or profession as their fathers before them but are acquiring new skills or insights into entrepreneurial possibilities that bring both increased remuneration and a new life-style. Upward social mobility, although still difficult to achieve, is also a realistic goal for those who can combine ingenuity and determination with more than an average share of good luck. Accordingly, the role models have changed and also the value systems associated with them. Traditional leadership in society and the life-styles associated with that leadership have undergone radical modification, and the place of the courtier and the cleric, the rural landlord and the tribal khan, has been taken by the civil servant and the engineer, the army officer and the successful businessman. For all who live above the subsistence level, an all-pervasive consumerism characterizes present-day Iranian society, reinforced by the mass media, which, while disseminating a comfortable sense of well-being, of national achievement, and of loyalty to the throne (exemplified by the coverage of the 1971 celebrations of 2500 years of Iranian monarchy), also intensify the hunger for new life-styles as a consequence of a heavy diet of foreign (mainly American) movies and television programs.

The outward signs of success—an expanding and more diversified economy, better living standards, an increasing range of consumer goods manufactured in Iran, the glitter of modern Tehran with its streets congested by cars assembled under patent in Iran—are very encouraging. The reverse of the coin is less obvious, but modernization is a process that involves perils as well as opportunities: the rapid growth of an urban labor force inadequately housed and serviced, rising expectations that cannot be fulfilled, inflation, a neglected agricultural infrastructure and a growing need to import basic foodstuffs, political cynicism and the alienation of an important segment of the educated young, a widening gap between the actual wealth, the life-styles, and value systems of different classes, and the confusion and anxiety resulting from the displacement of traditional values and from the pressures of modern urban life. But whatever the outcome, modernization in one form or another is a challenge to which virtually all Iranians today are compelled to respond.

2. CUMULATIVE FORCES FOR CHANGE IN MODERN SOUTH ASIA

In the preceding chapter it was stressed that nineteenth century India saw the introduction of modern education and professional life, movements to reform religion and society, and modern technology, medicine, and sanitation. At the same time, the intelligentsia provided a new psychological identity for India. Thus, many aspects of modernization dated from the colonial era, long before independence in 1947. In other areas—notably in industrial development—modernization in India was retarded. It was partly the awareness of India's backwardness under colonial rule and the organized effort to modify British policy in order to alleviate that backwardness that had given rise to nationalism.

Gandhi's leadership, however, while it appealed to large numbers of the rural masses, was based on an ideology of salvation which was strongly antimodernist. Gandhi's program of village reconstruction and revitalization, his liberal views on caste, his religious syncretism, and other features of his ideology suggest that he was more an indigenous modernizer than a traditionalist. But his opposition to industrialization and urbanization virtually negated his revitalization program and reduced his ideology to a vague form of indigenous populism. Gandhi's golden age of the Rama Raj was no adaptation of the Hindu past to modern conditions but was a defense of premodern agrarian traditions like those that were rapidly dying out in the industrialized West. In Gandhi's view it had been the collective wisdom of traditional India not to mechanize its economy, so as not to be seduced by materialism. Likewise, the village was elevated over the city, which was regarded as a place of unhappiness and degradation. But Jawaharlal Nehru (1889-1964), not Gandhi, assumed the leadership of India as a new nation in 1947. With Nehru the modernizing intelligentsia and the compradors came forward as India's new ruling elite. It is not without irony that after decades of being led by a man who continually reminded his followers that India could find itself again only by discarding "modern civilization," India turned for leadership to a man who openly declared his intention of making India secular, socialist, and industrial.

Nehru was born in Allahabad of a Kashmiri brahman family and of a father who was one of the most successful British-trained lawyers in India. In fact, so Westernized was Motilal Nehru that he sent Jawaharlal, at fifteen, to complete his schooling at Harrow in England; then entered him at seventeen for Cambridge University; and finally arranged for him, at twenty, to take his law degree at the Inns of Court. In 1912, after seven years in England, young Nehru returned to India to practice law with his father. Both Nehrus followed Gandhi after 1920 along with the great majority of the nationalist intelligentsia. Gandhi inspired them to discard their European manners and dress and to some extent even the use of English in day-to-day life and to tour the remotest villages and communicate directly with the peasantry. Gandhi gave to Jawaharlal Nehru a new sense of Indian identity which made him imbibe the spirit of the Indian renaissance. Nehru, the denationalized intellectual, slowly rediscovered India historically and culturally. In 1944, while in prison for nationalist activities, Nehru wrote *The Discovery of India,* which is perhaps the best account of India's past written by a nationalist in the twentieth century. Nehru's declared purpose in writing it was to comprehend "the spirit of India" and thereby provide foundations for the "house of India's future."

Although Nehru owed to Gandhi his new identity and his rediscovery of India, he owed far more to the universalist spirit of Rabindranath Tagore, the Brahmo Samaj, and the Bengal renaissance. Nehru was a modernist who wanted India to be in the mainstream of world progress. Nehru repudiated nation building based on religious definitions. In this sense he was close to the early moderate nationalists who saw the secular state as the only way of transcending communal strife and extending to all ethnic and religious groups a common identity in being Indian. Nehru was profoundly influenced both by Marxism and by the potentialities of modern science, which became two complementary components of his ideology. Several years prior to independence he issued a declaration proclaiming that the only solution to India's problems—the degradation of poverty, the autocratic political tradition, the subjection of the rural masses as a result of the land system, and the need to industrialize—lay in socialism. Although he criticized aspects of the Soviet model of socialism, he saw the October Revolution as an inspiration for creating a new civilization in which the profit motive would be replaced by a higher ideal of cooperative service.

Economic Development

An examination of economic practice in India since independence reveals that the socialist blueprint has operated largely as an ideal or a long-range goal. Part of the explanation for this lies in Nehru's Fabian socialist commitment to gradualism and the use of democratic means of persuasion. Nehru said that as much as he wished for the advancement of socialism he did not want to create difficulties by forcing the issue on the governing Congress Party. In the course of time he hoped to convert the Congress and the country as a whole to socialism. He was only too well aware of the limitations imposed by an illiterate and depressed peasantry, by the middle-class mentality of the Westernized intelligentsia, and by the growing power of former compradors converted into indigenous capitalists. Besides these factors, there was India's linguistic and regional diversity as well as the sinister influence of the Hindu extremists—one of whom had assassinated Gandhi. European-oriented Marxism had to be adapted to Indian conditions.

As with China, India launched her first five-year plan in 1951. The very idea of such a plan suggested that India was following not the West but the Soviet Union in the belief that the industrial revolution could be telescoped through careful planning. Thus a Planning Commission was created, which drew up a draft of the plan. But because India had chosen the democratic path, the states as well as special interest groups could and did draw up their own plans. Under the Constitution of India the states have jurisdiction over at least three areas essential to economic planning—agriculture, education, and health. This fact has necessitated a slow process of study, consultation, negotiation, and compromise between the state ministries and the center. Coordinated planning in pluralistic India proved far more difficult than in a regimented society like that of China but, as in China, the Indians focused on the problems of underdevelopment. Thus, planning had two sets of goals: the tactical, or specific, targets and the strategic, or ultimate, objectives. The basic idea was that all available resources should be mobilized and allocated to specific purposes. Each subsequent plan contained specific targets that the commission hoped would be achieved on the basis of the allocations made. These plans were not only specific in allocation of funds but comprehensive in covering many aspects of India's society and economy. Besides allocating funds for the more obvious sectors of agriculture, community development, heavy industry, and transport, the plan also gave relatively large sums to animal husbandry, land reform, domestic industries in rural areas, Gandhian-type cottage industries, the establishment of cooperatives, the development of natural resources, the development of electrical and nuclear power, irrigation, housing projects, public health, family planning, education, and social welfare.

To many social scientists who have studied India's developmental programs closely, the Indian task is like that of Sisyphus—tragically doomed to eternal failure. It is the harsh demographic reality of overpopulation that causes the Indian Sisyphus to roll his rock up the hill again and again. By 1965 the population of India was approximately 480 million, and the rate of increase since 1947 has been 2.4 percent annually. In other words, the number of India's inhabitants increased by more than 100 million since independence. The implication of such population growth was that production had to increase substantially even to maintain the existing low standard of living. Every year there was an increase of dependent children and of large numbers of young people entering the labor market searching for jobs that did not exist. The higher the proportion of nonearning dependent persons, the harder it became to save money and form capital, fundamental to economic development.

The first problem to be faced was that of feeding the ever-expanding population. The British had left India a stagnant agrarian society with very little in the way of modern tools or technical education for improving cultivation. There were no tractors, harvesters, and such like machinery—not even steel plows. There were no fertilizer factories, and no comprehensive effort had been made to replace the nitrogen annually lost from the soil, let alone to improve or restore it. The British had taken little interest in teaching Indian farmers new agricultural techniques. Moneylenders and rural indebtedness plagued the countryside, further exacerbating the evils of low investment per capita, minimal saving by the mass of the people, and exceedingly low productivity per person.

The land system at the time of independence was poorly suited to development. British colonial administration had made an uneven impact on the pattern of landholding, which was largely determined by local traditions and interest groups. In many areas under British jurisdiction the land revenue claimed by the state came to be assessed at a fixed level, while the rents paid to various landholders by the cultivators were determined by custom. Given increasing production and rising prices for agricultural products during most of the nineteenth century, these circumstances resulted in generally favorable conditions in most rural areas until the population increase outstripped production in the last decades of the century. Land was controlled at several different levels. Many landlords moved to the towns and cities and either depended on agents for collecting their rents or sold off the rent collection rights to intermediaries. In any case, the dominant figures in the countryside so far as the cultivators were concerned were not the absentee landlords but a class of intermediaries—relatively prosperous and powerful peasants who controlled access to large tracts of land. Through caste and kinship connections, these intermediaries could resist and moderate the demands of landlords, intervene or exert influence in the local administration, and wield a great deal of influence on those who actually worked the land. Under these circumstances the British administration could do little to affect agricultural production at the village level. In one area of the agrarian scene, however, the British were able to perform a positive role. In a country like India, which can raise two crops a year in many areas if sufficient water is available, irrigation is of crucial importance. Like the Mughuls before them, the British in northern India sought to divert the waters of the Ganges, the Jumna, and the tributaries of the Indus into irrigation projects. By independence, India had an estimated 50 million acres of land under irrigation—more than any other country in the world.

Modern industry in India got its start under British colonial rule, developing significantly from the 1870s, when manufactured items first began to be exported. The proportion of manufactured exports to total exports rose from 8 percent in 1879 to 22 percent by 1907-08, while the proportion of manufactured imports to total imports fell from 65 percent in 1879 to 53 percent in 1907. The earliest Indian industrial effort was the establishment of cotton mills in west India during the 1870s. The Tata family (who were Parsis) started India's first iron and steel industry in 1906. In 1921, still under British rule, the tariff policy was modified to assist the development of Indian industries. Slowly, many light industries under Indian ownership proliferated in such products as leather, glass, paper, soap, pharmaceuticals, and rubber. By 1939, India's industrial proletariat numbered 1.8 million. Nevertheless, India at independence was basically agrarian and underdeveloped, with half of the national income derived from agriculture and related nonindustrial occupations, which employed three-fourths of the labor force. When the British left India, manufacturing accounted for only about 6 percent of the national income and employed less than 2 percent of the working population. Thus, in 1948 India launched a program of economic development with the object of reaching self-sustaining growth.

Indian planners were well aware of the theoretical requirements for industrial takeoff: that is, that a country must invest about 15 percent of its national income in the production of capital goods, such as machine tools, factories, transportation facilities, and the like. These capital goods make it possible to produce other capital goods and thereby to accumulate larger sums—above those used for immediate consumption—for additional investment. In 1951 India invested 5 percent of its meager gross national income and at the time of Nehru's death in 1965 it was 10 percent. In that same year, Japan was investing 25 percent and the United States, 15 percent. In 1965, however, even after fourteen years of development in India, its 480 million people were producing an annual income of $35 billion, whereas some 190 million Americans at the same time were accumulating earnings of about $600 billion. Necessarily, therefore, India turned to external sources of financing for her economic growth. By means of foreign assistance and trade—mainly grants and loans through the aid-to-India consortium, led by the International Bank for Reconstruction and Development—India was able to accumulate billions of dollars. The sources and objectives of assistance considerably modified Nehru's paradigm of socialist development for India. Much of the $9.1 billion that the United States contributed as aid to India up to 1971 was used directly or indirectly to encourage the development of the private sector, whereas the Soviet Union's contribution of $2 billion was used principally in loans for the public-sector projects.

In launching its industrial revolution, India has been fortunate in having a substantial natural resource base for potential development, although this was another area that had been relatively neglected by the British. Since 1951 India has become one of the world's leading producers of mineral ores and a major supplier of mica and manganese. India has the largest known deposits of high-grade iron ore in the world, as well as coal reserves estimated at 44 billion tons. India also has the world's second largest reserve of bauxite for aluminum and ample atomic materials such as thorium. Developing India's energy potential was another vital consideration. Using the model of the multipurpose Tennessee Valley development in the United States, the Nehru government sanctioned projects designed for three purposes in varying combinations: irrigation, flood control, and hydroelectric power. One of the most important projects was the Damodar Valley complex in Bihar and Bengal, which lay at the heart of India's chief industrial area. When completed, it included four storage dams, several hydroelectric powerhouses, and three thermal power stations. These projects, although they have as yet done comparatively little to electrify the vast subcontinent, are nonetheless spectacular. The Bhakra Nangal project in the Panjab, for example, has a dam 740 feet high—one of the highest in the world—and 652 miles of canals designed to irrigate between 3.5 and 6.0 million acres. Nehru, who was deeply impressed with these projects, suggested that they be treated as the pilgrimage centers of modern India.

The Planning Commission gave high priority to increasing India's steel production. With the Tata Iron and Steel Works operating at full blast, the first five-year plan resulted in producing only 1.4 million tons. The Indian government therefore encouraged foreign assistance in building new steel plants. The U.S.S.R., West Germany, and Britain helped and by 1961 three new plants were in operation, boosting the steel capacity to 3.5 million tons. When Nehru died in 1965 the figure was 6 million tons and production has been increasing steadily ever since. On the other hand, India has a long way to go to catch up with major industrial powers such as the United States, which in 1965 was producing 100 million tons annually. Nevertheless, India is probably producing steel more cheaply than any other country in the world and this fact alone has stimulated many new industries.

India has made enormous progress industrially. From being a colony totally dependent on Britain and the industrial West for manufactured goods, India now produces its own motor vehicles, railway locomotives and coaches, bicycles, electrical equipment, radios, fertilizers, and aircraft. In 1974 India joined the small number of nations to have developed a nuclear device. All this has been accomplished by means of a "mixed economy," in which the government has generally assumed ownership of those industries requiring large concentrations of capital. There is public ownership of the railways, the telephone and telegraph systems, the airlines, life insurance companies, and banks.

Industrial expansion has led to industrial urbanization and India has been experiencing a mass exodus to the cities by people in search of factory-related jobs. Older cities like Calcutta and Bombay as well as the newer ones are attracting the rural masses of every caste and creed. New industrial cities have developed overnight around steel plants. Jamshedpur, Durgapur, and Asonsol in Bengal are such cities, and there are other examples in Madhya Pradesh and Orissa. Industrial opportunity and urbanization have spread radically in India until by 1970, 110 million people were encompassed by urbanization (or 10 million more people than the total population of Japan).

On the other hand, India has not neglected agricultural development. In the first three five-year plans (1951-66), heavy industry was the high priority item, but in 1965 the government decided to redistribute the budget to make India self-sufficient in food-grain production by the early 1970s. With the assistance of AID, the Ford Foundation, and other public and private agencies, the government pushed hard to increase production by providing farmers with better seeds, tools, credit, and services. To accomplish this India established twenty-four agricultural colleges, which have graduated tens of thousands of students since 1960.

Considering India's stagnant agrarian situation under the British, the change has been phenomenal. The radical increase in production has been called a "green revolution." After a monsoon season of good rainfall, the 1967-68 harvest totalled 95 million metric tons, or about 7 percent better than the best previous year on record. In the following year, with less than average rainfall, the harvest was 94 million tons; in 1970-71, the crop totaled more than 107 million tons. There is hope that the "green revolution" may represent a major breakthrough. Increased use of fertilizer has been a crucial factor. Production of nitrogeneous fertilizer rose to 800,000 tons by 1971, a tenfold increase in twelve years. Irrigation by means of tube wells has been another crucial factor. These deep-shaft wells go down two hundred feet or more and use a gasoline or diesel engine, wherever possible replacing the old Persian wheels, which bring up water in a long chain of tiny buckets. A tube well can irrigate one hundred times as large an area as can a Persian wheel and has become widespread as a consequence of village electrification. Land reform and the extension of credit to peasant farmers have also been contributing factors in the "green revolution," but there is a reverse side.

One of the consequences of the "green revolution" has been to distort social relationships in the countryside. Improved seeds, fertilizers, and mechanization have helped the wealthy farmer to become more wealthy. But the poor farmer who lacks the means to take advantage of these improvements may find himself correspondingly depressed, even becoming the hired labor of the wealthy farmer, working land that was formerly his own.

Despite industrial and agricultural developments in the direction of modernization, there still exists the agonizing problem of overpopulation, which represents a steady drag on economic development. While the "green revolution" was taking place, India's population was increasing by 12 million a year. Between 1961 and 1966 family planning clinics were increased from 1,800 to 10,000, and perhaps no other country in the world has spent so much time, effort, and money improving contraceptives and propagating the need for birth control. Some Indian family-planning experts predict that by 1980 the birth rate, which was 39 per thousand in the late 1960s, will be reduced to 23 per thousand, thus cutting the growth rate in half, but this projection is viewed by others as excessively optimistic.

Political Consolidation

When the British abdicated power in 1947, they left 1.2 million square miles of Indian territory divided between the imperial provinces of "British India" and the states. The nine provinces at the time of the British departure were Bombay, Madras, the Central Provinces, the United Provinces, Orissa, Assam, Bihar, and what became East Panjab and West Bengal. These were not homogeneous entities, for they contained within them people who spoke very different languages and maintained regionally distinct cultural traditions. There was, in addition, the problem of the princely states. The great majority of princely states were contiguous to British Indian districts. Though some princes desired independence, India consistently urged their assimilation even to the point of using military force to implement integration. Though Nehru was willing to grant the states some degree of autonomy as against the central government, at least to begin with, and was perhaps too willing to reshape provinces to accommodate linguistic and regional considerations, he adhered as much as possible to a policy of national integration.

In the fall of 1947 it looked very much as if the entire subcontinent would be convulsed by massacres brought about by religious fanaticism and mob violence and that both of the new nations would collapse. When the outbreaks had subsided more than 8 million refugees had crossed the India-Pakistan borders. It has been estimated that up to 5 million Hindus and Sikhs may have fled from the Panjab alone and that large numbers of them were butchered en route. Similar numbers of Muslims were likewise killed or forced to flee from Hindu areas, especially the provinces of Uttar Pradesh and Bihar. Three former princely states—Junagadh, Kashmir, and Hyderabad—decided to oppose the Indian assimilation policy and looked to Pakistan for moral and military support. All three were eventually integrated by force but Kashmir has remained a source of contention between India and Pakistan to the present day, with the Muslim majority there frequently agitating for union with Pakistan.

In the context of political consolidation, the year 1948 was perhaps the most crucial one of all for India. Over 600 former princely states containing 25 percent of the population had to be integrated smoothly into the Indian Union. Under the vigorous leadership of Sardar Patel, the Indian government laid down three basic principles to guide policy on the status of the princely states: (1) despotism must give way to democratic government; (2) the states must be subordinated to the central government; and (3) the British-imposed multiple-state system must integrate into larger and more viable units.

By 1950, 216 states had been merged with the former British provinces; 61 states had been taken over by New Delhi to be centrally administered; and 275 states had been joined together to form new political units or unions of states. According to the constitution that became the law of the land on 16 January 1950, the intricate divisions of the British period had been reduced to the 28 states or provinces of the Indian Union. Today, India is composed of 19 states and 9 union territories, and these conform fairly closely to the distribution of India's 16 major languages. Though Hindi is the official Indian language and English is still the *de facto lingua franca* among the elite, all the major regional languages are accorded official status, although Urdu, the language of northern Muslims, is discriminated against in practice.

With an electorate of 270 million, India was the largest democracy in the world until Mrs. Gandhi's assumption of emergency powers in the summer of 1975 threatened the fragile fabric of parliamentary institutions. It is still, however, governed under a federal constitution modeled in part on the practice of federalism in Canada, Australia, Switzerland, and the United States. The structure and function of the Supreme Court is American-influenced, but the Indians adopted the British parliamentary pattern for their legislature, and there is no separation of powers between executive and legislative bodies. Much of this system was intended to promote greater political consolidation. Yet the states have considerable power and the upper house (240 members) of the bicameral parliament is chosen by legislatures of the states and union territories, while the lower house is elected directly by the people for five-year terms and consists of 521 members. The national parliamentary pattern of bicameral legislatures has generally been followed on the state level. Normally, the most important executive figure in each state is the chief minister, who is responsible to the state legislature. The governor is a centrally appointed official with largely ceremonial functions, except during periods of internal crisis when he or she may assume complete power under central government rule. This has happened several times in troublesome states like West Bengal, demonstrating the center's ability to maintain tight national integration in crisis situations.

Aside from structural considerations, the workings of India's democratic system has greatly politicized Indian society as a whole by mobilizing mass support for party programs and objectives. Under Gandhi, nationalism and independence were the prime objectives; after independence and under Congress leadership, economic and social modernization have been the declared goals. This has been a very important consideration in a hitherto free society that has held regular elections and where politicians have owed their survival to a mass electorate. In a democratic situation, depending very much on the mood and ideological disposition of the voters, mass mobilization for modernization could easily have been offset and even obliterated by conservative opposition and by the face that the majority of voters are illiterate. Opposition parties representing religious sectarianism have always commanded a following, especially in the north, and most conspicuously the well-organized Jan Sangh (Indian People's Party), which espouses a Hindu-oriented nationalist political ideology and draws its strength from Hindi-speaking Uttar Pradesh.

In the general elections of 1953, 1957, and 1962, the Congress Party consistently held over 70 percent of the seats in the lower house and over 60 percent in the state legislatures. Following Nehru's death, the Congress Party finally lost its monopoly of political power in the general elections of 1967. It suffered severe reverses in state elections, and on the national level its share of seats in the representative lower house dropped to 55 percent. Clearly, the mas of people were turning against the Congress party bosses who stood behind Lal Bahadur Shastri, known as "The Syndicate." An analysis of the 1967 elections indicates not that the Indian masses had rejected modernization but that they had grown disenchanted with the post-Nehru dominant elite in the Congress Party, which was widely held to be highly conservative.

In 1969 Mrs. Gandhi launched a revolt against the Congress right wing, which led to a party split, and more than three-fourths of the members of the Congress in the lower house sided with her; the remainder sided with a group of old guard party leaders. Despite the fact

14.2 Crowds mourning the death of Jawaharlal Nehru, Delhi, 1964. The effective control and mobilization for development of an ever-increasing population is one of present-day India's most intractable problems. It has been estimated that by the early 1980s the population will have reached 700 million. Courtesy: Camera Press, London.

that her followers were reduced to a minority in Parliament, Mrs. Gandhi continued to rule with support from smaller parties. Then, in March 1971, she called an unscheduled national election, campaigning for radical modernization. She openly sought from the people a national mandate to develop and implement radical programs of economic and social reform. She won a two-thirds majority in the lower house, while the old party leaders who had split with her were routed. In the 1972 elections, as a result of her handling of the war against Pakistan and the independence of Bangladesh, she consolidated her power and her party obtained direct control of all but four state governments. In general, however, her direction of affairs did not result in any notable advances in the furtherance of socialism, and it may have been this failure, and the growing vociferousness of the opposition, that decided her to take the downhill (and probably irreversible) step towards more authoritarian rule.

One final note on political consolidation is the fact that the so-called steel frame of the British empire in India—the Indian civil service—still serves independent India as its bureaucratic structure. The Indian Administrative Service, as it is now called, has sometimes been looked upon as a mixed blessing in a new nation striving to democratize and modernize its political and social systems. The bureaucracy was never conceived as an integral part of an independent and democratic government. On the surface, it would appear that India was most fortunate to have a refined and effective bureaucratic structure to implement policy decisions on economic development. But the question is whether Indian bureaucrats since independence have been able to reorient themselves psychologically from being the agents of an alien rule to becoming servants of the Indian people. It is a matter of vital concern whether the civil servants are willing and able to interact with the mass of their countrymen to implement elaborate projects on the village level.

Social Mobilization

Central to this chapter is the question of the extent to which economic and political changes have penetrated Indian society. Without basic social change, governmental, constitutional, and legislative enactments or educational projects that look good on paper can have little actual impact. In 1950, for example, the Indian Constitution extended the Brahmo social reform program of the nineteenth century to every Indian citizen. At the stroke of a pen it proclaimed that "all citizens, irrespective of religion, race, caste, sex and place of birth, shall enjoy equality before the law and no disability shall be imposed on them in any respect." Moreover, the Constitution declared that untouchability was to be abolished. Thus, at least on the statute book, centuries of caste discrimination and untouchability were declared illegal, although in practice caste institutions and attitudes appear to be extraordinarily resilient.

Judging from the speeches and writings of the Nehru years, the ruling elite was acutely conscious of the need for full social mobilization to achieve a modernized society. It escaped no one's notice that all industrialized societies from the United States to Japan had compulsory systems of state education and high rates of literacy on a per capita basis. Thus, at the same time that India began to industrialize, she embarked on ambitious educational schemes designed to spread literacy far and wide among the millions of villagers of the subcontinent. Ideally, social mobilization should proceed in some coordinated relationship with economic development, land reform, and the politicization of the masses. Unfortunately, this has not been the case: great discrepancies have developed since 1951 between advanced states like the Panjab and backward states like Bihar. Here too can be seen a constitutional problem, since national priorities must be reconciled with state jurisdiction over education and agriculture. It is not perhaps the conservatism of the Indian peasant but ambiguities in the relations between the state governments and the center that account for so much lack of coordination in the multidimensional modernization process.

Where there is little evidence of increased social mobility or rising expectations (i.e., a desire to improve one's lot in life) in an underdeveloped society, it may be said that modernization is not really taking place. In rural India, however, the real drama since independence has been a marked increase in social mobility. Peasant groupings on the way up, rather than rejecting tradition have modernized it and translated their mobility in cultural terms. Basically, there are three components of mobility: physical, social, and psychological. In the Indian context, physical mobility refers to peasants actually moving from the stagnant countryside to cities or other places where developmental programs have created new opportunities. In early British times the exodus was from preindustrial cities to the countryside, whereas in postindependence times the exodus has been from the countryside to new industrial urban centers. In the cities, some former peasants may accumulate money and ultimately climb into the middle class. Less obvious, but perhaps more important in the rural areas of India, is the process some anthropologists call "Sanskritization," by which a lower caste or group adopts the customs of a higher caste and thereby claims a higher position in the hierarchy of prestige.

Sanskritization is not always symptomatic of modernization since there are cases of castes rising and other castes falling without the basic social structure in a given locale changing appreciably. But in those cases where *harijans* ("untouchables") have recently risen in status it is almost invariably a result of modernizing circumstances. Through the introduction of adult franchise and self-government at the village level, *harijans* and other low castes have been observed to experience a new sense of self-respect and power related also to the fact that *harijans* enjoy reserved seats in all elected bodies from the village to the federal parliament. Political mobilization is a very significant factor because often *harijans* and others begin to sway the local balance of power one way or the other. In the traditional land system it was possible for a small number of high caste families to own most of the arable land and exert great power in village affairs. But through the admittedly sluggishly imposed land reforms and such economic opportunities as have been available to poor cultivators and *harijans,* a more equitable distribution of land ownership has taken place in some parts of rural India.

The third component of mobility is psychological mobility—the liberation of the individual from his or her original self, giving the individual the opportunity and the means to shape a new and different personality. The urban environment plays a key role in this transformation. The change that has taken place among Indian peasants who have come to the great cities and joined labor organizations is remarkable. Working and trade union experiences have led to social mobility and a changing economic situation, while exposure to labor movement ideologies has served as an educational instrument leading to psychological liberation. Participation in voluntary associations or in modern urban society itself may be as effective in emancipating Indian peasants in the twentieth century as was formal schooling in emancipating the Indian intelligentsia in the nineteenth. Although the overall literacy rate is still only 29 percent, an estimated 50 percent—or over 50 million—of the urban people of India can read and write.

To others, the key to India's modernization lies not in her cities but in her 500,000 villages, containing the great bulk of the population. Recent village studies show that the isolation of the villages has broken down to the point where today there is greater emphasis on regional intercaste relations as against more restricted intracaste relations. The implication here is that it is not urbanization in itself but a process of social mobilization that provides the political and economic incentives to change. In the past, for example, lack of monetization in the village economy resulted in a barter (*jajmani*) system. Now economic development and political mobilization have not only supplanted the *jajmani* system in many places but have altered the traditional relationships within communities, so that the emphasis now is on open market competition and political rivalry for access to new kinds of power and prestige.

The picture presented here has stressed the goals and aspirations of India's national leadership and tried to suggest some of the kinds of change taking place. How India will develop in the future remains to be seen. Clearly, problems of population and food supply will remain critical for many years. Industrialization has still made only a modest impression on the society as a whole. It is less than clear how India's democratic institutions, dangerously eroded by Mrs. Gandhi's recent measures, will be affected by the stresses of regionalism and the hazards of an increasingly belligerent foreign policy, both of which were apparent in the transformation of East Pakistan into Bangladesh. Of particular interest in the future will be the continuing adaptation of India's cultural heritage and traditional social system to the demands of the modern world.

3. CUMULATIVE FORCES FOR CHANGE IN MODERN SOUTHEAST ASIA

With the exception of Thailand, the modern development of each of the nations of Southeast Asia was initiated under colonial rule and, in many cases, external influences have continued to play a very large part in changes taking place after independence. For this reason it is necessary to separate the question of modern change from the question of political independence, which was stressed in the last chapter, and to look at modernization processes in a time span that includes both the colonial era and independence.

Secularization—the desanctification of traditional patterns of thought and action—was hastened in Southeast Asia by the imposition of European ruling elites with foreign cultural values. The extension and rationalization of colonial control entailed increasing intervention in the affairs of the indigenous society and conscious efforts to transform that society. A significant change in the tempo of the processes occurred in the late nineteenth century, after about 1870, when European colonial control tightened, and there was a shift away from the early pattern of accommodation to traditional values and toward the imposition of European standards by professionalized European administrations. A second phase ensued after 1900 as an intermediate stratum of Asians emerged, possessed of sufficient European education to act as intermediaries between the ruling authority and the populace. From this perspective, to the extent that Western education—and here one may include the Western-educated modernizing leadership in Thailand along with colonial administrations—marked the displacement of traditional values, it corresponds to the pattern of secularization from the top downward and outward. The institution of modern educational systems in the postindependence period has continued this trend.

The economic development of Southeast Asian states was begun in the colonial era. One prominent feature of that process was the orientation of the economy toward exports and the world market. Port cities like Rangoon and Jakarta (Batavia under the Dutch) displaced older inland centers such as Mandalay, Surakarta, and Jogjakarta, and railway lines were developed to link the interior to the coast. A second feature of colonial economic policy, which continues to characterize many of the economies in the present, was the concentration of development on mineral resources (tin and oil), raw materials (hardwoods, rubber), and agricultural products (sugar, rice), which left the economies at the mercy of the world market and dependent upon the developed countries for manufactured items. A third effect of colonial policy was to disrupt the indigenous social order by interjecting new economic groupings. Often this took the form of encouraging the immigration of foreign groups to perform certain functions. Thus Indians entered Burma in large numbers, and Chinese settled in all parts of Southeast Asia, controlling a substantial share or even dominating the commerce of many nations.

Political consolidation in the new nation-states of Southeast Asia was everywhere complicated by the question of pluralism, the need to integrate newcomers and older indigenous elements into a single polity. By and large the new nations have conformed to the contours of the colonies that preceded them. This fact is a testament to the strength of the administrative arrangements that took hold in the first half of the twentieth century, since the demarcations of colonies had little to do with linguistic groupings or traditional polities. A particularly important factor in political consolidation has been the extent to which continuity of the indigenous elite was preserved during the colonial period. Elite continuity has generally fostered political stability, as manifested in Malaysia, Thailand, and the Philippines. While the forms of administration introduced in the colonial period have persisted in many areas, one of the most pronounced trends among the new nations has been the emergence of military dictatorships. In numerous cases—South Vietnam, Cambodia, Burma, Indonesia, Thailand, and perhaps the Philippines—this development has been at least partly the product of heavy external funding of the military sector, largely as a by-product of Cold War rivalries and the penetration of American power into the areas. This phenomenon may be viewed both as a continuation of foreign influence in the postcolonial era and as a form of economic and technological development through heavy investment in the military sector.

The mobilization of society has not progressed as rapidly in most parts of Southeast Asia as it has in many other areas of the world. This is due, no doubt, to the tardy integration of the area into the modern global economy and to the fact that industrialization and urbanization are only now beginning to intrude upon the village community. Administrative and economic development in the colonial period produced an Asian elite class as well as various groups of middlemen, often Indian or Chinese, who were both physically and socially mobile and fully responsive to trends in society at large. As these groups accommodated to Western institutions and acquired modern education, however, the distance between them and the rural peasantry tended to widen. Many peasants resisted opportunities to move to cities or to work for wages on plantations. In some cases, even in a phase of rapid economic development, such as the development of rice-exporting economies in the great river deltas of Burma, Thailand, and Cochin China, peasant producers could continue to apply traditional methods of production and preserve a good deal of their customary community organization. Often it was political developments, the struggle for independence or conflict in the postindependence period—notably the Indochina War—that broke open the village and linked the individual to wider social events, refocusing loyalties toward national symbols and organizations such as a political party or the armed forces.

The variations of the processes discussed here in general terms may best be illustrated by considering some of the differing patterns of modern change in Southeast Asia..

Malaysia

Malaysia stands out among the nations of Southeast Asia as an experiment in ethnic pluralism. Combining the southern third of the Malay peninsula and the northern portions of the island of Borneo into a single nation-state, Malaysia owes its definition more to the historical circumstances of British colonial administration than to the linguistic or ethnic cohesion of its population. The evolution of present-day Malaysia can best be understood in terms of the combined effects of the area's economic development and the heritage of British governmental institutions.

The mixed population of the Malay peninsula came about as the by-product of a growing export economy. Chinese merchants and entrepreneurs, organizing small-scale enterprises along guild or clan lines, entered the area in increasing numbers in the nineteenth century, supplying capital, labor, and managerial skills to what was in effect an expanding economic frontier. One important activity for the Chinese was tin mining, carried on by small, labor-intensive firms, which were outdistanced by better-equipped, capital-intensive Western firms after 1900. The major export item for Malaya in the twentieth century, however was rubber, much of which was grown on plantations. Since Malays were generally unresponsive to the opportunity to become agricultural wage laborers, English plantation owners arranged to import laborers from India. The majority of Indians contracting to work on Malayan plantations returned to India with their earnings, but enough elected to stay to constitute a substantial minority group within the population. The population of Malaya in 1931 was 3.75 million, of whom 34 percent were Chinese, 15 percent Indian, and the remainder, just about half, Malays.

British administration in Malaya was based on a complex set of arrangements with local sultans in which British "residents" were attached to each sultanate, first along the Malacca Straits and later in the rest of the peninsula and northern Borneo. The effect of these arrangements was to stabilize and perpetuate the indigenous ruling elite while at the same time imposing a network of British governmental agents, who exercised real power. Complementing the residents, the sultans also named Councils of Muslim Religion and Malay Custom, which were excluded from the sphere of British authority, to oversee local practices. Bolstering the traditional rulers was particularly important on the western side of the peninsula, where Chinese immigration and the proliferation of plantations threatened the old social order. In effect, there were now two societies existing side by side, the traditional Malay community, with its hereditary rule, and a burgeoning commercial establishment dominated by Western entrepreneurs and Chinese communal associations. Chinese predominated in the urban areas, where they rapidly accumulated capital and modern economic skills. British policy insulated the rural Malay population from the full impact of economic change by protecting Malay land ownership and providing a vernacular elementary school system.

This complex patchwork of direct rule in the developed areas and indirect rule in the more remote states, a classic application of the principles of divide and rule, faced serious handicaps when the colony neared independence after the Second World War. A degree of centralization did evolve over time under a resident-general and his secretariat at Kuala Lumpur, but the proposal in 1946 to unify Malaya by eliminating the sultanates met vigorous opposition from the Malays, who feared submersion in a state that would be dominated by a skilled and rapidly increasing Chinese population. The Malay elite formed a United Malays National Organization (UMNO) to represent its interests. In 1948 a Federation of Malaya was created, which protected Malay interests and made Malay the national language. Communist-led guerrilla forces, predominantly Chinese in membership, which had opposed the Japanese during the war, made a brief bid for power at the end of the war and carried on a prolonged insurgency during the 1950s. In the course of this emergency, as the British called it, the guerrilla movement did not win Malay support and was eventually suppressed. Meanwhile, more conservative elements in the three ethnic communities formed a Malayan Alliance, which made possible the inauguration in 1957 of an independent Federation of Malaya with Commonwealth status. The elements of the Alliance were the Malayan Chinese Association, formed by Chinese capitalists, the Malayan Indian Congress, and UMNO, headed by Tengku Abdul Rahman, a British-trained lawyer from the ruling house of one of the sultanates, who became the first prime minister. The new state was a constitutional monarchy in which the hereditary Malay rulers were to elect one of their number as a monarch every five years. Embodied in the state was the understanding that the Malays would continue to enjoy political control while Chinese dominance over the economy would not be threatened. Islam was designated the state religion, and Malay was eventually to become the sole national language, while the rights of Malays were given special protection and the citizenship and voting rights of non-Malays were initially curtailed.

In 1963, under the leadership of Tengku Abdul Rahman and Lee Kuan Yew, a Cambridge-educated lawyer who headed the Peoples' Action Party (PAP) of Singapore, the state of Malaysia was formed through the fusion of the Federation of Malaya, the island of Singapore, and the British colonies of Sabah and Sarawak on north Borneo. Just two years later, however, Chinese-Malay tensions were manifested in conflict between the Alliance and the PAP, which pushed for an end to the special status of Malays, and led to the withdrawal of Singapore from the Federation. The tiny island of Singapore, a city-state with a population of about 2 million (76 percent of whom are ethnic Chinese), became an independent state, relying on its highly developed commercial and industrial sectors and the largest port in Southeast Asia for its future. In Malaysia, racial tensions continued to run high as Chinese education and development outpaced the less advanced Malays and support for the conservative Malayan Chinese Association declined. In 1969 these tensions came to the surface in serious race rioting in Kuala Lumpur, which led to the temporary suspension of constitutional government.

Indonesia

The modern development of Indonesia has been influenced by the discontinuity between the colonial and independence periods. Unlike Malaya, the men who came to power in Indonesia were members of a Western-educated intelligentsia and not part of a traditional elite. It is interesting to note that this new leadership group fared far worse in guiding its country's economic development than did the sultans of Malaya or the royal court of Thailand. Declining exports, inflation, and seizures of foreign enterprises led to economic chaos in the 1950s. In addition to these problems, the physical fragmentation of the Indonesian islands and the ethnic diversity of the population severely hindered political consolidation. Western-style representative institutions were introduced after independence but failed to contain the tensions in a society that lacked the consensus needed to make them work. Conflicts between different ethnic groups, between hostile religious groups, and breakaway movements by some local military commanders threatened to tear the new nation apart in the late 1950s.

President Sukarno responded to this crisis by dispensing with constitutional government and replacing it with "guided democracy." Sukarno's strategy was to create national unity by focusing attention on foreign threats and by creating an official national ideology. He led the country into major "confrontations," with Holland in 1960 over control of New Guinea (West Irian) and with Malaysia in 1963. While the economy continued to deteriorate Sukarno received massive supplies of arms from the Soviet Union and support from the Communist Party (PKI), which emerged as the strongest political organization in the country. An unsuccessful coup by some army officers in 1965 provided the military leadership with a pretext to move against the PKI. Throughout Indonesia hundreds of thousands of villagers associated with the PKI were slaughtered as local antagonisms took a violent form. General Suharto, suppressor of the coup, came to power in 1966, displacing Sukarno and establishing a moderate military rule.

Thailand

Thailand's success in preserving its independence and guiding the development of its economy was made possible by the conjunction of favorable internal and external circumstances. Perhaps the most important single factor in Thai modernization has been effective and cohesive elite leadership. Following a devastating defeat by the Burmese in the mid-

14.3 Election poster in Singapore, 1955, illustrates the problems of social mobilization in a pluralistic society. The sign is written in Malay, Tamil, and Chinese, but it is English, the language of the colonial power, that serves as a *lingua franca*. Source: Victor Purcell, *Malaysia* (London, 1965).

eighteenth century, a new Thai royal line was established with its capital on the Chao-phraya (Menam) River, across from the present site of Bangkok. In the nineteenth century a series of able kings built a strong monarchy in which an open working relationship between the ruler and his ministers facilitated realistic and flexible decision making. The activities of Prince Mongkut in the first half of the nineteenth century are illustrative of royal receptivity to new ideas and of an openness within Thai elite culture, which contrasted sharply with other areas of Asia, particularly China, in the same period. Working within the intellectual framework of Thai Buddhism, Mongkut rejected a life of contemplation in favor of wide-ranging studies, which included foreign languages and science. Other princes studied such practical subjects as medicine, shipbuilding, and military affairs. This marked the beginning of royal initiative in the importation of foreign ideas, a trend that was accelerated when Mongkut took the throne in 1851 and more than a dozen Western advisers were hired.

In external affairs the Thais proved able to benefit from the demands of growing world trade. Early in the nineteenth century Chinese planters began commercial sugar produc-tion, and concessions were granted to British merchants trading in Bangkok, causing the volume of foreign trade to increase and allowing the Thais to begin importing foreign goods, including American weapons. In 1855 the British forced a commercial treaty upon Thailand, which opened the country to trade on conditions favorable to the Western merchants. Mongkut made this concession in the determination to avoid the sort of foreign encroachment then taking place in Burma and China. The Thai court itself had a vested interest in foreign trade and the king both promoted and invested in commercial develop-ment. The Chaophraya delta was one of the great economic frontiers of Southeast Asia, which when developed made Thailand a major rice-exporting nation. Chinese entre-preneurs, middlemen, and merchants played an important part in developing trade. The government took the initiative in building railway lines to tie its territory together.

One factor that favored Thailand was its location between a British sphere in Burma and French colonies in Vietnam. Skillful Thai diplomacy played the powers against one another so as to preserve an independent buffer zone between them. In constructing railways the Thais avoided the foreign loans that sapped the revenues of other states and employed the engineers of a country, Germany, that had no territorial ambitions in Southeast Asia. Later, during the Second World War, Thailand accommodated to the interests of Japan and declared war on the Western Allies. French and British weakness, together with Japanese support, enabled Thailand to expand its territory eastward into Laos and Cambodia and southward down the Malay peninsula. As Japanese power waned, the Thais replaced their military government with a civilian one and prepared to make a rapproachment with the Allies, the price of which entailed the surrender of their recent territorial gains. In the 1950s Thailand aligned itself with the United States, participating in the Korean War and later in the Indochina War and becoming a major base area for American armed forces.

Development, which in Thailand has proceeded from the top down, has inevitably transformed the nature of government. In the nineteenth century power was tightly held by the king and the royal family, which also happened to be the group most at home with Western education. As time passed the court structure was reformed under Chulalongkorn (r. 1868-1910), who established a system of functional ministries and extended central control into the provinces. As the governmental structure grew and a modern school system was created around the turn of the century, the body of civil servants and military officers with modern educations and value orientations expanded rapidly. In 1932 these new elements carried out a bloodless revolution, which established a constitutional monarchy, but in the end it was the military that took up the reins of government. In the next forty years nine constitutions came and went as governments were changed frequently by shifting alliances among a small and cohesive elite dominated by the military. Thailand has experi-enced a high rate of economic growth but wealth has not been shared equally, so that the distance between the richest and the poorest Thais has tended to increase. Discontent has found expression in two sectors of Thai society, both indicative of the progressive mobilization of a populace that is demanding a voice in political affairs. In the rural areas, particularly the underdeveloped northeast, where the influence of the Indochina War and the presence of American airbases have disrupted local affairs, armed insurgency has appeared. In the urban areas the demands of a growing educated middle class have been voiced by intellectuals and students. In 1973 massive student demonstrations demanding an end to corruption and a return to constitutional government led to violent clashes, which brought down the ruling military dictatorship and forced the leading figures into exile. The student revolution altered the direction of Thai political development by forcing many issues into the open and by renewing the commitment to the search for a viable and just constitution.

Vietnam

The dominant factor in the modern development of Vietnam has been the prolonged political and military struggles for independence and, subsequent to the French withdrawal in 1954, for reunification between the north and south. While the levels of violence and destruction have been noteworthy, it should not be assumed that the Indochina War has had an entirely negative impact in terms of the processes of modern change. Indeed, the fighting provided a strong stimulus to change, particularly in the mobilization of the populace and the consolidation of the nation-state. In the north, recruitment of personnel for war service, organization of civil defense in the face of American air raids, and ideological and production drives to support the war effort mobilized the population around a program of national goals formulated and popularized by the Communist Party (literally the Vietnam Labor Party). In the south the military competition between the Communist-led National Liberation Front (NLF) and the Army of the Republic of Vietnam (ARVN) drew a substantial portion of the population into military service or related militia organizations. Counterinsurgency programs in the south also frequently involved the forced resettlement or the destruction of villages in such a manner as to produce large numbers of refugees, many of whom entered urban areas in search of security and livelihood. The fighting itself provided many Vietnamese with the opportunity to acquire organizational and technical skills not found in the old society. Massive infusions of arms from China, the Soviet Union, and the United States required considerable expansion of the communications and transportation networks, including ports, roadways, airfields, pipelines, storage depots, and repair facilities, and the training of Vietnamese to operate and maintain the most modern military equipment.

The division of Vietnam at the seventeenth parallel left the north with a comparatively well developed industrial sector, while the south was primarily an agricultural region. In the Democratic Republic of Vietnam (DRV) a development program was launched which drew heavily on the experience of China and the Soviet Union. In the rural areas land was redistributed and agriculture and handicraft production were organized on the basis of village cooperatives in an ambitious program that provoked much resistance. While food production remained a problem in the north, the greatest emphasis was placed on industry. The leadership stressed science and technology in education to such an extent that by the 1970s North Vietnam possessed the best body of scientists and engineers in all of Southeast Asia. Discontent among the intellectuals was apparent in the 1950s, but in the following decade escalation of the war and appeals to patriotism encouraged acceptance of communist leadership. The ruling party may actually have been strengthened as a result of American bombing of the DRV because it necessitated a dispersal of units and a decentralization of authority, which gave substantial responsibility and power to lower level cadres.

An even more dramatic example of the influence of warfare on the transformation of the social order, here the desanctification of traditional social roles, can be seen in the changing status of women in North Vietnam. The Vietnamese women's movement got its start early in the twentieth century, well before the founding of the Communist Party. In the writings of the nationalist Phan Boi Chau, the point was made as early as 1913 that nationalism offered women an identity equal to men which could transcend the limited traditional roles of subservience in the family hierarchy. The Communist Party early accepted the concept of the equality of the sexes as a matter of principle but was slow to take forceful action toward implementation. In 1955-56, for example, when land reform was taking place, women were classified into the social classes of their husbands, regardless of their own family backgrounds. A marriage and family law enacted in 1959, however, attacked the old clan system and extended legal equality to women. It was the mobilization of the 1960s that brought the most dramatic changes. By 1970 women constituted 80 to 90 percent of the agricultural labor force, while female students made up half of the enrollment in elementary schools and more than half of the students in professional and technical fields of higher education. Women also made rapid advances in administrative and command positions. In 1966 the Central Committee directed that women replace men in many management organs. The percentage of women in the membership of village people's councils rose from 19 in 1965 to 44 in 1969. Similarly dramatic gains were made in the lower and middle levels of the party structure, suggesting that the changing status of women, although stimulated by the exigencies of war, is part of an irreversible transformation of Vietnamese society.

In South Vietnam political consolidation proceeded at a much slower pace than in the north. Ngo Dinh Diem, the American-backed power holder from 1954 to 1963, found solid support only among the Catholics, some 650,000 of whom fled south during the land reform. Rigidly anticommunist and partial to landlord interests, Diem found himself opposed by substantial sectors of Vietnamese society, most importantly the Buddhists. A revitalization of Vietnamese Buddhism began in the 1930s, when the Buddhists responded to the competition of Christianity by translating Buddhist texts into the vernacular, founding Buddhist studies associations, and increasing publishing activities. In 1951 a Buddhist congress was held in Hue, from which there developed a General Association of Vietnamese Buddhism. The Buddhists now began to organize themselves on a national scale with schools, youth groups, family groups, student groups, an academy for the clergy, and a network of cells in major urban areas. In this assertive mobilization the Buddhists of Vietnam departed radically from the passive and scripture-oriented style of Chinese Buddhism and strengthened their ties to the Theravada Buddhists of Burma, Thailand, and Ceylon. It was Buddhist-led protest, including public self-immolations, that led to the downfall of Diem, who was assassinated in 1963. Following Diem's demise the government of the Republic of Vietnam passed into the hands of the military, as American participation in the war escalated. The United States withdrew its combat forces from South Vietnam after 1972, making inevitable the collapse of the Saigon government which followed in 1975. This brought to power the Provisional Revolutionary Government, the administrative entity created by the NLF, and opened the way to cooperation with the DRV in the north and formal unification of the country in 1976.

The Philippines

It is appropriate to close this section with a brief consideration of the process of political consolidation in the Philippines, since at independence the Filipino elite possessed a depth of experience in self-rule unmatched in Southeast Asia. In the intervening years neither the cohesion of the Christianized Filipino elite nor the American-style constitution established in 1935 proved sufficient to guide the country smoothly through the processes of political consolidation and industrial development. One obstacle to development was the nature of the elite itself. Education expanded rapidly in the 1950s and 1960s, but the emphasis was on liberal arts and law degrees for children of the wealthy. Consequently, Manila was crowded with many who sought to live by their wits and their connections but who made no contribution to economic growth, while the influx from the countryside swelled the number of squatters in the capital to 800,000 by 1973. In the countryside the dominance of landlords over poor tenants persisted and the opposition to birth control by the hierarchy of the Catholic church inhibited any effort to deal with a rapidly expanding population.

Another factor that many Filipinos perceived as an obstacle to their national development was the continuation of an American presence after independence. Just prior to independence the United States prevailed upon the Philippine Congress to accept a "parity" arrangement, which extended to American citizens the same rights to residence, property, and occupation—and including the right to exploit natural resources—as were enjoyed by Filipinos. Between 1950 and 1973 American investment in the Philippines increased from $149 million to $1 billion. More important was a continuing military presence. The United States maintained major military bases in the Philippines and Filipino forces participated in the Indochina War. Through its military advisory group the United States shaped the development of the Philippine armed forces, assisted in the suppression of insurgency, and helped build the infrastructure for a police state. The Military Assistance Program provided helicopters, weapons, and communications equipment to support the Philippine Constabulary, while the AID program built up the police forces through training programs and the modernization of communications, record keeping, and identification systems.

Throughout the decade of the 1960s the political situation in the Philippines deteriorated. Student unrest and criticism of corruption and inefficiency in the government became increasingly strident, often erupting into demonstrations and clashes with authorities. In rural areas, communist-led insurgency of the New People's Army (NPA) began to spread in competition with the power of landed families, who controlled their areas almost as warlords through gangs of armed retainers. In the southern islands the pressure of Christian settlers on the land of Muslim tribesmen has provoked a heated confrontation, sharpening the division between the Christian-dominated government and the Muslim minority community. In September 1972 President Ferdinand Marcos took decisive action to meet these challenges by declaring a state of martial law. In reality, Marcos' action was a well-planned coup d'etat, which swept away most of the inherited American-style political structure and replaced it with what he called constitutional authoritarianism. Prior to this action Marcos had been nearing the end of his allowed tenure in office under the old constitution. This difficulty was met by forcing through the Constitutional Convention then in session a new constitution providing for a parliamentary form of government with a strong prime minister and transitory provisions allowing Marcos as the incumbent president to remain in power and decide on the timing of the transition of the new system. Marcos' seizure of power was accompanied by the arrest of thousands of political leaders, a blanket control of the news media, and an effort to disarm the civilian population. A New Society program was proclaimed, which included an attack on corruption, a renewed counterinsurgency effort, government seizure of key industries (airlines, steel), and a massive land reform program.

4. CUMULATIVE FORCES FOR CHANGE IN MODERN CHINA

Chinese society has been caught up in a pervasive and violent revolution since the first decade of the twentieth century. Any consideration of political and economic development or processes of modernization must take into account the primary and determining role that political factors have played in the Chinese scene. This assertion may be illustrated by noting that the economic development of various sectors of China has proceeded at differing rates and in different directions according to the policies of the dominant political forces. Urban commercial sectors were developed in the treaty ports, especially Shanghai, where the imperialist powers controlled concessions until the 1940s. Manchuria was extensively industrialized by the Japanese in the 1930s and 1940s. Taiwan, controlled by Japan until 1945, has been rapidly developed under the Nationalist regime since 1949, with intensive financial infusions from the United States. Hong Kong, an important commercial center since the middle of the nineteenth century, remains to this writing a British crown colony.

The roots of modern change in China can be traced back to the middle of the nineteenth century, when Chinese and Manchus, bent on rescuing the Ch'ing dynasty from collapse, initiated the first modest programs to introduce Western technology and industrial techniques into China. The weakness of the Manchu regime, a lack of capital, inefficient managerial arrangements, inadequate legal and financial protection, and traditional attitudes toward business antithetical to entrepreneurship or long-term investment all conspired to retard the growth of China's first industrial enterprises during those decades when Meiji Japan was laying the foundation for industrialization and sustained economic development. In the early twentieth century the modest revenues of the Peking government were committed largely to military purposes and the servicing of indemnities and loans owed to foreign powers and international banking interests. Warlord rivalry and civil war precluded the initiation of any program of national development until the establishment of the Nanking government in 1927. Known as the Republic of China, this Kuomintang government marked the maturation of Chinese nationalism. Despite the fact that they were driven from Nanking by the Japanese invasion in 1937 and from the mainland (to Taiwan) by the Communists in 1949, the Nationalist did succeed in giving China the forms of an independent nation-state. A modern government was organized and began to manage such matters as banking, currency, postal service, schooling, and diplomacy on a uniform national basis. Tariff autonomy was regained by 1930. China's nominal great-power status during the Second World War obliged China's allies to relinquish claims to extraterritoriality, to exchange with China ambassadorial-rank representatives, and to make China a permanent member of the Security Council of the United Nations. Substantial and effective programs of economic, social, and political development were not undertaken on a national scale until the Chinese Communist Party came to power in 1949.

The Trend toward Secularization

Some aspects of traditional Chinese culture, such as the notions that society should be ordered as it had been in the past, that agriculture was the most worthy and fundamental of economic activities, that the Confucian classics were the embodiment of the most essential truths known to man, and that heaven and earth were responsive to the morality of the Chinese ruler, were not conducive to the early acceptance of Western learning. The demonstration effect of foreign technology was important in changing Chinese views, and the notion of the cultural superiority of the emperor became more difficult to support once it was shown that Western guns and steamships could not be stopped. Some offered resistance to technological innovation on the grounds that telegraphs and railways would disturb the natural forces and spirits in the countryside, but the more serious objections stemmed from a fear for the social order, particularly the position of the Confucian scholar elite. The first schooling of dozens of young men in Western technology was undertaken as a necessary evil in the last decades of the nineteenth century. After 1900 students went abroad in the hundreds, the examinations in the Confucian orthodoxy were abolished, new schools for boys and girls were established, and the conviction spread that Western social and political forms, as well as Western science, were superior to China's traditional institutions. In 1911 the removal of the imperial state, which had always functioned as the patron and protector of orthodox belief, freed a new generation of youths to question all values.

The traditional elite culture was by no means lacking in values compatible with modern change. One important element was the emphasis on learning, which was the very cornerstone of the Confucian system. Once the subject matter to be mastered was changed, the Chinese turned their traditional respect for scholarship into a national asset in the struggle to master science and technology. Another positive feature was the human-centered view of the universe, in which human beings controlled the conditions of their existence and strove toward moral perfection in this world. European and American missionaries, whose schools played an important part in introducing Western learning into China before the 1930s, found Chinese students little interested in theology and other-worldly concerns, while natural science was eagerly accepted. A third traditional orientation that proved useful was the assumption that the ruler should play a leadership role in shaping social values. Just as the imperial state attempted to uphold the status quo, to most Chinese it seemed appropriate for the Communist Party and the government of the People's Republic to foster revolutionary change.

In traditional China there was no concept of an inner core to the personality or of a private sector of the individual's life (with the possible exception of obligations to one's family) that was beyond the reach of the authority of the state. Neither a religious notion of the sanctity of the soul or conscience nor any legal doctrine of individual rights proscribed a sacred sphere from rational manipulation. In part for this reason, the effort to extend control over the personality has been undertaken more directly in China than in Western countries. In Maoist practice this has taken the form of efforts to change the individual's political views and social ethics.

According to the Marxist perspective, political values, no less than art, grow out of the economic base. Political parties are the instruments by which economic classes control society. The Community Party is by definition the instrument of the working class and its mission is to establish a dictatorship to overthrow and suppress the former exploiting classes and establish socialism and communism. The problem that faced the infant Communist movement in China was the fact that China had no urban industrial proletariat to speak of. One of the crucial innovations in Maoism is the notion that one can take on a proletarian outlook through study. Thus the Chinese Communist Party, whose members were drawn largely from the bourgeoisie and the peasantry, could claim to embody the proletarian point of view.

The techniques the Chinese Communists have developed for changing the individual's point of view are described by the terms political study and thought reform. In the late 1930s and early 1940s the party had to absorb a massive influx of new members who joined during the war of resistance against Japan. Partially due to a high illiteracy rate and a lack of printed materials, new recruits were instructed in basic principles of Marxism, party organization, and guerrilla warfare, largely through group discussion. In group study the individual was helped to see the errors of his or her previous thought and action and gradually to acquire a correct point of view. In its most formal and rigorous application, group study may involve a fixed group of individuals in an intensive and prolonged process of thought reform. In thought reform each individual's thought and actions are scrutinized by the whole group and rigorously criticized from a proletarian or public viewpoint, which demands that the individual justify his or her actions in light of the common interest of society at large. Each person is compelled to engage in criticism of others, self-criticism, and often writing of a public confession. Since the thought-reform process is a group experience, the pressure for sincere and energetic participation is greatly increased by intimate contact and interaction among the members of the group, who may encourage the resistant individual through "struggle"—physical abuse or the more devastating psychological isolation. After 1949 the demand for thought reform was generalized over the whole population, and special attention was given to converting members of the intelligentsia to the communist outlook in special schools, courses, and thought-reform universities established around the country.

Because the demand for thought reform emanated from the Communist Party, it was official, universal, and persistent. The party claimed to embody the overall public interest. The demand that the individual bring thought and action into line with that broader interest touched upon the deepest centers of guilt and personal inadequacy within the psyche. Since 1949 virtually the entire adult population of China has been organized into small groups for the purpose of political study. One effect of this compulsory participation in public discussion has been to develop verbal and cognitive skills among a population that was largely illiterate and politically passive before liberation. People are now generally very articulate in analyzing their own and others' behavior in objective terms using concepts and vocabulary popularized by the Communist Party. This condition in itself must be viewed as a most important aspect of intellectual and psychic secularization, for it means that the broad mass of the Chinese people have been provided, within the last two decades, with the skills and tools necessary to analyze and modify not only their physical environment but their own patterns of thought and behavior. Perhaps it would not be incorrect to say that in China these processes have gone further, faster than in any other society. Virtually no area remains immune from consideration. The historical perspective of Marxism has acted to discredit many traditional taboos, with the result that any area of life is potentially open to scrutiny.

Political Consolidation in China
Due to the fragmentation of power which took place after 1911 and the invasion by Japan in 1937, the political unification of China took four decades of war to achieve. Two elements were required to consolidate power: military superiority and a disciplined political party. Sun Yat-sen, through repeated frustration, learned that without military power and tight control over his followers there was no hope of success. He early put forward the conception of a three-stage political development, starting with military government, to be followed by a period of political tutelage, which in turn would give way to an era of constitutional government. Sun's political dreams began to materialize after 1923, when Russian support built a modern military organization at Canton. Despite the fact that the Kuomintang party apparatus was structured like the Communist Party of the Soviet Union, the Nationalists had a poorly developed ideology in Sun Yat-sen's Three People's Principles and the party remained fragmented among factions. The northern expedition of 1927-28 resulted in the establishment of a new national government at Nanking, but in reality many areas were only nominally affiliated with the new center. In fact, most provinces in the north and west continued to be divided among jealous warlords, who gave only lip service to the supremacy of Nanking. The Japanese took over Manchuria and remnants of the Communist Party held out in mountain strongholds. Under Chiang Kai-shek the Nationalists prolonged the period of tutelage until 1948 in what was in effect military dictatorship.

The Chinese Communist Party, although it was richer in ideology and better disciplined than the Kuomintang, was forced in 1923 by the Comintern to subordinate itself to its stronger rival and therefore was unable to develop its own military establishment. During the first united-front period, its activists competed within the structure of the Kuomintang for influence in the labor and peasant movements. After Chiang Kai-shek purged the Communists in 1927, the Chinese labor movement was crushed and fragments of the Communist Party fled to the countryside to organize military resistance. For a number of years Soviet-trained leaders continued to dominate the Chinese party and to carry out Comintern orders to attempt the seizure of cities so that the proletarian party might have a proper urban base. These uprisings were uniformly disastrous and served eventually to discredit the pro-Soviet elements in the Chinese leadership.

The essential development that lay at the heart of what proved to be a viable Chinese form of Communist revolutionary organization was the grafting of the party apparatus onto a peasant mass base. Mao Tse-tung, who devised the new strategy, had worked in the peasant movement in the 1920s and lacked strong ties with the Soviet Union. In the discontent of the peasantry, particularly in the question of land and the tension between the remnants of the rural gentry and the agricultural workers, Mao found a potential revolutionary force far stronger than anything that existed in China's infant industrial system. In theory, Mao always insisted that the Communist Party was a proletarian party, but in fact he carried out his revolution among the peasants. Orientation toward the countryside freed the party of the need to control urban areas, where they were outclassed militarily by the modern army of the new Nationalist government. A second element in the Maoist formula was the development of a new model of participatory partisan warfare. Drawing on a rich heritage of popular literature about military strategy and peasant rebellion, as well as the practical experience of former bandits, warlord troops, and Kuomintang elements, Mao and his military associate Chu Teh built a partisan force in the mountains of south China in the early 1930s. Essential to their organization was the insistence that the military foster popular support by respecting property and persons, by paying for supplies, and by frequently helping with farming. The peasants, in turn, were encouraged to view the Red Army as their own army, to supply it, and to provide it with intelligence and sanctuary. It was well understood that the party could not survive in the countryside if it did not control its base area without popular support for its military arm. The notion of an army that would "serve the people" was an important element in the Communist image, well amplified by skillful propaganda.

In the Maoist model of revolutionary warfare there was no line between political and military elements, the two were always combined. Guerrilla warfare involved mobile action by lightly armed bands against heavily equipped conventional forces tied to supply lines and fixed urban bases. The guerrillas had to conceptualize war as an activity of fluid movement in an extended spacial plain in which the enemy could be drawn out from his sanctuary, isolated, and overwhelmed in a surprise attack. Great emphasis was placed on mobility and intelligence about the enemy's movements, often relayed to the guerrillas by children and old people in the villages. The essence of guerrilla warfare was the ability to disperse forces and avoid contact until conditions were favorable and then very quickly to assemble a force superior in numbers to that of the enemy and to strike. These tactics demanded much more than simple obedience from the Communist soldiers. The leaders of even the smallest units had to exercise considerable initiative in decision making. The recruiting and training of guerrilla forces involved extensive mobilization among the Chinese populace as innumerable individuals assumed new leadership roles and mastered skills of decision making, communication, and instruction. Mao Tse-tung himself became a tactician, lecturing to his officer corps on basic tactics and formulating the principles of mobile warfare in simple, pithy terms that could be understood, remembered, and applied by illiterate peasant soldiers. In the most famous statement of guerrilla strategy he reduced the basic principles to four sentences, each consisting of four Chinese characters:

(When the) enemy advances, we retreat.
(When the) enemy halts, we harass.
(When the) enemy (seeks to) avoid (battle), we attack.
(When the) enemy retreats, we pursue.[2]

On the political side of his thought, Mao displayed a genius for placing military considerations in a broader context of a long-range appraisal of foreign and domestic conditions at a strategic level. By keeping explicit the distinction between short-term and long-term goals, it was possible for Mao to maneuver party policy pragmatically without abandoning basic ideological values. The best example of Communist flexibility was the policy pursued during the war against Japan. By the summer of 1937, when the Japanese army launched a direct invasion of the central Chinese provinces, the Chinese Communist Party and the Kuomintang were obliged to suspend their hostilities and form a second united front in which the Communists pledged to support the Three People's Principles. During this period the Communist Party pursued a moderate policy with regard to property and other economic questions and stressed the need for cooperation against the foreign aggressor. A United Front Department was set up within the party to handle relations with nonparty groups. Party influence was extended by devices like the three-thirds system (1940), which allowed organizations to be made up of one-third Communist, one-third Kuomintang, and one-third unaffiliated members. Arrangements such as this gave the Communists an opportunity to compete legitimately with the Nationalists and to outperform them. The Communists appealed to all of the middle class and professional elements, consigning only the most exploitative of the big landlords, speculators, and collaborators to the category of those who had to be attacked or restrained.

So rapidly did party membership grow during the war years that the leadership had difficulty maintaining discipline in ideological matters. There were 40,000 party members in 1937 and 200,000 a year later. By 1943 membership swelled to 800,000; by 1945 it was 1.2 million. The growth was stimulated by the war and by the fact that the party was nominally at peace with the Nationalist government. Mao Tse-tung, emerging as an original theorist, called for a uniquely Chinese form of Marxism-Leninism. But those who were content to defend China in the name of the Three People's Principles were disabused. In his essay *On the New Democracy* (1940), Mao reiterated the conception of the Chinese revolution as a two-stage affair, involving first a democratic struggle for independence to be followed by a socialist revolution. The New Democracy was only a minimum program; the maximum program for the future was still socialism. Mao's explicit statement of the transitional nature of the moderate policy was part of an effort to tighten ideological control and indoctrinate new members. During the same period Liu Shao-ch'i wrote his booklet *How To Be A Good Communist,* stressing the importance of personal morality (with direct references to Confucianism) and submission to the authority of the party.

After 1940 relations between the Communist and Nationalist parties again became strained and armed clashes took place. The Nationalists, isolated in southwest China, held many of their best divisions out of battle against the day when the Japanese would be defeated and the civil war would recommence. Meanwhile, the Communists expanded their operations in the countryside throughout central China, where they moved around and between the Japanese strongpoints. By war's end they controlled better than 80 million people in more than a dozen liberated pockets scattered across north China. Their army (900,000 men and women in 1945), which was highly rated by American observers for its

2. Quoted in Edgar Snow, *Red Star over China* (Grove Press, 1968), p. 159. Repinted by permission of Grove Press, Inc. Copyright © 1938, 1944 by Random House, Inc.; © 1968 by Edgar Snow; 1961 by John K. Fairbanks (Introduction).

morale, discipline, and leadership, crushed the larger American-equipped Nationalist forces within four years.

The People's Republic of China established in October of 1949 embodied the transitional strategy of the New Democracy. Included at this initial stage in Mao's definition of the "people"—who enjoyed the right of electing their own government—were the working class, peasants, petty bourgeoisie, and national bourgeoisie (capitalists). Only the worst reactionaries were to be deprived of their rights by the people's democratic dictatorship. In institutional terms, the instability that has characterized Chinese government since the turn of the century has continued. The new government was established in 1949 by the Chinese People's Consultative Conference, a collection of representatives, selected under Communist Party influence, from many sectors of Chinese society, including political groups, racial minorities, army units, women, youth, workers, overseas Chinese, and the like. During the first five years, as the new government took shape, the country continued to be divided into six military regions, which had been set up during the civil war. By 1954 a constitution was enacted and the transition to civil government was complete. Authority was vested in an elected National People's Congress, which was supposed to be convened at regular intervals. The chairman of its Standing Committee was the chief of state. The central executive organ of the government is the State Council, headed by the premier, who oversees the massive administrative apparatus of staff offices, ministries and their subordinate departments, bureaus and sections out in the provinces. This bureaucratic core at Peking consists of more than 100,000 persons divided into numerous civil service grades, and through its service ministries (e.g., Machine Building), patterned after those of the Soviet Union, it employs more than 19 million persons.

Parallel to the government and interpenetrating it at all levels is the Communist Party. Through its own functionally differentiated departments the party can monitor and guide the direction of government policy. Party members, who may make up as much as 80 percent of the staff of higher government organs, assure that decision-making in their agencies will be responsive to party directives. Authority within the party flows in the manner of democratic centralism, from the membership to the elected Party Congress and again downward to the membership. The Central Committee of the Party Congress, consisting in 1973 of 195 members and 124 alternates, is the most powerful group in China. As its chairman, Mao Tse-tung was the party's leader. Within the Central Committee there is a Politburo of some two dozen members and alternates, and within that there exists a Standing Committee of about nine members. It is the Standing Committee and the Politburo that make the day-to-day decisions for the party. The Central Committee can be called together in plenary sessions for major decisions of policy, but this has happened with less than annual regularity. Congresses, which mark major junctures in the party's history, are very infrequent. A party constitution was adopted at the Seventh Congress in 1945 and modified by the Eighth Congress, which convened in 1956. In 1969 a Ninth Congress enacted a new constitution, which in turn was revised by the Tenth Congress in 1973.

The organization of the Communist Party, with a first secretary, a congress, an executive committee, a secretariat, and functional departments, is repeated at regional, provincial, district, and county levels. Membership increased from 1.2 million in 1945 to more than 28 million by 1973, drawn from all segments of Chinese society and organized into more than a million primary cellular units. The 500,000 members at the county level and above constitute the national political elite. They are active in a broad spectrum of national affairs and benefit from the information and reports that flow through party channels.

A notable aspect of political consolidation in China is the fact that since 1949 power has been shared by a triumvirate of national hierarchies—the party, the government, and the army—interacting in various combinations. From 1949 to 1952 the military, called the People's Liberation Army, dominated through the military administrative regions, which exercised a sort of martial law. The years 1953-57 saw the emergence of a bureaucratic government, which instituted centralized control of economic development through five-year plans. In the same period the army became professionalized, bureaucratic, and sharply stratified along the lines of the Soviet military. In 1958-60 the Communist Party seized direct control of economic policy, instituting a number of radical policies including the formation of communes and the Great Leap Forward, while the army underwent a shake-up that eventually eliminated ranks and returned the military to the more politically conscious but less professional model of the early guerrilla phase. The failure of the Great Leap Forward led to a moderate recovery policy in economic affairs presided over by Liu Shao-ch'i, who now replaced Mao Tse-tung as head of state. In the early 1960s the People's Liberation Army, under the command of Lin Piao, took the initiative in fostering a more radical ideological line than that of the Communist Party itself and in promoting the thought of Mao Tse-tung. From 1966 to 1969 China was swept by the Great Proletarian Cultural Revolution in which the Communist Party became the focus of criticism as Liu Shao-ch'i and many of his followers were attacked. In the confusion of the Cultural Revolution Mao Tse-tung was supported by the army, which literally took over administration of the country. In 1969 military men occupied a majority of provincial leadership positions and Lin Piao was named in the party constitution as the successor to Mao Tse-tung. There followed a period of party rebuilding in which the damage of the Cultural Revolution was repaired and Premier Chou En-lai (1898-1976) guided the affairs of the nation in the absence of a chief of state. In 1971 Lin Piao, later to be accused of plotting against Mao Tse-tung, was killed in a plane crash, and the top military leadership was promptly purged. The Tenth Party Congress in 1973 formalized the purge of the Lin Piao faction and restored many victims of the Cultural Revolution, but there were strong indications of persisting conflict among the top leaders. In 1975 a National People's Congress adopted a new state constitution embodying the lessons of the Cultural Revolution.

The significance of these political events from the perspective of political consolidation is that the new political order in China, despite the fact that it is a single-party state, is far from monolithic. There are in fact three power hierarchies, each one of which has shown itself capable of seizing the initiative. The Great Leap and the Cultural Revolution have established precedents for radical policy shifts and factional struggles within the existing framework of institutions short of internal warfare. Purges, with the exception of Lin Piao, have generally involved removal of an individual from office, discrediting his actions, and compelling him to undergo ideological reform and have frequently been followed by the individual's restoration to office.

The Mobilization of Chinese Society

The consolidation of authority in the hands of the Communist leadership has created a greater centralization of power in China than exists in perhaps any other nation, and certainly greater power than the imperial state exercised, because the new leadership concerns itself with a wider range of issues and extends its influence deeper into social and personal life. At the same time that authority has been centralized, the sphere of political participation has been drastically extended. The characteristic of political participation in China which contrasts most fundamentally with political participation in a democratic or representative system is the fact that in China participation follows rather than precedes decision making. In a representative system, people participate through voting, by electing representatives, and by lobbying with them to influence the determination of policy. In the Chinese system policies are determined by the leadership, which guides rather than follows public opinion, and are then relayed to the populace, which participates in the implementation.

The technique through which the Communist Party interacts with the populace is called the mass line. Developed in the 1940s, the mass line embodies the principle of "from the masses, to the masses." Party activists—cadres—study conditions from among the people, collecting information and soliciting opinions. This information is then relayed to higher authorities in the party, who use the unsystematic data in identifying problems and formulating new policies. Systematically stated in Marxist terminology, a decision then becomes part of the party line, to be relayed back down the party hierarchy for implementation. The carrying out of party policy involves an educational process in which the masses are informed of the policy, persuaded of its correctness, obliged to study it, and guided in its execution. The crucial element in the acceptance of the party line is the degree to which the population is convinced that what the party wants corresponds to its own real interests. The crucial element in the execution of policy is the delicate relationship between the cadres and the masses. These individuals must be both selfless and dynamic in their role so as to enjoy both respect from the populace and trust from the party. Being insensitive to public opinion (commandism) or following it too meekly (tailism) can diminish their effectiveness as leaders.

Participation is compulsory. All adults belong to small groups, which meet regularly either at their place of work or their place of residence. These discussion groups constitute a forum through which everyone in the society becomes linked up to the leadership. Group study, be it in basic literacy, political affairs, or hygiene, involves the individual in a public commitment to self-improvement along with his or her closest associates. Another of the transmission belts the party uses to communicate its messages to the population are mass organizations that reach specific sectors of the population, like women's organizations, labor federations, and youth groups. Often the policies the party leadership wishes to implement are orchestrated in the form of a campaign utilizing the press, radio, and posters to amplify the message and whip up interest to a fever pitch. During a big ideological campaign people are obliged to attend many meetings, to study new directives, and to change their habits or confess their mistakes. As pressure builds up people who have done things wrong or who hold an incorrect point of view may be selected as the targets for criticism and subjected to public humiliation.

Social mobilization in China has wrenched the individual out of the old particularistic ties of family, clan, village, and guild and refocused his or her loyalties to community and nation. Collectivization of agriculture and socialization of industry have taken ownership and management away from hereditary groups and made such matters public business. Consequently, the individual now finds that the work team and the street committee are the groups that hold power over his or her life. Status here is determined by achievement, industry, skill, and productivity, not by birth and age as it had been in the old society. Marriages are no longer arranged to maximize the economic interests of the older generation. With free choice in marriage protected by law and with the elimination of prostitution, concubinage, and the sale of children, the nuclear family of husband, wife, and children has been strengthened. The emancipation of Chinese women to full legal rights and their integration into the work force has been a dramatic transformation. While the liberation of the individual from the constraints of traditional institutions has meant an increase in both physical and occupational mobility, it has not meant the development of individualism. The sanctions for social change in China have been the national and the communal good and a strong preoccupation with social justice. The standards of goodness and justice in contemporary China remain collective standards, much as they were in Confucian China. Whereas a young couple is now free to marry if the partners so choose, they may be obliged by peer pressure to delay their marriage until they are in their late twenties so that their early years may be devoted to public service.

One interesting aspect of the social transformation in China revolves about the question of social mobility. Since the Communist leadership identifies itself with the proletarian

14.4 Small group discussion by women in a Chinese factory. Group discussion has played an important part in mobilization and education in China. Courtesy: Magnum Photos.

class, it conceives its mission to involve the destruction of the remaining power of feudal and capitalist elements. Consequently, class background has been retained as a label adhering to people in the second and third generation, inhibiting the careers of those who belong to landlord families and aiding those from the working class. In another context, mobility is limited by the extensive use of group pressure and public opinion to assure political conformity in a manner that echoes the traditional concern with "face." Mao Tse-tung's use of his own thought and personal authority to encourage criticism of his opponents during the Cultural Revolution made an authoritarian appeal reminiscent of the old patriarchal values enshrined in Confucian doctrine. Elements such as these raise questions about the degree to which traditional orientations may survive in new guises.

Economic Development in Agriculture and Industry

China's economic development was severely retarded during the first half of the twentieth century by internal disorder, foreign exploitation, and lack of investment. The population, which numbered 583 million in 1953, was one of the poorest and worst fed segments of humankind before the Communist Party came to power. The Nationalist government during its brief tenure in Nanking (1927-37) was unable to improve the economic situation. The Kuomintang territorial base included only the central provinces along the Yangtze, especially Kiangsu and Chekiang on the coast. Tax collections were severely limited by the government's inability to control many areas. Fundamental tax reform was never carried out, and large portions of the government budget were met through borrowing. Governmental control of key economic sectors like banking, and the division of these enterprises among various cliques in the leadership, led to the manipulation of bond flotation for private gain. Military expenditures were given first priority by Chiang Kai-shek, who was intent on crushing his opponents. Consequently, more than half of the budget was devoted to debt service and the military. A number of small-scale developmental projects in health, education, agriculture, and industry (e.g., the Chinese industrial cooperatives) were attempted during the Nationalist period on a demonstration basis with little impact on the overall economy. Experience gained in these token efforts was put to use after 1949.

More important than governmental programs in China's early industrial development was the accumulated heritage of a century of foreign enterprises and programs in China. In the treaty ports and coastal centers much technical and managerial expertise was acquired and light industrial equipment was inherited in substantial quantities, which contributed directly to industrial growth after 1949. In Manchuria the Japanese developed China's largest coal, iron, and steel complex and invested in railroads and heavy industry. Taiwan, too, was developed by the Japanese, who improved the railways, port facilities, and power industry, but primarily to facilitate the export of agricultural products, notably rice and sugar. Another influence that deserves mention is that of military organizations. European military advisers were active in China from the middle of the nineteenth century. During the decades from the 1920s through the 1950s, however, hundreds of thousands, even millions, of Chinese were exposed to foreign military advisers, soldiers, equipment, and techniques of organization. In the 1920s, Soviet advisers trained the new Kuomintang armies. In the 1930s, German officers and equipment were used against the Communists, while in the 1940s the Japanese and American armies recruited and trained vast numbers of Chinese and left behind the mountains of equipment that were used in the Chinese civil war. The Korean War of the early 1950s provided the Soviet Union with an opportunity to outfit, train, and reorganize the armed forces of the People's Republic of China. The experience thus accumulated in the use of aircraft, motor vehicles, radios, and other equipment must be seen as an important infusion of technology.

Centrally directed economic development was not undertaken in China until the establishment of a new order in 1949. The Communist leadership was able to institute effective economic programs because it had the power to drive out foreign influences and to enforce its policies and because it raised capital internally by eliminating vested interests. The first step in mobilizing China's economic resources was a transformation of the property system. This involved a prolonged social revolution that assaulted the privileged positions of the property owning classes while at the same time utilizing elements of those classes in programs of reconstruction.

Class struggle was a common element in both urban and rural development. In the cities, industrial and commercial establishments were taken over by the government but their former owners and managers, recognized as part of the "people" under the democratic dictatorship, were kept on, often with compensation, because their expertise was essential. The power of the urban bourgeoisie was broken by mass campaigns aimed at corrupt practices. Inflation, long beyond the control of the corrupt Nationalist government, was brought in line by drying up the money supply. Businessmen were organized into groups to raise money and meet quotas for buying bonds. This set them to watching each other and to identifying hidden wealth and tax evasion. At the height of the struggle against corrupt elements, "tiger hunts" were launched in the cities to expose the worst abuses, and many businessmen were driven to suicide or were tried in makeshift people's courts.

In the countryside the population was categorized into six strata: landlords, rich peasants, middle peasants, poor peasants, agricultural laborers, and vagrants. Land reform got underway in 1946 when the Central Committee declared a return to a radical land policy. By 1950 the rural revolution had swept the entire country in a social upheaval that released the pent-up frustrations of the peasantry with explosive violence and on a scale greater than any other revolution. In the first phase the landlords were designated as a class to be eliminated. As the Red Army secured an area, cadres moved in and began the work of classifying the population by surveying the land and setting up a peasant association and a militia unit to exercise control. Peasants were called together in emotion-charged meetings to verbalize their grievances against the old landlords and their agents. In these "speak bitterness" sessions, the peasants decided the fates of their old tormentors, sometimes putting them to death, usually dividing their grain and possessions. Land held by clans, temples, schools, and landlords was measured out and divided among the entire village population so that every family had some land. Mutual-aid teams were organized to make more efficient use of manpower, share tools and equipment, and to give the peasants experience in group enterprise.

The developmental significance of land reform was that it eliminated rent and tax evasion and allowed the central government for the first time in more than a century to efficiently collect the excess product from agriculture. The rate of investment grew rapidly, from 9 percent in 1950 to more than 25 percent of the gross domestic product by 1955. China launched an ambitious industrialization program stressing heavy industry and drawing on the technical assistance of Soviet advisers. Alarmed that China was drifting in the same direction as the Soviet Union, toward a situation in which a bureaucratic managerial class would prevail at the cost of revolutionary values, Mao shifted course. The problems were, first, that the urban areas were developing more rapidly and at the expense of the rural areas, and second, that the educated bourgeois elements in the cities and the rich peasants in the countryside were increasing their influence at the expense of workers and peasants.

In response to these trends the Communist Party intervened vigorously in economic affairs, particularly in the transformation of agriculture. In the years 1955-57 agricultural workers' cooperatives were formed in rural areas. In an effort to extend central political control into the countryside, the number of administrative villages was reduced and the work force was organized into brigades (twenty to forty families) and teams (seven to eight families) for collective labor. Land parcels were now combined into large fields and agricultural labor was performed by teams so that economies of scale could be attained. The state set production targets centrally, and purchasing agreements, loans, and tools were used to encourage villagers to form cooperatives. Although land plots were joined, rewards were initially based on the shares contributed; later, reward was calculated on labor alone. This shift reduced the advantage earlier enjoyed by the rich peasants.

The middle peasants and poor peasants became the target in 1958 when the party moved to a still more radical policy and combined China's 752,000 cooperatives to form 24,000 giant people's communes. Each commune was a multipurpose social cell with a full range of functions: agriculture, industry, education, and trade. In an effort to fully mobilize the labor potential of the people, private plots of land were eliminated and housekeeping efficiencies like dining halls, dormitories, and nurseries were introduced on a large scale to free more women for work in the fields. The communes were the agricultural side of the Great Leap Forward, a heroic and willful effort to defy the conventional wisdom of economic development by making a maximum infusion of labor and ideological incentives into an equation that was short of capital, equipment, raw materials, and technical expertise. In some projects, like dam and canal building, massed laborers performed impressively, using tools and techniques little changed from imperial times. In other areas, notably the local production of iron and steel, the technology was too complex and the products were often unuseable. In agriculture, the effort to centralize control and the intense pressure to overreport production statistics led to massive confusion, which was compounded by local resistance and natural disasters. The result was catastrophic. Crop failures were of such magnitude that the entire population was forced to reduce food consumption to bare subsistence levels for two years. Only rationing and tight discipline staved off famine. Economic development was set back as much as ten years, although precise measurement is impossible because statistics have not been issued since the falsifications of the Great Leap enthusiasm.

Retreat from the Great Leap led to the restoration of private plots and various incentives in agriculture. The communes were reduced in size, and while they remain as administrative entities, it is the work team, a segment of the old natural village, that became the most basic decision-making unit, returning considerable local autonomy to the peasantry. In the 1960s a better balance between industry and agriculture—"walking on two legs"—emerged, and more regional and local initiative could be discerned in economic planning. By the 1970s a substantial rise in the standard of living was apparent to all observers. Chinese clearly enjoy a level of security in terms of basics like food, clothing, shelter, and medical services which is in marked contrast to comparable Asian states like India and Indonesia. Technical achievements like atomic weapons, missiles, satellites, and computers are indications that China is on the road to building an advanced industrial sector.

The basic division over which development model China should follow has animated Chinese politics for the last two decades: either toward greater political consciousness and continued social revolution of the Maoist model or toward all-out industrialization under the expert management of a Soviet-style bureaucracy. One formulation of the debate has been the controversy over the proper balance between "redness"—that is, political consciousness—and "expertness." The Maoist view, which grows out of Mao Tse-tung's personal identification with the peasantry and the party's early experience in Yenan, reflects the concern that the peasantry, which still constitutes some 80 percent of the Chinese population, not be left behind in the process of development. In Yenan during the darkest days of the war against Japan, the party survived a blockage and Japanese offensive by mobilizing the peasantry to increase production by innovation and maximum utilization of meager resources. In this model of self-reliant, participatory development, greater emphasis is placed on the cultural and political advancement of the masses than on the further elaboration of the advanced industrial sector.

Strenuous efforts have been made in China to bridge the gap between the city and the country. Road building, advances in communications, the creation of a national market, and the improvement of organization at all levels have ended the economic isolation of the rural villages alluded to in Chapter 12. However, even a drastic expansion of the educational system, restructuring it to provide a basic rudimentary education to the widest possible number of students, and a vigorous attack on illiteracy, which has included the standardization of a limited vocabulary of simplified characters, have not yet sufficed to raise China's massive rural population to the literacy levels of Japan or other industrialized countries. Rather than allow laborers to move freely from the countryside to the cities in the classic pattern of industrialization, the Chinese have chosen to curtail such movement. Numerous programs have sent urban students and office workers to the countryside to experience rural conditions but also to diffuse expertise outward and downward. If this approach does indeed prove to be a viable alternative to unchecked urbanization, and not simply a transitional effort to reduce the costs of housing an urban population, the Chinese experience will have the most profound implications for development elsewhere in Asia, Africa, and Latin America.

A central concern in the Great Proletarian Cultural Revolution was criticism of authority and the opening of decision making to popular participation. Leading figures in the party were accused of "taking the capitalist road," and throughout China "two lines" emerged as people debated the social implications of the different strategies of development. Although Mao Tse-tung's views prevailed in the Cultural Revolution, it remains to be seen whether his preference for participatory activism will continue to have powerful advocates long after his departure from the scene.

5. CUMULATIVE FORCES FOR CHANGE IN MODERN JAPAN

Of all the areas in Asia, Japan stands out as the earliest and, at least until the Communist revolution in China, the most striking case of a society responding to the challenge of the modern era through a radical restructuring of institutions and reorientation of human attitudes. Efforts to explain Japan's rapid transformation focused initially on the wholesale reforms of the Meiji period (1868-1912), which created the political structure for a modern nation-state and mobilized the populace behind a concerted effort at industrialization. Recent historical scholarship, however, has produced considerable evidence that would push the beginnings of this transformation back into the preceding Tokugawa period, thereby rendering the pace of modernization somewhat less rapid than it was previously thought to be. It is thus important to stress the positive legacy of the Tokugawa "feudal" tradition when examining the success of the Meiji reforms. World War I was a convenient watershed for marking the beginning of a second major stage in this modern transformation. In the decades following 1918 the forces set in motion by the Meiji leaders gathered great momentum, carrying Japanese society along channels and through currents only dimly foreseen by the early modernizers and with a speed that was very often bewildering to their successors who were caught up in them. The confrontation with American military might in the Pacific War of the 1940s proved a disaster of cataclysmic proportions, and it is common to view the Occupation of 1945-52 as beginning yet a third stage in Japan's modernization. Without denying the very great changes wrought by Occupation reforms, it can be noted that the most lasting of these were those that built upon well-developed prewar trends with Japanese social and cultural life.

The Trend toward Secularization

In discussing the origins of modern Japanese nationalism (see Chapter 13), we have seen the process by which the status quo was desanctified as political thinkers and samurai activists liberated themselves from orthodox principles. A similar long-term trend toward reducing the realm of the sacred and expanding the sphere believed amenable to human control can be seen at work within the larger society during the late Tokugawa period.

The cultural value system of Tokugawa Japan, while originally heavily oriented toward tradition in many areas, had long given ample sanction to this-worldly action in the economic sphere. It stressed the obligation to strive toward long-range improvement through the manipulation of the environment in a planned, goal-oriented fashion. Some analysts have seen in this achievement orientation a strong analogy with the Protestant ethic as described by the German sociologist Max Weber. In the Japanese case, however, the emphasis was on the individual's repayment of obligations owed to the family and community rather than on the salvation of the individual soul. It was to this norm of achievement for the sake of the collectivity that statesmen, editorialists, and schoolmasters sought to appeal in their efforts to mobilize the nation behind the Meiji reforms. Western values as exemplified in Benjamin Franklin's *Autobiography* and Samuel Smiles' *Self-Help* helped to stir ambitious youth in the 1870s, but the ideas of the modernizers won their greatest audience when couched in more readily understandable, traditional terms of duty to society.

While the abstract concept of progress remained for the most part unarticulated in the Tokugawa period, it, too, was easily grasped when introduced in the Meiji period. The long experience in many villages as well as cities with economic growth achieved through innovations in agriculture and business had prepared the ground for the acceptance of more widespread social change. This is not to say that there was no conservative reaction against the Meiji reformer's attack on tradition. The Meiji modernizers blunted the reaction against their policies by invoking even more ancient historical myths, notably the Shinto religious sanctions for the imperial will, while the most entrenched ideological opponents to Western science—the Buddhist and neo-Confucian establishments—proved vulnerable to the charge that they after all were alien in origin. Beginning in the 1890s and reaching a crescendo in the 1930s, there were vehement nationalist attacks on trends within Japanese society, charging that Japan was in danger of losing its cultural identity and becoming a poor imitation of the West. But the most influential of these critics proclaimed a faith in progress and in modernity, their quest being not to turn back the clock or freeze change but rather to find that particular mix of modern institutions that would be most appropriate to Japan's cultural heritage. Like the Meiji leaders themselves, they sought a uniquely Japanese path to the future.

While the Meiji leaders appealed to indigenous values to gain support for national goals, they turned to Western knowledge for the means to national progress. From the 1840s Japan had been importing Western technology to bolster its military defenses; after the 1868 Restoration this trickle became a flood and determined efforts were made to acquire the broad scientific base as well as knowledge of the political, social, and economic principles underlying Western advancement. The small pool of Japanese specialists in things Western—some of whom had come to be employed by the Tokugawa shogunate in its final years—was mobilized by the new Meiji government, and foreign specialists in a wide range of fields from engineering to music were hired to advise on policy and teach in the educational system. An elite state institution of higher education—now the University of Tokyo—was created shortly after the Restoration, with a curriculum devoted primarily to Western learning. Its top graduates were assured positions in the various government bureaus, while the most outstanding were sent abroad at state expense for advanced training. A number of private colleges, especially Fukuzawa Yukichi's Keio Academy and Okuma Shigenobu's Waseda, acquired great prestige for the quality of their Western education, but the Imperial University of Tokyo and its sister institution in Kyoto remained preeminent. In the early years the textbooks, teachers, and even the languages of instruction were predominantly foreign. With the return of the first group of trainees from overseas the Meiji leaders soon phased out this early dependency, and by the turn of the century Japan had a substantial reservoir of domestic expertise with a growing sophistication in the style of scholarship pioneered in the Western world. Indeed, it began re-exporting Western knowledge through the Chinese students who came there to study. It should be pointed out that the neo-Confucian heritage of the Tokugawa period, far from being a necessarily inhibiting factor, must be seen in a positive light, for the majority of this new educated elite in the first generation was drawn from samurai families where the neo-Confucian stress on reason and study were formative elements.

The assimilation of Western knowledge among the new elite took place with remarkable speed. Equally significant, however, was the establishment of a compulsory, tax-supported coeducational elementary school system through which these ideas could be disseminated to the middle and lower classes. By 1907, 97 percent of all children six to eleven years old were enrolled in school. In addition to basic literacy, practical lessons in arithmetic, science, and hygiene were combined with the teaching of patriotic morality. Education beyond the primary stage remained limited. The bulk of those who did gain access to secondary schools were trained to fill the ranks of intermediate technicians or lower echelon administrative roles in private enterprises and public organizations. Only a small percent, almost exclusively males, reached the level of higher education. In public education the Meiji leaders were again building on the Tokugawa legacy. It is estimated that by 1868 some 40 percent of all males and 10 percent of females had received formal schooling either in the various domain academies or in the commoners schools in the villages and urban neighborhoods.

Political Consolidation in the New Nation-State

Public education is an excellent example of the manner in which the Meiji leaders utilized the power of the new central government to reshape key institutions within their society. The process of consolidating political power and creating a central government out of the old Tokugawa decentralized system, however, was not an easy one despite the rapid pace with which the transition was made. Governmental power under the old system was divided among over two hundred domains, the larger of which had a long tradition of autonomy under the overall hegemony of the shogunate. Moreover, many of the participants in the Restoration movement expected the integrity of the domains to be preserved in some form or another. The new leaders were quite sensitive to such domain loyalties, and in the initial phase immediately after the fall of the Tokugawa a system of representation based on domain units was experimented with.

In 1869, however, the first step was taken toward the creation of a unified central administration capable of directing national reforms. Key men from Satsuma and Choshu, conscious of the difficulties of coordination and fostering national unity given the existing political structure and aware of the centralized bureaucratic models in the West, in China, and in Japan's own historical tradition, persuaded their domain leaders to relinquish their legal claims to autonomy in the name of imperial authority. Once the other powerful domains had followed suit, the Meiji reformers maneuvered carefully behind a facade of the throne and figureheads drawn from the old elite to create an administrative apparatus designed to extend central control into local and regional areas. The rural communities, which had performed many of the actual functions of social control and tax collection in the Tokugawa period, were reorganized into administrative villages, which in turn were grouped with nearby towns into counties. The country as a whole was divided into prefectures, with prefectural governors and important functionaries at lesser levels owing their appointments directly to the Home Ministry in Tokyo. By the end of the century an elaborate system of ministries, bureaus, and offices had evolved to oversee such matters as police, health, transportation, and education, as well as critical aspects of economic life.

The long tradition of bureaucratic administration in the Tokugawa period, despite its decentralized character, and the large pool of former samurai officials made this transition less formidable than it might otherwise have been. In Japanese political theory the ruler had always properly concerned himself with all facets of his subjects's life: religious, cultural, economic, and social. The major change lay in the fact that the new Meiji state was far more systematic and efficient in practice. The health, welfare, and education of the populace as a whole were now directly affected by policy formation and administrative supervision from the center.

Parallel to the establishment of a national civil service was the creation of a central military system. In the early years the new government had to rely on the samurai armies of the loyalist domains. The danger of such dependency was clearly revealed in 1873 when Saigo Takamori (1828-77) of Satsuma, Itagaki Taisuke (1836-1919) of Tosa, and other restorationist leaders bolted from the coalition government and were followed home from Tokyo by a significant proportion of the Imperial Guard, which had formed the core of the government's forces. In the next three years there were several major local rebellions led by samurai reacting in large part to their loss of privileged status and the government's decision to create a conscript army. In 1877 Saigo led his Satsuma supporters into a full-scale battle with the Tokyo government, hoping to pitch the country into a civil war that would bring about change in leadership. By this time, however, the proponents of a modern conscript army had succeeded in building a military force both loyal enough and strong enough to destroy Saigo's rebel samurai. The new government, while seriously tested in the nine-month struggle, proved that it had the coercive force to back its policies. Two decades later it was powerful enough to win Meiji Japan's first international conflict by defeating the Chinese army and navy in 1895.

The critical political issues after 1877 had less to do with the dismantling of the old political structure than with the question of what segments of society were to participate in the new system of central decision making and how that system was to be structured on a more formal basis. Defections and natural attrition had reduced the loose collective leadership of early Meiji to a smaller group of influential individuals functioning as an informal oligarchy overseeing in the name of the emperor the growing bureaucracy. In opposition, Itagaki Taisuke and others who felt shut out of positions of power agitated vigorously for the creation of a popularly elected national assembly on the model of Western parliaments. In 1881 Okuma Shigenobu (1838-1922) precipitated a crisis within the inner circle by advocating the immediate adoption of English-style government; and after forcing Okuma to withdraw into the opposition camp, the Meiji leaders announced their intention of formulating a written constitution. Ito Hirobumi (1841-1909) and Yamagata Aritomo (1838-1922), who had emerged as the two most powerful members of the ruling circle, shared their opponents' view that Japan required a set of basic constitutional guidelines, primarily because of their belief that this would promote political stability and facilitate the task of of mobilizing the populace behind a national effort. Ito in particular apparently also shared the opposition's conviction that constitutional government with popular participation represented a higher stage of social evolution and thus a source of strength to Western societies. Yet another consideration was the prestige to be gained in foreign relations by adopting Western-style political forms.

On the other hand, Yamagata and others within the government were opposed to entrusting the masses with ultimate power and to turning over national leadership to partisan politicians, who might place regional interests or personal ambition above the good of the country. Hence, the Meiji Constitution, when finally promulgated in 1889, carefully combined German political practices with English parliamentary principles to curtail the amount of power to be exercised by the new bicameral Diet. Crucial was the absence of any provision for cabinet responsibility to the majority of the elected members of the lower house, thus permitting a small group acting in the name of the throne to appoint the prime minister and the heads of the ministries. Moreover, suffrage was extended only to those males who met certain limited qualifications as taxpayers.

Despite these precautions, once the new Diet received imperial sanction the stubborn determination of Itagaki's Liberal Party and Okuma's Progressive Party, plus the astute use of the limited budgetary power that had been granted the lower house, gradually expanded the influence of Asia's first elected parliament. After a decade of frustrated efforts to overwhelm the opposition in the Diet, Yamagata and his faction were persuaded by Ito to compromise and attempt to work through the Diet itself.

While it was true that the Meiji political parties were on the whole elitist with only a very limited popular base, nevertheless, by 1914, some significant segments of the larger populace had been integrated into the new political system. Rural landowners, some of whom had provided crucial support to the original movement for an elected assembly, utilized the franchise and their position as local elite to directly influence government agricultural policy. The new business community, while small and heavily dependent upon government aid, worked behind the scenes of Diet politics to further the interests of commerce and industry. Through the new media—the press—journalists and intellectuals participated in the often heated political debate. Thus by the eve of the First World War the foundations of a modern political community within the framework of a centralized nation-state had been laid.

Economic Development: Early Industrialization

The preoccupation of the Meiji leaders with consolidating power in a central government was in part due to their perceptions of the need for a concerted national effort at industrialization. The governmental machinery of the modern nation-state was to play a crucial role in the mobilizing and allocating of economic resources in the effort. For the most part those resources were internal. Except for two occasions in the first twenty-five years, the Meiji leaders were deterred from looking outside for capital by high interest rates and the fear of intervention should they default in repayment. Indeed, one important spur to industrialization was the need to repay shogunate and domain debts to foreigners accumulated during the decades of the Tokugawa period. Given the impoverished state of the shogunate and domain treasures in 1868, it was also clear to the Meiji leaders that they could not continue to purchase the Western armaments essential to national defense unless they could expand exports. Nor, in the absence of tariff barriers to Western imports, could they hope to stabilize the economy unless competitive goods could be produced at home. Finally, the Meiji leaders were quite sensitive to the social instability and the threat to their continuance in power caused by the economic plight of the lower peasantry and the lower samurai class. Gainful employment had to be found for this work force.

Modern factories were seen as a solution to all these problems. From 1873, after a large segment of the Meiji leaders returned from an inspection tour of the Western world, they committed much of their energies to a broad-based program of industrial development.

The initial hurdles were great. Meiji Japan had inherited from the previous period a highly productive agricultural sector capable of yielding a sizeable surplus beyond basic consumption needs, but the old tax system was ineffectual. In 1873 the government initiated a sweeping land tax reform, funneling taxes directly to Tokyo and assuring the government of a predictable annual revenue in cash based on more realistic and uniform assessments of land values. While the resulting pattern of land ownership and tax burden favored the affluent peasant over the rural poor and served to further increase tenancy, the new tax system did enable the central government to tap the one major source of internal capital for investment in industrial development.

In the initial phase, which extended into the 1880s, the government also found it necessary to import industrial technology, both in the form of machinery and foreign advisers, and to manage the new factories itself. It also took the lead in establishing modern banking facilities, constructing new railroads, and building a merchant marine. The Tokugawa commercial elite, for all its economic power under the old system, failed to meet the immediate need for entrepreneurial leadership in the new era. In part this was due to conservatism. Industrial technology, international trade, and maritime shipping were activities for which the Osaka and Tokyo merchant class had little background. The initial outlays of capital required in such ventures were also very large relative to available liquid assets. Moreover, prospects for short-term return on such investments were not good, given competition from the more advanced nations. Many merchant houses therefore preferred to remain in older types of business or simply to take advantage of the high interest rates on money lending. Yet commercial growth in the Tokugawa period had prepared some of the ground. The "putting-out" system, by which tools, spinning wheels, and raw materials were provided by merchant capitalists, was already well known, and some rural landlord capitalists had moved beyond it to an embryonic factory system in which labor in such industries as textile weaving and sake wine brewing were concentrated in work sheds as part of an integrated process of production. Once the government took the lead, some traditional merchant houses—for example, Mitsui and Sumitomo—did successfully reorganize to make the transition. From the ranks of the upper peasantry also came new entrepreneurs. An outstanding, if not representative, case was Shibusawa Eichi (1840-1931), whose family's success in indigo dyestuffs had given him springboard to leap into the samurai class during the turmoil of the 1860s and who then launched a career in investment banking which was to make him one of the half dozen most prominent businessmen in Japan. Other prominent entrepreneurs came out of the samurai class, which had the benefit often of close connections with members of the Meiji ruling circles. In the 1860s Iwasaki Yataro (1834-85) founded the Mitsubishi Shipping Company, the heart of what was to become a huge economic empire, as part of an effort to strengthen the Tosa domain's economic position. After the Restoration many young samurai, newly convinced that business was both a lucrative and a respectable means of serving their society, trained for the commercial wars at Fukuzawa's Keio Academy.

By the 1890s the private sector of the economy, led by the modernized textile industry, had become strong enough to take over much of the role of leadership from the government. The government factories for glass, woolens, cement, and other new products were sold off and government management was thereafter limited primarily to arsenals, although government subsidies and other types of aid continued and the policy of direct intervention was invoked where needed, as in the case of creating modern steel plants and the nationalization of the railroads. With this combination of government and private initiative, Japan experienced by 1914 a remarkable industrial growth, particularly in textiles, mining, shipping, railroads, and the light electrical industries. After 1895 Japanese capitalists also expanded abroad, competing with the West for raw materials and profitable markets in the treaty ports of coastal China, the leased territories in southern Manchuria, and in the new colonies of Taiwan and Korea.

Social Mobilization and the Meiji Revolution

The Meiji policies of political consolidation and industrial development offer ample evidence of a preoccupation with national strength rather than abstract concerns with natural rights or economic justice. The Meiji Constitution carefully hedged all individual rights with legal provisions bolstering the authority of the state and giving the working classes little protection against exploitation by rural landowners or urban factory managers. Nevertheless, the Meiji leaders also aimed at mobilizing the Japanese people and freeing their energies for national progress. The cumulative effects of their efforts in this direction produced a social transformation that well warrants the designation revolution.

The first objective was to tear down the Tokugawa barriers to geographical and occupational mobility. The legal strictures on leaving the agricultural village or the occupation of one's father had never been effectively enforced in practice, but the Meiji reformers were intent on removing all such inhibiting factors so that labor resources might be utilized wherever and in whatever manner needs of the economy dictated. Since the bulk of the new industry came to be located in the coastal cities—especially the Tokyo-Yokohama and Osaka-Kobe regions—these cities received new growth stimuli from the influx of rural labor. The concentration of higher education in these same urban centers also attracted those ambitious for access to elite positions and served to break down regional isolation. As the Meiji railroad building program progressed, transportation for the common people improved. Military conscription also meant that segments of the rural peasantry and the urban proletariat were exposed to new vistas.

Upward mobility tended to increase in the fluid conditions of the new Meiji society. The most dramatic single step in the direction of opening up opportunity was the termination of all legal privileges for the samurai as a hereditary class. Here the Meiji reformers were motivated by a number of considerations, not the least of which was the economic burden of hereditary stipends. After much internal debate, the government compromised in 1873 by offering samurai the option of commuting their annual stipends into lump sums. In 1876 this became mandatory. The creation of a national conscript army, to which the government committed itself in 1873, struck a parallel blow to the samurai as a hereditary military elite. The experience with units recruited from among commoners in the battles of the Restoration and the model of European armies convinced the reformers that a tradition-oriented samurai military could not compete internationally or be effective in domestic social control. At the same time, traditional sumptuary restrictions designed to identify and reinforce distinctions in social status, which included dress and the right to use a legal surname, were abandoned, and the new civil and criminal codes that came into effect in the 1890s instituted legal equality at least in theory to all imperial subjects.

Beyond the considerations of fiscal solvency and military expediency, however, was a larger commitment to a new social structure in which individual ability exercised in loyal service to the state was to be the highest criteria for social rewards. Leaders such as Itō Hirobumi and Yamagata Aritomo, both from the bottom rung of the old samurai class, had good reason to disdain the old system and to be suspicious of the vested interests and subversive loyalties of upper samurai. Western ideologies supporting citizen participation in the nation-state also played a role, but one of the common themes struck by late Tokugawa critics and participants in the Restoration movement had been the demand to open up positions of importance to "men of talent." Now, in the desire to mobilize the support of the larger populace, the Meiji leaders extended that principle to incorporate commoners into a new national community. Given that this commitment was to social mobilization rather than social security, it was not contradictory that in 1885 a new peerage was created to reward service to the state. The principle of hierarchical authority was to remain strong, and beyond compulsory primary education little was done to promote upward mobility for the disadvantaged.

Japan in the 1920s and 1930s

The First World War proved a tremendous stimulus to economic growth to Japanese industries because of Western demand for products. New markets in the Western colonies of Asia also opened up temporarily as European competition lessened. Japanese exports tripled in value during the war years and the gross national product jumped 20 percent in the 1918-19 period alone. The Japanese economy was becoming even more tightly integrated into the international system of trade while becoming more highly industrialized at home. The number of workers employed in factories doubled between 1910 and 1920, and the percentage of the total work force engaged in agriculture and fishing, which had accounted for 81 percent in 1880 and 60 percent in 1900, dropped to 50 percent by 1930. A similar shift of population from rural areas to towns and cities was taking place over the same period. A new round of growth took place in the 1930s in heavy industries—automobiles and aircraft, metal and machinery, as well as chemical and electrical.

Japan had become an urban industrial society. As such it suffered from the tensions and dilemmas familiar to similar societies elsewhere in the world—problems made more serious, however, by the rapidity of the pace of change and the fact that Japan's position as a power in the international world was tenuous (see Chapter 11). Too often the blame for domestic evils was placed on the international scene or on alien influences within Japanese institutions and values.

Economically, the 1920s was a decade of turbulence, as the boom of the war years was followed by an extended recession in agriculture, widely fluctuating business cycles, and large-scale umemployment. A monetary panic in 1927 precipitated a slide into what was to become a worldwide depression after 1929. The tariff policies of the United States, Great Britain, and other Western nations, aimed at protecting their own economies, heightened Japanese fears that without the economic base provided by the British empire or the United States' position in Latin America, Japan could not continue to grow.

Internally, the poverty of the urban laborer and the tenant farmer stimulated a reaction from both the left and the right in the Japanese political spectrum. Although bitter enemies, both identified the exploitation of big business and the bankrupt social policies of the Diet parties as the primary causes of urban unemployment and the collapse of the agrarian economy. For the left wing, led by older Meiji socialists and young university intellectuals inspired by such worldwide trends as the victory of the democracies in 1918 and the Bolshevik Revolution, the problem was seen in the context of a universal stage of social evolution. On the far left, an underground Communist Party was formed with Soviet support to work toward eventual revolution. Although the left was continually frustrated at the ballot box, its activities stirred heated political debate throughout the nation as the incidence of labor strife, tenant conflicts, and student demonstrations soared.

For the right wing, which enjoyed at least tacit support from a wide range of the conservative elite, including the upper echelons of the military, the emergence of a vigorous left was in itself evidence of the corrupting influences of Western culture on Japan. Invoking the slogans of Meiji nationalism, the right insisted that the government protect Japan's national identity by rooting out alien influences. The more radical elements sought solutions in a chauvinistic foreign policy abroad and a Showa restoration at home, a renovation of Japanese politics that would restore unity to the family-nation by removing evil advisers from around the throne and substituting government by a paternalistic elite for the corruptness of parliamentary politics. On the extreme fringe of the radical right were small groups of activists, including young officers in the military services, who increasingly after 1930 resorted to terrorist tactics in the hope of precipitating a military coup d'etat.

The primary target for both the left and the right was the parliamentary party structure, which had enhanced the power of the Diet without building a solid popular base for parliamentary democracy. The other major target for political dissidents in the 1920s and early 1930s was the constellation of *zaibatsu* firms—in particular, Mitsui, Mitsubishi, Sumitomo, and Yasuda. These large combines had taken advantage of the turbulent conditions of the 1920s to strengthen further their positions of dominance over the modern sectors of the economy, positions gained through the systematic integration of highly diverse enterprises in banking, foreign trade, shipping, mining, and manufacturing. Although the actual degree to which these companies were able to directly influence Diet policies is still debated, there was ample evidence of financial contributions, personal ties with Diet politicians, and occasional exposures of corruption to have made the conspiracy theory convincing and further erode faith in Western-style parliamentary government.

Caught in the cross fire of intellectual alienation and lower-class unrest on the left and military demands and political assassination on the right, the Diet party leaders gradually succumbed to political paralysis in the early 1930s. Power shifted from their hands into the control of an often uneasy coalition of civil bureaucrats and military elite. These men sought solutions abroad by aggressive diplomacy backed by armed force. Manchuria, seized in 1931 after a group of right-wing field officers had conspired to set off armed clashes with Chinese troops, was systematically exploited as a source of vital raw materials and a potential frontier for resettling excess population. A buffer zone was set up in northern China between Manchuria and the areas to the south being brought under the effective rule of the Nanking government. When war broke out in China in 1937, the Japanese government turned toward a diplomatic alliance with Germany as a means of blocking Soviet, British, or American intervention.

Internally, the coalition governments of the 1930s stepped up suppressive measures against the left wing and intensified the propagation of nationalist ideology to counter alien liberalism. After the February 1936 rebellion in Tokyo of the young officers in the First Division, the upper echelons of the army cooperated with the government to eradicate right-wing extremism. Simultaneously, government supervision over the life of the nation was extended under the slogan "new economic structure," thereby circumscribing the power of the *zaibatsu* firms. Although urgent armament production combined with the entrenched position of the *zaibatsu* to prevent control measures from being fully implemented, Japan like other industrial societies in the 1930s continued to move in the direction of a more planned economy under greater central coordination.

The American Occupation and Postwar Japan

The devastating defeat in 1945 and the American-authored reforms of the Occupation period constitute a watershed of tremendous importance in Japanese history. Parliamentary government has taken firm root with a marked shift in the direction of guaranteed civil rights and greater concern for social justice. The old military establishment was destroyed and the nationalist ideology of the prewar right was largely discredited for the generation of the 1950s and 1960s, although the 1970s have seen a renewed debate over Japan's role in international politics. The extensive land reforms, which received wide support from Japanese who had been debating the agrarian problem for two decades, radically altered the nature of rural life by virtually eliminating the landlord class. In the cities, the labor union movement was revitalized, initially with the encouragement of the Occupation.

Nevertheless, strong continuities with the prewar period—continuities often unperceived amidst the innovative zeal of the Occupation period—can also be identified. The vigor of the left wing, a source of anxiety to the U.S. Occupation authorities as the Cold War deepened, owed much to ground broken in the interwar years. Parliamentary democracy also had behind it a long period of incubation. The Liberal-Democrat Party, whose leaders have dominated the government since the 1950s, traces its origins directly to the prewar parties. The elite traditions of the civil service have been maintained, and as in the prewar period former bureaucrats such as Yoshida Shigeru, Kishi Shinsuke, and Sato Eisaku—the three strongest prime ministers since the war—have held the balance of power within the party. Charismatic politicians with large electoral bases have been a rare phenomenon, and leadership has remained collective in style. Despite Occupation attempts at strengthening local government by opening such posts as governor and mayor to election, political power remains highly centralized in the capital of Toyko. Local control over police and education were hotly disputed political issues in the 1950s and 1960s, but both have gravitated back toward central bureaucratic supervision.

Big business, which has supported the policy of retaining close ties with the United States, achieved in the postwar years a position of full partnership with the ruling party. This has actually furthered rather than reversed prewar trends toward a planned economy and bureaucratic supervision of industrial growth. This interdependency of government and business has been accepted, in part because of the critical role of international trade in the Japanese economy as well as because of the phenomonal success in generating industrial growth in the postwar era. By the end of the 1960s, Japan had surpassed her European rivals, Britain and Germany. In the process it has also come face to face with the ecological consequences of such industrial growth.

The surface of daily life in the larger society, especially in the cities where the majority of Japanese now live, has come to resemble greatly that of North America and Western Europe. In part this is due to yet another wave of conscious borrowing stimulated by the Occupation and sustained in a mid-twentieth century context of mass media and jet communications. Beneath the surface, quite apart from direct Western influences, have been deeper, socioeconomic currents pushing Japan in the direction of modernity. The net effects of the Meiji legal reforms, the industrial transformation in the interwar period, and national mobilization for the Pacific War have brought about great changes in human relations. Individual ties to the extended family and neighborhood community have lessened considerably as these primary and secondary groups have lost much of their educational and economic functions. The Occupation-directed expansion of facilities for higher education has promoted greater equality of opportunity, while the spread of democratic norms has also influenced the reduction of social distance between the upper and lower classes. Perhaps more profound has been the cumulative impact of the proliferation of economic roles calling for new specialized skills. Young men (and to a lesser extent, young women) have entered occupations quite different from those of their parents. Increasingly, these roles have had to be learned in achievement-oriented school systems or in on-the-job training, thus eroding the relevancy of family status and reducing the reliance on the expertise of elders. Geographical mobility has also reduced the relevance of the extended family. These trends were already apparent in the 1920s and 1930s and contributed to the turbulence of those decades. In the 1960s and 1970s they continue to cause severe tensions, especially among the younger generations.

Yet, the ideology of Western individualism has not supplanted the norms of subordination to the group, and the importance of vertically organized lines of authority has remained stronger than in other industrial societies. The nuclear family relationship has remained very close in the face of the impersonality of modern life. Japanese workers, both assembly line and white collar, have tended to manifest a personal identification with the firm that employs them, a sense of community with management as well as fellow employees which companies have fostered through a variety of paternalistic practices aimed at frustrating union solidarity and holding down the demands of labor. Some sociologists have seen this and other deviations from American or European social patterns as vestiges of traditional culture that are destined to pass away with "full" modernization. Others have challenged this assumption that all industrial societies must converge toward a single cultural model and have argued persuasively that such differences should be seen as lasting consequences of Japan's historical path toward modernity.

14.5 Increasingly in the twentieth century
Japanese students, workers, and other social
groups have used mass rallies and street
demonstrations as techniques to mobilize
political protest. Shown here is a "demo" by
the radical student association, the Zengakuen.
Courtesy: Mainichi Newspapers, Tokyo, Japan,
from Hisashi Uno "Zengakuren," *New Japan,*
Vol. 21 (1969).

CONCLUDING REMARKS

Clearly, the types of change described in the process section of this chapter have not affected Asian societies in any uniform fashion. Japan and China, albeit in different ways, have undergone the greatest alterations in their political, social, economic, and intellectual life, while in West Asia and parts of Southeast Asia—especially in the rural village—the twentieth century has not brought nearly as great a change in familiar patterns. Nor is it possible to speak of a political or social revolution in South Asia comparable to those of East Asia. As emphasized at the outset of the chapter, however, the study of Asian societies is highly colored by different assumptions about the defining characteristics of modernity or whether industrialization is incompatible with preindustrial values and institutions and will lead inevitably to convergence in Asian as well as other societies. Thus, a number of questions for comparison arise. Why did Japanese society respond earlier and have more immediate success in economic development than its neighbor China? Was the Islamic religion more of an obstacle to the spread of scientific method in Arab nations than Buddhism was in Japan? What was the role of colonialism in "arresting" economic development or political unity in South Asia?

Political scientists and historians have investigated the factors that could be interpreted as accelerating or retarding progress toward the formation of parliamentary parties or the coming of socialist revolutions. One might better ask why parliamentary forms of government have appeared anywhere outside of this original Western context. Such an inquiry might focus more on the question of how the patterns of the past in these civilizations have been adapted to accommodate the appeal of modern concepts of social egalitarianism, the demand for political independence, or the desire to utilize modern technology for material well-being. How is it that hierarchical authority and group-centeredness in Japanese social organization proves so compatible with economic innovation and industrial growth? Is the caste system in India hindering or facilitating mobility from countryside to urban areas? To what extent are the old patterns of bureaucratic political administration providing the institutional framework for centralized party direction of social change in China?

Yet a third approach might compare the cumulative effects of change on specific institutions or particular aspects of social structure without regard to whether they are converging. For example, how have the socializing or economic functions of the nuclear family as it existed in Mughul India or Ottoman Turkey—without assuming they are identical in "traditional" or in "modern" societies—undergone change in the twentieth century? What is the difference between the manner in which villagers under the Manchus or the Tokugawa collectively dealt with community interests and the dynamics of a Chinese agricultural commune or a Japanese farmers' cooperative? How does the role of a member of the *ulama*, brahman, or samurai contrast with the roles of the managerial elites of twentieth century Asia? What have been the changes in the status of women in the same time period? Such topics are, of course, more open ended than many suggested for earlier sections, because in a very obvious sense this last chapter treats changes still very much in progress.

BIBLIOGRAPHY

14.P CUMULATIVE FORCES FOR CHANGE IN MODERN ASIA: PROCESSES

Black, Cyril E., *The Dynamics of Modernization: A Study in Comparative History* (Harper Torchbook paperback, 1967), 206 pp. Although many of the underlying assumptions can be challenged, an interesting attempt by an historian to emphasize the role of politics and ideas in bringing about socioeconomic change.

Coleman, James S., ed., *Education and Political Development* (Princeton University Press paperback, 1968), 620 pp. One of a series of "Studies in Political Development," which includes both analytical introduction and case studies of various societies in Asia and elsewhere.

Hall, John W., "Changing Conceptions of the Modernization of Japan," in Marius B. Jansen, ed., *Changing Japanese Attitudes toward Modernization* (Princeton University Press paperback, 1965), 546 pp. A summary of a conference exploring the concept of modernization and its usefulness in studying Japanese history.

Moore, Wilbur E., *The Impact of Industry* (Prentice-Hall paperback, 1965), 117 pp. Introductory volume to a series of concise essays on the "Modernization of Traditional Societies"; emphasizes social change resulting from economic development.

Ward, Robert E., and Dankwart A. Rustow, eds., *Political Modernization in Japan and Turkey* (Princeton University Press paperback, 1968), 502 pp. Another in the series of "Studies in Political Development," which applies the concept of political modernization in explicit comparison of two Asian societies.

Weinberg, Ian, "The Problem of the Convergence of Industrial Societies," *Comparative Studies in Society and History* 11.1:1-15 (1969). A sophisticated questioning of the assumption that all fully modern societies converge toward similar patterns in their basic institutions and social values.

14.1 CUMULATIVE FORCES FOR CHANGE IN MODERN WEST ASIA

Avery, Peter W., *Modern Iran* (New York, 1965), 527 pp. An extended history of modern Iran from the beginning of the nineteenth century.

Banani, Amin, *The Modernization of Iran, 1921-1941* (Stanford, 1961), 159 pp. The only book available in English that concentrates on the reign of Riza Shah Pahlavi.

Bayne, E. A., *Persian Kingship in Transition* (New York, 1968), 249 pp. Wide-ranging discussions between the author and the present shah.

Lambton, Ann K. S., *The Persian Land Reform, 1962-1966* (Oxford, 1969), 386 pp. An in-depth inquiry and analysis by the author of *Landlord and Peasant in Persia*.

Pahlavi, H. I. M. Mohammed Reza Shah, *Mission for My Country* (London, .961), 328 pp. The present shah of Iran discusses his plans for the future of his country, as well as describing his early life and the turbulent history of Iran since the beginning of the twentieth century.

Upton, Joseph M., *The History of Modern Iran: An Interpretation* (Cambridge, Mass., 1970), 134 pp. A brief introduction, emphasizing those factors that have been critical for shaping the course of events during the past half century.

14.2 CUMULATIVE FORCES FOR CHANGE IN MODERN SOUTH ASIA

Crane, Robert I., ed., *Transition in South Asia* (Duke University Program in Comparative Studies on Southern Asia, 1970), 178 pp. Essays dealing with language change, political modernization, and population problems.

Hardgrave, Robert L., Jr., *India: Government and Politics in a Developing Nation* (Harcourt, Brace and World paperback, 1970), 211 pp. Descriptive account of Indian governmental institutions.

Rudolph, Lloyd I., and Susanne H., *The Modernity of Transition: Political Development in India* (Chicago, 1967), 306 pp. A sophisticated approach to modernity, which takes account of the peculiarities of the Indian pattern.

Shils, Edward A., *The Intellectual between Tradition and Modernity: The Indian Situation* (The Hague, 1961), 120 pp. Cultural orientation of intellectuals in the context of modern change.

Singer, Milton, *When a Great Tradition Modernizes: An Anthropological Approach to Indian Civilization* (Praeger paperback, 1972), 430 pp. Chapters approaching continuity and change from various directions with some consideration given to the comparative study of civilizations.

Srinivas, Mysore N., *Social Change in Modern India* (University of California Press paperback, 1966), 194 pp. Analysis of caste mobility in modern India.

14.3   CUMULATIVE FORCES FOR CHANGE IN MODERN SOUTHEAST ASIA

Asian Survey, monthly (University of California Press, Berkeley). The best source of articles on recent events in South, Southeast, and East Asia.

Bastin, John, and Harry J. Benda, *A History of Modern Southeast Asia* (Prentice-Hall paperback, 1968), pp. 153-201. A section dealing with the era since World War II political development.

Fitzgerald, Frances, *Fire in the Lake: The Vietnamese and Americans in Vietnam* (Random House paperback, 1972), 491 pp. This account of the American participation in the Vietnam War examines that intervention in the context of the structure and history of Vietnamese society.

Selden, Mark, ed., *Remaking Asia: Essays on the American Uses of Power* (Pantheon paperback, 1974), pp. 21-199, 257-78. A selection of radical scholarship critical of the American role in Asia including essays touching on Vietnam, Indonesia, The Philippines, and Thailand.

Steinberg, David J., *In Search of Southeast Asia: A Modern History* (Praeger paperback, 1971), pp. 169-235, 337-413. Two sections of this integrated comparative work deal generally with the processes of modern change. An excellent annotated bibliography is attached.

14.4   CUMULATIVE FORCES FOR CHANGE IN MODERN CHINA

Fairbank, John K., *United States and China* (Harvard paperback, 1971), pp. 219-58, 324-400. A brief and readable account of modern China by a leading authority; contains an excellent bibliography.

Myrdal, Jan, *Report from a Chinese Village* (Signet paperback, 1965), 397 pp. This book records the vivid impressions of the Chinese revolution by villagers near Yenan, as told to a young Swedish interviewer. A sequal, *China: The Revolution Continued* (Vintage paperback, 1970), 201 pp., records impressions of a return trip to the village after the Cultural Revolution.

Schurmann, Franz, *Ideology and Organization in Communist China* (University of California Press paperback, 1968), 642 pp. A massive and provocative analysis of the revolutionary transformation of Chinese society.

Snow, Edgar, *Red China Today* (Vintage paperback, 1971), 749 pp. A wide-ranging set of descriptions by an American reporter who enjoyed special trust and entree with the Chinese Communist leadership.

Solomon, Richard H., *Mao's Revolution and the Chinese Political Culture* (University of California Press paperback, 1971), 604 pp. This is a highly controversial work which attempts to explain the Maoist revolution in terms of changing authority in Chinese society.

Yang, C. K., *Chinese Communist Society: The Family and the Village* (M.I.T. paperback, 1959), 276 pp. Descriptions and analysis by a Chinese social scientist of changes at the local level of rural society in the early stages of liberation.

14.5   CUMULATIVE FORCES FOR CHANGE IN MODERN JAPAN

Dore, Ronald P., *City Life in Japan* (University of California Press paperback, 1958), 472 pp. A detailed but very readable description of a Toyko neighborhood in the early 1950s which raises many provocative questions regarding tradition and modernity.

————, *British Factory–Japanese Factory: The Origins of National Diversity in Employment Relations* (University of California Press paperback, 1973), 432 pp. An explicit rejection of the thesis that all industrial societies converge toward a common pattern of modernity, with very clear summaries of major points.

Fairbank, John K., *et al., East Asia: Tradition and Transformation* (Boston, 1973), 969 pp. Chapters 18, 22, 23, and 26 provide the best available introductory survey of Japan in the modern era.

Jansen, Marius B., ed., *Changing Japanese Attitudes toward Modernization* (Princeton University Press paperback, 1969), 546 pp. First in a six-volume series that offers some of the best scholarship on Japanese modernization; includes an important essay on the problems of conceptualization by John W. Hall.

Livingston, Jon, *et al.,* ed., *The Japan Reader* (Pantheon paperback, 1973), 2 vols. A potpourri excerpted from scholarly monographs, journalism, novels, and other sources, both Japanese and Western, on the modern period; notes are useful if often dogmatic in interpretation.

Morley, James W., ed., *Dilemmas of Growth in Prewar Japan* (Princeton, 1971), 527 pp. A collection of papers on the problems generated by rapid social change with an explicit focus on the relationship between these and Japanese aggression in the 1930s.

GLOSSARY

Caliph (Arabic, **khalifa**). Originating with the title of the Prophet Muhammad's successor, Abu Bakr, Khalifat Rasul Allah, "Successor of the Messenger of God." The Caliph was the head of the Islamic *umma,* "the community of believers," and was referred to as *amir al-muminin,* "commander of the faithful."

Choshu. A large *tozama,* or "outer domain," at the southern tip of the island of Honshu which supplied such leading Meiji Restoration figures as Ito Hirobumi and Yamagata Aritomo.

Communes. Local units of management and government formed in China in the late 1950s, consisting of several thousands of persons in groups of villages, intended as complete social units with agricultural, industrial, educational, and other organs, now chiefly a unit of economic planning and development.

Dervish. A Sufi; either a religious mendicant or a member of a Sufi brotherhood *(tariqa)* attached to a dervish convent *(khanqah).*

Ferdinand Marcos (b. 1917). Filipino lawyer and politician who as president set aside American style constitution for a form of military dictatorship called "constitutional authoritarianism," trying to carry out reforms and development policies in the face of extreme corruption and popular insurgency.

Great Leap Forward. Extreme radical phase of the Chinese revolution in late 1950s, when communes were formed and people mobilized to make rapid gains in industrialization through maximum use of human labor; resulted in economic chaos, severe setback of agriculture, temporary loss of influence by Mao Tse-tung.

Jawaharlal Nehru (1889-1964). English-trained lawyer from wealthy family, became a follower of Gandhi and leader of the Indian National Congress. After 1947 he became prime minister of India, advocating development along state-directed lines within parliamentary democracy.

Mass line. The program of the Chinese Communist Party developed through contact with the people and carried out through the mobilization of the masses.

New Democracy. An interim program of the Chinese Communist Party during the 1940s, which aimed at carrying out a bourgeois revolution through an alliance of classes which would achieve national independence, to be followed later by a more radical phase.

Ngo Dinh Diem (1901-63). Nationalistic Vietnamese from Catholic family who served as American-backed power holder in South Vietnam; misrule aroused opposition, especially among Buddhists; assassinated with American approval in 1963, making way for military puppets.

Politburo. Short for Political Bureau, a select group of the leadership of the Chinese Communist Party that makes daily decisions on behalf of the Central Committee, which convenes only for major changes of policy.

Republic of China. The Kuomintang-controlled regime known as "Nationalist China"; established at Nanking in 1927, it was the nominal government of China, forced to take refuge in Chungking during the Japanese invasion and expelled from the mainland by the Communists in 1949; it survived on the island of Taiwan with support from the United States, which recognized it as the only legitimate government of China until it was forced out of the United Nations in 1971.

Resident. British agents in South and Southeast Asia who exercised effective control over indigenous rulers.

Samurai. Members of the hereditary class of military retainers who served as political elite under the Tokugawa and from which many of the modern Japanese leaders were drawn.

Sharia. The Law of Islam, derived from the Quran, the *Hadith,* or *Sayings of the Prophet,* and the analogical interpretations of the jurists.

Shiis. Those who follow the *shia* (or "party") of Ali, Muhammad's son-in-law and the fourth caliph of the Muslims. The Shiis, although subdivided into a number of sects, constitute the largest minority group (as opposed to the Sunni majority) within Islam and are today chiefly to be found in Iran and Iraq.

Sukarno (1901-1970). Dutch-trained engineer who played central role in forming a national identity among the Malay-speaking people of the Indonesian archipelago, later president following independence.

Tengku Abdul Rahman. British-trained lawyer who led coalition in early years of the Federation of Malaysia.

Tosa. A large former *tozama,* or "outer domain", later incorporated into Kochi Prefecture which supplied many of the leaders in the Restoration and Meiji periods.

Ulama. The Arabic plural of *alim,* meaning a scholar trained in the Islamic "sciences." Collectively, the *ulama* enforced the Sharia and determined the social norms that governed the life of the Muslim community as a whole.

Index

Note: Volume 1 includes pages 1–474, while Volume 2 contains pages 404–797. (Pages 404–474 are included in both volumes.) Bold numerals in the index indicate a glossary entry, and italic numerals indicate a map or an illustration.